P. 115

58
THE ANNALS OF TACITUS
BOOK 4

THE ANNALS
OF TACITUS

BOOK 4

EDITED WITH A COMMENTARY

BY

A. J. WOODMAN

CAMBRIDGE
UNIVERSITY PRESS

CAMBRIDGE
UNIVERSITY PRESS

University Printing House, Cambridge CB2 8BS, United Kingdom

One Liberty Plaza, 20th Floor, New York, NY 10006, USA

477 Williamstown Road, Port Melbourne, VIC 3207, Australia

314–321, 3rd Floor, Plot 3, Splendor Forum, Jasola District Centre,
New Delhi – 110025, India

79 Anson Road, #06–04/06, Singapore 079906

Cambridge University Press is part of the University of Cambridge.

It furthers the University's mission by disseminating knowledge in the pursuit of
education, learning, and research at the highest international levels of excellence.

www.cambridge.org
Information on this title: www.cambridge.org/9781108419611
DOI: 10.1017/9781108303682

© Cambridge University Press 2018

First published 2018

Printed in the United Kingdom by Clays, St Ives plc

A catalogue record for this publication is available from the British Library.

Library of Congress Cataloging-in-Publication Data
NAMES: Tacitus, Cornelius, author. | Woodman, A. J. (Anthony John),
1945– editor.
TITLE: The annals of Tacitus book 4 / edited with a commentary by A.J.
Woodman.
OTHER TITLES: Annales. Liber 4 | Cambridge classical texts and commentaries ; 58.
DESCRIPTION: Cambridge : Cambridge University Press, 2018. | Series:
Cambridge classical texts and commentaries ; 58 | Includes
bibliographical references and indexes.
IDENTIFIERS: LCCN 2017054704 | ISBN 9781108419611 (alk. paper)
SUBJECTS: LCSH: Tacitus, Cornelius. Annales.
CLASSIFICATION: LCC PA6705.A6 B4 2018 | DDC 937/.07–dc23
LC record available at https://lccn.loc.gov/2017054704

ISBN 978-1-108-41961-1 Hardback

TO TED COURTNEY

Basil L. Gildersleeve Professor of Classics 1993–2002
University of Virginia

Quo non praestantior alter

CONTENTS

PREFACE

This volume of commentary completes the sequence on *Annals* 1–6 which was begun by F. R. D. Goodyear forty-five years ago in 1972. Two decades previously, in 1952, Bessie Walker had published her important contribution to the study of Tacitus, which was followed six years later by Syme's incomparable volumes; E. Koestermann began publishing his big commentary on the whole of the *Annals* in 1963, and by 1967 an Oxford colleague of Syme's was asking whether another book on Tacitus was really needed. Yet, if Goodyear's commentary was thus a product of its time, it was also a product of its place. We hear a great deal these days about the current interest in imperial Latin literature, as if this interest were something new, but as long ago as the 1950s three Cambridge Latinists – E. J. Kenney, A. G. Lee and L. P. Wilkinson – were working on the 'silver age', as it used to be called. Goodyear's own first book (1965) was an edition of the *Aetna*, and in the second half of the decade he supervised doctoral work on Velleius Paterculus and the *Ciris*. Other imperial authors on whom work was being done at this time in Cambridge included Lucan, Persius, Statius, Valerius Flaccus and Valerius Maximus; and those of us who were lucky enough to belong to that generation will have affectionate memories of 'Argentea Proles', an informal group which was set up by Kenney so that research students, as we were then known, could comment on one another's work and exchange views. It is always disappointing when recognition fails to be accorded to those who deserve it.

Frank Goodyear published the second volume of his commentary on the *Annals* in 1981, and, as in the first, paid handsome tribute to Ronald Martin for reading and commenting on his work in draft. It so happened that in the previous year I had had the good fortune to join Ronald as a colleague, and in due course, given our shared interests in early imperial historiography, he and I conceived the notion of writing a collaborative commentary on Book 4 of the *Annals* for the 'green-and-yellow' series. Initially Goodyear wanted us to wait until his own commentary on that book had been written, but, when we assured him that our purpose was significantly different from his in the 'orange' series, he gave us his blessing and our volume duly appeared in 1989. Recently it was suggested to me that I should return to Book 4 for the 'orange' series, and I am extremely grateful for the opportunity of looking again at this compelling narrative. It should be noted that I have generally not acknowledged the many occasions on which I have revised my views or now think that our earlier commentary was mistaken: this omission is not designed in any way to mislead readers but merely to save them the tedium of repeated confessions. The present book should be read on the assumption that its contents are more or less entirely new.

As always I am in the debt of my scholarly friends. In addition to frequent borrowings from their famous library, I have been in ongoing conversation with J. E. Lendon and E. A. Meyer, often conducted in the convivial context of the alcove table at our favourite downtown bistro. I have also sought and received advice from J. N. Adams, J. D. Dillery, F. K. Drogula, D. S. Levene, S. J. V. Malloch, K. S. Myers, J. Nelis-Clément, M. Peachin, H. Pinkster, N. K. Rutter, K. E. Shannon, B. D. Shaw, J. B. Solodow, P. Thonemann, R. S. O. Tomlin and V. Nutton. Special mention must be made of E. J. Champlin, who has kept me supplied not only with drafts of his published articles but also with valuable personal communications; his full-length study of Tiberius is eagerly awaited. As Editors of the 'orange' series S. P. Oakley and M. D. Reeve read my typescript with the greatest care and attention and made numerous comments and suggestions for which I am most grateful. Once again I prevailed upon S. Bartera, A. R. Birley, E. Courtney and R. Seager to read the whole of my commentary in draft, a task which they carried out with their customary acumen and good humour and for which I cannot express adequately the full extent of my gratitude and appreciation.

It is always an honour to be published by Cambridge University Press, and this is my fifth volume in the series Cambridge Classical Texts and Commentaries. When I started out, the Classics Editor at the Press was Pauline Hire (who delightfully arranged for my first volume to be published on the day of my wedding) and my typescripts were copy-edited by the legendary Susan Moore; the esteem in which they are held is rivalled only by that for their seamless successors, Michael Sharp and Muriel Hall, and I am greatly indebted to all of them for support and expertise stretching back more than four decades.

The book was written during my last two years at the University of Virginia, where I have had the privilege and pleasure of working in the Department of Classics since 2003. I shall always remain profoundly grateful to my wonderful colleagues for inviting me to succeed Ted Courtney as Gildersleeve Professor of Classics and thereby giving me the chance to prolong a career of teaching Latin which had seemed to be reaching an enforcedly premature conclusion.

Charlottesville   A. J. W.
Spring 2017

REFERENCES AND ABBREVIATIONS

References to the Cambridge commentaries on *Annals* 1–3 and 5–6, the *Agricola*, and Velleius are usually given in the forms 1.24.2n., *Agr.* 20.1n. and Vell. 97.1n. (or W. on Vell. 97.1) respectively.

As a general rule, works cited more than once are referred to by author's name and page-number; where an author is responsible for several works, these are distinguished either by an abbreviation or by a date. Full details will be found in (C) below.

(A) ABBREVIATIONS

AA	Syme, R. (1986). *The Augustan aristocracy.* Oxford
AE	*L'année épigraphique*
AHC	Kraus, C. S., Marincola, J. and Pelling, C. (edd.) (2010). *Ancient historiography and its contexts: studies in honour of A. J. Woodman.* Oxford
Ann. 3 or *Ann. 5–6*	Woodman, A. J. and Martin, R. H. (1996), *The Annals of Tacitus: Book 3* or Woodman, A. J. (2017), *The Annals of Tacitus: Books 5 and 6.* Cambridge
BA	Talbert, R. J. A. (2000). *Barrington Atlas of the Greek and Roman world.* Princeton [references are given both to the Atlas and to the two-volume Directory]
BNP	Cancik, H. and Schneider, H. (2002–9). *Brill's New Pauly.* Vols. 1–15. Leiden/Boston
CCT	Woodman, A. J. (ed.) (2009). *The Cambridge companion to Tacitus.* Cambridge
CIL	*Corpus Inscriptionum Latinarum*

CLE	Buecheler, F. and Lommatsch, E. (1895–1926). *Carmina Latina Epigraphica.* Vols. 1–3. Leipzig
CT	Pagán, V. E. (ed.) (2012). *A companion to Tacitus.* Malden/Oxford/Chichester
EJ	Ehrenberg, V. and Jones, A. H. M. (1955). *Documents illustrating the reigns of Augustus and Tiberius.* 2nd edn. Oxford
FRH	Cornell, T. J. (ed.) (2013). *The fragments of the Roman historians.* Oxford
G.	Goodyear, F. R. D. (1972–81). *The Annals of Tacitus.* Vols. 1–2. Cambridge
G–G	Gerber, A. and Greef, A. (1962). *Lexicon Taciteum.* Repr. Hildesheim
H.	Heubner, H. (1963–82). *P. Cornelius Tacitus. Die Historien.* Vols. 1–5. Heidelberg
IG	*Inscriptiones Graecae*
ILS	*Inscriptiones Latinae Selectae*
JCS	Gibson, A. G. G. (ed.) (2013). *The Julio-Claudian succession: reality and perception of the 'Augustan model'.* Leiden/Boston
K–S	Kühner, R. and Stegmann, C. (1971). *Ausführliche Grammatik der lateinischen Sprache.* Vol. 2 *Satzlehre.* Parts 1 and 2. 4th edn. Repr. Hanover
LH	Woodman, A. J. (2015). *Lost histories. Selected fragments of Roman historical writers. Histos* Suppl. Vol. 2
L–H–S	Leumann, M., Hofmann, J. B. and Szantyr, A. (1972). *Lateinische Grammatik.* Vol. 2 *Syntax und Stilistik.* Revised edn. Munich
LTUR	Steinby, E. M. (ed.) (1993). *Lexicon topographicum urbis Romae.* Vols. 1–6. Rome
MRR	Broughton, T. R. S. (1951–60). *The Magistrates of the Roman Republic.* Vols. 1 and 2 (with Supplement). New York

N–H	Nisbet, R. G. M. and Hubbard, M. (1970, 1978). *A commentary on Horace.* Vol. 1 *Odes I*, Vol. 2 *Odes II*. Oxford
NLS	Woodcock, E. C. (1959). *A new Latin syntax.* London
N–R	Nisbet, R. G. M. and Rudd, N. (2004). *A commentary on Horace. Odes Book III.* Oxford
OLD	*Oxford Latin dictionary*
OLS	Pinkster, H. (2015). *The Oxford Latin syntax.* Vol. 1. Oxford
PH	Woodman, A. J. (2012). *From poetry to history: selected papers.* Oxford
PIR	Groag, E., Stein, A., Petersen, L. et al. (1933–2015). *Prosopographia Imperii Romani.* 2nd edn. Vols. 1–8. Berlin
RE	*Paulys Realencyclopädie der classischen Altertumswissenschaft*
RIC	Sutherland, C. H. V. and Carson, R. A. G. (1984). *Roman imperial coinage.* Vol. 1 (revised edn). London
RICH	Woodman, A. J. (1988). *Rhetoric in classical historiography.* Portland
RP	Syme, R. (1979–91). *Roman Papers.* Vols. 1–7. Oxford
SCPP	*Senatus Consultum de Cn. Pisone Patre*
TLL	*Thesaurus Linguae Latinae*
Tac. Rev.	Woodman, A. J. (1998). *Tacitus reviewed.* Oxford
W.	Woodman, A. J. [see also above]

(B) EDITIONS AND COMMENTARIES CONSULTED

Bach, N. (1834). Leipzig
Borzsák, S. (1991/92). Stuttgart/Leipzig
Doederlein, L. (1841). Halle

Draeger, A. and Heraeus, W. ([7]1914). Leipzig/Berlin
Fisher, C. D. (1906). Oxford
Formicola, C. (2013). Naples [Book 4]
Fuchs, H. (1946). Frauenfeld
Furneaux, H. ([2]1896). Oxford
Heubner, H. (1983, [2]1994). Stuttgart
Jackson, J. (1931–7). London/Cambridge, MA
Jacob, E. (1885). Paris
Kiessling, Th. (1829). London
Koestermann, E. (1965). Heidelberg [Books 4–6]
Koestermann, E. (1965). Leipzig [Teubner edition]
Lenchantin de Gubernatis, M. (1940). Rome
Malloch, S. J. V. (2013). Cambridge [Book 11]
Martin, R. H. and Woodman, A. J. (1989). Cambridge [Book 4]
Nipperdey, K. and Andresen, G. ([11]1915). Berlin
Orelli, J. C. (1848, [2]1859). Zurich
Pfitzner, W. (1892). Gotha
Ritter, F. (1848). Cambridge/London
Ruperti, G. A. (1834). Hanover
Walther, G. H. (1831). Halle
Wuilleumier, P. (1978–89). Paris

(C) OTHER WORKS

Adams, J. N. (1972). 'The language of the later books of Tacitus'
  Annals', *CQ* 22.350–73
  (1973). 'The vocabulary of the speeches in Tacitus' historical
  works', *BICS* 20.124–44
  (2016). *An anthology of informal Latin, 200 BC–AD 900.*
  Cambridge
Bauman, R. A. (1967). [*CM*] *The crimen maiestatis in the Roman
  Republic and Augustan principate.* Johannesburg
  (1974). [*IP*] *Impietas in principem. A study of treason against the
  Roman emperor with special reference to the first century A.D.*
  Munich

Bernecker, A. (1981). *Zur Tiberius-Überlieferung der Jahre 26–37 n. Chr.* Bonn

Birley, A. R. (2000). 'The life and death of Cornelius Tacitus', *Historia* 49.230–47

    (2007). 'Sejanus: his fall', in N. Sekunda (ed.), *Corolla Cosmo Rodewald* 121–50. Gdańsk

Braund, D. C. (1984). [*RFK*] *Rome and the friendly king.* London/New York

Brunt, P. A. (1971). [*IM*] *Italian manpower 225 BC–AD 14.* Oxford

(1983). 'Princeps and Equites', *JRS* 73.42–75

    (1984). 'The role of the senate in the Augustan regime', *CQ* 34.423–44

    (1990). [*RIT*] *Roman imperial themes.* Oxford

Campbell, J. B. (1984). *The emperor and the Roman army.* Oxford

Carmody, W. M. (1926). *The subjunctive in Tacitus.* Chicago

Carter, M. J. and Edmondson, J. (2015). 'Spectacle in Rome, Italy, and the provinces', in C. Bruun and J. Edmondson (edd.), *The Oxford handbook of Roman epigraphy* 537–58. Oxford

Champlin, E. (2008). 'Tiberius the wise', *Historia* 57.408–25

    (2012). 'Seianus Augustus', *Chiron* 42.361–88

    (2013). 'The Odyssey of Tiberius Caesar', *C&M* 64.199–246

    (2015). 'Mallonia', *Histos* 9.220–30

Chausserie-Laprée, J.-P. (1969). *L'expression narrative chez les historiens latins.* Paris

Crawford, M. H. (1996). *Roman Statutes.* Vols. 1–2. London

Damon, C. (2012). *Tacitus: Annals.* (Penguin Classics.) London

Demougin, S. (1988). [*OE*] *L'ordre équestre sous les Julio-Claudiens.* Rome

    (1992). [*PCR*] *Prosopographie des chevaliers romains julio-claudiens.* Rome

DiLuzio, M. J. (2016). *A place at the altar: priestesses in republican Rome.* Princeton/Oxford

Draeger, A. (1882). [*SS*] *Über Syntax und Stil des Tacitus.* 3rd edn. Leipzig

Drogula, F. K. (2011). 'Controlling travel: deportation, islands and the regulation of senatorial mobility in the Augustan principate', *CQ* 61.230–66

Eck, W., Caballos, A. and Fernández, F. (1996). [Eck et al.] *Das senatus consultum de Cn. Pisone patre.* Munich

Fantham, E. (1972). *Comparative studies in republican Latin imagery.* Toronto

Garnsey, P. D. A. (1970). *Social status and legal privilege in the Roman empire.* Oxford

Ginsburg, J. (1981). *Tradition and theme in the Annals of Tacitus.* New York

Gradel, I. (2002). *Emperor worship and Roman religion.* Oxford

Hahn, E. (1933). *Die Exkurse in den Annalen des Tacitus.* Borna/ Leipzig

Halm, K. (1846). [*Beiträge*] *Beiträge zur Kritik und Erklärung der Annalen des Tacitus.* Speyer

Handford, S. A. (1947). *The Latin subjunctive.* London

Hänlein-Schäfer, H. (1985). *Veneratio Augusti: eine Studie zu den Tempeln des ersten römischen Kaisers.* Rome

Hardie, P. (2012). *Rumour and renown: representations of* Fama *in western literature.* Cambridge

Hartman, J. J. (1905). *Analecta Tacitea.* Leiden

Häussler, R. (1965). *Tacitus und das historische Bewusstsein.* Heidelberg

Hennig, D. (1975). *L. Aelius Seianus.* Munich

Herkommer, E. (1968). *Die Topoi in den Proömien der römischen Geschichtswerke.* Diss. Tübingen

Hollis, A. S. (2007). *Fragments of Roman poetry c. 60 BC–AD 20.* Oxford

Houston, G. W. (1985). 'Tiberius on Capri', *G&R* 32.179–96

Jackson, J. (1937). *Tacitus.* (Loeb edn.) Vol. 3. London/ Cambridge, MA

Kaster, R. A. (2005). *Emotion, restraint, and community in ancient Rome.* Oxford

Keitel, E. (1984). 'Principate and civil war in the Annals of Tacitus', *AJP* 105.306–25

Keppie, L. (1984). *The making of the Roman army*. London

Kienzle, E. (1936). *Der Lobpreis von Städten und Ländern in der älteren griechischen Dichtung*. Kallmünz

Lausberg, H. (1998). *Handbook of literary rhetoric*. Eng. trans. Leiden

Lendon, J. E. (2017). 'Battle description in the ancient historians. Part I: structure, array, and fighting', *G&R* 64.39–64

Levick, B. M. (1976). *Tiberius the politician*. Rev. edn 1999. London

Madvig, J. N. (1873, 1884). *Adversaria critica*. Vols. 2–3. Copenhagen

Magie, D. (1950). *Roman rule in Asia Minor*. Vols. 1–2. Princeton

Maltby, R. (1991). *A lexicon of Latin etymologies*. Leeds

Marincola, J. (1997). *Authority and tradition in ancient historiography*. Cambridge

Mekacher, N. (2006). *Die vestalischen Jungfrauen in der römischen Kaiserzeit*. Wiesbaden

Millar, F. (1992). *The emperor in the Roman world*. 2nd edn. London

Miller, N. P. (1968). 'Tiberius speaks', *AJP* 89.1–19

Moles, J. L. (1998). 'Cry freedom: Tacitus *Annals* 4.32–35', *Histos* 2.95–184

Müller, J. (1873–75). *Beiträge zur Kritik und Erklärung des Cornelius Tacitus*. Vols. 3–4. Innsbruck

Neue, F. (1836). *Observationum ad Tacitum specimen*. Dorpat

Norden, E. (1959). *Die germanische Urgeschichte in Tacitus Germania*. 4th edn. Darmstadt

Noreña, C. (2001). 'The communication of the emperor's virtues', *JRS* 91.146–68

Oakley, S. P. (1991). Review of Martin and Woodman, *CR* 41. 341–5

(1997, 1998, 2005). *A commentary on Livy Books VI–X*. Vols. 1–4. Oxford

Opelt, I. (1964). *Die lateinischen Schimpfwörter und verwandte sprachliche Erscheinungen*. Heidelberg

Orth, W. (1970). *Die Provinzialpolitik des Tiberius*. Munich

Otto, A. (1890). *Die Sprichwörter und sprichwörtlichen Redensarten der Römer*. Leipzig

Peachin, M. (2015). 'Augustus' emergent judicial powers, the "crimen maiestatis", and the Second Cyrene Edict', in J.-L. Ferrary and J. Scheid (edd.), *Il princeps romano: autocrate o magistrato? Fattori giuridici e fattori sociali del potere imperiale da Augusto a Commodo* 3–59. Pavia

Pernot, L. (1993). *La rhétorique de l'éloge dans le monde gréco-romain*. Vols. 1–2. Paris

Pfitzner, W. (1869).[*AT*] *Die Annalen des Tacitus kritisch beleuchtet*. Part 1. Halle

Price, S. R. F. (1984). *Rituals and power: the Roman imperial cult in Asia Minor*. Cambridge

Questa, C. (1963). *Studi sulle fonti degli Annales di Tacito*. 2nd edn. Rome

Raepsaet-Charlier, M.-T. (1987). *Prosopographie des femmes de l'ordre sénatorial*. Louvain

Rawson, E. (1991). *Roman culture and society: collected papers*. Oxford

Rigsby, K. J. (1996). *Asylia: territorial inviolability in the Hellenistic world*. Berkeley/Los Angeles/London

Rogers, R. S. (1935). *Criminal trials and criminal legislation under Tiberius*. Middletown, CT

Rougé, J. (1981). *Ships and fleets of the ancient Mediterranean*. Middletown, CT

Rüpke, J. (2008). *Fasti sacerdotum. A prosopography of pagan, Jewish, and Christian religious officials in the city of Rome, 300 BC to AD 499*. Oxford

Rutherford, R. B. (1989). *The* Meditations *of Marcus Aurelius: a study*. Oxford

Rutledge, S. H. (2001). *Imperial inquisitions*. London/New York

Santoro L'Hoir, F. (2006). *Tragedy, rhetoric, and the historiography of Tacitus' Annales*. Ann Arbor

Seager, R. (2005). *Tiberius*. Rev. edn. Oxford

Shatzman, I. (1974). 'Tacitean rumours', *Latomus* 33.549–78

Sörbom, G. (1935). *Variatio sermonis Tacitei aliaeque apud eundem quaestiones selectae*. Uppsala

Starr, C. G. (1960). *The Roman imperial navy*. 2nd edn. New York

Suerbaum, W. (1990). 'Zweiundvierzig Jahre Tacitus-Forschung: Systematische Gesamtbibliographie zu Tacitus' Annalen 1939–1980', *ANRW* 2.33.2.1032–1476

Sutherland, C. H. V. (1951). *Coinage in Roman imperial policy 31 BC–AD 68*. Oxford

Syme, R. (1958). [*Tac.*] *Tacitus*. Oxford
  (1970). [*TST*] *Ten studies in Tacitus*. Oxford
  (1979–91). [*RP*] *Roman Papers*, Vols. 1–7. Oxford
  (1986). [*AA*] *The Augustan aristocracy*. Oxford

Talbert, R. J. A. (1984). *The senate of imperial Rome*. Princeton

Thomas, R. F. (1982). *Lands and peoples in Roman poetry: the ethno-graphical tradition*. *PCPS* Suppl. 7. Cambridge

Tosi, R. (2007). *Dizionario delle sentenze latine e greche*. Repr. Milan

Treggiari, S. (1991). *Roman marriage: iusti coniuges from the time of Cicero to the time of Ulpian*. Oxford

Vanggaard, J. H. (1998). *The flamen. A study in the history and sociology of Roman religion*. Copenhagen

Vielberg, M. (1987). *Pflichten, Werte, Ideale: eine Untersuchung zu den Wertvorstellungen des Tacitus*. Stuttgart

Vogel-Weidemann, U. (1982). *Die Statthalter von Africa und Asia in den Jahren 14–68 n. Chr.* Bonn

Walker, B. (1952). *The* Annals *of Tacitus: a study in the writing of history*. Manchester

Wallace-Hadrill, A. (1981). 'The emperor and his virtues', *Historia* 30.298–323

Weinstock, S. (1971). *Divus Julius*. Oxford

Wilkes, J. J. (1969). *Dalmatia*. London

Wills, J. (1996). *Repetition in Latin poetry*. Oxford

Wisse, J. (2013). 'Remembering Cremutius Cordus: Tacitus on history, tyranny and memory', *Histos* 7.299–361

Woodman, A. J. (2004, ²2008). [Woodman] *Tacitus: The Annals*. Indianapolis
  (2015). 'Tacitus and Germanicus: monuments and models', in R. Ash et al. (edd.), *Fame and Infamy. Essays for Christopher*

Pelling on Characterization in Greek and Roman Biography and Historiography 255–68. Oxford

Yardley, J. C. (2008). *Tacitus: The Annals*. With Introduction and notes by A. A. Barrett. (Oxford World's Classics.) Oxford

Zimmermann, M. (1889). *De Tacito Senecae philosophi imitatore*. Breslau

INTRODUCTION

INTRODUCTION

INTRODUCTION

'The dichotomy which the tradition asserts in the reign of each
Caesar may appear suspect and artificial. Yet it reflects facts.'[1]
Syme's verdict is complicated by the fact that in the case of
Tiberius' reign the tradition asserts more than one dichotomy:
in Dio's opinion deterioration starts with the death of
Germanicus in AD 19,[2] which seems also to have been the belief
of Suetonius,[3] but Tacitus dates the change four years later, to
the death of Drusus in 23, which is described near the start of
Book 4 (7.1 'donec morte Drusi uerterentur'). Tacitus' date is
a reflection of, and perhaps caused by, his perception of the
princeps' life as falling into five periods, of which the last four –
those comprising his principate – are demarcated by the successive deaths of his partners in power (6.51.3):[4] evidently Tacitus
took the view that, since in the years after his accession Tiberius
was partnered by both of his sons jointly, Germanicus' death
had less impact on the *princeps*' life than did that of the son who
died later (cf. 6.51.3 'donec Germanicus ac Drusus superfuere').
It is a double irony that Tacitus, commonly regarded as
Tiberius' most successful critic, allows him four extra years of
benevolent rule and devotes as many books to the earlier years

---

[1] Syme, *Tac.* 420 n. 2.
[2] Dio 57.7.1, 57.13.6 ταῦθ' οὕτω πάντα μέχρι γε καὶ ὁ Γερμανικὸς ἔζη ἐποίει·
μετὰ γὰρ τοῦτο συχνὰ αὐτῶν μετέβαλεν, εἶτ' οὖν φρονῶν μὲν οὕτως ἀπὸ
πρώτης ὡς ὕστερον διέδειξε, πλασάμενος δὲ ἐφ' ὅσον ἐκεῖνος ἐβίω, ἐπειδήπερ
ἐφεδρεύοντα αὐτὸν τῇ ἡγεμονίᾳ ἑώρα, εἴτε καὶ πεφυκὼς μὲν εὖ, ἐξοκείλας δ'
ὅτε τοῦ ἀνταγωνιστοῦ ἐστερήθη, 57.19.1. In general see C. Pelling,
'Biographical history? Cassius Dio on the early principate', in
M. J. Edwards and S. Swain (edd.), *Portraits: biographical representation in the
Greek and Latin literature of the Roman Empire* (1997) 117–44.
[3] Suet. *Cal.* 6.2 'cunctis nec temere opinantibus reuerentia eius [sc.
Germanici] ac metu repressam Tiberi saeuitiam, quae mox eruperit'.
[4] The deaths are those of Drusus (23), Livia (29) and Sejanus (31). See
6.51.3nn. for the interpretation of Tiberius' obituary notice on which this
and the following statements are based.

3

(14–22) as he does to the significantly longer span which followed (23–37).

The continued existence of Drusus after Germanicus' death represented a substantial obstacle to the illimitable ambition of Sejanus, the murderous Prefect of the Praetorian Guard, who, after fleeting appearances in Books 1 and 3,[5] dominates the beginning of Book 4 (1–2). The book opens with a statement of what is to come: 'repente turbare fortuna coepit, saeuire ipse aut saeuientibus uires praebere' (1.1). The well-known allusion to Sallust (*C.* 10.1 'saeuire fortuna . . . coepit') functions as a kind of 'motto', reaffirming the Sallustian nature of Tacitus' narrative at this halfway point in the Tiberian hexad. Immediately after this statement Tacitus promises both a formal character sketch of Sejanus and an account of the *facinus* by which he embarked on seizing power (1.1 'quo facinore dominationem raptum ierit'): not only is the language Sallustian (cf. *H.* 1.55.20 'raptum ire') but there is perhaps an echo of the preface to the *Bellum Catilinae*, where a reference to Catiline's conspiracy ('id facinus') is followed by a formal sketch of the conspirator (*C.* 4.4–5). The distinction which Sallust draws between Catiline's physical attributes and his revolutionary temperament (*C.* 5.3 'corpus . . . animus audax') is exactly matched by Sejanus in the words of Tacitus (1.3 'corpus . . . animus audax'); and, although Sallust does not there mention the kind of homosexual rumours which Tacitus now attributes to Sejanus (1.2; cf. 10.2), they are not absent from the later narrative (*C.* 14.7); what Sallust does include is a reference to Catiline's ultimate ambition (*C.* 5.6 'dum sibi regnum pararet'), which Tacitus makes the climax of his sketch of Sejanus (1.3 'parando regno').[6]

Despite the uncertainty of his enterprise (*C.* 17.6 'incerta pro certis', 20.2 'incerta pro certis'; cf. 41.2), Catiline gathered

---

[5] See 1.24.2, 69.5; 3.16.1, 29.4, 35.2, 66.3, 72.3.

[6] For further details on the passages adduced here and below see the Commentary. For a comparative study see E. Arnold, *Zum Bild des Verschwörers: Catilina und Seian – ihre Darstellung bei Sallust und Tacitus* (1972), whose work is less concerned with stylistic details than this Introduction.

supporters around him by personal approaches and bribery (*C.* 17.1 'appellare', 20.1 'appellare', 21.2 'polliceri ... magistratus, sacerdotia'), techniques which were followed almost to the letter by the Tacitean Sejanus (2.2 'appellando ... neque senatorio ambitu abstinebat clientes suos honoribus aut prouinciis ornandi'). But Sejanus' ambitions nevertheless faced the challenge of the imperial house, which was well supplied with young family members and potential rivals. Evidently his plan was to eliminate them all, starting with Drusus (3.1–2), of whom he was afraid (7.1 'metuebatur') and with whom he had come to blows (3.2 'intenderat Seiano manus et contra tendentis os uerberauerat', a Sallustian sequence: cf. *H.* 5.27 'manum in os intendens'). Trying every means to bring this about (3.3 'cuncta temptanti': cf. Sall. *J.* 70.2 'omnia temptando'), he seduced Livi(ll)a, the wife of Drusus, and urged her to murder her husband (3.3 'necem mariti'); she for her part acquiesced in an uncertain future with Sejanus rather than an honourable present with Drusus (3.4 'pro honestis ... incerta'), while her lover, to convince her of his affection, banished his own wife from their house (3.5 'pellit domo'). Sejanus' manoeuvres here echo those of Catiline, whose desire to marry Aurelia Orestilla had been thwarted by the latter's fear of his son (*C.* 15.2 'timens'): he was believed therefore to have killed his son in order to leave his house empty for his new bride ('creditur necato filio uacuam domum ... fecisse').

To emphasise the deterioration in Tiberius' principate which he is about to describe in the remainder of Book 4 (6.1 'mutati in deterius principatus'), Tacitus now inserts into his narrative a double digression (5–6), in which he summarises the state of the empire up to AD 23 (6.1 'rei publicae partes, quibus modis ... habitae sint'); Sallust had structured his work similarly but for different reasons: in order to emphasise the social and political deterioration of which the Catilinarian conspiracy was symptomatic, he inserts a summary history of Rome (6–13), tracing the change for the worse which had taken place (*C.* 5.9 'quo modo rem publicam habuerint ... immutata'). Sallust was of the opinion that Catiline's alleged murder of his son and his involvement with Aurelia Orestilla constituted the reason why he decided to speed up his crime (*C.* 15.3 'maturandi'), and, while Sejanus was initially compelled by the *magnitudo facinoris* (another Sallustian expression: cf. *J.* 70.5) to act slowly (3.1, 3.5), eventually speed was forced upon him (8.1 'maturandum') because of the antagonism of Drusus.

Drusus' elimination was only the first. In the following year Sejanus manoeuvred against C. Silius and Titius Sabinus (18.1), and, although the case of the latter was temporarily deferred (19.1), the former was put on trial in the senate and compelled to listen to the *princeps* as he emphasised the consul's right and intoned the words of the *senatus consultum ultimum* (19.2): 'nec infringendum consulis ius, cuius uigiliis niteretur ne quod res publica detrimentum caperet'. Not only does this sentence evoke Sallust (*C.* 29.2–3 'darent operam consules ne quid res publica detrimenti caperet. ea potestas per senatum more Romano magistratui maxuma permittitur … aliter sine populi iussu nullius earum rerum consuli ius est') but Tacitus in his own voice adds this comment: 'proprium id Tiberio fuit scelera nuper reperta priscis uerbis obtegere'. The phrase *prisca uerba* was used of Sallust both by Asinius Pollio (Suet. *Gram.* 10.2 'nimia priscorum uerborum adfectatione') and by Lenaeus (ibid. 15.2 'priscorum … uerborum ineruditissimum furem'): the authorial comment confirms beyond all doubt that we are intended to see an allusion to Sallust's account of the Catilinarian conspiracy. The difference, of course, is that in the *Annals* it is not the conspirator at whom the senate's decision is aimed.

Silius anticipated the verdict of the senatorial court by committing suicide (19.4), but the subsequent distribution of his property underlined the rewards that would befall anyone who brought a successful prosecution (20.1–2). In mid-year a father was accused of treason by his son (28.1 'reus pater accusator filius'), and, when the case collapsed and the son left Rome in fear, he was dragged back to face the consequences (29.2 'retractus'). Remarkably a somewhat similar incident is recorded by Sallust: a young man who had left to join Catiline's band was dragged back to Rome by his father and ordered to be killed (*C.* 39.5 'filius quem retractum ex itinere parens necari iussit'). This repetition, however, is quite spectacularly outdone by an episode at the end of the following year. Tacitus' narrative of AD 25 concludes with an account of a 'facinus atrox in citeriore Hispania' (45.1), where L. Piso, the governor of the province ('praetorem prouinciae'), was ambushed on a journey ('in itinere') and killed by a local horseman. Likewise Sallust tells us that in 65 BC a Cn. Piso, who may or may not be an ancestor of the man in Tacitus, was sent as governor to Nearer Spain (*C.* 19.1 'Piso in citeriorem Hispaniam quaestor pro praetore missus'), where local horsemen killed him while travelling (*C.* 19.3 'iter faciens'). There are those who say, comments Sallust by way of explaining *tale facinus*, that the barbarians were unable to tolerate the governor's orders (*C.* 19.4 'imperia eius iniusta, superba, crudelia barbaros nequiuisse pati'), a not dissimilar reason to that provided by Tacitus: the barbarians were unable to tolerate the harshness with which the namesake had tried to retrieve money diverted from the public purse (45.3 'acrius quam ut tolerarent barbari').

'There is perhaps in all things a kind of cycle', remarked Tacitus in Book 3 (55.5 'nisi forte rebus cunctis inest quidam uelut orbis'), and it seems clear not only that he saw Sejanus as a second Catiline but also that in structure and diction he intended to recall and even to assimilate into his own annalistic narrative the monograph of his illustrious predecessor.[7] Since the relevant part of Book 5 has not survived,[8] we do not possess his accounts either of the senatorial meeting at which Sejanus' fate was sealed by a letter from Tiberius or of the minister's

---

[7] In other words the *Bellum Catilinae* is, in the terms of G. B. Conte, Tacitus' 'code model' as well as 'exemplary model' (*The rhetoric of imitation* (1986) 31).

[8] In the Introduction to my commentary on Books 5 and 6 I should have mentioned R. Drews, 'The lacuna in Tacitus' *Annales* Book Five in the light of Christian traditions', *AJAH* 9 (1984) 112–22, a reference I owe to the kindness of Davide Paolillo.

subsequent execution: hence we cannot know whether the Sallustian motif was continued into the final narrative; but the likelihood is that it was. We know that during the reading of Tiberius' letter Sejanus was abandoned by those sitting next to him (Dio 58.10.4 καί τινες καὶ ἐξανέστησαν τῶν συγκαθημένων αὐτῷ), that he was declared *hostis* (*ILS* 157), and that he was led down to the prison by the consul for execution (Dio 58.10.8 ἐς τὸ δεσμωτήριον ... κατήγαγεν). This is strikingly reminiscent of what had happened in the case of the Catilinarian conspiracy, when the benches were deserted on Catiline's entrance to the senate (Cic. *Cat.* 1.16), he was declared *hostis* (*C.* 36.2), and his representative Lentulus was led down by Cicero as consul to the prison for execution (*C.* 55.2 'in carcerem deducit'), Catiline himself having by now left the city. It is difficult to think that Tacitus would not have capitalised on the similarities. Be that as it may, the reader's mind is constantly directed towards Sallust by regular – albeit sometimes fleeting – allusions to the *Bellum Catilinae* both in Book 4 (7.2 'dominandi spes' ~ *C.* 17.5 'dominationis spes'; 14.3 'foeda ... temptari' ~ *C.* 26.5 'temptauerat ... foeda'; 38.5 'altissima cupere' ~ *C.* 5.5 'nimis alta cupiebat'; 44.3 'per decretum senatus' ~ *C.* 51.36 'per senatus decretum'; 65 'haud ... absurdum' ~ *C.* 3.1 and 25.5 'haud absurdum'; 66.2 'suum sanguinem perditum ibat' ~ *C.* 52.12 'ne illi sanguinem ... perditum eant') and in Books 5–6 (5.3.2 'rerum nouarum studium' ~ *C.* 37.1 'nouarum rerum studio' and 57.1 'nouarum rerum studium'; 5.6.2 'per dedecora' ~ *C.* 37.5 'per dedecora'; 6.4.4 'inter ganeam et stupra' ~ *C.* 13.3 'lubido stupri, ganeae'; 6.8.4 'summum ... iudicium' ~ *C.* 29.2 'iudicium summum'; 6.8.6 'consilia caedis' ~ *C.* 18.6 'consilium caedis'; 6.16.3 'culpa uacuus' ~ *C.* 14.4 'a culpa uacuus'; 6.22.1 'sed mihi ... audienti' ~ *C.* 53.2 'sed mihi ... audienti'; 6.22.4 'ne nunc incepto longius abierim' ~ *C.* 7.7 'ni ea res longius nos ab incepto traheret'; 6.24.2 'quasi per dementiam' ~ *C.* 42.2 'ueluti per dementiam'; 6.27.2 'dignationem addiderat' ~ *C.* 54.2 'dignitatem addiderat'; 6.38.1 'quo requiesceret animus a domesticis malis' ~ *C.* 4.1 'ubi animus ex multis miseriis atque

periculis requieuit'; 6.38.3 'ueritatis ... cui adulatio officit' ~
C. 51.2 'uerum ... ubi illa officiunt').

Whether this evidence justifies the perception of further
Sallustian reverberations in Book 4 is perhaps a more open
question. Sallust's story of Cn. Piso is told during his digressive
account of the so-called First Catilinarian Conspiracy, which is
framed by first-person statements designed to underline his
historian's authority (18.1 'de qua quam breuissime potero
dicam' ~ 19.5 'nos eam rem in medio relinquemus'). It may
be pressing matters too far to suggest that Tacitus had this
passage in mind when in a similar digression he discussed the
rumours which had grown up around Drusus' death; but the
first-person statements with which the discussion is framed serve
exactly the same purpose (10.1 ~ 11.3). Likewise the central
excursus in the *Bellum Catilinae* (36.5–39.4), designed to illustrate
the wretched state of the empire at the time of Catiline's conspiracy (C. 36.4 'mihi imperium ... multo maxume miserabile
uisum est'), somewhat resembles in purpose the famous digression on the current state of affairs (32.2 'maestae urbis res') with
which Tacitus concludes his narrative of AD 24 (32–3): there is
certainly some similarity of detail, since the careful manage-
ment of the people is mentioned by both Sallust (C. 39.2 'quo
plebem ... placidius tractarent') and Tacitus (33.2 'plebe ...
quibus modis temperanter haberetur'); but Tacitus' digression
has a historiographical focus which that of Sallust entirely lacks.

Whatever the Sallustian structuring of the narrative, it does
not compromise the more strictly annalistic format evident from
Tacitus' other books and which in Book 4 generates a 'ring'
pattern. The two opening years (23: domestic affairs ~ 24:
domestic/foreign/domestic) are mirrored by the two closing
years (27: domestic ~ 28: domestic/foreign/domestic), while
the two central years are arranged chiastically (25: domestic/
foreign ~ 26: foreign/domestic).[9] The ring is reinforced

---

[9] For the arrangement of these narrative years see Ginsburg 133–5 and
138–41.

thematically: the section at the very start of the book (1–3 'Sejanus and a seduction') is mirrored by a similar section at the very end (74–5 'Sejanus and a wedding'). At the beginning Sejanus is predicted to be a force for destruction even after his death (1.2 'pari exitio uiguit ceciditque'), assembles about him a crowd of clients (2.3), and is so successful in manipulating Tiberius that the *princeps* allows his statues to be worshipped in theatres, market-places and legionary headquarters (2.3); at the end of the book an Altar of Friendship is voted to both Sejanus and Tiberius, and the Campanian shore is filled with the crowds of those hoping for a glimpse of their leaders (74. 2–4), unaware that an equal destruction awaits the losers and winners respectively before and after Sejanus' death (74.5 'quibus ... grauis exitus imminebat'). At the beginning of the book, in order to compass the murder of Drusus, Sejanus seduces Livi(ll)a and leads her to hope of marriage (3); at the end the marriage is that of Cn. Domitius and Agrippina, parents of the murderous Nero (75). Nor is this framing merely formal; it resonates with some of the principal themes of the book. Sejanus' request to Tiberius for the hand of Livi(ll)a (39) introduces the pivotal section where Tiberius' refusal (40) prompts Sejanus to the thought of persuading the *princeps* to leave Rome: in this way he would control access to Tiberius and dispense with the need for his own *clientela* (41).[10]

Sejanus' successful manipulation of Tiberius and his consequent responsibility for the deterioration in the *princeps'* reign are above all manifested in accounts of trials, of which those for *maiestas* have already been brought to the reader's attention (cf. 4.6.2 'maiestatis quaestio'). But here the narrative contains something of a surprise, since the first half of Book 4 is markedly different from the second. There are four cases in AD 23, all minor (13.2, 15.2), and roughly three times as many the following year, including the set trials of C. Silius and his wife Sosia Galla

---

[10] For further discussion of the book's structure see Graf 25–77, G. Wille, *Der Aufbau der Werke des Tacitus* (1983) 416–45 (and 618–23).

(18–20.1) and of the elder and younger Vibius Serenus (28–30.1). In the famous digression at the end of this year Tacitus warns his readers that matters can only get worse from now on (32–3), and, sure enough, the year 25 begins dramatically with the famous set trial of Cremutius Cordus (34–5), which is followed by half a dozen or so other cases (36.1–3, 42.1–3); but, although we have been led to expect the trend to continue and even to worsen, this does not happen: there is one case in 26, involving an allegedly adulterous couple (52.1–3), and another in 27, where the defendant escaped condemnation (66). It is true that the final year of the book begins with the longest and perhaps most memorable trial of all, that of Titius Sabinus (68–71.1), but that is the only trial of the year. How is this sudden and somewhat paradoxical abatement to be explained?[11]

Although the frequency of trials illustrates Sejanus' pretence that Roman society was riven as if in a civil war (4.17.3 'diductam ciuitatem ut ciuili bello'), his larger ambition, as conceived during the course of the book, was to persuade Tiberius to leave Rome (41). This he achieves in AD 26 (57.1), but Tacitus, by means of an elaborate ring composition,[12] distributes the departure between the two years 26–27 and emphasises the significance of the event both at the very start, where there is an extended discussion of the *princeps'* motivation (57.1–3), and at the very end, where there is a geographical description of Capri as a 'foreign' country (67.1–3). The imperial departure constitutes the most important development of the reign; the final year of Book 4, which starts with the trial of Titius Sabinus and ends with Sejanus and Tiberius as virtual co-

---

[11] Book 4 as a whole nevertheless has a larger number of trials than any book apart from 6, which has almost twice as many, and AD 24 has many more trials than any other Tiberian year apart from AD 32: see the statistics in L. Bablitz, 'Tacitus on trial(s)', in L. L. Brice and D. Slootjes (edd.), *Aspects of ancient institutions and geography* (2014) 65–83, who acknowledges the difficulty of deriving precise totals from Tacitus' text.

[12] See *Tac. Rev.* 142–9.

regents (74), shows how things will be in the future and suggests that they can only get worse.

Book 4 comprises the central period of the five into which Tacitus divides the *princeps'* life (above, p. 3). It is the period in which Tiberius begins to change and Sejanus emerges as the false friend determined to seize power for himself; not until the end of the following period, in AD 31, does Tiberius at last recognise Sejanus for what he is, whereupon the minister is executed and the fifth and final period of the *princeps'* life begins. It is perhaps no coincidence that classical drama was conventionally divided into five 'acts' and defined by moments of change (περιπέτεια) and recognition (ἀναγνώρισις).[13] If Augustus could see his own life as a comedy (Suet. *Aug.* 99.1), it may be that his successor's life was seen by Tacitus as a tragedy, of which the last four acts are described in the first six books of the *Annals.* Whether or not that is the case, the narrative of Book 4 is without doubt dramatic. Warfare takes the reader south to Africa (23–6), east to Thrace (46–51) and north to Germany (72–3); a disillusioned veteran leads a slave revolt in southern Italy (27) and a dissident native kills the governor of Nearer Spain (45); there are two parricidal attempts, one fictional (10–11) and the other a failure (28–9), and each rebounds on the perpetrator; a jerry-built amphitheatre collapses at Fidenae (62–3) and the Caelian Hill burns down at Rome (64–5); there are pleas for marriage from Sejanus (39–41) and Agrippina (53) and pleas for cult from Asia (15.3, 55–6) and Further Spain (37–8); and, while some of these various topics suggest continuity with the narratives of Books 1–3, the machinations of Sejanus and Tiberius' withdrawal from Rome look forward to the changed future which is headlined at the start (1.1, 6.1, 7.1) and re-emphasised in the famous digression (32–3). Not without reason did Syme describe this pivotal book as 'the best that Tacitus ever wrote'.[14]

---

[13] For the five-act structure of drama see Brink on Hor. *AP* 189–90, R. J. Tarrant, *HSCP* 82 (1978) 218–21.

[14] Syme, *RP* 3.1031.

TEXT

SIGLA

M	Codex Mediceus siue Laurentianus 68.1 (saec. ix)
M^{mg}	Lectiones in margine codicis scriptae, quarum plerae-que Beroaldo adsignandae sunt
M^{c}	Emendationes additae supra uersum codicis quae pos-terioris manus esse dicuntur

Veteres emendationes suo quamque auctori haud facile quis adsignauerit; de Philippo Beroaldo, qui primus *Annales* I–VI Romae anno 1515 edidit, disputauit Goodyear (1.3–6).

CORNELII TACITI
AB EXCESSV DIVI AVGVSTI
LIBER QVARTVS

1 C. Asinio C. Antistio consulibus nonus Tiberio annus erat AD 23 compositae rei publicae, florentis domus (nam Germanici mortem inter prospera ducebat), cum repente turbare fortuna coepit, saeuire ipse aut saeuientibus uires praebere. Initium et causa penes Aelium Seianum, cohortibus praetoriis praefectum, cuius 5 de potentia supra memoraui; nunc originem, mores et quo facinore dominationem raptum ierit expediam.

2 Genitus Vulsiniis patre Seio Strabone, equite Romano, et prima iuuenta C. Caesarem, diui Augusti nepotem, sectatus, non sine rumore Apicio diuiti et prodigo stuprum ueno dedisse, 10 mox Tiberium uariis artibus deuinxit, adeo ut, obscurum aduersum alios, sibi uni incautum intectumque efficeret, non tam sollertia (quippe isdem artibus uictus est) quam deum ira in **3** rem Romanam, cuius pari exitio uiguit ceciditque. Corpus illi laborum tolerans, animus audax; sui obtegens, in alios crimina- 15 tor; iuxta adulatio et superbia; palam compositus pudor, intus summa apiscendi libido, eiusque causa modo largitio et luxus, *8gv* saepius industria ac uigilantia, | haud minus noxiae quotiens parando regno finguntur.

2 Vim praefecturae modicam antea intendit, dispersas per 20 urbem cohortes una in castra conducendo, ut simul imperia acciperent numeroque et robore et uisu inter se fiducia ipsis, in ceteros metus oreretur. Praetendebat lasciuire militem diductum; si quid subitum ingruat, maiore auxilio pariter subueniri; et seuerius acturos, si uallum statuatur procul urbis inlecebris. 25

INCIPIT LIBER IIII AB EXCESSV DIVI AVGVSTI   **1**   C. Asinio *Beroaldus*: G.
asino *M*   **7**   ierit *Pichena*: perit *M* (captauerit *M^{mg}*)   **8**   Vulsiniis *Beroaldus*
(*M^{mg}*): uulgus sinis *M*   **23**   oreretur *Haase* (oriretur *Faërnus*): credetur *M*:
crederetur *Beroaldus* (*M^{mg}*): *alii alia*   diductum *Beroaldus*: de- *M*

2 Vt perfecta sunt castra, inrepere paulatim militares animos AD 2
adeundo, appellando; simul centuriones ac tribunos ipse deli-
3 gere. Neque senatorio ambitu abstinebat clientes suos honoribus aut prouinciis ornandi, facili Tiberio atque ita prono ut
socium laborum non modo in sermonibus sed apud patres et 5
populum celebraret colique per theatra et fora effigies eius
interque principia legionum sineret.

3 Ceterum plena Caesarum domus: iuuenis filius, nepotes
adulti moram cupitis adferebant, quia ui tot simul corripere
2 intutum et dolus interualla scelerum poscebat. Placuit tamen 10
occultior uia et a Druso incipere, in quem recenti ira ferebatur.
(Nam Drusus impatiens aemuli et animo commotior orto forte
iurgio intenderat Seiano manus et contra tendentis os uerber-
3 auerat.) Igitur cuncta temptanti promptissimum uisum ad
uxorem eius Liuiam conuertere, quae soror Germanici, for- 15
mae initio aetatis indecorae, mox pulchritudine praecellebat. |
9or Hanc, ut amore incensus, adulterio pellexit et, postquam primi
flagitii potitus est (neque femina amissa pudicitia alia
abnuerit), ad coniugii spem, consortium regni et necem mariti
4 impulit. Atque illa—cui auunculus Augustus, socer Tiberius, 20
ex Druso liberi—seque ac maiores et posteros municipali
adultero foedabat, ut pro honestis et praesentibus flagitiosa et
incerta exspectaret. Sumitur in conscientiam Eudemus, ami-
5 cus ac medicus Liuiae, specie artis frequens secretis. Pellit
domo Seianus uxorem Apicatam, ex qua tres liberos genuerat, 25
ne paelici suspectaretur. Sed magnitudo facinoris metum,
prolationes, diuersa interdum consilia adferebat.

4 Interim anni principio Drusus ex Germanici liberis togam
uirilem sumpsit, quaeque fratri eius Neroni decreuerat senatus
repetita. Addidit orationem Caesar multa cum laude filii sui 30
quod patria beneuolentia in fratris liberos foret. Nam Drusus,

8–11 Ceterum ... ferebatur *de interpunctione edd. inter se dissentiunt* **9** et
quia *M* (et *transpos. ante* dolus *Woodman, secl. Nipperdey*): *post* et *lacunam statuit
Fuchs* **10** tamen *M* (*secl. Harlaeus*): tandem *J.F. Gronovius*: itaque *Ruperti
olim* **11** occultior *M*: -re *Ritter* **23** <ad>sumitur *Gerber*

quamquam arduum sit eodem loci potentiam et concordiam AD 23
esse, aequus adulescentibus aut certe non aduersus habebatur.

2   Exin uetus et saepe simulatum proficiscendi in prouincias
consilium refertur. Multitudinem ueteranorum praetexebat
imperator et dilectibus supplendos exercitus: nam uoluntarium 5
militem deesse ac, si suppeditet, non eadem uirtute ac modestia
agere, quia plerumque inopes ac uagi sponte militiam sumant.

3 Percensuitque cursim numerum legionum et quas prouincias
tutarentur; quod mihi quoque exsequendum reor, quae tunc
90v Romana copia in armis, qui socii reges, | quanto sit angustius 10
imperitatum.

5   Italiam utroque mari duae classes Misenum apud et
Rauennam, proximumque Galliae litus rostratae naues praesidebant, quas Actiaca uictoria captas Augustus in oppidum
Foroiuliense miserat ualido cum remige. Sed praecipuum 15
robur Rhenum iuxta, commune in Germanos Gallosque subsidium, octo legiones erant; Hispaniae recens perdomitae tribus

2 habebantur. Mauros Iuba rex acceperat donum populi
Romani; cetera Africae per duas legiones parique numero
Aegyptus, dehinc initio ab Syriae usque ad flumen Euphraten, 20
quantum ingenti terrarum sinu ambitur, quattuor legionibus
coercita, accolis Hibero Albanoque et aliis regibus qui magnitudine nostra proteguntur aduersum externa imperia.

3 Et Thraeciam Rhoemetalces ac liberi Cotyis, ripamque
Danuuii legionum duae in Pannonia, duae in Moesia attinebant, 25
totidem apud Delmatiam locatis, quae positu regionis a tergo illis
ac, si repentinum auxilium Italia posceret, haud procul accirentur, quamquam insideret urbem proprius miles, tres urbanae,
nouem praetoriae cohortes, Etruria ferme Umbriaque delectae

4 aut uetere Latio et coloniis antiquitus Romanis. At apud idonea 30
prouinciarum sociae triremes alaeque et auxilia cohortium,
neque multo secus in iis uirium; sed persequi incertum fuerit,

---

9 <ut noscatur> quae *Novák*   **20** Suriae *Muretus*: suria *M*
25 attinebant *M*: obtinebant *Reeve* **30** coloniis *Lipsius*: -nis *M*   **32** fuerit
Lipsius: fuit *M*

cum ex usu temporis huc illuc mearent, gliscerent numero et AD 23
aliquando minuerentur.

6 Congruens crediderim recensere ceteras quoque rei publicae
9ʳʳ partes, quibus modis | ad eam diem habitae sint, quoniam
Tiberio mutati in deterius principatus initium ille annus attulit. 5

2 Iam primum publica negotia et priuatorum maxima apud
patres tractabantur, dabaturque primoribus disserere et in adulationem lapsos cohibebat ipse; mandabatque honores nobilitatem maiorum, claritudinem militiae, inlustres domi artes
spectando, ut satis constaret non alios potiores fuisse. Sua con- 10
sulibus, sua praetoribus species; minorum quoque magistratuum exercita potestas; legesque, si maiestatis quaestio

3 eximeretur, bono in usu. At frumenta et pecuniae uectigales,
cetera publicorum fructuum societatibus equitum Romanorum
agitabantur. Res suas Caesar spectatissimo cuique, quibusdam 15
ignotis ex fama mandabat, semelque adsumpti tenebantur prorsus sine modo, cum plerique isdem negotiis insenescerent.

4 Plebes acri quidem annona fatigabatur, sed nulla in eo culpa
ex principe: quin infecunditati terrarum aut asperis maris
obuiam iit, quantum impendio diligentiaque poterat. Et ne 20
prouinciae nouis oneribus turbarentur utque uetera sine auaritia aut crudelitate magistratuum tolerarent prouidebat.
Corporum uerbera, ademptiones bonorum aberant. Rari per
Italiam Caesaris agri, modesta seruitia, intra paucos libertos
domus; ac, si quando cum priuatis disceptaret, forum et ius. 25

7 Quae cuncta non quidem comi uia, sed horridus ac plerum-
9ʳᵛ que formidatus, retinebat tamen| donec morte Drusi uerteren-
tur: nam, dum superfuit, mansere, quia Seianus incipiente
adhuc potentia bonis consiliis notescere uolebat, et ultor metuebatur non occultus odii set crebro querens incolumi filio adiu- 30

2 torem imperii alium uocari; et quantum superesse ut collega
dicatur! primas dominandi spes in arduo; ubi sis ingressus,
adesse studia et ministros; exstructa iam sponte praefecti castra,

---

4 quoniam *uulg.*: qũo *M*   **18** acri *Rhenanus*: agri *M*   **30** odii *Lipsius*,
set *Doederlein*: odiis et *M*

datos in manum milites; cerni effigiem eius in monimentis Cn.   AD 23
Pompei; communes illi cum familia Drusorum fore nepotes:
3 precandam post haec modestiam, ut contentus esset? Neque
raro neque apud paucos talia iaciebat, et secreta quoque eius
8 corrupta uxore prodebantur. Igitur Seianus maturandum ratus 5
deligit uenenum quo paulatim inrepente fortuitus morbus adsimularetur. Id Druso datum per Lygdum spadonem, ut octo post
annos cognitum est.

2   Ceterum Tiberius per omnes ualetudinis eius dies nullo
metu an ut firmitudinem animi ostentaret; etiam defuncto 10
necdum sepulto curiam ingressus est, consulesque sede uulgari
per speciem maestitiae sedentes honoris locique admonuit et
effusum in lacrimas senatum uicto gemitu simul oratione con-
3 tinua erexit: non quidem sibi ignarum posse argui quod tam
recenti dolore subierit oculos senatus; uix propinquorum adlo- 15
quia tolerari, uix diem aspici a plerisque lugentium; neque illos
imbecillitatis damnandos; se tamen fortiora solacia e com-
92r plexu rei publicae peti | uisse. Miseratusque Augustae extre-
mam senectam, rudem adhuc nepotum et uergentem aetatem
suam, ut Germanici liberi, unica praesentium malorum leua- 20
4 menta, inducerentur petiuit. Egressi consules firmatos adloquio adulescentulos deductosque ante Caesarem statuunt.
Quibus adprensis 'Patres conscripti, hos', inquit, 'orbatos
parente tradidi patruo ipsorum precatusque sum, quamquam
esset illi propria suboles, ne secus quam suum sanguinem 25
5 foueret, attolleret, sibique et posteris confirmaret. Erepto
Druso preces ad uos conuerto disque et patria coram obtestor:
Augusti pronepotes, clarissimis maioribus genitos, suscipite,
regite, uestram meamque uicem explete. Hi uobis, Nero et
Druse, parentum loco: ita nati estis ut bona malaque uestra ad 30
rem publicam pertineant.'

---

10 *post* ostentaret *sententiam concludit Woodman, continuant alii*   **24** parenti
(*suprascr.* e) *M*   **26** attolleret *M*: ac tolleret *Beroaldus*   confirmaret *Lipsius*:
conformaret *M* (*primo* –irm- *dein* –orm- *scripsisse librarius uidetur*)

9 Magno ea fletu et mox precationibus faustis audita; ac, si AD 2?
modum orationi posuisset, misericordia sui gloriaque animos
audientium impleuerat; ad uana et totiens inrisa reuolutus, de
reddenda re publica utque consules seu quis alius regimen
susciperent, uero quoque et honesto fidem dempsit. 5

2 Memoriae Drusi eadem quae in Germanicum decernuntur,
plerisque additis, ut ferme amat posterior adulatio. Funus imaginum pompa maxime inlustre fuit, cum origo Iuliae gentis Aeneas
omnesque Albanorum reges et conditor urbis Romulus, post
Sabina nobilitas, Attus Clausus ceteraeque Claudiorum effigies 10
longo ordine spectarentur.

92v 10 In tradenda | morte Drusi quae plurimis maximaeque fidei
auctoribus memorata sunt rettuli; sed non omiserim eorundem
temporum rumorem ualidum adeo ut nondum exolescat:

2 corrupta ad scelus Liuia Seianum Lygdi quoque spadonis ani- 15
mum stupro uinxisse, quod is [Lygdus] aetate atque forma carus
domino interque primores ministros erat; deinde, inter conscios
ubi locus ueneficii tempusque composita sint, eo audaciae
prouectum ut uerteret et occulto indicio Drusum ueneni in
patrem arguens moneret Tiberium uitandam potionem quae 20
3 prima ei apud filium epulanti offerretur; ea fraude captum
senem, postquam conuiuium inierat, exceptum poculum
Druso tradidisse, atque illo ignaro et iuueniliter hauriente auctam suspicionem tamquam metu et pudore sibimet inrogaret
mortem quam patri struxerat. 25

11 Haec uulgo iactata, super id quod nullo auctore certo firmantur, prompte refutaueris. Quis enim mediocri prudentia,
nedum Tiberius tantis rebus exercitus, inaudito filio exitium
offerret, idque sua manu et nullo ad paenitendum regressu?
Quin potius ministrum ueneni excruciaret, auctorem exquir- 30
eret, insita denique etiam in extraneos cunctatione et mora
aduersum unicum et nullius ante flagitii compertum uteretur?

---

12 maximaeque fidei *Ritter*: maxime que fideis *M*: maximeque fidis
Beroaldus **16** Lygdus *secl. Ernesti* **21** ei *Rhenanus*: et *M* captum
Muretus: cum *M*: deceptum *uel* inlectum *Heinsius* **32** unicum <filium>
Prammer

2 Sed, quia Seianus facinorum omnium repertor habebatur, ex AD 23
nimia caritate in eum Caesaris et ceterorum in utrumque odio
93ʳ quamuis fabulosa et immania credebantur, atroci|ore semper
fama erga dominantium exitus. Ordo alioqui sceleris per
Apicatam Seiani proditus, tormentis Eudemi ac Lygdi patefactus 5
est; neque quisquam scriptor tam infensus extitit ut Tiberio
3 obiectaret, cum omnia alia conquirerent intenderentque. Mihi
tradendi arguendique rumoris causa fuit ut claro sub exemplo
falsas auditiones depellerem peteremque ab iis quorum in manus
cura nostra uenerit <ne> diuulgata atque incredibilia auide 10
accepta ueris neque in miraculum corruptis antehabeant.

12 Ceterum laudante filium pro rostris Tiberio senatus populus-
que habitum ac uoces dolentum simulatione magis quam libens
induebat, domumque Germanici reuirescere occulti laetaban-
tur. Quod principium *** fauoris et mater Agrippina spem male 15
2 tegens perniciem adcelerauere. Nam Seianus, ubi uidet mortem
Drusi inultam interfectoribus, sine maerore publico esse, ferax
scelerum et quia prima prouenerant, uolutare secum quonam
modo Germanici liberos peruerteret, quorum non dubia suc-
cessio. Neque spargi uenenum in tres poterat, egregia custodum 20
3 fide et pudicitia Agrippinae impenetrabili. Igitur contumaciam
eius insectari, uetus Augustae odium, recentem Liuiae conscientiam exagitare, ut superbam fecunditate, subnixam popularibus
4 studiis inhiare dominationi apud Caesarem arguerent. Atque
haec callidis criminatoribus, inter quos delegerat Iulium 25
Postumum, per adulterium Mutiliae Priscae inter intimos auiae
93ᵛ et consiliis suis peridoneum, quia Prisca in animo Aug|ustae
ualida anum suapte natura potentiae anxiam insociabilem
nurui efficiebat. Agrippinae quoque proximi inliciebantur prauis
sermonibus tumidos spiritus perstimulare. 30

---

10 ne *suppl. hic Rhenanus, ante* auide *Ritter* incredibili (*suprascr.* a) M (*secl.*
Nipperdey) 15 *lacunam statuit Woodman* 17 inultam *Beroaldus*: mul-
tam M ferax *Hartman*: ferox M 23 superbam *Muretus*: -iam M
24 Atque M: alitque *Madvig*: agitque *Fuchs*: adque *Muretus* 26 auiae M:
aulae *J. Müller*: Liuiae *Ritter*

CORNELII TACITI

13   At Tiberius nihil intermissa rerum cura, negotia pro solaciis AD 2?
accipiens, ius ciuium, preces sociorum tractabat; factaque auctore eo senatus consulta ut ciuitati Cibyraticae apud Asiam,
Aegiensi apud Achaiam motu terrae labefactis subueniretur
2 remissione tributi in triennium. Et Vibius Serenus pro consule 5
ulterioris Hispaniae de ui publica damnatus ob atrocitatem
temporum in insulam Amorgum deportatur. Cars<id>ius
Sacerdos, reus tamquam frumento hostem Tacfarinatem iuuis-
3 set, absoluitur, eiusdemque criminis C. Gracchus. Hunc comi-
tem exilii admodum infantem pater Sempronius in insulam 10
Cercinam tulerat. Illic adultus inter extorres et liberalium
artium nescios, mox per Africam ac Siciliam mutando sordidas
merces sustentabatur; neque tamen effugit magnae fortunae
pericula. Ac, ni Aelius Lamia et L. Apronius, qui Africam
obtinuerant, insontem protexissent, claritudine infausti generis 15
et paternis aduersis foret abstractus.

14   Is quoque annus legationes Graecarum ciuitatium habuit,
Samiis Iunonis, Cois Aesculapii delubro uetustum asyli ius ut
firmaretur petentibus. Samii decreto Amphictyonum nitebantur, quis praecipuum fuit rerum omnium iudicium ea tempes- 20
tate qua Graeci conditis per Asiam urbibus ora maris
94r 2 potiebantur. | Neque dispar apud Coos antiquitas, et accedebat
meritum ex loco: nam ciues Romanos templo Aesculapii indux-
erant cum iussu regis Mithridatis apud cunctas Asiae insulas et
urbes trucidarentur. 25
3 Variis dehinc et saepius inritis praetorum questibus, postremo Caesar de immodestia histrionum rettulit: multa ab iis in
publicum seditiose, foeda per domos temptari; Oscum quondam ludicrum, leuissimae apud uulgum oblectationis, eo flagitiorum et uirium uenisse ut auctoritate patrum coercendum sit. 30
Pulsi tum histriones Italia.

7   temporum *M*: morum *Lipsius*   Cars<id>ius *Reinesius*   **20–1**   ea qua
tempestate *M, transpos. Rhenanus* (*qui et de* ea *secludendo cogitauit*)   **30**   ut *M^{mg}*,
om. M   **31**   tum *Beroaldus* (*M^{mg}*): dum *M*

15 Idem annus alio quoque luctu Caesarem adfecit alterum ex AD 23
geminis Drusi liberis exstinguendo, neque minus morte amici. Is
fuit Lucilius Longus, omnium illi tristium laetorumque socius
2 unusque e senatoribus Rhodii secessus comes. Ita, quamquam
nouo homini, censorium funus, effigiem apud forum Augusti 5
publica pecunia patres decreuere, apud quos etiam tum cuncta
tractabantur, adeo ut procurator Asiae Lucilius Capito accusante prouincia causam dixerit, magna cum adseueratione principis non se ius nisi in seruitia et pecunias familiares dedisse;
quod si uim praetoris usurpasset manibusque militum usus 10
foret, spreta in eo mandata sua: audirent socios. Ita reus cognito
3 negotio damnatur. Ob quam ultionem et quia priore anno in C.
Silanum uindicatum erat, decreuere Asiae urbes templum
Tiberio matrique eius ac senatui. Et permissum statuere; egit-
94v que Nero grates ea causa patribus atque auo, laetas | inter 15
audientium adfectiones, qui recenti memoria Germanici illum
aspici, illum audiri rebantur. Aderantque iuueni modestia ac
forma principe uiro digna, notis in eum Seiani odiis ob periculum gratiora.

16 Sub idem tempus de flamine Diali in locum Serui 20
Maluginensis defuncti legendo, simul roganda noua lege disser-
2 uit Caesar: nam patricios confarreatis parentibus genitos tres
simul nominari, ex quis unus legeretur, uetusto more; neque
adesse, ut olim, eam copiam, omissa confarreandi adsuetudine
aut inter paucos retenta (pluresque eius rei causas adferebat, 25
potissimam penes incuriam uirorum feminarumque); accedere
ipsius caerimoniae difficultates, quae consulto uitarentur, et
quod exiret e iure patrio qui id flamonium apisceretur quaeque
3 in manum flaminis conueniret: ita medendum senatus decreto
aut lege, sicut Augustus quaedam ex horrida illa antiquitate ad 30
praesentem usum flexisset. Igitur tractatis religionibus placitum

---

1 adfecit *Ritter:* adficit *M* **23** <debere> nominari *Fuchs* **26** *par-
enthesin proferunt usque ad* uitarentur *edd. plerique* acceder& *M (puncto subiecto):*
accedere et *Jac. Gronouius* **27** *post* uitarentur *lacunam statuit Lipsius* **28** quod
Ritter olim: quõ *M:* quando *Beroaldus:* quoniam *Orelli, Ritter (lacunam post*
conueniret *statuens)*

instituto flaminum nihil demutari; sed lata lex qua flaminica AD 23
Dialis sacrorum causa in potestate uiri, cetera promisco femin-
4 arum iure ageret. Et filius Maluginensis patri suffectus. Vtque
glisceret dignatio sacerdotum atque ipsis promptior animus
foret ad capessendas caerimonias, decretum Corneliae uirgini, 5
quae in locum Scantiae capiebatur, sestertii uiciens et, quotiens
Augusta theatrum introisset, ut sedes inter Vestalium
consideret.

17 Cornelio Cethego Visellio Varrone consulibus pontifices eor- AD 24
95ʳ umque | exemplo ceteri sacerdotes, cum pro incolumitate prin- 10
cipis uota susciperent, Neronem quoque et Drusum isdem dis
commendauere, non tam caritate iuuenum quam adulatione,
quae moribus corruptis proinde anceps si nulla et ubi nimia est.
2 Nam Tiberius, haud umquam domui Germanici mitis, tum
uero aequari adulescentes senectae suae impatienter indoluit 15
accitosque pontifices percontatus est num id precibus
Agrippinae aut minis tribuissent. Et illi quidem, quamquam
abnuerent, modice perstricti (etenim pars magna e propinquis
ipsius aut primores ciuitatis erant); ceterum in senatu oratione
monuit in posterum ne quis mobiles adulescentium animos 20
3 praematuris honoribus ad superbiam extolleret. Instabat
quippe Seianus incusabatque diductam ciuitatem ut ciuili
bello: esse qui se partium Agrippinae uocent ac, ni resistatur,
fore plures; neque aliud gliscentis discordiae remedium quam si
unus alterue maxime prompti subuerterentur. 25

18 Qua causa C. Silium et Titium Sabinum adgreditur. Amicitia
Germanici perniciosa utrique, Silio et quod ingentis exercitus
septem per annos moderator partisque apud Germaniam tri-
umphalibus Sacrouiriani belli uictor, quanto maiore mole
2 procideret, plus formidinis in alios dispergebatur. Credebant 30
plerique auctam offensionem ipsius intemperantia, immodice
iactantis suum militem in obsequio durauisse, cum alii ad sedi-
95ᵛ tiones prolaberentur; | neque mansurum Tiberio imperium si

---

13 proinde *M*: perinde *Rhenanus*   **30** procideret *Rhenanus*: procederet *M*

3 iis quoque legionibus cupido nouandi fuisset. Destrui per haec AD 24
fortunam suam Caesar imparemque tanto merito rebatur. Nam
beneficia eo usque laeta sunt dum uidentur exsolui posse; ubi
multum anteuenere, pro gratia odium redditur.

19 Erat uxor Silio Sosia Galla, caritate Agrippinae inuisa prin- 5
cipi. Hos corripi dilato ad tempus Sabino placitum, immissus-
que Varro consul qui paternas inimicitias obtendens odiis
2 Seiani per dedecus suum gratificabatur. Precante reo breuem
moram dum accusator consulatu abiret, aduersatus est Caesar:
solitum quippe magistratibus diem priuatis dicere; nec infrin- 10
gendum consulis ius, cuius uigiliis niteretur ne quod res publica
detrimentum caperet. (Proprium id Tiberio fuit scelera nuper
3 reperta priscis uerbis obtegere.) Igitur multa adseueratione,
quasi aut legibus cum Silio ageretur aut Varro consul aut illud
res publica esset, coguntur patres. Silente reo uel, si defensio- 15
4 nem coeptaret, non occultante cuius ira premeretur, conscientia
belli Sacrouir diu dissimulatus, uictoria per auaritiam foedata et
uxor socia arguebantur. Nec dubie repetundarum criminibus
haerebant, sed cuncta quaestione maiestatis exercita, et Silius
imminentem   damnationem   uoluntario   fine   praeuertit. 20
20 Saeuitum tamen in bona, non ut stipendiariis pecuniae red-
96r derentur, quorum nemo repetebat, sed liberalitas | Augusti
auulsa, computatis singillatim quae fisco petebantur. Ea prima
Tiberio erga pecuniam alienam diligentia fuit.
    Sosia in exilium pellitur Asinii Galli sententia, qui partem 25
bonorum publicandam, pars ut liberis relinqueretur censuerat.
2 Contra M. Lepidus quartam accusatoribus secundum necessi-
tudinem legis, cetera liberis concessit. Hunc ego Lepidum temporibus illis grauem et sapientem uirum fuisse comperior: nam
pleraque ab saeuis adulationibus aliorum in melius flexit; neque 30
tamen temperamenti egebat, cum aequabili auctoritate et gratia
3 apud Tiberium uiguerit. Vnde dubitare cogor, fato et sorte

---

2 imparemque <se> *edd. nonnulli*   **12** proprium *Beroaldus* (M^{mg}): quo
prium *M*   **15** *alii sententiam ultra* patres *usque ad* premeretur *continuare*
malunt   **18** socia (*suprascr.* s) *M*

nascendi, ut cetera, ita principum inclinatio in hos, offensio in AD 20
illos, an sit aliquid in nostris consiliis liceatque inter abruptam
contumaciam et deforme obsequium pergere iter ambitione ac
4 periculis uacuum. At Messalinus Cotta haud minus claris
maioribus sed animo diuersus censuit cauendum senatus con- 5
sulto ut quamquam insontes magistratus et culpae alienae nescii
prouincialibus uxorum criminibus proinde quam suis
plecterentur.

21   Actum dehinc de Calpurnio Pisone, nobili ac feroci uiro. Is
namque (ut rettuli) cessurum se urbe ob factiones accusatorum 10
in senatu clamitauerat et spreta potentia Augustae trahere in ius
Vrgulaniam domoque principis excire ausus erat. Quae in
praesens Tiberius ciuiliter habuit; sed in animo reuoluente
iras, etiam si impetus offensionis languerat, memoria ualebat.
2 Pisonem Q. Veranius secreti sermonis incusauit aduersum 15
96v maiestatem habiti, adiecitque | in domo eius uenenum esse
eumque gladio accinctum introire curiam. Quod ut atrocius
uero tramissum; ceterorum, quae multa cumulabantur, receptus est reus neque peractus ob mortem opportunam.

3   Relatum et de Cassio Seuero exule, qui sordidae originis, 20
maleficae uitae sed orandi ualidus, per immodicas inimicitias ut
iudicio iurati senatus Cretam amoueretur effecerat; atque illic
eadem factitando recentia ueteraque odia aduertit, bonisque
exutus, interdicto igni atque aqua, saxo Seripho consenuit.

22   Per idem tempus Plautius Siluanus praetor incertis causis 25
Aproniam coniugem in praeceps iecit, tractusque ad
Caesarem ab L. Apronio socero turbata mente respondit tamquam ipse somno grauis atque eo ignarus, et uxor sponte
2 mortem sumpsisset. Non cunctanter Tiberius pergit in
domum, uisit cubiculum, in quo reluctantis et impulsae uestigia 30
cernebantur. Refert ad senatum, datisque iudicibus Vrgulania
Siluani auia pugionem nepoti misit. Quod perinde creditum

---

7 perinde *Beroaldus*   **15** Pisonem Q. Veranius *Syme*: pisonemque
grauius *M*: Pisonem Q. Granius *Lipsius*   **23** factitando *Woodman*: actitando *M*

quasi principis monitu ob amicitiam Augustae cum Vrgulania. AD 24

3 Reus frustra temptato ferro uenas praebuit exsoluendas. Mox Numantina, prior uxor eius, accusata iniecisse carminibus et ueneficiis uaecordiam marito, insons iudicatur.

23 Is demum annus populum Romanum longo aduersum 5 Numidam Tacfarinatem bello absoluit. Nam priores duces, ubi impetrando triumphalium insigni sufficere res suas crediderant, *97r* hostem | omittebant; iamque tres laureatae in urbe statuae, et adhuc raptabat Africam Tacfarinas, auctus Maurorum auxiliis, qui, Ptolemaeo Iubae filio iuuenta incurioso, libertos regios et 10 2 seruilia imperia bello mutauerant. Erat illi praedarum receptor ac socius populandi rex Garamantum, non ut cum exercitu incederet sed missis leuibus copiis quae ex longinquo in maius audiebantur; ipsaque e prouincia ut quis fortunae inops, moribus turbidus, promptius ruebant, quia Caesar post res a Blaeso gestas 15 quasi nullis iam in Africa hostibus reportari nonam legionem iusserat, nec pro consule eius anni P. Dolabella retinere ausus erat, iussa principis magis quam incerta belli metuens.

24 Igitur Tacfarinas disperso rumore rem Romanam aliis quoque ab nationibus lacerari eoque paulatim Africa decedere, ac posse 20 reliquos circumueniri si cuncti quibus libertas seruitio potior incubuissent, auget uires positisque castris Thubursicum oppi-2 dum circumsidet. At Dolabella contracto quod erat militum, terrore nominis Romani et quia Numidae peditum aciem ferre nequeunt, primo sui incessu soluit obsidium locorumque oppor- 25 tuna permuniuit; simul principes Musulamiorum defectionem 3 coeptantes securi percutit. Dein, quia pluribus aduersum Tacfarinatem expeditionibus cognitum non graui nec uno incursu consectandum hostem uagum, excito cum popularibus rege Ptolemaeo quattuor agmina parat, quae legatis aut tribunis 30 *97v* data; | et praedatorias manus delecti Maurorum duxere. Ipse consultor aderat omnibus.

---

6 ubi *Lipsius*: sub *M* **14** fortunae *Beroaldus*: -ne *M*: -na *Halm*
22 Thubursicum *Nipperdey*: Thubuscum *M* **25** sui *M*: sub *Heinsius*
30 rege Ptolemaeo *Beroaldus*: recepto leameo *M*

25 Nec multo post adfertur Numidas apud castellum semiru- AD 2
tum, ab ipsis quondam incensum, cui nomen Auzea, positis
mapalibus consedisse, fisos loco quia uastis circum saltibus
claudebatur. Tum expeditae cohortes alaeque, quam in partem
2 ducerentur ignarae, cito agmine rapiuntur; simulque coeptus 5
dies et concentu tubarum ac truci clamore aderant semisomnos
in barbaros, praepeditis Numidarum equis aut diuersos pastus
pererrantibus. Ab Romanis confertus pedes, dispositae turmae,
cuncta proelio prouisa; hostibus contra omnium nesciis non
arma, non ordo, non consilium, sed pecorum modo trahi, 10
3 occidi, capi. Infensus miles memoria laborum et aduersum
eludentes optatae totiens pugnae se quis<que> ultione et sanguine explebant. Differtur per manipulos Tacfarinatem omnes,
notum tot proeliis, consectentur: non nisi duce interfecto
requiem belli fore. At ille deiectis circum stipatoribus uinctoque 15
iam filio et effusis undique Romanis ruendo in tela captiuitatem
haud inulta morte effugit. Isque finis armis impositus.

26 Dolabellae petenti abnuit triumphalia Tiberius, Seiano tribuens ne Blaesi auunculi eius laus obsolesceret. Sed neque
Blaesus ideo inlustrior et huic negatus honor gloriam intendit: 20
quippe minore exercitu insignes captiuos, caedem ducis belli-
2 que confecti famam deportarat. Sequebantur et Garamantum |
98r   legati, raro in urbe uisi, quos Tacfarinate caeso perculsa gens
nec culpae nescia ad satis faciendum populo Romano miserat.
Cognitis dehinc Ptolemaei per id bellum studiis repetitus ex 25
uetusto more <honor>, missusque e senatoribus qui scipionem
eburnum, togam pictam, antiqua patrum munera, daret regemque et socium atque amicum appellaret.

27 Eadem aestate mota per Italiam seruilis belli semina fors
oppressit. Auctor tumultus T. Curtisius, quondam praetoriae 30

12 se quisque *Beroaldus* (M^{mg}): siquis *M*   **15** deiectis *J.F. Gronovius*: delectis
M: disiectis *Mercerus*   **16** offusis *Lipsius*: circumfusis *Haase*   **17** inulta *Beroaldus*:
multa *M*   **24** nec culpae nescia *Ryckius*: et c- nescia *M*: et c- conscia *Lipsius*: alii
alia   **26** honos *ante* missusque *suppleuit Doederlein*: o̧missusque *M*: ex uetusto
mos, missusque *Lipsius*: alii alia   **30** Curtisius *M*: Curtilius *Reinesius*

cohortis miles, primo coetibus clandestinis apud Brundisium et AD 24
circumiecta oppida, mox positis propalam libellis ad libertatem
uocabat agrestia per longinquos saltus et ferocia seruitia, cum
uelut munere deum tres biremes adpulere ad usus commean-
2 tium illo mari. Et erat isdem regionibus Cutius Lupus quaestor, 5
cui prouincia uetere ex more calles euenerant: is disposita
classiariorum copia coeptantem cum maxime coniurationem
disiecit. Missusque a Caesare propere Staius tribunus cum
ualida manu ducem ipsum et proximos audacia in urbem traxit
iam trepidam ob multitudinem familiarum, quae gliscebat 10
immensum, minore in dies plebe ingenua.

28 Isdem consulibus, miseriarum ac saeuitiae exemplum atrox,
reus pater, accusator filius (nomen utrique Vibius Serenus) in
senatum inducti sunt. Ab exilio retractus inluuieque ac squalore
obsitus et tum catena uinctus peroranti filio <pater> praepar- 15
2 atur. Adulescens multis munditiis, alacri uultu, structas principi
insidias, missos in Galliam concitores belli index idem et testis |
98v dicebat, adnectebatque Caecilium Cornutum praetorium min-
istrauisse pecuniam; qui, taedio curarum et quia periculum pro
3 exitio habebatur, mortem in se festinauit. At contra reus nihil 20
infracto animo obuersus in filium quatere uincla, uocare ultores
deos ut sibi quidem redderent exilium ubi procul tali more
ageret, filium autem quandoque supplicia sequerentur.
Adseuerabatque innocentem Cornutum et falso exterritum;
idque facile intellectu, si proderentur alii: non enim se caedem 25
principis et res nouas uno socio cogitasse.

29 Tum accusator Cn. Lentulum et Seium Tuberonem nominat, magno pudore Caesaris, cum primores ciuitatis, intimi
ipsius amici, Lentulus senectutis extremae, Tubero defecto corpore, tumultus hostilis et turbandae rei publicae accerserentur. 30
Sed hi quidem statim exempti; in patrem ex seruis quaesitum et
2 quaestio aduersa accusatori fuit. Qui scelere uecors, simul uulgi

3 ferocia uel ferociora Beroaldus (M^{mg}): feroricia M   6 Cales Lipsius
euenerant Haase: -erat M   13 utrique Chifflet, Lipsius: uiriq; M   15 pater
suppl. Martin et Woodman: peroranti filio pater comparatur Madvig: pater oranti
filio comparatur Halm: alii alia   24 falso Ursinus: -sa M   25 si M, secl.
Hartman: ni Neue   30 arcesserentur Lipsius

rumore territus, robur et saxum aut parricidarum poenas mini- AD 2
tantium, cessit urbe. Ac retractus Rauenna exsequi accusationem adigitur, non occultante Tiberio uetus odium aduersum
3 exulem Serenum. Nam post damnatum Libonem missis ad
Caesarem litteris exprobrauerat suum tantum studium sine 5
fructu fuisse, addideratque quaedam contumacius quam
tutum apud aures superbas et offensioni proniores. Ea Caesar
octo post annos rettulit, medium tempus uarie arguens, etiam si
tormenta peruicacia seruorum contra euenissent.

30   Dictis dein sententiis ut Serenus more maiorum puniretur, 10
99r quo molliret | inuidiam intercessit. Gallus Asinius Gyaro aut
Donusa claudendum <cum> censeret, id quoque aspernatus
est, egenam aquae utramque insulam referens dandosque uitae
usus cui uita concederetur. Ita Serenus Amorgum reportatur.
2 Et, quia Cornutus sua manu ceciderat, actum de praemiis 15
accusatorum abolendis, si quis maiestatis postulatus ante per-
fectum iudicium se ipse uita priuauisset. Ibaturque in eam
sententiam, ni durius contraque morem suum palam pro accusatoribus Caesar inritas leges, rem publicam in praecipiti conquestus esset: subuerterent potius iura quam custodes eorum 20
3 amouerent. Sic delatores, genus hominum publico exitio repertum et <ne> poenis quidem umquam satis coercitum, per
praemia eliciebantur.
31   His tam adsiduis tamque maestis modica laetitia intericitur,
quod C. Cominium equitem Romanum, probrosi in se carminis 25
conuictum, Caesar precibus fratris, qui senator erat, concessit.
2 Quo magis mirum habebatur gnarum meliorum et quae fama
clementiam sequeretur tristiora malle. Neque enim socordia
peccabat; nec occultum est quando ex ueritate, quando adumbrata laetitia facta imperatorum celebrentur. Quin ipse, compo- 30
situs alias et uelut eluctantium uerborum, solutius promptiusque
3 eloquebatur quotiens subueniret. At P. Suillium, quaestorem

12 cum *suppl. hic Muretus, ante* Gyaro *Nipperdey* **14** Amorgum *Rhenanus:*
amor cum *M* **18** ni durius *Beroaldus* (*M^{mg}*): medurius *M* **22** <ne>
Bekker (et poenis quidem numquam *Beroaldus*)

quondam Germanici, cum Italia arceretur conuictus pecuniam AD 24
ob rem iudicandam cepisse, amouendum in insulam censuit,
99v tanta contentione animi ut <se iur>e iurando | obstringeret e
re publica id esse; quod aspere acceptum ad praesens mox in
laudem uertit regresso Suillio, quem uidit sequens aetas prae- 5
potentem, uenalem et Claudii principis amicitia diu prospere,
4 numquam bene usum. Eadem poena in Catum Firmium
senatorem statuitur, tamquam falsis maiestatis criminibus sor-
orem petiuisset. Catus (ut rettuli) Libonem inlexerat insidiis,
deinde indicio perculerat. Eius operae memor Tiberius, sed 10
alia praetendens, exilium deprecatus est; quominus senatu
pelleretur non obstitit.

32 Pleraque eorum quae rettuli quaeque referam parua forsitan
et leuia memoratu uideri non nescius sum; set nemo annales
nostros cum scriptura eorum contenderit qui ueteres populi 15
Romani res composuere. Ingentia illi bella, expugnationes
urbium, fusos captosque reges aut, si quando ad interna
praeuerterent, discordias consulum aduersum tribunos, agrari-
as frumentariasque leges, plebis et optimatium certamina libero
2 egressu memorabant. Nobis in arto et inglorius labor: immota 20
quippe aut modice lacessita pax, maestae urbis res et princeps
proferendi imperi incuriosus erat. Non tamen sine usu fuerit
introspicere illa primo aspectu leuia, ex quis magnarum saepe
33 rerum motus oriuntur. Nam cunctas nationes et urbes populus
aut primores aut singuli regunt. (Delecta ex iis et conflata rei 25
publicae forma laudari facilius quam euenire uel, si euenit,
2 [haud] diuturna esse potest.) Igitur ut olim, plebe ualida uel
100r cum patres pollerent, noscenda uulgi natura | et quibus modis
temperanter haberetur, senatusque et optimatium ingenia qui
maxime   perdidicerant   callidi   temporum   et   sapientes 30

---

3 ut <se iur>e *Woodman* (*iam* <se> *Doederlein*, <iur>e *Ritter*): uteiurando *M*   **9** Libonem *Beroaldus* (*M^mg*): tib- *M*   **10** indicio *Vertranius*:
iudicio *M*   **15** ueteris *Freinsheim* **16** composuere *Beroaldus*: cōpossiuere *M*
20   immota *Beroaldus* (*M^mg*): immo ita *M*   **25**   ex iis <iii> *E. Harrison*:
conflata *Kiessling*: consciata *M*: consociata *Ernesti*: *alii alia*   **27**   haud *secl.*
Madvig

credebantur, sic, conuerso statu neque alia <fiducia> rerum AD 2'
quam si unus imperitet, haec conquiri tradique in rem fuerit,
quia pauci prudentia honesta ab deterioribus, utilia ab noxiis
3 discernunt, plures aliorum euentis docentur. Ceterum, ut profutura, ita minimum oblectationis adferunt. Nam situs gentium, 5
uarietates proeliorum, clari ducum exitus retinent ac redintegrant legentium animum; nos saeua iussa, continuas accusationes, fallaces amicitias, perniciem innocentium et easdem
exitii causas coniungimus, obuia rerum similitudine et satietate.
4 Tum <adnotatum> quod antiquis scriptoribus rarus obtrecta- 10
tor, neque refert cuiusquam Punicas Romanasne acies laetius
extuleris; at multorum qui Tiberio regente poenam uel infamias
subiere posteri manent; utque familiae ipsae iam extinctae sint,
reperies qui ob similitudinem morum aliena malefacta sibi
obiectari putent. Etiam gloria ac uirtus infensos habet, ut 15
nimis ex propinquo diuersa arguens. Sed ad inceptum redeo.
34 Cornelio Cosso Asinio Agrippa consulibus Cremutius AD 2'
Cordus postulatur nouo ac tunc primum audito crimine, quod
editis annalibus laudatoque M. Bruto C. Cassium Romanorum
ultimum dixisset. Accusabant Satrius Secundus et Pinarius 20
2 Natta, Seiani clientes. Id perniciabile reo et Caesar truci uultu
100v defensionem accipiens, | quam Cremutius, relinquendae uitae
certus, in hunc modum exorsus est: 'Verba mea, patres conscripti, arguuntur, adeo factorum innocens sum. Sed neque
haec in principem aut principis parentem, quos lex maiestatis 25
amplectitur: Brutum et Cassium laudauisse dicor, quorum res
gestas cum plurimi composuerint, nemo sine honore memor-
3 auit. Titus Liuius, eloquentiae ac fidei praeclarus, in primis Cn.
Pompeium tantis laudibus tulit ut Pompeianum eum Augustus

---

1 neque alia rerum *M* (fiducia *post* alia *suppl. Woodman*, salute *post* rerum
Bringmann): neque alio rerum *Ryckius* (sic conuerso neque alio rerum statu
Acidalius): neque alia re Rom<ana> *Lipsius*   **4** euentibus *Ritter*   **9** exitii
Pichena: exitu *M*   **10** tum quod *M* (quod *secl. Nipperdey*): adnotatum *uel*
adnotandum *suppl. Woodman*: tumque *Ritter*   **11** Romanasne *Nipperdey*:
-asue *M* **12** infamiam *Lipsius*   **16** nimis *Muretus*: animis *M*   ad inceptum
Halm: ancepto *M*: ad incepta *Beroaldus*   **28** *post* praeclarus *interpunxit
Woodman, post* in primis *alii*

appellaret; neque id amicitiae eorum offecit. Scipionem, AD 25
Afranium, hunc ipsum Cassium, hunc Brutum nusquam
latrones et parricidas, quae nunc uocabula imponuntur, saepe
4 ut insignes uiros nominat. Asinii Pollionis scripta egregiam
eorundem memoriam tradunt; Messala Coruinus imperatorem 5
suum Cassium praedicabat; et uterque opibus atque honoribus
peruiguere. Marci Ciceronis libro quo Catonem caelo aequauit,
quid aliud dictator Caesar quam rescripta oratione uelut apud
5 iudices respondit? Antonii epistulae, Bruti contiones falsa quidem in Augustum probra, set multa cum acerbitate habent; 10
carmina Bibaculi et Catulli referta contumeliis Caesarum
leguntur; sed ipse diuus Iulius, ipse diuus Augustus et tulere
ista et reliquere, haud facile dixerim moderatione magis an
sapientia: namque spreta exolescunt; si irascare, adgnita uiden-
35 tur. (Non attingo Graecos, quorum non modo libertas, etiam 15
10ʳʳ libido impunita; aut si quis aduertit, dictis dicta ultus est.) | Sed
maxime solutum et sine obtrectatore fuit prodere de iis quos
2 mors odio aut gratiae exemisset. Num enim armatis Cassio et
Bruto ac Philippenses campos obtinentibus belli ciuilis causa
populum per contiones incendo? An illi quidem septuagesimum 20
ante annum perempti, quo modo imaginibus suis noscuntur,
quas ne uictor quidem aboleuit, sic partem memoriae apud
3 scriptores retinent? Suum cuique decus posteritas rependit;
nec derunt, si damnatio ingruit, qui non modo Cassii et Bruti
4 sed etiam mei meminerint.' Egressus dein senatu uitam absti- 25
nentia finiuit.

Libros per aediles cremandos censuere patres; set manserunt,
5 occultati et editi. Quo magis socordiam eorum inridere libet qui
praesenti potentia credunt exstingui posse etiam sequentis aeui
memoriam. Nam contra punitis ingeniis gliscit auctoritas, 30
neque aliud [externi reges aut] qui eadem saeuitia usi sunt nisi
dedecus sibi atque illis gloriam peperere.

3 uocabulum ponuntur *M*, *corr. Beroaldus* **4** insigni *M*, *corr. Beroaldus*
6 opibus *Acidalius*: opibusque *M* **18** enim *Halm*: eum *M* **22** ne *J.F.*
Gronovius: nec *M* **23** rependit *Beroaldus*: -unt *M* **25** sed& &iam *M*
27 set *Lipsius*: et *M* **31** externi reges aut *secl. Woodman* (aut *secl. Hartman*)

36 Ceterum postulandis reis tam continuus annus fuit ut feri- ᴀᴅ 2
arum Latinarum diebus praefectum urbis Drusum, auspicandi
gratia tribunal ingressum, adierit Calpurnius Saluianus in
Sextum Marium; quod a Caesare palam increpitum causa exilii
2 Saluiano fuit. Obiecta publice Cyzicenis incuria caerimo- 5
niarum diui Augusti, additis uiolentiae criminibus aduersum
ciues Romanos; et amisere libertatem quam bello Mithridatis
meruerant, circumsessi nec minus sua constantia quam praesi-
3 dio Luculli pulso rege. At Fonteius Capito, qui pro consule |
101v Asiam curauerat, absoluitur, comperto ficta in eum crimina per 10
Vibium Serenum. Neque tamen id Sereno noxae fuit, quem
odium publicum tutiorem faciebat. Nam ut quis destrictior
accusator, uelut sacrosanctus erat; leues, ignobiles poenis
adficiebantur.

37 Per idem tempus Hispania ulterior missis ad senatum legatis 15
orauit ut exemplo Asiae delubrum Tiberio matrique eius
exstrueret. Qua occasione Caesar, ualidus alioqui spernendis
honoribus et respondendum ratus iis quorum rumore arguebatur in ambitionem flexisse, huiusce modi orationem coepit:
2 'Scio, patres conscripti, constantiam meam a plerisque desider- 20
atam quod Asiae ciuitatibus nuper idem istud petentibus non
sim aduersatus. Ergo et prioris silentii defensionem et quid in
futurum statuerim simul aperiam.

3 'Cum diuus Augustus sibi atque urbi Romae templum apud
Pergamum sisti non prohibuisset, qui omnia facta dictaque eius 25
uice legis obseruem, placitum iam exemplum promptius secutus
sum quia cultui meo ueneratio senatus adiungebatur. Ceterum,
ut semel recepisse ueniam habuerit, ita per omnes prouincias
effigie numinum sacrari ambitiosum, superbum; et uanescet
Augusti honor, si promiscis adulationibus uulgatur. 30

38 'Ego me, patres conscripti, mortalem esse et hominum officia
fungi satisque habere si locum principem impleam et uos testor
et meminisse posteros uolo; qui satis superque memoriae meae

---

12 destrictior *M*: districtior *Beroaldus*   **28** per oᷗs per *(alterum* per
del.) M sacrari *Lipsius*: sacra *M*   **31** esse & | & *M*

tribuent, ut maioribus meis dignum, rerum uestrarum proui- AD 25
102r dum, constantem in periculis, | offensionum pro utilitate pub-
2 lica non pauidum credant. Haec mihi in animis uestris templa,
hae pulcherrimae effigies et mansurae: nam quae saxo struuntur, si iudicium posterorum in odium uertit, pro sepulchris 5
3 spernuntur. Proinde socios, ciues et deos et deas ipsas precor,
hos ut mihi ad finem usque uitae quietam et intellegentem
humani diuinique iuris mentem duint, illos ut, quandoque concessero, cum laude et bonis recordationibus facta atque famam
nominis mei prosequantur.' 10
4 Perstititque posthac secretis etiam sermonibus aspernari
talem sui cultum. Quod alii modestiam, multi quia diffideret,
5 quidam ut degeneris animi interpretabantur: optimos quippe
mortalium altissima cupere: sic Herculem et Liberum apud
Graecos, Quirinum apud nos deum numero additos; melius 15
Augustum, qui sperauerit; cetera principibus statim adesse;
unum insatiabiliter parandum, prosperam sui memoriam:
nam contemptu famae contemni uirtutes.

39 At Seianus nimia fortuna socors et muliebri insuper cupidine
incensus, promissum matrimonium flagitante Liuia, componit 20
ad Caesarem codicillos (moris quippe tum erat quamquam
2 praesentem scripto adire). Eius talis forma fuit: beneuolentia
patris Augusti et mox plurimis Tiberii iudiciis ita insueuisse ut
spes uotaque sua non prius ad deos quam ad principum aures
conferret; neque fulgorem honorum umquam precatum: | 25
102v excubias ac labores ut unum e militibus pro incolumitate imperatoris malle; ac tamen, quod pulcherrimum, adeptum ut con-
3 iunctione Caesaris dignus crederetur: hinc initium spei, et,
quoniam audiuerit Augustum in conlocanda filia non nihil
etiam de equitibus Romanis consultauisse, ita, si maritus 30
Liuiae quaereretur, haberet in animo amicum sola necessitudi-
4 nis gloria usurum: non enim exuere imposita munia; satis aestimare firmari domum aduersum iniquas Agrippinae

---

1 ut *M*: si *uel* ubi *Ernesti* **5** posterorum *Rhenanus*: posteriorum *M*
6 & deos & deas ipsas *M*ᶜ: & deos & deos ipsos *M*: et deos ipsos *Pichena*

offensiones, idque liberorum causa: nam sibi multum superque AD 2
uitae fore quod tali cum principe expleuisset.

40 Ad ea Tiberius laudata pietate Seiani suisque in eum bene-
ficiis modice percursis, cum tempus tamquam ad integram
consultationem petiuisset, adiunxit ceteris mortalibus in eo 5
stare consilia quid sibi conducere putent; principum diuersam
2 esse sortem, quibus praecipua rerum ad famam derigenda: ideo
se non illuc decurrere, quod promptum rescriptu, posse ipsam
Liuiam statuere nubendum post Drusum an in penatibus isdem
tolerandum haberet; esse illi matrem et auiam, propiora con- 10
3 silia; simplicius acturum, de inimicitiis primum Agrippinae,
quas longe acrius arsuras si matrimonium Liuiae uelut in partes
domum Caesarum distraxisset; sic quoque erumpere aemulationem feminarum, eaque discordia nepotes suos conuelli: quid
si intendatur certamen tali coniugio? | 15

103r 4 'Falleris enim, Seiane, si te mansurum in eodem ordine
putas, et Liuiam, quae C. Caesari, mox Druso nupta fuerit, ea
mente acturam ut cum equite Romano senescat. Ego ut sinam,
credisne passuros qui fratrem eius, qui patrem maioresque
5 nostros in summis imperiis uidere? Vis tu quidem istum intra 20
locum sistere, sed illi magistratus et primores qui <ad> te
inuitum perrumpunt omnibusque de rebus consulunt excessisse
iam pridem equestre fastigium longeque antisse patris mei amicitias non occulti ferunt, perque inuidiam tui me quoque incu-
6 sant. At enim Augustus filiam suam equiti Romano tradere 25
meditatus est. Mirum (hercule!) si, cum in omnes curas distra-
heretur immensumque attolli prouideret quem coniunctione
tali super alios extulisset, C. Proculeium et quosdam in sermonibus habuit insigni tranquillitate uitae, nullis rei publicae negotiis permixtos. Sed, si dubitatione Augusti mouemur, quanto 30
7 ualidius est quod Marco Agrippae, mox mihi conlocauit? Atque
ego haec pro amicitia non occultaui; ceterum neque tuis neque

21 ad *ante* te *suppl. Woodman* **22** inuitum *Heinsius: prius* inuitu, *dein* –e *M:* o *suprascr. M^c* perrumpunt *M:* <sem>per ambiunt *Fuchs* **23** longeque *Rhenanus:* legeque *M*

Liuiae destinatis aduersabor. Ipse quid intra animum uolu- AD 25
tauerim, quibus adhuc necessitudinibus immiscere te mihi
parem, omittam ad praesens referre; id tantum aperiam, nihil
esse tam excelsum quod non uirtutes istae tuusque in me animus
mereantur, datoque tempore uel in senatu uel in contione non 5
reticebo.'

41 Rursum Seianus, non tam de matrimonio sed altius metuens,
103v tacita suspicionum, uulgi | rumorem, ingruentem inuidiam
deprecatur; ac, ne adsiduos in domum coetus arcendo infringeret potentiam aut receptando facultatem criminantibus prae- 10
beret, huc flexit ut Tiberium ad uitam procul Roma amoenis
2 locis degendam impelleret. Multa quippe prouidebat: sua in
manu aditus litterarumque magna ex parte se arbitrum fore,
cum per milites commearent; mox Caesarem uergente iam
senecta secretoque loci mollitum munia imperii facilius tramis- 15
surum; et minui sibi inuidiam adempta salutantum turba, sub-
3 latisque inanibus ueram potentiam augeri. Igitur paulatim
negotia urbis, populi adcursus, multitudinem adfluentium
increpat, extollens laudibus quietem et solitudinem, quis abesse
taedia et offensiones ac praecipua rerum maxime agitari. 20

42 Ac forte habita per illos dies de Votieno Montano, celebris
ingenii uiro, cognitio cunctantem iam Tiberium perpulit ut
uitandos crederet patrum coetus uocesque quae plerumque
2 uerae et graues coram ingerebantur. Nam postulato Votieno
ob contumelias in Caesarem dictas, testis Aemilius e militaribus 25
uiris dum studio probandi cuncta refert et, quamquam inter
obstrepentes, magna adseueratione nititur, audiuit Tiberius
probra quis per occultum lacerabatur, adeoque perculsus est
ut se uel statim uel in cognitione purgaturum clamitaret, pre-
104r cibusque proximorum, adulatione | omnium aegre componeret 30
3 animum. Et Votienus quidem maiestatis poenis adfectus est;
Caesar obiectam sibi aduersus reos inclementiam eo

---

7 tam *M*: iam *Muretus* *post* metuens *nullum signum interpunctionis indicauit*
Doederlein **11** flexit *Beroaldus*: elexit *M* **17** inanibus *Beroaldus*: manibus
M ueram potentiam augeri *Marcilius*: –a –a augere *M*: –a –a augeri *Rhenanus*:
–am –am augere *Muretus*: –a –ae augeri *Heinsius*

peruicacius amplexus, Aquiliam adulterii delatam cum Vario AD 2
Ligure, quamquam Lentulus Gaetulicus consul designatus lege
Iulia damnasset, exilio puniuit, Apidiumque Merulam quod in
acta diui Augusti non iurauerat albo senatorio erasit.

43 Auditae dehinc Lacedaemoniorum et Messeniorum lega- 5
tiones de iure templi Dianae Limnatidis, quod suis a maioribus
suaque in terra dicatum Lacedaemonii firmabant annalium
memoria uatumque carminibus, sed Macedonis Philippi, cum
quo bellassent, armis ademptum ac post C. Caesaris et M.
2 Antonii sententia redditum. Contra Messenii ueterem inter 10
Herculis posteros diuisionem Peloponnesi protulere, suoque
regi Denthaliatem agrum, in quo id delubrum, cessisse; mon-
3 imentaque eius rei sculpta saxis et aere prisco manere; quod si
uatum, annalium ad testimonia uocentur, plures sibi ac locupletiores esse; neque Philippum potentia sed ex uero statuisse; 15
idem regis Antigoni, idem imperatoris Mummii iudicium; sic
Milesios permisso publice arbitrio, postremo Atidium
Geminum praetorem Achaiae decreuisse. Ita secundum
4 Messenios datum. Et Segestani aedem Veneris montem apud
Erycum, uetustate dilapsam, restaurari postulauere, nota mem- 20
104v orantes de origine eius et laeta Tiberio:| suscepit curam libens
5 ut consanguineus. Tunc tractatae Massiliensium preces probatumque P. Rutilii exemplum: namque eum legibus pulsum
ciuem sibi Zmyrnaei addiderant. Quo iure Volcacius Moschus
exul in Massilienses receptus bona sua rei publicae eorum et 25
patriae reliquerat.

44 Obiere eo anno uiri nobiles Cn. Lentulus et L. Domitius.
Lentulo super consulatum et triumphalia de Getis gloriae fuerat
bene tolerata paupertas, dein magnae opes innocenter paratae
2 et modeste habitae. Domitium decorauit pater ciuili bello maris 30
potens, donec Antonii partibus, mox Caesaris misceretur; auus

---

12 regi *Rhenanus*, Denthaliatem *Nipperdey* (Dentheliatem *iam Lipsius*): reci-
dent heliatem (*suprascr.* a) *M* **17** postremo *Beroaldus*: -rem *M*
20 dilapsam *Ernesti*: del- *M* **21** suscepit *M*: suscepit<que> *Ritter*
24 Volcacius *A. Kiessling*: uulcatius *M*: Vulcacius *uulgo* **29** paratae *M*:
partae *Lipsius*

Pharsalica acie pro optumatibus ceciderat; ipse delectus cui AD 25
minor Antonia, Octauia genita, in matrimonium daretur, post
exercitu flumen Albim transcendit, longius penetrata Germania
quam quisquam priorum, easque ob res insignia triumphi adep-
3 tus est. Obiit et L. Antonius, multa claritudine generis sed 5
improspera. Nam patre eius Iullo Antonio ob adulterium
Iuliae morte punito hunc admodum adulescentulum, sororis
nepotem, seposuit Augustus in ciuitatem Massiliensem, ubi
specie studiorum nomen exilii tegeretur. Habitus tamen supre-
mis honor, ossaque tumulo Octauiorum inlata per decretum 10
senatus.

45 Isdem consulibus facinus atrox in citeriore Hispania admissum a quodam agresti nationis Termestinae. Is praetorem
prouinciae L. Pisonem, pace incuriosum, ex improuiso in itinere adortus uno uulnere in mortem adfecit; ac pernicitate equi 15
105r profugus, | postquam saltuosos locos attigerat, dimisso equo per
2 derupta et auia sequentes frustratus est. Neque diu fefellit: nam
prenso ductoque per proximos pagos equo, cuius foret cognitum. Et repertus, cum tormentis edere conscios adigeretur, uoce
magna sermone patrio frustra se interrogari clamitauit: adsis- 20
terent socii ac spectarent; nullam uim tantam doloris fore ut
ueritatem eliceret. Idemque cum postero ad quaestionem retraheretur, eo nisu proripuit se custodibus saxoque caput adflixit ut
3 statim exanimaretur. Sed Piso Termestinorum dolo caesus
habe<ba>tur, qui pecunias e publico interceptas acrius quam 25
ut tolerarent barbari cogebat.

46 Lentulo Gaetulico C. Caluisio consulibus decreta triumphi AD 26
insignia Poppaeo Sabino contusis Thraecum gentibus, qui
montium editis inculti atque eo ferocius agitabant. Causa
motus, super hominum ingenium, quod pati dilectus et ualidis- 30
simum quemque militiae nostrae dare aspernabantur, ne regibus quidem parere nisi ex libidine soliti aut, si mitterent auxilia,

---

1 delectus *Pichena*: deiectus *M*   3   <cum> exercitu *Prammer*   6 Iullo
Andresen: Iulio *M*   25   habe<ba>tur *Pluygers*: habetur *M*   qui *M*:
qui<ppe>   *Bezzenberger*:   qui<a>   *Pichena*   29   <in>   montium
Bezzenberger   inculti *Beroaldus*: incultu *M*

suos ductores praeficere nec nisi aduersum accolas belligerare. AD 2⟨
2 Ac tum rumor incesserat fore ut disiecti aliisque nationibus
permixti diuersas in terras traherentur. Sed antequam arma
inciperent, misere legatos amicitiam obsequiumque memoraturos, et mansura haec, si nullo nouo onere temptarentur; sin ut 5
uictis seruitium indiceretur, esse sibi ferrum et iuuentutem et
3 promptum libertati aut ad mortem animum. Simul castella
105v rupibus indita conlatosque illuc parentes | et coniuges ostenta-
bant bellumque impeditum, arduum, cruentum minitabantur.

47 At Sabinus, donec exercitus in unum conduceret, datis miti- 10
bus responsis, <post>quam Pomponius Labeo e Moesia cum
legione, rex Rhoemetalces cum auxiliis popularium qui fidem
non mutauerant uenere, addita praesenti copia ad hostem pergit, compositum iam per angustias saltuum. Quidam audentius
apertis in collibus uisebantur, quos dux Romanus acie suggres- 15
sus haud aegre pepulit, sanguine barbarorum modico ob pro-
2 pinqua suffugia. Mox castris in loco communitis ualida manu
montem occupat angusto et aequali dorso continuum usque ad
proximum castellum, quod magna uis armata aut incondita
tuebatur. Simul in ferocissimos, qui ante uallum more gentis 20
cum carminibus et tripudiis persultabant, mittit delectos sagit-
3 tariorum. Ii dum eminus grassabantur, crebra et inulta uulnera
fecere; propius incedentes eruptione subita turbati sunt recep-
tique subsidio Sugambrae cohortis, quam Romanus promptam
ad pericula nec minus cantuum et armorum tumultu trucem 25
haud procul instruxerat.

48 Translata dehinc castra hostem propter, relictis apud priora
munimenta Thraecibus quos nobis adfuisse memoraui; iisque
permissum uastare, urere, trahere praedas, dum populatio
106r lucem intra sisteretur | noctemque in castris tutam et uigilem 30
capesserent. Id primo seruatum; mox uersi in luxum et raptis
opulenti omittere stationes lasciuia epularum, aut somno et uino

---

10 conduceretur *Pichena* **11** <post>quam ... uenere *Jac. Gronouius*: quam
... uenire^t *M* (dum *M^{mg}*): dum ... ueniret *Pichena* **18** angusto *Courtney*:
-um *M* **32** stationes *Beroaldus*: -ne *M*: -nem *Ritter*

2 procumbere. Igitur hostes incuria eorum comperta duo agmina AD 26
parant, quorum altero populatores inuaderentur, alii castra
Romana adpugnarent, non spe capiendi sed ut clamore, telis
suo quisque periculo intentus sonorem alterius proelii non acciperet. Tenebrae insuper delectae augendam ad formidinem. 5
3 Sed qui uallum legionum temptabant facile pelluntur;
Thraecum auxilia repentino incursu territa, cum pars munitionibus adiacerent, plures extra palarentur, tanto infensius caesi
quanto perfugae et proditores ferre arma ad suum patriaeque
seruitium incusabantur. 10

49   Postera die Sabinus exercitum aequo loco ostendit, si barbari
successu noctis alacres proelium auderent. Et postquam castello
aut coniunctis tumulis non degrediebantur, obsidium coepit per
praesidia, quae opportune iam muniebat; dein fossam loricamque contexens quattuor milia passuum ambitu amplexus est. 15
2 Tum paulatim, ut aquam pabulumque eriperet, contrahere
claustra artaque circumdare; et struebatur agger unde saxa,
3 hastae, ignes propinquum iam in hostem iacerentur. Sed nihil
aeque quam sitis fatigabat, cum ingens multitudo bellatorum,
imbellium uno reliquo fonte uterentur; simulque armenta (ut 20
106v mos | barbaris) iuxta clausa egestate pabuli exanimari; adiacere
corpora hominum quos uulnera, quos sitis peremerat: pollui
cuncta sanie, odore, contactu.

50   Rebusque turbatis malum extremum discordia accessit, his
deditionem, aliis mortem et mutuos inter se ictus parantibus; et 25
erant qui non inultum exitium sed eruptionem suaderent.
2 Neque ignobiles, quamuis diuersi sententiis, uerum e ducibus
Dinis, prouectus senecta et longo usu uim atque clementiam
Romanam edoctus, ponenda arma, unum adflictis id remedium disserebat; primusque se cum coniuge et liberis uictori 30
permisit. Secuti aetate aut sexu imbecilli et quibus maior uitae
3 quam gloriae cupido. At iuuentus Tarsam inter et Turesim

14   iam muniebat *M*: immuniebat *Freinsheim*   20   simulque *Danesius*:
simul eque *M*: simul equi *Lipsius*   27   Neque ... sententiis *secl.*
Ritter quamuis *M*: tantum his *Madvig*

distrahebatur. Vtrique destinatum cum libertate occidere, sed AD 2
Tarsa properum finem, abrumpendas pariter spes ac metus
clamitans, dedit exemplum demisso in pectus ferro; nec
4 defuere qui eodem modo oppeterent. Turesis sua cum manu
noctem opperitur, haud nescio duce nostro. Igitur firmatae 5
stationes densioribus globis.

Et ingruebat nox nimbo atrox, hostisque clamore turbido,
modo per uastum silentium incertos obsessores effecerat, cum
Sabinus circumire, hortari ne ad ambigua sonitus aut simulationem quietis casum insidiantibus aperirent, sed sua quisque 10
51 munia seruarent immoti telisque non in falsum iactis. Interea
barbari cateruis decurrentes nunc in uallum manualia saxa,
107r praeustas sudes, | decisa robora iacere, nunc uirgultis et crati-
bus et corporibus exanimis complere fossas; quidam pontes et
scalas ante fabricati inferre propugnaculis eaque prensare, 15
detrahere et aduersum resistentes comminus niti. Miles contra
deturbare telis, pellere umbonibus, muralia pila, congestas lapi-
2 dum moles prouoluere. His partae uictoriae spes et, si cedant,
insignitius flagitium; illis extrema iam salus et adsistentes plerisque matres et coniuges, earumque lamenta addunt animos. 20
Nox aliis in audaciam, aliis ad formidinem opportuna; incerti
ictus, uulnera improuisa; suorum atque hostium ignoratio et
montis anfractu repercussae uelut a tergo uoces adeo cuncta
miscuerant ut quaedam munimenta Romani quasi perrupta
3 omiserint. Neque tamen peruasere hostes nisi admodum 25
pauci; ceteros, deiecto promptissimo quoque aut saucio, adpetente iam luce trusere in summa castelli, ubi tandem coacta
deditio. Et proxima sponte incolarum recepta; reliquis quominus ui aut obsidio subigerentur praematura montis Haemi et
saeua hiems subuenit. 30
52 At Romae, commota principis domo, ut series futuri in
Agrippinam exitii inciperet Claudia Pulchra sobrina eius

18 partae M: partae <prope> *Greef:* paratae *Gross:* pariter *Fuchs:*
patratae *Koestermann* **26** deiecto *Orelli:* delecto M **28** incolarum
Muretus: incorum M

postulatur accusante Domitio Afro. Is recens praetura, modicus   AD 26
dignationis et quoquo facinore properus clarescere, crimen
impudicitiae, adulterum Furnium, ueneficia in principem et
2 deuotiones obiectabat. Agrippina semper atrox, tum et periculo
107v propinquae accensa, | pergit ad Tiberium ac forte sacrifican- 5
tem patri repperit. Quo initio inuidiae non eiusdem ait mactare
diuo Augusto uictimas et posteros eius insectari: non in effigies
mutas diuinum spiritum transfusum; se imaginem ueram, cae-
lesti sanguine ortam; intellegere discrimen, suscipere sordes;
frustra Pulchram praescribi, cui sola exitii causa sit quod 10
Agrippinam stulte prorsus ad cultum delegerit, oblita Sosiae
3 ob eadem adflictae. Audita haec raram occulti pectoris uocem
elicuere, correptamque Graeco uersu admonuit non ideo laedi
4 quia non regnaret. Pulchra et Furnius damnantur. Afer primoribus oratorum additus, diuulgato ingenio et secuta adseuera- 15
tione Caesaris qua suo iure disertum eum appellauit; mox
capessendis accusationibus aut reos tutando prosperiore eloquentiae quam morum fama fuit, nisi quod aetas extrema
multum etiam eloquentiae dempsit, dum fessa mente retinet
silentii impatientiam. 20

53   At Agrippina peruicax irae et morbo corporis implicata, cum
uiseret eam Caesar, profusis diu ac per silentium lacrimis, mox
inuidiam et preces orditur: subueniret solitudini, daret mari-
tum; habilem adhuc iuuentam sibi, neque aliud probis quam ex
matrimonio solacium; esse in ciuitate * * * Germanici coniugem 25
2 ac liberos eius recipere dignarentur. Sed Caesar non ignarus
quantum ex re publica peteretur, ne tamen offensionis aut
metus manifestus foret, sine responso quamquam instantem
108r reliquit. (Id ego, a scriptoribus | annalium non traditum,
repperi in commentariis Agrippinae filiae, quae Neronis princi- 30
pis mater uitam suam et casus suorum posteris memorauit.)

---

8 se imaginem *Muretus*: sed ⁱmaginem *M*   **13** arreptamque *Martin et*
Woodman   **24** probris *Petersen*   **25** *post* ciuitate *deest tertia fere pars uersus in*
M: qui diuo Augusto ortam *suppl. Haase* (*cf. 1.40.3*): *alii alia*   **27** ex re
publica *M*: ex se *Wurm*: ea re *Madvig*

54 Ceterum Seianus maerentem et improuidam altius perculit, AD 2
immissis qui per speciem amicitiae monerent paratum ei uenenum, uitandas soceri epulas. Atque illa simulationum nescia,
cum propter discumberet, non uultu aut sermone flecti, nullos
attingere cibos, donec aduertit Tiberius, forte an quia audi- 5
uerat; idque quo acrius experiretur, poma, ut erant adposita,
laudans nurui sua manu tradidit. Aucta ex eo suspicio
2 Agrippinae et intacta ore seruis tramisit. Nec tamen Tiberii
uox coram secuta, sed obuersus ad matrem non mirum ait si
quid seuerius in eam statuisset a qua ueneficii insimularetur. 10
Inde rumor parari exitium, neque id imperatorem palam
audere: secretum ad perpetrandum quaeri.

55 Sed Caesar, quo famam auerteret, adesse frequens senatui
legatosque Asiae ambigentes quanam in ciuitate templum sta-
tueretur plures per dies audiuit. Vndecim urbes certabant, pari 15
ambitione, uiribus diuersae. Neque multum distantia inter se
memorabant, de uetustate generis, studio in populum
Romanum per bella Persi et Aristonici aliorumque regum.
2 Verum Hypaepeni Trallianique Laodicenis ac Magnetibus
simul tramissi ut parum ualidi; ne Ilienses quidem, cum par- 20
entem urbis Romae Troiam referrent, nisi antiquitatis gloria
108v pollebant. Paulum addubitatum | quod Halicarnasii mille et
ducentos per annos nullo motu terrae nutauisse sedes suas
uiuoque in saxo fundamenta templi adseuerauerant.
Pergamenos (eo ipso nitebantur) aede Augusto ibi sita satis 25
adeptos creditum. Ephesii Milesiique, hi Apollinis, illi Dianae
3 caerimonia occupauisse ciuitates uisi. Ita Sardianos inter
Zmyrnaeosque deliberatum.

Sardiani decretum Etruriae recitauere ut consanguinei: nam
Tyrrhenum Lydumque Atye rege genitos ob multitudinem 30
diuisisse gentem; Lydum patriis in terris resedisse, Tyrrheno
datum nouas ut conderet sedes; et ducum e nominibus indita

---

7 sua *Rhenanus*: suae *M* **19** hypae penitrali tanique *M, corr.*
Beroaldus **20** nellienses *M, corr. Beroaldus* **25** aede ... sita *Lipsius*: aedē ...
sitam *M* **31** diuise *M, corr. Beroaldus*

uocabula illis per Asiam, his in Italia; auctamque adhuc AD 26
Lydorum opulentiam missis in Graeciam populis cui mox a
4 Pelope nomen. Simul litteras imperatorum et icta nobiscum
foedera bello Macedonum ubertatemque fluminum suorum,
temperiem caeli ac dites circum terras memorabant.   5

56 At Zmynaei repetita uetustate, seu Tantalus Ioue ortus illos
siue Theseus diuina et ipse stirpe siue una Amazonum condidisset, transcendere ad ea quis maxime fidebant, in populum
Romanum officiis, missa nauali copia non modo externa ad
bella sed quae in Italia tolerabantur; seque primos templum 10
urbis Romae statuisse M. Porcio consule, magnis quidem iam
populi Romani rebus, nondum tamen ad summum elatis, stante
2 adhuc Punica urbe et ualidis per Asiam regibus. Simul L.
1ogr Sullam testem adferebant, | grauissimo in discrimine exercitus
ob asperitatem hiemis et penuriam uestis, cum id Zmyrnam in 15
contionem nuntiatum foret, omnes qui adstabant detraxisse
3 corpori tegmina nostrisque legionibus misisse. Ita rogati sententiam patres Zmyrnaeos praetulere; censuitque Vibius Marsus ut
M. Lepido, cui ea prouincia obuenerat, super numerum legar-
etur qui templi curam susciperet. Et quia Lepidus ipse deligere 20
per modestiam abnuebat, Valerius Naso e praetoriis sorte missus est.

57 Inter quae diu meditato prolatoque saepius consilio tandem
Caesar <proficiscitur> in Campaniam, specie dedicandi templa
apud Capuam Ioui, apud Nolam Augusto, sed certus procul 25
urbe degere. Causam abscessus quamquam secutus plurimos
auctorum ad Seiani artes rettuli, quia tamen caede eius patrata
sex postea annos pari secreto coniunxit, plerumque permoueor
num ad ipsum referri uerius sit, saeuitiam ac libidinem, cum
2 factis promeret, locis occultantem. Erant qui crederent in senec- 30
tute corporis quoque habitum pudori fuisse (quippe illi praegracilis et incurua proceritas, nudus capillo uertex, ulcerosa

2 in Graeciam *M*: in insulam *Urlichs*: in Graecia<e regione>m *Fuchs* **3** icta
Rhenanus: dicta *M* **18** Marsus *Rhenanus*: Marcus *M* **24** in
Campaniam *M*: proficiscitur *suppl. hic Woodman, alia post* in Campaniam *alii*:
iit Campaniam *Lipsius* **30** occultantem *Rhenanus*: -tis *M*

facies ac plerumque medicaminibus interstincta); et Rhodi ᴀᴅ ₉
3 secreto uitare coetus, recondere uoluptates insuerat. Traditur
etiam matris impotentia extrusum, quam dominationis sociam
aspernabatur neque depellere poterat, cum dominationem
109v ipsam donum eius | accepisset. Nam dubitauerat Augustus 5
Germanicum, sororis nepotem et cunctis laudatum, rei
Romanae imponere, sed precibus uxoris euictus Tiberio
Germanicum, sibi Tiberium adsciuit; idque Augusta exprobrabat, reposcebat.

58 Profectio arto comitatu fuit: unus senator consulatu functus, 10
Cocceius Nerua, cui legum peritia; eques Romanus praeter
Seianum ex inlustribus Curtius Atticus; ceteri liberalibus studiis
2 praediti, ferme Graeci, quorum sermonibus leuaretur. Ferebant
periti caelestium iis motibus siderum excessisse Roma Tiberium
ut reditus illi negaretur, unde exitii causa multis fuit properum 15
finem uitae coniectantibus uulgantibusque: neque enim tam
incredibilem casum prouidebant ut undecim per annos libens
3 patria careret. Mox patuit breue confinium artis et falsi,ueraque
quam obscuris tegerentur. Nam in urbem non regressurum
haud forte dictum; ceterorum nescii egere, cum propinquo 20
rure aut litore et saepe moenia urbis adsidens extremam senec-
59 tam compleuerit. Ac forte illis diebus oblatum Caesari anceps
periculum auxit uana rumoris praebuitque ipsi materiem cur
amicitiae constantiaeque Seiani magis fideret. Vescebantur in
uilla cui uocabulum Speluncae, mare Amunclanum inter <et> 25
Fundanos montes, natiuo in specu. Eius os lapsis repente saxis
2 obruit quosdam ministros: hinc metus in omnes et fuga eorum
qui conuiuium celebrabant. Seianus genu utroque et manibus
110r super Caesarem suspensus opposuit sese | incidentibus atque
habitu tali repertus est a militibus qui subsidio uenerant. Maior 30
ex eo et, quamquam exitiosa suaderet, ut non sui anxius cum
fide audiebatur.

1–2 et Rhodi ... insuerat *post* locis occultantem *transposuit Cron*
20 ceterorum *M*: ceteri *Hartman* **26** et *suppl. hic Bezzenberger*, -que *post*
Fundanos *Beroaldus* **29** genu *M*: sinu *Probst* utroque *Woodman*:
uultuque *M*

46

3   Adsimulabatque uindicis partes aduersum Germanici stir-   AD 26
pem, subditis qui accusatorum nomina sustinerent maximeque
insectarentur Neronem, proximum successioni et, quamquam
modesta iuuenta, plerumque tamen quid in praesentiarum con-
ducteret oblitum, dum a libertis et clientibus, apiscendae poten-   5
tiae properis, exstimulatur ut erectum et fidentem animi
ostenderet: uelle id populum Romanum, cupere exercitus;
neque ausurum contra Seianum, qui nunc patientiam senis et
60 segnitiam iuuenis iuxta insultet. Haec atque talia audienti nihil
quidem prauae cogitationis, sed interdum uoces procedebant   10
contumaces et inconsultae, quas adpositi custodes exceptas
auctasque cum deferrent neque Neroni defendere daretur,
2 diuersae insuper sollicitudinum formae oriebantur. Nam alius
occursum eius uitare, quidam salutatione reddita statim auerti,
plerique inceptum sermonem abrumpere, insistentibus contra   15
inridentibusque qui Seiano fautores aderant.
    Enimuero Tiberius toruus aut falsum renidens uultu: seu
loqueretur seu taceret iuuenis, crimen ex silentio, ex uoce; ne
nox quidem secura, cum uxor uigilias, somnos, suspiria matri
Liuiae atque illa Seiano patefaceret. Qui fratrem quoque   20
110v Neronis Drusum traxit in partes, spe obiecta principis loci, | si
3 priorem aetate et iam labefactum demouisset. Atrox Drusi
ingenium super cupidinem potentiae et solita fratribus odia
accendebatur inuidia, quod mater Agrippina promptior
Neroni erat. Neque tamen Seianus ita Drusum fouebat ut non   25
in eum quoque semina futuri exitii meditaretur, gnarus praeferocem et insidiis magis opportunum.
61   Fine anni excessere insignes uiri Asinius Agrippa, claris
maioribus quam uetustis uitaque non degener, et Q. Haterius,
familia senatoria, eloquentiae—quoad uixit—celebratae; mon-   30
umenta ingeni eius haud perinde retinentur: scilicet impetu

1 dissimulabatque *Kritz*   uindicis *Shackleton Bailey*: iudicis *M*: indicis
Muretus   **4**   in praesentia *Ritter*   **4–5**   conducet *M, corr.*
Beroaldus   **6** animum *Pichena*   **17** uultu *secl. Ritter*   **24** promptior
M: pronior *Ernesti*   **28** insignes *Mᶜ*: insignis *M*   **29** et Q. *Beroaldus*: &
que *M*   **30** quoad *Beroaldus*: qua (*suprascr.* o) ad *M*

magis quam cura uigebat, utque aliorum meditatio et labor in AD 2
posterum ualescit, sic Haterii canorum illud et profluens cum
ipso simul exstinctum est.

62   M. Licinio L. Calpurnio consulibus ingentium bellorum cla- AD 2
dem aequauit malum improuisum; eius initium simul et finis 5
exstitit. Nam coepto apud Fidenam amphitheatro Atilius quidam libertini generis, quo spectaculum gladiatorum celebraret,
neque fundamenta per solidum subdidit neque firmis nexibus
ligneam compagem superstruxit, ut qui non abundantia pecuniae nec municipali ambitione sed in sordidam mercedem id 10
2 negotium quaesiuisset. Adfluxere auidi talium, imperitante
Tiberio procul uoluptatibus habiti, uirile ac muliebre secus,
omnis aetas, ob propinquitatem loci effusius: unde grauior
iiir pestis | fuit, conferta mole, dein conuulsa, dum ruit intus aut
in exteriora effunditur immensamque uim mortalium, specta- 15
culo intentos aut qui circum adstabant, praeceps trahit atque
3 operit. Et illi quidem quos principium stragis in mortem adflixerat, ut tali sorte, cruciatum effugere; miserandi magis quos
abrupta parte corporis nondum uita deseruerat, qui per diem
uisu, per noctem ululatibus et gemitu coniuges aut liberos 20
noscebant. Iam ceteri fama exciti, hic fratrem, propinquum
ille, alius parentes lamentari; etiam quorum diuersa de causa
amici aut necessarii aberant, pauere tamen; nequedum com-
63 perto quos illa uis perculisset, latior ex incerto metus. Vt coepere
dimoueri obruta, concursus ad exanimos complectentium, 25
osculantium; et saepe certamen si confusior facies, sed par
forma aut aetas, errorem adgnoscentibus fecerat.

Quinquaginta hominum milia eo casu debilitata uel obtrita
sunt; cautumque in posterum senatus consulto ne quis gladia-
torium munus ederet cui minor quadringentorum milium res 30
neue amphitheatrum imponeretur nisi solo firmitatis spectatae.

---

6 amphitheatrū *M* **7** celebraretur *Wex* **10** sordidam mercedem *Pichena:*
-a -e *M* **13** effusius *Lipsius:* -sus *M* **17** staragis *M, corr.*
Beroaldus **18** <felices> ut tali sorte *Wex: alii alia* **19** qui<que> *uel* <aut>
qui *Pluygers* **21** noscebant *M:* poscebant *Neue* **24** perculisset *Beroaldus:*
periculis sed *M*   **26**   sed *Bekker.* et *M* **30** munus *Beroaldus:* manus *M*

2 Atilius in exilium actus est. Ceterum sub recentem cladem AD 27
patuere procerum domus, fomenta et medici passim praebiti,
fuitque urbs per illos dies, quamquam maesta facie, ueterum
institutis similis, qui magna post proelia saucios largitione et
cura sustentabant.   5

64 | Nondum ea clades exoleuerat cum ignis uiolentia urbem
ultra solitum adfecit, deusto monte Caelio; feralemque annum
ferebant et ominibus aduersis susceptum principi consilium
absentiae, qui mos uulgo, fortuita ad culpam trahentes, ni
Caesar obuiam isset tribuendo pecunias ex modo detrimenti. 10
2 Actaeque ei grates apud senatum <et> ab inlustribus, famaque
apud populum, quia sine ambitione aut proximorum precibus
3 ignotos etiam et ultro accitos munificentia iuuerat. Adduntur
sententiae ut mons Caelius in posterum Augustus appellaretur,
quando cunctis circum flagrantibus sola Tiberii effigies sita in 15
domo Iunii senatoris inuiolata mansisset: euenisse id olim
Claudiae Quintae, eiusque statuam uim ignium bis elapsam
maiores apud aedem matris deum consecrauisse; sanctos accep-
tosque numinibus Claudios, et augendam caerimoniam loco in
quo tantum in principem honorem di ostenderint.   20

65 Haud fuerit absurdum tradere montem eum antiquitus
Querquetulanum cognomento fuisse, quod talis siluae frequens
fecundusque erat, mox Caelium appellitatum a Caele Vibenna,
qui dux gentis Etruscae, cum auxilium [appellatum] tulisset,
sedem eam acceperat a Tarquinio Prisco, seu quis alius regum 25
dedit (nam scriptores in eo dissentiunt). Cetera non ambigua
112r sunt, | magnas eas copias per plana etiam ac foro propinqua
habitauisse: unde Tuscum uicum e uocabulo aduenarum
dictum.

66 Sed, ut studia procerum et largitio principis aduersum casus 30
solacium tulerant, ita accusatorum maior in dies et infestior uis

---

6 nondum *M*: Nam dū *M*   **8** ominibus *Beroaldus* (*M*^*mg*): omnibus *M*
11 gratis *M*   et *suppl. Stein*   **20** ostenderint *Lipsius*: -erent *M*
24 appellatum *M, secl. Lipsius*: appellatus *Faernus: alii alia*   tulisset *Lipsius*:
tauisset *M*: <por>tauisset *Doederlein*   **30** casus *Heinsius*: -um *M*   **31** tulerant *Beroaldus*: tel- *M*

sine leuamento grassabatur; corripueratque Varum AD 2
Quintilium, diuitem et Caesari propinquum, Domitius Afer,
Claudiae Pulchrae matris eius condemnator, nullo mirante
quod diu egens et parto nuper praemio male usus plura ad
2 flagitia accingeretur. Publium Dolabellam socium delationis 5
extitisse miraculo erat, quia claris maioribus et Varo conexus
suam ipse nobilitatem, suum sanguinem perditum ibat. Restitit
tamen senatus et opperiendum imperatorem censuit, quod
unum urgentium malorum suffugium in tempus erat.

67 At Caesar dedicatis per Campaniam templis, quamquam 10
edicto monuisset ne quis quietem eius inrumperet, concursusque oppidanorum disposito milite prohiberentur, perosus
tamen municipia et colonias omniaque in continenti sita
Capreas se in insulam abdidit, trium milium freto ab extremis
2 Surrentini promunturii diiunctam. Solitudinem eius placuisse 15
maxime crediderim, quoniam importuosum circa mare et uix
modicis nauigiis pauca subsidia; neque adpulerit quisquam nisi
gnaro custode. Caeli temperies hieme mitis obiectu montis, quo
saeua uentorum arcentur; aestas in fauonium obuersa et aperto
circum pelago peramoena; prospectabatque pulcherrimum 20
112v sinum, antequam Vesuuius mons ardescens | faciem loci uer-
teret. Graecos ea tenuisse Capreasque Telebois habitatas fama
3 tradit; sed tum Tiberius duodecim uillarum †nominibus et
molibus† insederat, quanto intentus olim publicas ad curas,
tanto occultior in luxus et malum otium resolutus. Manebat 25
quippe suspicionum et credendi temeritas, quam Seianus
augere etiam in urbe suetus acrius turbabat non iam occultis
4 aduersum Agrippinam et Neronem insidiis. Quis additus miles
nuntios, introitus, aperta, secreta uelut in annales referebat,
ultroque struebantur qui monerent perfugere ad Germaniae 30
exercitus uel celeberrimo fori effigiem diui Augusti amplecti

6 conexus *Rhenanus*: conixius *M* **14** addidit (*suprascr.* b) *M* **18** gnaro
Beroaldus (*M^{mg}*): grano *M* **23–4** nominibus et molibus *M, obelis not. Martin
et Woodman* (*separatim* nominibus et *secl. Martin,* amoenitatibus et m- *tempt.
Woodman*): moenibus et m- *Kaster. alii alia* **25** occultior *M*: occultos *J.F.
Gronouius*: occultiores *Weissenborn*

populumque ac senatum auxilio uocare. Eaque spreta ab illis, ᴀᴅ 27
uelut pararent, obiciebantur.

68 Iunio Silano et Silio Nerua consulibus foedum anni princi- ᴀᴅ 28
pium incessit, tracto in carcerem inlustri equite Romano Titio
Sabino ob amicitiam Germanici: neque enim omiserat coniu- 5
gem liberosque eius percolere, sectator domi, comes in publico,
post tot clientes unus eoque apud bonos laudatus et grauis
2 iniquis. Hunc Latinius Latiaris, Porcius Cato, Petilius Rufus,
M. Opsius praetura functi adgrediuntur cupidine consulatus, ad
quem non nisi per Seianum aditus; neque Seiani uoluntas nisi 10
scelere quaerebatur.

Compositum inter ipsos ut Latiaris, qui modico usu Sabinum
contingebat, strueret dolum; ceteri testes adessent, deinde accu-
3 sationem inciperent. Igitur | Latiaris iacere fortuitos primum
sermones, mox laudare constantiam quod non, ut ceteri, flor- 15
entis domus amicus adflictam deseruisset; simul honora de
Germanico, Agrippinam miserans, disserebat. Et postquam
Sabinus (ut sunt molles in calamitate mortalium animi) effudit
lacrimas, iunxit questus, audentius iam onerat Seianum, saeuitiam, superbiam, spes eius; ne in Tiberium quidem conuicio 20
4 abstinet; iique sermones, tamquam uetita miscuissent, speciem
artae amicitiae fecere. Ac iam ultro Sabinus quaerere Latiarem,
uentitare domum, dolores suos quasi ad fidissimum deferre.

69 Consultant quos memoraui quonam modo ea plurium auditu
acciperentur. Nam loco in quem coibatur seruanda solitudinis 25
facies; et, si pone fores adsisterent, metus uisus, sonitus aut forte
ortae suspicionis erat. Tectum inter et laquearia tres senatores
haud minus turpi latebra quam detestanda fraude sese abstru-
2 dunt, foraminibus et rimis aurem admouent. Interea Latiaris
repertum in publico Sabinum, uelut recens cognita narraturus, 30
domum et in cubiculum trahit praeteritaque et instantia,
quorum adfatim copia, ac nouos terrores cumulat. Eadem ille

---

8 Latinius *M*: Lucanius *Andresen* Petilius *Lipsius*: petitius *M* **22** fecere
Faernus, Muretus: facere *M* **27** erat *Rhenanus*: erant *M*

et diutius, quanto maesta, ubi semel prorupere, difficilius AD 2
reticentur.

3 Properata inde accusatio, missisque ad Caesarem litteris
ordinem fraudis suumque ipsi dedecus narrauere. Non alias
magis anxia et pauens ciuitas, <cautissime> agens aduersum 5
113v proximos: | congressus, conloquia, notae ignotaeque aures
uitari; etiam muta atque inanima, tectum et parietes
circumspectabantur.

70 Sed Caesar sollemnia incipientis anni kalendis Ianuariis epistula precatus uertit in Sabinum, corruptos quosdam libertorum 10
et petitum se arguens, ultionemque haud obscure poscebat. Nec
mora quin decerneretur; et trahebatur damnatus, quantum
obducta ueste et adstrictis faucibus niti poterat, clamitans sic
2 inchoari annum, has Seiano uictimas cadere. Quo intendisset
oculos, quo uerba acciderent, fuga, uastitas: deseri itinera, fora. 15
Et quidam regrediebantur ostentabantque se rursum, id ipsum
3 pauentes quod timuissent: quem enim diem uacuum poena, ubi
inter sacra et uota, quo tempore uerbis etiam profanis abstineri
mos esset, uincla et laqueus inducantur? non <im>prudentem
Tiberium tantam inuidiam adisse; quaesitum meditatumque, 20
ne quid impedire credatur quo minus noui magistratus, quo
modo delubra et altaria, sic carcerem recludant.

4 Secutae insuper litterae grates agentis quod hominem infensum rei publicae puniuissent, adiecto trepidam sibi uitam, sus-
pectas inimicorum insidias, nullo nominatim compellato; neque 25
71 tamen dubitabatur in Neronem et Agrippinam intendi. (Ni mihi
destinatum foret suum quaeque in annum referre, auebat animus antire statimque memorare exitus quos Latinius atque
114r Opsius ceterique flagitii eius repertores | habuere, non modo
postquam Gaius Caesar rerum potitus est sed incolumi Tiberio, 30
qui scelerum ministros, ut peruerti ab aliis nolebat, ita

---

1 quanto *M*: quando *Manutius*　　**4** ipsi *Beroaldus*: ipse *M*　　**5** <cautis-
sime> agens *Martin*: egens *M*: tegens *Lipsius*: *alii alia*　　**15** acciderent
Rhenanus: acciperent *M*　　**19** <im>prudentem *Rhenanus*: pru- *M*　　**20** adis-
set (*sed* t *deletum*) *M*　　**24** adiecto *Beroaldus*: -ti *M*　　**28** Latinius *M*:
Lucanius *Andresen*

plerumque satiatus et oblatis in eandem operam recentibus AD 28
ueteres et praegraues adflixit. Verum has atque alias sontium
2 poenas in tempore trademus.) Tum censuit Asinius Gallus,
cuius liberorum Agrippina matertera erat, petendum a principe
3 ut metus suos senatui fateretur amouerique sineret. Nullam 5
aeque Tiberius, ut rebatur, ex uirtutibus suis quam dissimula-
tionem diligebat: eo aegrius accepit recludi quae premeret. Sed
mitigauit Seianus, non Galli amore uerum ut cunctationes
principis opperiretur, gnarus lentum in meditando, ubi prorupisset, tristibus dictis atrocia facta coniungere.   10
4   Per idem tempus Iulia mortem obiit, quam neptem Augustus
conuictam adulterii damnauerat proieceratque in insulam
Trimerum, haud procul Apulis litoribus. Illic uiginti annis exilium tolerauit, Augustae ope sustentata, quae florentes
priuignos cum per occultum subuertisset, misericordiam erga 15
adflictos palam ostentabat.
72   Eodem anno Frisii, transrhenanus populus, pacem exuere,
nostra magis auaritia quam obsequii impatientes. Tributum iis
Drusus iusserat modicum pro angustia rerum, ut in usus militares coria boum penderent, non intenta cuiusquam cura quae 20
firmitudo, quae mensura, donec Olennius e primipilaribus,
114v regendis Frisiis impositus, | terga urorum delegit quorum ad
2 formam acciperentur. Id, aliis quoque nationibus arduum,
apud Germanos difficilius tolerabatur, quis ingentium
beluarum feraces saltus, modica domi armenta sunt. Ac primo 25
boues ipsos, mox agros, postremo corpora coniugum aut liber-
3 orum seruitio tradebant. Hinc ira et questus et, postquam non
subueniebatur, remedium ex bello. Rapti qui tributo aderant
milites et patibulo adfixi; Olennius infensos fuga praeuenit,
receptus castello cui nomen Fleuum; et haud spernenda illic 30
ciuium sociorumque manus litora Oceani praesidebat.

9 opperiretur *Muretus*: aperirentur *M* **13** Tremetum *Freinsheim* **22** delegit
Beroaldus: deiegit *M* **28** subueniebatur *Rhenanus*: -ebat *M*

73 Quod ubi L. Apronio inferioris Germaniae pro praetore AD 2
cognitum, uexilla legionum e superiore prouincia peditumque
et equitum auxiliarium delectos acciuit ac simul utrumque
exercitum Rheno deuectum Frisiis intulit, soluto iam castelli
obsidio et ad sua tutanda degressis rebellibus. Igitur proxima 5
aestuaria aggeribus et pontibus traducendo grauiori agmini
2 firmat, atque interim repertis uadis alam Canninefatem et
quod peditum Germanorum inter nostros merebat circumgredi
terga hostium iubet; qui iam acie compositi pellunt turmas
sociales equitesque legionum subsidio missos. Tum tres leues 10
cohortes ac rursum duae, dein tempore interiecto alarius eques
immissus, satis ualidi si simul incubuissent; per interuallum
aduentantes neque constantiam addiderant turbatis et pauore
115r fugientium | auferebantur.
3 Cethecio Labeoni legato quintae legionis quod reliquum 15
auxiliorum tradit; atque ille dubia suorum re in anceps tractus
missis nuntiis uim legionum implorabat. Prorumpunt quintani
ante alios et acri pugna hoste pulso recipiunt cohortes alasque
fessas uulneribus. Neque dux Romanus ultum iit aut corpora
humauit, quamquam multi tribunorum praefectorumque et 20
4 insignes centuriones cecidissent. Mox compertum a transfugis
nongentos Romanorum apud lucum (quem Baduhennae
uocant) pugna in posterum extracta confectos, et aliam quadringentorum manum occupata Cruptorigis quondam stipen-
diari uilla, postquam proditio metuebatur, mutuis ictibus 25
procubuisse.
74 Clarum inde inter Germanos Frisium nomen, dissimulante
Tiberio damna ne cui bellum permitteret. Neque senatus in eo
cura, an imperii extrema dehonestarentur: pauor internus occu-
2 pauerat animos, cui remedium adulatione quaerebatur. Ita, 30
quamquam diuersis super rebus consulerentur, aram

---

4 castelli *Rhenanus*: -o *M* **5** digressis *Beroaldus* **7** Canninefatium
Aschbach **9** pelluntur (ur *deletum*) *M* **11** alarius *Freinsheim*:
acrius *M* **15** Cethecio *M*: Cethego *Lipsius* **23** confeltos (*suprascr.*
c) *M* **24** Cruptorigis *Otto*: -oricis *M* **29** internus *Rhenanus*: -nos *M*

clementiae, aram amicitiae effigiesque circum Caesaris ac AD 28
Seiani censuere; crebrisque precibus efflagitabant, uisendi sui
3 copiam facerent. Non illi tamen in urbem aut propinqua urbi
degressi sunt: satis uisum omittere insulam et in proximo
Campaniae aspici. Eo uenire patres, eques, magna pars plebis, 5
115v anxii erga Seianum, cuius durior | congressus atque eo per
4 ambitum et societate consiliorum parabatur. Satis constabat
auctam ei adrogantiam foedum illud in propatulo seruitium
spectanti: quippe Romae sueti discursus, et magnitudine urbis
incertum quod quisque ad negotium pergat; ibi campo aut litore 10
iacentes nullo discrimine noctem ac diem iuxta gratiam aut
5 fastus ianitorum perpetiebantur, donec id quoque uetitum. Et
reuenere in urbem trepidi quos non sermone, non uisu dignatus
erat, quidam male alacres, quibus infaustae amicitiae grauis
exitus imminebat. 15

75   Ceterum Tiberius neptem Agrippinam, Germanico ortam,
cum coram Cn. Domitio tradidisset, in urbe celebrari nuptias
iussit. In Domitio super uetustatem generis propinquum
Caesaribus sanguinem delegerat: nam is auiam Octauiam et
per eam Augustum auunculum praeferebat. 20

---

2 *fort.* <ut> uisendi **5** uenere *Borzsák* **6** eo *secl. Doederlein* **8** illud in
propatulo *Beroaldus*: illum in propatibulo *M* **9** magnitudine *Rhenanus*:
-ni *M* **12** id quoque *Muretus*: idque *M* **14** infaustae *Beroaldus*:
infastae *M* FINIT LIBER IIII · INCI PIT LIBER · V · *M*

COMMENTARY

COMMENTARY

BOOK 4
1–16 THE YEAR AD 23

Since T. divides his narrative of Tib.'s reign into two halves of three books each, the start of Book 4 is marked out in various ways as a new beginning (esp. 1.1 *coepit*, 6.1 *initium*; also 4.3nn., 6.1n.). The narrative of AD 23 is devoted entirely to home affairs, in this respect being paralleled only by AD 27 in Book 4 and by relatively few other years in Books 1–6 as a whole (Ginsburg 53–4, 140–1). This concentration not only underlines the importance of the year's domestic events but also anticipates the later remarks which T. will make about the lack of foreign affairs and the difference from republican historiography of the 'Livian' type (32–3: see nn.).

1–3 Sejanus and a seduction

The opening allusion to Sallust (1.1n.) suggests that this is going to be a Sallustian narrative; and the sketch of Sejanus in the sequel is so clearly modelled on that of Sallust's Catiline (1.3nn.) that we are invited to see Sejanus as a second Catiline and his conspiracy in terms of Catiline's. See further the Introduction (pp. 3ff. above). The climax of the section is Sejanus' plot to murder Tib.'s son, Drusus, through the agency of the latter's wife, whom he seduces; the stages of the plot are also conceived along Sallustian lines, although in this case the allusions are to Sallust's second monograph (3.5n.).

1.1 C. Asinio C. Antistio consulibus C. Asinius Pollio, whose brother will be consul in 25 (34.1n.), was son of Asinius Gallus (6.23.1n.) and grandson of the famous C. Asinius Pollio, consul in 40 BC: see *RE* 2.1602–3 = Asinius 26 (Schwartz), *PIR* 1.253–4 no. 1242, *BNP* 2.161 [II 12]. C. Antistius Vetus, whose brother will be suffect consul in 28, was son and grandson of the homonymous consuls of 6 and 30 BC respectively: see *RE* 1.2559 = Antistius 49 (von Rohden), *PIR* 1.148 no. 772, *BNP* 1.790 [II 8]; Rüpke 533 no. 643. The family is praised at Vell. 43.4 (see Syme, *AA* 425–6, 428). For the consular dating see 3.2.3n., 5.1.1n.

nonus Tiberio annus erat The tense of the verb ('was in progress') both accommodates the fact that Tib.'s ninth year had already begun in the preceding August and prepares for the inverted *cum*-clause which follows below (see Chausserie-Laprée 594). Dating by regnal year is only here in the *Annals* and is used 'for abnormal emphasis' (Syme, *Tac.* 390 n. 2); the synchronism with the consular date adds to the effect and invites the question of

59

their relative importance (on synchronism in general see D. Feeney, *Caesar's Calendar* (2007) 7–42). The dat. *Tiberio* (cf. 6.45.3) facilitates the defining gen. which follows (next n.).

compositae rei publicae, florentis domus The defining genitives are dependent upon *annus* (last n.), like *ambitu . . . ornandi* at 2.3 below (see further 3.63.3n.). The former phrase (again at *D.* 36.2) is found before T. only at Cic. *Leg.* 3.42 ('nihil est enim exitiosius ciuitatibus, nihil tam contrarium iuri ac legibus, nihil minus ciuile et immanius quam composita et constituta re publica quicquam agi per uim'), a passage which, given the role of *uis* in Sejanus' career (3.1 below), T. perhaps has in mind. The latter expression (again at 4.68.3) is a favourite of Cicero (*II Verr.* 1.55, *Orat.* 142, *ND* 1.6), though also at Sen. *Phaedr.* 435–6 'prospero regnum in statu est | domusque florens sorte felici uiget'. Whether the two participles here combine to form a single image, perhaps of a well-tended garden or field of crops before being wrecked by a storm, is hard to say. For *domus* of the imperial family (also at 3.1 below) see R. P. Saller, '*Familia, domus*, and the Roman conception of the family', *Phoenix* 38 (1984) 336–55, at 345–9.

nam Germanici mortem inter prospera ducebat For this theme see 3.2.3 'laetam Tiberio Germanici mortem male dissimulari', Dio 57.18.6. *ducere inter* seems uncommon but cf. Plin. *NH* 2.159, 7.33, 7.144, [Quint.] *Decl.* 268.12, 329.10 (*TLL* 5.1.2156.84–2157.9).

cum repente turbare Fortuna coepit, saeu̲i̲r̲e̲ ipse aut saeuienti- bus u̲i̲r̲e̲s̲ praebere The first of the various turning points in Tib.'s reign (cf. 6.51.3) is emphasised by being presented in terms of the one cardinal turning point in Roman history as seen by Sallust, namely, the destruction of Carthage in 146 BC (*C.* 10.1 'sed, ubi . . . reges magni bello domiti, nationes ferae et populi ingentes ui subacti, Carthago aemula imperi Romani ab stirpe interiit, cuncta maria terraeque patebant, *saeuire Fortuna* ac miscere omnia *coepit*'). The clarity of the reference is programmatic for the allusions to Sallust which follow below (nn.). But, whereas Sallust at *C.* 10.1 had seen Fortuna as a savage beast coming upon the scene after Rome had tamed or subdued all the other wild animals, T. has transferred the savagery to Tib. and his fellows and has presented Fortuna as a disruptive force like a storm (*fortuna turbat* is seemingly unparalleled, but cf. Apul. *Met.* 8.31.4 'in ultimo fortunae turbine'). It is relevant that Sejanus, who is about to be introduced, cultivated Fortuna and had a statue of her, which turned its back on him before his fall (5.6.2n.).

saeuitia is one of the principal vices of the archetypal tyrant (6.19.3n.): hitherto T. has sometimes associated Tib. with the vice by means of other voices (as 1.4.3, 1.10.7, 1.72.4, 3.22.4), but authorial statements have been relatively rare (1.53.3, 1.74.2), no doubt because T.'s view of the period AD 14–23 is almost entirely benign (6.2–4 below). Nor, on the evidence of Book 4, is there any indication that Tib. himself 'suddenly began to turn savage' now: perhaps, therefore, *aut* here has a corrective function and means 'or rather' (*OLD* 6b) and it is only later, after his withdrawal from Rome in 26 (cf. 4.57.1), that Tib.'s personal savagery comes to the fore (see *Tac. Rev.* 164–5). In the intervening years it is others, principally the *delatores* and/or Sejanus' henchmen, who act savagely (e.g. 19.1 Visellius Varro, 28.1 Vibius Serenus, 34.1 Satrius Secundus and Pinarius Natta); whether the *saeuientes* include Sejanus himself depends upon whether one thinks he is able simultaneously to be, as T. is about to say that he is, their *initium et causa*.

The repetition *saeuire* ~ *saeuientibus* belongs to the type broadly called 'category-shift', although 'participial resumption', as here, more normally retains the same subject (Wills 311–28). For *cum repente* see 6.2.2n.

Initium et causa penes Aelium Seianum For L. Aelius Seianus see, in addition to the standard works (Seager and Levick) and notes immediately below, *RE* 1.529–31 = Aelius 133 (v. Rohden), *PIR* 1.41–3 no. 255, *BNP* 1.205–6 [II 19]; Hennig; A. D. Heinrichs, *Sejan und das Schicksal Roms in den Annalen des Tacitus* (diss. Marburg/Lahn 1976); Demougin, *PCR* 234–7 no. 272; Syme, *AA* 300–12, 470 (index), and Table XXIII; Birley (2007); M. Hausmann, *Leserlenkung durch Tacitus in den Tiberius- und Claudiusbüchern der Annalen* (2009) 97–112; Champlin (2012); and my notes on Vell. 127–8.

Historiography regularly demonstrates a keen interest, derived from epic, in causation and 'firsts', of which the ἀρχή κακῶν motif (below, 6.1n.) is a common manifestation (see e.g. Häussler, 368ff.): see esp. *H.* 1.4.1. *initium* and *causa* (sing. and plur.) are combined before T. 3× in Cicero (who only has the terms in this order), 2× in Livy (the opposite order), and 2× in the younger Seneca (both orders, like T. elsewhere: see e.g. H. on *H.* 1.51.1 (quoted below, n. *nunc*)). For *initium penes* cf. *G.* 31.3, Gell. 16.17.2 (quoting Varro); *causa p.* is at 4.16.2 (below), Liv. 28.27.11, Juv. 14.226 (at Apul. *Flor.* 18 it means *coram*).

cohortibus praetoriis praefectum Sejanus had been appointed to this post, presumably in AD 14, alongside his father (1.24.2); when his father became prefect of Egypt in 15, Sejanus held the post alone (Dio 57.19.6; Birley (2007) 126 and n. 27). T. characteristically avoids the standard term *praefectus praetorio*, which he never uses. See further 2.1nn. below.

cuius de potentia supra memoraui Cf. 3.66.3 'Seiani potentia' (n.). His influence with Tib. is mentioned at 1.24.2 (n.), and the senate's vote in 22 to erect a statue of him in Pompey's Theatre is mentioned at 3.72.3 (nn.); he is also referred to at 1.69.5, 3.16.1, 29.4 and 35.2 (he is not mentioned in Book 2): see further Graf 27–30. His *potentia* will recur below at 7.1, 41.2 and 6.8.4: 'How strongly Tacitus is drawn to the word needs little documentation' (Syme, *Tac.* 413). For cross-references see 3.18.1n., and for *memorare* see 3.24.3n.; for the precise form *supra memoraui* see *Agr.* 18.3n.

nunc originem, mores et quo facinore dominationem raptum ierit expediam Just as Sallust prefaces his narrative of Catiline's conspiracy with a biographical sketch of the central, villainous character (*C.* 4.4 'de quoius hominis moribus pauca prius explananda sunt quam initium narrandi faciam'), so T. begins the second half of the first hexad with a similar sketch of Sejanus.[1] A key difference is that, so far as we can judge from the surviving text, Sejanus at no point overshadows Tib., who remains the central personality; but the sketch is a guide to Sejanus' importance, which is already impressive (2.3 below) and in later years saw him rise almost to the level of *princeps* (cf. Dio 58.4.1 ὁ δὲ δὴ Σεϊανὸς καὶ μείζων καὶ φοβερώτερος ἀεὶ ἐγίγνετο, ὥστε καὶ τοὺς βουλευτὰς καὶ τοὺς ἄλλους ἐκείνῳ μὲν ὡς καὶ αὐτοκράτορι προσέχειν, τὸν δὲ Τιβέριον ἐν ὀλιγωρίᾳ ποιεῖσθαι).

T.'s sketch of Sejanus, as will be seen (below), is heavily Sallustian, but its introduction here is differently worded. Although there are two exs. in Varro (*LL* 5.7, 5.57), the formula *nunc . . . expediam* + direct object or object noun clause 'takes us in the direction of poetry' (R. F. Thomas, *CCT* 62) and specifically to Lucretius (8×) and Virgil (4×); cf. also Sil. 11.1–3. T. uses the formula twice elsewhere (*G.* 27.2 'haec in commune de omnium Germanorum origine ac moribus accepimus; nunc singularum gentium instituta ritusque, quatenus differant quae<que> nationes e Germania in Gallias commigrauerint, expediam', *H.* 1.51.1 'nunc initia causasque motus Vitelliani expediam'). *origo* (γένεσις) and *mores* (ἐπιτηδεύματα), elsewhere combined only by T. (at *G.* 27.2, quoted), are two of the standard elements expected in a biographical description such as that which follows; a third is *facta* (πράξεις), to which *facinore* alludes.

Whether Sejanus' ultimate political goal was *dominatio*, as T. repeats at 3 below ('parando regno') and as other ancient authors seem to have believed (cf. Jos. *AJ* 18.179–82, Suet. *Tib.* 65.1 'res nouas molientem'), is controversial: modern scholars are generally sceptical (but see esp. Birley (2007), including a most helpful survey of scholarly opinion, and Champlin (2012)).

For M's *raptum perit* Pichena's *raptum ierit* is universally accepted: the expr. has Sallustian precedent (*H.* 1.55.20 'qua raptum ire licet') and is used by T. elsewhere (*H.* 2.6.2 'res Romanas raptum ire'). The *facinus* in question is the murder of Tib.'s son, Drusus (cf. 3.1 'magnitudo facinoris'). For *dominationem rapere* cf. Suet. *DJ* 30.5.

1.2 Genitus Vulsiniis, patre Seio Strabone Sejanus' date of birth is unknown but assumed to be the late 20s BC: he was therefore an exact contemporary of Velleius Paterculus, who is assumed to have been born

---

[1] Graf (30) remarks that T. in the *Annals* normally prefers the so-called 'indirect method' of characterisation, noting that the only parallel for so Sallustian a sketch is that of Poppaea Sabina at 13.45.

around 20/19 BC. For L. Seius Strabo, described by Velleius as 'princeps equestris ordinis' (127.3), see *RE* 2A.1.1125–6 = Seius 15 (Stein), *PIR* 7.2.121–3 no. 322, *BNP* 13.209 [2]; Demougin, *PCR* 181–3 no. 207; Syme, *AA* 300ff. and Table XXIII. Strabo was succeeded as Prefect of Egypt (above, 1.1n. *cohortibus*) by C. Galerius after only a year; it is assumed that he died in post. Volsinii (mod. Bolsena) in Etruria lay roughly 80 miles NNW of Rome; a fragmentary inscription recovered there honours Strabo as Praetorian Prefect (*CIL* 11.2707). For *genitus* see 3.61.1n.

prima iuuenta C. Caesarem ... sectatus At the turn of the century Gaius Caesar had been in the east, where he died prematurely in AD 4 from the after-effects of a wound (1.3.3). In his entourage was Velleius Paterculus, who later reported that, as Gaius' mind and body deteriorated after his wound, the young prince did not lack for 'the company of those who fostered his flaws by their flattery' (102.3); E. Badian (ap. G. V. Sumner, 'The truth about Velleius Paterculus: Prolegomena', *HSCP* 74 (1970) 267 n. 67) suggested that this was a covert refence to Sejanus, who is assumed also to have been with Gaius at the time (Syme, *RP* 1.313). For other members of the entourage see F. E. Romer, 'Gaius Caesar's military diplomacy in the East', *TAPA* 109 (1979) 202 n. 11, but without reference to Apicius (next n.), who may also have been a member (R. Syme, *Anatolica* (1995) 322 and n. 35).

Although Sejanus' birth and young manhood (standard biographical elements) are each referred to at the head of their respective cola (*genitus* ~ *prima iuuenta*), the cola themselves are arranged chiastically (*genitus*/proper name + appositional phrase ~ proper name + appositional phrase/*sectatus*), while *prima iuuenta* also looks forward to *mox* below (as 12.29.1 'prima imperii aetate ... mox'). Similar complexity characterises the remainder of the sentence (see below). For *iuuenta* see 3.8.2n.; for its qualification by *prima* see Malloch on 11.22.3.

non sine rumore Apicio diuiti et prodigo stuprum ueno dedisse That is, Sejanus was rumoured to have turned himself into what is described by Cicero (*Phil.* 2.105) as a *puer meritorius*, taking the passive role, which was regarded as disgraceful. Dio is more forthright (57.19.5 παιδικὰ δέ ποτε Μάρκου Γαβίου Ἀπικίου γενόμενος, Ἀπικίου ἐκείνου ὃς πάντας ἀνθρώπους ἀσωτίᾳ ὑπερεβάλετο), whereas Sallust was circumspect about the homosexual rumours attaching to Catiline (*C.* 14.7). M. Gavius Apicius became proverbial for his wealth and gourmanderie (Otto 29): he is mentioned by Seneca (*Cons. Helv.* 10.8–9, *Ep.* 95.42, 120.19) and Juvenal (4.23, 11.3) and very frequently by the elder Pliny and Martial (see e.g. Williams on 2.69.3, and, for general discussion of 'prodigal pleasures', see C. Edwards, *The politics of immorality in ancient Rome* (1993) 173–206). It is thought that some of the recipes of this Apicius found their way into the famous cookbook attributed to a later

Apicius, with whom Gavius is inevitably confused (*BNP* 2.893–4). For *diuiti et prodigo* cf. *H.* 1.66.2 (Fabius Valens); for *stuprum* see 6.1.1n. See also 3.3n. and 10.2n. below.

non sine (11× in T.) is common in all periods and types of language, esp. Horace's *Odes* and Suetonius' *Lives* (where it is almost a mannerism); Livy occasionally varies *non sine* (20×) by *haud sine* (5×), otherwise found only in verse in classical Latin (3×). The predicative dat. *ueno* is confined to T. (again at 13.51.1, 14.15.2), as is the form *uenui* to Apuleius (3×); but T. also has the more orthodox *uenum dare* (see Malloch on 11.22.6).

mox Tiberium . . . uiguit ceciditque Some idea of the extreme difficulty of this passage may be gathered from the extensive list of differing interpretations and translations provided by D. Wiesen, '*Isdem artibus victus est*: Tacitus, *Annales* IV 1,3', *Mnem.* 23 (1970) 402–7.[2] In my view the correct interpretation may be paraphrased as follows: 'Sejanus was so successful in subjugating Tiberius by various means that he rendered the *princeps* uniquely vulnerable to him – but the reason was not so much Sejanus' cleverness (after all, his defeat was brought about by the same means) as the anger of the gods against the Roman state, for which his prosperity and downfall were equally destructive.' The key element in this interpretation is that a distinction has to be made between *artibus* and *sollertia*. The former includes all the ways, especially guile and cunning, in which Sejanus manipulated Tib. and which Tib. deployed against Sejanus at the very last moment. The latter is a much broader quality, whose potential as a causative agent was almost completely nullified by the anger of the gods (as shown by Sejanus' ultimate defeat by Tib.).

Tiberium uariis artibus deuinxit The verb is a favourite of T., which he uses only in the *Annals*, always metaphorically, and 'often to give a negative expression to relationships' (Malloch on 11.28.2); here it is difficult to know whether the meaning is 'subjugated' (as 1.3.4) or 'bound <to himself>' (as 12.42.1): the former is perhaps more likely in view of the clause which follows and the absence of an expressed dative. The combination with *artes* is pointed, since for Cicero, to whom it is otherwise confined, it is a positive expression (*Off.* 1.22, *Fam.* 13.29.1, 15.4.16).

obscurum aduersum alios sibi uni *in*cautum *in*tectumque The description is characterised by alliteration, chiasmus and the *uariatio* of prep. ~ dat. (as *Agr.* 22.4, *H.* 1.35.2); for the dat. after *incautus* see 11.26.2. *obscurus* here refers to secretive behaviour, as at 6.24.3 'tegendis sceleribus obscurum' (*TLL* 9.2.172.35–45). *intectus* is only here in the

---

[2] Wiesen's list, despite its extent, is not comprehensive: it omits the extraordinary interpretation of Ritter, which is repeated verbatim by Doederlein.

metaphorical sense of 'unguarded' (*TLL* 7.2071.13–15). For the form *aduersum* see 3.14.1n.

non tam sollertia . . . quam deum ira The ablatives are causal and not, like *uariis artibus* and *isdem artibus*, instrumental; the same distinction is to be seen at e.g. Liv. 3.6.5 'urbem Romanam subita deum ira morbo populari'.

isdem artibus uictus est Each of these phrases has been contested (see Wiesen's paper, cited on *mox Tiberium* above). (a) [i] Many, perhaps the majority, think that *isdem artibus* refers to *sollertia*, just mentioned: 'i.e. *sollertia*', says Furneaux. [ii] Some think that *isdem* means 'identical': in other words, Tib. defeated Sejanus by using identical means to those which Sejanus had used against him. [iii] Others think that *isdem* is equivalent to *suis*: that is, Sejanus' *artes* brought about his own defeat.

As we have already seen, [i] should be ruled out. If *isdem artibus* refers to *sollertia*, the latter must mean something like 'cunning'; but, since *uariis artibus* is bound to include cunning, it makes no sense to say both that Sejanus subjugated Tib. through cunning and that his results were achieved 'not so much by cunning'. Between [ii] and [iii] there is little practical difference, since the techniques (cunning and the like) are the same in each case; but the clear relationship (denied by Wiesen) between *uariis artibus* and *isdem artibus* suggests that the reciprocal reversal of [ii] is preferable. This conclusion is supported by the meaning of the verb.

(b) [i] Many, again perhaps the majority, think that *uictus est* means 'was defeated by ~ '; [ii] others think that the meaning is 'was surpassed in ~ '. There can be little doubt that [i] is correct. *uinco* seems an unnatural verb to use = 'surpass' in this context, and a preparatory reference to Sejanus' fall (*ceciditque*) is welcome. It is also the case that T.'s sentence exemplifies a regular form of words which in Latin expresses the proverbial idea of 'hoist with one's own petard': that is, X finds that Y is using against him the *artes* which he himself had previously used against Y (e.g. Sall. *J.* 48.1 'Iugurtha ubi . . . se suis artibus temptari animaduortit', Liv. 22.16.5 'nec Hannibalem fefellit suis se artibus peti': see R. Renehan, 'A proverbial expression in Tacitus', *CP* 68 (1973) 114–15, with numerous other exs.; also Otto 154, 342).

Hence the meaning is: 'he was defeated by the same means [sc. as he had used against Tib.]'. It illustrates the commonplace that the tyrant is surrounded by men like himself (see *Agr.* 41.1n.), which was esp. applicable to Tib. and Sejanus (cf. Dio 57.19.7 τῆς τῶν τρόπων ὁμοιότητος). It is striking that the contemporary Philo should describe Tib. as τῶν κατ' αὐτὸν ἁπάντων δεινότατος ὢν ἀφανὲς ἀνθρώπου βούλημα συνιδεῖν (*Leg. Gai.* 33).

deum ira in rem Romanam It has been suggested that T. invokes divine anger to explain the anomaly that the 'manifestly intelligent and unremittingly suspicious' *princeps* could be fooled by the less astute Sejanus

(J. P. Davies, *Rome's religious history* (2004) 194 n. 161), but this interpretation takes no account of the fact that, as the following clause makes clear, divine anger caused Sejanus to have a malign influence on the *res Romana* even after his death (next n.). Rather, T. resorts to the *ira deum* to explain and emphasise the horror of the remainder of Tib.'s reign in its entirety: since this period comprises the second half of the first hexad of the *Annals*, the divine anger is mentioned very appropriately at the beginning of Book 4, casting a baleful shadow over everything that follows.

Syme described T.'s reference as 'A striking and ominous phrase, but no confession of a creed' (*Tac.* 521), while in Goodyear's opinion T.'s references to fate and the gods are 'nothing more than devices of style, calculated to enhance his presentation of particular scenes' (n. on 1.39.6, where the phrase *deum ira* recurs). Divine anger as a motivating force is as old as the *Iliad* (see Horsfall on Virg. *Aen.* 11.233 'ira deum'), and, although both *de(or)um ira* and *res Romana* are common expressions in both verse and prose, they lend themselves to epic (e.g. Enn. *Ann.* 156 'moribus antiquis res stat Romana uirisque') and their choice perhaps heightens the tone here. For the plur. *deum* see 3.57.1n.

cuius pari exitio uiguit ceciditque Since predicative datives are almost never qualified by an adj. (K–S 1.343), *pari exitio* must be abl. of attendant circumstances: his prosperity and fall were each accompanied by a similar destructiveness for the Roman state (cf. Liv. 25.16.11 'res . . . Romana quae prope exitium clade Cannensi uenisset'). The references are to the deaths which Sejanus brought about during his lifetime and to the vengeance which Tib. wrought on Sejanus' perceived associates after his death and which T. recalls, ring-fashion, at the ominous close of the book (74.5 'quibus infaustae amicitiae grauis exitus imminebat'). For *uiguit ceciditque* cf. Ov. *Met.* 15.426–8; for sentence-final *–que* see 3.34.5n.

1.3 Corpus illi laborum tolerans, animus audax . . . quotiens parando regno finguntur T.'s formal sketch of Sejanus needs to be seen in the light of two others: Velleius' sketch of the same man and Sallust's of Catiline.

Ti. Caesar Seianum Aelium, principe equestris ordinis patre natum, materno uero genere clarissimas ueteresque et insignes honoribus complexum familias, habentem consulares fratres, consobrinos, auunculum, ipsum uero *laboris* ac fidei capacissimum, sufficiente etiam uigori *animi* compage *corporis*, singularem principalium onerum adiutorem in omnia habuit atque habet, uirum priscae seueritatis, laetissimae hilaritatis, actu otiosis simillimum, nihil sibi uindicantem eoque adsequentem omnia, semperque infra aliorum aestimationes se metientem, uultu uitaque tranquillum, animo exsomnem.   Vell. 127.3–4

Corpus patiens inediae, algoris, uigiliae supra quam quoiquam credibile est. *animus audax*, subdolus, uarius, quoius rei lubet simulator ac dissimulator,

66

alieni adpetens, *sui* profusus, ardens in cupiditatibus; satis eloquentiae, sapientiae parum. Vastus animus inmoderata, incredibilia, nimis alta semper cupiebat. Hunc post dominationem L. Sullae *lubido* maxuma inuaserat rei publicae capiundae, neque id quibus modis adsequeretur, dum sibi *regnum pararet*, quicquam pensi habebat.   Sall. *C.* 5.3–6

Contrary to much scholarly opinion, T. was familiar with Velleius' history (*CCT* 2–4) and knew the above passage (*insignes . . . complexum familias* recurs in T. at 15.48.1 'insignesque familias . . . complexus'), which no doubt reflects the official image which Sejanus wished to project; but he has re-presented this image through the dark lens of Sallust, to whose sketch of Catiline he alludes with particular clarity at the beginning and end in the manner of a frame.

Corpus illi laborum tolerans, animus audax The (standard) contrast between body and mind is taken directly from Sallust, as the presence of *audax* shows. For *patiens* T. has substituted *tolerans* (a favoured verb: cf. 3.1.1n.), which he uses only here with the genitive (otherwise a feature only in Columella, e.g. 6.22.2 'frigoris tolerantior'). Reference to the toleration of hunger and cold is as appropriate to Catiline, who led an army in the field, as it is to Hannibal (Liv. 21.4.6), whose sketch by Livy is likewise modelled on that of Catiline by Sallust (see J. J. Clauss, *MD* 39 (1997) 169–82); but, since Sejanus, though wishing to be seen as a military man (39.2n.), operated almost exclusively in the domestic sphere, the more generalised *laborum* is more appropriately applied to him, as it is by Velleius. *audax* is code for 'subversive' or 'revolutionary' (C. Wirszubski, *JRS* 51 (1961) 12–22), and there seems no doubt that T. saw Sejanus in such terms (see further below).

sui obtegens, in alios criminator Sallust's contrast had been between an acquisitive and prodigal *animus* (above); T. transfers the contrast to Sejanus himself and applies it to his personality and programme. *obtegens* + gen. seems unparalleled (*TLL* 9.2.269.76–7); *criminator*, echoing and perhaps substituting for Sallust's paired nouns in –*ator* (above), is found again only at 4.12.4 below and Plaut. *Bacch.* 826 in classical Latin: for such nouns and T.'s fondness for them see Malloch on 11.19.2, with much further detail and bibliography. The sentence illustrates a double *uariatio* of *sui* ~ *in alios* (cf. e.g. 2.76.3 'sui . . . in Caesares', 14.9.2), which is an allusion to Sallust's *alieni* ~ *sui*, and of part. ~ noun (as 6.38.3 'ostentans et contemptor', 12.4.1 'obtegens . . . prouisor').

iuxta adulatio et superbia *iuxta* underlines the paradoxical coexistence of such opposite capabilities (the two nouns are co-ordinated only here) within the same person (cf. 11.21.3 'aduersus superiores tristi adulatione, adrogans minoribus', of Curtius Rufus). Presumably the former was more prominent in the earlier stages of Sejanus' career, when his lowly origins required sycophancy towards his social superiors; but his increasing power saw him come to treat these same individuals with arrogance and contempt (74.3–4 below; cf. 40.5). It is tempting to see *adulatio* as a reinterpretation of Velleius' *semper . . . infra aliorum aestimationes se metientem.*

palam compositus pudor, intus summa apiscendi libido The contrast between outer and inner (*palam ~ intus* recurs only at Varro, *LL* 5.131) resembles Velleius' *uultu uitaque tranquillum, animo exsomnem* but recasts it in the light of Sallust's *nimis alta semper cupiebat* and *lubido maxuma* (*summa* is neut. plur., as 11.26.3 'summa adeptus'). It is difficult to know whether *compositus* means 'contrived' or 'composed' (*OLD compono* 10b, 11, 13a); for *pudor* see Kaster 28–65, though our passage is not mentioned. For T.'s preference for *apiscor* over *adipiscor* see 3.31.2n.

modo largitio et luxus, saepius industria ac uigilantia *largitio* represents Sallust's *sui profusus*; *luxus* is the negative interpretation of Velleius' *laetissimae hilaritatis* (for the association of *hilaritas* and luxury see Vell. 105.2, Val. Max. 6.9 *ext.* 1, Stat. *Silv.* 5.2.73–4). *uigilantia* picks up both Velleius' *exsomnem* and Sallust's *uigiliae*. Industry and watchfulness are irreproachable qualities in themselves (Vell. 88.2n. (p. 241)) and natural partners (Sen. *Cons. Pol.* 7.2 'omnium somnos illius [sc. Caesaris] uigilia defendit, . . . omnium delicias illius industria', Fronto p. 175.20 vdH[2] 'industria et uigilantia'): thus Sejanus' *labor* and *uigilantia* are praised by Tib. at 3.72.3. In the sketch, however, they are misapplied (next n.). *modo . . . saepius* (again at 11.16.2, 14.10.1) seems strictly unprecedented, but for *saepius . . . modo . . . modo* cf. *Bell. Afr.* 6.5, Liv. 41.20.12; and for *modo . . . modo . . . saepius* cf. Cels. 1.1.1, Plin. *NH* 3.6. For *luxus* see 3.52.1n.

haud minus noxiae quotiens parando regno finguntur sc. *quam largitio et luxus*. Though *regnum parare* occurs elsewhere (e.g. Luc. 1.34–5), the context guarantees that *parando regno* is an allusion to Sallust's *dum sibi regnum pararet* (curiously not mentioned in the comparison of the two texts by B.-R. Voss, *Der pointierte Stil des Tacitus* (1963) 76–9). The point about Sejanus' industry and watchfulness was not that they were feigned (rather, the opposite) but that they were misapplied: the meaning is 'whenever they are moulded for the purpose of obtaining a kingdom' (for *finguntur* in this sense see 6.51.3 (n. *occultum*)). For the dat. gerundive construction, a favourite of T.'s (3.25.1n.), cf. Plaut. *Asin.* 250 'argento conparando fingere fallaciam' (though there the verb means 'devise').

2.1 Vim praefecturae . . . metus oreretur Dio 57.19.6 relates the consolidation (in almost identical terms) under AD 20 but implies that Sejanus had started it as soon as his father had left for Egypt, i.e. in AD 15. The whole of 1.2–3.5 is digressive and includes information about Sejanus' earlier career which T. has deliberately withheld until now for maximum effect; only at 4.1 ('anni principio') do we return to the beginning of AD 23.

modicam antea Nevertheless the prefect of the praetorian guard (Sejanus' father) had been preceded only by the two consuls in taking the oath of allegiance to Tib. (1.7.2). This was some measure of the prefecture's importance.

dispersas per urbem cohortes sc. *praetori(an)as*; Suetonius is a little more specific (*Tib.* 37.1): 'cohortes . . . per hospitia dispersae'. At this time there were nine cohorts in all (5.3 below), each thought to comprise 500 men. Only three of the cohorts were actually stationed in the city, the remaining six dispersed 'circa finitima oppida' (Suet. *Aug.* 49.1). At some later point, perhaps in Tib.'s reign but perhaps later, the number of cohorts was increased to twelve (*AE* 1978, no. 286, p. 78). See Keppie 153–4, Campbell 109–20, J. Coulston, '"Armed and belted men": the soldiery in imperial Rome', in J. Coulston and H. Dodge (edd.), *Ancient Rome: the archaeology of the Eternal City* (2000) 76–118, esp. 82–6, and in general M. Jallet-Huant, *La garde prétorienne dans la Rome antique* (2004), S. Bingham, *The Praetorian Guard: a history of Rome's elite special forces* (2013).

una in castra The camp was built into the city walls, between the Colline and Viminal Gates: see *LTUR* 1.251–4 (convenient map in e.g. J. R. Patterson, 'The city of Rome', *JRS* 82 (1992) 211). Its remains are still visible beneath the Biblioteca Nazionale.

ut simul imperia acciperent numeroque . . . fiducia ipsis, in ceteros metus oreretur The three genuine reasons for building the new camp undermine in advance the three pretexts which Sejanus will offer in the next sentence.

　　Commentators say that *in ceteros* is equivalent to a dative, comparing 59.2 'hinc metus in omnes et fuga eorum', 11.8.2 'unde metus . . . in ceteros'; but these exs. are different in that they have no expressed verb, which it is relatively easy to supply (e.g. 'terror settled/descended upon ~ '). If *oreretur* is right,[3] the natural meaning of *metus* is not 'fear' but 'ground for alarm' or 'threat' (*OLD* 5a): 'in order that . . . their size, strength and sight of one another should result in confidence for themselves and a threat to others'. *numerus* is a technical term for a military complement (*OLD* 5a); for *uisu inter se* see e.g. Liv. 28.19.14 'accendebantur animi . . . ipso inter se conspectu'. For the antithesis between *fiducia* and *metus* see 12.31.2, *H.* 2.66.2, Liv. 6.33.10, Val.

---

[3] To explain the corruption Furneaux compares 1.49.2 (*cremari* > *ore mari*), which is not quite the same.

Max. 7.4.1, Stat. *Theb.* 6.393, Plin. *Ep.* 9.13.8. For the *uariatio* of dat. ~ *in* + acc., here chiastic, see 9.2, 12.55.1.

Praetendebat . . . inlecebris Sejanus' first words in the *Annals* are specious, pretexts cleverly directed at the two different categories of praetorian cohorts (see below). The last two pretexts constitute an elegant chiasmus (*si*-clause + main clause ~ main clause + *si*-clause), but his compressed manner of expression (next n.) perhaps hints that he wants to get his false allegations out of the way as quickly as possible.

lasciuire militem diductum; . . . pariter subueniri *diductum* (= *qui* (or *si*) *diductus esset*) and *pariter* (= *si pariter miles subuenisset*) indicate that these two arguments are directed primarily at the six cohorts dispersed outside the city (above, n. *dispersas*). The vagueness of *si quid subitum ingruat* adroitly implies that an emergency is unlikely to happen under his command, but it is better to be safe than sorry. For the collective sing. *miles* see Malloch on 11.9.1, adding Austin and Horsfall on Virg. *Aen.* 2.20.

si uallum statuatur procul urbis inlecebris 'The antithesis between rustic virtue and urban corruption . . . was deeply rooted in ancient thought' (Courtney on Juv. 3, intro. (p. 154)). Since *procul* may, but need not, refer to a great distance (*OLD* 2, 1), Sejanus cleverly suggests that the three cohorts now stationed within the city will enjoy a much greater isolation than was in fact the case: the new camp was integral with the city walls (above, n. *una*). He blithely ignores the objection that the other six cohorts, previously dispersed in outlying towns, will now be nearer the city than before.

2.2 inrepere paulatim militares animos The verb is used literally of poison at 8.1 below and metaphorically of disease at 1.73.1 (n.; *PH* 163–4). Its transitive use is rare; there are two further metaphorical exs. at Gell. 1.6.4 'animos . . . inrepere' (quoting his teacher T. Castricius), Apul. *Met.* 7.1.6.

adeundo, appellando; simul . . . ipse deligere Each of these activities is characteristic of the ideal leader (see respectively 3.45.2n., Oakley on Liv. 8.39.4, and *Agr.* 19.2n.): the sentence illustrates T.'s 'familiar trick of making something normal sound somehow sinister' (as Mr Seager aptly puts it). T. is alluding to the 'battle for the principate' on which Sejanus has now embarked; Catiline had done the same (Sall. *C.* 17.1 'singulos appellare', 20.1 'appellare et cohortari').

T. is extremely fond of two-element asyndeton of various types (e.g. *compositae rei publicae, florentis domus* at 1.1 above or *frumenta et pecuniae uectigales, cetera publicorum fructuum* and *spectatissimo cuique, quibusdam ignotis* in quick succession at 6.3 below), but asyndeton bimembre involving two unqualified words, as here, is most frequent in the first hexad and more frequent in Book 4 than in any other book except the first (Adams (1972) 355): e.g. 36.3 'leues, ignobiles', 37.3

'ambitiosum, superbum', 43.3 'uatum, annalium', 48.2 'clamore, telis', 49.1 'bellatorum, imbellium', 50.4 'circumire, hortari', 57.3 'exprobrabat, reposcebat', 63.1 'complectentium, osculantium', 70.2 'fuga, uastitas', 'itinera, fora'. See also Malloch on 11.12.3 (nouns) and 11.16.2 (verbs); Vell. 100.3n.; Adams (2016) 78–83 and 690–1 (index: note the frequency of alliterating pairs, as here). For exs. elsewhere with gerunds see e.g. Plaut. *Poen.* 223 'lauando, eluendo', Cic. *Off.* 1.22 'dando, accipiendo'; no such example is given for Sallust by E. Wölfflin ('Zum Asyndeton bei Sallust', *ALL* 11 (1900) 29–30), though he quotes threefold asyndetic gerunds at *C.* 52.29 and 54.3. For the archaising *deligere* see Malloch on 11.22.4.

2.3 Neque senatorio ambitu abstinebat clientes suos ... ornandi Lit. 'nor did he refrain from a courtship of senators which consisted of honouring his own clients with offices or provinces': *ornandi* is a genitive of definition after *ambitu* (exs. of the genitive are quoted at *TLL* 1.1862.25–33 but they vary in nature). *clientes*, normally used of social inferiors, illustrates the paradoxical nature of Tiberian Rome: here they are senators, and their patron merely an *eques* (see R. P. Saller, *Personal patronage under the early empire* (1982) 10, 77–8). Examples are Iunius Otho, who entered the senate thanks to Sejanus' *potentia* (3.66.3), and Iunius Blaesus, who, as Sejanus' uncle 'atque eo praeualidum', became proconsul of Africa (3.35). See further 34.1, 40.5, 68.2. Catiline promised magistracies and priesthoods to his supporters (Sall. *C.* 21.1 'polliceri ... magistratus, sacerdotia') but was of course in no position to carry out his promise; women, dogs and horses were another matter (*C.* 14.6 'aliis scorta praebere, aliis canes atque equos mercari').

facili Tiberio atque ita prono The paradoxical nature of the times (last n.) extends even to the *princeps*. Normally he was difficult (1.2 *obscurum*) and aloof (*Ann. 3*, p. 583; *Ann. 5–6*, p. 325); but in the case of Sejanus he was exactly the opposite, complaisant and submissive: *prono* (cf. Ov. *Met.* 1.375–6, Juv. 6.47–8) almost suggests prostration (cf. Dio 58.11.2 ὅν [sc. Σεϊανόν] <τε> προσεκύνουν ᾧ τε ὡς θεῷ ἔθυον). The combination of the two adjs. has an odd distribution (Sall. *J.* 80.4, [Quint.] *Decl.* 18.2, 339.8, Juv. 9.43, 13.75).

socium laborum Whether this description, which is above all Ciceronian (5×), was actually used of Sejanus is unclear. The contemporary Velleius refers to him as 'singularem principalium onerum adiutorem' (127.3; cf. 127.1 'magnis adiutoribus'); Dio under AD 20 describes him as σύμβουλον καὶ ὑπηρέτην πρὸς πάντα (57.19.6) and under AD 30 as κοινωνὸν τῶν φροντίδων (58.4.3); Drusus is made to refer to him as 'adiutorem imperii' (7.1 below). Despite the varying nomenclature, however, there can be no doubt that Tib. used such terminology of Sejanus, and almost as an official title; it was a manifestation of his need for help in administering the empire

71

(1.11.1 'sociatis laboribus'), which was so important an element of Tib.'s principate that T. in his obituary notice of the *princeps* uses his successive helpers to demarcate the various stages of his rule (6.51.3 and nn.). The date at which Tib. began to refer to Sejanus in such terms is unclear; I have suggested elsewhere that, when Germanicus' death in 19 deprived Tib. of an earlier helper, Sejanus saw his chance and began successfully to assert himself alongside Drusus (*Ann. 5–6*, Appendix, p. 310). In general see E. Kornemann, *Doppelprinzipat und Reichsteilung im Imperium Romanum* (1930), P. Grenade, *Essai sur les origines du principat* (1961) 444ff. ('Les charges du pouvoir et la théorie des "adiutores imperii"'), F. Hurlet, *Les collègues du prince sous Auguste et Tibère* (1997).

apud patres et populum Cf. Dio 57.21.3 πολλοὶ δὲ καὶ ἔπαινοι καὶ παρὰ τῷ δήμῳ καὶ παρὰ τῇ βουλῇ ἐγίγνοντο, 58.4.3 πρός τε τὴν βουλὴν καὶ πρὸς τὸν δῆμον.

colique per theatra et fora effigies eius After Sejanus' sterling work in the fire of AD 22, 'censuere patres effigiem Seiano quae apud theatrum Pompei locaretur' (3.72.3 and n.; cf. 7.2 below); other images are mentioned by Dio 58.4.4. See Gradel 225–7.

interque principia legionum 'The *principia* consisted of an open court-yard with a sanctuary for the standards, enclosed by the grouping of the legion's administrative buildings, arsenal and assembly rooms for the officers' (*BNP* 11.863). After Sejanus' death Tib. rewarded the Syrian legions 'quod solae nullam Seiani imaginem inter signa coluissent' (Suet. *Tib.* 48.2); perhaps, as Prof. Birley suggests, they were ultra-cautious after their experiences under Piso (2.55.5, 2.76.1; *SCPP* 53–7).

3.1–2 Ceterum . . . ferebatur Not surprisingly the logic, and consequently the punctuation, of this passage have caused trouble. (a) Although numerous editors (most recently Heubner and Borzsák) make *Caesarum domus, iuuenis filius* and *nepotes adulti* the subjects of *adferebant*, it seems unlikely that these three elements can be on an equal footing since the son and grandsons are subsumed within the house of the Caesars. Conversely it seems unlikely that *iuuenis filius* and *nepotes adulti* are in apposition to *Caesarum domus* (as Jackson's translation would have it), because this would strictly require a singular verb. The likeliest interpretation is that *Ceterum plena Caesarum domus* is a sentence in its own right and is explained by *iuuenis . . . adferebant*.

(b) The extent and reference of the *quia*-clause are disputed. [i] Some editors begin a new sentence with *et quia*, assume that the *quia*-clause comprises two asyndetic cola, and understand *placuit tamen . . .* as the main sentence (so e.g. Walther, disputing with his predecessors whether or not there should be a comma after *et*). Yet no obvious sense can be derived from a *quia*-clause followed by *tamen*; it seems much more likely that *placuit tamen* begins a new sentence. [ii] Numerous editors have therefore seen the *quia*-clause as part of the sentence which precedes *placuit tamen*; but what exactly is this sentence? The majority, who retain *et*, make *dolus interualla scelerum poscebat* the preceding sentence, explained by *quia . . . intutum*. The difficulty with this is that *dolus . . . poscebat* seems entirely redundant after *moram cupitis adferebant*, which it appears simply to repeat. Nipperdey deleted *et*, thereby making the *quia*-clause the explanation for *moram cupitis adferebant*: 'a young son and grown-up grandsons put the brake on his desires, because the simultaneous seizure of so many by violence was unsafe (and) guile demanded intervals between the crimes'. This makes good sense; the only question is how *et* (or, more precisely, *&*) arose. My suggestion, preferable to Nipperdey's deletion, is that *et* was wrongly anticipated and that, although T. undeniably likes asyndetic cola at the start of Book 4, it should be transposed to precede *dolus*. Either way, the removal of *et* from its transmitted position has significant benefits when we come to consider the next sentence (3.2n. *Placuit*).

3.1 Caesarum domus is favoured by T. to describe the imperial family (40.3, 1.10.5, 14.7.4, 16.7.2; elsewhere only at Suet. *Galba* 2.1); in this case it is possible that the genitive is also felt with *plena*, as Jackson's translation perhaps suggests ('the imperial house with its plenitude of Caesars'). See also next n.

iuuenis filius, nepotes adulti The young son is Drusus Iulius Caesar, Tib.'s biological son, who was born in the autumn of 14 or 13 BC (3.56.4n.). The grown-up grandsons are the eldest sons of Germanicus and Agrippina, namely, Nero Caesar (b. AD 6) and Drusus Caesar (b. AD 7 or 8): there is some irony in T.'s recalling and recording their respective advancements immediately below (4.1 and nn.). Germanicus' third son, Gaius Caesar (the future emperor Caligula), was still a child (born 31 August AD 12); Tib.'s other grandsons, the twins Germanicus and Tiberius Gemellus (the sons of Drusus Iulius Caesar and Livi(ll)a), were even younger, though their exact birthdate is disputed (2.84.1n., 6.46.1n.).

moram cupitis adferebant is picked up at the end of the episode in ring composition (5 'magnitudo facinoris . . . prolationes . . . adferebat'). *moram adferre* is an expr. found often in Cicero but also elsewhere. *cupitum* is at Plaut. *Poen.* 1271, Sall. *H.* 4.47 and Sen. *Ep.* 88.29 before T. (again at 13.13.4): see *TLL* 4.1431.51–64.

quia ui tot simul corripere intutum *ui corripere* is a rare expr. first found at Lucr. 4.1210 'femina uim uicit subita ui corripuitque' in a biological context, then twice in Virgil of seizing up an object (*Aen.* 5.641, 12.93). Here the primary meaning of the verb is 'to destroy' (*OLD* 4b) but, since Sejanus' first victim will die of poisoning, it perhaps foreshadows the nature of the illness from which Drusus will die (cf. Val. Max. 1.7.4 'subita ui morbi correptus', evidently an echo of Lucretius; *OLD corripio* 5a). *intutum* = 'unsafe' is a meaning first found in T. (1.38.2n.).

3.2 Placuit tamen occultior uia et a Druso incipere The words *placuit tamen occultior uia* have caused considerable difficulty. If the main clause of the previous sentence is *dolus interualla scelerum poscebat* (as in the editions of e.g. Furneaux, Koestermann, Heubner and Borzsák), guile is a precondition of Sejanus' actions; and, since the present sentence shows Sejanus adopting a guileful method, there is no contrast to explain the presence of *tamen*, which some older editors either emended (*tandem* or *itaque*) or deleted altogether.[4] If, however, we accept the deletion or transposition of *et* in §1 above (see 3.1–2n.), the main clause of the preceding sentence is *moram cupitis adferebant*, and this does provide a contrast with the present sentence: the circumstances put a brake on his ambitions, *but nevertheless* he decided to go ahead with a more devious approach (i.e. rather than rushing ahead regardless or abandoning his ambitions altogether).

For Tib.'s son see *RE* 10.431–4 = Iulius 136 (Gardthausen), *PIR* 4.173–6 no. 219, *BNP* 4.726–7 [II 1]; Rüpke 35–6 no. 2005; D. Kienast, *Römische Kaisertabelle. Grundzüge einer römischen Kaiserchronologie* (²1996) 82–3. That he is chosen by Sejanus as his first victim is tragically ironical when we recall that in AD 14 Sejanus had been ordered by Tib. to accompany his son to Pannonia as his protector (1.24.2 'rector iuueni'): see Graf 27.

For the *uariatio* of noun ~ infin. see e.g. *H.* 3.76.1; Sörbom 110. Earlier exs. of *occulta uia* seem non-metaphorical (Horsfall on Virg. *Aen.* 3.695).

animo commotior orto forte iurgio The former phrase seems to be a unique variant on the more regular *animus commotus* (but note Claud. Quadr. F41 'animo tenus commoti'); the latter (again at 13.9.2) recurs only at [Quint.] *Decl.* 296.10. For the assonance of *–or or–* see below, 13.2n. (*ob*). For Drusus' depiction by T. see 1.76.3n., and note J. Bellemore, 'The identity of Drusus: the making of a *princeps*', *JCS* 79–94.

intenderat Seiano manus et contra tendentis os uerberauerat 'had brandished his fists at Sejanus and had struck his face when he offered resistance'; Dio has Sejanus as the aggressor (57.22.1). T. seems to be alluding to Sall. *H.* 5.27 'manum in os intendens', the context of which is unfortunately unknown. For *contra tendere* cf. 3.10.1n.; for compound verb followed by simple see 6.31.2n.

---

4 The only way out of this difficulty is to assume that the meaning is 'But he decided on an even more devious approach' (so Damon and Yardley in their translations); but there is no *etiam* or equivalent in the Latin.

3.3 Igitur After the brief digression on their mutual hatred ('nam ... uerberauerat') *igitur* returns us to Sejanus' decision to kill Drusus and explains how he proposed to go about it. For the resumptive use of *igitur* see G–G 550b–1a; for its position in T. see 3.2.2n.

ad uxorem eius Liuiam conuertere 'to have recourse to his wife, Livia' (*OLD conuerto* 6c). For Livi(ll)a see 6.2.1n. and P. Sinclair, 'Tacitus' presentation of Livia Julia, wife of Tiberius' son Drusus', *AJP* 111 (1990) 238–56.

adulterio pellexit Sejanus now adds adultery to his passive homosexuality of earlier (1.2n.), as was also alleged of Julius Caesar (Suet. *DJ* 52.3 'omnium mulierum uir et omnium uirorum mulier'): such combinations were typical of political invective (Opelt 154–7); see also 10.2n. below. Walther suggested that *adulterio* is dat., for which there is no parallel anywhere (*TLL* 10.1.999.39–41); it must be abl. (as 1.2.1, 13.45.4, *H.* 4.15.1).

postquam primi flagitii potitus est If we except the phrase *rerum potiri* as a special case (6.30.3n.), the verb is overwhelmingly constructed with the abl. rather than the gen.: according to the statistics in *TLL* 10.2.334.16–46, the only exceptions are *Rhet. Herenn.* (3:0) and Curtius (4:1). T. has two other exs. of the gen. (3.73.3 *ducis*, 13.6.1 *regni*) as against 23 of the abl. His present expr. seems rather unusual, but *flagitii* refers to his seduction of Livi(ll)a, the kind of context in which *potiri* often occurs (Malloch on 11.12.2).

neque femina amissa pudicitia alia abnuerit Rhenanus noted that T. is echoing the words uttered by Livy's Lucretia when she tells her husband and father that she has been raped by Tarquin (1.58.7): 'quid enim salui est mulieri amissa pudicitia?' Since there is no other example of *amittere pudicitiam* in classical Latin, it seems certain that T. is alluding to Livy.[5] Lucretia saw her rape as a reason for suicide and as an outrage demanding vengeance, which her family promptly exacts by abolishing the monarchy and establishing the republic; Livi(ll)a hopes to capitalise on her adultery to get rid of her husband and establish herself as regent alongside her seducer.

The clarity of the allusion belies the obscurity of the sentence. Draeger (*SS* 13), with whom Furneaux and Koestermann agree, included *abnuerit* in his long list of exs. (such as *contenderit* at 32.1 below) where the 'aoristic' use of the perfect potential subjunctive refers to the present. If that is correct, the

---

[5] Zimmermann (41–2) argued that Jer. *Adv. Iovin.* 1.49 ('pudicitiam in primis esse retinendam, qua amissa omnis uirtus ruit') is based on Seneca's lost *De Matrimonio*, and he suggested (without mentioning Livy) that T., as often, is alluding to Seneca. Sinclair (cited above) 240–2 quotes Livy but seems to prefer Seneca as T.'s source. See also R. Langlands, *Sexual morality in ancient Rome* (2006) 332–6.

meaning here will be: 'and a woman who has lost her virtue would not reject other things'. Sometimes, however, the perfect potential subjunctive is used to refer to the past and, in a form of *repraesentatio*, to express what is likely to have been the case at the time (*NLS* §120). Draeger's only ex. of this in T. (*H.* 2.47.2) is denied explicitly by Heubner and implicitly by Ash ad loc., but, if our passage is nevertheless an illustration of it, the meaning would be: 'and a woman who had lost her virtue would not have rejected other things'. It is very difficult to know which of these two meanings is correct. The misogynism of the former is tempered by the fact that it may allude to, or be a variant of, the proverbial notion which is found at Hdt. 1.8.3 Ἅμα δὲ κιθῶνι ἐκδυομένῳ συνεκδύεται καὶ τὴν αἰδῶ γυνή (on which see D. L. Cairns, *CQ* 46 (1996) 78–83). The attraction of the latter is that, although expressed as a generalisation, *femina* clearly alludes to Livi(ll)a, in the same way as the equally generalised *mulieri* at Liv. 1.58.7 applies to Lucretia. For the various uses of *femina* see J. N. Adams, 'Latin words for "woman" and "wife"', *Glotta* 50 (1972) 234–55.

ad *coniugii* spem, *consortium* regni et necem mariti impulit Sejanus' characteristic pressuring (cf. 41.1 *impelleret*) is arranged elaborately (ABBABA), alliteratively, and persuasively: he places first that which was most likely to appeal to the victim of his seduction; he places last that which was most likely to be distasteful to her (but which for him is the point of the whole masquerade). *consortium regni* (again at *HA Tyr. Trig.* 30.23, Just. 21.1.7, 24.2.4) is here pregnant for *spem consortii regni* (cf. also 51.2 and n.).

3.4 auunculus 'great-uncle' (*OLD* 2), as 75 below.

seque ac maiores et posteros municipali adultero foedabat *municipali* and *adultero* illustrate the charges of social inferiority and sexual impropriety which were commonplace in Roman political invective (e.g. Mart. 4.66. 1–2, Juv. 8.237–8 with Courtney; Cic. *Pis.* fr. 18, *Cat.* 2.23): see Nisbet's edn of Cic. *Pis.*, App. 6 (pp. 194–5), Opelt 149–51 and 266 (index). Prof. Birley suggests that Val. Max. may have been influenced by the career of Sejanus, his contemporary, to include amongst his *exempla* the stories about third-century BC debauchery at Vulsinii (9.1 *ext.* 2). J. H. D'Arms ('Upper-class attitudes towards *viri municipales* and their towns in the early Roman empire', *Athenaeum* 62 (1984) 458–60) has argued that T.'s 'scathing dismissal of Sejanus' is focalised by the imperial family and does not represent the historian's own view; yet T. would not be the first or last non-metropolitan figure who felt that his success entitled him to adopt a superior attitude to things provincial. See also 6.27.1 and n.

T.'s tricolon is the third in an ironic series (see *ad coniugii . . . necem mariti* and *auunculus . . . liberi* above). *–que ac*, much rarer than *–que et*, occurs in prose first at Liv. 26.24.6 and is found elsewhere in T. only at *H.* 3.63.2 (see H.; also K–S

2.37). For *foedaret* cf. Plaut. *Trin.* 656 'ut rem patriam et gloriam maiorum foedarim meum'.

ut pro honestis et praesentibus flagitiosa et incerta exspectaret In order to form his favourite kind of comparative aphorism (cf. e.g. 1.2.1 'tuta et praesentia quam uetera et periculosa') T. has added the contrasting elements of *honesta* ~ *flagitiosa*, which he perhaps remembered from Sallust (*H.* 3.48.13 'si uera et honesta flagitium superauerit'), to the proverbial *praesentia* ~ *incerta* (for which see e.g. Otto 81, Tosi 773 §1731). The latter appealed also to the supporters of Catiline (Sall. *C.* 17.6 'quibus in otio uel magnifice uel molliter uiuere copia erat incerta pro certis, bellum quam pacem malebant' and Vretska ad loc.).

medicus 'Quid . . . uenenorum fertilius?', asks the elder Pliny in his discussion of doctors (*NH* 29.20). Doctors appear regularly in the poisoning cases mentioned by rhetorical writers (Quint. 7.2.17, 7.2.25, [Quint.] *Decl.* 321, Calp. *Decl.* 13; cf. Mart. 6.31); the doctor Glyco was accused of having poisoned the consul Pansa in 43 BC (1.10.2n.); and a similar story to ours is told of Claudius' doctor, Xenophon, who is said to have poisoned the emperor on the instructions of his wife, Agrippina (12.67.2). Eudemus, who according to Pliny (loc. cit.) had an adulterous affair with Livi(ll)a, was presumably a Greek and a freedman. For a summary of Roman medicine in the empire see *BNP* 8.579–80; I. Israelowich, *Patients and healers in the High Roman Empire* (2015) 23–7.

specie artis frequens secretis Since T. uses *secretum* (*-a*) frequently and in a range of different meanings (G–G 1442b–43b), it is very difficult to know what exactly is meant by the last two words here. The likeliest rendering is perhaps 'under the pretext of his profession having frequent access to her privacy', which makes good sense of *specie artis* (*arte* alone would imply that Livi(ll)a was a chronic invalid). On this view *secretis* is either dat. (on the analogy of *frequens adesse*), as Draeger–Heraeus suggested, or local abl., as Nipperdey preferred, but there is admittedly no parallel for a dat. anywhere, and the exs. with an abl. (*H.* 4.69.3 'frequens contionibus', Plaut. *Mil.* 662 'benefactis frequens') are clearly different. On the other hand there is an odd gen. after *frequens* at 4.65 below.

3.5 Apicatam, ex qua tres liberos genuerat For Apicata see 5.6.2n., 6.2.1n.; it has sometimes been suggested that she was daughter of the Apicius mentioned earlier (1.2n.): see Birley (2007) 124 and n. 12. For Sejanus' two sons and a daughter see 5.8.1n., 9.1n. *pellere domo* (above) can have as object either men (e.g. Cic. *Dom.* 111–12) or women (e.g. Ov. *F.* 3.559 'pellitur Anna domo'), but in the present context the expr. is assumed to refer to divorce (but see 11.2n. below).

ne paelici suspectaretur 'to prevent his mistress from suspecting him' (of duplicity: cf. *ut amore incensus* at §3 above). In ordinary imperial usage *paelex*, a word thought to be associated with *pellicio* (cf. *pellexit* above), indicated no more than a woman who had intercourse with a married man, but originally the term stressed the status of the mistress in relation to the wife, not to the husband (J. N. Adams, 'Words for "prostitute" in Latin', *RhM* 126 (1983) 355): this is exactly the circumstance here, where Sejanus does not want his *paelex* Livi(ll)a to think that he is still in a relationship with his wife. It is unclear whether *paelici* is dat. of agent (cf. 2.50.3n.) or dat. of the person concerned (as in *alicui suspectus esse*); either way, the use of the verb to mean 'to suspect, be suspicious of' seems to have been introduced by T. (see *OLD* 2).

magnitudo facinoris metum, prolationes, diuersa interdum consilia adferebat The first section of the year's narrative ends with a final tricolon; *facinoris* looks back to *quo facinore* (1.1), as does *prolationes . . . adferebat* to *moram . . . adferebant* (3.1). *magnitudo facinoris* recurs at Curt. 8.2.1 but, esp. in view of other verbal and motival similarities in the passage, T. almost certainly has in mind a comparable passage of Sallust, where he describes Bomilcar enlisting Nabdalsa's help in killing Jugurtha (*J.* 70.1–5): '*suspectus regi* et ipse eum *suspiciens*[6] nouas res *cupere*, ad perniciem eius *dolum* quaerere . . . denique *omnia temptando* socium sibi adiungit Nabdalsam . . . qui . . . *omnis res exequi solitus erat* . . . is postquam *magnitudine facinoris* perculsus ad tempus non uenit *metusque rem impediebat*, Bomilcar, simul cupidus incepta patrandi et timore soci anxius, ne *omisso uetere consilio*[7] *nouum quaereret . . .*'.

4–6 The start of the year and the state of the empire

4.1 Interim anni principio Nowhere else in Latin is the formulaic *anni principio* (3.31.2n.) combined with *interim*: the combination suggests that in 1–3 T. has given us material which both precedes and follows the start of the year.

Drusus ex Germanici liberis togam uirilem sumpsit Drusus Iulius Caesar is described as Germanicus' son to distinguish him from the Drusus of 3.2–5 above; he had been born in AD 7 or 8. See *RE* 10.434–5 = Iulius 137 (Gardthausen), *PIR* 4.176–8 no. 220, *BNP* 4.727; Rüpke 735 no. 2004. Ginsburg has observed that after Germanicus' death it is often 'the family and friends of Germanicus which occupy the historian at the year's inception' (26).

quae . . . fratri eius Neroni decreuerat senatus See 3.29.1 and nn.; Rüpke 736–7 no. 2008. 'There is dramatic irony in the honoring of the

[6] The meaning 'suspecting' seems unique to this passage of Sallust, in much the same way as *suspectare* = 'to suspect' is an innovation of T.

[7] *uetus consilium*, though not uncommon, occurs at 4.2 immediately below.

younger Drusus, Germanicus' son, immediately after a chapter devoted to the scheme of Sejanus against the elder Drusus, Tiberius' son. The younger Drusus, together with his brother Nero, will be the next victims of Sejanus' (Ginsburg 25).

patria beneuolentia in fratris liberos For similar expressions cf. Hor. *C.* 2.2.6 'notus in fratres animi paterni', where N–H compare 4.4.27–8 'paternus | in pueros animus Nerones', Cic. *Rosc. Am.* 46 'qui animus patrius in liberos esset'; the last ex. is esp. noteworthy, since T. often places Ciceronian elements in Tib.'s mouth (see *Ann. 3*, p. 513; *Ann. 5–6*, p. 325) and *beneuolentia* is a strikingly Ciceronian term. For the form *foret* see 3.14.4n.

quamquam arduum sit eodem loci potentiam et concordiam esse As emerges from the main clause, the point seems to be Drusus' fear that he might be eclipsed by the two grandsons in the same way that his father had been eclipsed by Gaius and Lucius Caesar. The incompatibility of power and harmony was a cliché esp. applicable to the Triumvirate (Vell. 47.2 'ex inuidia potentiae tam male cohaerentis ... concordiae') but also in other circumstances (e.g. 13.2.1 'rarum in societate potentiae, concordes'). The language (*arduum, eodem loci*) suggests a precariously high and narrow ledge, where an increase in *potentia* is liable to dislodge *concordia* (see further 7.2n. *primas*); by contrast Drusus (below) was 'level' (*aequus*) with his nephews (cf. Hor. *C.* 2.3.1–2 'Aequam memento rebus in arduis | seruare mentem'). For *quamquam* + subjunctive see 1.3.5n.; for *eodem loci* = 'in the same place' cf. K–S 1.430.

4.2 Exin uetus et *s*aepe simulatum *pr*ŏficiscendi in *pr*ŏuincias consilium refertur T. has mentioned this plan twice before (1.47.3, 3.47. 2–3 (nn.)); Suetonius says that it was an almost annual occurrence (*Tib.* 38). The hesitancy is typical of Tib. (6.1.1n.), but staying in the city rather than venturing abroad was also a Claudian trait (Oakley on Liv. 9.29.5–11 (p. 359)). For *exin* see 3.13.1n., adding Adams (2016) 8–9; *refertur* = 'was revived' (*OLD* 16).

Multitudinem ueteranorum 'He means that his presence was required to induce the veterans to be content with their reward on dismissal', says Furneaux: this was a long-standing issue (see 1.36.3, 1.78.3; Campbell 172–3), but T. may simply mean that, given problems of recruitment, there was too high a proportion of veterans.

dilectibus supplendos exercitus That the proposed levies would involve conscription is implied by the following reference to the dearth and unsuitability of volunteers; yet Velleius, evidently referring to this same occasion, praises Tib. for reinforcing the army 'without the fear one normally associates with a levy' (130.2 'supplementum sine trepidatione dilectus'). There is no

79

discrepancy between these two statements: recruitment in the provinces (T.'s subject) rendered it unnecessary to hold the dreaded levies in Italy (see Brunt, *IM* 241, 414–15, 636–7, and 'Conscription and volunteering in the Roman imperial army', *RIT* 188–214, esp. 194–5). We know of levies in Narbonensis (*ILS* 950) and Thrace (46.1 below).

For the *uariatio* of noun ~ acc. and infin. see 3.47.2n.

uirtute ac modestia 'courage and discipline' (*OLD modestia* 2), as *H.* 3.11.2.

quia plerumque inopes ac uagi sponte militiam sumant 'because it was mostly the destitute and vagrants who were taking up a military career voluntarily.' *sumo* is often used of taking up an occupation etc. (*OLD* 12a), but *s. militiam* recurs only at *H.* 2.94.1, where the meaning is slightly different. *inopes ac uagi* is a Ciceronian doublet (*Phil.* 12.15) and thus appropriate on the *princeps'* lips (above, 1n.).

4.3 quas prouincias tutarentur By the late republic the frequentative form *tutor* was no longer in use. 'Before T. the only writers of prose who use the frequentative with any freedom are Sallust and, in particular, Livy' (Adams (1972) 369, who notes that its use almost disappears in *Ann.* 11–16). For the *uariatio* of noun ~ indir. qu. see 3.10.3n.

quod mihi quoque exsequendum reor 'Relativpronomen mit nachfolgender Epexegese', says Koestermann, comparing 3.65.1 and 6.7.3. The former passage is controversial (*Tac. Rev.* 86–103), while the latter happens to highlight what is different – and difficult – about our passage: at 6.7.3 the relative pronoun *quod* clearly refers back to the preceding words *suscepitque Cestius accusationem*, but what does *quod* refer back to in our passage? It seems unlikely to refer to *numerum legionum et quas prouincias tutarentur*, because these words comprise two elements and would lead one to expect the plural *quae . . . exsequenda*. The only alternative is *percensuit*, but this is awkward because the verb appears to be synonymous with *exsequendum*: it makes no sense to say 'he surveyed briefly the number of legions and which provinces they guarded, a survey which I think I too should survey'.[8] This awkwardness can be avoided if we assume that *exsequendum* does not mean 'survey' or 'enumerate' (*OLD* 6) but 'carry out' (*OLD* 5: ' . . . <a survey> which I think I too should carry out'), but this in turn deprives us of a suitable verb to introduce the indirect questions which follow. We thus appear to be thrown back on the explanation which at first seemed unlikely, namely that *quod* refers to *numerum . . . tutarentur*,

---

[8] It was for this reason that Martin–Woodman proposed as an alternative that *quod* be an adverbial accusative (cf. Cic. *Phil.* 2.21, Gell. 9.3.5) and *exsequendum* an impersonal gerundive: 'In view of which I think I too should survey what . . .'. But it is admittedly very difficult to separate *quod* from *exsequendum*.

which must therefore be regarded as a single idea: ' ... <a subject> which I think I too should survey, <namely> what ...'.

Tib. had already surveyed the state of the empire at the start of Book 1 (1.11.4 'quantum ciuium sociorumque in armis, quot classes, regna, prouinciae, tributa aut uectigalia, et necessitates ac largitiones'); the fact that he does so again here emphasises the division of the hexad into two halves and that this is the start of the second half. The difference is that on the present occasion T. makes the emperor's survey an excuse for a survey of his own (see below), supplying the details which, in the case of the emperor's survey, he had merely summarised; for a similar move see 3.25.2 'ea res admonet ut ... altius disseram'. For *reor* see 3.22.4n.

quae ... copia ..., qui socii reges, quanto ... Such sequences 'are characteristic of proemium-style, both poetic and historical' (Horsfall on Virg. *Aen.* 7.37–8 'qui reges ..., quae tempora ..., quis ... status', comparing, in addition to our passage, Hes. *Theog.* 105ff., Thuc. 6.2.1, Plb. 1.1.5, Dion. Hal. *Ant. Rom.* 1.5.1, Virg. *G.* 1.1ff., *Aen.* 7.642–4 'qui ... reges, quae ... acies ...', Liv. *praef.* 9). The appropriateness of such sequences for introducing a catalogue was shown as early as the *Iliad* (2.487 οἵ τινες ἡγεμόνες ..., 492 ὅσοι ...).

quae tunc Romana copia in armis 'what Roman forces were then under arms'; the singular *copia*, again at e.g. 47.1 and 56.1, 'is not common, but found in a variety of earlier prose' (2.52.2n.). *tunc* is used, as often by Livy (cf. R. B. Steele, 'The historical attitude of Livy', *AJP* 25 (1904) 36–8), to contrast past and present; the adv. has to be supplied with the two following clauses, as *sit/sint* with the two preceding.

qui socii reges See below, 5.2n. (*accolis*).

quanto sit angustius imperitatum sc. *quam nunc*. Comparison (σύγκρισις, *comparatio*) is a standard mode of eulogy (Vell. 126.2n.), and, by comparing the 'narrowness' of the Tiberian empire with the empire of his own day, to whose greater extent he had already referred at 2.61.2, T. is implicitly praising a century of imperialist expansion (see further 32.2n.). According to Cicero, the legend *fines imperii propagauit* was inscribed on the monuments of Rome's greatest generals (*Rep.* 3.24);[9] Augustus in his forum set up statues of those 'qui imperium populi Romani ex minimo maximum reddidissent' (Suet. *Aug.* 31.5); and Claudius extended the *pomerium* of the city of Rome 'more prisco quo iis qui protulere imperium etiam terminos urbis

---

[9] This passage is downplayed by J. Richardson in his argument that during the republic the Romans tended not to view the empire in geographical terms (*The language of empire* (2008) 75–6 and 191–3).

propagare datur' (12.23.2), a ritual symbolising the relationship between Rome and the world (cf. Ov. *F.* 2.684 'Romanae spatium est urbis et orbis idem').[10] No doubt T. is thinking in particular of the current emperor, Trajan, who in 106 added Arabia as a province, in 113 dedicated his Column celebrating the subjugation of Dacia, in 114 made a province of Armenia, and was at present engaged in a campaign against Parthia.[11]

As Augustus' *Res Gestae* makes clear, lists are a particularly effective method of presenting imperial power (see esp. C. Nicolet, *Space, geography and politics in the early Roman empire* (1991) 171–87): elsewhere T. describes Egyptian inscriptions which itemise in list-form territorial holdings and imperial revenues (2.60.3–4); and Velleius uses a list to illustrate the extent and number of Roman provinces (38.2–39.3). Since much of the present list involves the numbers and stations of legions, it resembles those catalogues of forces which are a feature of epic and other genres since the *Iliad* (2.484ff.): thus Herodotus has catalogues of the Persian forces (7.61–99) and the Greek fleet (8.43–8), Thucydides of the Athenian allies (7.57–59.1: see Hornblower ad loc. (pp. 654–60)). Many authors follow Homer in arranging their catalogues geographically, and this is also true of T., who, after a reference to the fleets, starts with Germany and moves in a generally anti-clockwise direction through the Roman world. Scholars recognise too that many catalogues have a structural function, dividing one section of narrative from another or constituting a 'build-up' to the narrative which follows; this is also true of T.'s catalogue, which serves to emphasise both the start of the second half of the hexad and the deterioration in Tib. that is about to take place (1.1 above, 6.1 below).[12]

The impersonal use of *imperitare* occurs previously at Liv. 21.1.3 'quod superbe auareque crederent imperitatum uictis esse' and, in imitation, Curt. 4.7.1 'auare et superbe imperitatum sibi esse credebant'; the verb's 'archaic and grandiloquent tone' (1.64.4n.) is complemented here by the 'heroic

---

[10] Whether Augustus also extended the *pomerium*, as T. says (12.23.2), is debated (see Swan on Dio 55.6.6).

[11] In addition, Britain had become a province in 43, Thrace in 46.

[12] The bibliography on catalogues is vast: see e.g. W. Kühlmann, *Katalog und Erzählung: Studien zu Konstanz und Wandel einer literarischen Form in der antiken Epik* (diss. Freiburg, 1973); W. P. Basson, *Pivotal catalogues in the Aeneid* (1975); E. Courtney, 'Vergil's military catalogues and their antecedents', *Vergilius* 34 (1988) 3–8; Horsfall on Virg. *Aen.* 7.641–817 (pp. 414–22); C. Reitz, 'Does mass matter? The epic catalogue of troops as narrative and metapoetic device', in G. Manuwald and A. Voigt (edd.), *Flavian epic interactions* (2013) 229–43.

clausula' (for the pentasyllabic ending see Vell. 95.2n.). See also 3.4.1n., Malloch on 11.8.1.

5.1 Italiam . . . proximumque Galliae litus . . . praesidebant The acc. after *praesidere* (again at 72.3 below and twice elsewhere in the *Annals*) is in imitation of Sallust (*H.* 2.94, 3.97), the only other author in whom it is found (see 3.39.1n.); the verb is not elsewhere used of fleets, but for *naues* see Curt. 3.1.20. For the fleets and their ports see Starr 13–24, Rougé 120–30 (map on p. 123), M. Reddé, *Mare nostrum: les infrastructures, le dispositif et l'histoire de la marine militaire sous l'Empire* (*BEFAR* 260, 1986) 171–97 (map on p. 312).

utroque mari is to be taken distributively: '(one) in each sea'. *utrumque mare*, here referring to the Tyrrhenian and Adriatic Seas (as at *H.* 2.62.1), is a natural form of expression for the ancient inhabitants of lands such as Italy and Greece which are bordered by sea on two sides: see e.g. Liv. 5.33.9, Mela 2.37; also 5.10.3n. For the anastrophe of *apud* (below) see 1.60.3n., 2.41.1n.; *Ann. 3*, p. 499; *Ann. 5–6*, p. 316; Malloch on *Ann.* 11, Index 1 s.v. 'word order'.

quas . . . ualido cum remige Mark Antony's warships will have been a valuable asset if the stories of their reputed size (Watson on Hor. *Epod.* 1. 1–2) were true. As *remige* is collective singular (*OLD* b),[13] *ualido* indicates that the crews were at full strength (*OLD* 6a); but there is perhaps also the suggestion that Augustus replaced with his own strongmen the allegedly effeminate troops on Antony's and Cleopatra's side (Watson on Hor. *Epod.* 9.13–14, N–H on *Odes* 1.37.9–10). Forum Iulii (mod. Fréjus), to which T. refers with a typical circumlocution (cf. also *H.* 2.14.1, 3.43.1), was where T.'s father-in-law came from (*Agr.* 4.1), which perhaps explains why the detail of the relative clause has been added (in a form of Sallustian 'verbal hyperbaton': cf. 3.1.1n.). For the place see A. L. F. Rivet, *Gallia Narbonensis* (1988) 226–38.

praecipuum robur Rhenum iuxta . . . octo legiones erant There were four legions in northern Germany (Germania Inferior): I, stationed first at Ara Ubiorum (Cologne) and then at Bonna (Bonn); V Alaudae, at Vetera (Xanten); XX, at Ara Ubiorum and then Novaesium (Neuss); and XXI

---

[13] 'Although *remex* and *nauta* might appear in official documents and the historians, it is clear that the ordinary seaman preferred the designation of *miles*' (D. Saddington, 'Problems in the nomenclature of the personnel and the question of marines in the Roman fleets', *BICS* 52 (2009) 126, basing his point on epigraphic evidence). Thus a Briton who served in the German fleet is commemorated by a tombstone at Cologne (*AE* 1956, 249) which describes him as 'mil(iti) ex classe G(ermanicae) p(iae) f(idelis)'.

Rapax, at Vetera. There were another four in southern Germany (Germania Superior): II Augusta, stationed at Argentorate (Strasbourg); XIII Gemina, at Vindonissa (Windisch); and XIV Gemina and XVI Gallica, at Moguntiacum (Mainz). See e.g. *BNP* 7.358–71, with a helpful map of the legionary distribution. For the strategy ('commune . . . subsidium'), similar to that at §3 below ('quae . . . accirentur'), see Syme, *Tac.* 454. Under Trajan there were only four legions in Germany (I Minervia, VI Victrix, VIII Augusta, XXII Primigenia).

Hispaniae recens perdomitae tribus habebantur sc. *legionibus* (probably dat. of agent: cf. 2.50.3n.). For *habere* = *tenere* or *occupatum tenere* see *TLL* 6.3.2401.29ff., esp. 47–69.

Spain was first declared conquered in 25 BC after a campaign in which Augustus himself participated; but further trouble required the attention of Agrippa and it was not until 19 BC that the region was finally 'tamed' (see Vell. 90.1 and n.). Although the metaphor is commonly applied to the subjugation of foreign tribes and the like (e.g. 1.1n.), *perdomitae* here perhaps recalls Livy's reference to the Augustan conquest of Spain (28.12.12 'postrema omnium nostra demum aetate ductu auspicioque Augusti Caesaris perdomita est'), but whether Livy is referring to 19 BC (as T. obviously is) or to 25 BC (which *ductu* perhaps makes more likely) is not clear (similar unclarity at Vell. 90.4: see n.).

At the time of which T. is speaking, Spain was divided into the three provinces of Citerior, Lusitania and Baetica, the first of which held the three legions: IV Macedonica, possibly stationed at Herrera de Pisuerga, VI Victrix, and X Gemina, possibly stationed at Petavonium (Rosinos de Vidriales). *recens* refers back more than 40 years but helps to explain why three legions were required, as opposed to the single legion of T.'s own day; at 11.25.3 *recens* refers back almost 80 years (see Malloch ad loc., and also for T.'s use of adv. *recens*).

5.2 Mauros Iuba rex acceperat donum populi Romani In 25 BC (Dio 53.26.2 with Rich's n.). For Juba II see e.g. *BNP* 6.1205–6 [Juba 2]; D. W. Roller, *The world of Juba II and Kleopatra Selene: royal scholarship on Rome's African frontier* (2003). He died around AD 23/24.

cetera Africae per duas legiones . . . coercita The verb has as its subjects also *Aegyptus* and *quantum . . . ambitur*. There were two African provinces: Africa proconsularis and Cyrenaica. Normally the region required only one legion, III Augusta, stationed at Ammaedara; but IX Hispana had been sent from Pannonia in 20 to assist in the war against Tacfarinas (3.9.1 and n.): it would return to Pannonia in 24 (23.2 below). For *cetera* + gen. (G–G 166b) see 3.24.3n.

parique numero Aegyptus The two Egyptian legions were III Cyrenaica and XXII Deiotariana, both stationed at Nicopolis. For the importance of Egypt see 2.59.3.

dehinc ... ambitur '(and) next the area enclosed by the large sweep of land from the tip of Syria up to the River Euphrates': *initio ... Euphraten* defines *ingenti terrarum sinu*, and *terrarum* is perhaps to be taken ἀπὸ κοινοῦ with *quantum* as well as *sinu*; for *ambire* = 'to include within' see *OLD* 10, *TLL* 1.1848.67–71 (our passage wrongly listed at 49–50). T. stresses the extent of territory because in his day it required defending by eight legions, rather than the four of Tib.'s time (next n.), although such 'sweep of empire' statements are a feature of imperialist inscriptions and the like (e.g. 2.60.3 'quasque terras ... colunt', *RG* 27.3 'prouincias omnis quae ... uergunt ad orientem', *OGIS* 54.13–14 κυριεύσας δὲ τῆς τε ἐντὸς Εὐφράτου χώρας πάσης).

quattuor legionibus The four Syrian legions were III Gallica, VI Ferrata (perhaps stationed at Raphaneae), X Fretensis (recorded as being at Cyrrhus in AD 17) and XII Fulminata (at Raphaneae).

accolis Hibero Albanoque et aliis regibus qui magnitudine nostra proteguntur aduersum externa imperia The Iberians and Albanians, or their respective kingdoms, are a regular pairing, esp. in the elder Pliny (e.g. *NH* 6.29). Both peoples lived in the area west of the Caspian Sea (*BA* Map 88; see 2.68.1n. and Malloch on 11.8.1) and later will play a major role in an episode of Book 6 (33–6: see nn.). Their mention here has a particular relevance to the time at which T. was writing (see further below), since in the summer of AD 114, at a meeting at Elegeia in Armenia, Trajan 'apparently installed a new king over Albania and received formal submission both from the Iberians and from the Sarmatian peoples beyond the Caucasus' (A. B. Bosworth, 'Arrian and the Alani', *HSCP* 81 (1977) 227 with n. 41). The *alii reges* are likely to be those of minor kingdoms (as indeed *magnitudine* implies), esp. in the Caucasus area; but they will almost certainly include the king of Osroene, Abgar VII, whose guest Trajan was during the winter of 114/15 (see further Magie 1.607, 2.1465 n. 32). Although T. here stresses the protective role of the *imperium Romanum*, such kings also protected the Roman empire against external threats (cf. *Agr.* 14.1 'uetere ac iam pridem recepta populi Romani consuetudine ut haberet instrumenta seruitutis et reges'; also Suet. *Aug.* 48): see Braund, *RFK* 91–103, and B. H. Isaac, *The limits of empire: the Roman army in the East* (²1993) 500 (index).

This passage, as is generally recognised, provides key evidence for the date at which T. was writing; the elements of primary importance are (a) the tense of the verb and (b) the absence of any reference to Armenia.

(a) Every other verb in T.'s survey is in a past tense (*praesidebant, erant, habebantur, acceperat, coercita, attinebant, accirentur, insideret*), as is to be expected in a paragraph whose explicit purpose is to contrast the past with the present (4.3 and n.). *proteguntur* is the only exception, and, since the historic present would be inappropriate in a survey of this nature, its tense must be genuinely present and have the meaning 'who have been and still are protected'. (b) In AD 23 Armenia was a client kingdom of Rome (cf. 2.56.2–3), and it remained so until the summer of 114, when at the meeting at Elegeia (see above) it was annexed as a province. This status lasted no longer than two years, however, since in the autumn of 116 Armenia reverted to being a client kingdom once more (see J. Bennett, *Trajan: Optimus Princeps* (²2001) 194–200 for a summary account of these events). Since Armenia's role as a buffer state between Rome and Parthia was crucial (cf. 2.56.1), T.'s failure to mention it here alongside the lesser kingdoms of Iberia and Albania very strongly suggests that he was writing this passage between the years 114 and 116, during which time its role as a buffer state was suspended and there was no truth in the statement that its king was one of those 'who have been and still are protected against foreign empires'. See the clear statement of Syme, *RP* 3.1445.

T.'s reference to 'foreign empires' supports this conclusion. It is generally accepted that this is a reference to Parthia, the one nation which according to our sources qualified to be called an 'empire' alongside the Roman (see 6.31–7, intro. n. (pp. 220–1)). In 116, however, Trajan conquered Parthia: he was given the title 'Parthicus', and coins were issued bearing the legend *Parthia capta* (*CCT* 41). Thus T.'s description of Parthia as an *externum imperium* (the plural seems to be rhetorical) would no longer be true after 116, providing a *terminus ante quem*. Given the time it would take for news of Armenia's annexation in 114 to reach Rome, we may venture to say, with more precision, that T. is likely to have written our passage in 115.

There remains the question of how, or whether, this conclusion comports with the three other passages in the Tiberian hexad which have been invoked for dating purposes; since each of them precedes our passage, it is natural to assume that they will have been written earlier. (i) Since at 2.56.1 the Armenians are expressly described as a buffer between the Roman and Parthian empires ('maximisque imperiis interiecti'), the passage must have been written in or before 114. (ii) Since at 2.60.4 Parthia's power is given equal status with that of Rome ('haud minus magnifica quam nunc ui Parthorum aut potentia Romana iubentur'), the passage must have been written before 116. (iii) The famous passage at 2.61.2 ('Elephantinen ac Syenen, claustra olim Romani imperii, quod nunc rubrum ad mare patescit') has been interpreted by some scholars to refer to Trajan's triumphal arrival at the Persian Gulf, the southernmost limit of the new province of Parthia, in 116. If this interpretation is correct, it means that, two books before our passage, there is a singular reference to the conquest of Parthia.

But the interpretation cannot be correct, since it is flatly contradicted by 2.60.4: Parthia cannot be referred to as a foreign empire 'nunc' at 2.60.4 and then, within ten lines, be referred to as a Roman province 'nunc' at 2.61.2. This contradiction is easily avoided, however, if we assume that *rubrum mare* at 2.61.2 refers not to the Persian Gulf but to the Red Sea and that T. is referring to the annexation of Arabia as a province. Although the annexation was effected in 106, public commemoration was deferred for five years until there came into existence its 'most conspicuous monument' (G. W. Bowersock, *Roman Arabia* (1983) 83). This was the Via Noua Traiana, which stretched south from Damascus to Aila at the northern tip of the Red Sea and was celebrated as follows on one of the many surviving milestones (*ILS* 5834): 'Imp. Caesar ... Traianus ... redacta in formam prouinciae Arabia uiam nouam a finibus Syriae usque ad mare Rubrum aperuit'. The opening up of the road symbolised the acquisition of the new province, and it is not too fanciful to suggest that T.'s *patescit*, a verb applicable to roadways (Stat. *Silv.* 3.3.27, Plin. *Ep.* 2.17.3), is an allusion to this very achievement.[14]

For the co-ordination *A Bque et C* see *Agr.* 12.5n., adding J. B. Solodow, 'The copulative particles in Livy' (diss. Harvard, 1971) 151–7.

5.3 Thraeciam Rhoemetalces et liberi Cotyis ... Cf. 2.67.2 'Thraecia in Rhoemetalcen filium ... inque liberos Cotyis diuiditur' (AD 19) and G. ad loc.

ripamque Danuuii legionum duae in Pannonia, duae in Moesia attinebant T.'s move from Pannonia to its eastern neighbour Moesia strictly disrupts the anti-clockwise arrangement of his survey, but the fronting of *ripam ... Danuuii* indicates that he is more interested in presenting the Danube frontier as a unit: from the first century AD 'the Romans labelled the whole area between the Middle Danube and Macedonia as Illyricum' (Wilkes 161). Dalmatia is placed in third position (below) because it facilitates the return to Italy and Rome. The two legions in Pannonia were VIII Augusta, stationed at Poetovio (Ptuj), and XV Apollinaris, probably at Carnuntum; those in Moesia were IV Scythica and V Macedonica, stationed at Oescus (Gigen). See Wilkes 92–4.[15]

legionum duae is presumably equivalent to the Eng. 'two of the legions', meaning 'two of Rome's legions', i.e. two out of the total number that

---

[14] The most extensive discussion of the dating of the composition of the *Annals* is G.'s long note on 2.61.2 (pp. 387–93), with which the above is largely in agreement. See also Syme, *RP* 3.1037–40 and 4.203–4; Birley (2000) 241–7.

[15] J. Dzino, *Illyricum in Roman politics 229 BC–AD 68* (2010), is largely concerned with the period before that to which T. refers here.

Rome possessed (for exs. of cardinal numerals + partitive gen. see K–S 1.426). *attinere* used of military possession is either unique (so *OLD* 2c) or very unusual (*TLL* 2.1143.14–18 quotes only metaphorical exs. at *Trag. Incert.* fr. 195 R and Cic. *Inv.* 2.169, where the text is uncertain), but in the *Annals* it is a favoured verb of T., who 'uses it more variously than Sallust' (1.35.4n.); Prof. Reeve's suggested *obtinebant* is nevertheless attractive.

totidem apud Delmatiam locatis VII at Tilurium (Gardun) and XI at Burnum (Šuplja Crkva): the two centres, roughly 60 miles apart from each other in the immediate hinterland of central Dalmatia, 'lie on a road that was employed as a *limes* by the army in their attacks on the peoples beyond the Dinaric Alps' (Wilkes 97).

quae positu regionis a tergo illis ac, si repentinum auxilium Italia posceret, haud procul accirentur The clause is a varied chiasmus (*a tergo ~ haud procul, illis ~ si . . . posceret*); *illis* refers back to Pannonia (where there had been mutiny as recently as AD 14: cf. 1.16–30) and Moesia; *repentinum auxilium* (to judge from Liv. 3.4.11 'dare Quinctio subitarios milites – ita tum repentina auxilia appellabant – iussi') means 'emergency reinforcement' (*OLD auxilium* 4). The imperfect subjunctives represent 'the past point of view of someone looking forward' (*NLS* §99).

quamquam insideret urbem proprius miles, tres urbanae, nouem praetoriae cohortes For the three urban cohorts, assumed to be a kind of police force, see C. J. Fuhrmann, *Policing the Roman Empire: soldiers, administration, and public order* (2012) 116 (and 123ff. for 'military policing in Rome and Italy under Augustus's successors'); also Keppie 154, 188–9. For the praetorian cohorts see 2.1n. above. *insido* presumably means 'occupy' (*OLD* 2).

5.4 apud idonea prouinciarum In this favoured construction (3.1.3n.) it is often difficult to gauge the degree to which the partitive nature of the genitive is felt (1.17.1n.); here the meaning seems more likely to be 'at suitable points in the provinces' rather than 'in suitable provinces'. For subst. *idonea* elsewhere cf. *Rhet. Herenn.* 4.3, Hor. *S.* 2.2.111, *AP* 334 (none of them constructed with the gen.).

sociae triremes See Starr 106–66, Rougé 121–3 (map of their bases on p. 123).

auxilia cohortium is a Tacitean variation (again at *H.* 2.4.4) on the regular *cohortes auxiliariae* (for which see e.g. Keppie 182–6).

neque multo secus in iis uirium *secus* is here uniquely treated as a noun, like some other adverbs which are found with a partitive gen. such as *affatim* (*OLD* b) or *abunde* (*OLD* 2): see L–H–S 52. When the term implies a comparison, as here, an abl. of comparison may be used (e.g. Liv. *praef.* 12 'quanto rerum minus').

sed persequi incertum fuerit Furneaux and Koestermann print the transmitted *fuit* and think that *persequi* means 'to track down, find by searching, trace' (*OLD* 4); but 'tracing them was uncertain' is not the best of sense and in any case implies an ellipse, '<so I did not do it>'. It is greatly preferable to adopt Lipsius' *fuerit* and to assume that *persequi* means 'to go through, enumerate' (*OLD* 8): in this sense the verb is regularly used absolutely (e.g. Sall. *J.* 95.2) and in contexts where, as here, a list is cut short or omitted (*TLL* 10.1.1692. 51–61). The sense is 'enumeration would be unreliable'; the subjunctive is potential and has a future aspect (*NLS* §119): it is greatly liked by T. for similarly programmatic statements (e.g. 32.2, 65.1, 15.41.1 'numerum inire haud promptum fuerit', *H.* 2.2.2, *Agr.* 9.4). See also Damon, *AHC* 355.

ex usu temporis 'according to the demands of the moment' (G–G 1711b); *ex usu* more normally means 'to the advantage of ~' (*OLD usus* 11c), as 6.42.2.

gliscerent For this Tacitean favourite see 3.19.2n.; for the contrast with *minuerentur* cf. 3.69.4.

6.1 Congruens crediderim recensere . . . sc. *esse* ('I am inclined to believe that it is fitting to review . . .'): *congruens est/uidetur* + infin. is found first in Pliny and T. (again at *H.* 5.2.1 'congruens uidetur primordia eius aperire', at the start of a comparable passage) but is not common: see *TLL* 4.302.67ff. For the technique whereby one digressive section of narrative is made to arise out of another see e.g. 6.20.2–21.3 ~ 22, *Agr.* 10–13.1 ~ 13.1–17, Sall. *C.* 53.2–5 ~ 53.6–54, Vell. 1.14–15 ~ 16–18. *recensere* is used also by Velleius for his review of Tib.'s reign (129.1).

quibus modis ad eam diem habitae sint For this use of *habere* = 'to handle, manage' (as again at 33.2 'quibus modis temperanter haberetur' and e.g. Sall. *C.* 5.9 'quo modo rem publicam habuerint') see 3.13.1n. The use of *dies* = *tempus* implies that the change in Tib.'s reign could be traced to a specific moment, and is perhaps influenced by the frequent appearance of the word in the ἀρχή κακῶν motif (next n.).

quoniam Tiberio mutati in deterius principatus initium ille annus attulit The clause repeats and therefore underlines the point made at the opening of the book (*Tiberio . . . ille annus ~ nonus Tiberio annus, initium ~ coepit . . . initium, mutati in deterius ~ turbare . . . saeuire*); on this occasion the point is expressed in terms of the ἀρχή κακῶν motif (e.g. Thuc. 2.12.3 ἥδε ἡ ἡμέρα τοῖς Ἕλλησι μεγάλων κακῶν ἄρξει, Virg. *Aen.* 4.169–70 'ille dies primus leti primusque laborum | causa fuit'; some other exs. at *RICH* 63 n. 186), and it is interesting that, even more than at 1.1 (where *fortuna* is invoked), Tib.'s deterioration is attributed to an external agency, here *annus* (as often: cf. 6.45.1n.). For *initium adferre* cf. Cic. *TD* 1.91, *Att.* 12.7.1, Cels. 1 *praef.* 18. A. A. Lund wished to emend *mutati* to *mutandi* (*Mnem.* 42 (1989) 126–7), but his emendation takes no account of the fact that in Latin 'the noun together with the predicative participle forms an abstract noun-phrase wherein the leading idea is conveyed by the participle' (*NLS* 75 §95; cf. K–S 1.762).

Suetonius famously divided Caligula's principate into two halves (*Cal.* 22.1) and did the same with Nero's (*Nero* 19.3), a division which is perhaps mirrored in T. (14.52.1). Syme maintained that 'The dichotomy which the tradition asserts in the reign of each Caesar . . . reflects facts' (Syme, *Tac.* 420 n. 2), though of course he derived those 'facts' from 'the tradition' – which in the case of Tib. is complicated, because Suetonius and Dio place the dichotomy in 19 (see above, p. 3). Cf. 6.46.4n. on Sulla.

6.2 Iam primum publica negotia et priuatorum maxima apud patres tractabantur

Similarly Suetonius (*Tib.* 30 'neque tam paruum quicquam neque magnum publici priuatique negotii fuit de quo non ad patres conscriptos referretur') and Dio (57.7.2 πάντα δὲ δὴ καὶ τὰ σμικρότατα ἔς τε τὴν γερουσίαν ἐσέφερε καὶ ἐκείνῃ ἐκοίνου). The point is that T. 'seems to have regarded the freedom of the Senate as freedom *par excellence*' (C. Wirszubski, *Libertas as a political idea at Rome* (1950) 163; cf. M. P. O. Morford, 'How Tacitus defined liberty', *ANRW* 2.33.5.3420–50 (1991), Oakley in *CCT* 184–94); see also next n. *Iam primum*, the words with which Livy's narrative begins, = 'to begin with' (*OLD iam* 8b), as 12.68.2, 14.31.1.

dabaturque primoribus disserere Since the denial of free speech was the mark of the slave (*Agr.* 2.3n.), the senators' ability to speak, amply attested by Dio (57.7.3–5), confirmed their free status (last n.): cf. esp. T.'s famous description of his own day: 'ubi sentire quae uelis et quae sentias dicere licet' (*H.* 1.1.4). For some exs. see 1.74.4, 1.77.3, 3.60.1 ~ 3; this is one of the areas in which Tib. was following Augustan practice (Brunt (1984) 443). For the impersonal use of *dari*, of which T. is fond, see 3.67.2n.

in adulationem lapsos cohibebat ipse For some exs. of senatorial *adulatio* see 1.7.1, 1.8.4, 2.32.2, 3.47.3–4, 3.57.1, 3.69.1; for Tib.'s reaction see 2.87, 3.47.4 and 3.65.3 'O homines ad seruitutem paratos!'. For *adulatio* see Syme, *Tac.* 573–4, Brunt (1984) 443–4, Vielberg 80–112.

mandabatque honores nobilitatem maiorum, claritudinem militiae, inlustres domi artes spectando *mandare honorem/-es* (again at 11.22.4) is a regular expr. for assigning magistracies (e.g. Cic. *Verr.* 4.81, *Pis.* 2, *Leg. Man.* 2, Hor. *S.* 1.6.19–20, Liv. 4.3.4, 24.8.1; *OLD mando*[1] 4b); Tib. did not of course personally assign magistracies, but by means of *commendatio*, to which T.'s use of the verb in this context perhaps alludes, he could ensure the appointment of those he favoured. For this subject and bibliography thereon see 1.14.4–15.1n., 1.81.1-2nn., Vell. 124.3n.; Seager 104–6.

Under the republic, as Syme remarked (*The Roman revolution* (1939) 374), 'nobility of birth, military service, distinction in oratory or law, these were the three claims to the consulate'. During the years surveyed by T. here, AD 15–23, the position of *consul ordinarius* was occupied by a *nobilis* on 12 out of 13 possible occasions:[16] the one exception is L. Pomponius Flaccus in 17 (2.41.2), who had campaigned with distinction in Moesia in AD 12 and had probably served with Tib. in Germany or Illyricum earlier (*RP* 3.1094). For, as Syme again remarked, 'military merit, oratory, and proficiency in legal studies, such were the channels of advancement for *novi homines* according to the traditional prescription at Rome' (*Tac.* 580, quoting Liv. 39.40.5 'ad summos honores alios scientia iuris, alios eloquentia, alios gloria militaris prouexit'). Of the *noui* who became suffects, C. Vibius Rufus (AD 16) was an orator, frequently cited by the elder Seneca and praised by Asinius Pollio (*RP* 3.1087); C. Pomponius Graecinus (16) was praised by Ovid for his *artes* and *militiae labor*, perhaps in Illyricum (*Ex P.* 1.6.7–10; R. Syme, *History in Ovid* (1978) 74–5); C. Vibius Marsus (17) is likely to have had a military record (*RP* 3.1353) and in any case was significant enough to rise to the proconsulship of Africa in 26/7–29/30 (6.47.2n.); L. Seius Tubero (18), a relative of Sejanus (29.1n.), had served as a legate under Germanicus (2.20.1); C. Vibius Rufinus (21 or 22) had probably served under Tib. in 6–9 (*RP* 3.1434) and proceeded to the proconsulship of Asia in 36/7. No pre-consular distinction in *militia* or *domi artes* seems to be attested for the remaining *suffecti*, but this may simply be due to the vagaries of the historical record. Some form of personal distinction may be inferred at least for C. Rubellius Blandus (18), who married Drusus Caesar's daughter in 33 (6.27.1 and n.) and became proconsul of Africa in 35, and P. Petronius (19), who held an 'exorbitant tenure' of Asia from 29 to 35 (*RP* 3.1354). Although the context of T.'s statement implies a change after AD 23, there are no clear signs of it. For example, of the four men who in 28 conspired to ruin Titius Sabinus through their *cupido consulatus*, 'ad quem non nisi per Seianum aditus' (68.2), only M. Porcius Cato was successful, and his suffect consulship came in 36, when Sejanus was dead and earlier friendship with him was more likely to have hindered advancement. For general discussion of the consuls under Tib. see Seager 106–9, Levick 96–9, and esp. Syme, *RP* 3.1350–63 (on those of AD 15–19); for Tib.'s characteristic regard for the senate on such issues see esp. Brunt (1984) 423–4, 429.

Despite their traditional implications, *nobilitas maiorum* is found elsewhere only at Quint. 6.1.21, *claritudo militiae* is unexampled altogether, and *domi artes*

---

[16] The *suffecti* have a converse distribution, all but three of a comparable number being *noui homines*.

recurs only at 3.70.3 above; for his preference for *claritudo* over *claritas* in the *Annals* see 1.28.1n.

ut satis constaret non alios potiores fuisse There is general agreement that this clause is consecutive; the notion that it may be purposive is described as 'refutable' by Oakley (1991: 343), who quotes several allegedly 'analogous *ut*-clauses', in each of which 'the sense is self-evidently consecutive'. But the majority of his examples are not analogous at all; and, while it is true that Cic. *Red. Quir.* 17 and Liv. 24.40.11 are 'self-evidently consecutive', the whole point is that this cannot be said of the present case. A purpose clause would testify to Tib.'s known determination, inherited from Augustus, to rule by senatorial consent.

potior is almost a technical term for being better qualified for office (*OLD potior²* 3a, cf. 1b; Oakley on Liv. 9.30.1).

Sua consulibus, sua praetoribus species *species* here = 'prestige' (*OLD* 4a), as Cic. *Pis.* 24 'magnum nomen est, magna species, magna dignitas, magna maiestas consulis'; *sua* = 'proper' (*OLD* 12a; cf. 10a, 11), as Plin. *Pan.* 93.1 'manet manebitque honori [i.e. the consulship] ueneratio sua'. Tib. made a point of deferring to the consuls (Suet. *Tib.* 31.2, Dio 57.8.5), and on Augustus' death in 14 the praetorian elections had been transferred from people to senate, thereby increasing the latter's self-esteem (cf. 1.15.1 and n.; Seager 105–6, Levick 95–6). In general see T. C. Brennan, *The praetorship in the Roman Republic* (2000) and F. Pina Polo, *The consul at Rome: the civil functions of the consuls in the Roman Republic* (2011).

exercita potestas An uncommon phrase for the exercise of power (as 6.11.3, [Quint.] *Decl.* 372.11).

legesque, si maiestatis quaestio eximeretur, bono in usu 'The emperor's judicial function was a core element of his civic role, and the popular conception of the *princeps* as a source of justice was fundamental to the emperor's public image' (Noreña 157, with further references; note also 15.2n. and ref. there to Tuori). For Tib. and the law see esp. Levick 180–2; he is the only Julio-Claudian emperor on whose coinage *iustitia* appears (in 22): see Sutherland 97–8, Weinstock 247, Wallace-Hadrill 323, and in general B. Lichocka, *Justitia sur les monnaies impériales romaines* (1974). *bono in usu* is an unparalleled expr. but presumably means that, *maiestas* apart, the laws were exercised well or appropriately.

By the Lex Cornelia de maiestate of 81 BC Sulla established a permanent court to try cases of alleged treason (the *quaestio de maiestate*, as it was called: cf. Cic. *Phil.* 1.22). Although some scholars infer from T.'s reference to a praetor at 1.72.3 that the court was still operating in AD 15 (see Talbert 466), it is known that by the early years of Tib.'s principate the senate had gradually come to take over the role and powers of the various individual *quaestiones* (Talbert 46off., Rutledge 21–2), and it is generally accepted that the treason court was a victim of this process and by the 20s had fallen into disuse. If that is correct, then *quaestio* in our passage must be non-technical = 'judicial investigation' (*OLD* 3, not 4a), or even 'issue', 'question' (*OLD* 6a); the 'distorted' use of language would be entirely typical (see *Ann. 3*, p. 503; *Ann. 5–6*, p. 319: s.v. 'technical ... language'). Yet the very phrase *quaestio maiestatis* at 19.4 below seems almost certainly to be a reference to the treason court (see n.), and, if that is the case, it is very difficult to believe that the words have a different meaning here. The two passages together constitute evidence that the court was still in active existence. For *eximo* see *OLD* 3b; the subjunctive appears to be a generalising potential (as 2.30.2 'si mollius acciperes'): see G–G 1488a, Carmody 131.

For *maiestas* in Tib.'s reign see, in addition to Seager 125–38 and 226–7 and Levick 182ff., Rogers, Bauman, *CM* and *IP*, Garnsey 19–25, 39, Rutledge *passim* and Peachin.[17] The first cases were in AD 15 (1.73–4), but all three defendants were cleared of the charge.

6.3 At frumenta et pecuniae uectigales . . . societatibus equitum Romanorum agitabantur

at was seen by Pfitzner as marking a transition from Rome to the provinces, but the sequence *apud patres* ~ *equitum Romanorum* ~ *plebes* may suggest that T.'s perspective is rather socio-political. Since *societas* is the technical term (*OLD* 2b) for a company of tax-gatherers or *publicani* (cf. 13.50.3 'uectigalium societates ... publicanorum cupidines'), T.'s evidence implies that a significant number of *publicani* were *equites* (*contra BNP* 12.182). On *publicani* in general see Brunt, *RIT* 354–432.

Most matters concerning Roman taxation are controversial (see e.g. *Agr.* 19.4n.); for the three kinds of state income mentioned here see P. Erdkamp, *The grain market in the Roman Empire: a social, political and economic study* (2005) 220. *pecuniae uectigales*[18] are usually taken to include harbour fees (*portoria*) and grazing taxes (*scriptura*); *publicorum* indicates revenues (usually assumed to be those from e.g. quarries and mines) that were paid into the *aerarium* (for which cf. M. Corbier, *L'aerarium Saturni et l'aerarium militare: administration et prosopographie sénatoriale* (1974)). In general on taxation and the like see e.g. Brunt, *RIT* 324–46, and, on our passage in particular, 391–3. For *agitare* = 'to manage', as 41.3 below, see *OLD* 13.

---

[17] I have not seen A. von Schilling, *Poena extraordinaria: zur Strafzumessung in der frühen Kaiserzeit* (2010).

[18] The only other occurrence of the expr. is Cic. *II Verr.* 1.89 'decem enim naues iussu L. Murenae populus Milesius ex pecunia uectigali populi Romani fecerat', which I take to mean that the money with which the ships were built would normally have gone in taxes.

Res suas Caesar . . . cum plerique isdem negotiis insenescerent It seems generally assumed that T. is referring to the equestrian procurators whom the emperor appointed to manage the revenues in the imperial provinces (e.g. A. N. Sherwin-White, 'Procurator Augusti', *PBSR* 15 (1939) 14), and apparent contrasts with the previous sentence (*res suas ~ publicorum fructuum, cuique* and *quibusdam ~ societatibus*) suggest a continuity of theme. But T.'s point about growing old in the same occupations has hitherto – and famously – been made about *proconsular governors* (1.80.1 'id quoque morum Tiberii fuit, continuare imperia ac plerosque ad finem uitae in isdem exercitibus aut iurisdictionibus habere'; cf. 6.39.3). It seems unlikely that there is an abrupt change of subject with *adsumpti*, and in any case the equestrian context (esp. *quibusdam ignotis ex fama*) seems to rule out a reference to the same category of person as mentioned at 1.80.1. When Josephus refers to the same phenomenon, he applies it not only to governors but also to ἐπίτροποι (*AJ* 18.170 ἡγεμόσι τε ἢ ἐπιτρόποις ὑπ' αὐτοῦ σταλεῖσιν οὐδεμία ἦν διαδοχή, ὁπότε μὴ φθαῖεν τετελευτηκότες), a term which covers praesidial procurators and prefects,[19] who governed certain of the provinces such as Judaea and Egypt. And in fact Judaea was a case where successive prefects, Valerius Gratus (AD 15–26) and Pontius Pilatus (26–36), governed for eleven and ten years respectively (cf. Jos. *AJ* 18.33, 35), while C. Galerius governed Egypt for even longer (16–31). Since the tenures of Gratus and Galerius began near the start of Tib.'s reign, it seems likely that the historian is referring to this type of governor as well as to financial procurators. *res suas* could as well mean 'possessions' as 'wealth'. 'His words', as G. remarks of 1.80.1, 'cannot be made to yield a precise connotation.'

In general see Brunt (1983) and, on the imperial *fiscus* to which the imperial revenues went, *RIT* 134–62 and 347–53. See also nn. below.

spectatissimo cuique looks back to *spectando* above and implies that Tib. was as demanding of the *equites* as he was of the senators: cf. the advice on *equites* which 'Maecenas' is made to offer Augustus in the speech put into his mouth by Dio (52.19.4, 25.1–5). Equestrians tended to attract appreciatory epithets according to their perceived rank within the order (Demougin, *OE* 591–9; see e.g. Vell. 88.2n. for *splendidus*); *spectatissimus* (the superl. is only here in T.) is above all a Ciceronian adj. (6×) and used by him of *equites* (e.g. *II Verr.* 1.137 'spectatissimus ordinis sui', 3.65).

quibusdam ignotis ex fama 'Of most candidates below the top levels of administration at Rome the emperors probably did not have much personal

---

[19] Cf. H. J. Mason, *Greek terms for Roman institutions* (1974) 49. Dio is unhelpful on the question of terminology (58.23.6 τί γὰρ ἄν τις ἔχοι τοὺς αἱρετοὺς ὀνομάζειν, οἷς καὶ ἀπὸ πρώτης ἐπὶ πλεῖστον ἄρχειν ἐδίδου;).

knowledge. In the absence of any formal mechanisms for application, such candidates relied on their patrons – perhaps the emperor's *amici* or members of his household – to bring them to the emperor's attention and praise them for their virtues' (R. P. Saller, 'Promotion and patronage in equestrian careers', *JRS* 70 (1980) 56).

cum plerique isdem negotiis insenescerent For Tib.'s policy in this respect, here and at 1.80.1 described in terms similar to those used by Josephus (above), see esp. Orth 71–81 and 127–32, adding L. Munatius Plancus Paulinus (cos. AD 13), who governed Pannonia for seventeen years (Syme, *RP* 3.1355 and n. 43); also Brunt, *RIT* 76, 490–1. Whether *negotiis* is abl. or (more likely) dat. is unclear; the verb is very rare.

6.4 Plebes acri quidem annona fatigabatur A fragment of Sall. *H.* (2.45 M = 2.41 R) reads: *<annonae intolerabil>is saeuitia. qua re fati<ga>ta plebes …* If the fragment has been restored with anything like correctness, T. has alluded to it both here and at 2.87 'saeuitiam annonae incusante plebe statuit frumento pretium' (an example of the literary phenomenon known as 'distribution'). In our passage the meaning 'grain supply' (*OLD* 2a) is suggested both by the verb (cf. 49.3 'sitis fatigabat', 1.68.5 'ciborum egestas fatigaret') and by the adj. (cf. Lucr. 3.65 'acris egestas'). For T.'s preference for the archaic form *plebes* see 3.2.2n.

quin infecunditati terrarum aut asperis maris obuiam iit Tib., whose first public act had been to help ease a grain crisis in 23 BC (*RG* 15.1, Vell. 94.3), intervened to control the price of grain in AD 19 (2.87, quoted last n.) and in 22 delivered a brilliant speech (3.53–4: see nn.) in which he had declared that his priority was keeping his people fed (3.54.5 'hanc, patres conscripti, curam sustinet princeps, haec omissa funditus rem publicam trahet'). Although the provision of grain was officially supervised by a *praefectus annonae* (a position created by Augustus late in his principate), *obuiam iit* suggests the personal concern which is emphasised in the *princeps'* speech in Book 3. See esp. *PH* 345–50. *infecunditas*, first in Sall. *H.* 3.46 M = 3.12 R, is another very rare word but it recurs in T. at 12.43.2; for the gen. cf. Col. 1 *praef.* 1 'agrorum infecunditatem'. T. has varied the common *aspera maria* by means of his favourite substantival adj. + gen.: cf. Man. 4.678, Sil. 6.359 'aspera ponti'. For famine, grain crises and the problems of transport see 3.54.4n.

quantum impendio diligentiaque potuit Tib.'s well known devotion to Augustan precedent is here underlined by means of an allusion to his adoptive father's boast that in 22 BC he resolved the recurring food crisis 'impensa et cura mea' (*RG* 5.2); but T. typically prefers a choicer synonym for the former noun, and a non-technical one for the latter. Velleius praises Tib.

for keeping down the price of grain in 14–29 (126.3); for pricing in general see G. E. Rickman, *The corn supply of ancient Rome* (1980) 143ff.

ne prouinciae nouis oneribus turbarentur *prouinciae* = 'provincials' by metonymy (*OLD* 3d). Tib. famously declared that 'boni pastoris esse tondere pecus, non deglubere' (Suet. *Tib.* 32.2; cf. Dio 57.10.5), and in any case he hated provincial disruption (2.65.1 'nihil aeque Tiberium anxium habebat quam ne composita turbarentur'). In 17 tribute was waived for the cities of Asia struck by an earthquake (2.47.2), and reduced for Cappadocia on its annexation as a province (2.56.4). Velleius praises Tib.'s *munificentia* in this regard (126.4). On Tib.'s provincial policy in general see G. Alföldy, 'La politique provinciale de Tibère', *Latomus* 24 (1965) 824–44; Seager 138–47 and 225–6; Levick 125–47; Brunt, *RIT* 75–6; and esp. Orth.

utque uetera sine auaritia aut crudelitate magistratuum tolerarent prouidebat Although provincials in this period could still be made by T. to voice traditional complaints (3.40.3 'continuatione tributorum, grauitate faenoris, saeuitia ac superbia praesidentium', AD 21), the contemporary Velleius said that the provinces were freed from the wrongdoing of magistrates (126.4 'uindicatae ab iniuriis magistratuum prouinciae'). Scholars (last n.) are generally sceptical but T. concurs (next n.). For the contrast between new and old burdens cf. Plin. *Pan.* 29.4 'nec nouis indictionibus pressi ad uetera tributa deficiunt'. *prouidebat* alludes to Tib.'s *prouidentia*, perhaps advertised for the first time on the coinage of the previous year (further details at 3.69.1n.); for a list of prosecutions during AD 14–22 see Brunt, *RIT* 90–1. For *tolerare* see 3.1.1n.

Corporum uerbera, ademptiones bonorum aberant These two elements (themselves chiastically arranged) pick up *utque . . . tolerarent* chiastically and are intended to prove that the emperor's *prouidentia* was successful. Brunt, however, notes apropos of this sentence that 'the contemporary Philo gives a very different impression of conditions' and, quoting *Flacc.* 105–7, says that 'governors were commonly guilty of corruption, plunder, and the punishment of innocent men of rank' (*RIT* 489).

Rari per Italiam Caesaris agri presumably means not that Caesar's lands were widely scattered across Italy but that he had very few of them (*rarus ager* at Ov. *Am.* 2.16.8 is usually taken to have a similar meaning, though McKeown ad loc. prefers 'porous soil'). Commentators suggest that T. is contrasting both the Tiberian age with later times and domestic estates with provincial; for the imperial estates, acquired through inheritances or confiscations, see D. J. Crawford, 'Imperial estates', in M. I. Finley (ed.), *Studies in Roman property* (1976) 35–56 (with a list of those attested in Italy on pp. 67–70), Millar 175–89.

modesta seruitia, intra paucos libertos domus Slaves and freedmen together made up what is known as the 'familia Caesaris' (see P. R. C. Weaver, *Familia Caesaris* (1972), esp. 299–300 for definitions). *modesta* = 'well behaved' or 'unassuming' (*OLD* 2, 4), in contrast with the arrogance on display later at e.g. 74.4 below; the fewness of the freedmen contrasts with what is implied later in the reign (cf. 6.38.2 and n.) but esp. with the reign of Claudius. For the common *uariatio* of adj. ~ prep. phrase see Sörbom 92–3.

si quando cum priuatis disceptaret, forum et ius There is no example of Tib.'s personal dispute with a private citizen, although he implied that, given the right circumstances, he would act as a private citizen against the elder Piso (3.12.2 'priuatas inimicitias non ut princeps ulciscar'). He was ready to support his mother's friend Urgulania in a private-citizen capacity (2.34.2 'hactenus indulgere matri ciuile ratus'), and he insisted that procurators, his own representatives, should be treated no differently from private citizens (Dio 57.23.5 περὶ τῶν διαφορῶν ἕν τε τῇ ἀγορᾷ καὶ κατὰ τοὺς νόμους ἐξ ἴσου τοῖς ἰδιώταις δικάζεσθαι, wording which closely resembles our passage). That Tib. was in general anxious to be seen acting as a *priuatus* or *ciuis* is attested by Vell. 124.2, Suet. *Tib.* 26.1 and Dio 57.11.7: see in general A. Wallace-Hadrill, '*Ciuilis Princeps*: between citizen and king', *JRS* 72 (1982) 32–48, esp. 39. Surprisingly, *forum et ius* is otherwise an unexampled pairing; *disceptaret* is a frequentative subjunc. (*NLS* §196).

7–12 The death of Drusus

This section begins with a paragraph on Drusus' quarrel with Sejanus (7) and ends with another on Sejanus' designs against a future victim, Agrippina (12). In between are two central panels (8–9 and 10–11), in the former of which, though the subject is nominally that of Drusus' death (cf. 10.1 'in tradenda morte Drusi'), the death itself is dismissed obliquely in two sentences (8.1) and T. concentrates instead on Tib.'s speech to the senate (8.2–9.1) and Drusus' funeral (9.2). This treatment allows T. to return to Drusus' death at greater and more insidious length in the second panel, which is presented in the form of an excursus (the funeral of 9.2 being resumed at 12.1).

7.1 Quae cuncta ... retinebat tamen, donec morte Drusi uerterentur *non quidem comi uia* contrasts with *sed horridus ac plerumque formidatus*, and both phrases together contrast with *retinebat tamen*. Since Suetonius and Dio make similar statements but with reference to the death of Germanicus in 19 (above, Introduction, p. 3), the probability is that in making Drusus' death the turning point of the reign T. was countering an established view. *uerterentur* perhaps connotes the technique of *peripeteia*, which was defined in terms of

97

change or reversal (Arist. *Poet.* 1452a22–3 Ἔστι δὲ περιπέτεια μὲν ἡ εἰς τὸ ἐναντίον τῶν πραττομένων μεταβολή); for some other exs. of similar self-reflexivity see *Agr.* 15.5n. (*deliberare*).

When T. deploys *comitas* contrastively elsewhere, its opposites manifest themselves through speech and looks, *sermo* and *uultus* (1.33.2, 6.50.1), which is presumably the case with *horridus ac plerumque formidatus* here: Tib.'s words were worryingly obscure (1.11.2, 13.3.2) and his demeanour terrifying (3.15.2, 4.60.2).[20] *horridus* probably means simply 'grim', since more active meanings ('causing fright') are almost exclusively poetical (*TLL* 6.3.2994.5ff.); *formidatus* (a verb T. uses nowhere else) illustrates the fear from which the subjects of a tyrant conventionally suffer (see e.g. 69.3, 70.2, 74.1, Xen. *Hiero* 6.4–8, Plato, *Rep.* 578A, Arist. *Pol.* 1311a25–7; Heinz 32–5):[21] for the coupling with *horridus* cf. Sil. 12.122–3 'horrens | et formidatus' (of Lake Avernus). For *cuncta* see 3.18.4n.; for the common *uariatio* of abl. of manner ~ adj./part. see Sörbom 89; for the subjunc. after *donec* without any sense of intention see e.g. Malloch on 11.22.4.

incipiente adhuc potentia See 1.1n. (*adhuc* = 'still <only>': *OLD* 1a). For *notescere* (below) see 1.73.3n.

ultor metuebatur non occultus odii set crebro querens The potential avenger is Drusus (a slightly awkward change of subject). The paradosis reads *odiis et*, which gives a wrong sense ('hidden by hatreds'?): Lipsius' *odii et* was improved by Doederlein to *odii set* (cf. 3.7.1, where the correct text is perhaps 'ultioni *set crebro questu*');[22] the gen. of reference, like *Agr.* 43.3 'securus iam odii', is found with *occultus* only in T. (it recurs, differently deployed, at 6.36.2: see n.). On fear and hatred see Braund on Sen. *Clem.* 1.12.4. For *metuo* see 3.10.2n.

incolumi filio adiutorem imperii alium uocari For Sejanus' title(s) see 2.3n. above. Drusus' indignant point is that he and Germanicus *already* enjoyed the title of 'assistants in power' (cf. Strabo 6.4.2 οἱ παῖδες αὐτοῦ Γερμανικός τε καὶ Δροῦσος ὑπουργοῦντες τῷ πατρί, c. AD 18) and that, although his brother was now dead, he himself was still alive (*OLD incolumis* 1c) and entitled (cf. 3.56.4 'laboris participem' and n.). *incolumi filio* is of course dramatic irony ('safe and sound': *OLD incolumis* 1a), since, thanks to his rival,

[20] For more on Tib.'s appearance see 57.2 and nn.

[21] E. Mastellone Iovane, *Paura e angoscia in Tacito: implicazioni ideologiche e politiche* (1989), concentrates on the Neronian books of the *Annals* but has a useful table of T.'s many words for fear and the like (p. 9).

[22] Where an emendation is involved, it seems helpful to print *set*, a form which is found quite frequently in M (e.g. 34.5 below). See C. F. Neue and C. Wagener, *Formenlehre der lateinischen Sprache* (3rd edn, 1892–1905) 2.961.

Drusus will very soon also be dead. *adiutores imperii* at Suet. *Cal.* 26.1 (its only other occurrence) refers to those who had assisted Caligula *to* power.

et quantum superesse ut collega dicatur! Drusus' continuing indignation (last n.) is more vividly expressed by an ironical exclamation (W. S. Watt's suggested punctuation) than by a rhetorical question. Sejanus at last became Tib.'s *collega* in 31, when he was declared *consul ordinarius* alongside the emperor (cf. 5.6.2n.). For the impersonal construction see *OLD supersum* 6b; also next n.

7.2 primas dominandi spes in arduo When a person fixes his eyes on the summit (*dominatio*), even the first stages seem out of reach (*in arduo*, again at 12.15.2, is a favourite Senecan metaphor, e.g. *Ben.* 4.33.2, but cf. esp. Quint. 1.10.8 'in arduo spes est'); but, once you embark on the ascent ('ubi sis ingressus'), you make progress until there is very little left between you and the top ('quantum superesse . . . !').[23] The generally Sallustian patterning of the Sejanus story (1–3n. above) suggests also an allusion to Sall. *C.* 17.5 'quos magis dominationis spes hortabatur', with the more emphatic gerund substituted for the abstract noun (which T. retains at 12.8.2, 14.2.2).

ubi sis ingressus The indefinite second-person subjunctive (below, 11.1n.) is here retained in the *oratio obliqua* (as e.g. 14.20.2 'si uetustiora repetas', *H.* 1.50.3 'scires'). See L–H–S 419.

adesse studia et ministros 'there was support from sympathetic assistants'.

exstructa . . . Cn. Pompei Cf. above, 2.1–3 and nn.

communes . . . nepotes In AD 20 (cf. 3.29.4) a daughter of Sejanus – presumably Junilla, who was still a very young child (cf. 5.9.1nn.) – was betrothed to Drusus, a son of the future emperor Claudius. According to Suetonius he died within 'a few days' of the betrothal by choking on a pear (*Claud.* 27.1), but the reference here to projected offspring suggests that Drusus was still alive in 23. Ritter solves the problem by assuming that T. has assembled complaints uttered at widely different times.

precandam post haec modestiam, ut contentus esset? If these words are printed as a statement, as they usually are, they are anticlimactic and do not fit easily into the context. If they are formulated as a rhetorical question ('After all this, must restraint be begged for [sc. from Sejanus], that he

---

[23] For the Romans' acquaintance with mountaineering see A. S. Pease, 'Notes on mountain climbing in antiquity', *Appalachia* 132 (1961) 289–98; for a description of rock-climbing see e.g. Curt. 7.11.13–17.

be content?'), they are transformed into a threat – simultaneously justifying Sejanus' description of Drusus as an 'avenger' (*ultor*, above) and explaining the sudden need for haste in killing him (*igitur*, below). The *ut*-clause is probably epexegetic of *modestiam*, but possibly one has to understand *precandum* from *precandam* (cf. 33.2); if the latter, the words could effectively be printed as two separate questions.

7.3 Neque raro neque apud paucos talia iaciebat The words look back chiastically to *non occultos* and *crebro*, framing Drusus' speech by ring composition.

corrupta uxore The position of the phrase next to the verb suggests an instrumental abl. (for which cf. 2.79.2n.) rather than an abl. abs.: now that Sejanus has seduced Livi(ll)a into an adulterous affair, she is viewed merely as an instrument.

8.1 maturandum ratus The expression is Livian (24.12.3, 35.50.6, 36.42.4) but the need now for haste may constitute a further element in the 'Sallustian' plot (cf. *C.* 17.3 'uidetur causa fuisse facinus maturandi').

deligit uenenum, quo ... fortuitus morbus adsimularetur Although Suetonius (*Tib.* 62.1) and Dio (57.22.1–2) agree with T. that Drusus was poisoned, modern scholars are sceptical (Syme, *Tac.* 402, Levick 161–2, Seager 155–7, 227). Stories of poisoning attached themselves to premature deaths in the imperial family (e.g. Gaius Caesar at 1.3.3, Germanicus at 2.73.4) and were often an element in stories of adultery (e.g. 52.1 below; see 3.22.1n.). Drusus had been ill two years previously (3.49.1) and, until the revelations of AD 31 (below), his death was thought by Tib. to have been caused by his notoriously intemperate way of life (*Tib.* 62.1; cf. Dio 57.14.9–10). *fortuitus* is used of idiopathic conditions such as fever (Suet. *Tib.* 73.2) or spontaneous bleeding (Cels. 2.8.18); for *deligere* see Malloch on 11.22.4.

Lygdum spadonem He was the ideal administerer of the poison since Drusus was fond of him and regarded him as one of his principal servants (10.2), perhaps using him as *praegustator*. For the term *spado* see 6.31.2n.

octo post annos In 31, after the downfall of Sejanus (Dio 58.11.6).

8.2 Ceterum Tiberius per omnes ualetudinis eius dies nullo metu an ut firmitudinem animi ostentaret A verb such as *agebat* ('acted') has to be understood in this sentence. Other edd. extend the sentence to *curiam ingressus est* and understand *curiam ingrediebatur* with *per omnes ... dies* (a form of 'gapping': see 3.3.3n.), but this interpretation seems precluded by Tib.'s speech below, where his appearance in the senate (*subierit oculos senatus* ~ *curiam ingressus est*) is specified as having taken place after his son's death (*tam recenti*

dolore ~ defuncto). The expressions *curiam ingressus est, consulesque . . . admonuit et . . .
senatum . . . erexit* all refer to the same occasion, whereas *Tiberius . . . ostentaret* is
a manifestation of his general behaviour. For the *uariatio* of abl. ~ purpose
clause (again at 48.2, 71.3) see Sörbom 114, R. H. Martin, *Eranos* 51 (1953) 92;
for the use of *an* see 1.13.6n. The alternatives thus expressed are not immediately clear: perhaps T. means that Tib. acted with no fear (sc. that Drusus
would die) or to display his fortitude (sc. since it was possible that Drusus might
die);[24] the latter is in contrast with Agricola at *Agr.* 29.1 'neque . . . ambitiose'.
firmitudo animi (again at 14.49.3; cf. 3.6.2) occurs once each in Plautus (*Asin.* 320)
and Caesar (*BC* 3.28.4) but otherwise only in Cicero's letters (3×); *firmitas animi*
is much commoner, esp. in Seneca.

defuncto necdum sepulto Drusus was buried on 14 September (EJ p. 52;
see further 14.1n., below); the date of his death is unknown.

sede uulgari i.e. among the other senators instead of on their normal seats
(*sellae curules*) on a raised platform (*tribunal*: cf. 16.30.3); there was a similar
gesture during the mourning for Augustus (Dio 56.31.3). See Talbert 121–2.

per speciem maestitiae 'It is implied that the mourning was insincere',
says Furneaux, and Koestermann agrees; but the expr. is almost certainly
objective (as Liv. 23.25.2 'ut . . . maestitiae publicae speciem urbi demi
iuberent').

honoris locique It is difficult to know whether these words refer respectively to the consuls' office and seats, as Cic. *Sull.* 5 'in locum atque in . . .
sedem' (where, however, *locus* refers to the office), or are a hendiadys, 'their
place of honour' (i.e. instead of e.g. *sedes honoris*, as at Cic. *Cat.* 4.2).

**et effusum in lacrimas senatum uicto gemitu simul oratione con-
tinua erexit** It is difficult to be certain of the scene which these words depict.
Most, though not all, scholars think that the *gemitus* is that of the *princeps*, but it
seems very odd that he showed no sign of distress when addressing the consuls
in the first part of the sentence. This is a strong argument that the *gemitus* is that
of the senators and is a varied way of referring to their mourning, of which we
have just been told in the preceding phrase ('effusum in lacrimas'). Although
one might expect *uincere gemitum* to refer to one's own *gemitus*, there seems no
reason why the expression should be any different from *uincere silentium*, which

---

[24] It is a misreading of our original note to say that 'Martin and Woodman
suggest the possibility that Tiberius' lack of fear could imply his participation in the plot' to kill Drusus (A. Feldherr, 'The poisoned chalice: rumor
and historiography in Tacitus' account of the death of Drusus', *MD* 61
(2009) 178).

can refer to overcoming another's silence (as Curt. 4.6.28) as well as one's own (as 11.2.1). On the other hand, the position of *simul* between two chiastically arranged abl. phrases suggests that it has a co-ordinating function and is equivalent to *et*. This usage is common in T. (see 3.24.3n.) and, for its joining abl. abs. and instrumental abl., see 11.9.1 and *H*. 3.45.2. If that is also the case here, it constitutes an argument in favour of the majority view that *uicto gemitu* refers to the *princeps'* own groaning.

oratio continua appears to be a regular expr. meaning something like 'a set speech' (cf. *H*. 4.7.1, Sen. *Ep*. 89.17, Quint. 6.1.46, 6.4.1, 7.10.17, 10.3.30, Suet. *Tib*. 27): it is not therefore contradicted by Tib.'s deliberately interrupting his speech so that the consuls can fetch Germanicus' sons (§§3–4). For *erexit* cf. *H*. 4.74.4 'tali oratione grauiora metuentes composuit erexitque', Cic. *Phil*. 5.1 'oratio consulum animum meum erexit'.

8.3 non quidem sibi ignarum Another Tiberian speech begins identically (3.69.2), and cf. 3.54.1 'nec ignoro'. For the form of words, often defensive and introductory, see 6.7.5n.

posse argui The subject is the following *quod*-clause ('the fact that he had submitted to the senate's gaze could be criticised').

quod tam recenti dolore subierit oculos senatus Ciceronian elements are a recognised feature of the speeches which T. puts into Tib.'s mouth (above, 4.1n.): for *oculos senatus* cf. Cic. *Leg. Agr*. 2.90 'in oculis senatus populique Romani'. The combination with *subire* appears to be unparalleled, but the Tacitean Tib. likes striking expressions (3.12.4n.). For other references to eyes and vision in the senate see 3.53.1 and *Agr*. 45.2 and nn.

diem aspici A Senecan expr. (*Cons. Helv*. 13.2, *Ep*. 93.6).

imbecillitatis The noun recurs in T. only at 15.56.3 but is found nearly fifty times in Cicero.

fortiora solacia e complexu rei publicae petiuisse Although the exact phrasing seems unparalleled, T. may derive the metaphor from Cicero (*Sest*. 53 '<e> complexu patriae', *Phil*. 13.9 'res publica . . . suo . . . sinu complexuque recipiet'), who likes personifications of the state (e.g. *Cat*. 1.27 'si omnis res publica sic loquatur', *Planc*. 92) and who constructs his second-favourite clausula with variants of *petiuisse* four times in the *Verrines* (*II Verr*. 1.16, 1.145, 2.54, 3.72). Tib. is alluding to the role which actual embraces played in consolatory situations (e.g. *Agr*. 45.4 'satiari uultu complexuque' and n.). For *solacia . . . petiuisse* cf. Ov. *Tr*. 5.2.41, Luc. 9.878–9, [Quint.] *Decl*. 12.26, 368.10; for *fortiora* cf. Plin. *Ep*. 5.16.10.

Augustae extremam senectam Livia was born in 58 BC (5.1.1n.). For *senecta* see 3.23.1n.

nepotum Usually identified with Nero Caesar and Drusus Caesar (3.1n.), the sons of Germanicus whose presence is required just below, but a good case for Drusus' twins, Germanicus and Tiberius Gemellus, is made by S. J. V. Malloch, *CQ* 51 (2001) 628–31. If the latter are meant, *rudem* will not mean 'inexperienced' (*OLD* 3a) but will be a reference to 'tender years', as 13.16.4 'rudibus annis' (*OLD* 3a): the twins had been born in AD 19 (and Germanicus will die at 15.1 below).

uergentem aetatem suam Tib. was born on 16 Nov. 42 BC and was now 63. For *uergentem* see 2.43.1n.

unica praesentium malorum leuamenta *malorum leuamenta* constitutes a medical metaphor, as at 1.30.3 (*PH* 304, 310); see also Sen. *Ira* 3.16.1 'unum est leuamentum malorum ingentium' and Plin. *Ep.* 8.19.1 'unicum doloris leuamentum'. For *unicus* cf. also *H.* 2.44.2 (and with *leuamen* at Sen. *Phoen.* 1–2); for *malorum* cf. also Liv. 6.35.1 'leuamen mali'. For T.'s preference for *leuamentum* over *leuamen* see 3.28.4n.

8.4 firmatos adloquio adds a nice touch of sympathetic verisimilitude, which the diminutive *adulescentulos* maintains. For the expr. cf. 1.71.3, *H.* 3.36.1.

orbatos parente Germanicus had died in 19 (2.72.2). The sentence of which this is the beginning is strikingly alliterative, another feature of Tiberian speech (3.53.4n.): '*p*arente . . . *p*atruo . . . *p*recatusque . . . *p*ropria *s*uboles . . . *s*ecus . . . *s*uum *s*anguinem . . . *s*ibique et *p*osteris'. It seems likely that, in composing this speech for Tib., T. had at the back of his mind the speech in which Micipsa presses upon Jugurtha the care of the brothers Adherbal and Hiempsal, who will soon be fatherless (Sall. *J.* 10): there is some of the same vocabulary (*tradidi, sanguinem, obtestor, uobis, bona malaque*), a similar use of asyndetic imperatives (*suscipite, regite*), and an identical change of address (to the brothers in question) at the end.

propria suboles Principally the twins Germanicus and Tiberius Gemellus (above and 3.1n.). For the choice noun see Oakley on Liv. 6.7.1.

foueret, attolleret, sibique et posteris confirmaret Since these three exhortations seem parallel to the three imperatives below (5 'suscipite . . . explete'), and since the imperatives are asyndetic, it seems very likely that these subjunctives are also in asyndeton and hence that *–que et* = 'both . . . and', a construction in which, as here, *–que* is usually attached to a personal pronoun (see 1.4.1n., *Agr.* 18.4n.).

confirmaret, apparently the original reading of M, has been changed in the MS to *conformaret*. Although the latter verb is not used elsewhere by T., the meaning is appropriate ('train', 'educate') and an exceptional use could be defended by the context of a Tiberian speech (cf. Syme, *Tac.* 710). But 1.71.3

('cunctos *adloquio* et cura *sibique et* proelio *firmabat*'; cf. *H.* 5.4.1 'quo *sibi* in *posterum* gentem *firmabat*') strongly suggests that T. wrote *confirmaret* in our passage; for the repetition *firmatos* ~ *confirmaret* see Sörbom 42. The meaning is 'that he should strengthen them both for his own sake and for that of posterity'. *attolleret*, greatly favoured by T. in its metaphorical usages, refers to moral improvement (*OLD* 11a); for the combination with *foueret* cf. Plin. *Pan.* 44.6.

8.5 preces ad uos conuerto Cf. [Quint.] *Decl.* 6.23 'ad te, uxor, preces conuertam'.

Augusti pronepotes Their mother, Agrippina, was the daughter of Agrippa and Julia, Augustus' daughter.

clarissimis maioribus Perhaps another Ciceronianism (cf. *Rep.* 1.71), since the expr. is surprisingly not found elsewhere. T.'s use of superlatives is relatively sparing and mostly confined to speeches (Adams (1973) 134 and n. 89).

suscipite, regite, uestram meamque uicem explete *suscipere* is technical of a father acknowledging his own new-born child or of persons adopting another's child into their own family (*OLD* 4a); *uicem* here = 'the place or part filled (in rotation, succession, etc., by a person)': hence virtually 'role' or 'function' (*OLD* 4a): for *explete* cf. Curt. 8.6.18, Sen. *HO* 948.

bona malaque uestra 'your good and bad fortune' (see *OLD bonum* 3).

9.1 fletu et . . . precationibus seems to be a Tacitean variant on *fletu precibusque* and the like (Caes. *BC* 2.4.3, Virg. *Aen.* 3.599, Apul. *Met.* 10.6.2). *faustis* = 'bringing good fortune' (5.4.2n.).

gloriaque animos . . . impleuerat *gloria* = 'a feeling of pride' (*OLD* 4a). *animos (-um) implere* (again at 1.31.4, *H.* 4.39.4) is common elsewhere.

ad *u*ana et totiens inrisa re*u*olutus, de reddenda re publica utque consules seu quis alius regimen susciperent, *u*ero quoque et honesto fidem dempsit This sentence is generally passed over by commentators, yet it is both difficult and important.

When Augustus died, Tib. at the so-called 'accession debate' first proposed that he himself should not succeed at all but that the 'munia rei publicae' should be administered by a consortium of distinguished men (1.11.1: see *Tac. Rev.* 46ff., esp. 50–1). This proposal was so strongly rejected by the senators that in mid-debate Tib. came up with an alternative plan, namely, that he should be given only part of the empire (1.12.1). This led to a series of statements and questions from protesting senators, some of which were – or were interpreted by Tib. as being – offensive (1.12.2–13.4).

Eventually the debate fizzled out (1.13.5), and, although in T.'s account Tib. never in fact agreed formally to be *princeps*, he reconciled himself to the unwelcome *fait accompli* by adopting various helpers or associates, of whom the two most prominent were his sons, Germanicus and Drusus (cf. Strabo 6.4.2). But, now that death had unexpectedly deprived him of the two young men on whom he had principally relied,[25] it was hardly surprising that his thoughts should turn again to resigning: indeed, in Suetonius' version of the succession, Tib.'s acceptance of the principate was conditional upon his laying down his office at some point in the future (*Tib.* 24.2 'recepit imperium, nec tamen aliter quam ut depositurum se quandoque spem faceret. ipsius uerba sunt: "Dum ueniam ad id tempus quo uobis aequum possit uideri dare uos aliquam senectuti meae requiem"'). That point had now come, and in the latter part of his present speech Tib. reverted (*reuolutus*) to the themes of the accession debate:[26] he spoke 'about giving up the state' (*de reddenda re publica*) and said that either the consuls or others should take up the reins in his stead (*utque . . . susciperent*).[27] These two interdependent notions are described by T. as unrealistic (*uana*) because there was no prospect of their ever being fulfilled: Tib. was a prisoner of circumstance and, if he could not escape the responsibility of rule on Augustus' death in AD 14, he was even less likely to do so nearly a decade later.[28] *totiens inrisa* refers to the disrespectful way in which Tib.'s proposals had been rejected by successive senators in the accession debate.

---

[25] Tib.'s only remaining family helper was Livia (4.57.3), who was now a great age. Sejanus was still new to the role (4.2.3 and nn.) and had all the problems of not being an aristocrat (see e.g. 6.27.1n.).

[26] *reuolutus* is *OLD reuoluo* 4b 'to fall back on a plan or idea'.

[27] (a) The exact meaning of the (uncommon) expression *reddere rem publicam* will depend upon the context in which it is used. A friend of Cicero in 43 BC credits the orator with 'returning the state' to the people (ap. Cic. *Fam.* 12.13.1 'nobis . . . rem publicam . . . reddidit'). When Suetonius says that Augustus 'de reddenda re publica bis cogitauit' (*Aug.* 28.1), he means the same thing; but, since Augustus had been responsible for constitutional change, the expression in this case is equivalent to 'restoring the Republic'. Our passage is *OLD reddo* 11b 'to give up, resign'. (b) The elliptical *seu quis alius* (sc. e.g. *deligeretur* or *uellet possetque*) presumably constitutes an oblique reference to individuals such as the 'tot inlustres uiri' whom Tib. mentioned at 1.11.1 and envisaged as working in a group ('sociatis laboribus').

[28] When he withdrew to Capri a few years later, he did not stop being *princeps*; he was simply avoiding responsibilities of which he could not be disburdened officially.

The impracticality and unpopularity of the latter part of Tib.'s speech caused the listening senators to have second thoughts about the reality (*uero*) and honourableness (*honesto*) of the earlier part: *fidem demere* means 'to deny the credibility of' or 'to deny credence to' (*G.* 3.3, *H.* 2.50.2, Ov. *Am.* 2.2.38, *RA* 290, Suet. *Gramm.* 25.8), while *uerus* ('real' or 'actual') is a regular opposite of *uanus* (e.g. Sen. *Ep.* 13.7, *Oed.* 700–1), esp. in Livy (e.g. 6.14.11, 7.14.10, 31.49.11, 34.12.4, 35.40.8, 37.42.1). In drawing this conclusion, T. was no doubt writing with the benefit of hindsight, since, thanks to the secret machinations of Sejanus (cf. 12.2 below), Tib. will soon appear to undermine the teenagers whom he has just urged the senators to adopt (cf. 59.3–60.3).

uanus and *inrisus* are coupled elsewhere only at *H.* 2.22.3. There seems to be no precise parallel elsewhere in T. for the *uariatio* of prep. + gerundive ~ indir. command: Sörbom (114–15) quotes only 3.63.4, where the clause is purposive. *regimen* commonly refers to 'direction of government' (3.47.2n.), but surprisingly there is no parallel for its combination with *suscipere*. The combination of *uerus* and *honestus* is esp. common in Cicero but is found elsewhere too, e.g. Sall. *H.* 3.48.13, Sen. *Contr.* 9 *praef.* 1, Quint. 5.11.37, 12.1.11; for the juxtaposition of identical syllables (*–dem dem–*) see 13.2n. (*ob*).

9.2 eadem quae in Germanicum decernuntur Cf. 2.83 and nn.

ut ferme amat posterior adulatio Cf. 6.42.3 'quos recens aetas largius inuenit'; Vielberg 99–100. For *ferme* see 3.16.2n.

imaginum pompa See H. Flower, *Ancestor masks and aristocratic power in Roman culture* (1996) 243, 253–4.

Iuliae gentis Tib. had been adopted by Augustus, who was himself the grandson of Caesar's sister, Julia, and had been adopted posthumously by Caesar in his will. According to Suetonius, when Caesar in 67 BC delivered the funeral oration for his aunt Julia, he said 'a Venere Iulii, cuius gentis familia est nostra' (*DJ* 6.1).

Sabina nobilitas, Attus Clausus For the family background see Suet. *Tib.* 1.1 'Patricia gens Claudia . . . orta est ex Regillis oppido Sabinorum. Inde Romam recens conditam cum magna clientium manu conmigrauit auctore Tito Tatio consorte Romuli uel (quod magis constat) Atta Claudio gentis principe, post reges exactos sexto fere anno'.

longo ordine is a very common phrase in epic (e.g. 7× in the *Aeneid*) and very occasionally too in prose, but the context of Drusus' *pompa* makes it tempting (see *Tac. Rev.* 233) to think that T. has in mind *Aen.* 6.754, where Aeneas observes the passage of Alban kings and others which itself is described in terms of a funeral procession (see Horsfall on 756–846 (§7 (b) (iii), p. 517), with further refs.).

10–11 Excursus on the death of Drusus: rumour and refutation

T. is renowned for his use of the 'loaded alternative': usually the alternative is restricted to an insidious phrase or sentence (e.g. 3.64.1 'siue occultis odiis'), but in the case of Drusus' death the alternative is a rumour which takes up a whole paragraph (10) and is then refuted point by point at even greater length (11). Not only is the scale unparalleled elsewhere in the *Annals* but 'the unequivocal rejection of the rumour . . . is unique in Tacitus' handling of rumours' (Hardie 289–90, referring to Shatzman 558).

Rumours were one of the standard items of evidence in a Roman lawcourt (e.g. *Rhet. Herenn.* 2.9, Quint. 5.1.2): they could be attacked as false or supported as true, but, no matter how successful the attack, there might always be the lingering suspicion that a rumour 'is not generally created recklessly and without some foundation' and that there is 'no reason for anybody wholly to invent and fabricate one' (*Rhet. Herenn.* 2.12). The anonymous author of the *Rhetorica* later referred to *rumor populi*, 'quem ex argumentis natum necesse est uerum' (4.53), and this positive attitude was that which was generally adopted by historians. Hence the frequency with which Livy introduces material by the expression *fama est* and the like: a good example is the story of poisoning at 8.18.1–11, which he would prefer to disbelieve (2) but nevertheless relates (3 'sicut proditur tamen res . . . exponenda est'). T. had adopted exactly the same procedure in the case of Calpurnius Piso (3.16.1 'neque tamen occulere debui narratum ab iis qui nostram ad iuuentam durauerunt': see ad loc.).

The method of killing Drusus was poison (8.1), one of the favourite topics of the declaimers (M. Winterbottom, *The Elder Seneca* (Loeb edn, 1974) 2.640 s.v. 'poison'). Declaimers also liked to put a different complexion or *color* on a given situation (S. F. Bonner, *Roman declamation* (1949) 55–6), exactly as T. does here (10.2–3), and, since his alternative version of events involves attempted parricide on Drusus' part and actual filicide on Tib.'s part, it should be remembered that the murder of close relatives was also a favourite topic of the declamatory schools (see again Winterbottom, ibid. 2.640 s.v. 'parricide'). Indeed the substitution of the one crime for the other is just the kind of bizarre twist on which declaimers thrived: there are close parallels in the declamatory literature, when a son who has been preparing poison receives orders to drink it himself from the father, who thinks his son was intending to kill him (Sen. *Contr.* 7.3 (cf. 3 'aut patri pereundum est aut filio'), [Quint.] *Decl. Mai.* 17, *Decl. Min.* 377), a motif which has also left its mark on Suet. *Vit.* 6, where a similar story is told of Vitellius and his son ('hunc . . . interemit, insimulatum insuper parricidii et quasi paratum ad scelus uenenum ex conscientia hausisset').

T. refutes the rumour on four grounds: (a) it is not properly attested (11.1, 11.2), (b) the action imputed to Tib. would be uncharacteristic of him (11.1),

(c) the atmosphere of the times gave credence to the fantastic (11.2), (d) the true sequence of events was revealed later by witnesses (11.2). Of these four, (b) is treated at the greatest length and in a manner appropriate to a lawcourt or declamation (rhetorical questions and legal language). In (c) it is explained why, despite the arguments of (b), the rumour was nevertheless believed. Although the contents of the rumour are here described only fleetingly as 'fabulosa et immania' (11.2), this description is picked up and elaborated in T.'s conclusion (11.3), where he explains why he has gone to such lengths to transmit and then refute this particular rumour: it is paradigmatic ('claro sub exemplo') for material which is foreign to the genre of historical writing ('incredibilia . . . in miraculum corruptis'). The whole excursus thus serves to enhance T.'s authority and credibility.

10.1 quae plurimis maximaeque fidei auctoribus memorata sunt rettuli T. makes a similar statement later in Book 4 (57.1 'secutus plurimos auctorum'), and elsewhere he says that, although any alternative versions of events will be attributed to historians by name, his general policy is to follow the authorial consensus (13.20.2 'nos consensum auctorum secuturi, quae diuersa prodiderint sub nominibus ipsorum trademus'): according to Josephus, universal agreement is the sign of true history (*Ap.* 26 τῆς μὲν γὰρ ἀληθοῦς ἐστι τεκμήριον ἱστορίας, εἰ περὶ τῶν αὐτῶν ἅπαντες ταὐτὰ καὶ λέγοιεν καὶ γράφοιεν). For other references to '(very) many authors' cf. also *H.* 5.3.1 and *Agr.* 10.1 (n.); for other historians' references to 'the majority' and 'most credible' of sources see Marincola 282–3 (App. IV §§2–3). For the *uariatio* of *tradenda* ~ *memorata sunt* ~ *rettuli* see Sörbom 35; that of adj. ~ descriptive gen. is common in other authors as well as T. (J. L. Catterall, *TAPA* 69 (1938) 304 (cf. 306–7), Oakley on Liv. 7.5.2). For *memorare* see 3.24.3n.

non omiserim eorundem temporum rumorem, ualidum adeo ut nondum exolescat T. justifies his excursus into rumour on two grounds: its contemporaneity, which is a virtue in historiography (e.g. 2.88.1, 5.9.2 (n.), 12.67.1, 13.17.2, Plb. 3.9.1–5, Liv. 6.12.2, 22.7.4, 29.14.9; Marincola 281–2, App. IV §1) and corresponds to the majority support of the preferred version (*eorundem temporum* ~ *plurimis . . . auctoribus*), and its persistence, which corresponds to the other's credibility (*ualidum* ~ *maximae . . . fidei auctoribus*); to these will later be added its dissemination (11.1 'uulgo iactata'). For *non omiserim* in a comparable context see 6.20.2 (n.). For T.'s use of rumour see esp. Shatzman and B. J. Gibson, 'Rumours as causes of events in Tacitus', *MD* 40 (1998) 111–29, with further refs.

10.2 corrupta ad scelus Liuia Readers are hereby reminded of what was said at 3.3–4 above.

Lygdi . . . animum stupro uinxisse *stuprum* is illicit sex (6.1.1n.): although Lygdus seems to have been a slave (cf. *domino* below) and therefore strictly lacking any rights at all, the illicitness presumably resides in the fact that he had the affection of Drusus and was one of his chief attendants, as T. proceeds to describe. The suggestion is of active homosexuality, which Sejanus is thus rumoured to have added to passive (1.2n.), as well as having committed adultery with Livi(ll)a (3.3n.). This comprehensive sexual censure resembles that which Suillius levelled against Valerius Asiaticus (11.2.1 'Suillio corruptionem militum, quos pecunia et stupro in omne flagitium obstrictos arguebat, exin adulterium Poppaeae, postremum mollitiam corporis obiectante': see Malloch ad loc.) and which was characteristic of political invective in general (see J. Pigón, 'Sejanus and the death of Drusus: one rumour or two?', *Antiquitas* 25 (2001) 147–52, at 150–1, and note also Champlin (2012) 379–81, who refers to P. Guyot, *Eunuchen als Sklaven und Freigelassene in der griechisch-römischen Antike* (1980)).

Pigón also goes further and, following Hennig (36), says that the allegation about Lygdus 'stands in a loose relation only to what follows . . . It should have belonged, rather, with Tacitus' first (and approved of) version of the poisoning: after all, it explains how it occurred that Lygdus decided to act against his master' (148). Pigón argues that, since in 11.1–3 T. refutes only the rumour about Tib. and says nothing further about Lygdus, his dual purpose was to lend credibility to the story of Lygdus' seduction and hence to enhance the denigration of Sejanus by means of additional sexual slurs. This seems to me to be a misreading. T. wishes to highlight as much as possible the elaborate preparations for the original plot so that he can emphasise by contrast Sejanus' great daring in allegedly changing plans entirely and involving the *princeps* in so risky and brazen a bluff ('eo audaciae prouectum ut uerteret'). The two principal participants in the original plot were Livi(ll)a and Lygdus; but, whereas we have been told in some detail at 3.3–4 about Livi(ll)a's seduction by Sejanus (last n.), we were told nothing about Lygdus' (8.1): that is the omission which T. makes good here.

Elsewhere T. uses the expression *animum deuincire* (12.64.3), a combination which in its various nuances is more common in prose (Cic. *Brut.* 276, Caes. *BC* 1.39.4, Val. Max. 5.8.2, Sen. *Ep.* 83.16) than verse (Ter. *Heaut.* 208); the only other exs. of *a. uincire* are Acc. *Trag.* fr. 45 R = 314D and Lucr. 3.416 (the text is uncertain at Phaedr. *App.* 13(15).24), but cf. also Cic. *TD* 2.48 'pars animi . . . uinciatur . . . amicorum propinquorumque custodiis'.

quod is [Lygdus] . . . erat Since T. often retains the indic. in subordinate clauses in indirect speech (1.10.2n.), we cannot be certain of the status of this clause; but it seems most likely to be authorial comment. *Lygdus* is implausible after *Lygdi* immediately above and was deleted by Ernesti as a gloss.

aetate atque forma The point of the two nouns, which are often combined, is that a 'youthful appearance' (hendiadys) is a key characteristic of eunuchism (cf. Ter. *Eun.* 375 'forma et aetas ipsast facile ut pro eunucho probes'; in general K. M. Ringrose, *The Perfect Servant: Eunuchs and the Social Construction of Gender in Byzantium* (2007) 78).

inter conscios Primarily Livi(ll)a and Lygdus, their participation in the original plot being the point of their mention in the previous sentence.

eo audaciae prouectum ut uerteret Either *uerteret* is intransitive, as the verb frequently is in various of its meanings (see *OLD*), or we must understand an object (e.g. *rem* or *consilium*). *audaciae* looks back to *audax* in the introductory sketch of Sejanus at 1.3 (n.).

occulto indicio Drusum ueneni in patrem arguens moneret Tiberium uitandam potionem quae prima ei apud filium epulanti offerretur Although other interpretations are possible, it seems likely that *occulto . . . arguens* is explained by *moneret . . . offerretur*: that is, the warning that Tib. should avoid the first drink at his son's banquet was itself the 'oblique information' that Drusus was intending to poison him: for this sense of *occultus* (as 2.30.2) cf. *TLL* 9.2.367.67–84, *OLD* 4b. *ueneni* (*OLD* 2b) = *ueneficii*, and *in* + acc. is used for the intended victim (as 2.88.1 'uenenum in Pyrrhum regem').

10.3 ea fraude captum senem It is impossible to know exactly what T. wrote here. Most modern editors print *captum* for the transmitted *cum*: the phrase *fraude captus* is common in Livy and the younger Seneca, both being authors whom T. imitates, and T. generally (although not invariably) prefers simple verbs to compound. On the other hand, *de–* could easily have been omitted after 'frau*de*', and Heinsius suggested *fraude deceptum*, a combination which occurs in a range of Augustan and post-Augustan authors, both prose and verse (the earliest ex. is Virg. *Aen.* 5.851). Heinsius' alternative, *inlectum*, is printed as their own suggestion by Nipperdey–Andresen, who quote the same expr. at *H.* 4.57.1; that would avoid the repetition *deceptum . . . exceptum* (below), but the phrase is otherwise unexampled. I have opted for *captum* largely because it seems the simplest change. The description of Tib. as *senem* here suggests the stock figure of the gullible old man, familiar from Roman comedy (cf. esp. Cic. *Amic.* 99–100, *Senec.* 36).

tamquam metu et pudore . . . struxerat As often, it is unclear whether *tamquam* = 'that', giving the substance of the suspicion, or 'as if', giving T.'s own explanation of what the suspicion was. *metus* and *pudor* are a frequent combination, esp. in T. (see 6.51.3n. and n. 140); *struo* is often used of evil designs and the like (*OLD* 6a) and is favoured by T. for Tib. and informers (Walker 159).

11.1 Haec uulgo iactata ... prompte refutaueris According to Quintilian (3.9.1), the *refutatio* was one of the five traditional parts of a forensic speech, although, apart from Cic. *Top.* 93, he is the only extant classical author to use the term (which he does frequently): *refutaueris* is therefore self-reflexive (for this device see above, 7.1n.). The second-person potential subjunctive 'invites the reader's active thought' (K. Gilmartin, 'A rhetorical figure in Latin historical style: the imaginary second person singular', *TAPA* 105 (1975) 119), as at *Agr.* 3.1 (see nn.), not only preparing for the following series of rhetorical questions but anticipating the reader's agreement with the author's arguments: for this notion of an 'insight shared' see C. Pelling, 'Tacitus' personal voice', in *CCT* 155–8. *uulgo iactata* (for the expr. cf. Cic. *Fam.* 8.1.4, Liv. 9.45.8, Quint. 6.3.47, Suet. *Otho* 12.2) will be picked up in the conclusion by *diuulgata* (3) and is concessive, adding a further aspect in favour of the rumour: widespread dissemination was a reason for including a rumour in one's narrative (*H.* 2.50.2 'uulgatis traditisque demere fidem non ausim'); for the antithesis with *refutaueris* cf. Cic. *Mil.* 7 'ea mihi esse refutanda quae . . . iactata sunt'.

super id quod nullo auctore certo firmantur Since we are told below (2) that no *writer* accused Tib. of poisoning his son, the present clause is capable of more than one meaning: *either* the story was an exclusively oral transmission but did not rest on a reliable source (such as the *seniores* who passed on the rumour about Piso and Tib. at 3.16.1: see n. ad loc.) *or* the story was indeed found in one or more written sources but, as with T. himself, none of them endorsed it. Since these meanings are not mutually exclusive, it is perhaps best to render *auctore* as 'authority' (the plain abl. denotes a lack of intention: see *NLS* §44). Either way, the phrase contrasts with *plurimis maximaeque fidei auctoribus* at 10.1 above.

super = 'besides' is regular (*OLD* 7) and greatly liked by T. (again at e.g. 44.1, 46.1, 60.3, 75; G–G 1595a–96a), but this alternative for the common *praeterquam quod* (which T. does not use) seems unique.

Quis ... inaudito filio exitium offerret ... ? 'Who ... would have offered ... ?' (the question is used at *NLS* §121 to illustrate the use of the imperf. potential subjunctive). Walther sees irony in the verb, on the grounds that it is the *mot juste* for offering someone a drink (e.g. 10.2 above, Curt. 7.5.12); but the evidence suggests that it is more commonly used of unpleasant things such as death (*TLL* 9.2.500.43–9 ~ 500.77–501.5). *inauditus* is used esp. of accused persons (*OLD* 1; *TLL* 7.1.837.22–41).

mediocri prudentia Ciceronian (*De Or.* 2.120, *Div.* 2.130, *ND* 1.61, *Fam.* 5.20.4).

nedum Tiberius tantis rebus exercitus The points which follow are based on the *persona* of the accused, as would be the case in a court of law (it is the converse of Quint. 7.2.31 'incredibile esse a filio patrem occisum'). The *princeps'* vast experience is stressed at both the beginning and end of the Tiberian *Annals* (1.4.3, 6.48.2).

nullo ad paenitendum regressu No doubt the idea is conventional (e.g. Liv. 24.26.15, 42.13.3), but there is a similar notion in the very declamation with which the present poisoning has so much in common: see [Quint.] *Decl.* 17.12 'non habent proximorum odia regressum'.

Quin potius ministrum ueneni excruciaret . . . ? 'Would he not rather have . . . ?'; the only other ex. of *quin* so used in the *Annals* is at 1.28.5, in a speech. The reference to a wine-waiter, when combined with *sua manu* above, helps to shade in the detail of the alleged context: the *princeps'* first drink was offered to him by a servant but then he handed it personally to his son. The point of torturing the servant would be to discover who had ordered him to offer the drink to Tib. ('auctorem exquireret').

insita denique etiam in extraneos cunctatione et mora Tib. is regularly described as hesitant (e.g. 42.1 'cunctantem', 57.1, 71.3 'cunctationes'; also above, 4.2n.), but T. can also portray him as forthright (1.7.5 'nusquam cunctabundus') and feigning hesitation (1.46.1 'cunctatione ficta'). For *cunctatione et mora* cf. 6.48.1n.; *insita . . . cunctatione* is Livian (28.40.7).

unicum is elliptical for *unicum filium*, 'proverbial as an expression of deepest sorrow' (Shackleton Bailey on Cic. *Fam.* 9.20(193).3). The ellipse is common (e.g. [Quint.] *Decl.* 17.6), including on inscriptions (see E. Löfstedt, *Syntactica* (1933) 2.241–2).

nullius ante flagitii compertum The gen. after *compertus* is regular (e.g. 1.3.4 'nullius tamen flagitii compertum', Liv. 7.4.4 'filium iuuenem nullius probri compertum'; *TLL* 3.2055.16–20). It is not clear whether *ante* qualifies *compertum* or is being used adjectivally with *flagitii*; there is a similar issue at Virg. *Aen.* 1.198 'neque enim ignari sumus ante malorum' (see Austin's n.).

11.2 facinorum omnium repertor Edd. compare Virg. *Aen.* 2.164 'scelerumque inuentor Vlixes'; cf. also Cic. *Vat.* 22 'facinorum . . . inuentor nouorum'.

quamuis fabulosa et immania credebantur The point is that the fabled was by definition incredible: hence the elder Pliny's argument *ad absurdum* that, if we are persuaded by their frequency to think that stories about werewolves are true, we shall be forced to believe all such tall tales (*NH* 8.80 'debemus . . . credere omnia quae fabulosa tot saeculis comperimus'). *immanis* suggests monstrousness and abnormality, and, while appropriate to an action as unnatural as filicide, is also a regular component of myths and legends (e.g. Liv. 26.19.7 'famam in Alexandro Magno prius uolgatam, et uanitate et fabula parem, anguis immanis concubitu conceptum', 29.17.12 'pestis ac belua immanis, quales fretum quondam quo ab Sicilia diuidimur ad perniciem nauigantium circumsedisse fabulae ferunt'). T.'s language is chosen as preparation for the generic conclusion which he will draw at 3 below (n.).

atrociore semper fama erga dominantium exitus 'rumour always being more shocking in the case of the deaths of one's masters'. As in so many other respects, the pattern had been established by Augustus, who was rumoured to have been murdered (1.5.1: see Shatzman 560–3); but T. is above all thinking of Drusus' brother, Germanicus, the narrative of whose recent death is shot through with rumours of various types (e.g. 2.69.3, 73.4, 77.2–3, 82.1–5, 3.10.2, esp. 19.2 'Germanici morte non modo apud illos homines qui tum agebant, etiam secutis temporibus uario rumore iactata'), including a story of dinner-time poisoning very similar to that alleged here (3.14.1–2). T. himself lived at a time when *exitus illustrium uirorum* constituted a sub-genre of historical literature (cf. Plin. *Ep.* 3.10.1, 5.5.3, 8.12.4, with Sherwin-White's nn.).

atrociore . . . fama seems first to be found at Sall. *H.* 1.107 M = 1.97 R (if the generally accepted supplement is correct), then Liv. 8.20.2. *erga* = 'in the case of' seems to originate in T. (*OLD* 3; see also G–G 357b and 2.2.3n.); its more usual meaning of 'towards' (*OLD* 2) seems more difficult here, though cf. 15.58.3 'atrox aduersus socios'. For subst. *dominans* see 3.54.3n.

Ordo alioqui sceleris per Apicatam Seiani proditus The revelation came eight years later, after the death of Sejanus (8.1n.). Since Apicata and Sejanus were certainly divorced by AD 25 (cf. 39.1–4), the ellipse of *uxorem* here may mean that she is being seen from the viewpoint of 23 rather than that of 31;[29] on the other hand, Dio under 31 has the expressions ἡ γυνὴ Ἀπικᾶτα and τῆς Λιουίλλης τῆς γυναικὸς αὐτοῦ almost side by side in the same sentence (58.11.6); see also 5.6.2n., 6.2.1n. *ordo* = 'the steps or stages (in an action or process)', as 69.3 'fraudis', 2.27.1 'negotii', Curt. 6.11.32 'cogitati sceleris' (see *OLD* 9a).

tormentis Eudemi The torture of the doctor, probably a freedman (3.4n.), exceeds the normal practice of the late republic, when only slaves were tortured (J. A. Crook, *Law and life of Rome* (1967) 274–5).

neque quisquam scriptor tam infensus extitit ut Tiberio obiectaret With *obiectaret* we have to understand e.g. *hoc* (which it is tempting

---

[29] If the viewpoint is that of 23, a further question is whether the ellipse means that Apicata and Sejanus were not yet divorced or is justified by the fact that the divorce was only recent (see above, 3.5n.).

to insert after *Tiberio*) or *haec* or *scelus*.[30] Although T.'s statement recalls his complaint in the preface that imperial affairs were narrated with hatred after the emperors in question had died (1.1.2), in fact no ancient author accuses Tib. of his son's murder apart from Orosius (7.4.9); Dio mentions the story but dismisses it as incredible (57.22.2–4). For *scriptor . . . extitit* cf. Quint. 8 *praef.* 3; for *infensus* see 3.15.2n.

cum omnia alia conquirerent intenderentque Although both verbs are used commonly of speech or writing etc. (see *OLD conquiro* 1c, 2b; *intendo* 7b), their combination perhaps suggests an image of stockpiling and aiming weapons (*OLD conquiro* 1a, *intendo* 7a). For sentence-final *–que* see 3.34.5n.

11.3 Mihi tradendi arguendique rumoris causa fuit The imminent closure of the excursus is indicated by the fronted pronoun (cf. 3.18.4) and verbal pick-up of 10.1 (~ *tradenda . . . rumorem*). *arguo* here = 'prove wrong' (*OLD* 5, cf. *TLL* 2.554.52–72); the language is again legal (cf. *Rhet. Herenn.* 2.12 'si rumor uehementer probabilis esse uidebitur, argumentando famae fidem poterimus abrogare'). *fuit* generates a sequence of imperfects ('depellerem peteremque') which show that the verb is analogous to an 'epistolary' tense, presenting matters from the point of view of T.'s readers, who are about to be mentioned explicitly ('quorum in manus'); but the sequence then changes to primary at the end ('uenerit . . . antehabeant'): see also next n. but one.

ut claro sub exemplo falsas auditiones depellerem The singularity of the example hints at the topos of the historian's selectivity (32.1n.); that *claro* means 'resounding' (*OLD* 1) is perhaps suggested by the choice of *auditiones* for 'hearsay, rumours' (*OLD* 2). For the word order see 5.1.3n.; for the use of *sub* see 3.68.1n. *depello* = 'to rebut' (*OLD* 7b).

quorum in manus cura nostra uenerit *cura nostra* is metonymical for the *Annales* (3.24.3n.): since the noun carries with it the inevitable suggestion that the author has taken pains, a topos of historiography (Marincola 148–57), it is esp. appropriate to a methodological excursus (again at 32.2 'labor'); *nostra* is an authorial plural (see e.g. Vell. 119.1n.) and hence *uariatio* after *mihi* above (as 32.1 'rettuli . . . annales nostros', 71.1 'mihi . . . trademus'; *Agr.* 43.2n. and reference there to Sörbom 74). *in manus* is a timely reminder that T. expected his work to be handled and hence read by individual readers (cf. Gell. *praef.* 2 'ut librum quemque in manus ceperam seu Graecum seu Latinum', Fronto, *Ep. Ant.* 4.1.1 (p. 105.7 vdH[2]) 'requies una librum in manus sumere'), rather

---

[30] This seems far more likely than to assume an absolute use, unique in classical Latin (so *TLL* 9.2.62.58–9).

than declaimed to the masses;[31] see further below, 33.3 'legentium animos'. It is impossible to tell whether *uenerit* is perf. subjunc. (influenced by the mood of the surrounding verbs) or fut. perf.: the former sees the action from the point of view of T.'s readers (now regarded as 'present' by means of *repraesentatio*), the latter from that of T. himself.

\<ne\> diuulgata atque incredibilia auide accepta ueris neque in miraculum corruptis antehabeant 'they should not prefer the eager reception of widely disseminated incredibilities to realism uncontaminated by the miraculous'. The concluding moral is presented as a contrast between two types of subject matter, and the type to be rejected is conveyed in language which picks up that used earlier in the excursus to criticise the rumour about Drusus' death: *diuulgata ~ uulgo iactata* (1), *incredibilia auide accepta ~ quamuis fabulosa et immania credebantur* (2). Statements defending one's own text against rival narratives are not of course restricted to historiography: thus Pindar promotes his account of Pelops 'through polemics against competing versions' (Z. Stamatopoulou, *Hesiod and classical Greek poetry* (2017) 22–3, quoting *Ol.* 1. 28–9 ἦ θαύματα πολλά, καί πού τι καὶ βροτῶν | φάτις ὑπὲρ τὸν ἀλαθῆ λόγον | δεδαιδαλμένοι ψεύδεσι ποικίλοις | ἐξαπατῶντι μῦθοι). But they are esp. at home in historiography, which often capitalises on the ancient threefold division of narrative into *fabula, argumentum* and *historia. Fabula* is that 'quae neque ueras neque ueri similes continet res', whereas *historia* 'est gesta res' (*Rhet. Herenn.* 1.13; cf. Cic. *Inv.* 1.27, Quint. 2.4.2): the former deals in myth, the latter in 'what really happened', and the contrast between the two is found in historical texts from Hecataeus (F1) onwards: see e.g. Thuc. 1.21.1 τὰ πολλά . . . ἀπίστως ἐπὶ τὸ μυθῶδες ἐκνενικηκότα ~ 22.4 ἐς μὲν ἀκρόασιν ἴσως τὸ μὴ μυθῶδες αὐτῶν ἀτερπέστερον φανεῖται, Liv. *praef.* 6 'quae . . . poeticis magis decora fabulis quam incorruptis rerum gestarum monumentis traduntur', Dion. Hal. *AR* 1.39.1, 40.6–41.1, Plut. *Thes.* 1.1–3; *PH* 7, J. Marincola, 'ἀλήθεια', *Lexicon historiographicum Graecum et Latinum* 2.23–4. Likewise T. in the

---

[31] There is much scholarly discussion of the ancient assimilation of literature. Some stress the individual handling and reading to which Horace famously referred (*Ep.* 1.20.11–12: see e.g. W. A. Johnson and H. N. Parker (edd.), *Ancient literacies* (2009) 164–8 and 190, D. Feeney in I. Du Quesnay and A. J. Woodman (edd.), *Catullus: poems, books, readers* (2012) 34–44); such reading will have been conducted in silence (A. K. Gavrilov, 'Techniques of reading in classical antiquity', *CQ* 47 (1997) 56–73, with a postscript by M. F. Burnyeat, pp. 74–6). Others stress aural and collective reception (T. P. Wiseman, *The Roman audience* (2015)). For more on historiography see J. Marincola in A. Feldherr (ed.), *The Cambridge Companion to the Roman Historians* (2009) 11–23.

Histories said that 'conquirere fabulosa et fictis oblectare legentium animos procul grauitate coepti operis crediderim' (2.50.2), although on that occasion he nevertheless repeated the story (above, 1n.); and later in the *Annals* he says that, although the story of Messalina's marriage to C. Silius will seem fantastic (11.27 'fabulosum uisum iri'), it was in fact true: 'sed nihil compositum miraculi causa, uerum audita scriptaque senioribus tradam' (see Malloch ad locc.). These are the contrasts with which T. is operating in our passage: having earlier characterised the rumoured events as *fabulosa* and disproved them to his own satisfaction, he here advocates prioritising the qualities which denote the narrative of a true historian such as himself. Indeed the very words *neque in miraculum corruptis* seem to combine allusions to two of his most illustrious predecessors, Thucydides (ἐπὶ τὸ μυθῶδες) and Livy ('incorruptis').

auidus (*–e*) is used of aural reception as early as Enn. *Scaen.* 63 J, but, since the only parallels for *auide accipere* are in the elder Pliny (*NH* 15.73, 18.196, though the contexts are quite different), perhaps this is another of T.'s echoes of that author (see *Tac. Rev.* 233). *antehabere* occurs in Latin only here and at 1.58.3 (n.).

12.1 Ceterum laudante filium pro rostris Tiberio *ceterum* returns us to the main narrative, as often (G–G 167a), *laudante . . . Tiberio* picking up *funus* at 9.2. Cf. Sen. *Marc.* 15.3 'Ti. Caesar . . . pro rostris laudauit filium stetitque in conspectu posito corpore, interiecto tantummodo uelamento quod pontificis oculos a funere arceret, et flente populo Romano non flexit uultum; experiendum se dedit Seiano ad latus stanti quam patienter posset suos perdere.' For *pro rostris* see 5.1.4n.

habitum ac uoces dolentum . . . induebat It was customary to wear mourning attire at funerals (3.2.2nn.), but *simulatione* perhaps indicates that *habitus* (which is regularly coupled with *uox*) here means 'attitude' or 'demeanour' (*OLD* 2) rather than 'style of dress' (*OLD* 3). For *induebat* cf. Stat. *Theb.* 2.95–7 'longaeui uatis opacos | Tiresiae uultus uocemque et uellera nota | induitur'; for the *uariatio* of *simulatione* ~ *libens* see 7.1n.

The gen. plur. of present participial forms in T. is usually *–ium* (as *audientium* at 15.3 below); other exceptions are *salutantum* (otherwise exclusively poetical) at 4.41.2 and 11.22.1, although he elsewhere prefers *salutantium*, and *gratantum* (elsewhere only at Sil. 10.627 and 13.798) at 6.50.4, although he has *gratantium* at 14.10.2. For *dolentum* cf. Sen. *Phaedr.* 1109, *Tro.* 1009; Seneca and Silius are two authors by whom T. was perhaps influenced. See also Malloch on 11.22.1.

domumque Germanici reuirescere pointedly recalls *florentis domus* at 1.1 above (cf. Curt. 10.9.5 'non ergo reuirescit solum, sed etiam floret imperium').

quod principium *** fauoris et *mater* . . . *male* tegens There is a seemingly unnoticed problem of logic here. The *fauor* in question can only be towards the *domus Germanici*, just mentioned, but the family of Germanicus has been the object of popular devotion ever since Germanicus' death four years previously (2.72.2). *principium fauoris* therefore makes no sense. The least difficult solution is to assume that something like *aucti* has dropped out by mistake ('the start of the increase in goodwill'), the same construction as 6.1 'mutati . . . principatus initium'.

The use of the pres. part. in the *ab urbe condita* construction recurs at 34.2, 51.2 and 67.2 in this book but is in general much rarer than the perf. (K–S 1.769).

12.2 sine maerore publico For the *uariatio* with *inultam* see 3.21.1n.; for *maeror publicus* see Val. Max. 3.3.2.

ferax scelerum was proposed by Hartman (172) and independently by S. J. Harrison (*CQ* 44 (1994) 557–9) for the transmitted *ferox scelerum*. In favour of the paradosis is the description of Jugurtha as 'sceleribus suis ferox' at Sall. *J.* 14.21; against is the fact that, apart from a very few special cases where the genitive is *animi* or *mentis* (as 1.32.2 (n.)), *ferox* is nowhere else constructed with a genitive with the possible exception of *H.* 1.35.1 'linguae feroces', where the text has been questioned (*lingua* Georges). Harrison, while admitting that T. sometimes has strange genitives elsewhere (e.g. 6.36.4 (n.)), largely rests his case on the anomalous genitive. Yet *ferax* also makes significantly better sense in the context. If *ferox* were correct, it would mean 'exulting in his crimes' and hence, as Hartman noted, would make redundant the following *quia*-clause, which is retrospective; *ferax*, however, not only produces a generalised reference to Sejanus' criminal fertility but, when combined with the *quia*-clause (in which the metaphor is sustained by *prouenerant*), is the perfect preparation for the main sentence, which is prospective ('uolutare secum quonam modo Germanici liberos peruerteret'). For *ferax* + gen. see 72.2n.[32]

et quia *prima prouenerant* 'and because his first crop [sc. of crimes] had burgeoned': for the metaphorical use of the verb see *TLL* 10.2.2310.21–38, and for the understood *scelera* cf. Luc. 2.60–1 'nouorum | prouentu scelerum'. For the *uariatio* with *ferax* see Sörbom 115.

Neque spargi uenenum in tres poterat Germanicus' youngest son, Gaius, is now added to his two elder brothers (3.1n., 4.1n.). *spargi uenenum*, first used of the Catilinarians by Cicero (*Cat.* 2.23), recurs at Ov. *M.* 2.801, 4.520 (cf. 14.403), Sen. *NQ* 6.28.1, [Quint.] *Decl.* 13.7, 13.14.

pudicitia Agrippinae impenetrabili Agrippina's sexual fidelity (*castitas*) is mentioned at 1.33.3; the metaphor is perhaps derived from body-armour

---

[32] *ferox* is defended by Formicola ad loc., referring to his paper in *Sileno* 26 (2000) 97–101.

(cf. 3.43.2, *H.* 1.79.3, Sil. 4.16; cf. Sen. *NQ* 4A.2.14, of crocodile skin). Remarkably '*penetrare* does not occur in a sexual sense in the Classical period' (J. N. Adams, *The Latin sexual vocabulary* (²1987) 151).

12.3 Igitur *contumaciam* eius insectari, uetus Augustae odium, recentem Liuiae *conscientiam* exagitare Pfitzner (*AT* 148) punctuates this sentence as two exclamations, regarding them as commands addressed by Sejanus to himself; but he produces no parallels and, although he retains the punctuation in his edition, the Latinity is surely impossible. The infinitives are historic, although it is difficult to grasp their precise meaning. The two verbs are otherwise combined only at Cic. *Att.* 1.16.8 'insectandis ... exagitandisque nummariis iudicibus', and the second of them seems clearly to stand in some relationship to Sall. *H.* 1.77.7 M = 67.7 R 'scelerum conscientia exagitati' (cf. *C.* 14.3 'quos ... conscius animus exagitabat'). Elsewhere in Cicero *insectari* is combined with the simple form *agitare* to refer to the hunt (*Leg.* 1.40 'eos agitant insectanturque furiae non ardentibus taedis ... sed angore conscientiae', *Div.* 2.144 'ista enim auis insectans alias auis et agitans'), so perhaps this is the image here: Sejanus targeted Agrippina's defiance and preyed upon the Augusta's longstanding hatred of her (cf. 1.33.3) and Livi(ll)a's recent complicity in Drusus' murder (3.3–4). *contumacia*, a favourite concept in T. (see Vielberg 168–77), occurs 4× in Book 4 alone (cf. 20.3, 29.3, 60.1) and is linked with *superbia* (next n.) at least half a dozen times in Cicero.

superbam fecunditate Cf. 2.43.6 'Agrippina fecunditate ... Liuiam, uxorem Drusi, praecellebat'.

subnixam popularibus studiis Cf. 3.4.2 'studia hominum accensa in Agrippinam'. *popularia studia* (again at Cic. *Sest.* 134) is an almost unique variant on the regular *studia populi* (7× in T. alone).

inhiare dominationi At 6.25.2 Agrippina is described as 'dominandi auida' (n.); metaphorical *inhiare*, though not uncommon, more often has money or treasure etc. as its object (*TLL* 7.1.1595.24ff.); see also Malloch on 11.1.1.

12.4 Atque haec callidis criminatoribus Madvig (2.545–6) agreed with those who wished to insert a verb: he proposed *a<li>tque* and was followed by Fuchs with *a<gi>tque*, although e.g. *<sustent>atque* (homoeoteleuton after *arguerent*) or *<ageb>atque* seems equally plausible. But is a supplement needed at all? It does not seem particularly difficult to understand a verb meaning 'he achieved' or 'he brought about' or, if *haec* is thought to be nominative, 'were done'. Some scholars think that *haec* is nominative singular and refers to Livi(ll)a, the second of the two female enemies mentioned in the previous sentence; but this seems unlikely both because of the plural *ut*-clause which precedes and

because of the references to Livia Augusta which follow. For the plain abl.
see 7.3n.

Iulium Postumum Scholars differ on whether this man is identical with
the homonym who was prefect of Egypt in 47 (see *RE* 10.780 = Iulius 403
(Stein), *PIR* 4.253 no. 482; Demougin, *PCR* 364 no. 441; R. E. Bennett,
'The prefects of Egypt: 30 BC–69 AD' (diss. Yale, 1970) 86–9): if the two were
the same, the man must have escaped successful prosecution after Sejanus'
fall.

Mutiliae Priscae At Dio 58.4.5–7, where a married couple commit suicide,
the transmitted names are conventionally emended in a way that makes
Mutilia Prisca the wife of Fufius Geminus, *ordinarius* in 29 (5.1.1n.), whose
own friendship with Livia will later attract Tib.'s criticism (cf. 5.2.2n.). Not
everyone, however, agrees with this identification (Raepsaet-Charlier 531
no. 659). See also *RE* 16.938–9 (Fluss), *PIR* 5.328 no. 763, *BNP* 9.376.

inter intimos auiae Nipperdey found this expression difficult and suggested deleting it: (a) *auiae* can only refer to Augusta, yet she was not
Agrippina's grandmother (Ritter emended to *Liuiae*); (b) *inter intimos* suggests
direct access to Augusta, whereas the following *quia*-clause implies that any
influence with Augusta belonged to Prisca. Neither of these grounds is decisive. (a) Since Augusta was grandmother to Agrippina's husband, and since
Agrippina herself was grandchild of Augusta's husband, there are two good
reasons why Augusta's relationship with Agrippina should be described as
that of grandmother. (b) *per adulterium Mutiliae Priscae* implies that Postumus'
access to Augusta depended upon his relationship with Prisca, and *consiliis suis
peridoneum* is explained by the fact that Prisca was able to influence Augusta:
the arrangement of ideas is chiastic, and, although the implication that
Postumus had access but not influence is perhaps odd, it does not seem
sufficient to justify athetesis. (c) There is a further consideration.
An interpolator is unlikely to have used an expression which is exclusively
Tacitean (*inter intimos* recurs only at 6.18.2, 6.21.3; cf. *H.* 1.71.2); nor, since the
point of interpolating is presumably to clarify, is he likely to have described
Livia by a term which itself requires explanation.

in animo . . . ualida This expr. recurs only at 14.51.3.

potentiae anxiam Cf. 2.75.1n.

prauis *ser*monibus tumidos *s*piritus *per*stimulare The verb, which
occurs nowhere else, perhaps suggests the metaphor of a proud animal (cf.
Sen. *Ira* 2.21.3 'sic . . . regendus est [sc. spiritus] ut modo frenis utamur, modo
stimulis'). The apparent allusion to Sen. *Ag.* 247–8 ('tamen superba . . . |
fortuna . . . spiritus tumidos daret') makes explicit the link back to *superbam*

119

(and to *contumaciam* beyond that). An infin. after *inlicio* seems to be paralleled only at 2.37.1 (see n.).

13–16 Events in the senate

Although it was conventional for the historian to end an annalistic year with a section on more or less miscellaneous events, loosely linked by vague temporal markers (14.1 'is ... annus', 3 'dehinc', 15.1 'idem annus', 16.1 'sub idem tempus'), those here have in common the fact that each of them is domiciled either explicitly or implicitly in the senate (13.1 'senatus consulta', 2 'damnatus', 14.1 'quoque ... legationes', 3 'praetorum questibus ... auctoritate patrum', 15.2 'patres decreuere', 3 'patribus', 16.1 'noua lege'). Tib.'s presence at most of them is headlined at the start (13.1 'negotia pro solaciis accipiens') and mentioned throughout (13.1 'auctore eo', 14.3 'Caesar', 15.2 'principis', 3 'auo', 16.1 'Caesar'). A striking feature of the section is that a significant number of the events echo those of the previous year or earlier: delegations from Greece or Asia (15.2–3), particularly concerning tax-relief (13.1) and asylum (14.1–2), and issues concerning the *flamen Dialis* (16.1–4); on two occasions the connection is made explicit (14.1 'quoque', 15.3 'priore anno'), on another it is implicit by its naming of the same individual (16.1). The general impression is one of continuity: indeed T.'s statement of senatorial activity (15.2 'apud quos [sc. patres] etiam tum cuncta tractabantur') seems designed to pick up his summary of the years 14–22 (6.2 'publica negotia et priuatorum maxima apud patres tractabantur') and to emphasise that, despite the statements of 1.1 and 6.1, nothing had changed after all. But the reference to Sejanus at 15.3 is a reminder that appearances were deceptive and that change was on its way.

13.1 nihil intermissa rerum cura is perhaps Livian terminology (10.29.20 'intermissa inde omnium aliarum rerum cura'), but cf. also Sen. *Ep.* 53.9 'curam intermisisses rei familiaris'. For *cura* see 67.3n., 1.19.2n., Vell. 106.3n.

negotia pro solaciis accipiens 'handling business as a way of consoling himself': see 8.1 and *Agr.* 29.1n.

preces sociorum For appeals such as these see Millar 346, Talbert 417.

ut ciuitati Cibyraticae apud Asiam, Aegiensi apud Achaiam ... subueniretur There had been a similar episode in 17 (2.47.1–3, where see n. for the commemorating of Tib.'s generosity). Cibyra was in SW Phrygia (*BA* Map 65: B3); Aegium was on the southern shore of the Corinthian Gulf (*BA* Map 58: C1).

13.2 Vibius Serenus pro consule ulterioris Hispaniae At 2.30.1 he is named as 'C. Vibius', but on the heading of *SCPP* his praenomen is given as

Numerius ('N. Vibio Sereno procos'). He had been governor of Baetica probably in 21/22 and was succeeded by Granius Marcianus (6.38.4n.). See further 28–30.1 below, and *PIR* 8.2.300–1 no. 575, *BNP* 15.387 [Vibius II 20].

de ui publica damnatus ob atrocitatem temporum in insulam Amorgum deportatur *uis publica* is 'the arbitrary execution or use of force against Roman citizens' (Seager 144; see 6.4 above); in the *Digest* the normal punishment for this offence according to the Lex Iulia de Vi was *aquae et ignis interdictio* (*Dig.* 48.6.10.2 'damnato de ui publica aqua et igni interdicitur').[33] The clear implication of *ob atrocitatem temporum*, however, is that Serenus was penalised more harshly than he otherwise would have been. Of what does this extra harshness consist? T. may mean simply that Serenus was deported to Amorgus rather than to some other island. Amorgus was the easternmost of the Cyclades, and no other exile is recorded as being deported there. On the other hand, solitary confinement is true of almost every other deportee (Drogula 265–6), and it is not obvious that Amorgus is appreciably more unpleasant than many other islands used for similar purposes. The selection of one island rather than another seems on the whole a relatively trivial matter and scarcely to justify the term *atrocitas*.

The alternative is to assume that Serenus was subjected to the harsher of the two types of exile available in the early empire: that is, to *deportatio* rather than to *relegatio*. The choice of capital rather than non-capital exile certainly makes good sense of the term *atrocitas* and may indeed be the inference from T.'s use of the verb *deportare*;[34] but, if this interpretation is correct, it would inevitably have to follow from *Dig.* 48.6.10.2 that *aquae et ignis interdictio* was as applicable to *relegatio* as to *deportatio*. This is something which seems not generally believed by modern scholars,[35] yet, since *interdictio* is not mentioned as one of the differences between *relegatio* and *deportatio* at *Dig.* 48.22.14.1 ('multum interest inter relegationem et deportationem: nam deportatio et

---

[33] Everything about the Lex Iulia de Vi seems controversial: see J. D. Cloud, *Athenaeum* 66 (1988) 579–95, 67 (1989) 427–65. For *aquae et ignis interdictio* see below, 21.3n.

[34] According to Berger, 'more severe punishment was inflicted in the later imperial legislation (deportation combined with confiscation of property became the normal penalty, and from the time of Constantine the death penalty was very frequent)', but the implication of this statement seems to be that deportation was not necessarily the normal penalty in the earlier imperial period (*Encyclopedic dictionary of Roman law* s.v. *vis* (p. 768)).

[35] In his note on Dio 56.27.2, however, P. M. Swan thinks that Dio's reference to interdiction may cover 'exiles more generally, including those merely relegated'.

ciuitatem et bona adimit, relegatio utrumque conseruat, nisi bona publicentur'; cf. 48.22.7.2), it may be possible to infer that interdiction applied equally to both forms of exile. For more on these confusing legal terms see 21.3n. below.

The reason given in M for Serenus' more severe punishment is the shocking times in which he lived ('ob atrocitatem temporum'): although the transmitted reading is retained by some editors such as Kiessling and Lenchantin, most have favoured Lipsius' *morum*, the alleged corruption being explained by dittography of *tem*. But the facts that *atrocitas temporis* is a Ciceronian phrase (*Phil.* 8.32, *Sest.* 11; cf. *Verr.* 4.108) and that *atrocitas temporum* is applied by Suetonius precisely to this period of Tib.'s reign (*Cal.* 6.2; also *Tib.* 48.1) suggest that the paradosis is correct.[36] For the repetition of *-tem tem-* see e.g. 3.2, 9.1 'fidem dempsit', 10.2, 25.2, 37.1, and *Agr.* 1.1n., adding J. Korpanty, 'Syllabische Homophonie in lateinischer Dichtung und Prosa', *Hermes* 125 (1997) 330–46.

Cars<id>ius Sacerdos See 6.48.4n.

reus tamquam frumento hostem Tacfarinatem iuuisset Since names were admissible as evidence in a Roman court of law (Quint. 5.10.30; Lausberg 175 §376 (14)), one hopes that the prosecution made something of the fact that grain would be needed by a leader who had flour inscribed in his name (cf. Vitr. 10.5.2 'subministrat molis frumentum et eadem uersatione subigitur *farina*'). For the war in Africa in AD 20 see 3.20–1 and 3.72.4–74 and nn. (3.20.1n. for Tacfarinas himself).

C. Gracchus Perhaps identical with the praetor of 33 (6.16.3) and the *delator* of 35 (6.38.4).

13.3 pater Sempronius See 1.53.3–6 and nn.

Cercinam An island off the eastern coast of Tunisia (Drogula 234, 237, 265).

inter extorres et liberalium artium nescios *extorris* (5× in T.) is an archaising alternative to the commoner *exul* (20× in T.), with which it is sometimes co-ordinated, as at *H.* 5.24.2 (see H. ad loc.; F. Kuntz, *Die Sprache des Tacitus und die Tradition der lateinischen Historikersprache* (1962) 135–6); for *nescius* see 3.1.1n., Malloch on 11.12.2.

---

[36] E. A. Meyer, however, follows Lipsius and notes that 'accusations of governors for wrongdoing can be enhanced by accusations of moral defect' ('The justice of the Roman governor and the performance of prestige', in A. Kolb (ed.), *Herrschaftsstrukturen und Herrschaftspraxis* (2006) 171). Formicola prints *poenarum*, which he had suggested in *Sileno* 20 (2000) 101–6.

mutando sordidas merces The disparaging adj. runs as a refrain through Cicero's discussion 'de artificiis et quaestibus, qui liberales habendi, qui sordidi sint' (*Off.* 1.150, with Dyck's nn.). *mutare merces* occurs first at Virg. *Ecl.* 4.39, whence it is perhaps picked up by Horace (*S.* 1.4.29); thereafter in Ov. *Tr.* 1.2.76.

Aelius Lamia L. Aelius Lamia (6.27.2n.), *ordinarius* in AD 3, had been proconsul of Africa in 15/16 or 16/17 (Vogel-Weidemann 59–66 no. 2).

L. Apronius had been *suffectus* in AD 8 (see 3.21.1n., 6.30.2n.) and proconsul of Africa in 18–21 (Vogel-Weidemann 73–9 no. 5). In 28 he was in charge of Lower Germany (4.73.1).

insontem See 3.67.2n., Malloch on 11.26.2, Oakley on Liv. 9.16.10.

claritudine infausti generis et paternis aduersis foret abstractus This chiastic verdict refers first to the deaths of Tiberius and Gaius Gracchus in 133 and 121 BC respectively, and secondly to the death of Gracchus' father in AD 14 (1.53.5); T. had earlier evoked the distant past in the case of another Roman in Africa, Furius Camillus (2.52.5nn.). In keeping with his preference for *claritudo* (1.28.1n.), *claritudo generis* is very frequent in T. (8×) but occurs nowhere else; other authors have *claritas generis* (Ascon. p. 20C, Plin. *Ep.* 4.9.4, *Pan.* 58.3, 70.2, Quint. 8.6.7 (cf. 3.7.19)). For *infausti* cf. Sen. *HF* 1135, Sil. 9.164. For *abstractus* = 'destroyed' cf. Sen. *Const. Sap.* 2.2, *Cons. Marc.* 24.5.

14.1 Is quoque annus . . . habuit *quoque* reminds readers that there had been similar delegations in the previous year (see 3.60–3, where add Rigsby 1–29 to the nn. on the cultural and historical background); it is not clear why the Samians and Coans arrive only now. The formulaic *(is) annus habuit* (again at 2.53.2, 13.33.1, 15.32.1) occurs a dozen times in Livy and thrice in Cicero; see also above, 6.1n.

Samiis Iunonis, Cois Aesculapii delubro uetustum asyli ius ut firmaretur petentibus There is fascinating evidence for this episode in a fragmentary inscription of 16 lines found on Samos (R. K. Sherk, *Roman documents from the Greek East* (1969) 183–4 no. 32): it is dated to the present year by the name (line 4) of C. Stertinius Maximus, the suffect consul, and even mentions (line 5) the Ides of September, the day before the funeral of Drusus (8.2n.). Lines 6–8 make it absolutely clear that the senate considered the cases of Samos and Cos together, although it is disputed whether lines 10–16 comprise the remains of the senatorial decree(s) which presumably resulted. For full discussion of the Samian temple of Hera (the largest temple in Greece in the classical period) and the Coan temple of Aesculapius and their respective asylum rights see Rigsby 106–11 (Cos) and 394–6 (Samos), the latter including text of and notes on the inscription. It is known from their surviving bases that two statues were erected in the Heraeum to the consuls of 23 by the people of Samos, and both places seem also to have honoured Tib. himself with statues.

It is important to remember that *asylum* has 'only one meaning, a sacred place in which one can take refuge from pursuers. The noun is concrete, not abstract' (Rigsby 30). Perhaps surprisingly, and contrary to the impression given by Rigsby, there is no parallel for the expression *asyli ius*: whether it means 'the right belonging to a sanctuary' or 'the right of <being> a sanctuary' is unclear; Rigsby says it is 'a genitive of analogy, "the right of an asylum," comparable to *ius Latii*'. For more on terminology see Rigsby 30–3. *uetustum . . . ius* (also at Val. Max. 7.8.9) is perhaps Livian (1.52.1, 27.8.8, 33.20.7).

decreto Amphictyonum nitebantur Amphictyonies were religious associations of Greek city-states, usually with a shrine or temple as the focal point (see e.g. V. Ehrenberg, *The Greek state* (²1969) 108–11). The Samians' claim 'may have rested on an anecdote from a local history or on a forged document from such a book' (Rigsby 394).

ea tempestate qua Graeci . . . ora maris potiebantur 'This appears to invoke the time after the Ionian migration in the Dark Ages, rather than the Hellenistic period' (Rigsby 394). M reads *ea qua tempestate*: all recent edd. delete *ea*, and it is true that *qua tempestate*, a relatively common phrase which drew a remark from Cicero (*De Or.* 3.153), is used to 'date' matters of ancient history at 2.60.1, 6.34.2, 12.62 and *H.* 5.2.1; but *ea tempestate qua* seems adequately defended by the recurrence of the same phrase at 6.8.1, although otherwise it does not occur until later Latin (e.g. Just. 15.4.20).[37] See further 1.3.6n. for *tempestas* = 'time'.

14.2 Neque dispar apud Coos antiquitas 'What the Coans put before the Senate was claimed to date from the age of the great migrations', a date that 'excluded a genuine decree' (Rigsby 107 and n. 4), i.e. a forgery.

cum iussu regis Mithridatis . . . trucidarentur For the decree of Mithridates VI in 88 BC and its terrible consequences see Vell. 2.18.1–3, App. *Mithr.* 22–3; according to Appian, and contrary to the impression given by their reported claim here, the Coans in fact welcomed Mithridates (see also 3.62.1n. *Magnetes*): see S. M. Sherwin-White, *Ancient Cos* (1978) 138–9, B. C. McGing, *The foreign policy of Mithridates VI Eupator, King of Pontus* (1986) 111–13.

14.3 praetorum Praetors had been given charge of the games in 22 BC (Dio 54.2.3–4).

---

[37] Each of these proposals was made by Rhenanus, although the former is mistakenly attributed by most editors to Lipsius.

Caesar . . . rettulit For the emperor bringing a motion before the senate see Talbert 165–7 and 234–6. *immodestia* seems intended to cover both of the charges mentioned immediately below.

multa ab iis in publicum seditiose, foeda per domos temptari Tib.'s chiastic and varied statement is repeated by Dio (57.21.3 τοὺς δὲ ὀρχηστὰς τῆς τε Ῥώμης ἐξήλασε . . . ὅτι τάς τε γυναῖκας ᾔσχυνον καὶ στάσεις ἤγειρον) and the two charges are themselves repeated chiastically in the next sentence ('flagitiorum et uirium'). *seditio*, like *discordia* (1.54.2, Suet. *Tib.* 37.2), is esp. used of theatrical disturbances (1.77.2, Vell. 126.2 'compressa theatralis seditio'; cf. Dio 57.14.10 ὥστε καὶ στασιάζειν αὐτοὺς καὶ μηδ' ὑπὸ τῶν νόμων, οὓς ὁ Τιβέριος ἐπ' αὐτοῖς ἐσενηνόχει, καθίστασθαι, under AD 15) and may refer to political dissent as well as to disputes between rival actors and their supporters (cf. e.g. 1.77.1 'probra in magistratus et dissensionem uulgi', 6.13.1 'in theatro . . . aduersum imperatorem'). For further disturbances cf. 11.13.1 (and Malloch ad loc.), 13.24.1, 13.25.4, 13.28.1 and see N. Horsfall, *The culture of the Roman plebs* (2003) 39–42; Swan on Dio 56.47.2. *foeda . . . temptari* may be a distant echo of Sall. *C.* 26.5.

Oscum . . . ludicrum is a reference to Atellan farce (called 'Osci ludi' at Cic. *Fam.* 7.1.3); Suetonius preserves an insult directed against Tib. at such a performance (*Tib.* 45), though the story is not without its peculiarities (Champlin (2015); cf. C.T. Mallan, *Histos* 19 (2016) 15–16). *quondam* is explained by the fact that these farces had originally been performed in Oscan. See *BNP* 1.224–6, Oakley on Liv. 7.2.11–12.

leuissimae apud uulgum oblectationis T.'s attitude to the lower classes is consistently superior (Z. Yavetz, *Plebs and princeps* (1969) 141ff.). For the expr. cf. Cic. *De Or.* 2.21 'leuissimam delectationem'; for the acc. form *uulgum* see 3.76.1n.

auctoritate patrum *auctoritas* here = 'an informal decree of the senate' (*OLD* 4a; cf. Talbert 523).

Pulsi tum histriones Italia Also banished were the leaders of the rival actors' factions (Suet. *Tib.* 37.2). The actors themselves were recalled by Caligula (Dio 59.2.5). See further 62.2 and n.

15.1 Idem annus alio quoque luctu Caesarem adfecit T. customarily places obituary notices at or very near the end of an annalistic year (3.30.1n.); here he inserts into the middle of the year's final section two noteworthy deaths, each of which is more a simple record than a genuine obituary.

idem annus (5× in T.) is a connecting phrase of Livy's (4.8.2, 9.44.1), the latter ex. with a transitive verb, a construction with *annus* of which T. in the *Annals* is fond (6.1n.). *quoque* refers back to the death of Drusus, although Dio says that

Tib. continued with his customary duties exactly as he had done when Drusus himself died (57.14.6). The exact meaning of *luctus* ('grief', 'instance or cause of grief' etc.: see *OLD* 2) is often difficult to determine (*TLL* 7.2.1740.1ff., 1744.36ff.), which no doubt explains why no distinctions are offered in G–G 785a, where the present instance is simply listed last; for *luctu adficere* cf. Cic. *Pis.* 18, Sen. *Prov.* 4.8, Gell. 3.15.4, Fronto p. 236.12 vdH².

alterum ex geminis Drusi liberis i.e. Germanicus (3.1n.): cf. Vell. 130.3.

exstinguendo . . . morte The former is an instrumental abl. (the 'subject' of the gerund is *annus*), the latter a causal abl. going closely with *luctu*.

Lucilius Longus Suffect in AD 7 (*RE* 13.1645–6 = Lucilius 27 (Miltner), *PIR* 5.104 no. 389): 'a person not named by any other author', said Syme (*AA* 224), arguing elsewhere that the man 'should be held identical' with the Favonius who is recorded on *ILS* 9483 as proconsul of Asia in (?) 15/16 (*RP* 4.355–7).

unusque e *senatoribus* Rhodii *secessus* comes Tib. would likewise take only one senator with him to Capri (58.1 below); for his withdrawal to Rhodes (6 BC–AD 2) see 57.2n.

15.2 quamquam nouo homini 'To use and promote *noui homines* was good Claudian tradition. They supplied what was often lacking in their social superiors, namely integrity and competence. And above all, loyalty' (Syme, *AA* 100). See Levick 97ff. for Tib. and *noui homines*.

censorium funus The award of such a funeral (for which see 6.27.2n.) to a *nouus homo* 'was totally anomalous' (Syme, *AA* 363), but another example was P. Sulpicius Quirinius, consul in 12 BC, who resembled Lucilius Longus in that 'Tiberium quoque Rhodi agentem coluerat' (3.48.1: see nn.).

effigiem apud forum Augusti The forum was between the Capitol and Quirinal (*LTUR* 2.289–95 and Fig. 116, *BNP* 5.521–2) and the place where Augustus had set up statues of the heroes of old (Suet. *Aug.* 31.5, quoted above, 4.3n.).

etiam tum T.'s favourite 'temporal innuendo' (see 3.55.2n.) suggests a contrast with what might have been expected, given that this was the year in which Tib.'s principate changed for the worse (above, 6.1); Furneaux saw a specific contrast with 'the later prevalence of private trials', which came to be used for misbehaving procurators (cf. *D.* 7.1 'apud principem . . . procuratores principum tueri et defendere datur'): for such trials see 6.10.2n., adding K. Tuori, *The Emperor of Law: the emergence of Roman imperial adjudication* (2016) (pp. 177–82 on Tib.). See also next n.

Lucilius Capito Since Capito was Tib.'s own equestrian procurator, the choice of the senate for his trial was 'remarkable' (Talbert 467) and 'a special compliment to that body' (Garnsey 31; cf. 86, and also Brunt (1983) 52). Little else is known of Capito (*RE* 13.1642 = Lucilius 24 (Stein), *PIR* 5.100 no. 381, *BNP* 7.851 [Lucilius II 3]; Demougin, *PCR* 214 no. 246).

magna cum adseueratione principis For the emperor's speaking in senatorial debates see Talbert 163ff. The details here correspond to those in Dio 57.23.4–5. *adseueratio* is used by T. disproportionately often for a relatively uncommon word (6.2.2n.); the constr. with the acc. + infin. appears to be unique (*TLL* 2.874.32ff.).

uim praetoris *uis* here probably means simply 'function, capacity' (*OLD* 14a); less likely is that the sentence illustrates 'theme and variation' and that by a form of metonymy the word refers to the governor's troops, who are mentioned in terms of their physical capability just below: 'manibusque militum' (-*que* being epexegetic, as often). *praetor* (again at 43.3 and 45.1) is used for *proconsul*, even when, as here and 2.77.1, the position was consular: see 1.74.1n. and Syme, *Tac.* 343–4. Though such avoidance of technical terms is familiar in T. (see *Ann. 3*, p. 503; *Ann. 5–6*, p. 319: s.v. 'technical . . . language'), the usage had republican precedent and may be employed to recall an age which is long since past.

cognito Not 'having been discovered' (as *Bell. Hisp.* 32.5 'cognito hoc negotio') but 'having been investigated judicially' (*OLD* 4).

damnatur Exile (Dio 57.23.4).

15.3 quia priore anno in C. Silanum uindicatum erat See 3.66–9 and nn. For the *uariatio* with *ob* above see 6.39.3n.; for *uindicatum in* + acc. see *H.* 4.45 and H. (Cic. Caes. Sall.).

templum Tiberio matrique eius ac senatui When the temple was eventually built (at Smyrna, after competition from various rival cities: see 55–6 below), coins portrayed it as enclosing a statue of Tib. as pontifex, with draped busts of the senate and Livia on the other side (see A. Burnett et al., *Roman provincial coinage* (1992) 1.1.419 no. 2469); see also Price 64, 66, 185, and 258 no. 45.

permissum statuere Like other early imperial prose-writers, but unlike Cicero, T. regularly constructs *permitto* with the infin. (see Adams (1972) 371–2 for this trend); the only exception is 3.63.1, which is perhaps not a straightforward example (see n.).[38]

---

[38] T.'s words could in theory mean 'they decided on permission' (i.e. *statuēre*), but the expr. would be otherwise unexampled, whereas *templum statuere* (again at 4.55.1 and 56.1 below) is regular (e.g. Ov. *Met.* 14.128).

egitque Nero grates For Nero see 3.29.1nn.; for *grates* see 3.18.3n.

illum aspici, illum audiri rebantur It was a commonplace that children should resemble their parents (for refs. see Vell. 93.2n.), and such resemblances can produce powerful emotions (e.g. Liv. 21.4.2 'Hamilcarem iuuenem redditum sibi ueteres milites credere: eundem uigorem in uoltu uimque in oculis, habitum oris lineamentaque intueri'). Germanicus' 'reappearance' is esp. effective after the enthusiasm which greeted the false rumours of the man's survival in 19 (2.82.4–5: see Woodman (2015) 266–7). For the importance of seeing and hearing in such circumstances see e.g. Virg. *Aen.* 4.83–4 'illum absens absentem auditque uidetque | . . . genitoris imagine capta'.

forma principe uiro digna An actual or potential leader was supposed to look the part (e.g. Vell. 94.2 'iuuenis . . . forma . . . instructissimus . . . uisuque praetulerat principem' and n.). For *principe uiro digna* cf. *Cons. Liv.* 344.

16.1 Sub idem tempus See 6.20.1n.

de flamine Diali in locum Serui Maluginensis defuncti legendo Servius Maluginensis, suffect in AD 10, had featured in a prominent episode the previous year (3.58.1–59.1 and nn., adding Rüpke 638 no. 1349).

16.2 nam patricios . . . uetusto more *confarreatio*, the oldest and most solemn form of marriage, was exclusive to patricians and obligatory for a major priest, who must also have been the offspring of such a marriage (see Treggiari 21–4, Vanggaard 70–8, K. K. Hersch, *The Roman wedding: ritual and meaning in antiquity* (2010) 24–7, DiLuzio 20–2; *BNP* 3.688).

eam copiam 'the supply for it', namely, the production of a short-list of three.

pluresque eius rei causas adferebat . . . This is a very difficult section. (a) Older editors evidently saw *pluresque . . . adferebat* as parallel to *disseruit* above and as introducing a second passage of indirect speech, beginning with *potissimam* [sc. *causam esse*] *penes incuriam uirorum feminarumque*. This interpretation is highly unlikely. It is clear from the mention of men and women here that *eius rei* can refer only to the scarcity of confarreate marriage amongst the parents of potential *flamines*, whereas, by the time we reach *et quoniam . . . conueniret* below, the subject has changed to the marital problems of the *flamen* himself and his wife: these latter are quite inappropriate as part of a speech designed to explain something entirely different.[39]

(b) A further difficulty is that M reads *et quõ exiret*. Since *quõ* is the standard abbreviation for *quoniam* (although older edd. print *quando*),[40] this generates

---

[39] 'Manifesto haec inter eas causas refertur, ob quas multi a capessendo eo flaminio deterrebantur' (Orelli).

[40] It is also the abbreviation for *quomodo*, but that is not relevant here.

a difficulty over the *et* which precedes it. Many scholars have assumed that *accedere* is followed both by *ipsius caerimoniae difficultates* and by *quoniam/quando exiret* and that these two varied elements are co-ordinated by *et* in a seemingly Tacitean fashion; but *accedere* is only ever followed by *quod* or *ut* (*OLD* 17b), and never by *quoniam* or *quando*. To explain the presence of *et*, Lipsius therefore proposed a lacuna after *uitarentur*.

Madvig (2.546) avoided both of these difficulties by suggesting that the words *pluresque eius rei causas adferebat* are the start of a parenthesis which in his opinion extends as far as *uitarentur*. On this view [i] it is the parenthesis alone which explains the scarcity of confarreate marriage, to which *ipsius caerimoniae* must therefore refer; [ii] *et* co-ordinates the abl. abs. *omissa . . . retenta* before the parenthesis with *quoniam exiret* after it, a type of *uariatio* readily paralleled elsewhere (Sörbom 115). Madvig's proposal has been adopted by Furneaux, Fisher, Koestermann, Lenchantin, Fuchs and Heubner; Borzsák extends the parenthesis as far as *conueniret*. But there are two difficulties. (1) It is very awkward to understand *ipsius caerimoniae* as referring to marriage when the discussion concerns the flaminate, in the context of which *caerimonia* is a conventional term (see below). Moreover *ipsius* seems intended to mark a change of topic, redirecting us to that which preceded the reference to marriage, namely, the difficulty of producing a short-list of three ('eam copiam'). (2) The juxtaposition of *pluresque eius rei causas* and *potissimam* strongly suggests (but admittedly does not prove) that T. offered only one of Tib.'s various reasons for the unpopularity of confarreate marriage, namely, 'the most important one'; *accedere . . . uitarentur* looks out of place as a further reason. I therefore believe that, although Madvig was right in principle, the parenthesis consists of no more than *pluresque . . . feminarumque* and that with *accedere* we are returned to the original speech which was introduced by *disseruit*.

It has to be admitted that, if *accedere* is not part of the parenthesis, we are returned to the problem of explaining the transmitted *et quõ*. The likeliest explanation is that *quõ* is a mistaken abbreviation of *quod*, which was first printed by Ritter in 1834 and then by Doederlein, the former adding in his 1848 edition that *quo* (without its tilde) is written for *quod* at 39.2 below.[41] Although T. happens not to use *accedit quod* elsewhere, the resulting *uariatio* would be typical of him (e.g. *amicitia . . . et quod . . .* at 18.1 below).

potissimam penes incuriam *penes* is relatively rare with a non-personal noun and in the present sense possibly unique (*TLL* 10.1.1057.40–1); for its being preceded by *causa* see 1.1n.

---

[41] Ritter later abandoned this conjecture, not mentioning it in his 1864 edition, where he printed *et quoniam* and posited a lacuna after *conueniret*.

accedere ipsius caerimoniae difficultates In the interpretation of this passage given above (last n. but one), *accedere* resumes the *oratio obliqua* after the parenthetic interruption of *pluresque . . . feminarumque.* Gellius begins his lengthy discussion of the Flamen Dialis with the statement 'Caerimoniae impositae flamini Diali multae' (10.15.1), where it is clear that *caerimoniae* (repeated at §§18 and 26) means 'taboos' or 'rituals'. In the present passage it is rather *difficultates* which has these meanings, while *caerimonia* here and elsewhere 'comes almost to stand for the office itself', as noted by Furneaux on 1.62.2 ('imperatorem auguratu et uetustissimis caerimoniis praeditum'): another ex. is at 1.54.1. It is absolutely typical of T. to use a technical term in this way (see *Ann. 3*, p. 503; *Ann. 5–6*, p. 319: s.v. 'technical . . . language'). See further 1.62.2n. and, on the taboos and rituals themselves, Vanggaard 88–104, DiLuzio 32ff.

quod exiret e iure patrio qui id flamonium apisceretur quaeque in manum flaminis conueniret *exire* is technical for abandoning a legal status (*OLD* 6a); *ius patrium* (Cic. *Phil.* 2.46, Liv. 1.26.9, Sen. *Contr.* 1.7.14, Calp. *Decl.* 14) is a variant on *patria potestas*, which, though common in modern usage (e.g. *BNP* 10.604–6), is no more frequent in extant classical texts (Cic. *Inv.* 2.52, *Q.Fr.* 1.3.10, Sen. *Clem.* 1.14.2, [Quint.] *Decl.* 9.10). After a *flamen*'s inauguration he was no longer subject to his father's *potestas* (Vanggaard 66 quotes Gai. *Inst.* 1.130, 3.114, Ulp. *Reg.* 10.5), and the same was evidently true of the woman who married the *flamen* (*in manum conuenire* = 'to marry' and is used of a wife: see *OLD conuenio* 1e; Treggiari 16ff.): the change of status had important implications for rights, responsibilities and privileges (see e.g. Treggiari 28–36). For *apiscor* see 3.31.2n.

16.3 sicut Augustus quaedam ex horrida illa antiquitate ad praesentem usum flexisset Since *horridus* often suggests 'unbending' (*OLD* 5), there is a contrast with *flexisset* (as Sen. *HO* 574–5 'sed iecur fors horridum | flectam merendo'), and *horrida illa antiquitate* refers back to 3.71.2, where we were told of a priestly decree whereby in certain circumstances the ancient '*binoctium* rule' (for which cf. Gell. 10.15.14) could be relaxed at the discretion of the *pontifex maximus* (i.e. Augustus). It is of course highly characteristic of Tib. to introduce Augustus as an *exemplum* (see *Ann. 3*, p. 513; *Ann. 5–6*, p. 325). On *binoctium* see further Vanggaard 65–6, 90 and n. 6; for the extended sense of *antiquitas* ('ancient practice') see *OLD* 3.

tractatis religionibus See 3.71.2n.

nihil demutari The verb occurs 9× in Plautus, once each in the elder Cato (*Or.* fr. 115 Malc.) and Gellius (17.1.6), and 3× in Apuleius: the archaism suggests a Tiberian idiolect (Syme, *Tac.* 702).

lata lex qua flaminica Dialis ... ageret On the *flamen*'s wife see Vanggaard 22–3, 30–1, 66, DiLuzio 17–51 (also above, n. *quod*). It is clear from the rel. clause that *ago* is here being used intrans. = 'live' (*OLD* 34–5): *cetera* is therefore adverbial, as again at 6.15.1, 6.42.3 (*TLL* 3.973.38–64).

filius Maluginensis Otherwise unknown (Rüpke 638 no. 1348).

16.4 Vtque glisceret dignatio sacerdotum From the decree mentioned below, which relates only to Vestal Virgins, it is to be inferred that *sacerdotum* refers to priests and priestesses alike. Once again Tib. is following Augustan precedent (cf. Suet. *Aug.* 31.3 'sacerdotum et numerum et dignitatem sed et commoda auxit, praecipue Vestalium uirginum' (the nearest parallel for the expr.) and Wardle ad loc.). For *glisco* see 3.19.2n.

atque ipsis promptior animus foret ad capessendas caerimonias *ipsis* can only refer back to *sacerdotum*: if it therefore refers to those who are *already* priest(esse)s, *caerimonias* seems likely to mean 'taboos', as at Gell. 10.15.1, despite the fact that at 2 above it seemed to refer to the priestly office itself (n.); if this seems too confusing, even for T., we should have to assume that *ipsis* is being used in a somewhat pregnant sense = 'potential priest(esse)s'. *promptus animus* is a common phrase in a wide range of authors.

decretum Corneliae uirgini..sestertii uicies It was regular for Vestals to receive money from the state (see Mekacher 40), but two million sesterces is a very large sum: twice the amount awarded to an unsuccessful candidate in 19 (2.86.2) and twice the requirement for the senatorial census. 'The background to the rich dowry may also include the "bankruptcy" of Sex. Vibidius Virro ..., whom in 17 Tiberius excluded from the Senate on account of his self-induced poverty' (Rüpke 630 no. 1299, referring to 2.48.3, where see n.). Virro was probably father of the Vestal Vibidia (11.32.2, 34.3).

Scantiae Not otherwise known (Rüpke 879 no. 2988, Mekacher 104–5).

capiebatur This technical term for appointing a Vestal Virgin (again at 2.86.1) is discussed at Gell. 1.12 (see Mekacher 23ff.).

ut sedes inter Vestalium consideret This privilege (for which see A. A. Barrett, *Livia: First Lady of imperial Rome* (2002) 144; Mekacher 30–1, 51, 194; DiLuzio 141–3) was later extended to Caligula's grandmother Antonia, his sisters, and Messalina (Dio 59.3.4, 60.22.2). 'It seems likely that this was the only way in which prominent women could get a front seat' (Rawson 517–18). For the various ways of referring to Vestals, including the plain *Vestalis* as here, see Mekacher 20–1. For the anastrophe of *inter* see 5.1n.

17–33 THE YEAR AD 24

The deterioration in Tib.'s principate was announced at the start of Book 4 (1.1) and underlined early in the narrative of AD 23 by surveys of the empire abroad and at home (5–6) which themselves are linked by a reminder of that deterioration (6.1). In the narrative of the present year T. adopts a different technique, closing the year with a digression in which he apologises for the kind of bleak historiography to which he is reduced by the changed circumstances of Tib.'s reign (32–3). The apologia is based partly on a contrast between himself and 'traditional' – that is to say, republican – historians (32.1, 33.3–4) and is not without irony, since it follows a narrative pattern of *res internae—externae—internae* which, if Ginsburg is right (54, 133–4), is above all associated with republican historiography.[42] The crucial difference lies in subject matter: the two domestic narratives of the present year, which mirror each other, are concerned above all with criminal trials.

17–22 Domestic Affairs

The section begins with an introductory episode in which the priests, mindful of Tib.'s speech about Germanicus' children a little earlier (8.3–5), try to please the *princeps* by honouring the young men; but they find out that they have misread his intentions (cf. 3.22.2n.) and, like the senate, are treated to a stern lecture (17.2). The episode raises his suspicions about Agrippina, which in turn serves to sustain the ongoing theme of the plotting of Sejanus (17.3; cf. 15.3); and it is the complementary motifs of friendship with the house of Germanicus (18.1 'amicitia Germanici') and of Sejanus' hatred (19.1 'odiis Seiani') which set in motion the first trial of the year, which is described at length (18–20). C. Silius escapes condemnation by committing suicide (19.4), but his wife Sosia Galla is exiled (20.1); and a difference of opinion over the fate of her property leads T. into his famously approbatory sketch of M. Lepidus, who seemed able to pick his way safely between the extremes of recalcitrance and subservience (20.3): many readers have seen here a model of behaviour which is repeated in T.'s father-in-law, Agricola, and acts as a defence of that of T. himself. The remainder of the section comprises three shorter trials. In the first of them the defendant dies before the trial can be completed (21.2); in the second the defendant has his exile upgraded (21.3); and in the third (22), which echoes that of Silius and Sosia Galla, the principal defendant commits suicide before any verdict can be reached (22.2), while his former wife is cleared of inducing his madness (22.3).

---

[42] For brief discussion of this issue see introductory note to 6.1–14.

17.1 Cornelio Cethego In due course he became proconsul of Africa, seemingly in 36/37 or 37/38 (*RE* 4.1281 = Cornelius 99 (Groag), *PIR* 2.313–14 no. 1336, *BNP* 3.830 [II 5]; Vogel-Weidemann 115–17 no. 11). His praenomen Servius 'appertained to ancient Lentuli' (Syme, *AA* 297 n. 117).

Visellio Varrone L. Visellius Varro, whose father had been suffect consul in 12 and *legatus* of the Lower German army in 21 (3.41.2n.), will feature in the episode immediately below (19.1–3). For him see *RE* 9A.1.360–1 = Visellius 7 (Hanslik), *PIR* 8.2.390 no. 726.

pontifices eorumque exemplo ceteri sacerdote For the *pontifices* see below, 2n. (*pars*); for the other priests see Rüpke 168.

pro incolumitate principis uota Shortly after Tib.'s death the date of 3 January was settled upon for this annual custom (Weinstock 219 and n. 1); it is to be distinguished from the *uota pro salute rei publicae*, which took place on 1 January (70.1n.).

Neronem quoque et Drusum Germanicus' sons were last mentioned in Tib.'s speech at 8.3–5 (below, 2n.).

adulatione, quae moribus corruptis proinde anceps si nulla et ubi nimia est For *adulatio* and Tib.'s reaction to it see above, 6.2n.; this alliterative and assonantal *sententia* is the second generalisation on the subject in Book 4 (cf. 9.2). For the antithesis with *caritas* see Val. Max. 4.7 *init.*, Fronto p. 110.18 vdH[2]. The antithesis *nullus* ~ *nimius* more usually contrasts different nouns (e.g. Liv. 23.18.11, Plin. *NH* 18.205), but cf. Sen. *Ep.* 89.3 'idem enim uitii habet nimia quod nulla diuisio' (Zimmermann 62); for the *uariatio* of *si* ~ *ubi* cf. 1.44.5; Sörbom 121. For *proinde*, mistakenly emended to *perinde* by Rhenanus, see 6.7.3n. The abl. abs. *moribus corruptis* originated in Sallust (*C.* 11.8) and, though found elsewhere (Nep. *Att.* 6.2, [Sall.] *Ep. Caes.* 1.5.4, Gell. 17.19.3), is a Tacitean favourite (6.16.1, 6.27.4, 14.15.3).

17.2 aequari adulescentes senectae suae impatienter indoluit Tib. had made an earlier reference to this age difference in his speech of the previous year, when he voiced his support for the two young men, urged the senate to look after them, and said that their futures were bound up with that of the state (8.3–5); but the priests, in trying to ingratiate themselves on precisely these grounds, had forgotten how protective of his *maiestas* the *princeps* was (see *Ann. 3*, p. 512). The acc. + infin. after *indolesco* is found before T. only at Cic. *Phil.* 2.61, Ov. *F.* 2.377, *Met.* 9.261 (*TLL* 7.1.1222. 84–1223.6); for *impatienter* cf. Plin. *Ep.* 9.22.2 'dolet . . . impatientissime'.

num id precibus Agrippinae aut minis tribuissent This is not an alternative question: the *princeps* has no interest in whether Agrippina's influence took the form of pleas or threats; he is asking the single question whether

Agrippina, with her pleas and threats, influenced the pontiffs' action: hence *num . . . aut* (cf. K–S 2.529–30). Contrast the case of her daughter at 12.42.3 'nisi Agrippinae minis magis quam precibus mutatus esset'. For the *coniunctio* of *Agrippinae* see 52.1n.

pars magna e propinquis ipsius aut primores ciuitatis erant Amongst the *pontifices* (for whom see Rüpke 168) was Nero Iulius Caesar (3.29.3n.), Germanicus' son and hence Tib.'s grandson by adoption. Three of the others were consulars: L. Calpurnius Piso (15 BC: see 3.68.2n., 6.10.3n.), C. Antistius Vetus (6 BC), and Sisenna Statilius Taurus (AD 16: see 2.1.1n.). The four others would achieve the consulship in due course: P. Cornelius Lentulus Scipio (suff. 24), M. Licinius Crassus Frugi (27: see 4.62.1n.), L. Antistius Vetus (suff. 28) and Paullus Fabius Persicus (34: see 6.28.1n.). For the expr. *primores ciuitatis* see 3.65.2n.

in senatu oratione monuit These words imply that Tib.'s criticism of the priests was conveyed in private, in which case it is not clear how T. can have known about it. Suetonius refers only to the senate (*Tib.* 54.1 'ut comperit ineunte anno pro eorum quoque salute publice uota suscepta, egit cum senatu non debere talia praemia tribui nisi expertis et aetate prouectis').

mobiles . . . animos is a fairly common expr. in prose authors from Cicero to Quintilian and T.: for some exs. see H. on *H.* 3.64.2.

praematuris honoribus It is characteristic of Tib. to criticise honours which he considered excessive (e.g. 1.14.2, 5.2.1). The adj. is used by T. (8×) more than by any other author; its meaning is discussed by Gellius (10.11.8 'Cum significandum autem est, coactius quid factum et festinantius, tum rectius "praemature" factum id dicitur quam "mature", sicuti Afranius dixit in togata cui Titulus nomen est: "adpetis dominatum demens praemature praecocem"').

17.3 partium Agrippinae 'There is no evidence for a "party" of Agrippina' (Seager 229), despite e.g. R. S. Rogers, 'The conspiracy of Agrippina', *TAPA* 62 (1931) 141–68.

gliscentis discordiae remedium *remedium* shows that Sejanus is presenting his case by means of the familiar metaphor of the state as a body (Béranger 218–37). Ancient medicine saw health in terms of harmony and unity within the body and its system, as is made esp. clear in the parable told by Menenius Agrippa (Liv. 2.32.9–33.1), but Sejanus says that the state is rent (*diductam ciuitatem*) and that, unless there is some resistance (cf. Apul. *Pl.* 2.9 'quae uitiosis partibus pro remedio resistunt'), its condition will only worsen: they need a remedy for the growing discord (cf. Liv. 2.45.3 'simulationem intestinae discordiae remedium timoris inuentum', 9.20.5 'cum . . . pro remedio aegris rebus discordia intestina petissent' with Oakley's n.). For such metaphors see *PH* 162–80; for *glisco* see 3.19.2n.

18.1 C. Silium See 1.31.2n., adding *BNP* 13.459–60 [II 3], W. Eck, *Die Statthalter der germanischen Provinzen vom 1.-3. Jahrhundert* (1985) 3–6 no. 1, Syme, *RP* 4.167–8, 171–3. For bibliography on his case see Rutledge 366 n. 24.

Titium Sabinum See *RE* 6A.1569 = Titius 39 (Stein), *PIR* 8.1.83 no. 270, *BNP* 12.744 [II 4]; Demougin, *PCR* 222 no. 258. His case will be deferred (19.1) until AD 28 (68.1).

ami̱ci̱ti̱a **Germa̱ni̱ci̱ perni̱ci̱osa** The dangers of friendship are a Tacitean theme (5.6.2n. *ob amicitiam*), and Germanicus' friendship will recur prominently when Sabinus' case is resumed at 68.1 ('ob amicitiam Germanici'). See esp. R. Seager, '*Amicitia* in Tacitus and Juvenal', *AJAH* 2 (1977) 43–4.

Silio et quod ingentes exercitus septem per annos moderator . . . Sacrouiriani belli uictor *perniciosum* has to be understood from *perniciosa* above: 'to Silius was also fatal the fact that . . .'; the description of Silius as *moderator* and *uictor* has, as it were, been taken out of the *quanto*-clause (to which it properly belongs) and placed first for emphasis: for such inversion edd. compare 11.21.1 'sector quaestoris . . . dum in oppido . . . secretus agitat' (and see E. Courtney, *Archaic Latin Prose* (1999) 4–5). *moderator*, unexampled as a term for an army leader but picking up the first reference to Silius at 1.31.3 'quibus Silius moderabatur' (itself a most unusual expr.: see n.), not only illustrates T.'s characteristic avoidance of standard terminology but ironically sets up Silius' *im*moderate behaviour as described below (2). Silius' seven years of army command are reckoned as from AD 14 to his victorious campaign over Sacrovir in 21 (3.40–7 and nn.). His honorary triumph was in 15 (1.72.1, where see n. on substantival *triumphalia*, adding Vell. 116.3n.).

quanto *maiore mole* procideret, *plus* formidinis in alios dispergebatur The statement is variously precious: both the impf. subjunctive ('was to fall': see Handford 84–5) and the impf. indic. ('would be spread': cf. e.g. 14.45.2 'omne iter quo damnati ad poenam ducebantur ['would be led'] militaribus praesidiis saepsit') represent regular but infrequent uses to express futurity from a past point of view; and the correlative *tanto* is omitted, as often in T. (6.17.3n.). The metaphor of a falling building (*procideret*: cf. 15.40.1) echoes that used by Sejanus in his advice to Tib. (17.3 *subuerterentur*) and is appropriate in a monitory context (e.g. Hor. *C.* 2.10.10–11 'celsae grauiore casu | decidunt turres', with N–H's n.); for the abl. see e.g. Virg. *Aen.* 3.656 'uasta se mole mouentem' (with Horsfall's n.). *dispergebatur* (for which cf. Amm. 29.6.9 'dispersa formidine') is part of the metaphor: '*formido* is scattered like falling rubble' (Oakley (1991) 344). See further nn. below.

18.2 auctam offensionem Tib. was highly susceptible to affronts and the like (see 1.7.7, 1.12.3, 1.13.1, 1.69.5 (n.), 2.42.3, 3.24.4, 3.64.2, 4.21.1, 4.29.3, 4.71.3, 5.2.2, 6.9.2; cf. 3.24.4, 4.38.1, 6.15.2), but, on the evidence of §1 above, Silius has committed no offence and thus there is nothing which his boasting (below) can 'increase'.

immodice iactantis suum militem in obsequio durauisse Silius' boast about the soldiers of Upper Germany (*suum* is emphatic) does not quite square with T.'s version at 1.31.3 ('mente ambigua fortunam seditionis alienae speculabantur'), but cf. 1.40.1 'superiorem exercitum . . . ubi obsequia et contra rebelles animum' (also 1.37.3). From Tib.'s response (below, 3n.) it is clear that Silius' alleged boasting does not belong to the present year, AD 24, but to the time of the German mutinies ten years earlier in 14, with which the tense of *prolaberentur* in the following *cum*-clause is consistent. In other words, old charges are being dredged up against Silius in the same way as against Cremutius Cordus later (34.1). For *immodice* cf. Claud. *Cons. Stil.* 3.26 'non immodicus proprii iactator honoris'. *durare* is often used of the permanence of buildings (*TLL* 5.1.2299.47–53): since *prolabi* is regular for collapsing structures (e.g. 14.27.1; *OLD* 5b), the two verbs combine to continue the metaphor of §1 above.

neque mansurum Tiberii imperium Editors (e.g. Pfitzner, Draeger–Heraeus, Nipperdey–Andresen, Furneaux, Koestermann) are agreed that one should supply *fuisse* here ('would not have survived'); but, if it is right to date Silius' alleged boasting to AD 14 (last n.), *mansurum* is a genuine future: 'and Tiberius' *imperium* would not survive, if those legions too get the lust for revolution'.[43] The expr. seems originally Livian (1.3.1 'imperium . . . mansit') and recurs only in T. (again at *H.* 1.50.3, 4.54.2).

cupido nouandi Cf. Velleius' description of the mutinous soldiers (125.1): 'profunda confundendi omnia cupiditate nouum ducem, nouum statum, nouam quaerebant rem publicam'. T.'s phrase again seems Livian (32.5.3 'cupido nouandi res'), but the absolute use of the verb is Sallustian (*C.* 39.3 'nouandi spes'; cf. 55.1); its primary meaning here is 'to engage in revolutionary activity' (*OLD* 4b–c), but, since the verb can also be used of replacing one building with another (*OLD* 1), it contrasts metaphorically with *mansurum*, which is regular of durable structures (*OLD* 7a). For the contrast *nouare* ~ *manere* elsewhere cf. Trajan *ap.* Plin. *Ep.* 10.115, though the context there is quite different.

---

[43] *fuisset* represents a fut. perf. in direct speech. It is clear from *suum militem in obsequio durauisse* that Silius does not *expect* his soldiers to change their minds and join the mutineers; he is merely saying that Tib. will not survive if they do.

18.3 Destrui per haec fortunam suam Caesar imparemque tanto merito rebatur The majority of scholars believe that *fortuna* here refers to Tib.'s 'position': if they are right, as seems likely, *rebatur* must relate to AD 14 and be contemporaneous with *iactantis* at 2 above. It makes good sense for the *princeps* to have thought in AD 14 that 'his position was being undermined by these boasts', but it makes no sense whatsoever for him to have such thoughts in AD 24, when he had been secure in power for a decade and his position was unassailable.[44] *destrui* indicates that in his response Tib. pointedly used the same metaphorical terms as Silius (*OLD destruo* 1): the issue was not the stability of the legions but the man's own destructive boasting.

The two complementary elements of Tib.'s thought are strangely separated by the interposition of nomin. *Caesar*, which, however, makes the ellipse of *se* (as subject of *imparem*) easier to understand.[45] See also 3.8.2n.

nam beneficia ... odium redditur The *sententia* is chiastic and varied (*dum* ~ *ubi*); for *eo usque ... dum* see *OLD usque* 4a, *eo²* 3a (the more normal order is *usque eo* but see *Agr.* 14.1n.). *anteuenio* is archaic and very rare, being used by

---

[44] If *destrui per haec fortunam suam imparemque tanto merito* is assigned to Tib. in AD 24, the words make sense only if they are taken to mean the opposite of what they say. E.g. they started life as an example of the emperor's famously grim humour: in response to Silius' boasting, Tib. said, with characteristic irony, that 'he could not repay so great a service and his position was ruined'. The humour would lie both in the omnipotence of the *princeps* as opposed to the vainglory of Silius and in the fact that Silius seems to have done nothing personally to ensure the loyalty of his legions. But, apart from other problems, this interpretation requires T. to have taken an ironical statement at face value. Commentators are not esp. helpful on the passage. Furneaux makes no comment at all. Koestermann merely paraphrases the Latin. According to Orelli, Tib. believed 'nimis minui principatus sui splendorem et obscurari tanto Silii merito'. This is impossible, since *fortuna* cannot mean *splendor*; its closest meaning to this is 'good fortune' (*OLD* 9), which Tib. did not believe his *imperium* to be. Ruperti repeats Walther's long note: 'Caesar rebatur per haec effici ut non fortuna sua, sed Silii merito ad imperii fastigium euectus esse uideretur; quod si admittatur, Silii meritum maius uideri quam ut ipse pro fortuna sua rependere possit. Germanice: *Caesar glaubte, sein Glück müsse dadurch den Ruhm einbüssen und so grossem Verdienste etwas schuldig bleiben.*' But not only is this interpretation open to the same objection as Orelli's but Walther has translated as if T. had written *famam*, not *fortunam*.

[45] Pichena thought that *imparem* agreed with *fortunam*: 'eandem fortunam suam Caesar tanto merito imparem rebatur'.

T. elsewhere only literally (at 1.63.4: see n.); the metaphorical use as found here seems unparalleled. The pairing of *gratia* and *odium* is regular, esp. in T. (e.g. 4.35.1, 6.26.3 (n.). 14.62.2, *H.* 1.72.2): for the general sense edd. compare Sen. *Ben.* 2.11.1, *Ep.* 19.11 'cum quidam, quo plus debent, magis oderint; leue aes alienum debitorem facit, graue inimicum' (see also Zimmermann 43–4; F. Wilhelm, *Curtius und der jüngere Seneca* (1928) 29, mentions other passages in his illustration of Curt. 6.8.5–8 'quaedam beneficia odimus').

19.1 Erat uxor Silio Sosia Galla This introductory form of words (for which see 5.4.1n.) helps to confirm that we are returning to the main story after a flashback. For Silius' wife see Raepsaet-Charlier 574–5 no. 720.

caritate Agrippinae inuisa principi Scholars usually take the gen. as objective ('her affection for Agrippina'), comparing 16.14.1 'caritate Agrippinae inuisum Neroni', but at 11.2 above it is subjective ('caritate in eum Caesaris', 'Caesar's affection for him').

corripi See 2.28.3n.

dilato ad tempus Sabino Until AD 28 (4.68.1). *ad tempus* must here = 'for the time being' *vel sim.* (G–G 1639a).

paternas inimicitias obtendens odiis Seiani per dedecus suum gratificabatur 'T.'s penchant for asserting or implying a distinction between appearance and reality sees him use *obtendere*, especially of speech, more frequently than his predecessors and contemporaries' (Malloch on 11.17.2; also 3.17.1n.). The elder Varro's hostility to Silius was due to the latter's having been preferred for the command against Sacrovir (3.43.3 and n.), but avenging his father was only a pretext for the son's action: his real reason was to curry favour with Sejanus, which brought the same shame on him as it would on the accusers of Sabinus four years later (4.69.3 'suum . . . dedecus'). Jac. Gronovius saw here a 'manifesta imitatio' of Sall. *J.* 3.4 'potentiae paucorum decus atque libertatem *gratificari*', although the construction is different. For *paternae inimicitiae* (again at 1.10.3) cf. Cic. *Acad.* 2.1, Liv. 21.10.11 and esp. 44.25.1 'non tam quia paternae inter eos inimicitiae erant quam ipsorum odiis inter se accensae'.

19.2 breuem moram, dum accusator consulatu abiret This perhaps suggests that only a short time was to elapse before Varro gave way to one of the suffect consuls (Rogers 77 n. 237).

nec infringendum consulis ius, cuius uigiliis niteretur ne quod res publica detrimentum caperet The charges against Silius (listed at 4 below) all relate to the past and show clearly that the *senatus consultum ultimum*, whose formulaic language is repeated here, did not have 'the slightest relevance to the present situation' (Seager 160): there was no emergency, and the state was in no danger. Tib. mentions the *s.c.u.* simply because it was the most powerful means of illustrating the *consulis ius* and hence of supporting Varro's actions ('nec infringendum'): see esp. Sall. *C.* 29.3 'ea potestas per senatum more Romano magistratui maxuma permittitur . . . aliter sine populi iussu nullius earum rerum *consuli ius* est'. Nevertheless the reference to the *s.c.u.* almost inevitably invites thoughts of the Catilinarian conspiracy (see also next n.), thus allowing T. to proceed to the cynicism and sarcasm of the next two sentences.

Proprium id Tiberio fuit, scelera nuper reperta priscis uerbis obtegere What does *scelera nuper reperta* mean? Although the parenthetical statement is a generalisation, it has to be relevant to the case in hand. The words could mean 'crimes only now coming to light', but this interpretation, though pleasingly ironical, is strictly relevant only to Silius' boasting a decade previously (18.2), and, since the boasting was certainly provocative, the reference to 'crimes' loses its edge. It therefore seems more likely that the words mean 'recently discovered crimes', that is, factors previously considered innocent, praiseworthy or neutral were now being regarded as criminal, namely the friendship and hatred of the 'wrong' people (18.1, 19.1), and a successful military record (18.1).[46] The novelty of these 'crimes' (cf. 34.1n. *nouo*) is emphasised by its chiastic juxtaposition with the antiquity of the language (the last *s.c.u.* had been passed in 40 BC, more than sixty years previously).

Although the phrase *prisca uerba* (or sing.) is not uncommon (e.g. Cic. *De Or.* 3.153, *Brut.* 83, *Leg.* 2.18, Liv. 7.3.5, Sen. *Ep.* 108.35), it was famously used by Asinius Pollio in his criticism of Sallust (Suet. *Gram.* 10.2 'Sallustii scripta reprehendit ut nimia priscorum uerborum adfectatione oblita'), which was later repeated in identical terms by Lenaeus as quoted by Suetonius (ibid. 15.2 'priscorum . . . uerborum ineruditissimum furem'): this suggests that in the preceding sentence we are intended to see an allusion to Sallust's account of the Catilinarian conspiracy.

19.3 quasi aut legibus cum Silio ageretur aut Varro consul aut illud res publica esset The charade of Silius' trial is memorably emphasised by a counterfactual denial of three key points which were in fact true. (1) Silius was indeed involved in a due legal process (4 below), but his 'real' crimes (last n.) were beyond the law. (2) Varro was indeed consul (17.1), but he was not acting on his own authority (19.1 'inmissusque Varro consul'). (3) The imperial system was routinely referred to as the *res publica* (e.g.

---

[46] The words cannot of course refer to the crimes with which Silius was actually charged (4 below), since there is nothing novel about them.

above, 1.1, 6.1), but it was a different *res publica* from that invoked in the *senatus consultum ultimum* (19.2).[47] *illud* is here rendered contemptuous by the lack of attraction to *res publica* (for which see 1.49.2n.).

cuius ira premeretur The expr. is exclusively poetical (Ov. *Tr.* 1.5.78, Sen. *Med.* 462–3, *HO* 441, Val. Fl. 4.474); likewise *coeptaret* above is 'largely poetical' (1.38.1n.). *cuius* presumably refers to Sejanus.

19.4 conscientia belli Sacrouir *diu* dissimulatus 'The lengthy cover-up of Sacrovir through complicity in his war': for the substantival use of the nomin. perf. part., which features also in the next colon, see 3.24.1n. Ironically, it was Tib. who had procrastinated at the start of the war and had then embarked on a cover-up, not informing the senate until the war was successfully concluded (3.41.3, 3.47.1).

uictoria . . . foedata et uxor socia There is no trace of such misbehaviour in T.'s account. For *uictoria . . . foedata* cf. Flor. 1.1 (= 1.3.5).

Nec dubie repetundarum criminibus haerebant Latin, like English, can speak of a charge 'sticking' (Cic. *Cael.* 15 'crimen non haerebat'); the converse, of an accused 'sticking to' a charge, seems unparalleled. The nearest meaning is perhaps *OLD* 6b 'to be tied to ~ ', i.e. could not be separated from the charges; whether *criminibus* is abl. or dat. is unclear.

T. nowhere says that Silius was guilty of complicity with Sacrovir, despite Rutledge's repeated statements to this effect (141–2); on the contrary, *nec dubie* implies that in T.'s opinion the charge of complicity was *un*justified, which certainly seems borne out by Tib.'s statement to the senate at the time (3.47.1): 'fide ac uirtute legatos . . . superfuisse'.

sed cuncta quaestione maiestatis exercita Translators are unanimous in their rendering of this sentence: 'the entire case was handled as an impeachment for treason' (Jackson), 'everything was conducted on the basis of the treason question' (Woodman), 'everything was handled as a case of treason' (Damon), 'everything was conducted as a treason trial' (Yardley). The problem is that in the Latin there is no word for 'as' or 'on the basis of'; indeed it is difficult to see how the words can mean anything other than 'Everything was administered/enforced by the treason court' (for *exercita* see *OLD exerceo* 8a, and for the abl. *quaestione* cf. e.g. Cic. *Clu.* 155);[48] yet how can this be, since we have already been informed in §3 that the trial took place in

---

[47] *res publica* = 'the Republic' is interestingly rare in T., but our passage should be added to the three listed in G–G 1395a (top), from which 1.3.7n. derives.

[48] Furneaux renders 'the whole case was conducted on the charge of treason', but *quaestio* does not mean 'charge' and in any case it is difficult to make sense of his English.

the senate? The answer seems to emerge from a passage of the *SCPP*, where the senate's verdict of exile (on the elder Piso's associates) is to be administered by the praetor in charge of the treason court (lines 121–2): 'socis et ministris aqua et igne interdici oportere ab eo pr(aetore) qui lege maiestatis quaereret'. This passage has been discussed by J. S. Richardson ('The senate, the courts, and the *SC de Cn. Pisone patre*', *CQ* 47 (1997) 510–18, at 515–17), who envisages a two-stage legal process of which the first is the trial in the senate: 'Much, of course, remains uncertain about the working of such a process. We cannot know, for instance, whether the praetor had to empanel jurors for the *quaestio* or whether, once the court was in session, he took the decision of the senate as equivalent to the votes of the jurors' (517). T.'s account of the trial of Silius and his wife, with its reference to the *quaestio maiestatis*, suggests that the former possibility is correct. See also 6.2n. above and 22.2n. below. Here the contrast (*sed*) with the charges of *repetundae* may even imply that that *quaestio* too was still available for charges of extortion, although not used in Silius' case; or T. may simply have in mind the panel of *reciperatores* referred to at 1.74.6 (n.).

20.1 Saeuitum tamen in bona *tamen* suggests an expectation that Silius' property would remain untouched, as seems certainly to have been the case with pre-emptive suicides ten years later in 34 (6.29.1 'eorum qui de se statuebant . . . manebant testamenta'); yet a formal proposal to this effect later in the narrative of 24 would be quashed by Tib. (4.30.2), the property of Libo Drusus had been divided amongst his accusers in 16 (2.32.1 and n.), and a part of Cn. Calpurnius Piso's estate had ended up being confiscated in 20 (3.17.4 and n.). It is not clear what conclusions should be drawn from this apparently conflicting evidence. For the 'biting verb' *saeuitum* see Ash on *H.* 2.62.1.

stipendiariis i.e. those who paid tribute in the form of cash (*OLD* 2a).

sed liberalitas Augusti auulsa, computatis singillatim quae fisco petebantur On the assumption that the fiscus' demands were considerably more sweeping than, as opposed to coextensive with, Augustus' gift to Silius, we might have expected *computatis . . . petebantur* to be the main clause and *liberalitas . . . auulsa* to be an abl. abs.: as at 34.5 (n.) and 64.3 (n.), T. has evidently transposed two ideas. There is a similar singling out of Augustus' generosity, but to different effect, in the case of Piso (cf. *SCPP* 84–6 'utiq(ue) bona Cn. Pisonis patris publicarentur, excepto saltu qui esset in Hillyrico; eum saltum placere Ti. Caesari Augusto principi nostro, cuius a patre diuo Aug(usto) Cn. Pisoni patri donatus erat, reddi', with Eck et al. 202–7, esp. 203 and n. 588). For the more concrete sense of *liberalitas* = 'gift' see 2.37.1n. As with Piso and Libo Drusus (2.32.1n., 6.2.1n.), Silius' images were ordered to be destroyed (11.35.1 and Malloch's n.). For the fiscus see 6.2.1n. (*tamquam*).

Sörbom (128) notes that the transition from a consecutive clause to a main clause is unique, but *non ut stipendiariis pecuniae redderentur* is more naturally taken as purposive. For the simple *petebantur* after *repetebat* just above see 3.29.1n., 6.31.2n.

Ea prima Tiberio erga pecuniam alienam diligentia fuit This statement looks back to those at 3.18.1 'satis firmus . . . aduersum pecuniam' (on the occasion of Tib.'s returning the elder Piso's property to his younger son) and 2.48.2 'neque hereditatem cuiusquam adiit, nisi cum amicitia meruissset' (n.). In addition the senate had agreed not to confiscate the property of the exiled Lepida (3.23.2), while Tib. had assented to the concession proposed in the case of the exiled Silanus (3.68.2). For the recording of 'firsts' (again at 1.1 above) see 6.1.2n. The combination of *diligentia*, here used 'with some irony' (Furneaux), and *erga* is Ciceronian (*Verr.* 5.161, *Fam.* 10.12.5: both personal).

Asinii Galli See 6.23.1n.

partem bonorum publicandam, pars ut liberis relinqueretur The property is that of Sosia exclusively; *partem . . . pars* = 'half . . . half', as at 3.17.4, where there is the same variation of construction (n.).

20.2 M. Lepidus See 6.27.4nn.

legis The Lex Iulia de maiestate.

liberis One of them was the C. Silius who features prominently in Book 11 (see Malloch on 11.5.3).

Hunc ego Lepidum ... grauem et sapientem uirum fuisse comperior Although the combination of *grauis* and *sapiens* is restricted almost exclusively to Cicero, in whom it is very frequent (e.g. *TD* 3.48 'uir grauis et sapiens'), scholars infer from the sentence as a whole that T. is alluding to Sallust's description of Q. Metellus Numidicus, the consul of 109 BC, as he restores discipline in the Roman camp in Africa (*J.* 45.1): 'Metellum ... magnum *et sapientem uirum fuisse comperior*: tanta temperantia *inter* ambitionem saeuitiamque moderatum' (see further below).[49] The deponent form *comperior* (only here in T. and very rare elsewhere) also suggests Sallust (cf. *J.* 108.3 'sed *ego comperior*'), while *sapiens* is used nowhere else of an individual by Sallust or T. (except ironically in a speech of Nero's at 14.56.2). The Sallustian allusions continue into §3 and link the description of Lepidus here to the more generalised speculations there.

pleraque ab saeuis adulationibus aliorum in melius flexit *saeuis* seems to sustain the allusion to Sallust's description of Metellus (last n.); the

---

[49] Sallust's *moderatum* is deployed in T.'s obituary for Lepidus at 6.27.4 'moderatione atque sapientia'.

adj., paradoxical with *adulationibus*, implies that men sought to flatter Tib. or Sejanus by advocating *saeuitia* towards their victims. *in melius flectere* is Senecan (*NQ* 3. *pr.* 8, *HF* 1065): the verb, while indicating the direction of Lepidus' influence ('ab . . . in . . .'), also suggests the successful operation of one of the three *officia* of the ideal orator (Cic. *Orat.* 69): 'erit igitur eloquens . . . is qui in foro causisque ciuilibus ita dicet ut probet, ut delectet, ut flectat . . . flectere uictoriae [sc. est].'

neque t̲a̲m̲e̲n̲ temperamenti egebat, cum aequabili auctoritate et gratia apud Tiberium u̲i̲g̲u̲e̲r̲i̲t̲ 'nor yet did he lack moderation, since he prospered in consistent influence and favour with Tiberius': that is, although he objected actively to *adulatio* ('pleraque . . . flexit'), he was nevertheless consistently in the *princeps'* good books and so could be described as a man of moderation or balance, able to follow a middle way between the two extremes of behaviour elaborated below (3n.).[50] He resembled T.'s own father-in-law, Agricola (*Agr.* 42.3–4 and nn.), a comparison which has often been made.[51]

auctoritate et gratia probably refers above all to the speech of Lepidus at 3.50, which symbolises his *temperamentum*, is heavily Sallustian in style, and is praised by Tib. (see nn. ad loc.). *auctoritas* and *gratia* (each of which is regularly constructed with *apud*) are commonly combined, esp. in Cicero, but *aequabili*, like *tamen*, derives from Sallust's introduction of Metellus (*J.* 43.1): 'uiro . . . fama *tamen aequabili* et inuiolata' (for *temperamenti* see above). The gen. with *egeo* is also a feature of Sallust, Cicero much preferring the abl. (K–S 1.468).

20.3 fato et sorte nascendi, ut cetera, ita principum inclinatio in hos, offensio in illos, an sit aliquid in nostris consiliis *sit* needs to be supplied in the first alternative from the second. The (unparalleled) co-ordination of *sors nascendi* (a common phrase) with *fato* indicates that T. is referring to the Stoic belief in fatalism; the question he is asking himself is whether an emperor's attitude to individuals is predetermined at birth or whether there is a role for individuals' own decision-making. Although these are presented as alternatives, the latter is in fact also compatible with Stoic belief, since Stoics thought that our lives have an element of self-determination about them and that we have the freedom to change our

---

[50] Some scholars (e.g. G–G 338a, Pfitzner, Draeger–Heraeus, Nipperdey–Andresen) prefer the interpretation 'he did not need to be moderate', pointing to the use of the verb at 13.3.2; but this changes Lepidus' character entirely and does not square with *grauem et sapientem uirum* above.

[51] Agricola but not Lepidus features in the discussion of T.'s use of *moderatio* and the like by K. Scheidle, *Modus optumum: die Bedeutung des 'rechten Masses' in der römischen Literatur (Republik–frühe Kaiserzeit), untersucht an den Begriffen modus–modestia–moderatio–temperantia* (1993) 139–64.

dispositions, and hence our tendency to behave in certain ways, even though we are doing so within a universe where the overall constitution of our minds and the outcomes of our actions are both predetermined (for discussion see S. Bobzien, *Determinism and freedom in Stoic philosophy* (1998) 258–71, 290–301): see esp. Sen. *NQ* 2.38.3 'quemadmodum manente fato *aliquid sit in* hominis arbitrio' (and Zimmermann 14–15). T.'s alternative questions are thus not mutually exclusive, but the really interesting feature of his wording is the phrase *ut cetera*: if (as seems to be the case) his doubt is focussed on the relationship between *principes* and individuals, *ut cetera* indicates that in T.'s opinion other areas of life are predetermined. See further 6.22 and nn.

liceatque inter abruptam contumaciam et deforme obsequium pergere iter ambitione ac periculis uacuum It was a feature of popular as well as peripatetic philosophy to say that virtue was positioned in the middle of two extremes (e.g. Arist. *EN* 1109a21, Hor. *Epist.* 1.18.9 'uirtus est medium uitiorum et utrimque reductum'; N–H on *C.* 2.10.5, Tosi 783–4 §§ 1756–8), but, given the Sallustian context, the notion of picking one's metaphorical way between two extremes probably derives in this instance from Sallust's description of Metellus (above, 2n.): '*inter* . . . moderatum' (for the metaphorical path of virtue see e.g. Fantham 70–1, Rutherford 176 and n. 138, N–R on Hor. *C.* 3.24.44). *pergere iter*, though occasionally found elsewhere (see 3.66.4n.), is used by Sallust at *J.* 79.5 (though not of Metellus), and for the combination of *ambitio* and *periculum* see Sall. *H.* 5.23 M(19 R). *uacuus* is the *mot juste* for an unobstructed road (*H.* 3.16.2, Caes. *BG* 2.12.2, Curt. 5.4.16, Val. Fl. 2.454–5), which here has the precipitous cliff of *contumacia* on one side (*OLD abruptus* 1) and the wasteland of *obsequium* on the other (*OLD deformis* 2b): there is a similar contrast, but lacking the metaphor, at *H.* 4.74.4 'ne contumaciam cum pernicie quam obsequium cum securitate malitis' (cf. Fronto p. 53.20 vdH[2]); and note also *Agr.* 42.4n. *contumaciam et . . . obsequium* corresponds chiastically to *ambitione ac periculis* in a form of 'double zeugma' (for which see 5.4.4n.); for *contumacia* see 12.3n.

20.4 At Messalinus Cotta For the polyonymous Cotta, consul in 20, see 2.32.1n., 3.2.3n.; *BNP* 2.384–5 [II 13]; he will feature prominently in Books 5 and 6. *at* seems not to have a resumptive function; here it serves merely to contrast Cotta with Lepidus (further, next n.).

haud minus claris maioribus sc. *quam Lepidus*. Although Lepidus' ancestry was distinguished, as T. will point out in his obituary notice (6.27.4), it seems rather odd to introduce Cotta here by comparing an ancestry which has not been mentioned – especially since ancestry seems irrelevant to the issue of gubernatorial responsibility. Cotta was the younger son of the famous Messala Corvinus (cos. 31 BC), who himself was the son of the consul of 61 BC, and an

Aurelia (Syme, *AA* Table IX). Lepidus was the son of Paullus Aemilius Lepidus (cos. 34 BC), the son of the consul of 50 BC (*AA* Table IV).

censuit cauendum senatus consulto T. omits to say that the *s.c.* was passed (Talbert 439 no. 24), although his interest in questions affecting the wives of senatorial governors is already clear from 3.33–4 (see nn.).

insontes See 3.67.2n.

culpae alienae nescii *aliena culpa* is perhaps a legal expr. (H. on *H.* 2.39.1 with some further exs.), although T. has here uniquely transposed the two words. *culpae nescius* recurs only at 4.26.2 below, although it is found in the *recentiores* of Virg. *Aen.* 12.648; for *nescius* see 13.3n. above.

proinde See above, 17.1n.

21.1 Calpurnio Pisone Piso the Augur (cos. 1 BC) and brother of the treasonable Piso: see 2.34.1n., 3.11.2n.; Rüpke 593 no. 1053. His son is killed at 45.1 below (n.).

nobili ac feroci uiro Piso's father, Cn. Calpurnius Piso, had been suffect in 23 BC (*AA* Table XXV); from him Piso inherited his defiance (2.43.2 'insita ferocia a patre Pisone'), which placed him near the *contumacia* end of the spectrum described at 20.3 just above: cf. Sen. *Cons. Helv.* 17.1 'ferox enim et . . . contumax'.

namque 'A word of elevated style . . . In ordinary prose of the late Republic and early Empire it is found only rarely . . ., and then usually before vowels. However, the poets . . . and certain archaizers use it freely' (Adams (1973) 142 n. 78). T. uses it throughout the *Annals* but less often than in the *Histories*. Livy is the first to place it as second word; he is followed by various other authors.

ut rettuli See 2.34 for both stories. For cross-references see 3.18.1n.

ob factiones accusatorum . . . clamitauerat *factiones* is here taken by Furneaux and Koestermann to mean 'intrigues', as also in *TLL* 1.135.8–11, but the parallels quoted in the latter (Sall. *C.* 34.2, Sen. *Ben.* 4.12.2) do not bear out such a meaning, which is in fact not recognised in *OLD*. The alternatives seem to be 'cliques' (*OLD* 4a), as if mirroring the political divisions alleged to exist in society as a whole (17.3), or 'groups, companies' (*OLD* 3), as if forming rival professional bodies; the one parallel for the expr. (Cic. *Brut.* 164 'in accusatorum factionem') is not much help. Like Sallust (and Velleius) T. never uses *clamo* (see *TLL* 3.1249.21–9).

Vrgulania A friend of Livia (22.2, 2.34.2) and paternal grandmother of Plautius Silvanus below (22.1–2): see *PIR* 8.2.535–6 no. 1010.

Quae ... ciuiliter habuit Cf. 3.76.2 'quod ciuiliter acceptum'; further exs. at 3.12.2n.

animo reuoluente Senecan (*Ag.* 164, *Med.* 466, *Oed.* 764); Curt. 4.10.31 is different.

etiam si impetus offensionis languerat, memoria ualebat *impetus* is regularly used of the violence of an illness (*TLL* 7.1.608.36ff.; *OLD* 3b) and *offensio* can refer to the 'attack' of an illness (*TLL* 9.2.497.59–74; *OLD* 3); *languesco*, normally used of ill persons 'wilting' *vel sim.*, can also be used of a decrease in pain (Cic. *TD* 2.31; cf. *TLL* 7.2.923.56ff.), while *ualere* is commonly used in various medical contexts. Tib.'s characteristic reaction to slights (cf. 18.2n., above) is here described as an acute illness with a tenacious after-effect: 'even if the violence of the attack had abated, the memory of it remained strong'. Note also *Agr.* 39.3 (n.).

21.2 Q. Veranius See 2.56.4n. and 3.10.1n. (where the statement that 'nothing further is heard of Veranius' requires deletion); also *PIR* 8.2.201 no. 388 (but not listing the present passage), *BNP* 15.290 [2], Syme, *TST* 54–5.

secreti sermonis incusauit ... habiti For the 'verbal hyperbaton' see 3.1.1n.

gladio accinctum introire curiam It was forbidden to enter the senate house bearing arms (Talbert 157–60).

ceterorum ... receptus est reus neque peractus 'he was listed as a defendant on the other charges but not prosecuted': the language is legalistic (*OLD reus* 2c, 3). No details of the charges are known, but an inscription from Samos, in which the names of Piso and his wife have been erased, suggests 'rapacity in a province' (Syme, *AA* 376; cf. 337).

ob mortem opportunam alludes to the topos *opportunitas mortis* (*Agr.* 45.3n.). Editors compare Liv. 6.1.7 'iudicio eum mors adeo opportuna ut uoluntariam magna pars crederet subtraxit' (see Oakley's n.).

21.3 Cassio Seuero exule One of the principal orators of Augustus' day and famous for his aggression, he had been exiled in AD 8 or 12: it is usually thought that the charge was *maiestas* (1.72.3 and n.; Syme, *AA* 409–12, Rutledge 209–12), but see 4.34.2n. (below) for some doubts.

sordidae ... orandi ualidus The brief sketch is quasi-chiastic and varied. *sordida origo* is surprisingly rare (only Suet. *Vit.* 1.1); *malefica uita* is unparalleled; and *ualidus* + gen. seems to be an innovation of T.'s (L–H–S 77). For Cassius' strength as a speaker cf. Sen. *Contr.* 3 *praef.* 2 'oratio eius erat ualens'.

ut iudicio iurati senatus Cretam amoueretur effecerat The irony
that Severus brought his fate upon himself is underlined linguistically by the
anagram linking his actions and his destination. '*amouere* = "banish" is pecu-
liarly Tacitean' (1.53.4n.), in this case referring to *relegatio* (see n. *bonisque*
below). For senatorial oaths see Talbert 261–2; for *iuratus* ('having sworn an
oath') of the senate see Briscoe on Liv. 42.21.5, adding Cic. *Flacc.* 17.

illic eadem factitando M reads *actitando*, but in the sense of 'keep on
doing' this verb does not otherwise occur until very late Latin (*TLL*
1.444.78ff.).[52] *factitare*, on the other hand, has the right nuance (e.g. *H.* 2.10.1
'delationes factitauerat', Cic. *Brut.* 130 'accusationem factitauerit') and again
has the same object at 2.59.1 'eadem factitauisse apud Siciliam' and the same
adv. at 6.39.1 'carmina illic in principem factitata'.

recentia ueteraque odia aduertit *uetus odium*, first in Cicero (e.g. *Sest.* 46)
and then in a sprinkling of other authors, is esp. common in Livy and, tellingly,
T. (4.12.3, 4.29.2, 13.37.3, 15.2.1, 15.52.3, *H.* 1.72.3, 3.32.1); *recens odium* (again at
1.1.2, *H.* 4.1.2) is Livian (4.40.4). With *aduertit* we have to understand *in se*, 'he
drew upon himself'.

**bonisque exutus, interdicto igni atque aqua, saxo Seripho
consenuit** The regular phrase with *interdicere* is *aqua et igni*; although T.'s
frequent substitution of *atque* (for which see below) is not unique (cf. Caes. *BG*
6.44.3), and, although he is not alone in changing the order of water and fire
(cf. Lucil. 787), no other author combines both of these variations or uses an
abl. abs. (again at 6.30.1). See *TLL* 7.1.2174.47–59, and note also H. Heumann
and E. Seckel, *Handlexikon zu den Quellen des römischen Rechts* (1907) 279.[53]

Since the purpose of interdiction was 'to prohibit the re-entry of exiles into
Roman territory on pain of death' (Garnsey 112), *aquae et ignis interdictio* pre-
supposes, and is virtually a synonym of, *exilium*. There were, however, two
categories of exile in the early principate, non-capital (*relegatio*) and capital
(*deportatio*), and it can be difficult to decide which category is being referred to
in any given case (see further above, 13.2n.). T. refers to interdiction on nine

---

[52] The normal meanings of the verb are 'to plead frequently' and 'to act in
plays' (*OLD* 2–3).

[53] The nominal form *aquae et ignis interdictio* is sometimes found with an
ablative instead of a genitive, although the matter is complicated by variant
readings and editorial adjustments (*TLL* 7.1.2178.19–28). *interdictus* is quite
often used by modern scholars to refer to an exile, and is restored in the
Venafro fragment of the Lex Pedia (Crawford 1.459), but the form is
naturally extremely rare (*TLL* 7.1.2175.62–71). See also Y. Rivière,
'L'interdiction de l'eau, du feu . . . et du toit (sens et origine de la désigna-
tion du bannissement chez les romains)', *RPh* 87 (2013) 125–55.

occasions, all of them in the *Annals*. (a) On four occasions interdiction is mentioned without further qualification (3.23.2 'itumque in sententiam Rubelli Blandi, a quo aqua et igni arcebatur' (but see further (b) below), 6.18.1 'sorori eius Sanciae aqua atque igni interdictum', 12.42.3 'ut accusatori aqua atque igni interdiceret', 16.12.1 'aqua et igni prohibitus est'). (b) On one occasion interdiction is mentioned alongside loss of property (3.50.4 'cedat tamen urbe et bonis amissis aqua et igni arceatur'). Does this exhortation imply that loss of property was extra to, or an integral part of, interdiction? The passage at 3.23.2, quoted above, is followed by the statement *mox Scauro ... datum ne bona publicarentur*; the likely interpretation here is that interdiction did indeed involve loss of property but that on this occasion, thanks to Scaurus' intervention, the victim would be allowed to retain his property; but it is also possible that Scaurus was responding to a separate *sententia*, proposed subsequently, which T. has omitted to mention. (c) Banishment to an island is mentioned alongside interdiction on three occasions (3.38.2 'aqua et igni interdictum reo, adpositumque ut teneretur insula', 3.68.2 'aqua atque igni Silano interdicendum censuit ipsumque in insulam Gyarum relegandum', 6.30.1 'in insulas interdicto igni atque aqua demoti sunt'). The specifying of island exile implies that T. is here referring to *deportatio*, which automatically deprived the victim of citizenship and property (cf. Ulp. *Dig.* 48.22.14.1 'deportatio et ciuitatem et bona adimit').[54] (d) In the present case the explicit reference to loss of property, along with the implied reference to island banishment, again implies *deportatio*, from which it is to be inferred that Severus' previous and less severe banishment to the province of Crete fell into the category of *relegatio* (see above). For further discussion of the terminology see e.g. Garnsey 111–22 and Drogula 231–5 and the bibliography cited by each, adding M. Peachin, *HSCP* 96 (1994) 322–4. P. Treves has argued that *consenescere* is an almost technical verb meaning 'to die in exile' (*AJP* 63 (1942) 129–53, pp. 136–7 for our passage).

The plain abl. *saxo Seripho* varies the normal construction for appositional nouns as found at 2.85.3 'in insulam Seriphon abdita est' (evidently the only other record of banishment to this island: see Drogula 265). Seriphos is one of the Cyclades; its rockiness is perhaps implied by Seneca (*Cons. Helv.* 6.4), who describes Corsica (his own place of exile) as 'huius aridi et spinosi saxi' (ibid. 7.9), and by Juvenal (10.170 'Gyarae clausus scopulis paruaque Seripho').

22.1 Per idem tempus See 3.29.1n., 6.10.1n.

---

[54] The use of *relegare* at 3.68.2 presumably illustrates T.'s habit of 'misusing' technical terminology (see *Ann. 3*, p. 503; *Ann. 5–6*, p. 319: s.v. 'technical ... language').

Plautius Siluanus praetor Son of the homonymous consul of 2 BC and known from an inscription to be urban praetor: see *RE* 21.33 = Plautius 44 (Hofmann), *PIR* 6.195–6 no. 479, *BNP* 11.360–1 [II 13]; for his wife see Raepsaet-Charlier 101–2 no. 86.

Aproniam coniugem in praeceps iecit G. Maggiulli ('"Saevius Plautus" o "Plautius Silvanus"?', *GIF* 30 (1978) 73–8) and B. W. Hicks ('The prosecution of M. Plautius Silvanus', *Anc. Hist. Bull.* 27 (2013) 55–64) have suggested between them (i) that Plautius Silvanus is identical with the Saevius Plautus who is said by St Jerome to have been accused of incest with his son in this same year and committed suicide (*Chron.* p. 172 Helm), (ii) that incest came under the heading of *stuprum*, and (iii) that the accused was charged with *stuprum* as well as murder.

tractusque ad Caesarem ab L. Apronio socero 'Strictly speaking, charges against magistrates and holders of official posts, or those designated to them, were inadmissible unless the accused could be persuaded or forced to resign first. But . . . exceptional instances are known' (Talbert 481, quoting five exs. in addition to our passage; cf. also E. J. Weinrib, 'The prosecution of Roman magistrates', *Phoenix* 22 (1968) 32–56, at 48–9 n. 65). One of the exceptional instances occurred in AD 10, when a quaestor was due in court charged with murder; but, when the man's accuser heard that the popular Germanicus was due to appear on the man's behalf, he was afraid 'that he would lose his suit before the judges who regularly heard such cases' and he therefore wished the trial to be held before the *princeps* (Dio 56.27.4, with Swan ad loc.). Evidently Apronius too thought that a direct approach to Tib. would stand more chance of success (cf. 1.75.1 'multaque eo [sc. Tiberio] coram aduersus ambitum et potentium preces constituta'). Cf. 3.10.2 'petitumque est a principe cognitionem exciperet', where, however, the circumstances are unclear (see n.); note also 3.38.2, 3.70.1–3. For Apronius see above, 13.3n.

turbata mente is a set phrase for being 'of disturbed mind' (again at 13.3.2).

tamquam . . . uxor sponte mortem sumpsisset As elsewhere (e.g. 10.3), it is not clear whether *tamquam* = 'that' or 'as if'. For the method of suicide alleged here see 6.49.1 'iacto in praeceps corpore' and n.: the question 'did she fall or was she pushed?' is said by Quintilian to be popular with declaimers; he himself spoke in a genuine case involving the same issue (7.2.24 'quaesitum, praecipitata esset ab eo uxor an se ipsa sua sponte iecisset'). *uxor* varies *coniugem* above (Sörbom 17): for discussion of the two terms see 3.33.1n. The expr. *mortem sumere* (again at 2.66.1, 3.50.2, 14.7.6) seems peculiar to T.

22.2 Non cunctanter Tiberius . . . The role of Tib. as private investigator seems odd, but cf. 3.23.2 'aperuit Tiberius compertum sibi' (and 3.67.2).

Refert ad senatum As he did when asked to take on the case of Calpurnius Piso (see above, iii.): 3.10.3 'integramque causam ad senatum remittit'.

datisque iudicibus This expression, which is not uncommon (*TLL* 7.2.598.72ff.), is generally used of the empanelling of jurors for a *quaestio*. It used to be thought that from Tib.'s reign onwards charges of *maiestas*, *saeuitia* and *repetundae* were heard by the full senate without reference elsewhere, and Talbert stated that 'There is no parallel for the senate referring to a panel the murder charge against the praetor of 24, Plautius Silvanus' (465 and n. 36). But the evidence of *SCPP* now suggests that, at least in cases of *maiestas*, at this date there was a two-stage legal process of senate followed by *quaestio* (cf. 19.4n. above): evidently a similar process may have been in operation in the present case.

Vrgulania See 21.iii.

22.3 uenas praebuit exsoluendas sc. *seruo* (presumably: cf. 2.31.1). *uenas exsoluere* is peculiar to T. (again at 11.3.2, 14.64.2, 16.17.5).

Numantina Fabia Numantina was daughter of Paullus Fabius Maximus (cos. 11 BC), sister of Paullus Fabius Persicus (cos. AD 34: 6.28.1n.), and some-time wife of Sex. Appuleius (cos. AD 14: 1.7.2n.): see *AA* 418 and Table XXVII; *BNP* 5.286 [5]; Raepsaet-Charlier 308–9 no. 353.

accusata iniecisse . . . uecordiam marito She was accused under the Lex Cornelia de sicariis et ueneficiis (Garnsey 26 n. 5); *marito* = 'former husband'. *accusari* + infin. is found earlier only in *Rhet. Herenn.* 2.43 (*TLL* 1.352.23–6); *iniicere uecordiam* is unparalleled, but cf. *H.* 3.10.4 'furorem . . . inicerent', Liv. 21.48.3 'uelut iniecta rabie', *HA Comm. Ant.* 8.6 'furor . . . iniectus'. *carminibus et ueneficiis* (again at Ov. *RA* 290) is perhaps a more recherché version of the combination with *uenenum* (Hor. *S.* 1.8.19, Juv. 6.133, Apul. *Ap.* 69, 90).

23–26 Victory in Africa
War against the Numidian chief Tacfarinas had begun seven years earlier in 17 (2.52) and T. had given accounts of the fighting in 20 (3.20–1) and 22 (3.72.4–74). No doubt he could have dismissed the end of the war with a brief statement or two, in the same way as he reported on the fighting of 21 (3.32.1, 35.1), but, as the elder Pliny said, Africa was proverbially a place of interest (*NH* 8.42 'uulgare Graeciae dictum, semper aliquid noui Africam adferre').[55]

---

[55] Pliny's reference is to Arist. *Hist. Anim.* 606b20 and *Gen. Anim.* 746b7: see H. M. Feinberg and J. B. Solodow, 'Out of Africa', *Journal of African History* 43 (2002) 255–61.

From Africa had come Hannibal and Jugurtha, enemies immortalised by Livy and Sallust respectively, and the defeat of Tacfarinas provided T. with an excellent opportunity of returning to the subject from a new angle: he uses the victory to illustrate the ironic paradoxes of Tib.'s reign and to continue reminding readers of the growing influence of Sejanus.

The episode begins with reference to the three previous commanders who had failed to conquer the enemy but who had nevertheless received public recognition (23.1); it ends, ring fashion, with the present commander, Cornelius Dolabella, who successfully concluded the war but whom Tib., in deference to Sejanus, refused to reward (26.1). Conversely Ptolemy, the king whose initial lethargy had led to his Mauri swelling Tacfarinas' ranks (23.1), was decorated with full and ancient honours (26.2). Within this frame T. constructs a military narrative which above all evokes Sallust. Although there are occasional allusions to the *Bellum Catilinae* and *Historiae* (as indeed to Livy too), by far the majority of the allusions are to the *Bellum Iugurthinum* and to two episodes in particular: Jugurtha's fight against Adherbal near the start of the narrative (*J.* 20–1) and Marius' successful operations near the end (99–101). And Marius, as T.'s readers are expected to remember, was rewarded with a triumph (104 BC).

23.1 annus ... longo ... bello absoluit For earlier episodes of the war see nn. on 2.52.1, 3.20–1 and 3.72.4–74. T. regularly makes *annus* subject of a transitive verb (6.45.1n.), but this precise usage of *absoluere* ('release a person from ~ ') is hard to parallel: the nearest meaning is perhaps judicial, 'acquit a person of ~ ' (*OLD* 2; cf. 4).

hostem omittebant 'discounted the enemy' (*OLD omitto* 6a). The topos of fraudulent victories (3.74.4n.) was a natural source of sarcasm.

tres laureatae ... statuae Of Furius Camillus (2.52.5), L. Apronius (3.21, but no award mentioned) and Iunius Blaesus (3.72.4). For triumphal statues (again at *Agr.* 40.1) see M. Beard, *The Roman triumph* (2007) 70, referring to Dio 55.10.3 and Swan's n.; *laureata* is not elsewhere found with *statua*, but for *imago* cf. Cic. *Mur.* 88.

raptabat Africam Tacfarinas The verb, perhaps on the analogy of *trahere* (3.74.2n.), here = 'plundered, ravaged', for which the only parallels quoted are 12.54.3 and Stat. *Theb.* 6.115 (*TLL* 11.2.120.30–3, *OLD* 4).

auctus ... auxiliis See 6.34.1n.

Ptolemaeo Iubae filio The son of Juba II (5.2n.); on his execution in 40 (cf. Suet. *Cal.* 35.1, Dio 59.25.1) Mauretania became a Roman province. See *RE* 23.1768–87 = Ptolemaeus 62 (Hofmann), *PIR* 6.429–30 no. 1025, *BNP* 12.151 [24].

libertos regios et seruilia imperia bello mutauerant A chiastic hendiadys: 'had exchanged the servile orders of the king's freedmen for war'. *seruilia* is focalised from the viewpoint of the Mauri; the expr. is Sallustian (1.11b.3 M = 1.10.3 R 'seruili imperio'). For *bello mutauerant* see 3.44.3n.

23.2 praedarum receptor ac socius populandi rex Garamantum Another chiasmus: *receptor* is extremely rare (elsewhere only at Cic. *Mil.* 50 in classical Latin) but illustrates T.'s well-known partiality to nouns in –*tor* (*Ann. 3*, p. 502, s.v. 'nouns'). The Garamantes were already helping Tacfarinas in 22 (3.74.2 and n.). The name of their king is unknown; for their territory see *BA* Map 36: C4, Map 37: A3.

non ut cum exercitu incederet sed missis leuibus copiis The words explain *socius populandi*: 'not with the result that he marched forth with an army but by sending light-armed forces' (the *uariatio* of consecutive clause ~ abl. abs. seems unparalleled even for T.: see Sörbom 120).

quae . . . in maius audiebantur Another Sallustian allusion (*H.* 2.69 M = 2.56 R 'haec . . . in maius . . . audiuit').

prouincia Africa.

ut quis = *ut quisque* (see 6.7.3n.).

ruebant sc. *ad Tacfarinatem*.

Blaeso Q. Iunius Blaesus (suff. 10) was Sejanus' uncle (3.35.1n.).

quasi nullis iam in Africa hostibus In other words, Tib. is as guilty as his generals (1 above). *quasi* + abl. abs. occurs elsewhere in T. (e.g. 14.22.1, 15.8.2) but is also found in other authors from Cicero onwards (E. B. Lease, 'The ablative absolute limited by conjunctions', *AJP* 49 (1928) 348–53).

nonam legionem See 5.2n. (*cetera*).

proconsule eius anni P. Dolabella Dolabella was governor in the current year, but T. often uses *is* in chronological contexts where we might have expected *hic* (e.g. 1.72.1, 3.31.2, 16.3.1). On Dolabella see 3.47.3nn., adding Vogel-Weidemann 85–92 no. 7.

incerta belli is Livian (30.2.6, 39.54.7).

24.1 disperso rumore For the expr. see H. on *H.* 2.96.2, adding Amm. 28.1.27 (his 'u. ö.' is mistaken).

lacerari eoque . . . decedere ac posse reliquos circumueniri si cuncti . . . incubuissent *lacerari* (cf. e.g. Val. Max. 9.12 *ext.* 9 'lacerandum feris', Petron. 115.18 'ferae tamen corpus lacerabunt') and *incubuissent* (cf. e.g. Gratt. 226–7 'atque hic egressu iam tum sine fraude reperto | incubuit', of

152

a hunting dog) suggest a hunting metaphor: Tacfarinas presents the Romans as animals forced to retreat (*decedere*) after their expedition has been mauled, while those who remain (he means Legio III: see 26.1n.) can be trapped (*circumueniri*) if the Africans hunt them down. The metaphor will prove ironically misguided, once the actual fighting starts (25.2n.).

quibus libertas seruitio potior T. alludes to a passage of Sallust (*H.* 1.55.26 M = 1.49.26 R 'potiorque uisa est periculosa libertas quieto seruitio') to which Livy had also alluded (35.17.9 'si non libertas seruitute potior sit'); cf. also Cic. *Phil.* 10.19 'mors . . . seruitute potior'. On T.'s use of *seruitium / seruitus* see 3.45.2n.

Thubursicum 'There can hardly be any doubt that the place besieged by Tacfarinas was Thubursicu Numidarum. Most students of Roman Africa will concur. What should be the behaviour of an editor of Tacitus? Palaeographically, the emendation is easy and seductive: *Thubu<r>s<i>cum* or *Thubur<si>cum* for *Thubuscum*' (Syme, *RP* 1.218ff., at 221). Thubursicum was about 45 miles south of Hippo Regius (*BA* Map 31: H4; *BNP* 14.631 [2]), and Syme's arguments in favour of Nipperdey's emendation are persuasive;[56] it should nevertheless be noted that, since many African toponyms begin *Thu-* (see *BA* Maps 31–2 and 34–5), it is quite possible that the transmitted *Thubuscum* correctly refers to a town which as yet remains unidentified.

oppidum circumsidet The two words are common and the phrase is naturally not exclusive to Sallust and T. (cf. e.g. Liv. 10.9.8, 41.11.2), but, since the section contains several echoes of the *Bellum Iugurthinum*, cf. 21.3 'oppidum circumsedit'.

24.2 quod erat militum 'such soldiers as there were', a reminder that Dolabella had just been deprived of half his forces. For the expr. see Ash on *H.* 2.55.1.

terrore nominis Romani et quia Numidae peditum aciem ferre nequeunt The tense of *nequeunt* indicates that Numidians retained their reputation (Liv. 24.48.5 'rudem ad pedestria bella Numidarum gentem esse, equis tantum habilem') in T.'s day, when they were employed in the Roman army. The *uariatio* of abl. ~ causal clause is common in T. (Sörbom 115) but also in other authors (e.g. Kraus or Oakley on Liv. 6.1.2). Elsewhere T. writes *Romanum nomen* in that order, as other authors mostly do; the present order is regular in Sallust and preferred by Livy.

---

[56] Syme notes correctly that *r* and *s* are frequently confused in M; it is perhaps worth adding that in the MS the word is divided between lines, as if the name were *thubus* and followed by the Latin word *cum*.

primo sui incessu *sui* has been questioned (one might have expected *suo* or no adj. at all) and Heinsius proposed *sub*. But the gen. of the reflexive pronoun is favoured by T. and perhaps emphasises Dolabella's decisiveness in contrast with the abortive operations of others (see e.g. 2.13.1n.; K–S 1.598–9, *OLS* 1.977–8). The arrival of a new general was always potentially significant (*Agr.* 18.3n.).

soluit obsidium For the expr. see 3.39.1n.

locorumque opportuna This type of partitive gen. is a favourite of T.'s (see *Ann. 3*, p. 501): for *opportuna* so used the only other ex. in *TLL* is Liv. 30.12.10 'opportuna . . . moenium' (9.2.777.7–10).

Musulamiorum A subdivision of the Gaetuli, inland from Hadrumetum and Thapsus (Syme, *RP* 1.220; *BA* Map 33: B1). Despite being nominally ruled by Tacfarinas, some of them evidently acknowledged allegiance to Rome.

defectionem coeptantes is an unparalleled expr. but analogous to *seditionem coeptare* (1.38.1, 1.45.2, 2.81.1) or *rebellionem coeptare* (3.40.1); the verb 'is much in favour with T.' (1.38.1n.).

securi percutit 'A Republican and consecrated term' (Syme, *Tac.* 725; cf. *TLL* 10.1.1239.69–74). For similar punishments see G. R. Watson, *The Roman soldier* (1969) 119–21, and note Oakley on Liv. 6.6.4–5 and 7.19.3; in general E. C. Kiesling, 'Corporal punishment in the Greek phalanx and the Roman legion', *Historical Reflections* 32 (2006) 233–46.

24.3 graui 'heavily armed' (*OLD* 2c).

consectandum hostem uagum Cf. Liv. 31.36.9 'ad consectandos uagos frumentatores', Val. Max. 3.2.22 'pertinacia in consectandis hostibus'.

excito i.e. to help Dolabella, after the indifference of 23.1 above.

quattuor agmina parat This had been Jugurtha's tactic at Sall. *J.* 101.3 'copias in quattuor partis distribuerat'.

legatis After the withdrawal of Legio IX (23.2) only one legion – and hence only one *legatus legionis* – remained (26.1n.).

praedatorias manus The same phrase is used at Sall. *J.* 20.7 of Jugurtha's habitual tactics (later at Amm. 21.3.1).

Ipse consultor aderat omnibus It was conventional to describe the ideal general both as intellectually capable (cf. esp. Sall. *J.* 85.47 'in agmine aut in proelio *consultor* idem et socius periculi uobiscum *adero*' (of Marius); also Vell. 79.1 'consultisque facta coniungens' (of Agrippa) and n.) and as omnipresent (cf. esp. Sall. *J.* 100.3 'apud *omnis adesse* . . . *ipse*' (again of

Marius); also *Agr.* 35.4n.).[57] T.'s liking for nouns in *–tor* is well known (above, 23.2n.): *consultor*, regular in Sallust (6×) but by no means restricted to him, is again combined with *adesse* at *J.* 103.7.

25.1 castellum semirutum In extant Latin *semirutus* (again at 1.61.2) first appears in Sall. *H.* 2.64 M (25 R) and is frequent (8×) in Livy (e.g. 28.44.9 'semiruta . . . castella'); it recurs in Lucan (2×) and Statius (*Silv.* 5.3.104), then in a selection of later authors (e.g. Amm.: 2×).

cui nomen Auzea 'This is presumably the fort Auzia (Aumale) in Mauretania, over 200 miles to the west of Thubursicu' (Syme, *RP* 1.221 n. 5). See *BA* Map 30: G4. For the regularity of naming in foreign narratives see 73.4n.

mapalibus See 3.74.3n.

uastis circum saltibus claudebatur *saltus*, a standard element of geographical descriptions (see e.g. N. Horsfall, *PBSR* 50 (1982) 45–52), are registered in Africa by the elder Pliny (*NH* 5.26 'saltus repleti ferarum multitudine'), while *saltuosa loca* feature in Sall. *J.* (38.1, 54.3). *uastus* (on which see *Agr.* 38.2n.) is a natural epithet (Curt. 3.10.2, Luc. 6.331, Sil. 17.578). It is hard to say whether *circum* is to be taken with *claudebatur* (synchesis) or quasi-adjectivally (L–H–S 171).

cito agmine is an exclusively Tacitean variant (again at 1.63.4, *H.* 3.71.1) on the Livian *citato agmine*.

25.2 concentū tŭbarum ac truci clamore For the first element of this chiastic, varied, alliterative and assonantal phrase cf. Liv. 9.41.17, Juv. 10.214–15 (slightly different at Plin. *NH* 8.75 and Gran. Licin. 28.16 Criniti); for the second cf. Liv. 7.23.6, Curt. 3.10.1; for the juxtaposition of *concentus* and *clamor* cf. *D.* 15.3, Curt. 7.11.25; for other exs. of chiastic alliteration in T. see W. Renz, 'Alliterationen bei Tacitus' (Aschaffenburg 1905) 27–8. The repetition *–tū tŭ–* (for which see 13.2n.) here creates an onomatopoeic echoing effect. See also Sall. *J.* 99.1, quoted next n.

aderant semisomnos in barbaros Attacks on a somnolent enemy (again at 1.51.1) are a feature of Livian narrative (9.37.9, 25.39.3, 30.5.10, 37.20.13), and the tactic is used by Jugurtha against Adherbal (Sall. *J.* 21.2 'obscuro etiam tum lumine milites Iugurthini . . . semisomnos . . . fugant funduntque'); but T. surely has in mind Marius' attack at *J.* 99.1 'ubi lux aduentabat, defessis iam hostibus ac paulo ante somno captis, de improuiso . . . cohortium,

---

[57] The misinterpretation of T.'s words by D. Fishwick and B. D. Shaw (*Historia* 25 (1976) 493) has been refuted by D. B. Saddington (*CQ* 28 (1978) 330–1) but without reference to the topos illustrated here.

turmarum, legionum tubicines simul omnis signa canere, milites clamorem tollere ... iubet' (see further on *non arma* below and 48.1n.). The position of *semisomnos* emphasises the Africans' unpreparedness (5.1.3n.). For *adesse* = 'be upon ~ ' see *OLD* 15.

praepeditis Numidarum equis The dangers of this practice were spelled out by Xenophon (*Cyr.* 3.3.27 πεποδισμένους γὰρ ἔχουσι τοὺς ἵππους ἐπὶ ταῖς φάτναις, καὶ εἴ τις ἐπ' αὐτοὺς ἴοι, ἔργον μὲν νυκτὸς λῦσαι ἵππους, *Anab.* 3.4.35). The verb is rare in its literal sense.

Ab Romanis 'On the Roman side' (K–S 1.492). For the *uariatio* with dat. *hostibus* below see Sörbom 81–2.

dispositae turmae The appropriate deployment of troops (as at Hirt. *BG* 8.19.1 'dispositis turmis', 28.2 'turmas partim idoneis locis disponit') was naturally an essential quality of the ideal general (e.g. Front. *Strat.* 2.3; Oakley on Liv. 9.17.15). A *turma* was a cavalry unit of c. thirty men (*BNP* 15.34); here there is a contrast with the concentrated infantry of the preceding colon.

cuncta *proelio prouisa* The third element of the tricolon crescendo (AB-AB-BA) relates to the conventional foresight of the ideal general (cf. 2.14.1): see esp. Sall. *J.* 100.3 'omnia prouidere' (of Marius: above, 24.3n. *ipse*), *C.* 60.4 'omnia prouidere ... boni imperatoris officia simul exequebatur' (of Catiline). For *cuncta* see 3.18.4n., Malloch on 11.9.2.

non arma, non ordo, non consilium Each element contrasts with those in the preceding tricolon describing the Romans: cf. esp. Sall. *J.* 99.2 'neque fugere neque arma capere neque omnino facere aut prouidere quicquam poterant' (of the Mauri and Gaetuli); see also next n.

sed pecorum modo trahi, occidi, capi This final tricolon rounds off the sequence of three *and*, like *Agr.* 37.2, models its series of asyndetic infinitives on Sall. *J.* 101.11 'sequi, fugere, occidi, capi' (Marius' victory over Jugurtha's troops), which itself perhaps recalls Thuc. 7.71.4 ὀλοφυρμός, βοή, νικῶντες, κρατούμενοι (and Hornblower's n.). The animal simile first appears in Latin with Sall. (*C.* 58.21 'sicuti pecora trucidemini', *H.* 4.67 M = 2.96 R 'uicem pecorum obtruncabantur'), who again may have had Thuc. in mind (2.51.4 ὥσπερ τὰ πρόβατα ἔθνησκον), although T.'s precise wording *pecorum modo* is Livian (5×) and hence imitated by Curtius (2×); see also Vell. 119.2n. The simile is heavily ironical in that it was Tacfarinas who earlier saw as the hunter and the Romans in animal terms (24.1n.).

25.3 Infensus miles ... optatae totiens pugnae The soldiers' memory is not of the battle (which by definition had not happened) but of their desire for it, just as *negatus honor* at 26.1 below means 'the refusal of the honour' (the *ab urbe condita* construction: see above, 6.1n.): 'The soldiery, angry at the memory of their hardships and of their frequent desire for battle against the elusive <enemy>'. The words are a striking quotation of the opening of Caesar's speech at Luc. 7.251 *'miles*, adest *totiens optatae* copia *pugnae'* (also picked up by Sil. 11.517, 16.81). *infensus memoria* recurs only at 2.3.2 (for *infensus* see 3.15.2n.); for sing. *miles* see above, 2.1n.; for *eludentes* and 'foreign trickery' see 3.74.1n.; for the form *aduersum* see 3.14.1n.

se quis<que> ultione et sanguine explebant *explere* with *sanguine* is regular (H. on *H.* 4.1.2, 4.14.3) but unexampled with *ultione*: we seem to have a hendiadys, 'bloody vengeance'.

Differtur See 3.12.4n.

ruendo in tela This expr. (again at Liv. 7.15.3, 26.44.9) is a much rarer variant on *ruere in arma* (e.g. Liv. 7.12.10 'ruendo in arma'), which is frequent in epic (e.g. Virg. *Aen.* 2.353, Luc. 3.37). Other exs. of rushing into the midst of the enemy at Sall. *C.* 60.7 (Catiline) and *J.* 98.1 (Marius).

Isque finis armis impositus Although Tacfarinas' defeat was not followed by a lasting peace (Syme, *RP* 1.224), the metonymy of *armis* for *bello* (cf. Cic. *De Or.* 3.167; Oakley on Liv. 7.22.6) suggests a reference to 'fighting' in general. *finem imponere* is a generally common expression (see H. on *H.* 3.48.2 for a few exs.), and the *is finis* 'formula' is very common esp. in Livy (10×) and T. (7×): see 3.19.2n. But there is no parallel anywhere for their combination.

26.1 Seiano tribuens When Tib. awarded the *triumphalia* to Blaesus, 'dare id se dixit honori Seiani, cuius ille auunculus erat' (3.72.4). It was also awkward for Tib. personally that his decision to withdraw Legio IX (23.2) proved premature.

huic negatus honor gloriam intendit For the nomin. use of the *ab urbe condita* constr., used to express a similar sentiment at 6.27.2 'non permissa prouincia dignationem addiderat', see 3.24.1n.

minore exercitu Africa's original Legio III Augusta (5.2n.).

captiuos ... deportarat The verb is technical = 'bring back to Rome' (*OLD* 2a) and can be used of objects (2.26.4 'deportare lauream'), persons (*captiuos d.* is a Livian expr.: cf. 23.34.8, 30.43.8) and abstractions (e.g. Curt. 9.10.24 'gloriam ... ex illis gentibus deportauerat'; *famam* is unparalleled).

caedem ducis is compressed for *famam caedis ducis.*

26.2 nec culpae nescia M reads *&culpae nescia*, which, though retained by some editors, seems quite illogical and not improved by emending *et* to *set* (Halm). The choice lies between Lipsius' *et culpae conscia* and Ryckius' *nec culpae* *nescia*, either of which provides the necessary motivation for *ad satis faciendum.* T. wrote *culpae . . . nescii* at 20.4 just above (n.) and is fond of negativing *nescius* (with *non* at 32.1 below, *haud* at 2.55.3, 4.50.4, 15.68.3); *culpae conscius* is much the commoner expression, though not present in T. On the whole Ryckius' suggestion seems preferable, but it is very difficult to choose.

Ptolemaei . . . studiis Cf. 24.3.

repetitus ex uetusto more <honor> missusque e senatoribus qui . . . daret M reads *exu&usto more omissusque*, with dots above and below the *o* of *omissusque* to indicate that that letter should be deleted. The paradosis is otherwise retained by Borzsák on the grounds that the subject of *repetitus* is the same as that of *missus* (*Gnomon* 56 (1984) 403); but this is not so: the subject of *missus* is a specific individual senator, whereas the putative subject of *repetitus* would have to be a generalised or hypothetical figure.

Many older edd. were attracted by Lipsius' *ex uetusto mos*, the theory being that *mos* would easily have been changed to *more* on account of *uetusto*; but *repetitus ex uetusto* [sc. *more*] *mos* seems to make little, if any, sense, and C. Heraeus (*Studia critica in Mediceos Taciti codices* (1846) 150) pointed out that the full phrase *uetusto more* had occurred at 16.2 just above and that T. writes *uetere ex more* at 27.2 below and 14.42.2. Doederlein proposed to insert *honos*, which has found favour with many recent editors. The appearance of *honor* at §1 above, so far from being an objection (it recurs at 37.1 ~ 3), in fact serves to contrast Dolabella's treatment with that of Ptolemy; but I have preferred the form *honor* because it would help to explain the omission of the word after *more*. For *repetitus . . . honor* see e.g. Sall. *J.* 85.37, Liv. 39.32.6.

scipionem eburnum, togam pictam, antiqua patrum munera The presentation of these gifts to foreign rulers was 'a sign that the Romans recognised them as kings' (Oakley on Liv. 10.7.9): cf. Liv. 30.15.11 'Masinissam primum regem appellatum . . . scipione eburneo, toga picta et palmata tunica donat', 31.11.11, 42.14.10. For further discussion and other exs. see Rawson 181–3; Braund, *RFK* 27–9. Over seven hundred years later, Moorish envoys to Belisarius would request that the symbols of office be sent to them κατὰ δὴ τὸν παλαιὸν νόμον (Procop. *Bell.* 3.25.4).

regemque et socium atque amicum The sequence of titles is conventional (e.g. Cic. *Leg. Man.* 12, Liv. 31.11.14, 16, 34.62.14, 35.46.5).

27–31 Domestic Affairs

The last section of the year is an exact replica of the first. An introductory episode (27) is followed by a trial described at length (28–30) and then by three others (31).

The principal trial is 'an example of wretchedness and savagery' in that a father, already in exile, is dragged back to Rome ('retractus') to face new charges of treason introduced by his son (28.1): such violations of *pietas* figure prominently in that index of popular intellectual taste, the *Controuersiae* of the elder Seneca, and parricide, to which the case is expressly compared (29.2), was particularly relished (see above, intro. n. to 10–11). T.'s account is a classic example of vivid writing (ἐνάργεια) and features numerous reversals (περιπέτειαι). As the two protagonists (both are called Vibius Serenus) enter the senate, the son's exquisite attire and aggressive appearance seem to give him the advantage over his filthy and shackled father (28.1); but there are also indications that the son may have gone too far, while unkemptness was a regular way of evoking sympathy for a defendant. At any rate, the father is unbowed: rattling his chains, he challenges his son in ironical indirect speech (28.3). When the son responds by naming Lentulus and Tubero as his father's accomplices, his accusation misfires completely since the men are clearly innocent; and, to make matters worse for the son, the father fails to be indicted by his slaves (29.1). At this point the son fears for his life and flees to Ravenna, evidently hoping to escape abroad; but he is dragged back to Rome ('retractus') and forced to continue the case which he had abandoned (29.2). The *princeps*' long-standing hostility to the elder Serenus seems to guarantee his condemnation, but, in a final twist, Tib. twice intervenes to mitigate the proposed penalties and the father is returned to his original place of exile, evidently no worse off than before his trial (29.3–30.1).

The *princeps* also showed clemency in the next case, causing people to wonder why he did not do so more often (31.1–2); and, whereas he intervened on the side of severity in the penultimate case of the year (31.3), he again showed mercy in the last (31.4). These three cases conclude a domestic narrative which, like the first of the year, has consisted almost entirely of trials, thus providing the context for the digression which follows (32–3).

27.1 Eadem aestate mota per Italiam *seruilis* belli *semina* fors oppressit The 'seed(s) of war' (again at 16.7.2, *H.* 4.80.1) is a relatively common metaphor (Cic. *Phil.* 2.55, *Off.* 2.29, Liv. 28.32.10, 40.16.3, Luc. 1.158–9 with Roche's n., 3.150, Sil. 1.654, Stat. *Theb.* 1.243). *mouere* is the technical term for seeds starting to sprout up through the ground (Ov. *Am.* 3.1.59, Stat. *Theb.* 4.212), while *opprimere* refers to the stifling or choking of seeds or budding plants (as Ov. *RA* 81 'opprime, dum noua sunt, subiti mala semina morbi', Col. 5.6.18 'uitis . . . incremento opprimetur'). *aestate* applies equally to the season for plants and for campaigning. For the related *spargere bellum* see 3.21.4n. (of Tacfarinas). For *seruile bellum* see H. on *H.* 3.48.2.

T. Curtisius The name is not otherwise attested but is defended by Syme, *TST* 67–8.

positis propalam libellis For another example of posting inflammatory handbills (AD 6) see Dio 55.27.1 πλείω δὲ δὴ βιβλία νύκτωρ ἐξετίθεσαν. *positis* is simple for *propositis* (as 1.7.3, where see n.).

agrestia per longinquos saltus et ferocia seruitia 'rural and defiant slaves on the extensive [*or perhaps* far-distant] estates': the prepositional phrase, although it seems to illustrate the word-order known as *coniunctio* (52.1n. *in principem*), more naturally qualifies *seruitia* than serves to link the two adjs.

tres biremes adpulere ad usus commeantium illo mari W. Eck has suggested that *commeare* is a quasi-technical term for messengers and that T. is referring to the *cursus publicus* ('Tacitus, *Ann.* 4.27.1 und der *cursus publicus* auf der Adria', *SCI* 13 (1994) 60–6). It is true that the verb is used of letters at 41.2 (n.), but, like S. Crogiez ('Le *cursus publicus* et la circulation des informations officielles par voie de mer', in *L'Information et la mer dans le monde antique* (ed. J. Andreau and C. Virlouvet, 2002) 63–5), I can see no evidence for such a reference. The Latin surely means 'to meet the needs of those travelling on that sea'. Since the ships were manned by marines (2 *classiariorum*), they will have sailed down from the naval port of Ravenna (above, 5.1n.) to protect shipping in the Adriatic from pirates. They may have put in at Brundisium for a period of leave, as Crogiez suggests.

27.2 Cutius Lupus is otherwise unknown but he is well named to counter self-declared 'freedom-fighters': cf. Vell. 27.2 'Telesinus . . . adiiciens numquam defuturos raptores Italicae libertatis lupos, nisi silua in quam refugere solerent esset excisa'; cf. Ogilvie on Liv. 3.66.4 'The Romans, jealous of their descent from Romulus and Remus, were proud to be known as *lupi* but the term could rebound.' Note also what the German chief Bato is alleged to have said to Tib. in AD 9 about the Romans: ὑμεῖς τούτων αἴτιοί ἐστε· ἐπὶ γὰρ τὰς ἀγέλας ὑμῶν φύλακας οὐ κύνας οὐδὲ νομέας ἀλλὰ λύκους πέμπετε (Dio 56.16.3, quoted by Champlin (2008) 416–17).

cui prouincia . . . calles euenerant (a) According to *OLD callis* 2b, where our passage is quoted, the full expression is *siluae callesque* and refers to 'public pasture-lands in Italy allotted yearly to a magistrate as his *prouincia*'. This 'full expression' is found only at Suet. *DJ* 19.2, where it is said that the *optimates*, in their desire to slight Caesar and Bibulus, ensured 'ut prouinciae futuris consulibus minimi negotii, id est siluae callesque, decernerentur'. This statement is self-evidently extremely odd. Willems deleted the words *id est siluae callesque* altogether and was supported by J. C. Rolfe ('The so-called Callium Provincia', *AJP* 36 (1915) 323–31), but P. J. Rhodes supported the suggestion of J. P. V. D. Balsdon that Suetonius had misinterpeted the evidence and that the consuls of 59 BC were initially assigned a token province, leaving the senate free to delay a serious decision until the situation in Gaul became clearer ('Silvae callesque', *Historia* 27 (1978) 617–20). Though the latter is no doubt a more plausible reading of Suetonius, it does nothing to clarify the passage of T.

(b) Some editors of T., drawing attention to Cic. *Sest.* 12 ('Catilina, cum e pruina Appennini atque e niuibus illis emersisset atque aestatem integram nanctus Italiae calles et pastorum stabula praeoccupare coepisset'), have inferred that in south-eastern Italy there were tracts of land which produced valuable revenues and which, on the basis of our passage of T., were therefore administered by a quaestor. Since in that passage Cicero 'alludes to the fear of servile uprising' (Kaster ad loc.), it is perhaps pointed that T. directs our attention to the past ('uetere ex more').

coeptantem cum maxime coniurationem *cum maxime* (*OLD cum²* 13b), a very common combination in the younger Seneca, here emphasises that the conspiracy was broken up *just* as it was beginning (cf. Summers on Sen. *Ep.* 12.3).

audacia implies revolutionary designs, as often (1.3n. *corpus*).

urbem . . . iam trepidam ob multitudinem familiarum, quae glis-cebat immensum, minore in dies plebe ingenua In his great speech two years previously Tib. had made reference to the large number of slave-households (3.53.4 'familiarum numerum' and n.); whether they were grow-ing as the number of the free-born declined seems unknown, but it would be in keeping with a general trend: see Brunt, *IM* 131 (our passage is not mentioned in W. Scheidel's studies of the free and slave population in Italy, *JRS* 94 (2004) 1–26, 95 (2005) 64–79). *urbem . . . trepidam* (again at *H.* 1.50.1) is a poetic – and largely epic – expr. (Luc. 2.160, 3.372–3, Sil. 14.667, Stat. *Silu.* 3.5.73, *Theb.* 10.871); for the 'verbal hyperbaton' see 3.1.1n. For the adverbial *immensum* (again at 40.6 below) see 3.30.1n.: its combination with *gliscebat* (3.19.2n.) is from Sall. *H.* 3.56 M(77 R) 'immensum aucto mari et uento gliscente'. *plebs ingenua* (again at 16.13.2) is first in Ov. *Met.* 9.671, then Plin. *NH* 7.60.

28.1 Isdem consulibus See 6.13.1n.

miseriarum ac saeuitiae exemplum atrox Ancient literature was expected to be useful (*utile*), a function which in the case of historiography resided in its exemplary nature (33.2n.). Sometimes the point is made in a preface (e.g. *H.* 1.3.1 'bona exempla', Liv. *praef.* 10), sometimes the term *exemplum* appears explicitly in the narrative, as here and again at e.g. *H.* 3.51.2. *miseriarum* and *saeuitiae* dictate our sympathy for the father and against the son in the drama which follows. For T.'s characteristic deployment of a phrase in apposition to the sentence see 1.27.1n.

reus pater, accusator filius . . . in senatum inducti sunt T. will later introduce the episode of Cremutius Cordus with an allusion to the opening of Cicero's *Pro Ligario* (34.1n.); here is perhaps an ironical allusion to the conclusion of the *Pro Caelio* (80 'conseruate parenti filium, parentem filio'). For trials in the senate see Talbert 460–87; for the present case and bibliography thereon see Rutledge 282–3.

Vibius Serenus For the elder and his exile see 13.2n.; the younger (*RE* 7A.1984 = Vibius 55 (Hanslik), *PIR* 8.2.301 no. 576, *BNP* 15.387 [II 21]) reappears at 36.3 below.

inluuieque ac squalore obsitus Although the elder Serenus' condition was occasioned by his fate as an exile, advocates wishing to arouse the pity of their audience would ensure the shabby appearance of their clients (Quint. 6.1.30 'producere ipsos qui periclitentur squalidos atque deformes': see e.g. J. Hall, *Cicero's use of judicial theater* (2014) 40–63; also F. S. Naiden, *Ancient supplication* (2006) 59–60); this suggests that the son may not have things all his own way. For the coupling of *inluuies* and *squalor* see Liv. 21.40.9, Sen. *Ira* 3.17.3; *obsitus* with *squalore*, first attested at Liv. 2.23.3 and 29.16.6, becomes a mannerism of Val. Max. (4×); but with *inluuie* it is otherwise only at 6.43.2 (n.).

peroranti filio <pater> praeparatur Scholars have been troubled both by the fact that in M this sentence lacks an expressed subject, corresponding to *adulescens* below, and by the apparent inappropriateness of *praeparatur*, which some scholars (following Venturius) change to *praeparatus* and take with *adulescens*.[58] (See the discussion by D. Wardle, *CQ* 43 (1993) 346–8.) To provide a subject, scholars have sought to extract the word *pater* either from the prefix (abbreviated in M) of *peroranti* or from that of *praeparatur*, the latter simultaneously eliminating the allegedly troublesome *praeparatur*. But is the verb in fact a problem? Two difficulties have been seen: (i) to say that the father was 'prepared' seems contradicted by his description earlier in the sentence, where he is plainly *un*prepared; (ii) *praeparare* appears scarcely at all in the *Annals* and then only in speeches,[59] whereas the simple form is extremely common (176×, according to Wardle, who stresses these statistics). The first of these difficulties may be dismissed: the alleged contradiction is simply an example of Tacitean cynicism (for such deliberate incongruity

---

[58] The sentences at the start of ch. 28 have been variously divided and punctuated: see e.g. Walther's long n.

[59] The exact figure is hard to determine: Syme (*Tac.* 720) cites only 11.7.1 and 13.21.3, thereby discounting the present case and 11.8.2, where *praeparauerat* is retained by some older edd.

between participle(s) and main verb see E. Laughton, *The participle in Cicero* (1964) 9). The second difficulty is admittedly more substantial; yet, if T. can use *praeparare* once in the *Histories*, and that too in narrative (1.72.2), as opposed to numerous exs. of *parare*, presumably there is nothing to stop him doing the same in the *Annals*. The fact is that *praeparatur* is written out fully in M and makes excellent sense in the context; it seems rash to get rid of it (for the middle-passive sense cf. *TLL* 10.2.757.37ff.). We therefore need to find another way of providing the sentence with a subject, and, while it is true that the abbreviations for *pater* and *per* might easily be confused, the transmitted *peroranti* makes excellent sense (cf. 3.17.3n.) and is indeed used apropos of the elder Vibius at 2.30.1 (n.). It therefore seems preferable to insert *pater* at some point between the words *uinctus* and *adulescens*; Martin and Woodman believed that *pater* (esp. if abbreviated) could easily have dropped out before *praeparatur*, and, while an omission before *peroranti* would be equally plausible, there seems no cogent reason to disagree with the earlier decision.

28.2 multis munditiis, alacri uultu An orator's dress was important but should be 'splendidus et uirilis' (Quint. 11.3.137): hence Hortensius was the victim of verbal abuse because, when he spoke, he was 'multa munditia' and resorted to effeminate gestures (Gell. 1.5.2). The younger Serenus seems guilty of the same fault. Likewise an orator's facial expression (*uultus*: see 5.3.2n.) was not only important but 'dominatur . . . maxime' (Quint. 11.3.72); but *alacri uultu* is one of the phrases used by Cicero when describing an orator's behaviour which is 'in primis flagitiosum' (*De Or.* 2.184; see also 3.9.2n.).

structas . . . insidias To the exs. given by H. on *H.* 1.58.2 add Val. Max. 8.2.3, Sen. *Clem.* 1.9.2, Stat. *Theb.* 2.501–2.

missos in Galliam concitores belli At the time of the Gallic revolt (3.40–7 and nn.) the elder Vibius had been governor of Baetica (4.13.2n.). For *concitor belli* see H. on *H.* 1.68.2.

index idem et testis See 3.10.1n.

Caecilium Cornutum Frater Arvalis as well as ex-praetor: see *RE* 3.1200 = Caecilius 47 (Groag), *PIR* 2.5–6 no. 35, *BNP* 2.882 [II 10]; Rüpke 579 no. 972.

quia periculum pro exitio habebatur Scholars compare 16.14.3 'inter damnatos magis quam inter reos . . . habebantur', Sen. *Ep.* 70.10 'omnes enim necessarii deseruerant impie iam non reum, sed funus: habere coepit consilium, utrum conscisceret mortem an expectaret'. For the *uariatio* with abl. *taedio* see 24.2n.

28.3 nihil infracto animo Cf. Cic. *Red. Quir.* 19, Liv. 2.59.4 'nihil infractus . . . animus', 7.31.6, Curt. 9.2.30.

uocare ultores deos ut sibi quidem redderent exilium . . ., filium autem quandoque supplicia sequerentur The elder Serenus expects the obviousness of his innocence to be inferred from his calls for vengeance. For *ultores deos* see H. on *H.* 4.57.2, where many more exs. could be added, esp. from epic; the unparalleled expr. *supplicia sequi* seems to personify the noun and perhaps to evoke the Homeric Λιταί, who followed after Sin (*Il.* 9.504 μετόπισθε, 507 ὀπίσσω) and whose name belied their function as instruments of vengeance (510–12). For the use of *reddo* in an ironical context ('ut indicet quam mala praesentia sint') see *TLL* 11.2.482.1–2 and 485.33–8.

falso exterritum Ursinus' emendation is guaranteed by *H.* 2.8.1 'falso exterritae'. For the verb see 3.15.2n.

idque facile intellectu, si proderentur alii 'and the matter <of Cornutus' guilt or innocence> was easy to understand, if others were produced': Serenus makes the existence or otherwise of accomplices the decisive factor in proving that Cornutus had been wrongly accused (next n.). If *id* is taken as referring to the whole question of whether the man was innocent or not, the sentence does not present the difficulties of logic which Neue (5) and Hartman (35–6) eliminated by emendation.

non enim se caedem principis et res nouas uno socio cogitasse Serenus concludes by affecting to admit that he had planned murder and revolution and had had accomplices (*cogitasse* rather than *cogitaturum fuisse*). Since we know from his calls for vengeance (above) that he claims to be innocent, it is clear that he is adopting the strategy of irony (cf. Quint. 8.6.54–5; Lausberg 266–7 §§582–3) and means the exact opposite of what he says; but the more he can suggest the importance of accomplices, the better chance he has of Cornutus' innocence being confirmed by their non-existence. He is of course working on the confident assumption that there are no accomplices to be produced, although his son has other ideas (next n.).

29.1 Tum accusator Cn. Lentulum et Seium Tuberonem nominat The younger Serenus responds to his father's challenge by naming two alleged accomplices, although in a further twist they turn out to be self-evidently implausible conspirators.

Syme argued that all T.'s references to a Cn. (Cornelius) Lentulus (again at 1.27.1, 2.32.1, 3.68.2, 4.44.1) are not to the consul of 18 BC but to his namesake, 'the Augur', the consul of 14 BC. See *AA* 284–99; also *BNP* 3.833 [II 25] and 3.59.1n. L. Seius Tubero was suffect consul in AD 18 (with Germanicus) and half-brother, or son of a half-brother, of Sejanus (Syme, *AA* 300–12, esp. 307, and Table XXIII; Levick, Table D): see 2.20.1n., *PIR* 7.2.123 no. 324, *BNP* 13.209 [4].

164

cum primores ciuitatis ... *tu*multus hostilis et *tu*rbandae rei publicae accerserentur The men's description as *primores ciuitatis* (3.65.2n.) serves as a reminder that Serenus' trial is being held in the senate (28.1): the two accused are amongst its most distinguished members. *tumultus hostilis* is a Livian expression (10.20.11, 26.22.8, 44.5.2), but the noun often implied a specifically Gallic uprising (3.43.1n.): these two charges thus repeat (chiastically) those levelled against the elder Vibius himself at 28.2 above ('structas . . . belli'). For *turbare rem publicam* cf. Sen. *Contr.* 2.6.4, Sen. *Brev. Vit.* 12.3, [Quint.] *Decl.* 11.7; for the variation of construction see Sörbom 112 (assonantal play with the various affiliates of *tumultus* and *turbare*, as again at *H.* 1.55.4, is extremely common in numerous authors): while a gen. of the charge is common with *arcesso*, a gerundive seems unparalleled (*TLL* 2.452.30ff.).

intimi ipsius amici Cf. Dio 57.24.8 for Lentulus.

Lentulus sen*ec̣t̲u̲t̲is extremae, T̲u̲b̲e̲r̲o̲ def̲e̲c̲t̲o̲ corpore T. has named the two individuals just above, but such repetition instead of using pronouns is common (Müller 4.13 n. 2): 'It is either a mannerism or a way to get clarity and emphasis' (2.28.3n.). Lentulus, now in his 70s or early 80s, will die in the following year (44.1); the description of Tubero is perhaps an allusion to the man's name (see 3.75.1n.); for the *uariatio* of descriptive gen. ~ abl. (again at e.g. 61 below) see Sörbom 77.

exempti sc. *crimini* or *periculo* (the latter a fairly common combination in T.: see G–G 423b). For *quaesitum* ~ *quaestio* (below) see 6.10.1n.

29.2 scelere uecors The expr. recurs only at *H.* 2.23.5, but the notion that consciousness of one's crime leads to madness was common (e.g. 1.39.2, Cic. *Rosc. Am.* 67, Curt. 6.9.32 'conscientia sceleris . . . amens'; *PH* 313 and n. 66).

simul See 3.24.3n.

uulgi rumore seems taken from Sil. 4.9 and recurs at 41.1 below and 15.73.1; for *territus* cf. Caes. *BG* 6.20.2, Apul. *Met.* 3.27.7.

minitantium The plur. form illustrates *constructio ad sensum* (synesis) after the collective *uulgi*, as Liv. 1.41.1 'clamor inde concursusque populi, mirantium quid rei esset' (L–H–S 436, *OLS* 1.1292). For T.'s preference for the frequentative verb see 3.73.1n.

robur et saxum Respectively the Tullianum (6.40.1n.) and Tarpeian Rock (*LTUR* 4.237–8).

parricidarum poenas A parricide 'was subject to a gruesome and unique punishment' (Dyck's comm. on Cic. *Rosc. Am.* (2010), Intro. p. 1): he was sewn in a sack (along with a cock, a dog, a viper and an ape) and thrown into the sea. See *OLD culleus* 3; *BNP* 10.557–8.

retractus Rauenna exsequi accusationem adigitur Normally it is defendants and the like who are dragged back to the city (e.g. 6.14.2, Sall. *C.* 39.5, 47.4, 48.3); the reference to Ravenna suggests that Vibius had been planning to escape by sea (27.2n.). *exsequi accusationem* recurs elsewhere only in a famous letter from Pliny to T. (*Ep.* 7.33.4).

29.3 post damnatum Libonem For the case of Libo Drusus in AD 16 see 2.27–32.

litteris See 3.16.1n.

suum tantum studium sine fructu fuisse Vibius had played a key role in the prosecution of Libo Drusus (2.30.1), but, whereas the three other accusers had been awarded praetorships *extra ordinem* (2.32.1), he must either have been praetor designate or already held the office by this date, as he was proconsul of Baetica in (probably) 21/22. His complaint is thus likely to have been that he lacked comparable recognition.

contumacius quam tutum apud aures superbas et offensioni proniores T. is esp. fond of metonymical or similar references to ears (e.g. 1.31.5, 1.65.4, 2.39.3, 4.69.1, 4.69.3), particularly those of the *princeps* (e.g. 4.39.2, 11.28.2, 11.32.2, 13.14.2, 15.67.3; *Agr.* 41.4n.); and, since nothing is more lethal than the ears of a tyrant (Juv. 4.86 'Quid uiolentius aure tyranni?'), *aures superbae* symbolise tyrants or persons like them (Liv. 24.5.5 (cf. 34.5.13), Sen. *Ira* 2.21.7). *proniores* (again at *H.* 1.1.2, 1.54.1, Stat. *Silv.* 5.3. 58–9) suggests ears bent forward eagerly to catch every affront: for Tib.'s well-known propensity to take offence see above, 18.2n.; for *superbas et . . . proniores* cf. Sen. *Ira* 3.1.5. *apud* = 'in the presence of' (*OLD* 8), as Quint. 10.1.32, Fronto p. 166.15 vdH², Amm. 28.6.26. For *contumacia* see 12.3n. above.

Ea Caesar . . . rettulit For this characteristic of Tib. see 21.1n.

peruicacia seruorum The loyalty of slaves under torture was a popular topic (*H.* 1.3.1, Val. Max. 6.8.1).

30.1 more maiorum This phrase (again at 14.48.2, 16.11.3 and *H.* 4.42.6) is 'the standard term' (2.32.3n., where it is varied) for the punishment described by Suet. *Nero* 49.2: 'quaeri ut puniatur more maiorum . . . nudi hominis ceruicem inseri furcae, corpus uirgis ad necem caedi'.

quo molliret inuidiam intercessit 'he intervened to soften the resentment' (sc. which would have been caused by so drastic a punishment). Tib.'s *intercessio* (the verb is technical), which he repeats at 31.4 below, will have been made by virtue of his *tribunicia potestas* (Talbert 170–1); other exs. are collected by Rogers 202–3 and Ginsburg 125 n. 32. That *quo = ut* is not an archaism, as commonly stated (e.g. 3.8.1n.), is argued by Oakley on Liv. 9.10.9.

Gallus Asinius See 6.23.1n., and, on the inversion of names, 3.21.3n.

Gyaro aut Donusa claudendum <cum> censeret Gyarus in the northern Cyclades had been proposed for the exile of C. Iunius Silanus (3.68.2; cf. 3.66.1n.) but Tib. objected that the island was 'inmitem et sine cultu hominum' (3.69.5; cf. Plut. *Mor.* 602c Γύαρον . . . σκληράν). Donusa, a small island east of Naxos, seems otherwise unattested as a place of exile (Drogula 265–6).

egenam aquae Here, as at 15.3.2, T. is alluding to Sall. *J.* 89.5 'omnia . . . egentia aquae'; for *egenus* see Oakley on Liv. 9.6.4, with statistics.

dandosque *uitae* usus cui *uita* concederetur *uitae usus* is a relatively common expr. but found esp. often in Cicero, of whose locutions the Tacitean Tib. is particularly fond (see *Ann. 3*, p. 513; *Ann. 5–6*, p. 325); he is likewise partial to assonance (6.2.4n., 6.6.1n.), in this case polyptoton (35.1n.).

Amorgum reportatur See 13.2 for the elder Serenus' initial banishment to Amorgus. It seems from Dio 58.8.3 that Serenus (though not named there) was an enemy of Sejanus and that he was pardoned by Tib. in 31 when Sejanus was losing favour.

30.2 de praemiis accusatorum abolendis Since T. has told us earlier that Silius lost his property *despite* his having committed suicide (20.1 *tamen*; cf. 19.4), it seems natural to infer that the present proposal was intended merely to formalise an existing convention. Tib.'s objection (below) is therefore something of a surprise, esp. since we know that by AD 34 the estates of pre-emptive suicides were normally left untouched (6.29.1). Perhaps at some point during the intervening decade the present proposal, or one very like it, was reintroduced and passed.

contraque morem suum palam . . . conquestus esset The prepositional phrase is perhaps to be taken with *palam* and hence to constitute a reference to the *princeps*' typically obscure speech (the resulting arrangement would be pleasingly chiastic); on the other hand it may be taken with *conquestus esset*, in which case there is an authentically Tiberian tension between *clementia* and legalism (see *Ann. 3*, p. 513; *Ann. 5–6*, p. 325).

subuerterent potius iura quam custodes eorum amouerent 'Without volunteer prosecutors the whole legal system would have been rendered ineffective. This fact was seldom mentioned, though it was pointed out on one occasion by the emperor Tiberius' (J. G. F. Powell, 'Juvenal and the *delatores*', *AHC* 237). The statement (chiastic, like *inritas . . . in praecipiti* just preceding) is suggestive of Tiberian idiolects: *subuerti leges* occurs in a speech of his at 2.36.3, while *iuris custos* is a Ciceronian phrase (*Rab. Perd.* 12, *Leg.* 3.8).

30.3 genus hominum publico exitio repertum et <ne> poenis quidem umquam satis coercitum *poena coercere* is a standard (but not esp. common) legal expr.: the plur. *poenis* almost certainly alludes to the successive measures taken against *delatores* by Titus (Suet. *Tit.* 8.5), Nerva (Dio 68.1.2) and Trajan (Plin. *Pan.* 34–5).[60] There is a question over the text, however, since M's *et poenis quidem umquam satis coercitum* is clearly wrong. Should we agree with Beroaldus, who emended *umquam* to *numquam*, or with Bekker, who inserted *ne* after *et*? While *n* is perhaps more likely to have been omitted from the sequence –*em num-* than *ne* before *poenis, ne . . . quidem* makes for better sense ('and never sufficiently restrained, even by punishment') and the extending use of *et . . . quidem* (a form of words of which he is otherwise fond) does not occur elsewhere in T.[61]

genus hominum is an exceptionally common phrase in a wide range of authors; here its tone seems somewhat apocalyptic (as e.g. Cic. *Part. Or.* 91 'genus hominum ad honestatem natum, malo cultu prauisque opinionibus corruptum'), and the chiastic arrangement of its description underlines the almost inhuman nature of its activities (*hominum ~ publico*): even wild beasts do not attack their own species (Watson on Hor. *Epod.* 7.11–12, Tarrant on Sen. *Ag.* 738ff., Courtney on Juv. 15.159–64). For *publico exitio* (again at *H.* 1.33.2) cf. Cic. *Mil.* 3 'unum genus est aduersum infestumque nobis eorum quos P. Clodii furor . . . omnibus exitiis publicis pauit', Sen. *Ira* 2.9.3; contrasts between *poena* and (below) *praemium* are extremely common (e.g. Plin. *Pan.* 70.2 'nec poenis malorum sed bonorum praemiis bonos facias').

31.1 His tam adsiduis tamque maestis The adjs. prepare for the themes of the following digression (32.2 'maestae urbis res', 33.3 'nos . . . coniungimus, obuia rerum similitudine et satietate').

C. Cominium See *RE* 4.607 = Cominius 5 (Stein), *PIR* 2.300 no. 1261, *BNP* 3.619 [II 1]; Demougin, *PCR* 216 no. 248.

fratris, qui senator erat T. characteristically distinguishes the two brothers in terms of rank: see 1.75.2n., Talbert 249 n. 10. It has been suggested that the brother is to be identified with T. Cominius Proculus, governor of Cyprus

---

[60] T.'s *sententia* could almost be a comment on Pliny's praises: 34.2 'cauisti ne fundata legibus ciuitas euersa legibus uideretur', 35.2 'quos quidem non in praesens tantum sed in aeternum repressisti, mille poenarum indagine inclusos', 35.3 'exspectent paria praemio damna'.

[61] He has *et quidem* at 6.9.3 (by emendation) and *G.* 44.3.

early in Claudius' reign (*PIR* 2.302 no. 1270; G. Hill, *The history of Cyprus* (1940) 1.255 no. 11).

31.2 gnarum meliorum . . . tristiora malle Cf. Ov. *Met.* 7.20–1 'uideo meliora proboque, | deteriora sequor' (and Bömer ad loc. for earlier, esp. Euripidean, examples).

quae fama clementiam sequeretur *clementia* was one of the virtues of Tib.'s reign, probably advertised as recently as the coinage of 22 (3.68.2n.), but the *princeps* took a long view and was less interested in immediate fame than in his reputation amongst posterity (3.69.4n., 6.46.2n.). The puzzled reaction of his contemporaries here ('quo magis mirum habebatur') is repeated in similar circumstances at 38.4–5 below (nn.). For the *uariatio* of noun ~ indir. question see 3.10.3n. *fama sequitur* (again at *D.* 10.1) appears first in Sall. *H.* 4.69 M(60 R).22, then Virg. *Ecl.* 6.74, *Aen.* 10.679, Sen. *Ira* 3.41.1, *Ben.* 6.43.3, Plin. *NH* 35.105.

neque enim socordia peccabat Just as *nec occultum est . . . celebrentur* (below) corresponds to *quae fama clementiam sequeretur*, so the present sentence corresponds to the antithesis *gnarum meliorum . . . tristiora malle* (which in turn relates to Tib.'s support for *delatores* at 30.2 above). *socordia*, which occurs disproportionately often in Sallust, usually means 'lethargy' *vel sim.* but also has a non-physical sense, said to be associated with the elder Cato (*OLD* b), which here means something like 'carelessness', 'thoughtlessness', 'indifference'. *neque* applies both to *socordia* and to *peccabat*: he was neither thoughtless nor blundering; his actions were quite deliberate (for *peccare* = 'blunder' see *OLD* 1).

nec occultum est quando ex ueritate, quando adumbrata laetitia facta imperatorum celebrentur 'nor is it a mystery when emperors' actions are celebrated sincerely and when with spurious pleasure' (for *adumbrata laetitia* cf. Sen. *Cons. Pol.* 5.4). For an indir. question after *occultum est* (again at 11.28.1) see Sall. *J.* 24.5; for the *uariatio* of prepositional phrase ~ abl. see Sörbom 85–7.

compositus alias et u̲e̲l̲ut eluctantium u̲erborum solutius promp-tiusque e̲loquebatur quotiens subueniret *compositus*, used of Tib.'s appearance at 2.34.3 'compositus ore', is here a technical description of speech but transferred to the speaker (other exs. at *OLD* 4a): here it perhaps = 'deliberate' and seems to contrast with *promptius*. A chiasmus is completed by the seeming antithesis between Tib.'s halting words and his fluent delivery (*solute* is another technical term, frequent in Cicero's *Brutus*). The two adverbs together had earlier been used by Val. Max. to describe Demosthenes (8.7 *ext.* 1 'fertur quoque ori insertis calculis multum ac diu loqui solitus, quo uacuum promptius esset et solutius'). For other refs. to

Tiberian speech cf. 1.11.2 'suspensa semper et obscura uerba', 1.33.2 'sermone, uultu adrogantibus et obscuris', 4.52.3 'haec raram occulti pectoris uocem elicuere', 4.70.1, 13.3.2 'artem ... callebat qua uerba expenderet, tum ualidus sensibus aut consulto ambiguus'. The unusualness of his speaking out is here underlined by *eloquebatur*, used elsewhere in the *Annals* only at 3.65.3, again of Tib., and *eluctor*, only here in the *Annals* (see 6.12.2n.); *eluctantia uerba* is a unique combination, unless Wopkens was right to emend *inluctantia* at Stat. *Theb.* 4.790 (Statius has *uox eluctata* at *Ach.* 1.525). For the *uariatio* of adj. ~ descriptive gen. see 10.1n.

31.3 P. Suillium P. Suillius Rufus, son of the astonishing Vistilia (5.8.1n.) and half-brother of the general Corbulo and of Caligula's fourth wife Caesonia, was quaestor in (?) 15 and recalled from banishment after Tib.'s death, becoming suffect consul in (?) 41. See *RE* 4A.719–22 = Suillius 4 (Fluss), *PIR* 7.2.357–8 no. 970, *BNP* 11.927 [3]; Syme, *RP* 2.806–8, *AA* 182; Malloch on 11.1.1, who describes him as 'the most notorious *delator* of Claudius' reign'.

cum Italia arceretur . . ., amouendum in insulam censuit That is: *relegatio* was proposed (*arceretur* is condensed for *arcendus censeretur*) but Tib. intervened to ensure the harsher punishment of *deportatio* (for the terms see 13.2n., 21.3n.); for another case where he intervenes similarly see 42.3 below (and Rogers 203–4, Ginsburg 125 n. 32). For *amouendum* see 1.53.4n.

ob rem iudicandam is a set phrase in Cicero (12×), usually accompanied by *pecuniam accipere* (or, less usually, *capere*, as in T.): see esp. *Rab. Post.* 16. Elsewhere only at Quint. 5.10.87. For *conuincor* + infin. (below) see 3.46.2n. (§d).

tanta contentione animi ut <se iur>e iurando obstringeret M reads *uteiurando*, with a superscript *t* added as if to make three words, *ut et iurando*. Since *iure iurando obstringere* is a rare but invariable phrase (8× elsewhere in Latin), it is certain that Ritter's *iure* must be correct and that in this regard Doederlein's <*s*>*e iurando* is mistaken. On the other hand, *obstringere* is a transitive verb, as is clear in all but one of the other exs. of the phrase; the one possible exception is 1.14.1 'iure iurando obstrinxit se non excessurum', where *se* is both object of the verb and subject of the acc. + infin. (which depends on *iure iurando*, as often, not *obstrinxit*).[62] It therefore seems inevitable that we should insert *se* as well as *iure* here. For senatorial oaths see 21.3n.; for oaths from Tib. see 1.74.4, 2.31.3.

---

[62] Alternatively *se* is the expressed object of *obstrinxit* but has to be understood as the subject of the acc. + infin. (see 3.8.2n.). *OLD ius* 5 does not mention that *ius iurandum* can be followed by an acc. + infin., but the construction is common (*TLL* 7.2.704.2).

contentio animi is above all a Ciceronian expr. (7×); elsewhere at Curt. 8.1.33.

e re publica id esse The phraseology, again in a Tiberian speech at 3.53.1, is formulaic (Talbert 261 and n. 2).

quod aspere acceptum ad praesens mox in laudem uertit regresso Suillio 'The present rough reception of this changed later to praise on Suillius' return.' It is not known when or whence Suillius returned. For *aspere acceptum* (again at *H.* 3.56.3) cf. Cic. *Att.* 9.2a.1; *ad praesens* is used often by T. (10×) as an alternative to *in praesens* (12×); elsewhere only in the elder Pliny (5×) and Suet. *Tit.* 6.2.

quem uidit sequens aetas ... numquam bene usum For the rare anticipatory notice see 6.32.4n. Suillius was again banished, to the Balearic Islands, under Nero (13.42–3, where the charge of being *uenalis* is repeated). For the phrase *uidit ... aetas* see *Agr.* 2.3n.

31.4 Catus, ut rettuli, Libonem *in*lexerat *in*sidiis, deinde *in*dicio perculerat See 2.27–30; nothing else is known about Firmius Catus. For *perculerat* see 6.3.4n.

quominus senatu pelleretur non obstitit For withdrawal of senatorial status, and the emperor's role therein, see 42.3; Talbert 27–9.

32–33 Digression

To separate his account of AD 24 from that of AD 25, T. interposes a digression in which he apologises for, and defends, the foregoing and following narrative (32.1 'quae rettuli quaeque referam').[63] The digression is constructed on a 'ring' basis:

32.1–2a T.'s narrative compared unfavourably with others
　　32.2b Usefulness of T.'s narrative
　　　　33.1–2a The three types of political constitution
　　33.2b Usefulness of T.'s narrative
33.3–4 T.'s narrative compared unfavourably with others

---

[63] That these chapters constitute a digression is clear from the closural formula at the very end (33.4n.), although they are not treated by Hahn. For discussion see *RICH* 180–6, updated in *Tac. Rev.* 128–35; there is an extensive and characteristically bravura analysis in Moles 95–134; see also Wisse 330–6, who denies that the digression has a separative function and prefers to see it 'as standing outside the narrative altogether' (314 and nn. 49–50), thus contradicting what he says about a 'triptych' on the very next page. For further bibliography see Suerbaum 1361–2.

T.'s principal contention is that his narrative compares unfavourably with that of earlier, more traditional historiography (32.1–2a, 33.3–4). Most of the comparison relates to his unattractive subject matter and the effect it will have on his readers: whereas in the preface to the *Histories* he had listed the subjects which he knew would entice his readers and grip their imagination (*H.* 1.2–3), here he twice produces a similar list of subjects only to deny them, itemising by contrast the grim and monotonous themes to which the reign of Tib. compels him (32.1–2, 33.3). There is also a further disadvantage (33.4). Historians of bygone times do not arouse the passions of their readers, but Tib.'s reign is relatively recent and descendants of the protagonists are still alive, and, even when that is not the case, readers see in the text a coded criticism of themselves.

The programmatic nature of the digression is self-evident: many of the topics with which T. deals are those which might be expected in a historian's preface. So-called 'second prefaces' are of course characteristic of several ancient genres: thus Virgil begins the second half of the *Aeneid* by declaring that the more weighty part of his epic is under way (7.44–5 '*maior* rerum mihi nascitur ordo, | *maius* opus moueo'), while Livy is only one of several historians to deploy the device (21.1.1 'licet mihi praefari ... bellum *maxime omnium memorabile* quae umquam gesta sint me scripturum').[64] As will be clear, however, T. is fundamentally different in two related respects. Whereas second prefaces tend to advertise 'greater' or 'more important' material than hitherto, T. does exactly the opposite (32.1 '*parua* ... et *leuia* memoratu'); and, whereas in other authors second prefaces usually occur halfway through the text or at comparable points, T.'s equivalent is not placed (as might have been expected) at the start of Book 4 but concludes the second narrative year of the book. The reason for this is not hard to discern. Rhetorical convention dictated that, when a writer's material was unattractive, as T. now professes his to be, he should not use a direct opening but instead should adopt the technique of *insinuatio* or the 'disguised opening' (e.g. *Rhet. Herenn.* 1.9: see Lausberg 132–3 §§280–1). By adhering to rhetorical convention T. has underlined the main theme of the digression. Indeed his very choice of a digression to convey his apologetics is itself significant. We know from Cicero (*Inv.* 1.27, *Brut.* 322, *De Or.* 2.311; cf. Quint. 9.1.28) that digressions were a conventional means of entertaining one's readers, and we know from Quintilian (10.1.33)

---

[64] See in general G. B. Conte, 'Proems in the middle', *YCS* 29 (1992) 147–59 (= *The poetry of pathos* (2007) 219–31), S. Kyriakidis and F. De Martino (edd.), *Middles in Latin poetry* (2004); on *Aen.* 7.44–5 in particular note D. P. Nelis, *The Aeneid and the Argonautica of Apollonius Rhodius* (1998) ch. 7 §1. For historians see Herkommer 10.

and Pliny (*Ep.* 2.5.5) that digressions were a recognised feature of the historiographical genre: hence, by using a digression specifically to *deny* that his work contains any of the pleasurable elements of which traditional historiography was thought to consist, he could hardly have chosen a more ironically appropriate medium in which to emphasise the changed nature of his work.

Although the digression constitutes an effective vehicle for re-emphasising the deterioration in Tib.'s reign which began in AD 23 (4.1.1, 4.6.1), that is largely because T. devotes so much attention to the matter, twice detailing the disadvantages of his current narrative when compared with traditional historical writing (32.1–2a, 33.3–4). It is true that the usefulness of his narrative is also mentioned twice, but his treatment of the topic in no way proves a positive counterbalance. On the first occasion (32.2b) his apparently insignificant narrative is justified briefly by the commonplace that important developments can have small beginnings. Although the commonplace in its turn is formally explained by what follows (33.1 *Nam*), no explanation is in fact forthcoming. The reader is led to believe that the statements about democracy and oligarchy – surprising in themselves – will function merely as a foil for a comparable statement about monarchy (33.2 *ut . . . sic . . .*), which in turn will finally provide the explanation anticipated by *Nam* at 33.1; but this is not what happens: T. draws no conclusion about monarchy but simply repeats his earlier claim that his kind of narrative is useful (33.2b ~ 32.2b), now adding the quite different explanation that people learn from the experiences of others. Even by T.'s own high standards this seems at best indirect: the two brief references to usefulness respectively generate and are generated by a substantial constitutional section which, though forming the central panel of the ring composition, is essentially irrelevant to the main theme, namely, the disadvantages of his current narrative.[65]

Although the placing of the digression has its own justification, as we have seen, it is of course no accident that it is immediately followed by the trial of Cremutius Cordus – another trial in a sequence of trials and one in which, like T. himself in the digression, a historian discusses and defends his own history (see 34–5 and nn.).

32.1 Pleraque eorum quae rettuli quaeque referam Häussler sees the digression as the '"Methodenkapitel" der Annalen' (379), while for Levene it is a description of T.'s work 'as a whole' (*CCT* 227 n. 3). Such views fail to take account of (a) the placing of the digression at precisely this point in the narrative, as explained above, and (b) the words *Tiberio regente* at 33.4, which anchor T.'s discussion in Tib.'s reign. It seems to me far more likely that *quae*

---

[65] Attempts to deny that this is the digression's main theme, e.g. by Wisse, seem to me to fly in the face of the evidence of T.'s text.

rettuli refers to the foregoing narrative of Book 4, *quaeque referam* to the following narrative up to the end of Book 6.

parua forsitan et leuia memoratu uideri These words appear to allude to Thucydides' preface, combining a reversal of 1.1.1 μέγαν τε … καὶ ἀξιολογώτατον τῶν προγεγενημένων (*oppositio in imitatione*) with an echo of 1.22.4 ἴσως τὸ μὴ μυθῶδες αὐτῶν ἀτερπέστερον φανεῖται (the latter suggested by Moles 110 n. 24). Ancient authors were expected to use a preface for the purposes of αὔξησις or *amplificatio*, claiming that the forthcoming work will deal with great or important matters (e.g. *Rhet. Herenn.* 1.7, Cic. *Inv.* 1.23 'demonstrabimus ea quae dicturi erimus magna . . . esse', Quint. 4.1.33; Lausberg 118 §259, 125–6 §270); in the case of historiography such claims were often complemented by reference to the virtue of selectivity, whereby historians announced, usually in a preface or other programmatic section, that they were dealing with only the most memorable or deserving events: e.g. Hdt. pref., Plb. 1.2.1, Sall. *C.* 4.2 'memoria digna', *J.* 5.1 'magnum', Diod. 1.2.6, Liv. 21.1.1, Dion. Hal. *AR* 1.1.2–3, 1.2.1; Avenarius 128–9, Herkommer 164ff., Marincola 34–43. Cicero's reference to *rebus magnis memoriaque dignis* (*De Or.* 2.63) virtually amounts to a definition of the historiographical genre, and its terms are the exact opposite of those used by T. here. It is of course true that T.'s apologetics relate only to appearances (*uideri*), but he nevertheless creates the impression that his material actually *is* insignificant. For *leuis* as referring to trivial or unimportant material cf. Sen. *Med.* 48 'leuia memoraui', Plin. *Ep.* 8.6.5 'leuia haec et transeunda; illa memoranda' (the famous letter about Pallas), Juv. 4.11 'sed nunc de factis leuioribus' (the turbot satire); for the supine cf. Liv. 38.29.3 'leue dictu'. For *parua* see Liv. 25.1.5 'consul . . . multa proelia parua, haud ullum dignum memoratu fecit' (*haud magna memoratu* at 38.29.3); for both adjs. together cf. Hor. *Epist.* 2.1.179–80 'sic leue, sic paruum est, animum quod laudis auarum | subruit aut reficit'. See also *Agr.* 1.2n. For the adj. *paruus* see 3.31.2n.

non nescius sum The litotes is appropriate to a programmatic passage (6.7.5n.): see e.g. Xen. *Hell.* 2.3.56 καὶ τοῦτο μὲν οὐκ ἀγνοῶ, ὅτι ταῦτα ἀποφθέγματα οὐκ ἀξιόλογα (Moles 106–9 believes that an allusion to the whole Xenophontine episode is 'certain').

set nemo annales nostros cum scriptura eorum contenderit *annales* is a term often used = '(work of) history' (e.g. 34.1, 43.3, 53.2) and, when coupled with *nostri*, is a regular phrase to denote Roman historical texts in general (Varro, *LL* 5.101, Plin. *NH* 8.173, 19.87, Gell. 3.15.4).[66] Scholars have been reluctant to see in our passage a reference to the title of T.'s work, in the

---

[66] At Cic. *Brut.* 49 the phrase has something of the ambiguity of the Eng. word 'history' and could perhaps almost be translated 'our past'.

same way as no one thinks Livy refers to his own actual title when he uses the phrase 'meos annales' at 43.13.2; but Pliny had already referred to T.'s *Historiae* as 'historias tuas' (*Ep.* 7.33.1), and it is obviously possible that T.'s two major works of history had acquired in his lifetime the titles which were later given to them in the sixteenth century by Vertranius (for some discussion see Wellesley's edn of the *Historiae* (1989) 183–4). For general discussion see G. P. Verbrugghe, 'On the meaning of *annales*, on the meaning of annalist', *Philol.* 133 (1989) 192–230; on titulature see N. Horsfall, *BICS* 28 (1981) 103–14.

Various types of comparison or *syncrisis* were basic to literary evaluation in the ancient world (see e.g. F. Focke, 'Synkrisis', *Hermes* 58 (1923) 327–68, A. D. Vardi, '*Diiudicatio locorum*: Gellius and the history of a mode in ancient comparative criticism', *CQ* 46 (1996) 492–519), and *aemulatio* of one's predecessors was of course an integral part of being an author (A. Reiff, *Interpretatio, imitatio, aemulatio: Begriff und Vorstellung literarischer Abhängigkeit bei den Römern* (1959)). Thus historians too were expected to improve on their earlier counterparts (see e.g. Marincola 112–17, 241–57): e.g. 1.1.2–3, *H.* 1.1.1–3, *Agr.* 10.1 (n.), Hecataeus F1, Thuc. 1.20.3, Liv. *praef.* 2, Jos. *Ap.* 24–5. In our passage T. affects to do exactly the opposite: 'Let no one compare . . .' (for the relatively unusual perf. subjunc. to express a prohibition see Handford 49 §48). For the *uariatio* of plur. *nostros* after the preceding singulars *rettuli* and *referam* see 11.3n.

quī uĕtĕrēs pŏpŭlī Rōmānī rēs cōmpŏsŭērĕ Although the plural is maintained in the next sentence ('illi . . . memorabant'), it seems virtually certain that this is a reference to Livy, whose monumental work had ensured his reputation as the outstanding historian of the republic (34.3n.); indeed the phrase *populi Romani res* may even be an allusion to the opening sentence of Livy's preface (*praef.* 1 'Facturusne operae pretium sim si a primordio urbis *res populi Romani* perscripserim'), both authors dispensing with the participle *gestas*, which is found in Cato's *Origines* (F1) and Sallust (*C.* 4.2, *H.* 1.1). On this interpretation, Livy's *a primordio urbis* is replaced by *ueteres*, which therefore should not be emended to *ueteris* (as by Freinsheim) on the basis of 1.2.1 'ueteris populi Romani prospera uel aduersa claris scriptoribus memorata sunt'. For the convention whereby a plural form disguises a reference to a particular predecessor see Skutsch on Enn. *Ann.* 206.

On the basis of M's *cōpossiuere* Ritter proposed to read *conposiuere*, but this form of the compound verb is not found apart from *CIL* 1.584.2. For the appropriately archaising ending *–ere* see *Agr.* 10.3n.; for the pentasyllabic 'heroic' clausula see 4.3n. above. T. seems often to adopt an epic rhythm when referring to the remote past, although the present clause is one syllable too long for a perfect hexameter line (cf. 2.60.2 (and Woodman (2015) 258), 3.26.4n.; more generally see *PH* 378–84).

Ingentia . . . bella, expugnationes urbium For these defining topics of Roman historiography see respectively Lendon and G. M. Paul, '*Urbs capta*: sketch of an ancient literary motif', *Phoenix* 36 (1982) 144–55. For the contrast *illi* . . . [2] *nobis in arto* cf. Plin. *Ep.* 9.2.2–3 'illi . . . qua uarietas rerum qua magnitudo largissime suppetebat; nos quam angustis terminis claudamur . . . perspicis' (a reference I owe to Prof. C. S. Kraus).

fusos captosque reges For example, the defeat and capture of the African king Syphax in 203 BC (Liv. 30.12.1–2) or of King Perseus of Macedonia 168 (Liv. 45.6.10–7.5, where the fate of Syphax is compared). Both subsequently died in captivity in Italy.

si quando ad interna praeuerterent If *illi* (above) genuinely referred to a plurality of writers, T.'s wording here could in theory be taken to refer to historians such as Sisenna, who had concentrated on domestic affairs, i.e. a different category of historians from those (such as Coelius Antipater) who dealt with foreign affairs; but, if *illi* is in fact a disguised reference to Livy, as suggested, this theoretical possibility must be discounted. Indeed, even if *illi* were a genuine plural, the journeying metaphor of *praeuertere* is sustained by *libero egressu* below and strongly suggests a continuity of subject throughout. The reference, in other words, is to the kind of narrative written by Livy and by T. himself, in which there is an alternation between domestic and foreign affairs. *si quando* does not mean 'if ever' (i.e. 'on the rare occasions that . . .') but 'whenever' (i.e. 'on every occasion that . . .'). *praeuertere* is normally deponent in the sense of 'turn to' (*OLD* 5; *TLL* 10.2.1107.25 and also 1108. 8–9, where the statement about T. seems misleading).

discordias consulum . . . optimatium certamina T. adopts three different ways of describing the series of crises (many of them similar in nature) which characterised the later republic. A tribune of the people would seek to win popular support, and a reputation for himself as a *popularis*, by proposing agrarian or grain legislation (the former aimed at the redistribution of land in Italy and the provinces, the latter at the provision of cheap or free grain in Rome). Such proposals inevitably conflicted with the interests of the conservative aristocracy (*optimates*), from whose ranks the consuls were almost exclusively drawn and who sought to preserve the status quo. Well known exs. are the tribunates of Ti. Sempronius Gracchus (133 BC: *MRR* 1.493–4) and his brother Gaius (123, 122: *MRR* 1.513–14, 517–18), L. Appuleius Saturninus (103, 100: *MRR* 1.563, 575–6), P. Servilius Rullus (63: *MRR* 2.168) and P. Clodius Pulcher (58: *MRR* 2.195–6).

libero egressu memorabant *liber egressus* is found elsewhere only in Columella (4×), where it is used literally to refer to the free movement of animals and birds (6.23 'freti uiribus per nemora uagantur liberosque egressus et reditus habent' (of bulls), 8.8 (*bis*), 9.1); here in T. the phrase is being used metaphorically to explain that republican historians could move freely between and within domestic and foreign narratives: neither type of narrative deterred historians from embarking on it, and, once embarked, they found ample opportunity in both for drama and excitement.[67] See also C. Damon, *AHC* 356–7.

32.2 Nobis in arto et inglorius labor Scholars as far back as Muretus have seen here an allusion to Virg. *G.* 4.6 'in tenui labor; at tenuis non gloria', but, quite apart from the question of whether there actually is an allusion (the passages have only the two words *in* and *labor* in common), the Virgilian line has led to a misinterpretation of T.'s words. It is of course quite true that historians were expected to seek *gloria* through their works (e.g. Sall. *C.* 1.3, 3.2; Marincola 57–62, 149–50), but T. is not saying that his efforts will fail to bring him glory: (a) such a statement would contradict his remarks to the contrary at 3.55.5 (see nn.); (b) the author's glory has not been mentioned hitherto in the digression, it strikes an irrelevant note in the argument, and it does not feature in the digression again; (c) a reference to the author's glory would make no sense of *quippe* below. *inglorius* refers rather to the nature of T.'s subject matter and is explained by the next sentence (*quippe*): his efforts as an author are not devoted to glorious material such as foreign conquests. *inglorius* is (as it were) transferred from the author's material to his labours,[68] much as *compositus* at 31.2 is transferred from Tib.'s speech to the man himself: the adj. thus combines well with *in arto* (for the *uariatio* see Sörbom 92–3): his ability to move between domestic and foreign affairs is restricted by the nature of each (*in arto ~ libero egressu*), and neither offers him the desired scope. For the historian's *labor* see Marincola 148–58; also below, 61n.

immota quippe aut modice lacessita pax Compare the praise of a contemporary, Philo (*Leg. Gai.* 141 τρία πρὸς τοῖς εἴκοσιν ἔτη γῆς καὶ θαλάσσης ἀναψάμενον τὸ κράτος καὶ μηδὲ σπέρμα πολέμου μήτε κατὰ τὴν Ἑλλάδα μήτε κατὰ τὴν βάρβαρον ὑποτυφόμενον ἐάσαντα, τὴν δὲ εἰρήνην καὶ τὰ τῆς εἰρήνης ἀγαθὰ παρασχόμενον ἄχρι τῆς τοῦ βίου τελευτῆς), but T.'s statement reads oddly in the light of the Thracian campaign only two years later (4.46–51, where see intro. n.); perhaps the campaign is to be regarded as an example of 'modest disturbance'. For *immota* see 15.27.2, 46.2; for *lacessita* see 15.2.2, Sen. *Ep.* 66.40 (at Liv. 31.18.4 the object of the verb is presumably *me* rather than *pacem*).

---

[67] *egressus* is also used metaphorically at Quint. 4.3.12, where, however, the meaning is different and more concrete ('digression').

[68] Compare the transference described at Plut. *Glor. Ath.* 345E–F.

maestae urbis res The adj. suggests death (*maestam . . . urbem* at Virg. *Aen.* 11.26 and 147).

princeps proferendi *imp*eri *in*curiosus erat Tib. inherited from Augustus a 'consilium coercendi intra terminos imperii' (1.11.4) and famously abided by it (6.32.1 and n., *Agr.* 13.2n.). *proferre* is the *mot juste* for extending the empire or its boundaries (1.3.6, 12.23.2, Cic. *Rep.* 3.24, Liv. 1.33.9, Virg. *Aen.* 6.795, *al.*). *incuriosus* is used more often by T. (18×) than by any other classical author; he is also the first to use it with the genitive (e.g. *Agr.* 1.1, *H.* 1.49.3 and H.) and the only one to construct it with the gerundive (dat. at 14.38.2): see *TLL* 7.1.1082.21 and 46–7.

Non tamen sine usu fuerit introspicere illa primo aspectu leuia While *illa primo aspectu leuia* repeats in more precise terms *pleraque . . . leuia . . . uideri* at the start of the digression, rounding off temporarily the topic of triviality, *non . . . sine usu* introduces the new topic of usefulness by which T.'s subject matter will be defended and to which he will return after his account of constitutions (33.2 'haec conquiri tradique in rem fuerit'). On *introspicere* Malloch notes that 'T. uses this uncommon verb more than any other writer' (11.38.1n.): it is appropriate to his interest in psychology and behaviour (cf. *OLD* 3) and consistent with his distrust of appearances (C. Damon, *AHC* 357 and n. 14); see further I. Lana, 'Introspicere in Tacito', *Orpheus* 10 (1989) 26–57. For the etymological word play cf. Sen. *NQ* 6.5.2 'nec contentum exteriore eius aspectu introspicere', Quint. 10.2.16 'qui non introspectis penitus uirtutibus ad primum se uelut aspectum orationis aptarunt'. For the usefulness of historiography see e.g. Avenarius 22–6, Herkommer 128ff. *fuerit* is fut. perfect.

ex quis magnarum saepe rerum motus oriuntur Although the general idea of 'oaks from acorns' is a commonplace (e.g. Arist. *Pol.* 1303b17–18, Caes. *BC* 3.68.1, 3.70.2, Liv. 6.34.5 and Oakley's n., 10.23.4, 25.18.3, 27.9.1, Plin. *Ep.* 1.20.12; also 3.31.2n., 5.4.1n.; Tosi 381–3), the precise meaning of *motus* is not clear: perhaps 'the stirrings of great affairs'. For *quis* see 3.28.2n., Malloch on 11.20.3.

33.1 Nam cunctas nationes . . . regunt The statement acts as a 'foil' for the elaboration of the three constitutions which follows below (*ut . . . sic . . .*). Although T. seems to have Cicero's *De Re Publica* primarily in mind (next n.), Herodotus (3.80–2) and Polybius (6.3–10) provided precedents for the inclusion of constitutional material in a historical narrative. It is perhaps relevant that the three basic forms of constitution were also discussed in his *Kingship Orations* by Dio Chrysostom, T.'s contemporary, and in the fragmentary *De Monarchia* ascribed to Plutarch.

Delecta ex iis et conflata rei publicae forma laudari facilius quam euenire uel, si euenit, [haud] diuturna esse potest T.'s reference to the so-called 'mixed constitution' (*rei publicae forma* is a set expression = 'system of government': see Vell. 89.4n.; *OLD forma* 6b) is parenthetic to his main argument and poses numerous difficulties.

(1) *deligere ex* + abl. is a partitive expression and cannot be used of choosing the totality of a group or list *vel sim.* (cf. e.g. *TLL* 5.1.455.24–30): if the text is right (and no one appears to have questioned it), *delecta ex iis* must be elliptical for 'chosen from <elements of> those' (for the notion of 'elements' in a similar context see Cic. *Rep.* 1.69 'quiddam in re publica . . . regale'). E. Harrison (*CR* 37 (1923) 22) suggested that *iii* (i.e. *tribus*) had dropped out after *iis* and he quoted in support Cic. *Rep.* 1.45 'quartum quoddam genus rei publicae maxime probandum esse sentio, quod est ex his quae prima dixi moderatum et permixtum tribus':[69] although I have not printed it, the suggestion is attractive and, as will be seen, T. in this sentence is clearly alluding to Cicero's *De Republica*. (2) The transmitted *consciata* was emended to *consociata* by Ernesti, but this verb, though printed by Furneaux and Koestermann, has the wrong meaning (see *OLD* 2). Th. Kiessling proposed *conflata* without further comment; E. Harrison (loc. cit.) independently made the same proposal and suggested that T. was alluding to Cic. *Rep.* 1.54 'probo anteponoque singulis illud quod conflatum fuerit ex omnibus', a passage already adduced by Ritter and Doederlein. The allusion seems confirmed by the fact that T.'s subsequent wording picks up an immediately preceding sentence (*Rep.* 1.53 'qui eam *formam rei publicae* maxime *laudant* '); T. does not use *conflare* elsewhere but it is a favourite verb of Cicero. (3) The sequence *diuturna esse potest* also evokes Cicero (e.g. *Rep.* 2.62 'in hoc statu rei publicae, quem dixi iam saepe non posse esse diuturnum', 3.7 'eam rem publicam quae possit esse diuturna', *Off.* 2.25 'nec uero ulla uis imperii tanta est quae premente metu possit esse diuturna'), but Madvig (3.227) rightly argued that *haud* had been mistakenly added by someone who failed to perceive that the sentence as a whole pivots around *quam* and contrasts *laudari* with the two alternatives *euenire uel . . . diuturna esse* ('a system of government chosen from elements of those in combination is able to be praised more easily than to happen or, if it does happen, to be long-lasting').

There is a vast bibliography on the mixed constitution, e.g. K. von Fritz, *The theory of the mixed constitution in antiquity* (1954), A. W. Lintott, 'The theory of the mixed constitution at Rome', in J. Barnes and M. T. Griffin (edd.), *Philosophia Togata II* (1997) 70–85, C. Rowe and M. Schofield (edd.), *The Cambridge history of Greek and Roman political thought* (2000) 739 (index),

---

[69] Harrison believed that *tribus* in Cicero's text was out of place and should be transposed to follow *ex his*.

R. K. Balot (ed.), *A companion to Greek and Roman political thought* (2006) 626 (index), D. Hammer, *Roman political thought* (2014) 48–58. Although numerous earlier authors had praised this form of constitution (e.g. Thucydides (8.97.2), Aristotle, Polybius,[70] and Dionysius of Halicarnassus), T.'s allusions to Cicero suggest that *laudari* is primarily a reference to the *De Republica* (cf. 1.45, 1.54, 1.69–70, 2.41).

33.2 Igitur For the resumptive use of *igitur*, here picking up the main argument after the parenthetical *delecta . . . potest*, see 3.3n.

plebe ualida uel cum patres pollerent looks back to *populus aut primores* above (1). For the *uariatio* of abl. abs. ~ temporal clause see e.g. 71.1, 1.25.2, 2.33.2, 6.51.3. For *ualida* cf. Liv. 5.29.1 'plus suis comitiis plebs ualuit'; for the combination with *pollere* cf. Sall. *J.* 6.1 'pollens . . . ualidus', Sil. 16.296–7 'ualent . . . pollent'.

noscenda uulgi natura et quibus modis temperanter haberetur 'one had to become acquainted with the nature of the common people and by what means they would be maintained in a controlled manner': the use of *haberi* is similar to 6.1 above ('quibus modis ad eam diem habitae sint'), and, in order to introduce the indir. question, *noscendum* has to be understood from *noscenda*. Although there is no verbal similarity, perhaps T. is thinking of Sall. *C.* 39.2 'quo plebem in magistratu placidius tractarent'. *temperanter* is unique to T. (again at 15.29.1).

senatusque et optimatium ingenia qui maxime perdidicerant Cf. Plin. *NH* 29.27 'satis esse ingenia Graecorum inspicere, non perdiscere'. *senatus* and *optimates* are a Livian combination (24.23.10, 37.9.4; later at Vell. 2.3.2).

callidi temporum et sapientes credebantur Cf. Cic. *Inv.* 1.58 'sapiens et callidus' (also *Att.* 10.8.7). For *callidus* + gen. see H. on *H.* 2.32.1.

sic . . . haec conquiri tradique in rem fuerit, quia . . . plures aliorum euentis docentur Since *sic* is correlative with *ut* above, readers are led to expect that a similar point is about to be made here as there: just as in a democracy it is important to know the character of the people (*noscenda*) and in an oligarchy to learn the temperament of the rulers (*perdidicerant*), so too in an autocracy it is important to understand the *princeps*. But this is not what T. says. He reverts, ring fashion, to the point he made at 32.2, namely, that his apparently trivial material (*haec*) is useful; but, whereas earlier he saw usefulness in terms of deceptiveness (we should take notice of trivial events because they can have important consequences), here he sees it in terms of exemplarity: the majority of people learn from the experiences of others

---

[70] To whose name Moles (119–20) saw a punning allusion in T.'s *diuturna*.

('quia . . . plures . . . aliorum euentis docentur'). The expected reference to the *princeps* has been entirely elided. Since Tib. was famously inscrutable (3.22.2n.), this may not be surprising; but his elision transfers the emphasis from the *princeps* to his subjects (*aliorum*), who constitute the *exempla* for T.'s readers. Livy's normative view of exemplarity was that historiography offered examples of good behaviour to imitate and of bad behaviour to avoid (*praef.* 10); yet these are not at all the responses which *aliena malefacta* and *gloria ac uirtus* receive from readers when T. focusses on them in more detail below (4).

conquirere evidently means both 'to search out' and 'to investigate' (*OLD* 2 and 3): since *tradi* clearly looks back to *rettuli . . . referam . . . memoratu* at the start of the digression, it is natural to conclude that *conquiri* looks back to *introspicere* and hence that it means, at least primarily, 'to investigate' (as at Col. 1 *praef.* 29, where it is again combined with *tradere*); for the acc. + infin. after *in rem esse* cf. Liv. 44.19.3.

conuerso statu neque alia <fiducia> rerum quam si unus imperitet *hic rei publicae status* having been a common phrase in Cicero, *status* was appropriated by Augustus to describe the principate (Suet. *Aug.* 28.2, Gell. 15.7.3), as if to suggest continuity with the republic: T.'s reference to 'change' (as again at 1.4.1 'uerso ciuitatis statu') is therefore pointed. See further E. Koestermann, '"status" als politischer Terminus in der Antike', *RhM* 86 (1937) 225–40; Vell. 131.1n. For *conuerso* cf. [Quint.] *Decl.* 268.19 'ciuitatium status scimus ab oratoribus esse conuersos'.

T.'s words illustrate 'theme and variation', the first abl. abs. being explained by the second, which involves a favourite form of words (1.6.3 'ut non aliter ratio constet quam si uni reddatur', 1.9.4 'non aliud discordantis patriae remedium fuisse quam <ut> ab uno regeretur', 1.30.3, 4.17.3, 13.25.4); but the transmitted *alia* requires a noun with which it can agree. Most editors have followed Lipsius in emending *alia rerum* to *alia re Rom<ana>*, which is strongly supported by Moles (115–18) and Wisse (332 n. 115), but K. Bringmann (*Historia* 20 (1971) 376–9) suggested *alia rerum <salute>* and was followed by Heubner and Borzsák. Although each emendation makes good sense,[71] neither helps to explain how the corruption came about. I therefore suggest *fiducia* (homoeoteleuton); for the combination with *rerum* cf. *H.* 2.4.2 (and H. for other exs.): 'with the change in the constitution and there being no confidence in affairs other than if one man ruled'. *imperitet* is subjunctive because *neque . . . rerum* is equivalent to the

---

[71] Lipsius' text is translated as 'the Roman world is little else than a monarchy' by Jackson, an interpretation which seems universal; but the words could equally well mean 'there being no alternative Roman system to monarchy'. Lipsius himself did not offer an explanation of his emendation.

apodosis of an ideal future condition (= 'nor would there be any confidence unless one man were to rule'). For the sentiment cf. *H.* 1.1.1 'omnem potentiam ad unum conferri pacis interfuit', Quint. 3.8.47 'stare iam rem publicam nisi uno regente non posse', Flor. 4.3.5–6 [2.14.5–6] 'imperii corpus, quod haud dubie numquam coire et consentire potuisset nisi unius praesidis nutu quasi anima et mente regeretur', Sen. *Clem.* 1.3.5. For the frequentative *imperitare* see above, 4.3n.

pauci prudentia honesta ab deterioribus, utilia ab noxiis discernunt *prudentia* was commonly defined in terms of distinguishing between good and evil (e.g. Cic. *Off.* 1.153, *Fin.* 5.67): it seems odd to insist that it is a virtue possessed only by a few, but the point is of course rhetorically appropriate to T.'s argument (and for the alternative, *euentis docentur*, see Liv. 22.39.10, quoted next n.). The contrast between *honesta* and *deteriora* recurs at 11.38.4 (but the text is badly corrupt), that between *utilia* and *noxia* at 6.46.5.

plures aliorum euentis docentur Ancient historiography conventionally had a didactic or exemplary function (see also 28.1n., 32.2n.): classic examples are Livy (*praef.* 10) and esp. his older contemporary, Diodorus, much of whose preface is devoted to the subject: he calls historiography a 'schooling' which enables readers 'to distinguish each element of utility' (1.1.1 διδασκαλίαν, 1.1.2 τῶν χρησίμων ἕκαστα διαγινώσκειν). There is an extensive bibliography on *exempla* and exemplarity: see e.g. J. D. Chaplin, *Livy's exemplary history* (2000), C. S. Kraus, 'From exempla to exemplar? Writing history around the Emperor in Imperial Rome', in *Flavius Josephus and Flavian Rome* (ed. J. Edmondson et al., 2005) 181–200, R. Langlands, '"Reading for the moral" in Valerius Maximus: the case of *severitas*', *PCPS* [= *CCJ*] 54 (2008) 160–87, M. Roller, 'The exemplary past in Roman historiography and culture', in A. Feldherr (ed.), *The Cambridge companion to the Roman historians* (2009) 241–30, B. Tipping, *Exemplary epic: Silius Italicus' Punica* (2010), S. J. V. Malloch, 'Frontinus and Domitian: the politics of the *Strategemata*', *Chiron* 45 (2015) 77–100. See also 37.3n. below.

Ritter wished to emend to *euentibus*, a noun which is commonly combined with *docere* (e.g. Liv. 22.39.10 'nec euentus modo hoc docet, stultorum iste magister'), but cf. Cic. *Div.* 2.27 'docere . . . euentis'.

33.3 ut profutura, ita minimum oblectationis adferunt T. refers to the *utile* and *dulce* which historical writing was expected to provide (Cic. *Fin.* 5.51 'esse utilitatem in historia, non modo uoluptatem'), and he repeats in reverse (chiastic) order the point he made at 32.1–2: although his narrative is useful, as just demonstrated in §2, nevertheless, as he is about to explain, it offers his readers no pleasure (his superlative is even more unappealing than Thuc. 1.22.4 ἀτερπέστερον, compared by Lipsius). For the pleasure to be afforded by historiography see e.g. Duris F1 ἡδονῆς, Cic. *Orat.* 37

'delectationis causa', *De Or.* 2.59 'delectationis causa', *Fam.* 5.12.4–5 'uoluptatis ... ad delectationem lectoris ... iucundae ... delectationem ... iucunda ... delectat ... iucundissima lectionis uoluptate', Vitr. 5 *praef.* 1, Plin. *Ep.* 5.8.4 'historia quoquo modo scripta delectat' (cf. *PH* 232); Avenarius 26–8, Herkommer 135 (both perhaps misleading). *oblectationem adferre* may be Ciceronian (*Rep.* fr. dub. 2 Powell, where see app. crit.); for *delectationem adf.* see *Brut.* 13, *Fam.* 7.1.2, Quint. 2.13.11.

situs gentium, uarietates proeliorum These were the two elements which in Cicero's opinion defined the genre of historiography (*Orat.* 66 'historia ... in qua et narratur ornate et regio saepe aut pugna describitur'; cf. *De Or.* 2.63 'rerum ratio ... desiderat regionum descriptionem'), and he was thrilled to think that his brother had such material from his trip to Britain (*Q.Fr.* 2.16.4 'quos tu situs, ... quas gentes, quas pugnas ... habes!'). T. included ethno-geographical material in the *Agricola* (10–13.1: see nn.) and *Histories* (5.2–10: see A. C. Miravalles, '*Excursio per Orientem*: eastern subjects in Tacitus' *Histories* and *Annals*' (diss. Durham, 2004) 52–76), as did Sallust in his *Bellum Iugurthinum* (17–19) and *Histories* (3.61–80 M = 3.82–99 R) and Livy (*per.* 103–4); *situs* is the technical term for such material (Hor. *Epist.* 2.1.250–3, Vell. 96.3 and n.). *uarietates* refers to the suspense which historians were expected to engender in their readers (see esp. Cic. *Fam.* 5.12.4 'nihil est enim aptius ad delectationem lectoris quam temporum uarietates fortunaeque uicissitudines', 5 'uiri saepe excellentis ancipites uariique casus'): the classic ex. is the battle in the harbour at Syracuse as described by Thucydides (7.70–1).

clari ducum exitus may perhaps be an example of enallage, 'the deaths of distinguished leaders' (cf. *H.* 1.3.1 'supremae clarorum uirorum necessitates', Cic. *Div.* 2.22 'clarissimorum hominum nostrae ciuitatis grauissimos exitus'), but cf. e.g. *H.* 1.3.1 'laudatis antiquorum mortibus pares exitus', Cic. *Fam* 5.12.5 'si uero exitu notabili concluduntur, expletur animus iucundissima lectionis uoluptate', *Brut.* 43, *TD* 1.116 'clarae uero mortes pro patria oppetitae non solum gloriosae rhetoribus'.

retinent ac redintegrant legentium animum Like Sisenna (F130C = 127P 'ne uellicatim aut saltuatim scribendo lectorum animos impediremus') and Livy (*praef.* 4 'legentium plerisque', 9.17.1 'legentibus' with Oakley's n.), as well as other types of author (e.g. Plin. *NH* 2.241 'legentium animos per totum orbem ueluti manu ducere'), T. shows himself explicitly aware of his readership (6.7.5 'lecturos', *H.* 2.50.2 'oblectare legentium animos');[72] also below (n. *obuia*) and 11.3n. above. *retinere* is almost technical for holding the attention

---

[72] It may be inferred from the recurring presence of the word *animus* that the authors in question expected their texts to be read personally by individual readers rather than declaimed to them in public or recited to them in private.

(*OLD* 2b): see esp. Cic. *Fam.* 5.12.5 'cuius studium in legendo non . . . *retinetur?*' (as Ernesti says, and as these notes make clear, T. seems to have this whole passage in mind). For *redintegrant . . . animum* cf. Caes. *BG* 2.25.3, Front. *Strat.* 2.7.11 (neither refers to reading, however).

saeua iussa For an esp. telling example see 6.24.1 ('quo non aliud atrocius uisum'); for the expr. cf. Val. Fl. 3.47 'iussa . . . saeuissima'.

continuas accusationes The continuity is mentioned both immediately before and after the present digression (31.1 'His tam adsiduis . . .', 36.1 'postulandis reis tam continuus annus fuit'); see also e.g. 6.29.1 'caede continua', 6.40.1 'adsuetudine malorum'.

fallaces amicitias The outstanding example in Book 4 is the entrapment of Titius Sabinus in 28 (68.4 'speciem artae amicitiae'), but the falsity of Sejanus' friendship (cf. esp. 4.59.2 'quamquam exitiosa suaderet, ut non sui anxius cum fide audiebatur') would have dominated Book 5 and still resonates in Book 6 (see 5.6.2n.). *fallaces amicitiae* recurs only at 16.32.3, another instructive passage.

perniciem innocentium Cremutius Cordus will claim innocence at the very beginning of his speech below (34.2 'adeo factorum innocens sum'). For the expr. cf. Cic. *Clu.* 129, *Rosc. Am.* 141, Curt. 10.1.30.

easdem exitii causas coniungimus Pichena's emendation of the transmitted *exitu* produces a regular phrase which is common in the *Annals* (1.5.2, 4.52.2, 4.58.2, 16.14.1). For *coniungere* see 6.38.1n.

obuia rerum similitudine et satietate 'presented with a satiety of similar material' (*OLD obuius* 4), but the adj. perhaps suggests also a return to the metaphor of *libero egressu* at 32.1 (so Oakley (1991) 344): see *OLD obuius* 3 and, for similar metaphors, 6.22.4n. Works of rhetorical theory warned that monotony of one sort or another leads to satiety (Cic. *Inv.* 1.76, *De Or.* 2.177, Quint. 5.14.30, 9.4.143 'taedium ex similitudine ac satietatem creat'; *OLD satietas* 3b), a danger of which T. expresses himself well aware elsewhere (see 6.7.5n., 6.38.1n., 16.16.1).

33.4 Tum <adnotatum> quod . . . extuleris M reads simply *tum quod*, which is usually translated 'Then there is the fact that . . .'; yet there seems to be no parallel for *tum quod* in the sense of *adde quod* or *accedit quod*: in other instances where *quod* is preceded by *tum*, the conjunction habitually introduces a subordinate clause of cause, which would make no sense here.[73] It is

---

[73] This nevertheless seems to be close to what is argued by Müller (3.46–9), who invites us to imagine that *ingentia illi bella . . .* at 32.1 had been preceded by *primum quod*, which is now picked up by *tum quod*.

theoretically possible to regard *quod* as a concessive conjunction and correlative with *at* (= *tamen*) below, a construction for which only Lucr. 2.532–5 and Prop. 3.2.11–16 are cited (K–S 2.83; *OLD quod* 6c); but the sense of the single sentence which results is scarcely cogent. Nipperdey suggested deleting *quod*, but it is hard to see why the word came to be in the text; Ritter emended to *tumque*, a form found at *H.* 4.57.1, but with a different meaning. I suggest that a word such as *adnotatum* or *adnotandum* has dropped out after *tum*: 'Moreover, it has been [*or* must be] observed that . . .' (for the construction cf. Plin. *Ep.* 2.11.6 'adnotatumque experimentis quod fauor et misericordia . . . primos impetus habent', Front. *Aq.* 104.3 'crediderim adnotandum quod senatus . . . numerum uetuerit'). Whatever solution is adopted, *tum* (*OLD* 9) clearly introduces a new point – and one whose double focus brings the digression to a natural conclusion. The references to old writers and the Punic Wars take us back to 32.1, providing further reasons why republican historians have the advantage over T.; on the other hand, the contemporaries to whose disapproval T. refers can only be readers of his narrative, this being a continuation of the theme of disappointed readers at §3 just above.

neque refert cuiusquam Punicas Romanasne acies laetius extuleris Given the link back to 32.1, T. is presumably thinking of Livy's third decade rather than Coelius Antipater's monograph; but his choice of the Punic Wars as an example was perhaps prompted by the *Punica* of his older contemporary, Silius Italicus, with whose work he was familiar (*CCT* 37).

Nipperdey changed the transmitted *Romanasue* to *Romanasne*, thus producing an identical construction to that found at Hor. *S.* 1.1.49–51; without the change there is no word to indicate an indir. question at all. *laetius extuleris* is perhaps an allusion to Virg. *Aen.* 2.687–8, though the sense is quite different.

at introduces a contrast between the two preceding readerships (*rarus obtrectator* and *cuiusquam*) and the two following: [1] the enduring *posteri* and [2] guilty individuals with no family connections (cf. *utque . . . exsintctae sint*). The latter are then subdivided into two further categories: [2a] those who see themselves in the guilty characters of T.'s narrative (*qui . . . putent*) and [2b] those who resent the heroic characters of the narrative (*etiam . . . arguens*). The two categories are contrasted by *similitudinem* ~ *diuersa*.

multorum qui Tiberio regente poenam uel infamias subiere posteri manent Family members might naturally be inclined to favour their ancestors and thus be predisposed to think that a historian has not treated them fairly (see esp. Thuc. 2.35.2 ὅ τε γὰρ ξυνειδὼς καὶ εὔνους ἀκροατὴς τάχ' ἂν τι ἐνδεεστέρως πρὸς ἃ βούλεταί τε καὶ ἐπίσταται νομίσειε δηλοῦσθαι), but the singling out of Tib.'s *victims* suggests that their descendants' particular concern is guilt by association, worried that they may be seen as being as treasonable as their ancestors (in the way that Asinius Gallus and the elder Piso, for example, were thought to have inherited their fathers' intransigence: cf. 1.12.4, 2.43.2). T.'s statement assumes extra meaning if Syme was right to suggest that some of the names in the *Annals* 'look deliberate, revealing the forebears of senators known to Tacitus' and 'unmistakable to any contemporary' (*Tac.* 302, quoting numerous exs.; see also 6.7.2n., 6.47.1n.).

Tiberio regente is a perfectly normal way of saying 'in Tiberius' reign' (cf. 13.3.1 'regente eo', Quint. 3.8.47, quoted at 2n. above); the verb is used equally of democracy and oligarchy at §1 above. The plural *infamias* has been doubted, but there is one other classical occurrence (Plaut. *Pers.* 347) and T. likes the plural of abstract nouns, such as *audaciae* at 1.74.1 (*TLL* 7.1.1337. 31–2); *poenam subire* and *infamiam subire* are both regular expressions, though the latter is less common (13.21.2, Cic. *Q.Fr.* 3.4.3, Suet. *Aug.* 68.1, *Claud.* 5.1, Gell. 1.3.23). *posteri manent* recurs in T.'s version of Claudius' speech at 11.24.3; *manent* = 'are still alive' (*OLD* 7b).

utque 'and even if . . .' (as 40.4; *OLD ut* 35).

reperies qui *ob* similitudinem *morum* aliena *malefacta* sibi obiectari putent This danger is similar to that against which Phaedrus warns (3 *prol.* 45–50): 'suspicione si quis errabit sua | et rapiet ad se quod erit commune omnium, | stulte nudabit animi conscientiam. | huic excusatum me uelim nihilo minus: | neque enim notare singulos mens est mihi, | uerum ipsam uitam et mores hominum ostendere.' Ancient readers were accustomed to double meanings (Quint. 9.2.65–7, 81–5; Lausberg 408 §906); Pliny says that Domitian, in view of his affinity with Nero (*Agr.* 45.2n.), would have interpreted criticism of Nero as criticism of himself (*Pan.* 53.4 'ut in se dicta interpretaretur quae de simillimo dicerentur'). Cf. also 6.29.3n.

It is worth asking whether *reperies* is simply a *façon de parler* (cf. 6.22.1n.) or whether it is based on T.'s personal experience. Pliny in one of his letters (*Ep.* 9.27.1–2) tells an interesting story about an anonymous historian:

Recitauerat quidam uerissimum librum, partemque eius in alium diem reseruauerat. Ecce amici cuiusdam orantes obsecrantesque ne reliqua recitaret. Tantus audiendi quae fecerint pudor, quibus nullus faciendi quae audire erubescunt.

The context is not quite comparable, since Pliny (as in *Ep.* 5.8.12–13) seems to be referring to the recitation of a contemporary work, but his letter well illustrates the response to historiography at the time. T. could well have gathered reaction to the *Annals* from reciting parts of it, and indeed Pliny's anonymous historian has been thought by some to be T. himself (C. L. Whitton, *CT* 363–4).

For the preposition *ob* see 3.5.2n.; *putent* is subjunctive because the clause is generic, as e.g. *D.* 12.6 'plures hodie reperies qui Ciceronis gloriam quam qui Vergili detrectent'.

Etiam gloria ac uirtus infensos habet Rome's aristocratic society was based on a culture of rivalry and competition, a culture in which historiography played its part by offering examples of behaviour to imitate (above, 2n.): when Sallust compares historical writing to *imagines*, he remarks on how *memoria rerum gestarum* lights a flame in the breasts of outstanding men (*J.* 4.6): 'eam flammam ... crescere neque prius sedari quam uirtus eorum famam atque gloriam adaequauerit', a statement which is shortly followed by the formula to which T. alludes below (n. *sed*). Just as Sallust proceeds to lament that this culture has broken down in his own day (4.7–8), so T.'s words, reminiscent of points already made in the *Agricola* (1.4 'tam saeua et infesta uirtutibus tempora', 41.1 'infensus uirtutibus princeps'), illustrate his favourite topic of the reversal of the moral order (for which see Walker 81) and thus provide an appropriate conclusion to a digression whose main theme has been reversal.

gloria and *uirtus* seem to be used almost metonymically = 'examples of glory and *uirtus*' (cf. *uirtus ipsa* of Thrasea Paetus and Barea Soranus at 16.21.1). Although the reference to glory seems to contradict what was said about the lack of glorious material at 32.2 (n.), we should bear in mind that T.'s statements, though general, are not absolute (cf. 32.1 *pleraque*, 2 *modice*): there are a very few exs. of glory, such as Dolabella at 4.26.1 ('huic ... gloriam intendit'). It is well known that there is a scarcity of *uirtus* in the *Annals*, although Lepidus at 4.20.2 above is perhaps an example.

ut nimis ex propinquo diuersa arguens 'as demonstrating/criticising their opposites from too close at hand'. Quintilian stated that most things are proved by their opposites (12.1.35 'plurima contrariis probantur'), and by way of example said that the nature of *uirtus* is revealed by its antithesis, evil ('uirtus quid sit, aduersa ei malitia detegit'); T.'s statement is the converse of the latter: accounts of *gloria* and *uirtus* reveal infamy and evil. *nimis ex propinquo* perhaps relates to the circumstances under which the opposites of behaviour manifest themselves: the reader who, when faced with a crucial dilemma, has made an ignoble choice will resent the character in the text who, when confronted by an identical dilemma, chose nobly and thereby shows up the immoral nature of the reader for what it is. This is the *recti inuidia* to which T. refers in the preface to the *Agricola* (1.1 and n.; Kaster 182 n. 15); and, the closer the circumstances of comparison, the greater the contrast between good and evil. This way of looking at things was no doubt facilitated by the common ancient belief that for each virtue there was a corresponding vice (see e.g. Cic. *Inv.* 2.165).

Sed ad inceptum redeo Only two digressions in the *Annals* end with
a closural formula (for the other see 6.22.4 'ne nunc incepto longius abierim'
and n.); from the traces in M (*ancepto*) it is difficult to think that T. is not
alluding to the only two other exs. of *ad inceptum redeo* (Sall. *J.* 4.9, 42.5). For
some other closural formulae see Vell. 68.5n.

34–45 THE YEAR AD 25

The pattern of this year's narrative, in which a short section on foreign
affairs follows a much longer sequence of domestic events, has no parallel in
the Tiberian or Neronian books; yet this introspective emphasis follows on
naturally after the preceding digression (above, p. 172). The domestic section
falls into four subsections and is dominated by the three episodes of
Cremutius Cordus' trial (34–5), Tib.'s speech in the senate (37–8), and
Sejanus' exchange of letters with the *princeps* (39–40).[74] These three are
each linked with one another: Cordus' trial is instigated by Sejanus (34.1),
whose increasing power and influence are typified by his letter to Tib.;
Cordus' speech is themed by memory (35.2–5), which will recur in the
emperor's speech (38.1, 3).

34–44 *Domestic Affairs*

34–36 Cremutius Cordus and other trials
The trial of the historian Cremutius Cordus (34–5) precedes and entirely
eclipses the other cases in this section (36). It has attracted an enormous
amount of scholarly comment, partly because Cordus is seen as a surrogate
for T., his speech providing an insight into the author himself, partly because
he appears as a heroic figure, a defendant speaking up for freedom in the face
of certain death.[75]

34.1 Cornelio Cosso Asinio Agrippa For Cossus Cornelius Lentulus,
brother of the consul of the following year (46.1n.) and son of the consul of
1 BC, see *RE* 4.1365–6 = Cornelius 183 (Groag), *PIR* 2.335–6 no. 1381, *BNP*
3.833 [II 27]; after his consulship he probably became governor of Upper
Germany. For Asinius Agrippa, brother of the consul of 23 (1.1n.) and

---

[74] This arrangement was proposed in Martin–Woodman p. 16; Wisse's
objection that such arrangements 'are very insecure' (315 n. 55) does not
stop him adopting a different arrangement which he describes as 'significant' and 'clearly correct', despite its failing to take account of ch. 36.
[75] For the latest discussions see Moles 134–84 and Wisse, the latter with
extensive bibliography (356–61), to which add Suerbaum 1361–2.

grandson of Asinius Pollio (below, 4n.), see *RE* 2.1584 = Asinius 7 (von Rohden), *PIR* 1.243–4 no. 1223, *BNP* 2.160 [II 1]; he will die in the following year (61n.).

Cremutius Cordus was a historian and father to the Marcia for whom Seneca wrote his *Consolatio ad Marciam* on the death of one of her sons; Cordus is remembered in the work (see below). Whether or not he was a senator is uncertain; that his trial took place in the senate cannot be used as evidence, since the *eques* M. Terentius was likewise tried there (6.8.1): see further below, n. *Seiani*. The exact scope of his history is unknown: Seneca says 'ciuilia bella defleuit' and makes reference to 'unius . . . saeculi facta' (*Cons. Marc.* 26.1, 5); Dio refers to a history ἣν πάλαι ποτὲ περὶ τῶν τῷ Αὐγούστῳ πραχθέντων συνετεθείκει (57.24.2–3; cf. Suet. *Aug.* 35.2). Two allegedly verbatim fragments, on the death of Cicero, survive in Sen. *Suas.* 6.19 and 6.23: see, in addition to Feddern's commentary ad locc., B. M. Levick in *FRH* 1.497–501 (substantial bibliography on p. 497), 2.964–73, 3.592–3; *LH* 64–9, 127–9. See *RE* 4.1703–4 = Cremutius 2 (Cichorius), *PIR* 2.384 no. 1565, *BNP* 3.929. For his case and bibliography thereon see Rutledge 95–6.

nouo ac tunc primum audito crimine T. begins the episode with an allusion to the opening of Cicero's speech *Pro Ligario* ('*Nouum crimen*, C. Caesar, et ante hunc diem non *auditum*'), delivered in 46 BC and subsequently famous: it is mentioned or quoted innumerable times by Quintilian, who on one occasion discusses its opening words at some length (11.3.108–10; cf. 9.4.92). The *Pro Ligario* is the only extant defence speech of Cicero in which he acknowledges that his client is guilty (evidently of *perduellio* or treason); but at the same time Cicero argues inconsistently that Ligarius has committed no crime at all (cf. C. Craig, *CJ* 79 (1984) 193–9). These mutually contradictory claims are an appropriate introduction to the speech of Cordus, who acknowledges the words with which he is charged but denies that he has committed any crime. In addition, the background to Cicero's speech is the conflict between Pompey and Caesar, both of whom will feature prominently in Cordus' defence. For the abl. of the charge see 3.38.1n.

T. here adopts the convention whereby writers drew attention to the novelty of their subject matter (e.g. *Rhet. Herenn.* 1.7 'attentos [sc. lectores] habebimus si . . . de rebus . . . nouis', Sall. *C.* 4.4 'nouitate'); the recording of 'firsts' was also esp. popular (6.1.2n.). Whether, or to what extent, the charge laid against Cremutius Cordus was in fact novel is unclear (for a survey of the relevant evidence see Peachin 17–46). At some unknown date in Augustus' principate (14 BC has been suggested) a lawyer in Milan, defending a client accused of murder, was so incensed by the intervention of lictors 'ut . . . Brutum, cuius statua in conspectu erat, inuocaret legum ac libertatis auctorem et uindicem': for this outburst, adds Suetonius, 'paene poenas luit' (*Gramm.*

30.5). Nevertheless he was not actually charged, the potential punishment is not thought to have involved the *lex maiestatis* (see Kaster ad loc.), and it is difficult to believe that reporting of the incident has not been influenced by the fame of Cordus' trial. The Augustan declaimer and historian T. Labienus, known for his Pompeian sympathies, was notorious for his attacks on individuals of every type (Sen. *Contr.* 10 *praef.* 4–8), and the senate decreed the burning of all his books, presumably therefore including his now lost history (for which see T. J. Cornell, *FRH* 1.472–3, 2.900–5, 3.551). What seems to distinguish Cordus from these possible precedents is that his praise of the tyrannicides was written rather than oral and that he used the written word for eulogy rather than vituperation (see below, 2nn.).

tunc primum illustrates further the ἀρχὴ κακῶν motif (above, 6.1n.) and implies that other similar cases would follow: T. no doubt has in mind the eulogies of Thrasea Paetus and Helvidius Priscus by Arulenus Rusticus and Herennius Senecio respectively (*Agr.* 2.1 and nn.), which are always in the background of the present episode.

quod . . . dixisset This statement needs to be read in the light of two further considerations. (1) Both Suetonius (*Tib.* 61.3) and Dio (57.24.2–3) say that Cordus' history had been read to or by Augustus, the former associating his case with that of the poet Mamercus Scaurus, which T. mentions at 6.29.3 (see nn.). If Suetonius and Dio are right, the 'publication' of Cordus' *annales* had taken place many years previously and for malign purposes was being denounced only now. (2) Dio gives a similar range of charges to those listed by T. here (57.24.2–3 οὕτω γὰρ οὐδὲν ἔγκλημα ἐπαίτιον λαβεῖν ἠδυνήθη . . . ὥστε ἐπὶ τῇ ἱστορίᾳ . . . κριθῆναι, ὅτι τόν τε Κάσσιον καὶ τὸν Βροῦτον ἐπήνεσε, καὶ τοῦ δήμου τῆς τε βουλῆς καθήψατο), while Suetonius mentions only a variant on those relating to Brutus and Cassius (*Tib.* 61.3 'quod Brutum Cassiumque ultimos Romanorum dixisset'). Yet according to Appian (*BC* 4.114) and Plutarch (*Brut.* 44.1) it was Brutus who had called Cassius 'the last of the Romans': it is therefore very possible that Cordus' charge was at least partly based, not on his own words at all ('Verba mea' at §2 below), but on his repeating the words of a third party.

It is very striking that neither of these considerations, each of which would have increased the reader's sympathy for Cordus, is mentioned in T.'s text. (Of course he may have been unaware of them, or, if aware, believed them mistaken.)

Similar praise to Cordus' is recorded of Philopoemen by Plutarch (*Phil.* 1.7 Ῥωμαίων δέ τις ἐπαινῶν ἔσχατον αὐτὸν Ἑλλήνων προσεῖπεν, ὡς οὐδένα μέγαν μετὰ τοῦτον ἔτι τῆς Ἑλλάδος ἄνδρα γειναμένης οὐδ' αὐτῆς ἄξιον); for more on the concept of 'last' see Moles on Plut. *Brut.* 44.1.[76] For the 'afterlife' of Brutus

[76] J. L. Moles, *A commentary on Plutarch's* Brutus (*Histos* Suppl. 7, 2017) 354–5.

and Cassius see R. MacMullen, *Enemies of the Roman order: treason, unrest, and alienation in the Roman empire* (1966) 18ff., Rawson 488–507. For the term *annales* see 32.1n.

Satrius Secundus et Pinarius Natta For the former see 6.8.5n. and Rutledge 266; he was married to the promiscuous Albucilla (6.47.2). For the latter see *RE* 20.1401–2 = Pinarius 17 (Stein), *PIR* 6.163 no. 410, *BNP* 11.263 [II 2]; Rutledge 254–5.

Seiani clientes Seneca told Marcia that 'Seianus patrem tuum clienti suo Satrio Secundo congiarium dedit', explaining that Sejanus was angry because, when a statue in Pompey's Theatre was being voted to him in 22, Cordus had exclaimed 'tunc uere theatrum perire!' (*Cons. Marc.* 22.4; cf. 3.72.3 and n.). It is possible to read Seneca's account as implying that Cordus was actually present for the vote, which we know from T. took place in the senate (cf. 3.72.3 'censuere patres').

34.2 Id perniciabile reo The exceptionally rare adj. (otherwise only at Curt. 7.3.13) cannot fail to recall *pernicies innocentium* at 33.3, implying the innocence which Cordus claims (below).

Caesar truci uultu defensionem accipiens When Cicero had visited Julius Caesar to intercede for Ligarius, he had come away confident from the look on Caesar's face (*Fam.* 6.14.2 'ex uultu'); Tib., however, looks pitiless (*trux* is commonly found with *uultus*), as was conventional for tyrants (see *Agr.* 45.2n.). Neither he nor Sejanus is mentioned in Cordus' speech. For Tib.'s demeanour at other trials see 2.29.2, 3.15.2, 3.16.2 and 3.67.2 and nn. For the use of the present part. see 12.1n.

relinquendae uitae certus is almost universally taken to refer to suicide, but Moles (135) and Wisse (323 and n. 86, 327–8) favour 'sure of leaving life', comparing 1.27.2 'exitii certus' (and n.). T.'s precise construction seems unparalleled, though a gen. gerund (again at *H.* 4.14.1) is first found at Virg. *Aen.* 4.554 (*TLL* 3.911.52–4).

in hunc modum exorsus est Cordus is not the only historical writer in Latin historiography to deliver a speech: Sallust gives a speech to Julius Caesar in the *Bellum Catilinae* (51) and to Licinius Macer in the *Histories* (3.48 M = 3.15 R), while the elder Cato, who famously inserted his own speeches into his *Origines* (cf. Cic. *Brut.* 89, *De Or.* 1.227, Liv. 45.25.3, *per.* 49, Val. Max. 8.1 *abs.* 2), is given a speech by Livy (34.2–4) to which T. had alluded in Book 3 of the *Annals* (see intro. n. to 3.32–5).

Cordus' speech is placed by T. in the senate (35.4 'egressus . . . senatu') in the presence of Tib. (see above), but, in the view of Momigliano and some earlier scholars cited by Rogers (86 n. 275), 'we know from Seneca that

Cremutius Cordus committed suicide before he was tried in the senate (*Cons. Marc.* 22.6). It is hard to avoid the conclusion that Tacitus made Cremutius go before the senate because he had thought of a good speech to put into his mouth. But it is fair to add that this idea may already have occurred to a predecessor of Tacitus. In that case, Tacitus would have been at fault in trusting a predecessor instead of going to read the *acta senatus'* (A. Momigliano, *The classical foundations of modern historiography* (1990) 113). What is to be made of this?

No one would claim that Cordus' speech is in any sense authentic: like that of Terentius at 6.8, 'the speech is all Tacitus' (Syme, *Tac.* 337 n. 10). On the other hand, it is not certain that Seneca makes no reference to a trial: the use of the term *rei* ('defendants') may well imply a trial (*Cons. Marc.* 22.7), and Cordus would have had a precedent in the elder Piso for committing suicide while his trial was still in progress (cf. 3.15.3). Admittedly there is a difference between Piso's instantaneous self-stabbing and Cordus' self-starvation, which lasted several days and allowed the prosecutors time to complain twice to the consuls that their victim was escaping justice (*Cons. Marc.* 22.6–7): why was Cordus not forced back to the curia to face his accusers? We cannot know the answer (perhaps Tib. made it known that the historian was not to be interrupted); but at least the accounts of Seneca and T. do not seem absolutely incompatible. For another senatorial trial at the start of a year see 68–70.3 below (Ginsburg 27–8); for such formulae as *in hunc modum* see 6.8.1n.

Verba mea, patres conscripti, arguuntur, adeo factorum innocens sum This is a brilliant opening. The parataxis (instead of *adeo . . . ut . . .*) allows the fronting of *Verba mea*, which forms the basis of the whole case, while the antithesis with *factorum* reminds Cordus' listeners that until very recently there had been an important legal distinction between words and deeds (cf. 1.72.2 'facta arguebantur, dicta impune erant').[77] Further, the context of a senatorial trial means that *arguuntur* = 'are accused' (as if the words are personified, in the same way as Labienus' books at Sen. *Contr.* 10 *praef.* 5 'res noua et inusitata supplicium de studiis sumi'): there is therefore an additional contrast between the accused words and the historian, as if the former had an existence independent of their innocent author. Both *uerba . . . arguuntur* and *innocens* + gen. are unparalleled.

Sed neque haec . . . 'but not even my words . . .' (*OLD neque* 2b). A verb such as *composui* or *fuerunt* has to be supplied.

---

[77] Whether, or to what extent, malicious speech was catered for by the Twelve Tables is uncertain (Crawford 2.677–9 on Table VIII, 1).

in principem aut principis parentem, quos lex maiestatis amplectitur Although Cordus' statement makes good sense in itself,[78] it appears to conflict with 1.72.3: 'primus Augustus cognitionem de famosis libellis specie legis eius [sc. maiestatis] tractauit, commotus Cassii Seueri libidine, qua uiros feminasque inlustres procacibus scriptis diffamauerat'. Since we know that Severus was banished to Crete (21.3 above), probably in AD 8 or (cf. Dio 56.27.1) 12, the natural – and seemingly universal – inference from this passage is that he was successfully prosecuted for *maiestas* ('specie legis eius'). Yet (a) T. does not actually say that Severus was dealt with under the *lex maiestatis*, and no other source mentions the *lex* in connection with him. (b) It makes no sense that the defamation of noble men and women, which is essentially a personal matter, should be treated as equivalent to diminishing the majesty of the Roman People or of the *princeps* and his family.[79] (c) It is poor strategy if Cordus at the very beginning of his defence makes a statement which can be refuted easily by reference to the case of Cassius Severus a mere dozen years previously.[80] (d) Severus' form of banishment was *relegatio*, which, as even Bauman admits, was 'well below the statutory penalty for *maiestas*' (*IP* 49).[81] A more likely interpretation of 1.72.3 is that, in the troubled last decade of his principate, Augustus, alerted by Cassius Severus' extreme behaviour to the potential damage which defamation could do, extended the *lex maiestatis* to cover speech and writings

---

[78] It seems from 2.50.2 that *principis parentem* must be a reference to Augustus, not Livia.

[79] The text of Cic. *Fam.* 3.11(74).2, a passage which may offer contrary evidence, is highly uncertain and its interpretation much debated (see Shackleton Bailey's n.; Bauman, *CM* 247–50). Suetonius records that, at an unknown date, the appearance of *famosi libelli* directed against Augustus persuaded the *princeps* to propose measures 'de iis qui libellos aut carmina *ad infamiam cuiuspiam* sub alieno nomine edant' (*Aug.* 55), but there is no indication that these measures came under the heading of *maiestas*, a draconian development which Suetonius would surely have mentioned. The inapplicability of *maiestas* to cases restricted to private individuals is clearly implied in such passages as Quint. 5.10.39 and [Quint.] *Decl.* 252.5 (with Winterbottom ad loc.; cf. also Sen. *Contr.* 9.2.13ff.).

[80] The possibility that T. is deliberately making Cordus present a poor case is to be discounted.

[81] Bauman (*IP* 32–3) can quote no parallel case to that of Cassius Severus until Fabricius Veiento in 62 (14.50.1–2), but his case is not parallel at all since it clearly had a political dimension ('probrosa in patres et sacerdotes'). Bauman had discussed *famosi libelli* earlier in *CM* 246–65.

aimed at the imperial family but ensured that Severus himself was punished under some other law.

For the co-ordinated polyptoton of *principem aut principis parentem* (a version of the so-called 'Priam figure') see Wills 33–41 and 254–61.

Brutum et Cassium laudauisse dicor Cordus in his previous sentence takes it for granted that it is criticism or vituperation which was dangerous ('*in* principem aut principis parentem'), and this is the theme of §5 below (cf. also 31.1 'probrosi in se carminis', 1.72.3 'diffamauerat'); yet he is charged with the very opposite – but praise too could be dangerous, as Agricola discovered (*Agr.* 41.1), and T.'s recent reminder of the grounds on which *gloria* and *uirtus* could arouse hostility (33.4) was very relevant in the present context, since Brutus was proverbial for his *uirtus* (N–H on Hor. *C.* 2.7.11).

Some scholars believe that Cordus was actually charged with some quite different, and much more serious, offence; but there is no evidence for this. *dicor* perhaps has a legal tone (*OLD* 4).

quorum res gestas cum . . . Commentators explain that this is equivalent to *quos, cum eorum res gestas . . .*

34.3 Titus Liuius, eloquentiae ac fidei praeclarus Somewhat like Ovid in *Tristia* 2 (lines 363–468), Cordus invokes in his defence a list of earlier writers; but, whereas Ovid began with the Greeks before moving on to the Romans (as was more normal in such catalogues), Cordus begins with the Romans and mentions the Greeks only collectively at the end (35.1). His first defence witness is Livy. The monumental scale of Livy's history (142 volumes) placed him in a different class from other earlier historians: Pliny, who as a teenager was reading Livy while Vesuvius erupted (*Ep.* 6.20.5), tells the famous story of the man who journeyed all the way from Cadiz just to catch sight of the great historian, and, once he had done so, returned home again (*Ep.* 2.3.8). Livy was particularly famous for his eloquence (Sen. *Ira* 1.20.6, Quint. 8.1.3, 10.1.101), but Quintilian also made this well-known comment: 'neque illa Liuii lactea ubertas satis docebit eum qui non speciem expositionis sed fidem quaerit' (10.1.32). At *Agr.* 10.1~3 T. himself likewise testified to Livy's eloquence but implied that he lacked *fides* in the matter of British geography. Cordus is represented as disagreeing with these assessments of Livy and *fides*, a quality for which Cordus himself was praised by Seneca (*Cons. Marc.* 1.3). *praeclarus* is probably not found elsewhere with the gen. (*TLL* 10.2.486.1–7).

in primis Cn. Pompeium tantis laudibus tulit ut 'Pompeianum' eum Augustus appellaret Augustus, Tib.'s proclaimed *exemplum* (37.3), is implied (§4) or named (§5) pointedly throughout Cordus' speech.

While early imperial writers criticised the *Pompeiani* who under their leader's banner had resisted Caesar and Octavian, they tended to glorify Pompey himself as a heroic soldier-citizen whose death had been a tragedy (P. Grenade, 'Le mythe de Pompée et les Pompéiens sous les Césars', *REA* 52 (1950) 28–63, at 57–61). Thus Cordus himself was outraged when in 22 the statue of Sejanus had been erected in the Theatre of Pompey, 'in monumentis maximi imperatoris' (*Cons. Marc.* 22.5: see above). The point of his present remark seems to be that Augustus had suggested that Livy's praise of Pompey meant sympathy for his supporters too. Cordus has perhaps taken Augustus' remark more seriously than it had been intended; there is nevertheless the implication that Augustus could have responded differently to the 'exaltation' (*tulit*) of Pompey, an ironical reflection on T.'s recent observation that no one cares whether you 'exalt' (33.4 *extuleris*) the Punic or Roman armies. When Octavian in the triumviral period wrote verses attacking Pollio, the latter is said to have replied: 'at ego taceo. non est enim facile in eum scribere qui potest proscribere' (Macr. *Sat.* 2.4.21).

Modern editors punctuate in such a way that *in primis* is to be taken with *praeclarus* rather than with *Cn. Pompeium*, but *praeclarus* is already a superlative adj. and has no need of further qualification (contrast Cic. *Sen.* 39 'magni in primis et praeclari uiri'); *in primis* more naturally accompanies *Cn. Pompeium* as 'introducing the leading member of a group' and 'as the first item in a series' (*OLD imprimis* 1b, 2), as at Plin. *NH* 22.119 'in primis sapientissima animalium esse constat quae fruge uescantur'.

Scipionem Q. Caecilius Metellus Pius Scipio, consul in 52 BC with Pompey, who married his daughter, and an enemy of Caesar (*MRR* 2.234–5, *BNP* 2. 880–1 [I 32]).

Afranium L. Afranius, another Pompeian, was consul in 60 BC (*MRR* 2.183, *BNP* 1.289 [1]).

Cassium ... Brutum Syme noted that this order of the names occurs three times in Cordus' speech as well as in the narrative at 3.76.2: 'The author's hostility to convention and to "ideologies" could not be more emphatically paraded' (*Tac.* 557 n. 7); but the precedence of Cassius is common in some other ancient sources (Rawson 490ff.).

latrones et parricidas Like Cicero (*Mil.* 18, *Phil.* 4.5) and Lentulus (ap. Cic. *Fam.* 12.15.4), Cordus couples two regular terms of abuse (see Opelt 274 and 277–8 (index)), but each had a special point apropos of Brutus and Cassius: the former in Lycia and the latter on Rhodes had perpetrated terrible extortion and slaughter in 42 BC (*CAH* 10.7), and, when they murdered Caesar, he held the title *parens patriae* (Weinstock 200ff., Bauman, *IP* 219 and n. 183).

quae nunc uocabula imponuntur Ritter notes the frequency with which such nomenclature as 'parricide' is used by Cordus' contemporary, Valerius Maximus (1.5.7, 1.6.13, 1.7.2, 1.8.8, 3.1.3, 6.4.5). Since changes of vocabulary were emblematic of civil war (Thuc. 3.82.4–8, Isoc. *Antid.* 283–5), Cordus turns the tables on his opponents by implicitly associating them with a similar charge to that which they have brought against him (cf. 35.2). Although *uocabulum (–a) imponere* is a perfectly regular expr. = 'to give a name to ~ ' (e.g. Varro, *LL* 5.1.1), the verb inevitably has a sinister connotation here.

34.4 Asinii Pollionis scripta C. Asinius Pollio, the 'renaissance man' who was consul in 40 BC and *triumphator* in (?) 39, was orator, tragedian, historian, and patron of poets (including Virgil). *scripta* is a reference to his lost histories, the scope of which is much disputed: see A. Drummond in *FRH* 1.430–45 (substantial bibliography on p. 430), 2.854–67, 3.521–30; *PH* 129–44, *LH* 70–4. None of the surviving fragments mentions Brutus or Cassius. His grandson as consul no doubt listened to Cordus' speech.

memoriam tradunt Livian (8.10.8, 9.41.4).

Messalla Coruinus The consul of 31 BC and famous orator, who was second-in-command to Brutus and Cassius at Philippi but later joined and enthusiastically supported Augustus (see 3.34.2n.; Vell. 71.1n.). He was patron of Tibullus and wrote a history of uncertain scope which is now lost (see A. Drummond in *FRH* 1.463–71, 2.896–9, 3.546–50); the context here suggests that it is this work to which Cordus refers, though the matter is debated (*FRH* 1.467 and n. 33).

imperatorem suum Cassium praedicabat It was natural for a subordinate to address his commanding officer as 'imperator' (see e.g. Vell. 104.4; E. Dickey, *Latin forms of address from Plautus to Apuleius* (2002) 239, 331–2): the point of the remark is likely to be that Corvinus continued to refer to Cassius as 'imperator meus' in his history even when his reconciliation with Augustus meant that the latter was now his *imperator* (*praedicabat* is impf.). A charge levelled against another Cassius many years later was that his bust of the tyrannicide was inscribed 'duci partium' (16.7.2).

uterque opibus atque honoribus peruiguere Of these two nouns, which are commonly combined, the former applies esp. to Pollio, whose foreign campaigning brought him the immense wealth with which he founded a public library in Rome; the latter applies esp. to Corvinus, who, in addition to his consulship, was *praefectus urbi* (very briefly: see 6.11.3n.), augur and *frater arualis* (Rüpke 940 no. 3414).

It is impossible to believe that T. wrote the transmitted *opibusque*. He has the rare —*que ac* only twice elsewhere, and each time —*que* is attached to the pronoun *se* (see 3.4n., above); it seems obvious that *opibusque* had been influenced by the words on either side of it. The verb recurs only at Vict. *Caes.* 17.5 'pugnandique arte peruigens' (*TLL* 10.1.1871.63–7).

libro quo Catonem caelo aequauit After his suicide at Utica in 46 BC, the younger Cato was rapidly idealised and became the subject of several panegyrics, including one each from Cicero (cf. *Orat.* 35) and Brutus (*ORF* frr. 27–8, pp. 466–7): see M. Gelzer, *Caesar* (1969) 301–4, and in general P. Pecchiura, *La figura di Catone Uticense nella letteratura latina* (1965), R. J. Goar, *The legend of Cato Uticensis from the first century B.C. to the fifth century A.D.* (1987), Rutherford 60. Hints of superhumanity were appropriate in panegyric and esp. applicable to Cato, 'dis quam hominibus propior' (Vell. 35.2). *caelo aequare* is a regular phrase (*OLD aequo* 3c; *TLL* 1.1019.46–8), but the nearest parallel to T.'s figurative use is Virg. *Aen.* 11.125 'quibus caelo te laudibus aequem?' (see Horsfall ad loc.).

quid aliud dictator Caesar . . . respondit? The acc. (varied by *rescripta oratione*) allows for the possibility of a non-verbal response. *dictator Caesar* is nevertheless not pejorative but factual (sc. 'though' or 'when'):[82] for Caesar's various dictatorships see *MRR* 2.256–7 (49 BC), 272 (48), 294–5 (46) and 305–6 (45); in early 44 he was appointed dictator for life. See further O. Devillers, 'Permanence et transformations du modèle augustéen: le César de Tacite', in O. Devillers and K. Sion-Jenkis (edd.), *César sous Auguste* (2012) 209–15, esp. 213. *dictator Caesar* is T.'s preferred order of the words (9:3); the elder Pliny prefers the converse (5:23), as does Suetonius (0:2); Ammianus has no preference (1:1).

rescripta oratione The *Anticato* which Caesar produced in 45 BC: see H. Tschiedel, *Caesars Anticato: eine Untersuchung der Testimonien und Fragmente* (1981). Augustus too produced 'Rescripta Bruto de Catone' at some point (Suet. *Aug.* 85 with Wardle's n.).

uelut apud iudices is heavily ironical: the present speech is being delivered in an actual court of law, and Cordus himself is the accused. Readers are perhaps also intended to remember the trial of Silius the previous year (4.19.3): 'quasi . . . legibus cum Silio ageretur' (Wisse 322).

34.5 Antonii epistulae Traces are preserved in e.g. Suet. *Aug.* 7.1, 16.2, 63.2, 69.2: see Wardle ad locc., and also M. P. Charlesworth, *CQ* 27 (1933) 172–7.

Bruti contiones Nothing has survived.

falsa quidem in Augustum probra The name, bestowed on Octavian in 27 BC, is anachronistic for the time of the *epistulae* and *contiones*.

---

[82] According to C. Rubincam, the clear implication of the expression is that Caesar 'forbore to use the great power that was his', but she mistakenly attributes Cordus' speech to Tib. ('The terminology of power in the early Roman empire', *Cahiers des Études Anciennes* 26 (1995) 168–9).

carmina Bibaculi et Catulli referta contumeliis Caesarum leguntur Catullus attacked Julius Caesar (Poems 29, 54, 57, 93) but not Octavian: it has therefore been inferred from this passage that Bibaculus attacked Octavian but not Julius, although whether the inference is correct is uncertain (see Hollis 127–8 for discussion). None of the surviving fragments of Bibaculus displays any evidence of the *contumeliae* mentioned here (E. Courtney, *The Fragmentary Latin Poets* (²2003) 192–200, Hollis 118–45).

As *sed* (below) indicates, the emphasis of the present sentence falls upon *referta* rather than *leguntur* (cf. 64.3n.). The expr. as a whole (for which cf. Sen. *Ep.* 33.2 'eiusmodi uocibus referta sunt carmina, refertae historiae') is perhaps intended to hint at the genre of satire, in the definitions of which the word *refertus* features prominently: see Diomedes (ed. Keil) p. 485.36 and p. 486.7, although Diomedes himself (p. 485.17) links Bibaculus and Catullus with Lucilius and Horace as writers of 'iambic' (cf. Quint. 10.1.96 'cuius [sc. iambi] acerbitas in Catullo, Bibaculo, Horatio . . . reperietur').

haud facile dixerim moderatione magis an sapientia Like Caesar (Weinstock 237–40) and Augustus (Vell. 86.2n.), Tib. was famous for his *clementia* (31.2n. above; 3.68.2n.); but Cordus has adroitly substituted the quasi-synonym *moderatio* in an effort to name an even more favourite virtue of the *princeps* (see *Ann. 3*, p. 513; *Ann. 5–6*, p. 325). (*haud*) *facile dixerim* and variations thereon are common; here (unlike *D.* 35.2) the use is parenthetic or 'extra-syntactical', as is T.'s wont with such phrases (5.1.2n.): so too Plin. *NH* 36.50 'non facile dixerim secto an solidis glaebis polito'. The ellipse of *utrum* is very common (see G–G 77a–b); the combination of the two nouns is rare (6.27. 4n.).

namque spreta exolescunt; si irascare, adgnita uidentur Zimmermann (35) quotes Sen. *Ira* 2.32.2 'melius putauit non agnoscere quam uindicare', *Const. Sap.* 14.3 'non uindicauit iniuriam . . . sed factam negauit'. Since Cordus is about to end his speech by comparing literature with *imagines* and by referring to posterity and memory, T. perhaps remembered a letter of his friend Pliny to Vestricius Spurinna (*Ep.* 5.17.4–6 'posteris . . . imagines . . . agnoscere uidentur'). For the *uariatio* of *spreta* ~ *si irascare* see e.g. *H.* 4.18.4; Sörbom 119.

35.1 Non attingo Graecos Cordus means that he will not give individual examples, as he did in the case of the Roman authors; the characteristics of the Greeks are presented collectively.

non modo *libertas*, etiam *libido* impunita *libertas* (*OLD* 7) translates παρρησία, a typically Greek and esp. Athenian notion (e.g. Cic. *Flacc.* 16; C. Wirszubski, *Libertas as a political idea at Rome* (1950) 7, 13): although *libertas* was a quality for which Cordus himself was evidently well known (Sen. *Cons. Marc.* 1.4, 22.4, Quint. 10.1.104 'Cremuti libertas'), it is worth noting that its single appearance in his speech is in connection with the Greek past. For *libido* used of *maledicta* the only other exs. in *TLL* are 1.72.3 and 5.4.3 (7.2.1334.68–74). The two nouns naturally attracted word play, e.g. Cic. *De Or.* 3.4 'libidinem tuam libertas mea refutabit'; for the ellipse of *sed* see 3.19.2n.

si quis aduertit, *dictis dicta* ultus est *aduertit* is simple for compound *animaduertere*, 'to take punitive action' (2.32.3n.); for the polyptoton, a device which T. uses more normally in speeches than narrative (Adams (1973) 124 and n. 14), see Plaut. *Men.* 945, Virg. *Aen.* 10.448 'talibus et dictis it contra dicta tyranni'; G. Landgraf, 'Substantivische Parataxen', *ALL* 5 (1888) 184. It is not certain whom Cordus has in mind.

Sed maxime solutum et sine obtrectatore fuit prodere de iis quos mors odio aut gratiae exemisset After the brief parenthesis on the Greeks, *sed* returns us to the late-republican and Augustan periods exemplified at 34.3–5 (*fuit* is formally parallel to the series of historic verbs from *tulit* to *reliquere*); since the works mentioned there were based on partiality and hatred respectively (34.3–4 and 34.5), *odio* and *gratiae* bring chiastic closure to Cordus' list of examples, while *maxime* serves to contrast narratives about the dead – which are Cordus' primary concern – with the criticism of contemporaries illustrated immediately above at 34.5 ('Antonii epistulae . . . sapientia'). With *solutum* ('exempt') a word such as *poenā* has to be understood (see 14.28.1; *OLD solutus* 10b).

Since Cordus claims that in earlier days death removed individuals from the passions of writers and readers alike (*exemisset* is perhaps causal subjunctive), he implies that his accusers' reaction to his narrative of Brutus and Cassius has been manufactured for their own purposes; and his statement acquires added authority because his references to *odium* and *gratia* seem almost to quote the very many historians who in their prefaces or elsewhere had disclaimed such faults (a good selection of examples in Avenarius 49–54). The statement is nevertheless incomplete and disingenuous: incomplete, because Cordus cannot have failed to realise that it is not death alone which removes individuals from contemporary passions; there are other relevant considerations too, of which time is one. T. begins the *Annals* with a recognition of this very fact (1.1.3 'tradere . . . Tiberii principatum et cetera, sine ira et studio, quorum causas *procul* habeo'), and in the above digression he said that ancient writers are hardly ever criticised (33.4 'rarus obtrectator') and that no one cares about issues of ancient history such as the Punic Wars; but the events even of Tib.'s reign caused problems for some readers many decades later, as he also admitted (33.4), and the interval between Philippi and Cordus' trial was even less (below, 35.2). Cordus' statement is also disingenuous, because some individuals retain the capacity of rousing passions long after death, and Junia's funeral a mere three years previously will have confirmed for Cordus that Brutus and Cassius fell precisely into this category (3.76.2 and n.).

The *uariatio* of adj. ~ prepositional phrase is common (see Sörbom 92–3). For *mors . . . exemisset* cf. 12.51.2 'ut morte honesta . . . eximeretur', Lucr. 3.863 'mors eximit'; *odium* and *gratia* are regularly paired (6.26.3n.).

35.2 Num enim . . . populum per contiones incendo? The usual interpretation of this sentence is: 'For surely it is not the case that I am inflaming the people in support of civil war through public speeches at the very moment when Cassius and Brutus are holding the field in full armour at Philippi?' On this view the abl. abs. provides a date in the past and thus a clear connection (*enim*) with the preceding sentence, which referred to persons long since dead ('quos . . . mors exemisset'); the disadvantage is that it offers a poor defence, since it has Cordus denying something – insurrectionist oratory – of which he has not been accused. In 1989 I proposed a different interpretation: 'For surely it is not the case that, by having Cassius and Brutus holding the field in full armour at Philippi, I am inflaming the people in support of civil war through public speeches?' On this view the abl. abs. refers to the content of Cordus' history (for a somewhat similar case cf. Hor. *S.* 1.10.40–2) and distinguishes a historical narrative from insurrectionist oratory; the disadvantage is that we have to wait until the next sentence for the point that the protagonists are long since dead ('septuagesimum . . . perempti'). Critics have found it difficult to decide between these two interpretations (see Moles 141 n. 82; Damon, *AHC* 358–9), but on the whole I still favour the second. The abl. abs. is expressed in such a way (esp. *armatis* and *campos obtinentibus*) as to suggest the *enargeia* of historical narrative rather than simply a mere date, and the contrast with *per contiones incendo* gives the sentence as a whole more point.

incendo anticipates Cordus' talionic punishment of having his books burned (35.4). Moreover, if Håkanson were to be right in reading 'turba . . . quae paulo ante caluerat piis *contionibus*' (for the transmitted *coluerat*) in Cordus' surviving account of Cicero's death (F1C = 1P), it is possible that T. is alluding to an actual expression of the historian.

An illi quidem . . . perempti *quidem* both transfers the emphasis from Cordus ('num . . . incendo?') to the tyrannicides themselves and prepares for the contrasted fates of others, including Cordus himself, at §3 below: such a multipurpose usage is difficult to define (see e.g. J. B. Solodow, *The Latin particle quidem* (1978) 62–3, 69, 87). *septuagesimum ante annum* is both a round and a 'rhetorical' number (see A. Dreizehnter, *Die rhetorische Zahl* (1978) 81–90): the battle of Philippi had taken place in 42 BC, as T. had noted precisely at 3.76.1 (n.). For *perimere* see 6.23.1n.

quo modo imaginibus suis noscuntur, . . . sic partem memoriae apud scriptores retinent It is to be inferred from T.'s account of the funeral of Junia, wife of Cassius and sister of Brutus, that *imagines* of the tyrannicides were not allowed to be displayed in public (3.76.2 and n.); and in AD 65 Nero will accuse the jurist L. Cassius Longinus of keeping an *imago* of the earlier Cassius amongst those of his ancestors (16.7.2), from which it may be inferred that the display of Cassius' image was now forbidden even in private. On the other hand, Cordus' remark clearly implies that images of Brutus and Cassius were visible in some quarters; and the younger Pliny explicitly says that it was permitted to have their images at home (*Ep.* 1.17.3 'mirum est qua religione, quo studio imagines Brutorum, Cassiorum domi (ubi potest) habeat'). It is difficult to know what historical conclusions to draw from this conflicting evidence,[83] but Cordus' comparison between *imagines* and texts seems so phrased as to suggest the superiority of texts: whereas Sallust had intimated that *imagines* acted as a 'prompt' for viewers to recall their subjects' achievements (*J.* 4.6, quoted above, 33.4n.), Cordus chooses to restrict the function of *imagines* to the mere *facial recognition* of their subjects ('imaginibus suis noscuntur'; cf. Ov. *F.* 1.231 'noscere . . . imagine'), assigning – and in a most graphic manner (see below) – the role of memorialisation to texts. For other comparisons between images and texts see *Agr.* 46.3–4 and nn.; Pelling, *AHC* 366–7 and n. 3. See also below, 35.5n.

quas ne uictor quidem aboleuit Augustus ordered the preservation of a statue of Brutus in Milan (Plut. *Comp. Dion. Brut.* 5.1–2), presumably the same statue as mentioned by Suet. *Gramm.* 30.5 (above, 34.1n. *nouo*); but *ne uictor quidem* carries the clear implication that a conqueror might be expected to destroy images of the defeated and hence that Augustus could have ordered their destruction if he had wanted.

partem memoriae apud scriptores retinent If the point of this sentence is to transfer the focus from Cordus to the tyrannicides themselves, as seems to be the case (cf. *illi quidem* above), it is underlined significantly by Cordus' expression. *memoriam retinere* is a common phrase, and used of those who do the remembering (cf. 5.6.3, *H.* 3.68.2 and H.); here it is used – unusually and perhaps uniquely – of those who are remembered, as if the protagonists of history have power over their own memory, forcing themselves upon posterity and (so to speak) dictating to their memorialists how they shall be remembered in their texts ('apud scriptores'). *partem* is explained by the fact that, even so, authors' texts are a limited medium: they cannot reproduce a visual record in the way that images can.

---

[83] There seems nothing relevant in H. Flower, *Ancestor masks and aristocratic power in Roman culture* (1996) or *The art of forgetting: disgrace and oblivion in Roman culture* (2006).

35.3 Suum cuique decus posteritas rependit This is Cordus' version of the *pro meritis* theme which is common in epitaphs and the like (some exs. listed by D. Korzeniewski, *Gymn.* 79 (1972) 387 and n. 32).

si damnatio ingruit The present tense conveys the imminent likelihood of the *damnatio*: T. makes Cordus accept that the outcome of the trial is a foregone conclusion.

etiam mei meminerint Despite his disclaimer above (2n. *partem*), Cordus cannot deny that he has been partly responsible for preserving the memory of Brutus and Cassius; in just the same way his own memory will be preserved by T., who was always alive to the reception of his work by posterity (3.55.5, 3.65.1 and nn.). For some reflections see J. Grethlein, 'Ancient historiography and "future past"', in A. Lianeri (ed.), *Knowing future time in and through Greek historiography* (2016) 74–7.

35.4 uitam abstinentia finiuit There is a moving account of his suicide at Sen. *Cons. Marc.* 22.6. T.'s expr. recurs only at Sen. *Ep.* 70.8–9 ('utrum inuides carnifici tuo an parcis? Socrates potuit abstinentia finire uitam et inedia potius quam ueneno mori'), a letter on the right time to die with which T. was very familiar (*PH* 362). For *abstinentia* see 6.26.2n.

libros . . . cremandos As had happened with Labienus' books (Sen. *Contr.* 10 *praef.* 8; cf. Dio 56.27.1) and would happen again with those of Fabricius Veiento under Nero (14.50.1–2: see below) and Rusticus and Senecio under Domitian (*Agr.* 2.1, a very similar passage to this: see nn. ad loc., adding W. Speyer, *Büchervernichtung und Zensur des Geistes bei Heiden, Juden und Christen* (1981) 65, J. A. Howley, 'Book-burning and the uses of writing in ancient Rome: destructive practice between literature and document', *JRS* 107 (2017) 213–36). Not only is the punishment talionic (cf. 2 'incendo') but the choice of *cremare*, though a common verb for the burning of books (see esp. Liv. 40.29. 13–14), invites the thought that Cremutius' opponents subjected him and his books to the kind of punning abuse of which the Romans were fond (e.g. Suet. *Tib.* 42.1, 75.1). For a list of the verbs used for book-burning see Wisse 325 n. 93.

occultati et editi His daughter was one of those who hid his writings and hence facilitated their later re-emergence: cf. Sen. *Cons. Marc.* 1.3–4 (quoted below, 5n.) and Dio 57.24.4 ὕστερον δὲ ἐξεδόθη τε αὖθις (ἄλλοι τε γὰρ καὶ μάλιστα ἡ θυγάτηρ αὐτοῦ Μαρκία συνέκρυψεν αὐτά). Caligula revoked the embargo along with others (Suet. *Cal.* 16.1 'Titi Labieni, Cordi Cremuti, Cassi Seueri scripta senatus consultis abolita requiri et esse in manibus lectitarique permisit, quando maxime sua interesset ut facta quaeque posteris tradantur'), although Quintilian implies that the books of Cordus in circulation were expurgated (10.1.104 'habet amatores – nec inmerito – Cremuti libertas, quamquam circumcisis quae dixisse ei nocuerat; sed elatum abunde spiritum et audaces sententias deprehendas etiam in iis quae manent'). In general see R. J. Starr, 'The circulation of literary texts in the Roman world', *CQ* 37 (1987) 213–23, esp. 219.

35.5 socordiam eorum inridere libet Mockery is usually the resort of T.'s characters (P. Plass, *Wit and the writing of history* (1988) 15–25); here it is used of T. the author, ascribing to himself – and inviting his readers' participation in – one of the chief devices of the lampoons which, as Cordus has just argued (34.5), exemplified the free speech of earlier times. If readers of historical narrative were as sensitive to layers of meaning as T. suggested in the digression (33.4), it is not difficult to see here a tribute to the principate of Trajan, 'rara temporum felicitate, ubi sentire quae uelis et quae sentias dicere licet' (*H.* 1.1.4). R. H. Martin's remarks to the same end (*Tacitus* (1981, rev. 1994) 137) are rejected by Moles (149) and Wisse (356), although the former points out that Trajan reissued the *libertas* coinage of Brutus (on this see G. Seelentag, *Taten und Tugenden Traians* (2004) 468–84, esp. 468–71); and, since *libet* is etymologically connected with *libido*, T. is perhaps drawing a connection with the free speaking of the Greeks whom Cordus invoked in his defence (35.1).

socordia perhaps = 'stupidity' here, as opposed to the 'indifference' which Tib. failed to display at 31.2 (n.); but it is hard to resist the further contrast between the victim whose 'heart' was inscribed in his name (*cor* can refer to mind or spirit or intellect) and the heart-less nature of the tyrant (*socordia = sine + corde*: see Maltby 571–2).

qui praesenti potentia credunt exstingui posse etiam sequentis aeui memoriam *exstingui* keeps alive metaphorically the memorialisation which the unnamed authorities mistakenly think they have snuffed out by the book-burning above (for the 'flame of memory' see Sall. *J.* 4.6, quoted 33.4n.). Although the statement is general, the reference is esp. to Nero and Domitian (see above, 4n.). *etiam* means 'as well as of the present age' but is strictly illogical, since, although the authorities may appear to have succeeded temporarily with their destruction, the memory of future ages depends upon the survival of copies in the present: see esp. (and with numerous points of contact with T.) Sen. *Cons. Marc.* 1.3–4 'Vt uero aliquam occasionem mutatio temporum dedit, ingenium patris tui, de quo sumptum erat supplicium, in usum hominum reduxisti et a uera illum uindicasti morte ac restituisti in publica monumenta libros quos uir ille fortissimus sanguine suo scripserat. Optime meruisti de Romanis studiis: magna illorum pars arserat; optime de posteris, ad quos ueniet incorrupta rerum fides, auctori suo magno inputata; optime de ipso, cuius uiget uigebitque memoria quam diu in pretio fuerit Romana cognosci, quam diu quisquam erit qui reuerti uelit ad acta maiorum, quam diu quisquam qui uelit scire quid sit uir

Romanus, quid subactis iam ceruicibus omnium et ad Seianianum iugum adactis indomitus, quid sit homo ingenio, animo, manu liber. Magnum mehercules detrimentum res publica ceperat, si illum ob duas res pulcherrimas in obliuionem coniectum, eloquentiam et libertatem, non eruisses: legitur, floret, in manus hominum, in pectora receptus uetustatem nullam timet; at illorum carnificum cito scelera quoque, quibus solis memoriam meruerunt, tacebuntur'.

For *memoriam exstinguere* cf. Cic. *Cael.* 71, *Mil.* 73 (and note *Deiot.* 15), Val. Max. 5.6 *ext.* 4, 8.14.1, Sen. *Ep.* 49.1; for *sequentis aeui* cf. Virg. *Ecl.* 8.27, Luc. 8.623, Amm. 17.4.9, 30.4.6; for *aeui memoriam* cf. Liv. 26.11.12; for *potentia* cf. Curt. 10.10.18 'potentia exstinxit'.

punitis ingeniis gliscit auctoritas It has to be said that this did not quite happen with the writings of Fabricius Veiento under Nero (14.50.2): 'conuictumque Veientonem Italia depulit et libros exuri iussit, conquisitos lectitatosque donec cum periculo parabantur; mox licentia habendi obliuionem attulit.'

neque aliud . . . gloriam peperere There are three reasons for believing that T. did not write this concluding sentence as it is found in M: (a) the reference to foreign kings is quite irrelevant to anything in the preceding episode; (b) no foreign king is recorded as having punished writers or burned their books; (c) the words *aut qui eadem saeuitia usi sunt* are extraordinarily clunking; Hartman (172–3) objected to them on the different but related grounds that, after the contrastive reference to foreign kings, there should be no reversion to domestic rulers.

It is difficult to believe that the sentence as a whole is interpolated: (a) the combination of a regular phrase (*gloriam parere*) with an irregular (*dedecus parere* recurs only at Apul. *Met.* 10.15.4) is typical of T.'s manner; (b) the archaising form *peperere* is unlikely to be the work of an interpolator. I therefore suggest that *externi reges aut* has been wrongly added for some unknown reason.[84]

Although *saeuitia* is commonly used in connection with tyrannical behaviour (1.1n.), it is likely that T. is thinking esp. of Domitian, archetypally *saeuus*, whose treatment of the eulogists Arulenus Rusticus and Herennius Senecio ensured his own disgrace and their glory – the double process aided by T. himself in the *Agricola* (2.1) in just the same way as Tib. and Cordus are now being immortalised in the *Annals*. For the antithesis of *dedecus* and *gloria* cf. 3.21.1n.

---

[84] It is possible (but not obligatory) to speculate further that the mistaken addition led to the subsequent addition of *eadem*. Hartman deleted *aut*, but not only does this leave the resulting sentence open to objection (b) above but *aliud* is made falsely to appear to be retrospective rather than prospective.

36.1 postulandis reis tam continuus annus fuit In fact fewer prosecutions 'are recorded in this year than in the preceding or any of several others' (Rogers 86). It may be argued that T. has omitted those whom he did not deem worthy of record, but such an omission seems odd after such an introduction (cf. also 6.7.5 and n.). The use of the modal abl. gerundive with *continuus* is paralleled at 11.5.1 but nowhere else.

feriarum Latinarum diebus praefectum urbis For this ritual and the timing of the festival see 6.11.1n.

Drusum Germanicus' son was now 17 or 18.

adierit Calpurnius Saluianus in Sextum Marium; quod a Caesare palam increpitum causa exilii Saluiano fuit '[T]he enmity of Calpurnius Salvianus and Sextus Marius in AD 25 was rooted in an ancient provincial feud. This explanation of the incident of AD 25 draws attention to the salient feature of Tacitus' two-sentence account of the quarrel between the two men. Compact and elliptical, it is close to incomprehensible . . . Tacitus' omissions are extraordinary here, even for Tacitus . . . We get no hint whatsoever about the nature of Salvianus' grievance against Marius. We get no inkling of Tiberius' relationship with Sextus Marius . . . We get no hint of what the charge against Salvianus in his turn may have been, or who brought it, indeed it is not clear from the Latin exactly what Tiberius was complaining about and how it was the reason for exile. *Exilium*, voluntary or enforced, was the punishment for a crime, but interrupting a magistrate at a religious ceremony was hardly criminal. The historian's account of the affair is thin to the vanishing point' (E. J. Champlin, 'The richest man in Spain', *ZPE* 196 (2015) 290, q.v. for the story of the ancient feud). For more on the fabulously rich Marius see 6.19.1 and nn.; nothing else is known of Salvianus (see *RE* 3.1401 = Calpurnius 114 (Stein), *PIR* 2.76 no. 315).

36.2 Obiecta publice Cyzicenis incuria caerimoniarum diui Augusti, additis uiolentiae criminibus aduersum ciues Romanos; et amisere libertatem quam bello Mithridatis meruerant Dio agrees with T. (57.24.6 Κυζικηνῶν ἡ ἐλευθερία αὖθις, ὅτι τε Ῥωμαίους τινὰς ἔδησαν καὶ ὅτι καὶ τὸ ἡρῷον ὃ τῷ Αὐγούστῳ ποιεῖν ἤρξαντο οὐκ ἐξετέλεσαν, ἀφῃρέθη); Suetonius mentions only the latter charge (*Tib.* 37.3 'Cyzicenis in ciues Romanos uiolentius quaedam ausis publice libertatem ademit quam Mithridatico bello meruerant'). Dio's αὖθις is explained by the fact that Augustus had already deprived them of their *libertas* in 20 BC for violence against Roman citizens but had restored it five years later (54.7.6, 54.23.7). Since modern scholars infer that Cyzicus will have been a *ciuitas libera* since the second century BC, either from the Treaty of Apamea in

188 BC or from the establishment of the province of Asia in 133, *meruerant* seems to mean that the community had 'deserved' its freedom in the Third Mithridatic War of c. 74–72 BC (*MRR* 2.106–8): this seems to be the view of Magie 1.234 ('a privilege which it amply justified'), 2.1111 n. 4. If *meruerant* is thought to mean 'had won', however, we have to assume either that there had been an earlier deprivation or that one source or another is mistaken.

publice (again at 43.3) means 'as a community' (*OLD* 2). As at 3.73.2 (slightly different) T. has the gen. *Mithridatis* for the regular adj. *Mithridatico*, a characteristic substitution (1.3.7n.) in which he is unique. See also 55.4 below.

circumsessi nec . . . pulso rege 'after being besieged and with the king beaten off by their own resolve no less than by the support of Lucullus' (see App. *Mithr.* 75–6 for the details). For the *uariatio* see Sörbom 91.

36.3 Fonteius Capito, qui pro consule Asiam curauerat Capito, consul with Germanicus in AD 12, had been proconsul of Asia in 22/23 or 23/24: see Vogel-Weidemann 249–53 no. 34; also *RE* 6.2847–8 = Fonteius 21 (Kappelmacher), *PIR* 3.198 no. 470, *BNP* 5.492 [II 4]. His son or grandson would be consul in 59 (14.1.1). For *curare* of provincial administration see 1.31.2n.

comperto ficta in eum crimina per Vibium Serenum It is not known what the charges were: perhaps extortion, or perhaps indifference to the *incuria caerimoniarum* of the Cyzicenes. For the younger Serenus see 28.1nn. For the one-word abl. abs. *comperto*, a construction of which T. is fond (see *Ann. 3*, p. 499; *Ann. 5–6*, p. 316), see Malloch on 11.13.2 and 11.26.3.

ut quis destrictior accusator, uelut sacrosanctus erat For the transmitted *destrictior* ('more severe, uncompromising') Beroaldus suggested *districtior* ('busier'); the two words are very often confused in MSS (see *TLL* 5.1.771.6ff.). In classical Latin *destrictus* is only once used elsewhere of a person (Val. Max. 8.2.2 'ex amica obsequenti subito destrictam feneratricem agere coepit') and as a comparative adj. is unparalleled (the compar. adverb is at Apul. *Apol.* 79); *districtus*, though less common generally, is more regular of persons (*TLL* 5.1.1552.24–32), although the compar. adj. is found elsewhere only at Cic. *Q.Fr.* 2.16(15).1. It is a difficult choice, although the paradosis is self-evidently more vivid and perhaps better suited to the context (see also Halm, *Beiträge* 13–15).

sacrosanctus, not used by T. elsewhere, ironically gives to accusers the special prerogative of tribunes (for which see Weinstock 220–1). T.'s whole expr. seems related to the motif *deteriores sunt incolumiores* (Quadrig. F26C = 9P), for which cf. also Sall. *J.* 31.14 'quam quisque pessume fecit, tam maxume tutus est', *H.* 3.48 M(15 R).13 'omnis iniuria grauitate tutior est', Sen. *Ep.* 96.5. For *ut quis* see 6.7.3n.

leues, ignobiles 'the ineffectual and undistinguished'; for the asyndeton see 2.2n.

37–38 Tiberius and the imperial cult
The subjects of Asia and the imperial cult, with which this section begins (37.1), have each been trailed in the preceding chapter, where the people of Cyzicus were accused of neglecting the cult of Augustus (36.2) and a recent governor of Asia was obliged to face charges (36.3). But continuity between the two sections is established above all by the notion of memory. Cremutius Cordus' speech (34.2–35.3) arose from the memorialisation of Brutus and Cassius (34.2 *memorauit*, 34.4 *memoriam*, 35.2 *memoriae*), and his prediction that, if convicted, he himself would be remembered by posterity (35.3 *posteritas, etiam mei meminerint*) was fulfilled at the authorities' expense (35.5 *memoriam, sequentis aeui gloriam*). It is therefore with some irony that here in the very next section Tib. is given a speech in which he rejects ruler cult in his own case by saying that he is far more concerned for the preservation of his own memory by posterity (38.1 *meminisse posteros, memoriae*, 3 *recordationibus, famam nominis mei*).

Syme described the *princeps'* speech as 'a firm and noble discourse' (*Tac.* 315), its firmness emphasised by the conflicting popular talk by which it is introduced and concluded: the criticism which gives rise to his speech (37.1) is flatly contradicted by the reaction which it provokes (38.4–5), and that reaction is itself undermined by the terms in which the people express themselves (see nn.). Yet Tib. is himself guilty of a more significant inconsistency: he claims to follow Augustan precedent in all matters as if it were legally binding (37.3 'qui omnia facta dictaque eius uice legis obseruem'), but this is a claim whose falsity Cremutius Cordus has already proved with his life (cf. 34.3–5). Other critics have come to rather different views of the *princeps'* speech from that of Syme.[85]

37.1 exemplo Asiae The invocation of Asia, whose desire to set up a temple was motivated by gratitude for the punishment of their procurator (15.3), suggests that similar motivation is operating here: Vibius Serenus, the proconsul of Hispania Ulterior, had likewise been punished in 23 (13.2; cf. 30.1).

ualidus alioqui spernendis honoribus Tib.'s well-known attitude to divine honours (for which see Levick 139–40, Seager 121–3, Gradel 59, 143) has to be seen in the context of a culture where it was regular to divinise heroes

---

[85] See, most recently, Moles 168 n. 111, Pelling, *AHC* 377–8, Wisse 345–6.

(e.g. above, 34.4n. *libro*), benefactors (6.18.2n.) and the like (see also S. Cole, *Cicero and the rise of deification at Rome* (2013) and M. Koortbojian, *The divinization of Caesar and Augustus: precedents, consequences, implications* (2013), though neither refers to the work of I. M. Le M. Du Quesnay, *PLLS* 3 (1981) 97–113, or D. S. Levene, 'God and man in the classical Latin panegyric', *PCPS* 43 (1997) 66–103). For *ualidus* + abl. gerundive see 3.10.2n.; for *spernere honores* cf. Liv. 3.21.7, 3.70.14, 4.8.7, Vell. 2.13.3, Val. Max. 1.6.13, 2.8.3.

quorum rumore arguebatur in ambitionem flexisse These critics are to be contrasted with those who after his speech accuse Tib. of the very opposite (38.4–5). 'A world of constant talk and rumour is evoked, and a world . . . where, as far as his critics are concerned, Tiberius cannot do anything right' (Pelling, *AHC* 369; cf. 371, 375). In general see P. O'Neill, 'Going round in circles: popular speech in ancient Rome', *CA* 22 (2003) 135–66. For the repetition –*rum rum*– see 13.2n.; for *flexisse* see 1.13.5n.

huiusce modi orationem coepit is T.'s variant on the Sallustian *huiusce modi orationem habuit* (*C.* 20.1, 52.1, 57.6, *J.* 86.1). Koestermann alleged that the speech 'in der Hauptsache offenbar authentisch ist'. For such formulae as *in hunc modum* see 6.8.1n.

37.2 constantiam meam a plerisque desideratam *constantia* contrasts with the change which Tib.'s critics, who themselves are inconsistent (last n. but one), have accused him of making (*flexisse*; cf. Liv. 28.8.12 'flexisset . . . constantia'). *desiderare* occurs nowhere else in the *Annals* and may be intended to suggest a Tiberian idiolect (Syme, *Tac.* 701, Miller 16–17).

37.3 templum apud Pergamum In 29 BC (Dio 51.20.7): see Price 178, 182, 252 (and coin illustration at plate 2b); Hänlein-Schäfer 6ff., 166–8.

qui omnia facta dictaque eius uice legis obseruem The position of the clause before the main verb, and hence before the unexpressed antecedent of *qui*, is unusual (we might have expected *cuius* instead of *qui . . . eius*). For Tib.'s devotion to Augustus and his precepts see 1.77.3; Levick 223–4, Seager 147–50, Brunt (1984) *passim*, esp. 425 and n. 7, M. Peachin, 'Exemplary government in the early Roman empire', in O. Hekster et al. (edd.), *Crises and the Roman empire* (2007) 75–93, esp. 80–1. Augustus himself claimed to have fostered exemplarity (*RG* 8.5, a passage imitated by T. at 3.55.5 (see n.)), while Tib. was himself seen as an *exemplum* (Vell. 126.5 (see n.)). Given that Cremutius Cordus was condemned by a legal process despite his pleas to Augustan precedent (34.3–5), the phrase *uice legis* is esp. ironical; indeed Miller (16–17) has seen *uice* + gen. as intended to suggest Tib.'s manner, since the combination recurs only in a Tiberian context at 6.21.3.

placitum iam exemplum 'the precedent already approved' (i.e. by Augustus).

ueniam habuerit For this expr. cf. Hor. *Epist.* 2.1.169–70, Ov. *Tr.* 2.108.

effigie numinum sacrari For the plur. *numinum* see 1.10.6n.; for the verb see 3.18.2n.

ambitiosum, superbum Tib. thus refutes the charge of *ambitio* which had provided the cue for his speech (1). For the two adjs. cf. Mart. 9.64.

si promiscis adulationibus uulgatur This 'withering conclusion' is 'the true voice of the man who is so scornful of the *adulatio* which others pour upon him' (Pelling, *AHC* 369, quoting 3.47.4 and 3.65.3, where see nn.). For the expr. cf. Suet. *Aug.* 40.3 'uulgari honorem'.

38.1 Ego me . . . mortalem esse . . . With typically chiastic alliteration (3.53.4n.), Tib. repeats what he had already said after the funeral of Germanicus (3.6.3 'principes mortales . . . esse'). In 1622 L. Aurelius (Louis d'Orléans) detected an allusion to Homer's *Odyssey* (7.208–10 οὐ γὰρ ἐγώ γε | ἀθανάτοισιν ἔοικα, τοὶ οὐρανὸν εὐρὺν ἔχουσιν, | οὐ δέμας οὐδὲ φυήν, ἀλλὰ θνητοῖσι βροτοῖσιν), and it will be remembered that Odysseus was the *princeps'* favourite Homeric character (see below, 59.1n.), with whom he may even have identified (Champlin (2013)); in view of *habere* (just below) there seems also to be some similarity to Cic. *Rep.* 6.26 'tu uero . . . sic habeto non esse te mortalem . . . deum te igitur scito esse', a work already recalled at 33.1 (n. *delecta*). The remainder of Tib.'s speech is dominated by the themes of mortality, death and posthumousness (*meminisse posteros, memoriae meae*, 2 *posterorum, pro sepulchris*, 3 *ad finem usque uitae, quandoque concessero, recordationibus, prosequantur*). What Tib. is above all concerned about is his memory after death (cf. 6.46.2, quoted below).

hominum officia fungi The acc. after *fungor* is archaising (L–H–S 122) and, since it recurs in a Tiberian directive at 3.2.1 (n.), may be intended to suggest his manner, though of course we cannot be sure (Syme, *Tac.* 284, 700, Miller 16).

satisque habere si locum principem impleam The repetition of *satis* (below) recurs in Tiberian utterances at 2.26.2 and 3.69.4; the wording of the protasis recurs in a German speech at 11.16.3 'qui principem locum impleat' (and cf. 3.75.1).

et uos testor et meminisse posteros uolo Compare 6.46.2 'illi non perinde curae gratia praesentium quam in posteros ambitio' and n.

memoriae meae tribuent Cf. Vell. 2.16.2, Sen. *Ben.* 3.4.2. For the resumption of *meminisse* in *memoriae* see 6.10.1n.

ut . . . credant 'if they believe . . .': this use of *ut* = *si*, to be distinguished from the concessive use (in which the *ut*-clause usually precedes the main clause, as at 33.4 and 40.4: see nn.), is highly unusual (Draeger, *SS* 74 §183), but cf. e.g. Cic. *Amic.* 52 'qui uelit, ut neque diligat quemquam nec ipse ab ullo diligatur, circumfluere omnibus copiis' (quoted by Draeger), *Verr.* 3.112 'ager efficit cum octauo, bene ut agatur; uerum ut omnes di adiuuent, cum decumo' (quoted in *OLD ut* 31).

The context of memory and posterity (above), together with the references to stone statues and tombstones (below), suggests that the *princeps* is here inscribing his own epitaph; and the fact that he wishes to be remembered for *four* qualities suggests further that he is proposing his personal 'virtues' as his inscription. Greek philosophers had traditionally spoken of a canon of four (or sometimes five) cardinal virtues (bravery, temperance, justice and wisdom); and a series of four virtues, but with considerable variation as appropriate, was regularly claimed by great men or attributed to them by others (Weinstock 228–59, Wallace-Hadrill 300–7, Noreña 152–60). Thus Augustus was presented with a shield, testifying to his *uirtus, clementia, iustitia* and *pietas* (*RG* 34.2).

maioribus meis dignum In the competitive culture of ancient Rome it was natural that one should wish to rival, or at least to be judged worthy of, one's ancestors (see 3.55.5n. (p. 412); Oakley on Liv. 7.10.3, with *Addenda* at 4.550–1); but it is remarkable how Tib.'s phrase, though found elsewhere (12.12.1, Plin. *Ep.* 5.17.1), is domiciled almost exclusively in Cicero, the author whom he above all imitates in his speeches (e.g. *Fin.* 2.62, *Flacc.* 101, *Phil.* 3.25, 10.13, *Fam.* 2.18.3, esp. *Sest.* 21 'quia utile est rei publicae nobiles homines esse dignos maioribus suis, et quia ualet apud nos clarorum hominum et bene de re publica meritorum memoria, etiam mortuorum'). Tib. is no doubt thinking primarily of Augustus; coins advertising *pietas* had been issued in 22/23 (M. Grant, *Roman anniversary issues* (1950) 36).

rerum uestrarum prouidum *prouidentia* was another cardinal virtue of the reign, perhaps appearing on the coins of 22 (3.69.1n.).

constantem in periculis Although his critics accused him of a lack of *constantia* in the matter of imperial cult (2 above), Tib. implies that he displays the quality when it matters: 'in periculis'. In fact *constantia*, regular in a military context (e.g. Curt. 5.7.1 'illam in subeundis periculis constantiam'), was not a feature of the historical Tib. and was claimed as an official virtue only on the coinage of Claudius (Sutherland 129, 131, Levick 91, Wallace-Hadrill 321).

offensionum pro utilitate publica non pauidum *offensio* is a distinctively 'Tiberian' word (Miller 13), and here he echoes his great speech at 3.54.6 'offensionum . . . quas . . . graues et plerumque iniquas pro re publica suscipiam' (see n.); cf. also 6.15.2 'offensiones ob rem publicam <sus>ceptas' (a letter of Tib.), and also above, 18.2n. *non pauidum* suggests that the noun is passive, 'not afraid of being attacked', and that the emperor is referring to the virtue of *patientia*, one of the recognised aspects of *fortitudo* (cf. Cic. *Inv.* 2.163, *Part. Or.* 77, *Rhet. Herenn.* 3.5; R. A. Kaster, *CP* 97 (2002) 136–7, 143);[86] but Pelling argues strongly that the word must also refer to the giving of offence: 'for an emperor, the taking of offence readily leads to actions that cause further offence, and Tiberius is not "afraid" to behave as he must' (*AHC* 377 n. 42). *utilitas publica* (again at 14.44.4, 15.44.5) is a regular expr., though Cicero much prefers the variant *utilitas rei publicae* (which T. uses at *H.* 4.7.2).

38.2 Haec mihi in animis uestris templa, hae pulcherrimae effigies et mansurae The two demonstratives refer back to the four qualities to be elicited from Tib.'s 'epitaph' just above (1) and substitute them for the physical temple which, no doubt together with its statues, the Spanish envoys had asked to be erected. There is a somewhat similar transition in Pericles' funeral speech (Thuc. 2.43.3 οὐ στηλῶν μόνον ἐν τῇ οἰκείᾳ σημαίνει ἐπιγραφή, ἀλλὰ καὶ ἐν τῇ μὴ προσηκούσῃ ἄγραφος μνήμη παρ' ἑκάστῳ τῆς γνώμης μᾶλλον ἢ τοῦ ἔργου ἐνδιαιτᾶται); Maecenas, in the long speech invented for him by Dio, advises Augustus to reject physical images and temples but to construct ἄλλας ... ἐν αὐταῖς ταῖς τῶν ἀνθρώπων ψυχαῖς καὶ ἀκηράτους καὶ ἀθανάτους ἐξ εὐεργεσιῶν (52.35.3); and the elder Cato is alleged to have said that his fellow citizens carried about his images in their hearts (Plut. *Cat. Mai.* 19.5 αὐτοῦ δὲ καλλίστας εἰκόνας ἐν ταῖς ψυχαῖς περιφέρειν τοὺς πολίτας: see P. Sinclair, *CP* 86 (1991) 333–5).[87] The expr. attributed to Tib. here is more vivid than *Agr.* 46.4 'quidquid ex Agricola amauimus, quidquid mirati sumus, manet mansurumque est in animis hominum', which is unspecific, or Cic. *Cat.* 3.26 'in animis ego uestris omnis triumphos meos, omnia ornamenta honoris, monumenta gloriae, laudis insignia condi et conlocari uolo', where the physical is listed alongside the abstract; closer is Val. Max. 1.7 *ext.* 3 'melius illi et diuturnius in animis hominum sepulcrum constituens'. The Tacitean Tib. likes striking metaphors in his speeches (3.12.4n.).

quae saxo struuntur ... pro sepulchris spernuntur 'Observe the alliteration' (Syme, *Tac.* 701); the assonance is also noteworthy. *pro* = 'like' (*OLD* 9c): the neglect of gravestones was proverbial (e.g. *Anth. Pal.* 5.21.6 ὡς δὲ τάφον νῦν σε παρερχόμεθα, Lucian, *Tim.* 5), but Pelling (*AHC* 370) suggests that

---

[86] Tib.'s *patientia* is praised at the beginning of *SCPP* (17).

[87] It would be esp. interesting if similar phraseology appeared in the Alexandrian speech of Tib.'s adopted son Germanicus (*P. Oxy.* 2435 recto, lines 26–7), but there is doubt whether ψυχαῖς or εὐχαῖς should be read.

the *princeps*' strong language ('spernuntur') diplomatically hints at more than neglect (cf. Hor. *S.* 1.8.38–9 with Gowers' n. on 37–9, Pers. 1.112–14 with Kissel's n., Juv. 1.131 'ad effigiem non tantum meiere fas est' with the nn. of Mayor, Courtney or Braund, Petron. 71.8 'ne in monumentum meum populus cacatum currat' with Schmeling's n.; R. Lattimore, *Themes in Greek and Latin epitaphs* (1942) 119ff.). There is also perhaps an etymological contrast with the preceding, *pulcherrimae imagines* instead of *sepulchra*, as if the latter were compounded of *sine* + *pulcher* (cf. Val. Fl. 6.313–14 'iuueni sors pulchrior omnis: | et certasse manu decet et caruisse sepulchro'; Don. on Ter. *Andr.* 128 'quod sine pulchra re sit'; Maltby 561). In its literal sense *struere* is preferred by T. to *exstruere* in Books 1–6; like Cicero and Caesar, he prefers the compound in 11–16 (Adams (1972) 363–4).

si iudicium posterorum in odium uertit Tib. allegedly told the senate that, if they ever came to doubt him, he hoped it would be after his death, and he did not wish to receive any honour that they would come to regret (Suet. *Tib.* 67.4 'uobis autem exprobrabit . . . inconstantiam contrarii de me iudicii').

38.3 deos et deas ipsas M reads *deos et deos ipsos* with a superscript *a* over each of the last two words. Pichena was followed by some older editors in simply reading *et deos ipsos*, but Lipsius' acceptance of the MS correction, printed here, is supported both by the phrase *di . . . deaeque* in another Tiberian utterance at 6.6.1 (n.) and by the formulaic language, as Plaut. *Most.* 655 'malum quod isti di deaeque omnes duint'; *ipsas* agrees with the nearest noun, as 12.65.2 'conuictam Messalinam et Silium'.

hos ut . . . duint, illos ut . . . prosequantur The two clauses are balanced and varied: each begins with a temporal expression (*ad finem usque uitae* ~ *quandoque concessero*) and ends with a finite verb; the first clause has a single object (*mentem*) qualified by two adjs. (*quietam et intellegentem*), the second clause has two objects (*facta atque famam*), one of which has a single dependent genitive (*nominis mei*); *intellegentem* in the first clause has a dependent noun and two adjs. (*humani diuinique iuris*), the verb in the second clause has two nouns and a single adj. (*cum laude et bonis recordationibus*).

usque For the position see *Agr.* 14.1n.

quietam et intellegentem . . . mentem duint Tib. characteristically (see above, 1n.) adopts the archaising form *duint* (as Cic. *Cat.* 1.22 'utinam tibi istam mentem di immortales duint!') rather than *dent* (as Liv. 6.18.9, Mart. 7.67.16). For *quieta . . . mens* see H. on *H.* 3.12.1; the combination with *intellegens* seems unparalleled. *intellegens* + gen., first in Cicero (*TLL* 7.1.2103.4–8), recurs at 5.9.1, 12.26.2; for Tib.'s knowledge of human and divine law see Levick 89, 253 n. 33.

quandoque concessero Without *uitā*, as 13.30.2 and perhaps 2.71.1.

cum laude et bonis recordationibus _facta_ atque _famam_ nominis mei prosequantur *prosequor* in various senses is regularly accompanied by (*cum* +) an abl., but, since the *princeps* is talking about the period after his death, here the uppermost meaning, at the very conclusion of a speech dominated by death, is that of escorting a funeral (*OLD* 1b; *TLL* 10.2.2187.38–52). The clausula is Cicero's favourite. Various combinations of, and plays on, *facta* and *fama* are common from Plaut. *Bacch.* 64 'facta et famam'; *fama nominis* (again at 5.10.1) is a common expr. (Vell. 94.4n.), esp. in Livy (Liv. 1.2.5, 3.2.3, 28.46.11, 38.58.5). *prosequi* with *facta* recurs at Val. Max. 2.7.12, 9.8 *praef.*, Col. 8.16.3, but with *famam* is unique; *p.* with *laude* (*–ibus*) is a regular phrase (e.g. *D.* 32.2), but with *recordationibus* is unparalleled: such combinations are typical of T.

38.4 secretis . . . sermonibus is a common phrase for private conversations and the like; but, if they were private, how does T. know what was said? Furneaux notes that the *princeps'* refusal 'was not so persistent as Tacitus supposed', referring to a Cypriot temple of AD 29, inscribed to Tiberius without any addition of Rome or the senate (EJ 134). According to Gradel, however, 'refusals were important in the interplay between emperor and Senate in Rome, but they had little relevance to what took place at the municipal or civil level' (85).

Quod alii . . . multi . . . quidam . . . interpretabantur There is *uariatio* not only of pronoun and adj. but also of construction after the verb (Sörbom 32–3, 115): the predic. acc. is regular, *ut* (again at *H.* 1.27.1) is very rare (and the gen. unparalleled), and a *quia*-clause unparalleled (*TLL* 7.1.2259.8ff., 24–6, 37–9). The second and third allegations are more reprehensible counterparts of the first and second respectively, while the third is expanded by a passage of *oratio obliqua* whose various barbs seem to be blunted by the way in which they are expressed (see nn. below). For a brilliant analysis see Pelling, *AHC* 364–86, esp. 371–8.

modestiam is an aspect of the *moderatio* for which Tib. was famous (3.50.2n.) and is duly reflected in his letter to the people of Gythium in Laconia on divine honours (EJ 102 (b), lines 20–1): αὐτὸς δὲ ἀρκοῦμαι ταῖς μετριωτέραις τε καὶ ἀνθρωπείοις [sc. τιμαῖς]. Since *modestia* was the antithesis of *ambitio* (cf. 3.26.2 'pro modestia ac pudore ambitio et uis'), this first group of speakers directly contradicts those whose accusations of *ambitio* had given rise to Tib.'s speech in the first place (37.1).

quia diffideret 'on the grounds that he lacked confidence' (sc. that he was equal to such an honour; cf. Suet. *Tib.* 67.2). *diffidentia* is seen by Quintilian (9.2.72) as a negative version of *pudor*: hence this second group of speakers are placing a critical interpretation on the 'modesty' attributed to the *princeps* by the first group.

degeneris animi negates the *princeps*' hope that he would be thought 'worthy of his ancestors' (1). Although the expr. (again at *H.* 3.85) occurs elsewhere (Luc. 6.417 'degeneres trepidant animi', Sen. *Ep.* 107.12, Apul. *Plato* 2.14), the context suggests an allusion to Virg. *Aen.* 4.12–13 'credo equidem (nec uana fides) genus esse deorum. | degeneres animos timor arguit', where divine ancestry as well as fear is in play (Pelling, *AHC* 372). Tib.'s alleged degeneracy both means that he is not living up to his adoptive father (or to the latter's adoptive father) and proves that he is overcome by fear, an intensification of the lack of confidence attributed to him by the second group of speakers (cf. Gell. 1.11.18 'diffidentiae . . . et timori'). For Tib.'s fear of being compared to Augustus cf. 1.76.4 (a somewhat similar passage).

38.5 optimos quippe mortalium altissima cupere The words constitute a denial of Tib.'s claim to be known as *optimus princeps* (Vell. 126.5, Val. Max. 2 *praef.*, *CIL* 6.902, 904; cf. 6.93). *mortales* for *homines*, a usage of which T. is fond (6.22.1n.), here contrasts with the immortality to which the following three heroes passed when deified. *altissima cupere* is paralleled only at Sall. *C.* 5.5 'nimis alta cupiebat', where it is used of Catiline, thus taking some of the shine off the remarks of the *princeps*' critics.

sic Herculem et Liberum apud Graecos, Quirinum apud nos deum numero additos T. 'is mocking conventional opinions – hence allusion to Greek deifications and stock Augustan themes' (Syme, *Tac.* 315 n. 6, comparing Hor. *C.* 3.3.9ff.). *addere* is almost technical in such contexts (*OLD* 9; N–H on Hor. *C.* 2.19.13).

melius Augustum sc. *fecisse* or *egisse*, as 1.43.1 (n.). While the critics thus deny Tib.'s claim to follow Augustan precedent (37.3), their denial is inconsistent with earlier attacks on Augustus' own practice (1.10.6 'cum se templis et effigie numinum . . . coli uellet'): cf. Pelling, *AHC* 369.

cetera principibus statim adesse probably means 'everything else was available instantly for *principes*' (*OLD* 20 rather than 17b).

unum insatiabiliter parandum, prosperam sui memoriam The critics blatantly disregard Tib.'s words (cf. 1 'qui *satis* superque *memoriae meae* tribuent'): the one thing he wants is to bequeath a lasting and favourable memory of himself. The adv. recurs only in Lucr. 3.907, 6.978, Plin. *Ep.* 9.6.3 and [Quint.] *Decl.* 18.10. 'It was difficult to use the word seriously', according to Syme (*Tac.* 727 n. 3), who says that here it is 'exaggerated if not insincere'.

***contemptu* famae *contemni* uirtutes** The Roman ethos, esp. evident in Sallust (e.g. *C.* 1.4 ~ 2.9), was to display *uirtus* and thus guarantee one's *fama*:

it was therefore notable when someone achieved his reputation otherwise (Nep. *Lys*. 1.1 'Lysander Lacedaemonius magnam reliquit sui famam, magis felicitate quam uirtute partam'). Tib.'s critics turn this relationship on its head and, on the false grounds that he rejects *fama*, allege equally falsely that he rejects *uirtutes* – despite his enumeration of the virtues for which he wished to be remembered (1). For the resumption of a verbal noun by a verb see Wills 327.

39–41 Sejanus and Tiberius
In the central section of the year, and at the midway point in Book 4, T. introduces an exchange of letters between Sejanus and Tib. which will have momentous consequences. Sejanus' request for the hand of Livi(ll)a (39) is rejected by the *princeps* (40), a rejection which convinces Sejanus that, if his attempt on power is to succeed, he should try the alternative tactic of persuading Tib. to leave Rome (41). His persuasion is soon successful and Tib. withdraws from Rome (57.1), never to return.

Demetrius thought that the style of a letter was a reflection of the writer's soul (*Eloc.* 227 σχεδὸν γὰρ εἰκόνα ἕκαστος τῆς ἑαυτοῦ ψυχῆς γράφει τὴν ἐπιστολήν). Sejanus is genuine in his desire for marriage to Livi(ll)a but hides from Tib. the reasons why he wants to be married to her; Tib., though ignorant of Sejanus' ultimate ambitions and having the power to refuse his request outright, astutely counters his minister's points and couches his refusal in characteristically oblique terms. His reply is a 'masterpiece' of 'consummate craft' (Syme, *Tac*. 701–2), and it is not difficult to see in this exchange of correspondence an initial manifestation of the superior skill which T. attributed to the emperor at the beginning of the book (1.2). Although Sejanus will have the upper hand throughout the immediately succeeding years, when letters to and from Capri constitute the dominant form of communication (see 6.2–14 intro. n.), it will be another characteristically oblique letter from the *princeps* which condemns Sejanus to death in AD 31.

39.1 At Seianus ... These ominous words introduce both a change of focus and the central section of the narrative year (cf. Virg. *Aen*. 4.1 'At regina ...'). The sentence as a whole appears to be arranged chiastically: Sejanus' insensibility ('socors') leads him to write to Tib. ('componit ... codicillos'), while *muliebri ... incensus* is explained by *promissum ... Liuia* (next n.).

nimia fortuna socors et muliebri insuper cupidine incensus The dangers of excessive success (e.g. Publil. F8 'Fortuna nimium quem fouet stultum facit'; Ogilvie on Liv. 5.21.15 'nimia sua fortuna', Oakley on 10.13.6, Tosi 394 §843) and the madness of love (e.g. Publil. A15 'Amans quid cupiat scit, quid sapiat non uidet'; Tosi 632–3 §1399) are proverbial and constitute regular elements in tragic drama;[88] each features prominently in two of the famous stories with which Herodotus begins his history (1.8.1, 1.30). The reference to fortune here is pointed, since Sejanus kept a statue of Fortuna, a goddess whom he cultivated (5.6.2n.). Since his affection for Livi(ll)a was feigned (3.3 'ut amore incensus'), *muliebri . . . cupidine* must refer to her desire for him (cf. *OLD muliebris* 1a–b), not, as *incensus* might lead one to expect, his desire for her.

promissum Cf. 3.3 'ad coniugii spem . . . impulit'.

moris quippe tum erat quamquam praesentem scripto adire The custom of approaching office-holders by letter had started in the late republic and continued in T.'s own day (see Millar 240ff. and 537ff.):[89] as *tum* and *quamquam praesentem* suggest, T. directs attention to the custom because, after Tib. absented himself from Rome in 26 (57.1), there was generally no alternative to an epistolary approach (see 6.2–14 intro. n.). For the gen. *moris* see *Agr.* 33.1n.

39.2 eius talis forma fuit 'It is difficult to see what authentic record could have been known to Tacitus of this letter or the reply' (Furneaux). This seems to be the majority view (see Seager 228 and n. 118, though noting that Levick 'seems inclined to accept the correspondence as genuine': see Levick 117, 164–5).

patris Augusti Sejanus is presumably referring to his time in the entourage of Gaius Caesar, Augustus' grandson (1.2n.). As at 3 below, the reference to Tib.'s adoptive father constitutes a *captatio beneuolentiae* (cf. 37.3n.).

plurimis Tiberii iudiciis Cf. Vell. 128.1 'in huius [sc. Seiani] uirtutum aestimatione iam pridem iudicia ciuitatis cum iudiciis principis certant', although in our passage *iudiciis* = 'marks or instances of esteem' (*OLD* 10a).

ita insueuisse ut spes uotaque sua non *prius* ad deos quam ad *principum* aures conferret Since *ut . . . conferret* is not a consecutive

---

[88] The present passage nevertheless seems not to be mentioned by Santoro L'Hoir, while F. Galtier, *L'image tragique de l'histoire chez Tacite: étude des schèmes tragiques dans les Histoires et les Annales* (2011) 172 n. 153, says merely that Sejanus 'abandonne sa prudence habituelle' in asking to marry Livi(ll)a.

[89] Millar gives the impression that the normal term for such letters was *libelli*, whereas *codicilli* was reserved for imperial letters of appointment (288ff., 305ff.): if this distinction is correct, T.'s reference to *codicillos* (above) is characteristically distorted (see *Ann. 3*, p. 503; *Ann. 5–6*, p. 319: s.v. 'technical . . . language').

clause, *ita* must mean something like 'in this way' or 'thus' (his original words are imagined as being e.g. 'I have become accustomed, as I am doing now, to bringing . . .'). See also below, 3n. For *insuesco* + *ut* cf. Gell. 1.17.3.

spes and *uota* are a regular combination (*Agr.* 3.1n.) but in the context the reference to 'prayers' is pointed and renders Sejanus' flattery even more audacious: the gods were always supposed to take precedence over humans (Tosi 376–7 §805). *aures*, though appropriate to a *princeps* (e.g. Hor. *S.* 2.1.19 'Caesaris aurem', Ov. *Ex P.* 1.2.115 'Augustas . . . aures'; and above, 29.3n.), is also appropriate for the gods (Callim. *Epigr.* 25.4 οὔατ' ἐς ἀθανάτων, Cat. 63.75, Ov. *F.* 1.181 'aures . . . deum'); the conceit is maintained by *precatum* in the next sentence. Sejanus has already been shown to have a clever way with words (2.1nn.), but here he seems to have forgotten that Tib. tended to insist on his own mortality (38.1n.), an insistence of which the *princeps* will remind him in his reply (40.1n.). For the omission of *se* from the or. obl. see 3.8.2n.

neque fulgorem honorum umquam precatum *fulgor* with *honorum* (−*is*) is very rare (only Val. Max. 5.5.2): in view of his military image, Sejanus has perhaps chosen the word to imply an upcoming contrast with the proverbial glitter (*fulgor armorum*) associated with life in the Roman army (*Agr.* 33.1n.; cf. *Agr.* 26.1n.), a contrast which he then thwarts by referring to the more mundane 'watches and toils' in the next sentence. His contemporary, Velleius, describes Sejanus as 'nihil sibi uindicantem' (127.4). The most famous analogy is Maecenas, who never sought political advancement but remained an *eques* throughout his life (Vell. 88.2n. §1), but there were others both earlier (Nep. *Att.* 6.2 'honores non petiit') and later (Tac. *A.* 16.17.3 'petitione honorum abstinuerat').

excubias ac labores This unparalleled and more vivid variant on the common combination of *uigiliae* and *labores* corresponds to the description of Sejanus at 1.3 above ('laborum tolerans . . . industria ac uigilantia') and at Vell. 127.3–4 ('laboris . . . capacissimum . . . animo exsomnem'), and picks up Tib.'s own description of his minister at 3.72.3 'labore uigilantiaque' (n.). Indeed Sejanus' very 'title' was 'socius laborum' (4.2.3n.). He cultivated a military image of himself as the ideal general (4.2.2n.): he was a second Agrippa (Syme, *Tac.* 402–3), complementing his imitation of Augustus' other great minister, Maecenas (last n.).

ut unum e militibus An ideal general was supposed to be 'one of the men' (Vell. 79.1n., 114.1–3n.), but, given Sejanus' unique position as Tib.'s minister, he could never realistically play this role: *ut* is nicely ambiguous ('as', 'as if').

pro incolumitate imperatoris The regular phraseology was *pro incolumitate principis* (17.1n., 12.68.1; cf. 14.62.3) but Sejanus has substituted 'commander-in-chief' to underline their military relationship (cf. 34.4n.).

217

ac tamen . . . ut coniunctione Caesaris dignus crederetur Sejanus' daughter had been betrothed to Claudius' son, Drusus, in 20 (3.29.4n., 4.7.2n.).

It is very difficult to decide whether *quod pulcherrimum* is parenthetic or whether it is the object of *adeptum* and expanded by the *ut*-clause; the sense is much the same either way. I have decided on a parenthesis because clauses consisting of *quod* + superl. adj. very often are parenthetic; for *adipiscor* followed by *ut* cf. 6.8.1; *TLL* 1.692.1–5.

39.3 quoniam audiuerit Augustum . . . consultauisse Since any reference to his former wife would bring back painful memories for Tib. (6.51.2), Sejanus has to choose his words carefully: *audiuerit* is diplomatically disingenuous, since the matter was evidently well known (Suet. *Aug.* 63.2), and *equitibus Romanis* is a suitably vague plural. The *princeps* characteristically responds with precise details at 40.6 below.

Hartman, objecting that *quoniam* is never correlated with *ita* (below), proposed to read *quomodo* instead (173–4); but *ita* refers only to *Augustum . . . consultauisse*, not to the whole of the *quoniam*-clause. Note also Sejanus' use of *ita* at 2 above.

amicum sola necessitudinis gloria usurum The *amicitia* between Tib. and Sejanus is acknowledged in the *princeps'* reply (40.5, 7) and will be sealed by an altar and statues at the end of the book (74.2: AD 28), but it nevertheless seems bold for the subordinate to venture the term here (see 40.1n.). For the idea of 'reflected glory' see Plin. *Ep.* 5.11.2 'gaudeo primum tua gloria, cuius ad me pars aliqua pro necessitudine nostra redundat'.

39.4 non enim exuere imposita munia *imponere* is a regular verb for assigning responsibilities (*TLL* 7.1.657.67ff., *OLD impono* 11b), but T.'s favourite *exuere* (1.2.1n.) activates the metaphor of putting on clothes (*TLL* 7.1.654.77ff., *OLD impono* 6a): cf. Sen. *Cons. Helv.* 16.2 'inposita lugubria numquam exuerunt'.

satis aestimare firmari domum aduersum iniquas Agrippinae offensiones 'He thought it enough if the family [sc. of Tiberius] were/ would be strengthened . . .' (*OLD aestimare* 7a). The substitution of *domus* for *familia* (3.24.1n.) suggests the metaphor of an actual house being fortified against the onslaughts of a violent storm or tidal wave (for this sense of *offensio* see *TLL* 9.2.498.4ff.; for *iniquus* of natural conditions etc. see *OLD* 6c).

idque liberorum causa Although Sejanus' wording, exactly like that at Cic. *Dom.* 34 and [Quint.] *Decl.* 291.6, suitably alludes to the official formula of a Roman marriage contract (for which see Malloch on 11.27; Treggiari 8, 211, 458), the reference is not of course to the procreation of future offspring but to the protection of those already in existence. Several scholars think that

Sejanus' own children are meant, which in the context of his request seems highly implausible; Lipsius argued that the reference is to the surviving children of Drusus and Livi(ll)a, namely Ti. Gemellus and Julia, Tib.'s grandchildren;[90] but, since Julia was herself already married to Nero Caesar, Agrippina's son (3.29.3n.), Sejanus is perhaps referring primarily to Gemellus, who was still just a very young child (2.84.1n.; cf. 6.46.1n.): *liberi* can denote a single child (*TLL* 7.2.1303.41–64). It is typical of Sejanus' effrontery that it was he who had made Gemellus and Julia fatherless by murdering Drusus (above, 8.1).

sibi multum superque uitae fore quod tali cum principe expleuisset The common motif *satis uixi*, of which *multum superque uitae* is a unique and extravagant variant, can be used in a range of different contexts (6.48.1n.): here see esp. *El. Maec.* 2.11–12 ' "sed tamen hoc satis est: uixi te, Caesar, amico | et morior", dixit, "dum moriorque, satis"'. See also Fraenkel on Aesch. *Ag.* 1314; for *uitam explere* see *TLL* 5.2.1719.59ff.

40.1 laudata . . . percursis The chiastic abl. abs. at once establishes the hierarchical basis of Tib.'s relationship with Sejanus, thereby correcting the latter's use of the term *amicus* at 39.3.

cum tempus . . . petiuisset, adiunxit Numerous scholars think that Tib. is imagined as having written two letters, a brief note praising Sejanus' devotion and enumerating his own favours (above), and then, after the interval requested here, the longer letter presented below. Others think that only one letter is envisaged and that the request for a time of reflection is thus part of the letter. The Latin is capable of either interpretation, but *adiungere* is so common of 'adding in speech or writing' (*OLD* 9a) that it strongly suggests that only one communication is meant. A single reply to Sejanus' single letter is also more dramatic, while the reference to a definitive decision in the future is pleasingly and ominously Tiberian.

tamquam ad integram consultationem Tib. again picks up Sejanus' letter (39.3 'consultauisse'). *integra consultatio* is found elsewhere only in Livy (31.2.2, 39.7.7), where scholars seem agreed that a 'full' rather than an 'unprejudiced' deliberation is meant. Either meaning would be equally appropriate here and, as the authorial *tamquam* indicates, each is undercut by the letter itself, which is already very long and, despite what the *princeps* says in §7, almost entirely negative.

ceteris mortalibus succinctly underlines the point which Tib. has already made in his speech at 38.1 above, namely, that he is mortal like everyone else

---

[90] Germanicus, twin brother of Gemellus, had died in 23 (above, 15.1).

('me . . . mortalem esse'). Sejanus' implied attribution of divinity (39.2n. *ita*) was misconceived.

quid sibi conducere putent The implication is that, despite his protestations, Sejanus' request was motivated by self-interest; the reader knows this to be true, but whether Tib. intended the implication is debatable (cf. 59.2 'ut non sui anxius, cum fide audiebatur').

principum diuersam esse sortem contrasts with *ceteris mortalibus* above: it is characteristic of Tib. to distinguish between everyone else and *principes* such as himself (3.3.1n., 3.53.3n.).

quibus praecipua rerum ad famam derigenda Tib.'s reference to fame or renown in his preceding speech (38.3 'famam nominis mei') makes it seem likely that that is the meaning of *fama* here too: unlike other mortals, *principes* are obliged to take the long view. Several commentators, however, think that *fama* here refers to rumour or public opinion and that Tib. is deploying the topos that great men have to take into account what people think about them (Sen. *Clem.* 1.15.5 'principes multa debent etiam famae dare'; see also Mayor on Juv. 8.139, and, for a related topos, 67.1n. below). For *praecipua rerum* cf. 41.3n.

40.2 quod promptum rescriptu expands upon *illuc* (as Hor. *S.* 1.3.38 'illuc praeuertamur . . . quod . . .') and is itself expanded by the following acc. + infin. *rescribere* is the technical term for an imperial response (*OLD* 2a), but the supine form is unparalleled.

nubendum post Drusum an in penatibus isdem tolerandum haberet For this use of *habeo* in expressions of obligation ('I have to ~ ') see H. Pinkster on 'The so-called deontic value of the gerundive', *OLS* 1.298ff. (§5.41), esp. p. 300. The construction is common in T.: exs. of various types are *D.* 8.2 'quae non auditu cognoscenda sed oculis spectanda haberemus', 19.5 'nec exspectandum habent oratorem', 31.4 'dicendum habuerit', 36.7 'cum . . . respondendum haberent', 37.4 'dicendum habeas', *H.* 1.15.3 'in qua nihil praeteritum excusandum habeas', 4.77.3 'neque aliud excusandum habeo', *A.* 14.44.1 'si nunc primum statuendum haberemus'. Hence our passage means: 'whether she should have to [*or* ought to] marry after Drusus' death or to continue in the same household'. See further *TLL* 6.3.2422.59ff., K–S 1.732, L–H–S 372, *OLD habeo* 17a; J. N. Adams, *Social variation and the Latin language* (2013) 626. For the ellipse of *utrum* see 34.5n.; for such brachylogical expressions as *post Drusum*, common with *post* in T. (e.g. 1.16.1 'post Augustum') as well as other authors, see 1.68.5n., N–H on Hor. *C.* 1.18.5. For the absolute use of *tolerare* cf. 6.11.3.

matrem et auiam, propiora consilia The former is Antonia minor, widow of the elder Drusus (Tib.'s brother) and daughter of Octavia (Augustus' sister) and Mark Antony (cf. Raepsaet-Charlier 90–1 no. 73); the latter is Livia Augusta. The decision not to name them is deliberate (see below, 4n. *fratrem . . . patrem*). For the metonymical use of *consilium* for individual advisers see *OLD* 3a; cf. 15.61.2 'quod erat . . . intimum consiliorum'.

40.3 simplicius 'more frankly', 'more directly' (*OLD simpliciter* 4; cf. 3 and 5). *simplicitas* is of course the very last quality that one would associate with Tib., but note his own statement at *Tab. Siar.* IIb.16 'ipse se uelle non dissimulare eodem libello testatus' (cf. 71.3n.).

de inimicitiis primum Agrippinae, quas longe acrius arsuras si matrimonium . . . distraxisset The *princeps* turns first to the issue which Sejanus had left almost till the last; but, whereas the latter had described Agrippina's *offensiones* in terms of a storm or tidal wave (39.4n.), Tib. chooses fire (for *acrius* see *Agr.* 4.3n.), pointedly leaving the storm/wave metaphor to describe the marriage which Sejanus has requested (for *distrahere* of storms see 3.10.3n.). *in partes* means literally 'into factions' but metaphorically 'to pieces'. For the acc. + infin. in the relative clause (*quas = et eas*) see *NLS* §230 (6) *Note*, §289.

sic quoque erumpere aemulationem feminarum 'even as things were, . . .' (*OLD quoque* 4d, *sic* 9b), an ironical reference to 12.3 above, where the rivalry is exacerbated by Sejanus; for earlier divisions within the imperial household see 2.43.5–6. For *erumpere* of water bursting forth see 5.11.1n.; for *aemulatio* cf. Flor. 2.13.13 (4.2.13) 'aemulatio erupit'.

eaque discordia nepotes suos conuelli Tib.'s grandsons were Drusus' son, Ti. Gemellus (still a child), and the sons of Germanicus: Nero Caesar, Drusus Caesar and Gaius (Caligula). *conuelli* is perhaps vivid for *conuulsum iri* and thus an anticipation of rivalries that will soon develop (see esp. 60.3 below). The verb (for which see 6.40.2n.; *OLD* 3) maintains the metaphor.

quid si intendatur certamen tali coniugio? The question recalls *Aen.* 4.47–8 'quam tu urbem, soror, hanc cernes, quae surgere regna | coniugio tali', where Anna successfully persuades Dido to forget her dead husband Sychaeus and contemplate a marriage to Aeneas, which, while allegedly enhancing her own power, would have meant disaster for the future of Rome.

40.4 Falleris enim . . . cum equite Romano senescat Little does Tib. know that Sejanus has no intention of staying within his own rank and that it is Livi(ll)a who wants to marry him rather than the other way round (3.3–4 above). Such dramatic irony permeates the whole of the *princeps'* letter, whose change from indirect to direct speech at this point was found 'notably effective' by Syme (*Tac.* 317); for the same technique elsewhere see 3.12.2, 4.8.4 (though with an interruption), 16.22.2; for Livy's practice see Oakley 1.119; in general K–S 2.548 Anm. 5.

C. Caesari Augustus' grandson, Gaius Caesar, who had died in AD 4. Livi(ll)a must have been married to Gaius before he was sent to the east in 1 BC and when she was still a child, but the exact date, like the date of her marriage to Drusus, is unknown.

senescat For this ideal of marriage see Catull. 61.149–56/156–63, Plin. *Ep.* 4.19.5 (though with Pliny's own slant on it), Mart. 4.13.9–10.

Ego ut sinam 'Even if I should allow it' (*OLD ut* 35b): cf. 33.4.

fratrem . . . patrem Respectively Germanicus and the elder Drusus, who, like Antonia and Augusta above (2), are not named but referred to in terms of their family relationships. 'Perhaps the reason for the use of so many kin terms with respect to Livilla here is the special position of the women of the imperial family, who on the one hand derive their status mainly from their male family members, not being able to hold any public offices themselves, but on the other hand provide the essential dynastic links' (Y. Klaassen, 'Contested successions: the transmission of imperial power in Tacitus' *Histories* and *Annals*' (diss. Nijmegen 2014) 258 n. 919); see also R. Seager, 'Perceptions of the *domus Augusta*, AD 4–24', *JCS* 41–57. The verb *uidere* neatly combines the notions of 'to see ~ in a particular state' (*OLD* 8) and, since *maiores nostros* is one of its objects, 'to be alive at the time to see ~ ' (*OLD* 11c).

40.5 sistere is commonly intransitive in a variety of different senses (see *OLD* and e.g. Horsfall on Virg. *Aen.* 3.7).

illi magistratus et primores qui <ad> te inuitum perrumpunt omnibusque de rebus consulunt T.'s words are closely matched by those of Dio (57.21.4 ἔς τε τὴν οἰκίαν αὐτοῦ οἵ τε ἄλλοι οἱ ἐλλόγιμοι καὶ οἱ ὕπατοι αὐτοὶ ὑπὸ τὸν ὄρθρον συνεχῶς ἐφοίτων, καὶ τά τε ἴδια αὐτῷ πάντα, ὅσα τινὲς ἀξιώσειν παρὰ τοῦ Τιβερίου ἔμελλον, καὶ τὰ κοινά, ὑπὲρ ὧν χρηματισθῆναι ἔδει, ἐπεκοίνουν), with the striking exception of the problematic verb *perrumpunt*. M here reads *inuite* (which makes no sense), having first started to write *inuitu*. A second hand has suggested the correction *inuito*, but this leaves both verbs incomplete in sense (for ex., neither has an object). Heinsius' *inuitum*, favoured by most edd., remedies this deficiency but raises a question over the meaning of *perrumpunt*. The verb, if used transitively, means 'to burst apart/through', its object being e.g. a wall (as 3.46.3); there is a remarkable metaphorical use at 3.15.2, where Tib. cannot be penetrated by emotional appeals ('ne quo adfectu perrumperetur'), but such a meaning is clearly inappropriate here, where the subject is persons: the magistrates and leaders are not 'bursting through Sejanus'. What one expects T. to say is 'burst through *to* Sejanus': although this intransitive use + *ad* is not found elsewhere in T., it occurs several times in Livy (*TLL* 10.1.1667.32–9). The image recalls the siege tactics at Hor. *S.* 1.9.54–6, where the pest is told that he will have to get through the outer barriers ('aditus primos') if he is to succeed in achieving access to Maecenas. The insertion of *ad* before *te inuitum* does not seem unduly difficult, and it is relatively easy thereafter to supply *te* as the object of *consulunt*. The reader of course knows that *inuitum* is false and that Sejanus has been actively canvassing support (2.2–3 above); see further 41.1, 74.3–4.

excessisse ... fastigium The reference to height, to which Tib. will return at the end of his letter in conciliatory terms (7), generates his upcoming point about *inuidia*: '*inuidia*, like lightning, strikes the "peaks" – of achievement, fame, and so on – just because they are the peaks' (Kaster 88 and n. 15). For the expr. cf. Val. Max. 5.6.4, Curt. 5.1.28, 8.9.3, 9.2.28, Plin. *Pan.* 54.4, Suet. *Cal.* 22.2.

perque inuidiam tui me quoque incusant Hence it is Tib.'s treatment of Sejanus which is defended so elaborately by Velleius, who discusses the complementary issues of the minister's relatively humble background and his immense power (127–8, with W.'s nn.).

40.6 At enim Augustus ... *at*, as often (*OLD at¹* 4b), introduces another speaker's objection, which in this case is constituted by the point already made by Sejanus in his letter at 39.3; *enim*, though very frequently combined with *at* (esp. in comedy, Cicero and Livy), here perhaps indicates that Sejanus' reference to Augustus constituted an explanation of his own request (cf. *quoniam* at 39.3).

Mirum (hercule!) si, cum ... extulisset ... The sentence is an ironical exclamation, implying its opposite: 'What a surprise that, when he was distracted by every concern and foresaw that the one whom he raised above others by such a union would be elevated immeasurably ...' (i.e. the sense is 'It is no surprise that ...'). The meaning of the sentence has been explained by Ernesti as follows: Augustus realised that Julia's future husband, whoever he might be, would be catapulted to a position of such eminence that he would be a potential rival to himself, and, since the *princeps* had many other claims on his attention, the situation would be dangerous: he therefore considered individuals who were conspicuously non-political. Compare the time when Augustus was seeking the *tribunicia potestas* for Tib. (3.56.2 'modestiae Neronis et suae magnitudini fidebat'): the situation had the same theoretical potential for danger, but on that occasion Augustus had confidence in both Tib.'s diffidence and his own impregnability. For *in curas distrahi* cf. Liv.

22.7.10; for *immensum . . . attolli* cf. 6.37.2 (and 3.30.1n. for the adv. *immensum*).
attolli is varied by *extulisset* as *coniugio* (3) by *coniunctione* (Sörbom 17, 35).

C. Proculeium This is our only evidence that one of those under consideration for Julia's hand was the *eques* Proculeius, half-brother of Terentia (wife of
Maecenas) and of the Murena who conspired against Augustus in 23 or 22 BC
(see Dio 54.3.5). See *RE* 23.72–4 = Proculeius 2 (Hanslik), *PIR* 6.413 no. 985,
BNP 11.926; J. S. Arkenberg, 'Licinii Murenae, Terentii Varrones, and
Varrones Murenae I', *Historia* 42 (1993) 326–51 at 347–9. His fraternal devotion is celebrated by Horace (*C.* 2.2.5–6 with N–H's n.), but his conspiratorial
brother is not to be identified either with the Murena who was elected consul
for 23 BC or with the man who is addressed as Licinius at *C.* 2.10 (see Vell.
91.2n., Syme, *AA* 388–91, J. S. Arkenberg, 'Licinii Murenae, Terentii
Varrones, and Varrones Murenae II', *Historia* 42 (1993) 471–91; *contra* N–H
ad loc.). The period at which Augustus was considering Proculeius as his son-
in-law is disputed but was 'presumably after the death of Marcellus' (N–H on
Hor. *C.* 2.2.5; *contra* Wardle on Suet. *Aug.* 63.2): this is certainly the implication
of T. here.

tranquillitate uitae recurs elsewhere only in Cicero (*TD* 5.6, *Mur.* 55 'qui
remoti a studiis ambitionis otium ac tranquillitatem uitae secuti sunt'). Tib. of
course likes Ciceronian expressions in his speeches, but was he aware that
Proculeius and Cicero's client (Licinius Murena was consul in 62 BC) were
distantly related (see Arkenberg's discussions, cited above)?

nullis rei publicae negotiis permixtos Proculeius had no formal political career, although he received some special commissions from Octavian/
Augustus. *rei publicae negotia* seems another Ciceronian phrase (*Pis.* 82, *Font.* 18),
found also at Plin. *Ep.* 7.15.2.

Sed, si dubitatione Augusti mouemur The *princeps* turns Sejanus'
trump example on its head. For *dubitatio*, another Ciceronian abstract noun,
see 3.41.3n.

Marco Agrippae, mox mihi Julia married Agrippa in 21 BC, Tib. in 11 BC,
after Agrippa's death the previous year. Augustus forced Tib. to divorce Julia
in 2 BC (Suet. *Tib.* 11.4).

40.7 non occultaui picks up *simplicius acturum* (3 and n.) and rounds off the
principal section of argument; but T. no doubt intends his readers also to
recall Tib.'s habitual secretiveness (1.2). See also next n.

ceterum neque tuis neque Liuiae destinatis aduersabor Tib.
'seems here to fall back on the evasive reply which he had taken credit for
not making' (Furneaux), and his announcement 'comes as a distinct surprise
after such telling arguments against the marriage' (Seager 167); but it well

illustrates the difficulties of interpreting the *princeps'* speech (31.2n.; *Ann. 3*, p. 513; *Ann. 5–6*, p. 325). After the lengthy discussion of §§3–6, however, Sejanus knows he has no choice in the matter, as is clear from his reaction at 41.1 below; nevertheless at the time of his death Sejanus was almost certainly married to Livi(ll)a, though the matter is controversial (see 5.6.2n. *ille*). See also next n. but one.

intra animum recurs in another Tiberian utterance at 3.54.5 (elsewhere only at [Quint.] *Decl.* 347.9, Apul. *Deo Socr.* 16).

quibus adhuc necessitudinibus immiscere te mihi parem Tib.'s 'preparations' in the matter of Sejanus are referred to as a mystery by M. Terentius in his speech of self-defence at 6.8.4 ('abditos principis sensus, et si quid occultius parat, exquirere inlicitum'). *necessitudo* applies to any connection between persons, not excluding marriage (see last n. but one).

nihil esse tam excelsum quod non uirtutes istae tuusque in me animus mereantur With *uirtutes istae* Tib. mentions last the points which Sejanus in his letter had mentioned first (39.2 'excubias ac labores'), while *tuus . . . in me animus* picks up *pietate Seiani* at the start of Tib.'s letter in ring composition. *excelsum* – a word which recurs in the *Annals* only at 3.53.3, another utterance of Tib. (Miller 16) – suggests that in the future Sejanus will receive a reward commensurate with the peak of his achievement (5 above).

datoque tempore picks up *cum tempus . . . petiuisset* (1) in a further ring and adds to the suspense in which Sejanus is to be kept: the *princeps* is toying with his minister as he in his turn would toy with others (59.3n.).

uel in senatu uel in contione non reticebo 'The closing words of Tiberius are intended (there can hardly be a doubt) to foreshadow what happened in the Senate when the "verbosa et grandis epistula" was read out on October 18 of the year 31, conveying the doom of Aelius Seianus' (Syme, *AA* 170; cf. Juv. 10.71, Suet. *Tib.* 65.1, Dio 58.10.1–7). There is similar fore-shadowing at 70.1 (n. *sollemnia*).

41.1 Rursum 'In his turn' (*OLD* 4).

non tam de matrimonio sed altius metuens Muretus' *iam* has been universally accepted but makes no sense, since there was no hint that Sejanus was 'afraid' when he wrote to Tib. (quite the opposite, in fact: cf. 39.1). *tam* has to be correct: for *non tam . . . sed* cf. Lucr. 3.613–14, Cic. *De Or.* 3.56, *Brut.* 58, *Fin.* 1.1, *al.*[91] The comparative *altius metuens* is explained by Sejanus' reaction to the *princeps'* letter: despite the promises issued at 40.7 ('neque tuis neque Liuiae

[91] *tam* was defended by J. H. Waszink ('Tacitea', *Mnem.* 10 (1942) 235), although not for reasons of logic but on mistaken grounds of style.

destinatis aduersabor'), Tib.'s generally negative response made Sejanus fearful about the proposed marriage – but he was *even more* fearful about some of the individual points that Tib. made, which he attempts to counteract in the following sentence. For *altius metuens* cf. Apul. *Met.* 8.31.2; *metuere de* + abl. is relatively rare (*TLL* 8.904.47–53) and only here in T., though he has *metus de* at 3.69.2.

tacita suspicionum, uulgi rumorem, *in*gruentem *in*uidiam deprecatur Sejanus' almost synonymous tricolon (destroyed by Doederlein's repunctuation) is largely bluster, but it is clear from his change of tactic, described in the next sentence, that he has been particularly stung by Tib.'s remarks about his *clientes* and is worried that the resulting unpopularity is rubbing off on the *princeps*, upon whom his entire future still depended (40.5 'sed illi ... non occulti ferunt'; note esp. *inuidiam tui* there ~ *ingruentem inuidiam* here).

The sentence (ABBABA) is characteristically varied. T. has substituted his favoured partitive gen. construction (1.17.3n.; *Ann. 3*, p. 501) for the more regular *tacitas suspiciones* (*Rhet. Herenn.* 4.41, Liv. 28.20.10, Apul. *Apol.* 98); *uulgi rumorem* (above, 29.2n.) is a possessive gen.; *ingruentem inuidiam* (unparalleled) substitutes an adj. for the gen. For *inuidiam deprecari* cf. Cic. *Rep.* 6.8 Powell (quoted by Gell. 7.16.11 in a discussion of *deprecari*), Suet. *Cal.* 9.1, but in our passage the verb has the different meaning of 'deprecated' (*OLD* 1c).

in domum coetus arcendo As Seneca was to do (14.56.3). *in domum* goes closely with *coetus* (cf. Liv. 4.25.9 'coetus indicere in domos tribunorum plebis').

infringeret potentiam is an expr. peculiar to the *Annals* (13.12.1, 14.1.3, 14.52.1).

huc flexit ut Tiberium ad uitam procul Roma amoenis locis degendam impelleret *procul* is naturally to be found in contexts of retreat from city life (e.g. 57.1, Hor. *Epod.* 2.1 and Watson ad loc.). No destination is specified, and the countryside is not even mentioned (though no doubt implied by *amoenis locis*, a regular expr. since the time of Cicero, who used it often): the deliberate vagueness here and below reflects Sejanus' attempts at being as persuasive as possible. In fact Tib. will first spend a year in Campania (57.1), which was proverbially attractive (3.59.3n.), and then spend the remainder of his life on Capri (67.1–3 and nn.). *huc* perhaps expresses not so much direction as degree (*OLD* 2b): 'he changed to this degree, that ...'. Tib.'s withdrawal from Rome was, after all, the major change of his principate.

41.2 sua in manu aditus Thus Horace warns that his patron, Maecenas, 'difficiles aditus primos habet' (*S.* 1.9.56).

cum per milites commearent The tense indicates that the use of soldiers was current practice: commentators quote Plut. *Galba* 8.4 τῶν δ' ὑπάτων οἰκέτας δημοσίους προχειρισαμένων τὰ δόγματα κομίζοντας τῷ αὐτοκράτορι, καὶ τὰ καλούμενα διπλώματα σεσημασμένα δόντων, . . . οὐ μετρίως ἠγανάκτησεν ὅτι μὴ παρ' αὐτοῦ καὶ σφραγῖδα καὶ στρατιώτας λαβόντες ἀνέπεμψαν. For *commeare* cf. Cic. *Att.* 8.9a(188).1 'crebro enim illius litterae ab aliis ad nos commeant'.

uergente iam senecta secretoque loci mollitum Sejanus repeats Tib.'s own description of his declining age at 8.3 above (n.); to it he adds chiastically the commonplace that persons could be affected by their localities (e.g. Sall. *C.* 11.5 'loca amoena, uoluptaria facile in otio ferocis militum animos molliuerant', with Vretska's n.): it will be not so much the isolation of Capri which softens Tib. but the opportunities for vice which the isolation offers (6.1.1). For the *uariatio* of abl. abs. ~ adj./participle see Sörbom 91; *secreto . . . loci* (as Sen. *Ep.* 41.3) substitutes for the more regular *secreto loco* (e.g. Liv. 44.31.10).

munia imperii See *Agr.* 13.1n.

minui sibi inuidiam adempta salutantum turba Towards the end of his reflections Sejanus returns to the matter which has been preoccupying him most (above, 1n.): for *minui . . . inuidiam* (*minui*, like *augeri* below, is vivid present for fut.) cf. Cic. *Leg. Agr.* 1.14, Liv. 3.9.12, Quint. 11.1.64. The *salutantum turba* is a recurring feature of Roman socio-political life (Cic. *Ep. Brut.* 2.4.1, Sen. *Ep.* 19.11, Juv. 5.21, Suet. *Galba* 17.1, Fronto p. 46.19–20 vdH²; cf. Tac. *A.* 13.18.3): see Watson on Hor. *Epod.* 2.7–8, *BNP* 12.909–10, both with bibliography. Sejanus' word order (verb→noun ~ verb→noun) generates a chiasmus with his final sentence (itself chiastic) below (verb→noun ~ noun→verb).

sublatisque inanibus ueram potentiam augeri Sejanus' *clientes* and the like are not literally 'trivialities' or 'inessentials' but he regards them as mere expedients on his route to real power (for the contrast see e.g. Ov. *Am.* 2.2.31 'huic, uerae ut lateant causae, finguntur inanes'), nuisances to be discarded once that power is achieved (for *inania*, a substantival usage of which T. is fond, cf. *TLL* 7.1.828.3ff.).

M here reads *uera potentia augere*: any emendation which involves an abl. (such as Rhenanus' *uera potentia augeri*, printed by Borzsák) is unlikely to be correct because of *sublatis . . . inanibus*; the choice is therefore between *ueram potentiam augeri* (Marcilius) and *ueram potentiam augere* (Muretus), the former providing a sharper contrast with *minui . . . inuidiam*. Heinsius proposed *uera potentiae augeri*: the idiom is certainly Tacitean (e.g. 6.45.3 'simulationum . . . falsa'; Malloch on 11.9.1), but *augere potentiam* at *H.* 3.45.1 is an argument against.

41.3 negotia urbis, populi *ad*cursus, multitudinem *ad*fluentium increpat The contrast between town and country was deep-rooted (see e.g. Hor. *S.* 2.6, *Epod.* 2, *Epist.* 1.10, 1.14, Juv. 3, with their respective commentators ad loc.), and the question of which locality was better was a rhetorical commonplace (Quint. 2.4.24 'rusticane uita an urbana potior'). Praise of the one (*extollens* below) inevitably involved criticism of the other (*increpat* here), and with the present passage one should compare the similar list at Liban. *Encom. Georg.* 262.18ff. πόρρω μὲν ἀγορᾶς καὶ τῆς ἐν ἀγορᾷ φιλονεικίας, πόρρω δὲ δικαστηρίων καὶ τῶν ἐν δικαστηρίοις συκοφαντιῶν, πόρρω δὲ ἐκκλησίας καὶ τῶν ἐπ' ἐκκλησίας θορύβων. Sejanus' mannered tricolon (ABBAAB) comprises both the general and the specific. *negotia* were emblematic of life in the city of Rome (e.g. 74.4, Hor. *Epod.* 2.1, *Epist.* 1.14.17 'trahunt inuisa negotia Romam', Plin. *Ep.* 7.30.2 'me huc quoque urbana negotia persequuntur'); but, although crowds are naturally an urban feature too (e.g. Sen. *Tranq. An.* 12.2–6, Juv. 3.243–8), the repeated prefix suggests those in particular which accost a great man or *princeps* (see *Agr.* 40.3n., Vell. 89.1n., 103.4n.). When Tib. left the Palatium to attend a trial, he was accosted by the people (2.34.3 'occursante populo'), and even when he was in Campania the townsfolk ran up, much to his displeasure (4.67.1 'concursusque oppidanorum'). In general see R. Jenkyns, *God, space and city in the Roman imagination* (2013) 143–77 on 'movement in the city'.

extollens laudibus quietem et solitudinem Virgil famously chose *quies* to identify country life (*G.* 2.467), while rural solitude naturally contrasted with the bustle of the city (e.g. Ov. *F.* 1.398): see H. Kier, 'De laudibus vitae rusticae' (diss. Marburg 1933) 33ff. (esp. 35, 37). But Sejanus is also employing flattery: since it was a commonplace of popular philosophy that the wise man profits from solitude (A. Oltramare, *Les origines de la diatribe romaine* (1926) 58, 85; cf. Powell on Cic. *Senec.* 49), there is also a tribute to Tib.'s implied wisdom (see also next n.).

Although *extollere laudibus* (again at 12.11.3, 14.14.2) seems something of a set phrase (earlier at Cic. *Har. Resp.* 47, Sall. *J.* 15.2), the noun perhaps refers self-reflexively to the rhetorical terms *laudes* ~ *uituperatio* with which Sejanus is operating (see previous n., and e.g. Quint. 3.7.1ff. for the contrasting terms). For *extollens* contrasted with *increpat* cf. Sen. *Tro.* 302.

quis abesse taedia et offensiones ac praecipua rerum maxime agitari *quis* is probably abl. (of separation with *abesse* and of 'place where' with *agitari*), but conceivably dat. with *abesse*, in which case *ubi* needs to be understood with *agitari*. Sejanus' wording is again carefully calculated. Tib. was prone to *taedium* (1.76.4 'taedio coetus', 1.80.2, 3.65.3 'tam proiectae seruientium patientiae taedebat') and sensitive to *offensiones* (18.2n., 38.1n.). *praecipua rerum* echoes the *princeps'* own words in his reply to Sejanus (40.1), but, whereas there Tib. was referring to important matters of state, Sejanus is perhaps implying, in the manner of a philosophical friend, that the *princeps* needs to get his priorities right: the *really* important things in life are to be found in the peace and quiet of the countryside (*maxime* is correctly taken with *praecipua rerum* by Doederlein: for the combination of *praecipuus* + adv. of degree cf. e.g. Cic. *Off.* 1.12 'ingeneratque inprimis praecipuum quendam amorem').

42–44 The end of the year
The final section of the year's domestic narrative consists of three parts, each of which is itself constituted of three items (42 three trials, 43 three embassies, 44 three obituaries). The first of the three trials continues the theme with which the previous narrative section ended: the withdrawal which Sejanus was urging on Tib. at 41.1–3 edges nearer when the *princeps* during the course of the trial is compelled to listen to the insults which people directed at him. The three men whose deaths are commemorated by obituaries serve to introduce the last section of the year's narrative, which records the death of a further individual in Spain (45). It is perhaps the central of the three parts which is the most interesting of all. We know from an extended episode in Book 3 (60–3) that embassies to Rome, especially those from the east dealing with religious issues, engaged the attention of both Tib.'s contemporaries and T.'s readers (see esp. 3.60.1–3). We have already had a brief example of such embassies under AD 23 (14.1–2); here under AD 25 not only is the scale rather more elaborate but the first of the three embassies, which is treated in some detail (43.1–3), deals with a temple dispute which happens to be recorded on a lengthy inscription which survives from Olympia. This is one of the very few cases where the literary and epigraphic evidence can be compared (see 43.3nn.).

42.1 Ac forte ... per illos dies These two favoured expressions, both absent from Livy as introductory formulae, are here combined to produce a unique variant on the Livian introductions *per eos forte dies* (10.21.2 etc.), *per eosdem forte dies* (23.41.10 etc.) and *per hos forte dies* (42.49.1).

de Votieno Montano A noted orator from Narbo in Gaul who is mentioned often by the elder Seneca (J. Fairweather, *Seneca the Elder* (1981) 408 (index)). T. does not name the accuser but Seneca reports that P. Vinicius (3.11.2n.), representing Narbo, laid an unspecified accusation against him in front of the *princeps* (Sen. *Contr.* 7.5.12 'accusauerat illum apud Caesarem'). Whether this was the same or a different occasion is unclear. See *RE* 9A.1.924 (Papenhoff), *PIR* 8.2.532 no. 998 (cf. 997), *BNP* 15.524; Rutledge 97, 351 n. 60.

cunctantem iam Tiberium 'already delaying': it is as if Sejanus' persuasion (41.3) had initially had its effect, but then Tib.'s *insita cunctatio* (11.1) took over. Votienus' trial caused him to change his mind back again, but only to the extent of *believing* that he should avoid the senate ('ut . . . crederet'), something which T. cannot in fact have known.

uocesque quae plerumque uerae et graues coram ingerebantur *uoces . . . ingerebantur* is perhaps from Luc. 8.433 'ingeret has uoces', although cf. also Liv. 3.68.4 'uocis uerborumque quantum uoletis ingerent'; *uerae et graues* seems to be principally a Ciceronian combination (*Phil.* 5.50, *Div.* 1.35, *Fin.* 4.7; also Gell. 18.4.10). *plerumque* is to be taken with *uerae*, as *coram* with *ingerebantur*.

42.2 postulato Votieno evidently refers to a preliminary arraignment before the formal trial (*cognitio*), as is indicated by *uel statim uel in cognitione* below.

testis Aemilius e militaribus uiris This is likely to be the same Aemilius as mentioned at 2.11.1–3; from the inscription quoted ad loc. it emerges that Aemilius was a tribune in the Praetorian Guard and perhaps therefore 'hand-picked by Sejanus' (D. C. A. Shotter, 'A crucial witness – a note on Tacitus *Annales* 4.42', *LCM* 16 (1991) 21). For the expr. *militares uiri* see *Agr.* 41.2n.; for the omission of *unus* cf. 2.60.3n.

dum studio *prob*andi cuncta refert et, quamquam inter obstrepentes, magna adseueratione nititur T. relishes the picture of a soldier struggling against his supposedly natural inarticulateness (*Agr.* 9.2n.) in order to perform his duty, and in the process causing consternation: see also 1.6.3 and 15.67.2–3; the episode at 6.24.1–2 is rather different but describes a similar reaction from the fathers (see n.).

***prob*ra quis per occultum lacerabatur, adeoque perculsus est** For the imagery cf. Liv. 31.6.5 'laceratusque probris', 43.8.3 'eum lacerarunt . . . multis obiectis probris'; also above, 31.4, and see 6.3.4n., 6.9.4n. For word play *probare* ~ *probra* cf. *H.* 1.48.3 'praepositus probatusque seruili deinceps probro respersus est', Cic. *Senec.* 42, Suet. *Claud.* 16.1 'iuuenem probri plenum, sed quem pater probatissimum sibi affirmabat'.

ut se uel statim uel in cognitione purgaturum clamitaret *purgaturum* may be used absolutely ('would clear his name') or, as Nipperdey argued, have *probra* (understood from above) as its object; but the likeliest interpretation is that it is being used reflexively, with *se* as the object ('would absolve himself': *OLD* 8a). Tib.'s outburst recalls that at 1.74.4.

42.3 maiestatis poenis St Jerome (*Chron.* p. 173.6 Helm) reports that he was exiled to the Balearic Islands and died in 27.

obiectam sibi aduersus reos inclementiam eo peruicacius amplexus 'embracing all the more persistently the mercilessness towards defendants that was imputed to him': see 31.1–2 and nn. *inclementia* has not hitherto been used in prose or applied to persons (later in Fronto p. 48.25 vdH²).

Aquiliam adulterii delatam Cases involving adultery *tout court* are hardly ever mentioned in the sources (Rutledge 61; cf. 338 n. 43). Appuleia Varilla was charged with *maiestas* as well as adultery but was released from the charge (2.50.1–3); Aemilia Lepida was accused of adultery with a slave (6.40.3). For the gen. after *deferor* (again at 6.47.2, 14.48.1) see K–S 1.464.

Vario Ligure Probably the son of a praetorian prefect under Augustus (for whom see Syme, *AA* 301), he recurs at 6.30.1 immediately before an episode involving the same Gaetulicus who is mentioned here.

Lentulus Gaetulicus consul designatus He had probably been elected no earlier than October, but 'there was no regular timetable for consular elections during the Julio-Claudian period' (Talbert 204). As consul designate he would have been invited to speak first (3.17.4n.). For him see 6.30.2–4nn.

exilio puniuit The implication seems to be that she lost all her property (i.e. *deportatio*), which would not have been the case under the Lex Iulia (see 2.50.3n.).

Apidium . . . Merulam Otherwise unknown.

quod in acta diui Augusti non iurauerat Such an oath was regular on 1 January each year (Talbert 201). In 66 Thrasea Paetus faced a similar charge (16.22.1).

albo senatorio 'The list of members of the senate in order of seniority, publicly displayed, and updated each year' (Talbert 523). For expulsion see 31.4n., 2.48.3n.

43.1 Auditae . . . legationes de iure templi Dianae Limnatidis Limnae and its temple were on the slopes of Mt Taygetus, on the border between Laconia and Messenia (Strabo 8.4.9 Τὸ δ᾽ ἐν Λίμναις τῆς Ἀρτέμιδος ἱερόν . . . ἐν μεθορίοις ἐστὶ τῆς τε Λακωνικῆς καὶ τῆς Μεσσηνίας): see *BA* Map 58: C3. *iure templi* = 'the right over the temple', as *iura libertorum* (*H.* 2.92.3) means 'rights over their freedmen'. For the background to the dispute and bibliography see S. L. Ager, *Interstate arbitrations in the Greek world 337–90 BC* (1996) 140–2, N. Luraghi, *The ancient Messenians* (2008) 16–27. For delegations seeking rulings from Rome on boundary disputes see Millar 434ff.; Talbert notes but does not discuss the fact that the present appeal emanated from the imperial province of Achaea but was evidently heard in the senate (418).

quod . . . dicatum . . . firmabant annalium memoria uatumque carminibus 'whose dedication they attested by . . .' (*OLD firmo* 9). *annalium* *memoria* is found elsewhere exclusively in prose (Cic. *Sull.* 27, *Q.Fr.* 1.1.7, Liv. 22.27.3, Plin. *NH* 2.140), whereas the more common *uatum carmina* (sing./plur.) is exclusively in verse (e.g. Prop. 4.1.51, the earliest ex.) apart from Sall. *H.* 1.77 M(67 R).3. For parallels to such appeals see Ager (above) 141 n. 2.

Philippi The father of Alexander the Great had moved into the Peloponnese after the decisive battle of Chaeronea in 338 BC.

C. Caesaris et M. Antonii sententia redditum Although documentation of similar decisions regarding asylum rights is mentioned and illustrated in the notes to 3.61–3, no evidence of this present *sententia* has survived; it is assumed that the Caesar referred to is Octavian rather than his adoptive father (Luraghi (above) 21).

43.2 ueterem inter Herculis posteros diuisionem Temenus, Cresphontes and the sons of Aristodemus took possession of Argos, Messenia and Laconia respectively (Apollod. 2.8.4).

suoque regi ... cessisse No ex. of *proferre* with the acc. + infin. is cited from classical Latin in *TLL* or *OLD*, but cf. Cic. *Inv.* 1.107 'res turpes et humiles et illiberales proferuntur et indigna esse ... quae passi perpessuriue sint', where there is a similar *uariatio* to that here (the general type is regular in T.: see Sörbom 110–11). *cessisse* = 'had become the property of, had passed into the possession of' (*OLD* 15a). The Denthalioi inhabited the disputed border area between the Spartans and Messenians.

monumentaque eius rei ... aere prisco manere The Messenians are keen to appeal to bronze memorials because bronze was associated with the sacred as well as the permanent (C. Williamson, 'Monuments of bronze', *CA* 6 (1987) 160–83). They underline their point by a learned etymology, since *memoria*, one of the supposed origins of *monumentum* (Maltby 392), was itself said to derive from *manere* (Varro, *LL* 6.49 'memoria a manendo'; Maltby 378).

43.3 si ... uocentur 'if they were being/to be challenged' (*OLD* 5).

locupletiores 'more reliable' (*OLD* 4).

neque ... potentia sed ex uero statuisse Madvig (2.547) declared that *potentia statuere* was not Latin and that, even if it were, the noun would not be a suitable antithesis of *uerum*. His first point seems nullified by Nep. *Cato* 2.2 'non potentia sed iure res publica administrabatur'; his second seems entirely arbitrary, since 'had decided not by virtue of his power but in accordance with reality/the truth' makes perfectly good sense. His proposed alternative (<*im*>*potentia*) is implausible, since T. reserves that term almost exclusively for women (the one exception is 14.31.3).

regis Antigoni ... imperatoris Mummii This is almost certainly Antigonus III Doson of Macedonia (see Ager (above) 141–2), who occupied Sparta in 222 BC (*BNP* 1.750–1). L. Mummius was in charge of Greece after the fall of Corinth in 146 BC (*MRR* 1.465–6); he is mentioned in lines 52–5 and 63–6 of the Olympia inscription (next n.): see Ager (above) 411–13 no. 150.

sic Milesios permisso publice arbitrio 'the arbitration having been granted to them as a community' (for *publice* cf. 36.2); the date is thought to be c. 138 BC. A long inscription from Olympia (*IOlympia* 52) is agreed to deal with this episode: 'this is one of the rare cases for which we have both epigraphic and literary evidence. The inscription was carefully engraved on the base of the impressive Nike of Paionios and is a striking example of the practice of publication in an international sanctuary ... The judgement was carried out in Miletos itself, by the largest court definitely attested in any case of interstate arbitration. A full assembly of the people was convened, with the agreement of the Spartan and Messenian representatives. Lots were then drawn to make up a panel of six hundred judges, taken from the citizen population at large ... The court found overwhelmingly in Messene's favour: 584 to 16' (Ager (above) 449–50, q.v. pp. 446–50 no. 159 for the full text of the inscription and further bibliography and discussion; Luraghi (above) 19–21).

Atidium Geminum praetorem Achaiae It is generally thought that he was praetorian proconsul at some point during Augustus' principate (*RE* 2.2075 = Atidius 6 (Klebs), *PIR* 1.271 no. 1343), though some prefer a date earlier in Tib.'s reign (Luraghi (above) 22). For *praetorem* see 15.2n.

Ita secundum Messenios datum This is legal terminology (*secundum* (*OLD* 6) = 'in favour of'): see H. on *H.* 3.7.1. The subject is *ius templi* or *iudicium*. 'Boundary stones in accordance with this award, and apparently belonging to this date, inscribed Ὅρος Λακεδαίμονι πρὸς Μεσσήνην, are still seen on the spot' (Furneaux); interestingly the decision reverses that made by Octavian many years earlier (1 above).

43.4 aedem Veneris montem apud Erycum The earliest mention is Thuc. 6.46.3 τὸ ἐν Ἔρυκι ἱερὸν τῆς Ἀφροδίτης. See 2.60.1n. for the placing of a prep. between two nouns in apposition.

uetustate dilapsam is a set phrase found esp. commonly on inscriptions (*TLL* 5.1.1158.4ff.).

suscepit curam libens ut consanguineus In AD 4 Tib. had been adopted into the *gens Iulia*, traditionally descended from Venus via her son Aeneas, who allegedly founded her temple on Mt Eryx (*Aen.* 5.759); see also Hornblower on Thuc. 6.2.3. On the Arch of Ticinum (*ILS* 107 = EJ 61), dating from AD 7 or 8, Tib. and Gaius and Lucius Caesar are all described identically as 'Augusti f. diui nepot.' As Seager has remarked, 'The desired effects of this are clear. All are ultimately legitimised by descent from the deified Julius Caesar. No distinction is drawn between their Julian or Claudian origins. All are alike sons of Augustus' (*JCS* 43). According to Suet. *Claud.* 25.5 the actual rebuilding of the temple belongs to Claudius' reign.

Koestermann, Fuchs and Heubner adopt Ritter's *suscepit<que>*, but Ritter printed simply *suscepit* in his edition and it is difficult to disagree with Borzsák that the addition is not necessary.

43.5 Tunc tractatae Massiliensium preces Two sets of delegations lead to mention of a third. There were perhaps two reasons why Marseille felt the need to appeal to the senate: (a) as a general rule (see below) towns did not receive inheritances (as opposed to legacies); (b) the benefactor in this case was an exile from Rome. The second of these difficulties was covered by the precedent of Rutilius Rufus (next n.).

probatumque P. Rutilii exemplum P. Rutilius Rufus (consul in 105 BC) was controversially convicted in 92 of extortion and went into exile at Smyrna, where he received the community's citizenship in place of that of Rome (Cic. *Balb.* 28): see G. P. Kelly, *A history of exile in the Roman republic* (2006) 181 and 258 (index).

Quo iure Volcacius Moschus . . . bona sua rei publicae eorum ut patriae reliquerat Halm's *Vulcacius* for M's *uulcatius* is accepted by almost all recent editors, including Heubner and Borzsák, but A. Kiessling (*Hermes* 26 (1891) 634–5), identifying the man as the orator from Pergamum who is mentioned by Porphyrio on Hor. *Ep.* 1.5.9, suggested that he derived his name and his citizenship from L. Volcacius Tullus, the consul of 33 BC and subsequently proconsul of Asia in the early 20s. On Latin inscriptions the name is almost always spelled *Volcacius*, as Syme pointed out (*TST* 78), approving that form in the edition of Lenchantin (although the credit should really go to Kiessling). According to the elder Seneca (*Contr.* 2.5.13), Moschus 'reus ueneficii fuit et, a Pollione Asinio defensus, damnatus Massiliae docuit'; another of his defenders was the Torquatus addressed by Horace in *Epist.* 1.5 (cf. Porphyrio, loc. cit.). On account of his exile to Marseille, Moschus substituted Massilian citizenship for Roman and on this basis bequeathed his estate to his new community. Bequests of this type to communities were very uncommon (see D. Johnston, 'Munificence and *municipia*: bequests to towns in classical Roman law', *JRS* 75 (1985) 105–25, esp. 106–8), and 'overt posthumous expressions of affection or patriotism', such as references to *patria mea* in inscriptions and the like, are 'extremely rare' (E. Champlin, *Final judgments* (1991) 162 and n. 21). See *PIR* 8.2.486 no. 933; Syme, *RP* 2.536–7.

44.1 Obiere eo anno uiri nobiles 'The aristocratic generals Cn. Lentulus the Augur and L. Domitius Ahenobarbus, victorious beyond the great rivers, echo back to a more expansive epoch, evoking nostalgia and pointing the contrast with the deep peace of Tiberius' reign' (Syme, *TST* 86). For Lentulus (cos. 14 BC) see 29.1n. Domitius (cos. 16 BC) was legate successively in Illyricum and Germany, and had been proconsul of Africa in 13/12 BC. He was grandfather of Nero (75n.). See Suet. *Nero* 1–5 for the family history; also *RE* 5.1343–6 = Domitius 28 (Groag), *PIR* 3.32–4 no. 128, *BNP* 4.644 [II 2]; Syme, *AA* 483 (index) and Table VIII.

triumphalia de Getis For Lentulus' victory on the lower Danube c. 9 BC see Syme, *RP* 3.879–80, 6.435–40; for the Getae in particular see Gaertner on Ov. *Ex P.* 1.2.76. For *triumphalia* see 1.72.1n., Vell. 116.3n.

bene tolerata paupertas Though 'poverty' was no doubt a relative concept, *paupertas tolerabilis* was something of a badge of honour, associated, for ex., with C. Fabricius (Cic. *TD* 4.56), a famous *exemplum* (e.g. Val. Max. 4.3.6a, 4.4.3).

magnae opes innocenter paratae Lipsius' *partae*, adopted by many edd., certainly has the right sense (e.g. Prop. 3.18.28, Tib. 2.4.40, Col. 12 *praef.* 6, Sen. *Vit. Beat.* 23.1, Amm. 22.4.7), but, despite Ritter's long note alleging a difference between the two verbs, so too does the transmitted reading (e.g. Prop. 1.8.36, Ov. *F.* 5.282, Sil. 17.61, Quint. 10.1.5): there seems no justification for the change. The two words are often confused (e.g. 11.10.3, 12.64.1): see *TLL* 10.1.412.54–8.

44.2 pater ciuili bello maris potens Cn. Domitius Ahenobarbus (cos. 32 BC) commanded a fleet in the Adriatic against the triumvirs in the late 40s (*MRR* 2.361, 365, 373, 382; *BNP* 4.641–2 [I 6]). The expr. *maris potens* is found at Hor. *C.* 1.5.15–16 and Virg. *Aen.* 3.528, if in those passages *potens* governs *maris*; otherwise only Liv. 27.30.16.

donec . . . misceretur He transferred his allegiance to Mark Antony in 40 and to Octavian just before Actium in 31. For the expr. cf. Vell. 86.3 'cum . . . partibus eius se miscuisset' (of Pollio, and in a similar context); for *donec* + subjunc. see 7.1n.

auus L. Domitius Ahenobarbus was consul in 54 BC (*MRR* 2.221, *BNP* 4.642–3 [I 8]).

minor Antonia 'Cornelius Tacitus was guilty of error or inadvertence', notes Syme, but 'the error was easy to make' (*AA* 309, 165): this is in fact Antonia maior, the elder daughter of Octavia (Augustus' sister) and Mark Antony (*BNP* 1.793; *AA* 473 (Index) and Tables III and VIII). The error recurs at 12.64.2.

exercitu flumen Albim transcendit is contextualised by *longius ...
priorum* immediately below (T.'s dependence on the elder Pliny's *Bella
Germaniae* (1.69.2n.) at this point was suggested by Norden 277). The crossing
is placed in AD 1 by Dio 55.10a.2 but may have been slightly earlier, c. 2 BC (see
Syme, *RP* 3.1100, 1102–3; also Vell. 106.2n.); and modern scholars think that
the river in question is more likely to have been the Saale than the Elbe itself
(see Swan on Dio loc. cit., and Rives on Tac. *G.* 41.2 'Albis ... flumen
inclutum et notum olim, nunc tantum auditur'). *transcendere* is rare of crossing
rivers but cf. Col. 6.29.1 'pontem flumenque transcendit' (of a horse), Plin. *NH*
6.49 'transcendit eum amnem Demodamas', Apul. *Met.* 7.18.1 'cum fluuium
transcenderemus', *Deo Socr.* 19. Prammer reasonably proposed to insert *cum*
before *exercitu*, but T. takes liberties with the 'abl. of military accompaniment'
at 6.44.2 (n.; cf. 6.37.3n.) and so perhaps here too.

insignia triumphi See 1.72.1n., Malloch on 11.20.2.

44.3 Obiit et L. Antonius Antonius is one of only three Roman men to
whom, though not senators of consular rank, T. gives an obituary notice
(Syme, *TST* 80), the others being Sallustius Crispus (3.30.2–3) and Asinius
Saloninus (3.75.1). For the addition of a third obituary to an earlier pair
see 3.76.

multa claritudine generis sed improspera Antonius' mother was
Marcella maior, elder daughter of Octavia (Augustus' sister) and her first
husband, C. Claudius Marcellus (cos. 50 BC), and hence half-sister to
Domitius' wife Antonia maior (above), who was therefore Antonius' aunt.
The unfortunate element in Antonius' distinguished lineage derived from his
grandfather and father (next n.). See *RE* 1.2590 = Antonius 24 (von Rohden),
PIR 1.154 no. 802, *BNP* 1.806 [II 2].

patre eius Iullo Antonio The second son of Mark Antony and his third
wife, Fulvia, Iullus Antonius was spared by Octavian and proceeded to the
consulship in 10 BC. After his adultery with Augustus' daughter, Julia, he
committed suicide in 2 BC (Vell. 100.4). See *RE* 1.2584–5 = Antonius 22
(Groebe), *PIR* 1.153–4 no. 800, *BNP* 1.806 [II 1]; Syme, *RP* 2.912–36.

sororis nepotem sc. *suae* (i.e. Augustus').

seposuit 'banished' (*OLD* 2b), a favourite usage otherwise confined to the
Histories (G–G 1472b).

ubi specie studiorum nomen exilii tegeretur Ancient Marseille was
a 'university town'; it is curious that it is mentioned so soon after the episode
at 43.5 above, but it was where Agricola, T.'s father-in-law, was brought up
(*Agr.* 4.2 and nn.). For *nomen ... tegeretur* cf. Nep. *Dion* 1.4, Sen. *Tro.* 272, Plin.
Ep. 9.13.3.

tumulo Octauiorum Is this, as Syme supposes (*AA* 118), Augustus' mausoleum, for which T. has a variety of expressions (3.4.1 't. Augusti', 3.9.2 't. Caesarum', 16.6.2 't. Iuliorum')? *Octauiorum* seems rather to denote the tomb of Antonius' grandmother's family, the Octavii.

per decretum senatus Sallustian (*C.* 51.36) for the regular *decreto*. As a case of the senate 'interesting itself in the last resting place of a more remote relative of the imperial family', our passage is compared by Hollis (313) with Dom. Marsus on the burial of Atia (182H = 9C 'genetrix hic Caesaris, hospes, | condita: Romani sic uoluere patres').

45 Death in Spain

Hitherto the narrative of the year has been devoted entirely to domestic affairs, as if confirming T.'s remarks at 32–3; but he ends the year by describing the murder of a Roman governor in Spain, an episode for which, as noted by Hartman (174), there is a very similar predecessor in Sallust (*C.* 19). The description is transitional in nature: while it continues the obituary theme of ch. 44 above, suggesting closure, the governor's harsh measures, which provoked his death (45.3), are mirrored in those to which the Thracians react violently at the start of the following year (46.1; cf. Syme, *Tac.* 310).

45.1 Isdem consulibus See 6.13.1n.

facinus atrox in citeriore Hispania admissum There is similar headlining of an episode at *Agr.* 28.1, where Sall. *J.* 79.1 is compared.[92] *facinus atrox* is above all a Livian expr. (5×), though also at Sen. *Tro.* 289.

nationis Termestinae Termes, their main town, was roughly 12 miles SW of Numantia and 80 miles due W of Bilbilis (*BA* 25: B4).

praetorem prouinciae 'Not a consular but a legate of praetorian rank, acting governor when L. Arruntius was detained at Rome' (Syme, *AA* 377). For the use of *praetor* see 15.2n.

L. Pisonem Syme infers from Sall. *C.* 19, a passage in which Cn. Piso (quaestor 65 BC) meets a similar death and to which T. alludes here, that L. Piso must be a descendant of his and hence son of L. Piso (the Augur), whose last activity and death are recorded at 21.1–2 above (n.). But this is not

---

[92] The technique is evidently called 'headline prolepsis' by J. Pigoń, *Ze studiów nad technikami narracyjnymi Tacyta: wypowiedzi proleptyczne* (2004): see J. F. Gaertner and B. C. Hausburg, *Caesar and the Bellum Alexandrinum* (2013) 120–1 and n. 184.

the universal view: see *RP* 3.1227, *AA* 377–8 and Table XXV; also *RE* 3.1383 = Calpurnius 75 (Groag), *PIR* 2.68–9 no. 292, *BNP* 2.1001 [II 19].

pace incuriosum Like the notorious Quintilius Varus (Vell. 117.4–118.1). *incuriosum* combines the notions of 'careless' and 'unsuspecting' (*OLD* b-c).

ex improuiso in itinere adortus *adorior* with either *ex improuiso* or *in itinere* are standard elements of military narrative (e.g. Liv. 25.9.11 for the former, Caes. *G.* 3.20.3 for the latter): for both together, as here, cf. *Bell. Afr.* 61.5 'in itinere praedatores equites Numidas Gaetulosque ex improuiso adorti'. Sallust's Piso likewise 'iter faciens occisus est' (*C.* 19.3).

uno uulnere in mortem adfecit *adficio* (or passive) with *uulnere* (or plur.) is very common, esp. in the Caesarian corpus, but on no occasion are the various phrases combined with *in mortem*. Hartman (174) wished to read *adflixit* on the basis of 62.3 'in mortem adflixerat', but there seems little reason to change, esp. since *adflixit* occurs at §2 below.

pernicitate equi Cf. 2.68.1, 12.51.1, *H.* 1.79.2, Sen. *Brev. Vit.* 18.4, Fronto p. 19.13 vdH², Amm. 29.5.14.

saltuosos locos The suffix *–osus* expresses the idea of 'abounding in', especially in reference to concrete features, and hence is suited to the description of landscape (Adams (2016) 68). For the phrase see 6.34.2n.

per derupta et auia See 6.21.1n.

45.2 uoce magna sermone patrio . . . clamitauit 'The assassin duly exhibits Spanish defiance when put to torture' (Syme, *Tac.* 729, comparing Liv. 21.2.6 'comprensusque ab circumstantibus haud alio quam si euasisset uultu, tormentis quoque cum laceraretur, eo fuit habitu oris ut superante laetitia dolores ridentis etiam speciem praebuerit').

cum postero ad quaestionem retraheretur sc. *die*, as at 15.57.2 'postero cum ad eosdem cruciatus retraheretur' (the heroic Epicharis).

proripuit se custodibus saxoque caput adflixit For such suicides see Vell. 120.6n. The plain abl. after *se proripere* is very rare (*TLL* 10.2.2148.68–71, though classifying our ex. differently).

45.3 sed Piso Termestinorum dolo caesus habe<ba>tur As W. G. Pluygers pointed out, the circumstances of Piso's death are extremely unlikely to have been a live issue amongst T.'s contemporaries (*Mnem.* 9 (1860) 61): his *habebatur* makes appreciably better sense, though he failed to support it by noting the frequency with which medial syllables are omitted in M. (Koestermann notes that at *TLL* 6.3.2449.24ff. only 12.15.2 and Sall.

H. 4.42 M (= 32 R) are quoted as parallels for this use of *haberi* with nomin. + infin., and it so happens that in both cases the verb form is *habebatur*.)

qui ... acrius quam ut tolerarent barbari At the very end of the passage comes the closest allusion to the episode in Sallust (*C.* 19.4 'imperia eius iniusta, superba, crudelia barbaros nequiuisse pati'). *cogebat* is probably conative: 'tried to collect'. All recent edd. (Fisher, Koestermann, Heubner, Borzsák) print the emendation *quippe*, but the plain relative clause seems explanatory enough.

pecunias e publico interceptas i.e. by the Termestini themselves (for the verb in a similar context cf. 15.43.4 'aqua priuatorum licentia inter-cepta'); scholars compare Cic. *Att.* 6.2(116).5 and Plin. *Ep.* 10.17A.3 (see Sherwin-White's n.).

46–61 THE YEAR AD 26

T. divides his narrative of the year into foreign and domestic events (46–51, 52–61), one of his commonest arrangements (Ginsburg 54, 136–40) but without parallel in Book 4. The warfare in Thrace, where there had been earlier trouble in AD 21 (3.38.3–39 and nn.), takes up almost forty per cent of the year's narrative and comes as something of a surprise after T.'s recent remarks about the absence of warfare from his work (chh. 32–3 above); but, despite his gripping account of the fighting, it is in the year's domestic narrative that the most ominous events occur.

The domestic narrative begins and – if we discount the formal closure of the year by the obituary notice at ch. 61 – ends with measures against the house of Germanicus. Tib.'s deteriorating relationship with his daughter-in-law Agrippina (52–4) is matched by Sejanus' machinations against Nero Caesar, her eldest son (59.3–60.3). Within this frame are two contrasting sections. To distract attention from unwelcome rumours about himself and Agrippina, Tib. is in regular attendance at the senate, where delegations from Asia are delivering speeches full of dignity and local pride, competing for the honour of building the temple to Tib. and his mother which had been agreed in the previous year (55–6). In the course of proceedings, however, the secretive *princeps* slips away and, in the most significant event of his principate so far, withdraws to Campania (57–59.2). The event is marked by discussions both of its motivation (57.1–3) and of the predictions which accompanied it (58.2–3). One of these predictions – that the *princeps* would never return to Rome – is confirmed by the historian (58.3), and the reader knows that the journey to Campania is merely the prelude to his permanent withdrawal to the island of Capri.

239

46–51 War in Thrace

'The Thracian campaign of C. Poppaeus Sabinus', writes Levene, 'is described with all the dramatic vicissitudes that one would associate with a major set-piece war' (*CCT* 234). T. begins with the causes of the revolt and the Thracians' initial overtures, backed up by threats (46); Sabinus' response is to temporise until he has gathered forces in sufficient numbers, at which point he establishes a camp and launches from it his first attack, which enjoys mixed fortunes (47). Next he sets up a second camp, leaving loyal Thracian auxiliaries to defend and operate from the first; but the Thracians' love of attacking only their neighbours, of which we have already been warned (46.1), here leads to disaster for the loyalists, whose pillaging of the defectors provokes a night-time reprisal (48). When the enemy decline battle the next day, Sabinus decides to embark on a siege (49.1–2).

Hitherto the narrative has tracked Sabinus' gradual closing in on the enemy (47.2 'usque ad proximum castellum', 48.1 'hostem propter'); now he encircles them with a cordon which he proceeds to draw ever tighter (49.2 'paulatim ... contrahere claustra'), until he is close up to them (49.3 'propinquum iam in hostem'). The siege tactics work, and T. gives a vivid picture of the death, despair and social breakdown which affected the besieged (49.3), who debate whether to surrender, commit suicide or risk a break-out (50.1–4). Those who favour this last option again choose night for their operation, and T. gives a brilliant account of the combat and confusion (50.4–51.2). In the darkness the Romans are bewildered by the echoes from the mountains, but the enemy fails to break through their lines and is eventually forced to surrender (51.3).

T.'s descriptions of the campaign and of the Thracian enemy are largely conventional, as the commentary illustrates; at the same time he writes in his most graphic manner, appealing to the reader's sense of hearing (47.2, 50.4, 51.2) and sight (46.3, 47.1, 50.4–51.1), even – horrifyingly – smell and touch (49.3). Suggestive forms of expression convey the immediacy of speech (50.3n., 51.2n.); the language extends to the choice (46.1–2nn.) or poetic (48.1nn., 50.4n.). The episode exhibits anaphora (49.3, 51.1), asyndetic tricola (48.1, 49.2, 49.3, 51.1) and a remarkable series of historic infinitives (51.1), the first two co-ordinated by anaphora, the last three asyndetic; and there are the expected borrowings from Sallust (nn. on 46.1, 47.1, 48.1, 49.3, 50.4, 51.3) and Livy (nn. on 47.1, 50.4, 51.2). Of particular interest are the sustained allusions to Sallust's account of P. Servilius' engagement with the Isaurians in 76/75 BC (*H.* 2.87 M = 2.74 R), which were first noted by W. Heraeus (*ALL* 14 (1906) 273ff.; cf. Syme, *Tac.* 729), and to Caesar's account of the siege of Alesia in 52 BC (*BG* 7.69–90).

It is obviously very striking that T. should include such an elaborate account of warfare so soon after the digression at 32–3, where he appeared to lament the absence of this kind of topic. It is therefore worth looking more closely at what is actually said on the two relevant occasions in the digression:

Nobis in arto et inglorius labor: immota quippe aut modice lacessita pax, maestae urbis res et princeps proferendi imperi incuriosus erat. (32.2)

Nam situs gentium, uarietates proeliorum, clari ducum exitus retinent ac redintegrant legentium animum; nos saeua iussa, continuas accusationes, fallaces amicitias, perniciem innocentium et easdem exitii causas coniungimus, obuia rerum similitudine et satietate. (33.3)

On the first occasion T. does not say that there were no wars at all but that peace was disturbed only 'moderately'; he seems more concerned about the absence of expansionist campaigns. On the second occasion he does not in fact state that his work lacks ethnographical descriptions and fluctuating battles; he merely *implies* their absence by listing the topics which his work *does* contain. Given that we are dealing with Tacitus and that 'we have to read him very closely indeed to perceive that he has in fact denied what one thought he had said',[93] it would seem that his account of the war in Thrace does not strictly conflict with the digression. In Thrace the Romans were suppressing a revolt, not expanding their empire, and, although T. indicates the *situs gentium* and describes the *uarietates proeliorum*, the action qualifies as an example of the 'moderate disruption of the peace' which was acknowledged in the digression.[94] The insurrection in Thrace goes unmentioned by Velleius, writing at the time, and by Dio, writing two hundred years later; that it looms so large in T.'s narrative is due entirely to the author whose recent disavowal of such topics now turns out to be more apparent than real.

46.1 Lentulo Gaetulico C. Caluisio consulibus For Cn. Cornelius Lentulus Gaetulicus, brother of the consul of the previous year (34.1), see 6.30.2n. A daughter of his was betrothed to a son of Sejanus (ibid.), while his sister is thought to have been married to the other consul, C. Calvisius Sabinus (Syme, *AA* 298 n. 120). For Calvisius see 6.9.3n.

decreta triumphi insignia ... contusis Thraecum gentibus The episode, like its predecessor, begins with a 'headline statement' (45.1n.). In the context of a triumphal award, the abl. abs. construction suggests an

---

[93] Irving Kristol, *Encounter* 6 (May 1956) 86, whose telling remark bears repeating.

[94] Levene sees the Thracian campaign in the context of Germanicus' successful war against the Germans in Book 2, arguing that T.'s description of Sabinus' 'comfortable win' was designed to highlight 'the success of Germanicus, who had made control of the Empire all too easy' (*CCT* 237).

official announcement, rather like its use for commemorative legends on coins. *contusis* perhaps contributes to this style (cf. *H.* 4.28.3 'contusis Ubiis', Liv. 40.52.6 'classis regis Antiochi . . . fusa, contusa fugataque est'), although the verb appears frequently too in poetry from Enn. *Ann.* 386 Sk. onwards (e.g. Sil. 4.706 'contundere gentem'): see *TLL* 4.806.12ff. For *insignia triumphi* see 44.2n.

Poppaeo Sabino He had been *ordinarius* in AD 9 and was grandfather of Poppaea, Nero's mistress and wife. He was governor of Moesia from 12 to 35 but was appointed to Macedonia and Achaea in addition in 15 (1.80.1): see 5.10.2nn.

qui montium editis inculti atque eo ferocius agitabant Thucydides (2.96.1–2) distinguishes between various groups of Thracians, including those who lived between Mt Haemus and the Black Sea and those whom he calls 'the mountain Thracians' (τῶν ὀρεινῶν Θρᾳκῶν); T. refers to Mt Haemus (*BA* 22: C6) at the very end of the episode (51.3n.).

M's *incultu* is retained by Fisher, Koestermann, Heubner and Borzsák, evidently on the grounds that the noun in its abl. form is found in Sallust (*C.* 55.4, *J.* 2.4); but the meaning there ('neglect') is different from that required here ('uncouthness'), and the alleged use of the plain abl. is difficult to explain and defend, as Furneaux observed. The adj. *incultus*, on the other hand, is very popular with Sallust, and for intrans. *agitare* = 'live' (a favourite usage of Sallust) + adj. see *J.* 19.5 'uagos agitare', 74.1 'uarius incertusque agitabat', and in T. again at 1.50.1 and 11.21.1; for *ferocius agitare* see *C.* 23.3, and for the *uariatio* of adj. ~ adv. see Sörbom 96–7. For the *ferocia* of barbarians see 3.40.2n.; for their mountainous life see 3n. below: for the connection between the two see e.g. Liv. 9.13.7 and Oakley ad loc. *edita montium* (again at 12.56.3), another ex. of one of T.'s favourite constructions (3.1.3n.), is found elsewhere only at Curt. 6.6.25.

Causa motus For historians' interest in causation see 1.1n. above.

super ingenium hominum Disparaging references to the *ingenium* of barbarians are conventional (*Agr.* 16.1n.).

ualidissimum quemque militiae nostrae dare aspernabantur 'Thracians contributed largely to the Roman army' (J. Spaul, *Cohors*[2] (2000) 353–82, at 353, with bibliography and further details). For this use of *nostrae* = *Romanae* (again in this episode at 50.4 below) cf. 3.42.1; Marincola 287–8. *aspernari* + infin. is found in prose only here and is exceptionally rare in verse (*TLL* 2.825.82–826.3).

ne regibus quidem parere This is an extreme illustration of the Thracians' notorious *discordia* (below, 50.1n.).

ductores The noun, extremely common in the *Aeneid*, is used by T. of or by non-Romans (cf. 2.10.1, 12.34.1, *H.* 3.47.2, 4.21.1 (this last of Civilis)): see the discussion by Oakley on Liv. 7.41.4.

belligerare For this 'mild archaism' see 2.5.2n.

46.2 rumor incesserat See 1.5.1n.

fore ut . . . diuersas in terras traherentur Cf. Percennius' speech at 1.17.3 'trahi adhuc diuersas in terras, ubi per nomen agrorum uligines paludum uel inculta montium accipiant'; but, whereas Percennius was referring to land assigned to legionary veterans, probably at Emona (see 1.17.3n.), the Thracians are complaining about being stationed far from home (see e.g. *Agr.* 32.2nn.).

antequam arma inciperent The metonymical substitution of *arma* for *bellum* with *incipere* is paralleled only at Stat. *Theb.* 10.690 (*TLL* 7.1.916.31).

misere legatos amicitiam obsequiumque memoraturos The Parthian king had acted similarly (2.58.1 'legati uenere. miserat amicitiam ac foedus memoraturos').

si nullo nouo onere temptarentur The complaint of (new) burdens is conventional (G–G 1025b–1026a). *temptari* here = 'to be troubled, harassed' (*OLD* 10c). For the *uariatio* of acc. + infin. after a direct object see Sörbom 110–11.

sin ut uictis seruitium indiceretur The Thracians' *oratio obliqua* is structured chiastically and expressed assonantally. For T.'s use of *seruitium* cf. 3.45.2n.

esse sibi ferrum et iuuentutem et promptum libertati aut ad mortem animum The barbarians' defiance is conveyed by an ascending tricolon, its third member varied (cf. Sörbom 83) and again quasi-chiastic. For *promptus* + dat. see *TLL* 10.2.1888.3ff., for *ad* ibid. 1889.20ff. (our passage at 1889.38–9).

46.3 castella rupibus indita Barbarians were often associated with mountain perches (Virg. *G.* 3.474–5 'aerias Alpes et Norica . . . |castella', Hor. *C.* 4.14.11–12 'arces | Alpibus impositas tremendis', *Epist.* 2.1.252–3 'arces | montibus impositas et barbara regna', Liv. 21.32.7 'tecta informia inposita rupibus', 27.39.8 'suas rupes suaque castella', Plin. *NH* 5.74 'inde Masada castellum in rupe', 6.30 'in rupe castello . . . communito'; Dauge 483), and the elevated positions with which the Romans are forced to contend are stated or implied throughout the episode (46.1 'montium editis', 47.1 'per angustias saltuum', 'apertis in collibus', 47.2 'montem . . . continuum', 49.1 'non degrediebantur', 51.1 'decurrentes', 51.3 'in summa castelli'). The Thracian narrative, says Levene, 'shows how topography has ceased to matter: the Romans can win comfortably even in the most alien terrain' (*CCT* 236–7). For *indita* cf. Flor. 1.36.14 (3.1.14) 'saxeo inditam monti . . . urbem'.

conlatosque illuc parentes et coniuges ostentabant The implication is that the Thracians would have an incentive to fight which the Romans, campaigning far from home, would lack: for this see *Agr.* 32.2n., G. Walser, *Rom, das Reich und die fremden Völker in der Geschichtsschreibung der frühen Kaiserzeit* (1951) 158; also 51.2 below.

bellumque impeditum, arduum, cruentum minitabantur *impeditum* and *arduum* transfer to the war adjs. which more normally are used of terrain (*OLD impeditus* 2a, *arduus* 4): *bellum impeditum* is otherwise unparalleled, *arduum* recurs only at Man. 5.637, *cruentum* is relatively common (Vell. 71.1n., adding e.g. Man. 3.632, *Anth. Lat.* 415.54). For *minitor* cf. 3.73.1n.

47.1 donec exercitus in unum conduceret is to be taken with *datis mitibus responsis*. Kiessling approved Pichena's emendation *conduceretur*, thinking that one should understand *locum* with *in unum*; but *in unum* is a set phrase meaning 'into one unit' *uel sim.* (*OLD unus* 4; cf. G–G 1704a), suggesting that *exercitus* is plural rather than singular.

mitibus responsis The language is Livian (8.21.3), but cf. esp. Sall. *H.* 2.87 M (= 2.74.4 R) 'mollia interim legatis ostentans'.

<post>quam . . . uenere Many scholars accept *postquam* as the likeliest conjunction, but Pfitzner (*AT* 52–4 and in his edition) also wished to retain the transmitted *uenire* on the grounds that T. often has an historic infin. in subordinate clauses. However, the only certain ex. of *postquam* + infin. in the whole of Latin is 3.26.2, where the infin. is co-ordinated, in T.'s usual manner, with a regularising indic. verb and is therefore not parallel to what is alleged here. (Pfitzner seems alone in wishing to print *postquam . . . accipere* rather than the superscript correction *accepere* at 1.20.1.)

Pomponius Labeo e Moesia cum legione The actual governor of Moesia was Poppaeus Sabinus (above, 46.1n.), but there was also a succession of deputies of praetorian rank, such as Labeo (for whom see 6.29.1n.). The legion was either IV Scythica or V Macedonica (5.3n.).

rex Rhoemetalces King of Thrace since 19 (5.3n.).

cum auxiliis popularium qui fidem non mutauerant i.e. as opposed to the Thracians described in 46.1–3 above.

addita praesenti copia 'adding his existing force' (i.e. to those of Labeo and the king).

compositum iam per angustias saltuum Compare the Dalmatians, on the opposite side of the Balkan Peninsula (Vell. 115.4 'situ locorum ac montium, ingeniorum ferocia . . . et praecipue angustiis saltuum paene inexpugnabiles'); but resorting to *saltus* is a typically barbarian manoeuvre (e.g. 1.63.1; N. Horsfall, *PBSR* 50 (1982) 45–52). *compositum* = 'deployed' (*OLD* 6); for the 'verbal hyperbaton' see 3.1.1n.

Quidam audentius apertis in collibus uisebantur The adv. has to be taken loosely: 'some, more daringly, showed themselves on the open hillsides' (Doederlein says instead that *agentes* has to be understood); for the verb cf. *OLD uiso* 2b. For *apertis . . . collibus* cf. Virg. *G.* 2.112–13, Liv. 27.41.6.

suggressus occurs exclusively in T. (5×) apart from Sall. *H.* 4.83 M = 75 R.

sanguine barbarorum modico 'the bloodshed of the barbarians being only moderate' (*OLD sanguis* 2b); for similar phrases see Vell. 90.2n., 95.2n.

47.2 castris . . . communitis Standard phraseology, esp. in Caesar and Livy. *in loco* = 'on the spot' (*OLD locus* 4b).

montem . . . angusto et aequali dorso continuum No other mountain is described as 'angustus' in Latin, and the allusion to Caesar suggests that the transmitted *angustum* should be emended, as Prof. E. Courtney suggests (Caes. *G.* 7.44.3 'dorsum esse eius iugi prope aequum, sed . . . angustum'; cf. Liv. 44.4.4 'iugum montis in angustum dorsum cuneatum'). For this kind of 'topography' see N. Horsfall, 'Illusion and reality in Latin topographical writing', *G&R* 32 (1985) 197–208. For the verbal hyperbaton see above.

more gentis applies to what follows ('cum . . . persultabant'); such phraseology is routine in ethnographical descriptions (3.43.2n.; also next n.).

cum carminibus et tripudiis persultabant For such typical barbarian behaviour cf. *H.* 5.17.3 'sono armorum tripudiisque (ita illis mos)', Liv. 21.42.3 'gaudio exultans cum sui moris tripudiis', 23.26.9 'erumpunt igitur agmine e castris tripudiantes more suo', 38.17.4 'cantus ineuntium proelium et ululatus et tripudia', Curt. 7.10.4 'carmen laetantium modo canere tripudiisque . . . gaudium quoddam animi ostentare coeperunt'. *persultare* = 'to prance about', as here, seems less common than its other principal meaning of 'to scour': see *TLL* 10.1.1773.58ff.

47.3 Ii dum eminus grassabantur 'for as long as they were advancing at a distance'; for some of the difficulties of an archery battle see 6.35.1 and nn., but relative distance could be a problem in any type of battle (e.g. Caes. *BG* 7.82.1 'dum longius ab munitione aberant Galli . . .').

crebra et inulta uulnera *inulta* has been questioned, and the expr. is indeed without parallel; but the usage seems not so different from e.g. 4.25.3 'haud inulta morte', 4.50.1 'non inultum exitium'.

propius incedentes eruptione subita turbati sunt For the close approach cf. e.g. 1.35.5, 15.13.1, Caes. *BG* 7.82.1 'posteaquam propius succes-serunt'; the 'sudden breakout' is very common (e.g. *H.* 3.26.2, 4.30.1, Caes. *BG* 3.6.1, 7.69.7, *Bell. Afr.* 23.2, Liv. 31.36.8, 38.29.2, Val. Max. 3.7.2, Suet. *DJ* 64.1, *Aug.* 96.2, Amm. 20.11.18).

Sugambrae cohortis The Sugambri were a tribe of the lower Rhine who had been defeated by Drusus in 12 BC and transplanted by Tib. probably in 8 BC (2.26.3n.); the cohort in question will have been the Cohors I Sugambrorum (see Spaul (cited above) 245–6).

promptam ad pericula It was naturally good practice to keep forces in reserve to deal with emergencies (*Agr.* 37.1n.).

nec minus . . . trucem sc. than the Thracians. The Sugambri were notor-iously fierce (Hor. *C.* 4.14.51 'caede gaudentes'); for *trucem* cf. Flor. 2.26.13 (4.12.13) 'Moesi quam feri, quam truces fuerint, quam ipsorum etiam barbari barbarorum horribile dictu est'.

cantuum et armorum tumultu 'An ethnographic commonplace stan-dard in writing about Celts and Germans' (Oakley on Liv. 7.10.8, q.v.).

48.1 relictis . . . memoraui T. mentioned the earlier camp at 47.2 and the loyal Thracians at 47.1. For cross-references see 3.18.1n.; for *memoro* see, besides 3.24.3n., Oakley on Liv. 6.9.3.

uastare, urere, trahere praedas Cf. *H.* 2.12.2 'urere, uastare, rapere', Cic. *Att.* 9.7.4 'uastare, urere, pecuniis locupletum <non> abstinere'; for successive infinitives see 51.1n., *Agr.* 38.1n. For *trahere praedas* see 3.20.1n.

dum populatio lucem intra sisteretur Cf. Sen. *Ep.* 110.9 'nec intra haec . . . sistitur'.

noctemque in *castris* tutam et uigilem *ca*pesserent The instruction is conveyed in incongruously poetic language: for *tutam* cf. Luc. 9.922 'nox tuta uiris', *Il. Lat.* 700; for *uigilem* cf. Sen. *HO* 647, Sil. 11.409. *noctem capessere* is unparalleled.

uersi in luxum et raptis opulenti The conventional susceptibility of non-Romans to loot (e.g. 1.65.6, 1.68.1; 3.20.1n.) is conveyed in a varied chiasmus. For *luxus* cf. 3.52.1n.

stationes See 6.34.1n.

somno et uino procumbere Another conventional circumstance (1.50.4; Oakley on Liv. 8.16.9) but no doubt alluding also to 'l'ivrognerie proverbiale des Thraces' (Dauge 643; see e.g. N–H on Hor. *C.* 1.27.2). Here the words conclude a second chiasmus and echo Nisus' conversation with Euryalus at Virg. *Aen.* 9.189–90 'somno uinoque soluti | procubuere'. See also 25.2n.

48.2 populatores See 3.39.2n.

alii . . . adpugnarent The verb is peculiar to T. and probably coined by him (2.81.1n.).

ut clamore, telis suo quisque periculo intentus sonorem alterius proelii non acciperet Although *sonor proelii/pugnae* seems an unparalleled expr.,[95] noise is a regular feature of ancient battle descriptions (e.g. Miniconi 166–7; Lendon 49–50 and n. 27) and an important consideration for commanders when, as here, a two-pronged engagement was planned (cf. e.g. Sall. *J.* 52.6 'accepit . . . ex Iugurthae proelio clamorem augeri, ueritus ne legatus cognita re laborantibus suis auxilio foret'). For shouting in particular see e.g. Mariotti on Sall. *C.* 60.2, Oakley on Liv. 8.38.10; note also *Agr.* 34.1n. *clamore . . . intentus* is causal with *non acciperet*: for the *uariatio* of causal abl. (*clamore, telis*) ~ adj./part. (*intentus*) see Sörbom 89; for the asyndeton bimembre see 2.2n. *periculo* is dat. with *intentus*, as Sen. *Brev. Vit.* 2.1.

tenebrae insuper delectae augendam ad formidinem Night both induced fear and was an unexpected time for fighting (Oakley on Liv. 9.24.8 and 7.33.15 respectively); but it was favoured by barbarians (cf. 2.12.1, *G.* 43.4 'insitae feritati arte ac tempore lenocinantur . . . atras ad proelia noctes legunt ipsaque formidine atque umbra . . . terrorem inferunt', Caes. *BG* 7.81.1), and their mixed fortunes here do not prevent them from trying again later (50.4 and n.). *augere* with *formidinem* is significantly less common (only *Rhet. Herenn.* 2.4, Curt. 8.2.26) than with *metum* or *terrorem*; for the unusual word order of the gerundival phrase see 1.64.5n.

48.3 repentino cursu Standard phraseology (see e.g. H. on *H.* 3.9.1), sometimes varied by *repentina incursio* (e.g. Caes. *BG* 6.23.3, Liv. 7.15.11).

plures extra palarentur Cf. 1.30.1 'pars extra castra palantes . . . caesi', Liv. 4.55.4 'palantes in agris caesos', 31.2.9, 33.19.4.

quanto perfugae et proditores ferre arma ad suum patriaeque seruitium incusabantur Auxiliary troops inevitably incurred accusations such as these: compare those levelled by Arminius against his brother, Flavus

---

[95] G.'s n. on 1.65.1 says that 'The poeticism *sonor* . . . was too precious to appeal to prose-writers generally', but it is in fact common in Cicero.

(2.10.1). *proditor* is a regular term of abuse (Opelt 279 (index)); for the addition of *perfuga* cf. *H.* 4.21.2 (Civilis), Cic. *II Verr.* 1.98, *Rosc. Am.* 117. For the very rare construction with *incusari* see 6.3.3n.; for the ellipse of a comparative with *quanto* see 1.57.1n.; for *seruitium* see 3.45.2n.

49.1 exercitum aequo loco ostendit si barbari ... proelium auderent His hope was that the barbarians would display collectively the boldness which some of them had shown earlier (47.1 *audentius*); if not, there was a boost to the Roman morale and humiliation of the barbarians. For such challenges see Oakley on Liv. 6.22.9; J. E. Lendon, 'The rhetoric of combat', *CA* 18 (1999) 310–11.

successu noctis alacres Cf. Liv. 26.45.4 'cum ... ipso successu audacia atque alacritas hostium cresceret', Front. *Strat.* 2.5.36 'alacres successibus uictoriarum'.

obsidium coepit per praesidia, quae opportune iam muniebat The evidence, though slight, suggests that *praesidia munire* is a regular expr. (cf. Cic. *Rab. Perd.* 3 (metaphorical), Vell. 120.6) and that Freinsheim was quite misguided to propose *immuniebat* on the strength of 11.19.2, where *praesidium immuniuit*, though retained by Malloch, should almost certainly be emended to *p. muniuit*.

fossam loricamque contexens quattuor milia passuum ambitu amplexus est 'linking a ditch and parapet, he incorporated four miles in its circumference' (i.e. the circumference of the construction was four miles long); compare Caes. *BC* 3.44.3 'castellis enim xxiv effectis xv milia passuum circuitu amplexus' (*OLD amplector* 10). Cf. Veg. *Mil.* 4.28.3 'obsidentes ultra ictum teli fossam faciunt eamque non solum uallo et sudibus sed etiam turriculis instruunt, ut erumpentibus ex ciuitate possint obsistere, quod opus loriculam uocant'; Florus describes the Numantines as 'fossa atque lorica quattuorque castris circumdatos' (1.34.13 = 2.18.13).

49.2 contrahere claustra artaque circumdare *claustra* is an alternative way of referring to the ditch-and-parapet system just mentioned (cf. 12.31.4; *OLD* 5b). The process described is that whereby a circumvallation of four miles in length was gradually reduced to a point from which they could build an *agger* within range of the enemy (below). *arta* is presumably substantival and refers to the increasingly confined area between the siege system and the enemy's position (the comparative *artiora* is used substantivally at *Agr.* 37.4): the whole expr. is chiastic.

saxa, hastae, ignes The same technique was used by Sentius Saturninus against Calpurnius Piso (2.81.2 'hastas, saxa et faces ingerere'); cf. also 12.16.2 'facibus atque hastis turbabant obsessos'.

COMMENTARY: 4.49.3

49.3 Sed nihil aeque quam sitis fatigabat The point of a siege was 'to reduce the enemy to *inopia*' (Front. *Strat.* 3.2), and commanders were expected to divert streams and contaminate water supplies in order to bring this about (ibid. 3.7); cf. also Veg. *Mil.* 4.7.2. The graphic scene which follows will be rounded off by thirst ('quos sitis peremerat') before the concluding statement. For T.'s expr. cf. Front. *Strat.* 2.1.1 'hostes inedia, siti, mora sub armis fatigati'; *nihil aeque quam* is a favourite turn of phrase (H. on *H.* 5.3.2 'sed nihil aeque quam inopia aquae fatigabat').

cum *in*gens multitudo bellatorum, *im*bellium *u*no reliquo fonte *u*terentur The polar opposites of combatants and non-combatants, their contrast here emphasised by the 'high-style' *bellator* (Adams (2016) 33), are the first of three others: the scarcity of water here ('uno reliquo fonte') will be followed by that of food ('egestate pabuli'), while the deaths of animals ('armenta ... exanimari') will be followed by those of humans ('corpora hominum'). At the same time the indiscriminate nature of the devastation is shown, as barriers are broken down (*uno, simul, iuxta*). For repetitions of the type *bellatorum ~ imbellium* see Wills 451–4; this particular instance is unique in classical Latin.

simulque armenta, ut mos barbaris, iuxta clausa M reads *simul eque*, which was emended to *simulque* by Danesius (followed by Fisher) and *simul equi* by Lipsius (followed by the Teubner editors).[96] The phrase *ut mos barbaris* indicates, as usual, that T. is dealing with an ethnographical topos (cf. 3.43.2n.), and the point is not that horses and herds were kept together but that the Thracians were living alongside their animals, as the Egyptians were said by Herodotus to do (2.36.2 Αἰγυπτίοισι δὲ ὁμοῦ θηρίοισι ἡ δίαιτά ἐστι). The classic example is Polyphemus, the archetypal barbarian, in the *Odyssey* (9.183–4, 298). *simulque*, a favourite connection in T., links the implied scarcity of water (above) with the lack of food (below).

egestate pabuli exanimari The description is borrowed from Sall. *J.* 44.4 'odor aut pabuli egestas locum mutare subegerat' (*odor* occurs below); Caesar prefers the expr. *inopia pabuli* (4× in the Corpus), which T. uses at 15.5.3.

quos uulnera, quos sitis peremerat Though *perimo* often has things as its subject (*TLL* 10.1.1475.61ff.), *uulnus* and *sitis* are otherwise unparalleled; see also 6.23.1n.

pollui cuncta sanie, odore, contactu Statements of 'unqualified assertion' involving terms like 'all' or 'nothing', especially when combined with one or more rhetorical figures (such as the tricolon and quasi-anagram here),

---

[96] Most edd. attribute *simulque* also to Lipsius, but Ursinus mentions Danesius, as Prof. Reeve points out to me.

are common and effective closural devices (3.11.2n.); in battle scenes and other vivid descriptions Caesar and Livy in particular are fond of neut. plur. *omnia* (Kraus on Liv. 6.3.5), for which T. has, as it were, here substituted his favoured *cuncta* (Malloch on 11.9.2), as at 51.2 below and 1.70.3 'cuncta pari uiolentia inuoluebantur'. *polluere* is relatively uncommon of disease etc., but the references to discharge and stench impart a spuriously medical tone (*sanies* and *odor* are commonly combined in Celsus, e.g. 7.27.1) and constitute a brief appeal to those readers who relished descriptions of illness or a gory death (see 3.20.2n.; J. Grimm, *Die literarische Darstellung der Pest in der Antike und in der Romania* (1965)). At Luc. 6.457 *mens . . . sanie polluta* refers to snake's venom.

50.1 malum extremum discordia The *discordia* of barbarians is a topos (3.38.4n., adding Malloch on 11.16.1), that of the Thracians being notorious since Hdt. 5.3.

deditionem . . . et mutuos inter se ictus . . . et . . . eruptionem The three options are identified with the three named leaders in turn below (2–4). For the first and third options cf. Caes. *BG* 7.77.2 'uariis dictis sententiis, quarum pars deditionem, pars . . . eruptionem censebat'.

mortem et mutuos inter se ictus Since this group is distinct from those who intend to die at the hands of the enemy in a break-out (below), *et* must be epexegetical ('theme and variation'). The collective suicide of barbarians is another topos (3.46.4n.).

50.2 Neque ignobiles, quamuis diuersi sententiis, uerum e ducibus Dinis . . . disserebat Although the passage is by no means straightforward, it seems not to require any of the emendations which have been proposed for it. The verb with *ignobiles* is *disserebant*, to be understood from *disserebat* below (an example of 'gapping', for which see 3.3.3n.): 'And it was not the commoners, although divided in opinion, but one of the leaders, Dinis, who said that they should lay down their arms.' The sentence is a twofold paradox: although one would have expected the *ignobiles* to be united in favour of giving up, like Thersites in the *Iliad* (2.236), it was in fact one of the leaders who took this line, while the *ignobiles* were as divided in their opinions as their leaders.

prouectus senecta et longo usu uim atque clementiam Romanam edoctus Elderly advisers of one type or another are a common feature of battle narratives (*Agr.* 25.3n.); here T.'s chiastic phrase seems to allude to the persons mentioned at Sall. *H.* 2.87 M (= 2.74.7 R) 'illi quibus aetas imbellior et uetustate uis Romanorum multum cognita erat cupere pacem' (cf. also Liv. 6.32.7 'longa societate militiam Romanam edoctae'). For *senecta* see 3.23.1n., Oakley on Liv. 6.8.2; for *uim atque clementiam* cf. Liv. 44.9.1 (an allusion to Sall. *J.* 32.5 'uim quam misericordiam'), Curt. 9.1.23.

unum adflictis id remedium The motif 'one remedy' (as Cic. *Div. Caec.* 9 'hoc unum his tot incommodis remedium esse') is perhaps more normally used in a battle context to encourage fighting (thus 1.67.1 'unam in armis salutem' (n.), Virg. *Aen.* 2.354 'una salus uictis nullam sperare salutem', with Horsfall's n.).

50.3 Tarsam . . . et Turesim Nothing else is known.

properum finem, abrumpendas pariter spes ac metus clamitans The writing is impressionistic: with *properum finem* we have to supply e.g. *petendum esse* or *optimum esse*. Although *spem abrumpere* is found occasionally elsewhere (*H.* 3.63.1 and H.'s n.), the verb more commonly has *uitam* as its object (*TLL* 1.141.18ff.): Tarsa is diplomatically alluding to the means by which the 'quick end' to their troubles is to be achieved.

qui . . . oppeterent Cf. 2.24.2n.

50.4 haud nescio duce nostro It was expected that a general would find out the enemy's plans (e.g. 2.20.1, *Agr.* 25.3,[97] Front. *Strat.* 1.2). For the use of *nostro = Romano* see 46.1n. above.

firmatae stationes A Livian expr. (4.27.7, 5.43.2).

densioribus globis Originally Virgilian (*Aen.* 10.373), then in Luc. 4.73–4, Sil. 4.518–19.

ingruebat _nox nimbo atrox_ Although night and difficult weather conditions offered obvious advantages for certain undertakings (cf. e.g. *H.* 3.69.4, 5.22.1, Caes. *BG* 7.27.1, Liv. 24.46.4–5), the Romans affected to claim that night-fighting was beneath them (Liv. 42.47.5 'non per insidias et nocturna proelia . . . bella maiores gessisse'); here it is the enemy who again desire to fight a night battle (cf. 48.2n.), and, since 'night' was a standard topic for rhetorical description (cf. Hermog. 16.20–2), T. unsurprisingly makes the most of the opportunity. His introductory phraseology is striking and unparalleled, though F. Urban compares Thuc. 3.22.1 νύκτα χειμέριον ὕδατι on the siege of Plataea (*Belagerungsschilderungen: Untersuchung zu einem Topos der antiken Geschichtsschreibung* (diss. Göttingen 1966) 202); *nimbus* = 'rain' is found predominantly in verse authors (H. Tränkle, *WS* 81 (1968) 117). The impf. tense, like that of *effecerat* below, prepares for the following inverted *cum*-clause.

clamore turbido, modo per uastum silentium The *uariatio* of instrumental abl. ~ prep. phrase (Sörbom 84, though not mentioning our passage)

---

[97] H. Allgeier on 'Das Bild des Feldherrn im Werk des Tacitus' says little (*Studien zur Kriegsdarstellung bei Tacitus* (diss. Heidelberg 1957) 197–201).

indicates that the latter = 'by means of an eery silence', i.e. a different meaning from Luc. 5.508 'per uasta silentia' ('through'). The silence, of course, is that kept deliberately by the enemy, as shown by *simulationem quietis* below; we are not to forget the noise of the rain (of which there is a vivid description at Liv. 24.46.5). *uastum silentium* is originally Livian (10.34.6, with Oakley ad loc.), repeated by T. at *Agr.* 38.2 and *H.* 3.12.2. For *clamore turbido* cf. 12.43.1, Plin. *Ep.* 9.13.4; for the omission of an initial *modo* see 6.32.1n.

cum Sabinus circumire For the historic infin. in an inverted *cum*-clause see 6.44.2n.

ne . . . casum insidiantibus aperirent *casus* = 'opportunity' (*OLD* 7), a probably Sallustian meaning (Malloch on 11.9.1); *aperire* is found with *occasionem* at Liv. 4.53.9 and 9.27.2 (its use with *casus* at Ov. *Met.* 15.559 refers to prophecy). This is the only certain example in T. of the substantival use of *insidians*, which starts with Caes. *BG* 8.19.3 and Sall. *J.* 113.5 and then becomes more common in Livy (J. N. Adams, *Glotta* 51 (1973) 128).

immoti telisque non in falsum iactis Contrast the Isaurians at Sall. *H.* 2.87 M (= 2.74.1 R) 'per obscuram noctem tela in incertum iacientes'. For the *uariatio* of part. ~ abl. abs. cf. Sörbom 91.

51.1 cateruis decurrentes '*Cateruae* often consist of barbarians and receive contemptuous treatment from Roman writers' (Tarrant on Sen. *Ag.* 601 'barbaricis . . . cateruis', to whose exs. add Sil. 9.77). *decurrentes* reminds readers that the barbarians have been occupying high ground (49.1). The abl. is modal, as *H.* 2.42.2 'cateruis . . . concurrebant'.

manualia saxa, praeustas sudes, decisa robora iacere Another allusion to Sall. *H.* 2.87 M (= 2.74.2 R) 'saxa, pila, sudes iacere', echoed also by Liv. 27.28.12 'saxis, sudibus, pilis absterrent hostem' (*sudibus et pilis* at Tac. *H.* 4.23.2, *ferratas sudes, grauia saxa* at ibid. 4.29.3). The verb is the first of nine successive historic infinitives, which is the second highest number in T. (ten at *Agr.* 38.1, where see n.): this is usually taken to be a Sallustian feature (there are eleven at Sall. *J.* 66.1: see further J. J. Schlicher, 'The historical infinitive II: its literary elaboration', *CP* 9 (1914) 374–94, esp. 374–8 and 386–92), although such clustering is not in fact unique to him (thus eight at Plaut. *Merc.* 46–52: see H. Rosén, 'The Latin infinitivus historicus revisited', *Mnem.* 48 (1995) 536–64, at 551–2; see also T. Viljamaa, *Infinitive of narration in Livy* (1983) 69). For *manualis* see Sisenn. F36C = 23P 'manualis lapides', Amm. 20.7.10 'manualium saxorum', 24.2.1; the Greek term is χειροπληθεῖς λίθοι (Xen. *An.* 3.3.17) or χερμάδια in Homer (*Il.* 16.774, *Od.* 10.121): much attention was paid to the use of stones in ancient warfare (e.g. Veg. *Mil.* 1.16, 4.8.3–4). For *praeustae sudes* cf. Caes. *BG* 5.40.6 (and see

n. *muralia* below) and Virg. *Aen.* 7.524 (with Horsfall on 506). *decisa robora* presumably refers to any hewn boughs, not necessarily oak trees.

nunc uirgultis et cratibus et corporibus exanimis complere fossas *complere fossas* is common esp. in Caesar, who on one occasion describes an incident in Gaul in 56 BC where the Roman commander shared the name Sabinus with the Thracian governor (*BG* 3.18.8 'laeti, ut explorata uictoria, sarmentis uirgultisque collectis, quibus fossas Romanorum compleant, ad castra pergunt'; cf. Front. *Strat.* 3.17.7). At Alesia hurdles were used (ibid. 7.79.4 'fossam cratibus integunt'); for the use of bodies, which might naturally pile up (Tac. *H.* 4.20.3), cf. Liv. 26.6.2 'corporibus cum oppleta fossa esset, uelut aggere aut ponte iniecto transitum hostibus dedit' (though these are of elephants). (See also next n.) Anaphora of *nunc*, common in Livy (Oakley on 9.18.15), is only here in T.

eaque prensare Cf. Amm. 19.5.6 'multitudini . . . iam propugnacula ipsa prensanti'. The verb is 'a mild poeticism' (1.68.2n.).

Miles contra deturbare telis T. seems to be thinking not only of the engagement at Alesia (Caes. *BG* 7.86.5 'multitudine telorum ex turribus propugnantes *deturbant*, aggere et *cratibus fossas* ex*plent*, falcibus uallum ac *loricam* rescindunt') but also of that at Isaura (Sall. *H.* 2.87 M (= 2.74.2 R) 'multos prope egressos *comminus* plagis aut omni re *deturbare*; qua repentina formidine pars <in> uallo transfixa, alii super *tela* sua praecipitati, ruinaque multorum *fossae* semi*pletae* sunt, ceteris fuga tuta fuit incerto noctis et metu insidiarum'). T. usually reserves unqualified *miles* for the Romans, but not always (12.33.1); for the collective sing. see 2.1n.

pellere umbonibus See *Agr.* 36.2n.

muralia pila, congestas lapidum moles prouoluere Since *pila* were throwing-weapons, it seems likely that *muralia pila* were deployed defensively from walls (see J. Kromayer and G. Veith, *Heerwesen und Kriegführung der Griechen und Römer* (1928) 524–5; *BNP* 11.259–60), although it is disputed whether the archaeological specimens traditionally identified as *muralia pila* were in fact this weapon (see J. Bennett, 'The Great Chesters "pilum murale"', *Archaeologia Aeliana* 10 (1982) 200–5, M. C. Bishop and J. C. N. Coulston, *Roman military equipment: from the Punic Wars to the fall of Rome* (²2006) 116–17 and fig. 68.1). They featured at Alesia (Caes. *BG* 7.82.1) but also elsewhere (ibid. 5.40.6).[98] *prouoluere*

---

[98] That the *pila muralia* at Curt. 8.10.32 are a different weapon, as stated in *TLL* 10.1.2146.21–2, is not at all clear. There are no other examples of the term apart from the four mentioned here, but cf. *H.* 4.29.3 'propellere umbone, pilo sequi'.

applies more naturally only to the stones (as *H.* 2.22.2 'molares . . . prouo-luunt'); with *pila* we have to understand (by zeugma) a verb such as (*e*)*mittere* (cf. e.g. Sall. *J.* 57.5 'saxa uoluere . . . pila . . . mittere'). For the stones cf. *H.* 2.21.3.

51.2 His partae uictoriae spes et, si cedant, insignitius flagitium There are various ways of taking this passage, the text of which has also been questioned. It is possible that *spes* and *flagitium* are two of the subjects of *addunt animos*, but the writing is more vivid if we simply understand *est* with *spes* ('the Romans had the expectation of gaining victory'). It would not make sense, however, to understand *est* also with *insignitius flagitium*: we must assume either the ellipse of *spes* ('and, if they yielded, the expectation of a more signal disgrace'), as at 4.3.3 above (n.), or an instance of so-called 'free indirect discourse' ('and, if they yielded, there would be a more signal disgrace'). For the type of *uariatio* involved (noun ~ conditional clause) see 6.34.3 (n.), *Agr.* 35.2 (n.); Sörbom 117–18.

Although *parta uictoria* and *uictoriae spes* are both extremely common phrases (note esp. Liv. 27.31.3 'uictoriae partae fama') and found elsewhere in T., doubt has been cast on *partae uictoriae spes*, evidently on the grounds that it cannot refer to a victory not yet achieved (hence Greef's *partae <prope> uictoriae spes*: see G–G 1536b).[99] Of the various conjectures which have been made, only E. Gross's *paratae* deserves serious consideration: the two words are often confused (44.1n.), the meaning is ideal ('hope of an easy victory'), and the Latin paralleled (Petron. 15.9 'nec uictoria mi placet parata'). But, if *mutati in deterius principatus initium* at 4.6.1 can mean 'the start of the deterioration in his principate', as most scholars agree (see n. and *NLS* there quoted), it is difficult to see why our phrase cannot mean 'the hope of the gaining of victory' (lit. 'the hope of a gained victory').

insignitum flagitium seems to be T.'s unique variant on *insigne flagitium* (Cato, *Or.* 60 M, Sen. *Ep.* 99.13, Plin. *NH* 35.119), although Prof. Reeve points to the possibility that the medial –*it*– in the adj. was caused by anticipation of *flagitium*.

illis extrema iam salus, et *a*dsistentes plerisque matres et con-iuges earumque lamenta *a*ddunt *a*nimos As in the previous sentence, *addunt animos* may have *extrema . . . salus* as one of its subjects, but, again, the writing is more vivid if we understand *est*: 'for the enemy it was now their final salvation, and the presence of their womenfolk . . . gave them extra courage' (*adsistentes* is another substantival participle: see 12.1n.). The laments of the attending women contrast with the confident role foreseen for them at 46.3 (n.); *extrema . . . salus* is a variant on the '*una salus* motif' (above, 50.2n.).

---

[99] Furneaux translates 'the hope that they had already won the victory', but this is rendered unlikely by *et . . . flagitium*.

Nox aliis in audaciam, aliis ad formidinem opportuna The darkness of night renders the daring and the coward equally invisible, spurring the former to even more perilous feats and allowing the latter to lie low without disgrace. This is the opposite of Caes. *BG* 7.80.5 'quod in conspectu omnium res gerebatur neque recte aut turpiter factum celari poterat, utrosque et laudis cupiditas et timor ignominiae ad uirtutem excitabat'. *nox . . . opportuna* is Livian (7.35.10): the adj. is regularly followed by *ad* + acc., but for *in* only Sen. *Brev. Vit.* 17.4 is quoted (*TLL* 9.2.779.21–3). It is not clear to which side *aliis . . . aliis* refers (perhaps the Thracians and Romans respectively, as Furneaux suggests) or whether both pronouns are applicable to both sides equally (so Pfitzner).

incerti ictus, uulnera improuisa The former element of the chiasmus is focalised by the striker of the blows (cf. Sil. 5.297),[100] the latter by the recipient of them.

suorum atque hostium ignoratio The classic example of this situation is the night battle on Epipolae (Thuc. 7.44.1–2 ἐν δὲ νυκτομαχίᾳ . . . τὴν μὲν ὄψιν τοῦ σώματος προορᾶν, τὴν δὲ γνῶσιν τοῦ οἰκείου ἀπιστεῖσθαι).

montis anfractu Again Livian (29.32.4, 32.11.2, 38.23.6).

51.3 deiecto promptissimo quoque aut saucio Cf. Sall. *C.* 61.7 'strenuissimus quisque aut occiderat in proelio aut grauiter uolneratus discesserat', *J.* 92.9 'optumus quisque cadere aut sauciari'. *deiecto* = 'struck down' (*OLD* 7a).

adpetente iam luce Though the expr. is found earlier in Livy and Curtius, its first recorded occurrence is in Caesar's Alesia narrative (*BG* 7.82.2): see Oakley on Liv. 10.20.9.

trusere in summa castelli This is presumably the *castellum* which was last mentioned at 49.1, but the meaning of the phrase is unclear: 'to the upper part of the fortress' (Church and Brodribb), 'to their stronghold on the height' (Jackson), 'to the heights of the stronghold' (Woodman). That the subject of *trusere* is the Romans has to be understood from the preceding sequence *neque tamen peruasere hostes nisi admodum pauci; ceteros . . .*

coacta deditio A final allusion to Sall. *H.* 2.87 M (= 2.74.3 R) 'coacta deditio est'.

proxima 'the immediate neighbourhood or vicinity' (*OLD* 2a).

sponte incolarum Cf. 13.39.5 'alia sponte incolarum in deditionem ueniebant'.

---

[100] Luc. 7.129 is different.

ui aut obsidio T. repeats these alternatives twice elsewhere, but, whereas at *H.* 2.23.1 he prefers the term *obsidium* (as here), at *A.* 14.24.2 he prefers *obsidio* (as at Cic. *Mur.* 20, Luc. 3.343): see 3.39.1n.

praematura montis Haemi et saeua hiems The Balkan Mountains range is nearly 8,000 ft at its highest point; winter there usually starts at the end of October or beginning of November. Thrace was regarded by the ancients as 'un pays exceptionnellement froid et fortement enneigé', and its ὄρεα νιφόεντα appear as early as Hom. *Il.* 14.227 (P.-J. Dehon, *Hiems Latina: études sur l'hiver dans la poésie latine des origines à l'époque de Néron* (1993) 48, with many refs. in n. 89; also Kienzle 25).

52–61 Domestic Affairs

52–54 Agrippina and Tiberius

This section amplifies and develops the relationship between Tib. and his daughter-in-law, in the same way as 39–41 above, to which it is the counterpart, did for the *princeps'* relationship with Sejanus. The section is tripartite, like the earlier one, and details three brief encounters between the two principal characters: each encounter is trivial in itself and anecdotal in nature, but all three illustrate and typify the events which Sejanus has been setting in train since AD 23 (12.2–4; cf. 17.2–3). In addition, Agrippina's pathetic request for a husband (53.1) contrasts with Sejanus' confident request for a wife the previous year (39), although each is rejected by Tib. Similarly the false rumour that Sejanus manoeuvred Tib. into poisoning his son (10.2–3) is here mirrored by Sejanus' false suggestion that Tib. intended to poison his daughter-in-law (54.1): although the falseness of the latter is an integral element of the plot (whereas in the earlier episode the falseness is attested by the author), nevertheless T.'s narrative offers a series of interpretative options which lend it the uncertain quality of rumour itself (54.1nn).[101] And the ironical result of the episode is the generation of a further rumour (54.2 'inde rumor . . .').

52.1 At Romae See 3.22.1n.

commota principis domo It is not clear whether T. is referring to the death of Drusus (8.1ff.) or Sejanus' initial moves against Agrippina (12.2–4) or his recent exchange with Tib. (39–41) or a combination of some or all of these. The metaphor is that of an earthquake (cf. Vell. 124.1n.), a domestic convulsion analogous to that just experienced in Thrace (46.1 *motus*).

ut series futuri in Agrippinam exitii inciperet This very strange clause has attracted little or no editorial attention, yet, when *series* is followed by a genitive, as here, the genitive is almost always plural. At *D.* 19.3 the transmitted

---

[101] For the defining characteristics of rumour see Hardie 8–9.

256

text reads *narrationis alte repetita series*, where Gudeman in 1894 accepted Spengel's *narrationum*; but in his 1914 edition he returned to the transmitted reading, referring to W. A. Baehrens on 'Bemerkenswerter Gebrauch des Singulars' ('Vermischtes über lateinischen Sprachgebrauch', *Glotta* 4 (1913) 271–3) and quoting a long list of exs. (but not our passage) where *series* is followed by a sing. genitive, to which one could add e.g. Luc. 4.823 'Caesareaeque domus series', Sen. *Tro.* 1065 'seriem caedis', Stat. *Theb.* 9.431 'belli series'. *narrationum* is mentioned but not printed by Peterson and Lenchantin; it is not even mentioned by Winterbottom (OCT) or Mayer, who also offers no comment on the singular. In most cases of the singular it is possible to understand a collectivity (e.g. individual family members at Luc. 4.823), but this is difficult at Stat. *Silv.* 4.3.145 'seriem . . . aeui', where Coleman comments that '*aeui* needs to be qualified by a word that will ease the phrase'; and, although she adopts Polster's *imminentis* for the transmitted *merentis*, she translates as a plural ('a series of forthcoming years').[102] Our passage is doubly difficult in that *exitium* is a once-for-all event that has not yet happened. If the text is correct (and no one seems to have questioned it), T. appears to be imagining Agrippina's destruction as a staged process which is beginning now and extending into the future.

A further awkwardness is the expression *in Agrippinam* instead of the more usual genitive. *in* seems to be used of the intended victim, as with *ueneficia in principem* below. There is perhaps a comparable use of a preposition at 6.8.6 'consilia caedis aduersum imperatorem' (n.). Hence: 'in order that the process of the future destruction intended for Agrippina should begin'. The clause suggests a preordained sequence of events (for which see 3.13.2n.) and is to be taken with what follows.

Claudia Pulchra, sobrina eius She was daughter of Augustus' niece, Marcella *minor*, and M. Valerius Messalla Appianus (cos. 12 BC), and hence second cousin ('sobrina') of Agrippina, the granddaughter of Augustus. She was the widow of the unfortunate general, Quintilius Varus. See *RE* 3.2898–9 = Claudius 434 (Groag), *PIR* 2.268 no. 1116 (stemma on p. 236), *BNP* 3.386 [II 11]; Syme, *AA* 147–9, 327 and Tables III, VI, VII. For her case, to which Dio alludes in a flashback under 39 without naming her (59.19.1), see Rutledge 142–3, 367 n. 32.

Domitio Afro Cn. Domitius Afer, who prosecuted Claudia Pulchra's son in the following year (66.1), became an outstanding orator (see 4 below), was suffect consul in 39 and was appointed *curator aquarum* in 49 (Front. *Aq.* 102.8, with Rodgers' n.). He died in 59 (14.19). For him see *RE* 5.1318–20 = Domitius 14 (Kappelmacher/Wissowa), *PIR* 3.29–30 no. 126, *BNP* 4.649–50 [III 1]; Rutledge 220–3.

---

[102] Liberman (2010) objects to *imminentis* and prints Heinsius' *uirentis*.

recens praetura 'fresh from the praetorship': i.e. he was praetor in the previous year, not (as Rutledge 221 supposes) the current year. For *recens* + abl. see 1.41.3n.

modicus dignationis et quoquo facinore properus clarescere The reference to his praetorship (above) indicates that *dignatio* must mean 'reputation, honour' here, not 'rank' (G–G 292b); for *modicus* see 2.73.2n. *properus*, a favourite of T.'s (Malloch on 11.26.2), is not elsewhere found + infin. (*TLL* 10.2.1988.34–5); he is also the first writer to apply *clarescere* to persons (Malloch on 11.16.2).

Furnium Unknown (*RE* 7.375 = Furnius 1 (Kappelmacher)), but presumably descended from the consul of 17 BC (*RG* 22.2; *RE* 7.377 = Furnius 4 (Kappelmacher)).

in principem is to be taken with *deuotiones* ('curses': *OLD* 2) as well as *ueneficia*; this device of joining two terms by the interposition of a third is known as *coniunctio* (cf. *Rhet. Herenn.* 4.38) or 'conjunct hyperbaton' (A. M. Devine and L. D. Stephens, *Latin word order* (2006) 586–91). The whole phrase constitutes the third element of a tricolon of accusations, balancing the three descriptions of Afer above. For *ueneficia . . . et deuotiones* see 3.13.2n.

52.2 semper atrox, tum et periculo propinquae accensa For *accensa* cf. *H.* 1.54.1 'pericula . . . accendebant animos', Liv. 3.62.8 'periculo . . . animos . . . accendunt'; for *atrox* see 60.3n.

sacrificantem patri Tib. was one of the *sodales Augustales* (1.54.1; Rüpke 169).

quo initio inuidiae non eiusdem ait mactare diuo Augusto uictimas et posteros eius insectari Agrippina's indignation (*OLD inuidia* 1a) leads her to attack first the devotion to Augustus which was Tib.'s guiding principle (37.3n.), and she frames it in a chiasmus which is introduced by, and bristles with, assonance. *non* is resumed in anaphora below.

non in ªeffigies mutas ᵇdiuinum ᶜspiritum ᵈtransfusum; se ªimaginem ueram, ᵇcaelesti ᶜsanguine ᵈortam Agrippina's point-by-point repudiation of Tib.'s actions throws into relief the two adjs. whose correspondence is only formal: he is confronted by a reality (*ueram*) who can talk back at him – and is doing so (~ *mutas*). Her proud self-description, more emphatic if we understand *esse* after *se*,[103] is given edge by *imaginem ueram*,

---

[103] M here reads 'sed ¹maginē', for which modern edd. read *se imaginem*. It is plausible to assume that, after *non in mutas . . .*, the scribe was expecting *sed*, although Lenchantin and Koestermann seem to imagine a different sequence of corruption (*seimaginem → setmaginem → sedmaginem*), *i* and *t* being often confused.

which is both a pun and a paradox: she is a likeness (*OLD* 9) but not a statue or bust (*OLD* 1), and one cannot have a statue which is real (*OLD uerus* 2). For the importance of family likeness see 15.3n.; for Agrippina's pride in her descent from Augustus see 3.4.2n. For various other exs. of *imago uera* cf. Sen. *Ben.* 7.27.1, Plin. *NH* 35.52, Petron. 60.9, Quint. 5.12.17; for *effigies mutas* cf. Quint. 6.1.32. *diuinus spiritus* is a very common phrase; *caelestis sanguis* is unparalleled.

intellegere discrimen, suscipere sordes 'she understood her danger and was adopting *sordes*' (probably a separate sentence: see previous n.). For the expr. cf. Cic. *Sest.* 145 'hae sordes susceptae sunt propter unum me'; for *sordes* (28.1n.) as a political gesture, as here, see Kaster on Cic. *Sest.* 25.

frustra Pulchram praescribi Scholars mostly take *praescribi* to mean 'was being used as a pretext', for which they compare 11.16.3 'frustra Arminium praescribi'; but the parallel is denied in *TLL*, where our passage is regarded as the only ex. of this meaning (10.2.826.41–3; cf. 35–6), although there is a comparison with the noun at Caes. *BC* 3.32.4 'ut honesta praescriptione rem turpissimam tegerent'. But the verb may also mean 'was the heading [sc. on the charge sheet]'; often *titulus* or *nomen* is used as the object of the verb (as 3.57.1 'ut . . . non consulum nomina praescriberentur'), but not always (cf. *H.* 2.65.1 'diplomatibus nullum principem praescripsisset'; *TLL* 10.2.826. 22–4). Both interpretations make good sense in the context.

quod Agrippinam stulte prorsus ad cultum delegerit 'that she had – foolishly no doubt – chosen Agrippina for her attentions' (*prorsus* is concessive and perhaps ironical: cf. 6.3.2n.). Agrippina pointedly substitutes her own name for (an ambiguous use of) *se*, capitalising on the various effects (such as pathos or arrogance) to which self-reference lends itself (see Rutherford 14–15; Tarrant on Virg. *Aen.* 12.11). For the construction cf. Plin. *Ep.* 6.6.5 'me . . . ad amorem . . . delegit'.

Sosiae Cf. 19.1 'Sosia . . . caritate Agrippinae inuisa principi'.

52.3 raram occulti pectoris uocem elicuere The *pectus* is a regular source of the voice (Quint. 10.7.15 'pectus est enim quod disertos facit'), esp. but not exclusively in epic, and *uocem* (*–es*) *elicere* is a relatively common expr.; but the only other occasion on which both are found together is Lucr. 3.57–8 'uerae uoces tum demum pectore ab imo | eliciuntur'.[104] It is therefore interesting that the unusual genitive *pectoris* (instead of the normal prepositional phrase) is also paralleled in Lucr. (1.731–2 'carmina quin etiam diuini pectoris eius | uociferantur'); perhaps coincidence (though Agrippina's words can be reassembled into a hexameter line: 'pectoris occulti raram uocem elicuere'). The gen. *occulta pectoris* at Sall. *J.* 113.3 seems rather different but

[104] Lambinus proposed *eiciuntur*.

may well have been in T.'s mind; cf. also Luc. 2.285 'arcano sacras reddit Cato pectore uoces'. For Tib.'s habitual reluctance to speak see 31.2n.; for his secretiveness see e.g. 4.1.1.

correptamque Graeco uersu admonuit nōn ĭdĕō lāedī quĭă nōn rēgnāret The same story occurs in Suet. *Tib.* 53.1 'nurum Agrippinam post mariti mortem liberius quiddam questam manu apprehendit Graecoque uersu "si non dominaris", inquit, "filiola, iniuriam te accipere existimas?"'. Most scholars (incl. G–G 230a) assume that *correptam* is T.'s equivalent of Suetonius' *manu apprehendit*, but *corripio* is normally used of more violent seizure (e.g. Curt. 10.2.30 'singulos manu corripuit nec ausos repugnare XIII adseruandos custodibus corporis tradidit'). This problem is avoided by Ritter's interpretation (also in *TLL* 4.1045.39) that *correptam* means 'rebuked': *corripio* in this sense is often followed by a reference to the medium by which the rebuke is conveyed (*dictis* etc.: cf. *TLL* 4.1045.10ff.), as here by *Graeco uersu*, and *admonuit . . . regnaret* specifies the nature of the rebuke ('theme and variation' again). On the other hand, *arripio* is the *mot juste* for taking a person by the hand, and it may be that *arreptamque* should be read here, as Martin and Woodman proposed. For Tib.'s use of Greek cf. 3.65.3, Suet. *Tib.* 70–1; it is unknown what Greek line the *princeps* quoted, but scholars have seen a similarity to Arist. *Pol.* 1277a24 Ἰάσων ἔφη πεινῆν ὅτε μὴ τυραννοῖ. Whether T.'s dactylic rhythm is intended to suggest epic is unclear.

damnantur The sentence is not known; the plural verb implies that the charge of *maiestas*, which had been directed against Pulchra alone, was dropped (so Seager 169).

52.4 additus suggests inclusion in a canon (38.5n.). Quintilian, a pupil of Afer's (5.7.7), described him as 'longe omnium quos mihi cognoscere contigit summum oratorem' (12.11.3), 'principem . . . fori' (ibid.), an orator 'quem in numero ueterum habere non timeas' (10.1.118). He is mentioned approvingly at *D.* 13.3.

suo iure Perhaps 'unconditionally', 'without qualification', although Pfitzner prefers 'a born orator'.

nisi quod aetas extrema multum etiam eloquentiae dempsit Cf. Quint. 12.11.3 'ualde senem aliquid ex ea quam meruerat auctoritate perdentem'.

dum fessa mente retinet silentii impatientiam Evidently contemporaries of Afer circulated the witticism that 'malle eum deficere quam desinere' (Quint. 12.11.3). *fessa mente* refers to failing powers (*OLD fessus* 3b, 5c). Pliny tells an amusing story about Afer and silence when the orator was at his peak (*Ep.* 2.14.10–12); Formicola sees an allusion to T. at Apul. *Flor.* 17 'impatientia linguae' (an 'Umkehrung').

53.1 peruicax irae et morbo corporis implicata *peruicax* + gen. (again at *H.* 4.5.2) is not found before T. (contrast Curt. 8.6.1 'peruicacioris irae'); *morbo implicari* is a set phrase (the verb occurs nowhere else in T.). The expr. is chiastic.

cum uiseret eam Caesar Visiting the sick was a characteristic of Tib. (Dio 57.11.7; cf. Vell. 114.1 and n.), as it had been of Augustus (Millar 112): such visits, for which *uiso* is the technical term (*OLD* 3b), were a responsibility of friendship (J. C. Yardley, *Phoenix* 27 (1973) 285–6).

inuidiam et preces 'indignation and pleas' (3.67.4n.).

subueniret solitudini 'he should remedy her widowhood', as Apul. *Apol.* 70 'tandem aliquando se quoque paterentur solitudini suae et aegritudini subuenire'.

habilem adhuc iuuentam sibi The truth of this statement is somewhat belied by *morbo corporis implicata* above, illustrating the pathetic desperation of Agrippina's request. She was now about 40.

neque aliud probis quam ex matrimonio solacium Petersen suggested *probris*, and aristocratic widows were indeed vulnerable to malicious gossip (Treggiari 500); but Agrippina was famous for her chastity (1.33.3 and esp. 4.12.2), *ex matrimonio solacium* looks back to *subueniret solitudini*, and the unqualified *probis* is perhaps Sallustian (cf. *C.* 25.2). The companionship of marriage was important, and the death of one's spouse could be a major disaster (Treggiari 250, 483ff.).

esse in ciuitate *** On the assumption that *esse* constitutes the beginning of a new sentence rather than the end of the previous one (which cannot be certain), the insertion of *qui* would restore sense; but the length of the gap in M (about a third of a line, or roughly 14–15 letters) suggests that more than a single word is missing. Many scholars assume that Agrippina made a further reference to her descent from Augustus (her 'Leit-motiv', as it is called by Questa 173 n. 60).

53.2 non ignarus quantum ex re publica peteretur 'not unaware of how much was being asked of the state' (i.e. by Agrippina). *tamen* (below) indicates that this phrase is concessive, which in turn indicates that the *princeps'* answer was immediate and negative.

peto is the regular term for asking for a marriage (*TLL* 10.1.1962.73ff.). Madvig believed (2.548) that *quantum ex* could only be understood partitively ('how much of the state was being asked for'), but the meaning of the expression depends upon its context (e.g. Cic. *Fam.* 3.8.1 'quantum ex tuis litteris intellegere potui'), and, though *ex aliquo petere* is not a common variant of *ab aliquo p.*, it is found from Cicero onwards (*TLL* 10.1.1975.73–4). Tib. might have said *ex se* (which indeed Wurm proposed to read), but he characteristically presents things from the state's point of view: 'to give a new husband to the grand-daughter of Augustus and mother of the natural heirs to the principate was a very grave matter' (Furneaux).

ne tamen offensionis aut metus manifestus foret Most scholars, e.g. Oakley (1991) 343, assume that *offensionis* is passive ('annoyance' *vel sim.*; cf. 3.64.2 'dissimulata offensione', 14.49.3 'offensione manifesta'), and it is indeed true that Tib. is regularly associated with the taking of offence (18.2n.); but *sine responso quamquam instantem reliquit* (below) suggests that, despite his bluntness at other times (52.3), on this occasion Tib. was concerned about the proprieties of his visit and that *offensionis* is active ('lest he should be caught out in giving offence [to Agrippina] or in being afraid [of introducing someone to rival his own power]'). For the alternatives cf. Ov. *Met.* 15.503 'indiciine metu magis offensane repulsae?' (though here *offensa* is passive). *manifestus* + gen. is Sallustian (2.85.3n.).

a scriptoribus annalium non traditum Ancient historians were faced with a dilemma: on the one hand, like writers in many other genres, they wished to claim for their work the authority of some sort of past tradition (3.16.1n.); on the other hand, also like other types of writers (e.g. Lausberg 125–6 §270; N–R on Hor. *C.* 3.1.2–3), they wished to parade the lure of novelty (e.g. Vitruv. 5 *praef.* 3 'historiae per se tenent lectores: habent enim nouarum rerum uarias exspectationes'). A convenient way out of this dilemma was provided if one could boast access to a new (and preferably recherché) source (see Marincola 107ff.). Here T.'s negative reference to mainstream predecessors (for *scriptor(es) annalium* cf. Val. Max. 4.2.1 'ueteres annalium scriptores . . . tradiderunt', Gell. 1.11.9, 15.29 *init.*, Fronto p. 124.11 vdH²) prepares for the privileged source to which he is about to refer (next n.). Cf. also 6.7.5 and nn.

in commentariis Agrippinae filiae Roman historians rarely name their sources. T. mentions the elder Pliny at 1.69.2 (the only other named reference in *Annals* 1–6), 13.20.2 and 15.53.3; Cluvius Rufus and Fabius Rusticus at 13.20.2 and 14.2.1–2 (and the latter alone at 15.61.3); and Corbulo at 15.16.1. Standard discussions are Questa; O. Devillers, *Tacite et les sources des Annales: enquêtes sur la méthode historique* (2003). Nothing further is known of Agrippina's *commentarii* and only one other so-called 'fragment' of her writing survives (Plin. *NH* 7.46): see A. A. Barrett, *Agrippina* (1996) 198–9; *FRH* 1.515–17, 2.996–9, 3.602. For Agrippina herself see, in addition to Barrett, *RE* 10.909–15 = Iulia 556 (Hasebroek/Lackeit), *PIR* 4.302–5 no. 641, *BNP* 1.394 [3]; Raepsaet-Charlier 365–7 no. 426; W. Eck, *Agrippina, die Stadtgründerin Kölns: eine Frau in der frühkaiserzeitlichen Politik* (1993), J. Ginsburg, *Representing Agrippina: constructions of female power in the early Roman Empire* (2006).

Neronis principis mater The insertion of these words is perhaps intended to indicate that Agrippina wrote her *commentarii* after her son had become *princeps*; if so, the time of composition was no doubt given within the work itself.

casus suorum Her brothers Nero Caesar and Drusus Caesar died in 31 and 33 respectively (5.3.3n., 6.23.2), the latter shortly followed by their mother (6.25.1–3).

54.1 Ceterum resumes the narrative after the brief parenthesis on Agrippina's *commentarii* (G–G 167a). The following story, like that at 52.2–3 above, is in Suetonius (*Tib.* 53.1 'quondam uero inter cenam porrecta a se poma gustare non ausam etiam uocare desiit, simulans ueneni se crimine accersi; cum praestructum utrumque consulto esset, ut et ipse temptandi gratia offerret et illa quasi certissimum exitium caueret').

inmissis qui ... monerent ... uenenum, uitandas soceri epulas An action replay of 10.2 'ueneni ... moneret ... uitandam ... epulanti' (see further below), but there is also an echo of the attack on Silius (19.1 'inmissus ...'). *soceri* interacts with *nurui* below and underlines the unnatural aspects to Sejanus' intrigues.

per speciem amicitiae The episode illustrates the *fallaces amicitiae* mentioned at 33.3 (n.); for the friendship theme see further 18.1n.

simulationum nescia The meaning 'knowing nothing of deceiving' is strongly suggested by the remainder of the sentence, but 'unaware of [Sejanus'] deceptions' is also possible. For *nescius* see 3.1.1n., Oakley on Liv. 9.3.12.

non uultu aut sermone flecti may mean either 'did not change in expression or conversation' or 'was not distracted by any look or conversation'. *uultus*, which tends to refer to one's expression at any given moment (5.3.2n.), is commonly combined with *sermo* (6.50.1n.).

an quia audiuerat 'or because he had been told' (*OLD audio* 8b). For the *uariatio* with *forte* see 24.2n.

quo acrius experiretur 'The sense is analogous to the frequent one of activity in research etc.' (Furneaux): cf. 6.20.2 'peritiam . . . expertus' (and n.).

ut erant adposita If the meaning is 'exactly as they had been served', the implication is that Tib. was demonstrating the wholesomeness of the fruit of which the diners were partaking; but, if *ut* = 'as soon as', the point is almost the opposite, in that Tib. was conspicuously offering the fruit before he or others had tasted it (so Doederlein). The fruit perhaps constituted the last course of the meal (cf. Mart. 10.18.18). For the verb see *OLD appono* 2.

Aucta ... suspicio A further development in the action replay of 10.3 'auctam suspicionem'.

intacta ore seruis tramisit If she expected the slaves to eat the fruit in due course, she must have been prepared for them to die from the poison which she thought had been aimed at herself (so R. G. Austin on Cic. *Cael.* 58). Perhaps her action was accompanied by some diplomatic remark to the effect that she would eat the fruit later. Her belief that the fruit was poisoned seems not to be taken account of by W. Allen et al. in their survey of the possible scenarios ('Imperial table manners in Tacitus' *Annals*', *Latomus* 21 (1962) 376).

54.2 obuersus ad matrem Livia 'is to be understood as placed on the other side of him' (Furneaux); her hatred of Agrippina (12.3) made her an obvious confidante.

parari exitium Germanicus on his deathbed had warned his wife to be afraid of Tib. (2.72.1). For the expr., first found in Enn. *Trag.* 327 J, see H. on *H.* 4.58.1.

secretum ad perpetrandum quaeri *secretum* = 'conditions in which no witnesses are present' (*OLD* 3a); *perpetrare* is a 'recherché compound' which occurs only here in *Annals* 1–6 but is more common in 11–16 (Adams (1972) 364). For *secretum . . . quaeri* cf. [Quint.] *Decl. Min.* 344.9, *Decl. Mai.* 17.15.

55–56 Temples in Asia
In 23 the senate had given permission to the cities of Asia that they could build the temple to Tib. and his mother which had been requested (15.3). In 25 the senate had received three further religious delegations: Spain quoted the example of Asia in the hope that they too could build a temple to Tib. and his mother (37.1), while communities from the Peloponnese requested the settlement of a boundary dispute concerning a temple to Diana (43.1–3) and Segesta asked for the restoration of a temple of Venus (43.4). Now in 26 the senate receives delegations from the eleven cities of Asia which were competing for the honour of building the temple agreed in 23.

55.1 quo famam auerteret The rumour is that just mentioned (54.2); for *famam auertere* cf. Plin. *Pan.* 28.1. For *quo* see 30.1n.

Vndecim urbes certabant For such rivalry see 3.63.1n.

per bella Persi et Aristonici aliorumque regum The war with Perseus, king of Macedonia, was 171–168 BC; that with Aristonicus of Pergamum was 131–129 BC. The 'other kings' include esp. Mithridates VI (14.2n.). Editors note that the gen. *Persi* (for *Persei*) is also at Sall. *H.* 1.8 M = 1.2 R 'ad bellum Persi Macedonicum', which T. may be imitating.

55.2 Hypaepeni Trallianique Laodicenis ac Magnetibus simul tramissi ut parum ualidi Hypaepa was in Lydia (*BA* Map 56: F5), Tralles in Caria (*BA* Map 61: F2). There was more than one city called Laodicea and Magnesia: it is assumed that Laodicea ad Lycum in Phrygia (*BA* Map 65: B2) and Magnesia-on-Meander (3.62.1n.; *BA* Map 61: F2) are meant here. *simul* is of course the preposition in anastrophe; *ualidi* refers more strictly to the cities' arguments (as 40.6) than to the people themselves (a form of hypallage: see *OLD* 7b; cf. a): the notion of some edd. that the word refers to wealth or resources is misguided.

Ilienses . . . antiquitatis gloria pollebant For Ilium (*BA* Maps 56: C2, 57: E2) see 2.54.2n., adding M. M. Sage, 'Roman visitors to Ilium in the Roman imperial and late antique period: the symbolic functions of a landscape', *Studia Troica* 10 (2000) 211–31. *antiquitatis gloria* is one of the phrases which T. shares with the elder Pliny (*NH* 5.61, 37.114: see further *Tac. Rev.* 233–4).

uiuo . . . in saxo is a phrase which originates with Virg. *Aen.* 1.167 and becomes popular with Ovid; this is the only ex. in prose (J. C. Plumpe, *Traditio* 1 (1943) 6). For the word order see 5.1.3n. Halicarnassus was on the western coast of Caria (*BA* Map 61: E3); Asia was notorious for its earthquakes (13.1).

aede Augusto ibi sita For the famous temple see 37.3n.; for Pergamum itself (*BA* Map 56: E3) see 3.63.2n. For such anagrams as *sita satis* see e.g. *Agr.* 1.1n.

Ephesii Milesiique For Ephesus (*BA* Map 61: E2) see 3.61.1n.; for Miletus (*BA* Maps 57: F4, 61: E2) see 3.63.3n. and 4.43.3n.

caerimonia occupauisse ciuitates Some idea of this may be gathered from *Ephesiaca* 1.2.2–3 by the novelist Xenophon of Ephesus (see J. Dillery, 'Xenophon, the military review and Hellenistic *pompaï*', in *Xenophon and his world* (ed. Tuplin, 2004) 266).[105]

55.3 Ita Sardianos inter Zmyrnaeosque deliberatum Both communities featured briefly in the asylum episode in 22, where their appeals were unsuccessful (3.63.3 and nn.). No reference was made there to their services to Rome, which are presented here and seemingly constitute the decisive factor (55.4, 56.1–2).

Sardiani Sardis (*BA* Map 56: G5) had suffered from a serious earthquake in 17 (the subject of an epigram by Bianor, *Anth. Pal.* 9.423); the extent to which it had recovered is disputed (2.47.2 and n.).

---

[105] Cf. also the mountain festival described by N. Douglas, *Old Calabria* (2007 edn (orig. 1915)) 149–57.

decretum Etruriae The reference is to the pre-conquest league of the twelve states of Etruria (for which see Ogilvie on Liv. 5.33.9). Nothing is known of any decree: 'entweder war es uralt oder gefälscht' (Draeger–Heraeus).

nam . . . rege genitos As becomes clear at §4 below (see nn.), the Sardians in presenting their case adopt the standard topics of the *laus locorum* and *laus urbium*, for which formalised rules are found in the work of Menander Rhetor, a native of the Laodicea to which reference was made above (2n.).[106] Praising a city by reference to its origin (τὸ γένος) was very important (Menand. 353.4ff.; Pernot 1.209–10): it was best if the founder was a god, but, if a man, then a king was acceptable (353.17–18). The Sardians' legendary history first appears in Hdt. 1.94.5–7 (where see Asheri's long note) and is explained by them here at some length, whereas their services to Rome are mentioned only briefly (4); the Smyrnaeans adopt the converse strategy (56.1–2). 'Chaque cité développe les points qui lui sont favorables' (Pernot 1.186). For the repetition *–ge ge–* (as of *ciuitate templum* and *nutauisse sedes* above) see 13.2n.

ob multitudinem diuissise gentem Menander deals with the question of whether a community resulted from 'colonisation or union or transference' etc. (355.13ff.), and he recognised the role that 'division' of one sort or another could play (357.21). Overcrowding is a standard element in foundation stories (e.g. Vell. 1.4.3 'magna uis Graecae iuuentutis abundantia uirium sedes quaeritans in Asiam se effudit', Sen. *Cons. Helv.* 7.4 'alios nimia superfluentis populi frequentia ad exonerandas uires emisit', Just. 24.4.1 'abundante multitudine'): Menander has no specific rules for this topic, although many of his references to 'growth' are relevant.

ducum e nominibus indita uocabula Naming and changes of name are essential ingredients of foundation legends (see e.g. N. Horsfall, 'Aeneas the colonist', *Vergilius* 35 (1989) 18 and 22), as Menander recognised (355.24ff.). Tyrrhenia, the alternative (Grecising) name for Etruria (Ov. *Met.* 14.452), indicates its establishment by Tyrrhenus.

---

[106] The praise of cities and the praise of countries tend to be mentioned alongside each other (e.g. Quint. 3.7.26–7, Menand. 332.9–10), and Menander recognised that the one is often subsumed in the other (344. 12–14; Pernot 1.203). In addition to the commentary on Menander by Russell and Wilson, and the older works by Kier (41.3n.) and Kienzle, see I. H. M. Hendriks et al., *ZPE* 41 (1981) 74–5, and Pernot 1.178–216, who notes (2.713 n. 240) the role played by encomium in the making of requests, including the present example.

cui mox a Pelope nomen The antecedent of *cui* is not strictly *Graeciam* but, as Pfitzner suggests, that part of Greece which later took its name from Pelops (a kind of *constructio ad sensum*).

55.4 litteras . . . bello Macedonum No evidence of the generals' letters or of the treaties during the war with Perseus seems to have survived, although we do have the text of an asylum document from Julius Caesar, dated 11 days before his murder (3.63.3n.; Rigsby 433–7). *Macedonum* is a unique and characteristically Tacitean variant on the regular *bellum Macedonicum* (see also above, 36.2n.).

ubertatemque fluminum suorum, temperiem caeli ac dites circum terras Each of these three elements was a standard encomiastic topos: water supply, including rivers (Menand. 345.2, 346.4–7, 347.7–8, 349.25–9); climate (345.30–1, 348.1–2, 383.12–13, 25–6); and (surrounding) countryside, especially if fertile (345.2–3, 12–13, 346.4–7). Since the principal river of Sardis was the Pactolus, it may be that *ubertatem* refers to the proverbial gold with which it flowed (see e.g. Watson on Hor. *Epod.* 15.20; Otto 261), although *OLD* refers simply to the river's inexhaustible supply of water (2): 'ancient taste, accustomed to river-beds that were nearly empty in summer, found all large rivers in imagination beautiful' (Mynors on Virg. *G.* 2.137). See further on this topic J. E. Lendon, *Chiron* 45 (2015) 127–32, with ample bibliography (145–9). A temperate climate (εὐκρασία) was naturally regarded as highly desirable, and 'the form *temperies* was frequently used . . . in the discussion of climatic perfection' (Thomas 12, q.v. pp. 3 and 11–12; Kienzle 16–17, 27–8; Pernot 1.206–7); the combination with *caeli* first appears in Ov. *Ex P.* 2.7.71 and is esp. common in the elder Pliny. Aeschylus' description of Sardis as πολύχρυσοι (*Pers.* 45) perhaps refers to its fame as the place where coinage was invented (I. Carradice and M. Price, *Coinage in the Greek World* (1988) 23–4, G. Le Rider, *La naissance de la monnaie* (2001) 47): this may also be the point of *dites* here, although the adj. may refer simply to natural fertility (cf. e.g. Virg. *G.* 2.136 'ditissima terra'), of which Strabo speaks highly in the case of the area around Sardis (13.4.5). *circum* (adjectival: cf. 25.1n.) implies the centrality of the city of Sardis itself (cf. Pernot 1.205–6).

56.1 Zmyrnaei repetita uetustate The tracing back of their antiquity is elaborated by the Smyrnaeans in the following alternative clauses (hence the subjunctive *condidisset*). For the Smyrnaeans (*BA* Maps 56: E5, 57: F3) see 3.63.3n.

diuina et ipse stirpe *et ipse* (= *item*) is a mannerism of T. (e.g. *Agr.* 25.4), as of Livy, the elder Pliny and Quintilian (Gudeman on *D.* 30.1).

una Amazonum The eponymous Smyrna (Strabo 11.5.4, 12.3.21, 14.1.4, Plin. *NH* 5.118).

267

transcendere 'passed on' (*OLD* 5a); the form is presumably historic inf., though perf. indic. clearly cannot be excluded.

in populum Romanum officiis As with Sardis (above), no epigraphical evidence of Smyrna's services to Rome survives. *officiis* is abl. because (oddly) in apposition to *quis*; the meaning is not that some services to Rome were more telling than others but that all their various services to Rome constituted the evidence on which they relied most.

non modo externa ad bella sed quae in Italia tolerabantur Respectively against Antiochus in 191–188 BC (see e.g. Liv. 37.16.1, 37.54.1, 38.39.11) and the Social War of 91–88 BC. For *bella . . . tolerabantur* cf. H. on *H.* 4.68.1.

M. Porcio consule Cato the Censor was consul in 195 BC.

stante adhuc Punica urbe St Augustine at *Civ. Dei* 2.18, after claiming to be reporting Sallust ('ipsum Sallustium testem potius adhibebo'), continues as follows: 'cum . . . causam . . . huius boni non amorem iustitiae sed stante Carthagine metum pacis infidae fuisse dixisset'. Since the phrases *infida pax* and *stantis . . . Carthaginis* occur in close proximity in Velleius (1.12.6–7), who often imitates Sallust, W. V. Clausen argued that Augustine's quotation of at least these two phrases was accurate and that Maurenbrecher was correct in restoring the sequence *stante Carthagine metus pacis infidae* at Sall. *H.* 1.11 M ('Notes on Sallust's *Historiae*', *AJP* 68 (1947) 300–1). Although *stare* is often used of cities (*OLD* 15), and although the abl. abs. *stante urbe* occurs 3× in Cicero, there can be little doubt both that T. is here echoing Sallust ('allusion with substitution') and that Maurenbrecher's hypothesis was correct.[107]

ualidis per Asiam regibus Asia did not become a Roman province until 133 BC.

56.2 L. Sullam The mention of Sulla indicates that the reference is to the First Mithridatic War of 89–85 BC (*MRR* 2.58).

56.3 patres Zmyrnaeos praetulere According to Aelius Aristides, a resident of the city, 400 senators voted in favour of Smyrna, the other ten cities receiving a combined total of only 7 votes (*Or.* 19.13: see Talbert 149 and 281, who assumes that 'the natural conclusion must be that the *sententia* in favor of Smyrna was put first, thereby resolving the matter without further ado'). The Smyrnaeans' success was celebrated by the issue of a coin bearing on the obverse the heads of the senate and Livia, together with the legend Σεβαστή Σύνκλητος, and, on the reverse, the name and figure of Tiberius in front of

---

[107] Reynolds in the OCT of Sallust (1.11) admits the words to his text, Ramsey in the Loeb (1.9R) does not.

a temple (B. V. Head and R. S. Poole, *Catalogue of the Greek coins of Ionia* (repr. 1964) p. 268).

Vibius Marsus See 4.6.2n. (*mandabat*), 6.47.2n.

M. Lepido See 20.2n.

templi curam For the temple see Price 185, 258 no. 45.

Valerius Naso A gentleman from Verona (Syme, *RP* 2.716): see *PIR* 8.2. 93–4 no. 151.

57–59.2 Tiberius leaves Rome
The building of a temple in Asia (55–6) leads to the dedicating of temples in Campania (57.1); but T. makes it clear that the dedications are just an excuse ('specie') for some more permanent withdrawal: 'certus procul urbe degere'. In anticipation of the *princeps*' eventual seclusion on Capri, to which the present departure from Rome is merely the prelude, T. discusses his motivation (57.1–3) and reports on the predictions by which his departure was attended (58.1–3). The one certainty was that Tib. would never return, although the famous episode in the seaside grotto at Spelunca convinced many people that he was soon to die (59.1). Their conviction was mistaken: the episode merely resulted in an increase in the power of Sejanus (59.2). As it happens, Sejanus does not feature in the account of these same events by Suetonius (*Tib.* 39–40), whose narrative is otherwise close to that of T.; but, whereas Suetonius deals with the *princeps*' protracted withdrawal in a single episode, T. is more diverse and, by means of an overarching ring composition, traces into the following year Tib.'s progress towards eventual retirement (see *Tac. Rev.* 142–9).

57.1 Inter quae suggests, if taken literally, that the *princeps* left Rome during the debate which he had been attending assiduously over several days in order to divert attention from the unwelcome rumour of his murderous intentions towards his daughter-in-law (54.2–55.1).

diu meditato prolatoque saepius consilio Suetonius says that, when Tib. became emperor in 14, he expressed the intention of retiring at some point in the future (Suet. *Tib.* 24.2 'recepit imperium, nec tamen aliter quam ut depositurum se quandoque spem faceret. Ipsius uerba sunt: "Dum ueniam ad id tempus quo uobis aequum possit uideri dare uos aliquam senectuti meae requiem"'). T. mentions no such intention at the time of Tib.'s accession (1.13.5) but appears to do so under AD 21, when the *princeps* had made an earlier departure for Campania (3.31.2 'Tiberius ... in Campaniam concessit, longam et continuam absentiam paulatim meditans'). On that occasion Tib. was forced to return in the following year because of an illness of his mother's (3.64.1), and it may be suggested that this 'abortive retirement' (so to speak) helps to explain the phrase *prolato ... saepius* here;

another occasion, when Tib. was evidently about to withdraw in the immediate aftermath of Sejanus' persuasion but had changed his mind, had arisen in AD 25 (see 42.1n. *cunctantem*). T. elsewhere uses *saepe* to refer to no more than two occasions (see 3.18.1n., 4.4.2n.).

tandem Caesar <proficiscitur> in Campaniam The text as transmitted has no verb. Syme believed that this gave a 'strong emphasis' to the crucial episode which follows (*Tac.* 524);[108] Furneaux, on the other hand, thought it very odd that 'the prominent thought of the whole passage' should be introduced by a verb which is missing. Is the transmitted text right? Among more recent edd. the omission is retained by Fisher, Fuchs, Koestermann, Heubner and Borzsák, the last of whom praises 'die kühne Auslassung' (*Gnomon* 56 (1984) 401). In defence of the omission it is conventional to say that T. is imitating Sall. *J.* 100.1 'dein Marius, uti coeperat, in hiberna', which is duly quoted by Koestermann; but, when Koestermann came to annotate that passage in his commentary on Sallust (1971), he had changed his mind and printed Dietsch's *in hiberna <pergit>.*[109] The issue is not easy, since ellipse in general, and of verbs in particular, is a recognised feature of T.'s style: see B. Clemm, *De breviloquentiae taciteae quibusdam generibus* (1881) 42ff. Elsewhere in T. the omission of a verb of motion is coupled with *in* + acc. at e.g. 4.59.1 'hinc metus in omnes' and 6.50.5 'pauor hinc in omnes', and, although Clemm (59) thought the latter sufficient justification for retaining the paradosis in our passage, many readers would accept that those passages are significantly easier. Numerous supplements have been proposed, but it is naturally impossible to know what T. wrote; if *proficiscitur* were to have been omitted after *Caesar*, it would provide a link with *profectio* at 58.1, where the main narrative resumes after the parenthetic *Causam abscessus . . . reposcebat.*[110]

specie dedicandi templa apud Capuam Ioui, apud Nolam Augusto The temple at Capua is assumed to have been dedicated on 13 September (the Ides was Jupiter's day); since only about 25 miles along the Via Popilia separate Capua from Nola, where Augustus had died on 19 August 14 (cf. 1.5.3, 1.9.1), the dedication there may have taken place later the same month (see Bernecker 9 n. 3, with further refs.). For the latter temple, evidently based on the house where Augustus had died (Dio 56.46.3), see Hänlein-Schäfer 129–30. T. returns to the dedications, ring fashion, at 67.1

---

[108] Syme also saw a parallel with Hadrian's journey to Campania in AD 119.
[109] One of the other passages quoted in defence of the ellipse is Liv. 41.3.5, where the omission of a verb is supported by Briscoe ad loc. but not by S. P. Oakley (*CQ* 44 (1994) 179–80).
[110] Seneca tells us that L. Piso was entrusted with secret orders by 'Tiberius proficiscens in Campaniam' (*Ep.* 83.14) but there is no indication whether he is referring to the present withdrawal or to that in 21 (3.31.2).

(AD 27); Suetonius agrees with him that they were a pretext for the *princeps'* departure (*Tib.* 40 'quam causam profectionis praetenderat'): for a schematic comparison of the two historians' narratives at this point see *Tac. Rev.* 142–5.

sed certus procul urbe degere Sejanus' plan had been 'ut Tiberium ad uitam procul Roma . . . degendam impelleret' (41.1). For intrans. *degere* see *OLD* 2a; *certus* + infin. occurs only in poetry before T. (*OLD* 10a).

Causam abscessus quamquam secutus plurimos auctorum ad Seiani artes rettuli, quia tamen caede eius patrata sex postea annos pari secreto coniunxit, plerumque permoueor num ad ipsum referri uerius sit Two explanations are given for Tib.'s retirement from Rome: the first is the wiles of Sejanus; the second is a predisposition on the part of Tib. himself (*ipsum*). The relationship between these two gives rise to various problems.

Since Syme believed that T.'s reference to Rhodes at §2 below was a later addition to the narrative (see ad loc.), it seems to follow, as outlined by T. J. Luce ('Tacitus' conception of historical change', in *Past perspectives* (ed. Moxon, Smart and Woodman, 1986) 154), that in Syme's view the present sentence must also be the result of T.'s second thoughts, since it negotiates the transition between what T. has hitherto believed to be the explanation for Tib.'s withdrawal ('Seiani artes') and what he now believes to be the explanation (*ipsum*). Yet there are two reasons why Syme's thesis cannot stand. (a) At 3.31.2 (quoted above) T. says that Tib. was already thinking about withdrawal in AD 21, four years before Sejanus applied his dark arts to the *princeps* at 4.41.1–3. (b) In the present passage T. says that he has 'often' been moved to consider whether the explanation for Tib.'s withdrawal was the man's own predisposition: *plerumque permoueor* is inconsistent with the notion that T. came to this explanation only at a late stage.

Although the two explanations are presented as contrasting alternatives (*quamquam ~ tamen*), the fact is that they are not mutually exclusive but rather complementary, as Luce pointed out (155). It is perfectly possible both that Tib. was predisposed to retirement and that he was encouraged in his predisposition by Sejanus. T.'s sentence may be paraphrased as follows: 'although I ascribed Tib.'s departure at this moment to the wiles of Sejanus, subsequent events showed that he was likely to have departed at some point anyway'. The six years of solitude after Sejanus' death (AD 31–37) are adduced as confirmation of the view which T. has held all along and to which he alluded four years earlier at 3.31.2, namely, that the *princeps* was destined to withdraw from Rome.

secutus plurimos auctorum Mention of 'the majority of authors' (for which convention see 10.1n.) acts as a foil not only for T.'s own view but also for those other, unnamed authors who lie behind *Erant qui crederent* and *Traditur etiam* below (2–3).

caede . . . patrata is an expr. not found before T. (H. on *H.* 4.61.1).

sex postea annos pari secreto coniunxit probably means 'afterwards he spent six continuous years in identical seclusion' (*OLD coniungo* 6) rather than that he joined six later years on Capri to those he had already spent there.

plerumque permoueor num . . . is extremely condensed for 'Often I am/have been moved to ask whether . . .'. Many scholars compare the use of *adducor = adducor ut existimem* (for which see Pease on Cic. *Div.* 1.35, Madvig on *Off.* 1.14; A. E. Housman, *Classical Papers* (1972) 1153–4); Draeger–Heraeus compare Caes. *BG* 4.14.2 'perturbantur copiasne . . . ducere an castra defendere an fuga salutem petere praestaret', which is easier because the same subject is effectively maintained in the subordinate clause. On the other hand, the presence of *num* makes our passage a much less difficult case than 6.22.3 (n.).

saeuitiam ac libidinem, cum factis promeret, locis occultantem In the years 29–31, according to his obituary notice (6.51.3), the *princeps* was encouraged in his *saeuitia* by his affection for Sejanus, while his fear of Sejanus compelled him to cover up his *libidines*; but, after Sejanus' death in 31, he had no further need to hide his *libidines*. The present passage means simply that, living on Capri, Tib. was distanced from the reign of terror in Rome and was able to satisfy his private lusts away from the public gaze. Many of the victims of the reign of terror were former associates of Sejanus: this explains why, at the start of Book 4, Sejanus' death is said to have been as murderous as his life (2.1). For *saeuitiam ac libidinem* cf. 6.6.2n.

57.2 Erant qui crederent in senectute corporis quoque habitum pudori fuisse . . . et Rhodi secreto uitare coetus, recondere uoluptates insuerat 'Something has gone wrong. The allusion to Rhodes and secret pleasures is not in the right place', says Syme (*Tac.* 695), adding that it ought to have come immediately after *locis occultantem* above. The sentence was indeed transposed there by three scholars independently: H. Cron (1874), K. Zacher (1883), and J. P. V. D. Balsdon (*CR* 61 (1947) 44–5, with further bibliographical details); Syme himself, however, preferred to think in terms of the author's second thoughts, mistakenly inserted in the wrong place (ibid.; cf. 286 and 425 n. 5).[111] Yet none of this is necessary, since nothing has gone wrong.

Erant qui crederent . . . insuerat is exactly parallel to *Traditur etiam . . . reposcebat* at §3 below: both passages begin by reporting the views of others, and within

---

[111] Unsurprisingly it is difficult to know exactly what Syme thought, since he uses a slightly different form of words on each occasion; and in any case the whole issue is bound up with his conviction that T. came to believe that he had started the *Annals* at the wrong point (see 3.24.3n.).

both passages T. produces evidence corroborating those views, on the first occasion introduced by *et* (= *et quidem*: see 5.10.1n.), on the second by *Nam*. Those designated by *Erant qui crederent* held the same view as just expressed by T. himself in §1, namely, that on Capri the *princeps* was hiding his savagery and lust, but they *also* believed that in his old age Tib.'s physical disadvantages were an *additional* reason for his withdrawal ('in senectute corporis *quoque* habitum'); and T. then corroborates their view by pointing out that *both* elements of their belief – one of which they share with T. himself – are paralleled (chiastically) by Tib.'s *two* habits on Rhodes: his avoidance of crowds is evidence that he may well have been ashamed of physical disadvantages even in his younger days (*uitare coetus ~ pudori fuisse*), while his hiding his pleasures is evidence that then too he was addicted to vices which required secrecy (*recondere uoluptates ~ libidinem . . . locis occultantem*). *saeuitia* is not mentioned because there was no suggestion that Tib. practised savagery during his sojourn on Rhodes.[112] Thus the passage is to be read as follows: 'There were those who believed that in his old age his physical appearance too had been a source of shame (for . . .); and indeed in the seclusion of Rhodes he had been accustomed to avoid crowds as well as conceal his pleasures.'[113]

quippe illi praegracilis ... interstincta This sentence constitutes a parenthetical explanation of *Erant . . . pudori fuisse*. The adj. *praegracilis* occurs only here.

[112] The references to *saeuitia* and *ira* at 1.4.3–4 are in *oratio obliqua*.

[113] Two alternative interpretations of this difficult passage may be registered. (a) M. R. Comber ('Parenthesis in Tacitus', *RhM* 119 (1976) 182–3) argued that *Erant . . . interstincta* forms a parenthesis, while the statement about Rhodes (below) 'is circumstantial evidence adduced in support of Tacitus' interpretation of the Emperor's retirement'. This view, with which R. H. Martin agreed, is difficult for two reasons. [i] *Erant qui crederent . . . interstincta* cannot be both parenthetic and parallel to *Traditur etiam . . .* below. [ii] The description of *Erant . . . interstincta* as a parenthesis does little to help the integration of *et Rhodi . . . insuerat*. (b) In 1989 I suggested that *Erant . . . pudori fuisse* is concessive and acts as a foil for the statement about Rhodes, the phrase *in senectute* being picked up by *Rhodi secreto*, referring to Tib.'s younger days: 'There were those who believed that in his old age his physical appearance too had been a source of shame (for . . .); and yet in the seclusion of Rhodes he had been accustomed to avoid crowds and conceal his pleasures.' This view avoids each of the objections to which (a) was vulnerable; the problem is that *et Rhodi* has to be regarded as adversative, and, although there are plenty of parallels for *et* = *et tamen* in T. (1.13.2n.; G–G 397b–8a), it cannot be denied that this would be an esp. difficult example.

incurua proceritas According to pseudo-Aristotle, the shameless man is μικρὸν ἔγκυρτος· . . . τῷ σχήματι μὴ ὀρθὸς ἀλλὰ μικρῷ προπετέστερος (*Physiog.* 807b30); Suetonius in his description of Tib. (see further n. 114) refers to 'statura quae iustam excederet' (*Tib.* 68.1).

nudus capillo uertex 'Bald men were common enough at Rome. Only one of them will be admitted to the dignified pages of the senatorial annalist, and the word *caluus* is eschewed: instead, a poetical periphrasis alludes to the denuded summit of a Roman emperor' (Syme, *Tac.* 343). *nudus uertex* first appears at Virg. *Aen.* 11.642 and then mostly in first-century epic (e.g. Sil. 4.751), in all of which places it refers to the absence of head-gear.

ulcerosa facies ac plerumque medicaminibus interstincta *medicamen* and *medicamentum* are synonyms, the latter being many times the more common in prose writers (exclusively so in the case of the technical authors Celsus and Scribonius Largus), though *medicamen* is the preferred form in verse (statistics in *TLL* 8.529.34–55). The only prose author in whom the two words are used roughly equally is Columella; for those who prefer *medicamen* the statistics are meaningless (Petronius 2:1; Florus 1:0). Though T. often likes the 'weighty ending' *–mentum* (Syme, *Tac.* 341), he predictably chooses *medicamen* exclusively and, apart from Florus, is the only prose author to do so (5:0). Twice he uses it of healing agencies (12.51.4, 14.6.3), twice of poison (12.67.1, 14.51.1); in our passage it is used either of salves or cosmetics, underlining the point that in the ancient world it was very often difficult to distinguish between the two (in general see K. Olson, 'Cosmetics in Roman antiquity: substance, remedy, poison', *CW* 102 (2009) 291–310, esp. 304–5): Juvenal capitalises on this ambiguity when he jokes about women who apply so much make-up that their face looks as though it is one big sore (6.473 'facies dicetur an ulcus?'). Tib. ought to have the look of a ruler (15.3n.); instead he resembles the slave Thallus in Apuleius (*Apol.* 43 'facie ulcerosus'), his face blotchy ('interstincta') with *medicamina*. That the *princeps* did indeed suffer from facial blemishes is also said by Suetonius (*Tib.* 68.2 'facie honesta, in qua tamen crebri et subiti tumores'),[114] and Galen mentions a medicine specifically for 'Tiberius Caesar's ἕρπητες' (*Comp. Med.* 13, p. 836 K).[115] For

---

[114] 'The description of Tiberius in Suetonius provides the most striking example of an emperor whose physical merits and defects correspond from a physiognomical point of view to the virtues and vices of his character' (E. C. Evans, 'Roman descriptions of personal appearance in history and biography', *HSCP* 46 (1935) 68–70, at 68).

[115] Syme suggested (*RP* 3.1376–7) that Tib. suffered from the *mentagra* described by Pliny (*NH* 26.2–4). The suggestion is attractive, but Pliny dates the arrival of the affliction in Italy to midway through Tib.'s reign,

the 'reality' cf. L. Polacco, *Il volto di Tiberio* (1955), D. Hertel, *Die Bildnisse des Tiberius* (2013).

et Rhodi secreto uitare coetus, recondere uoluptates insuerat This is the only occasion in *Annals* 1–6 on which there is arguably a direct contradiction between the main narrative and Tib.'s obituary. According to the obituary, the period before Tiberius' accession was 'egregium uita famaque' (6.51.3), whereas here Tacitus refers to hidden pleasures. To escape this contradiction, if such it is, one would presumably have to assume that the *uoluptates* of a middle-aged *priuatus* did not merit the censure of an elderly emperor's *libidines* on Capri.

For this episode in the *princeps'* life see now M. Peachin, 'Tiberius on Rhodes', in F. M. Simón et al. (edd.), *Autorretratos: La creación de la imagen personal en la antigüedad* (2016) 129–42.

57.3 matris impotentia extrusum The same reason for Tib.'s departure is given by Suet. *Tib.* 51.1 and Dio 57.12.6; see also e.g. 3.64.2n. *impotentia* is a common attribute of women (e.g. Liv. 34.2.2); for its application to Livia see 1.4.5n.

quam dominationis sociam aspernabatur neque depellere poterat For Livia as Tib.'s *socia* and the apparent paradox of T.'s statement see 6.51.3n. (*idem*).

dubitauerat Augustus Germanicum, sororis nepotem et cunctis laudatum, rei Romanae imponere 'Augustus had considered appointing …' (*OLD dubito* 4). Cf. Suet. *Cal.* 4 'sic probatus et dilectus a suis ut Augustus … diu cunctatus an sibi successorem destinaret, adoptandum Tiberio dederit'. Germanicus was the son of Antonia *minor*, daughter of Octavia's second marriage (to Mark Antony).

precibus uxoris euictus For a later occasion when Livia's *preces* were again effective see 3.17.1 and n. For the expr. cf. Liv. 38.9.7, Val. Max. 6.5 *ext.* 3, Sen. *Med.* 184, [Quint.] *Decl.* 9.8, Suet. *Tib.* 37.2.

Tiberio Germanicum, sibi Tiberium adsciuit The verb must here mean 'associated' (cf. *OLD* 1a), with *per adoptionem* understood in each case (cf. 1.3.5). The order of words is significant: Tib. had to adopt Germanicus before he was himself adopted by Augustus; 'he could not do so legally afterwards, as he was no longer *paterfamilias*' (B. M. Levick, '"Julians and Claudians"', *G&R* 22 (1975) 30). Both adoptions took place in AD 4 (1.3.3, 1.3.5): see Seager 30–1, 216.

whereas the above interpretation of *Erant qui crederent* . . . requires that Tib. was already disfigured during his sojourn on Rhodes many years earlier.

58.1 Profectio arto comitatu fuit T. now resumes his main narrative after the discursive discussion of the reasons for Tib.'s departure (57.1–3 'Causam abscessus . . . reposcebat'). The reference to a restricted entourage, though seemingly borne out by the short list that follows, is nevertheless misleading: once ensconced on Capri, Tib. had frequent visits from family members and others, and the upkeep of the court would require a substantial staff (Houston 183–5, 187–91). *artus* = 'containing few members, small in number' (*OLD* 7); the abl. is one of description.

Cocceius Nerua had been suffectus in 21 or 22 and was currently *curator aquarum* (Front. *Aq.* 102.4). See 6.26.1n.

eques Romanus . . . ex inlustribus Curtius Atticus Later we are told that Vescularius Flaccus (identified as an *eques* at 2.28.1) and Iulius Marinus, who had been with Tib. on Rhodes, were 'inseparable' from him on Capri (6.10.2, where Curtius Atticus' elimination by Sejanus is also referred to: see nn.). For the elliptical *ex inlustribus* see 2.60.3n.; for *inlustris* used of *equites* see the discussion in Demougin, *OE* 594–8 ('*Illustris* . . . conserve une très forte connotation personnelle, élargie au-delà de l'origine familiale ou de statut étatique').

ceteri liberalibus studiis praediti, ferme Graeci, quorum sermonibus leuaretur Suetonius refers to 'conuictores Graeculi, quibus uel maxime adquiescebat' (*Tib.* 56), and says that the *princeps* 'artes liberales utriusque generis studiosissime coluit' (70.1); he was fluent in Greek (71.1) and particularly liked to discuss mythology (70.3): see in general Houston 182–3; M. Billerbeck, 'Philology at the imperial court', *G&R* 37 (1990) 191–203, esp. 196–7; also below, 59.1n. Champlin (2008: 411) notes it as a folklore motif that 'the king prefers educated men as company' (Stith Thompson J146.1). We know that the astrologer Thrasyllus (6.20.2n.) and the doctor Charicles (6.50.2n.) were with Tib. on Capri; and it is conjectured that a third Greek, Tiberius Iulius Pappus, acted as librarian (Houston 186, 189). *studiis (-o) praediti* is a Ciceronian expr. (plur. at *Cael.* 24, 54, *Fam.* 13.30.1). Although *liberalia studia* occurs elsewhere (e.g. Cic. *De Or.* 1.11, Vell. 1.13.3), including the Vindolanda Tablets (*Tab. Vind.* 3.660, more or less contemporary with T.'s writing of the *Annals*), it is overwhelmingly Senecan (almost 30×). For *sermone (–ibus) leuare* cf. Cic. *Att.* 1.18.1, Varro, *Menipp.* 421 Cèbe, Virg. *Aen.* 8.309. For *ferme* (with which we must here understand *omnes*) see 3.16.2n.

58.2 periti caelestium *caelestia* = 'astronomy' (*OLD* 4c). Cf. Liv. 1.34.9 'Tanaquil, perita . . . caelestium prodigiorum mulier'. For Tib. and astrology see 6.20.2–21.3nn.

motibus siderum The professionals' quasi-technical language (H. on *H.* 2.78.1) forms a contrast with the false inferences which were drawn from their predictions (next n.).

multis . . . uulgantibusque Although *multis* could refer to a sub-group of the astrologers just mentioned, it seems more likely that T. is referring to those who jumped to rash conclusions from the astrologers' predictions (cf. Suet. *Tib.* 39 'constanti et opinione et sermone paene omnium quasi neque rediturus umquam et cito mortem etiam obiturus'). For the 'verbal hyperbaton' see 3.1.1n.

incredibilem casum Cf. Cic. *Fam.* 15.2.8. For *prouidebant* cf. [Quint.] *Decl.* 274.9.

ut . . . libens patria careret *patria carere* is a set expr. which is often associated with exile or means 'to be in exile' (*TLL* 3.453.3ff.), and it is so used of their own exiles by the famous outcasts Cicero (e.g. *Sest.* 49, 145, *Att.* 3.26) and Ovid (e.g. *Tr.* 1.5.39, 4.9.12). *libens* indicates the paradox that in Tib.'s case the 'exile' was his own choice.

58.3 Mox patuit breue confinium artis et falsi After his remarks on the misguided *multi*, T. now returns to the astrologers. *breue* here means 'narrow', as 6.33.3 'breuia litorum', and *patuit* means 'was visible' (*OLD* 6).

ueraque quam obscuris tegerentur The terms are natural opposites in the case of prophecies, oracles and the like (e.g. Cic. *Div.* 2.115 'oraculis . . . partim casu ueris . . . partim . . . obscuris'), but it is difficult not to think that T.'s mind is already on caves (59.1n., below) and hence on Virgil's Sibyl (*Aen.* 6.100 'obscuris uera inuoluens'). For the *uariatio* of noun ~ indir. qu. see 3.10.3n.

ceterorum nescii egere Hartman (175–6) proposed to read *ceteri* here, on the grounds that the astrologers had confined themselves to the statement that Tib. would never return to the city, as T. has just repeated ('in urbem . . . haud forte dictum'). But this is to mistake T.'s point, which is that, although the astrologers were right in their prediction, they were very nearly wrong: the meaning is 'but they acted in ignorance of other factors'. Besides, it is almost impossible to imagine *ceteri* being changed by mistake to *ceterorum*.

propinquo rure aut litore et saepe moenia urbis adsidens Cf. 6.1.1 'saepe in propinqua degressus, aditis iuxta Tiberim hortis', 15.3 'deuiis plerumque itineribus ambiens patriam et declinans', 39.1 'urbem iuxta', Dio 58.1 *init.* οὐκέτι τὸ παράπαν ἐς τὴν πόλιν ἀνεκομίσθη, καίτοι μέλλων τε ἀεὶ καὶ ἐπαγγελλόμενος. *adsidens* suggests 'besieging' (as 6.43.1 'adsidendo castellum'), as if Tib. kept returning from exile to lay siege to the walls of the very city from which he was supposed to govern.[116] There is some irony in the fact that the

---

[116] In Book 6 there develops the complementary notion that Tib. was waging war against his fellow citizens (Keitel 307, 317ff.).

wording here is picked up at the end of the book (74.3–4 'non tamen in urbem aut propinqua urbi degressi sunt . . . campo aut litore iacentes'), where the situation is exactly the opposite: the whole population of Rome has decamped to Campania to catch sight of Tib. and Sejanus. For the *uariatio* of abl. of place ~ adj./part. Sörbom (91) quotes only 15.43.4 'largior et pluribus locis'; for *senecta* see 50.2n. above.

59.1 oblatum Caesari anceps periculum auxit uana rumoris *uana rumoris* refers to the mistaken inference that Tib. would soon die (58.2): since the rumours were increased by the present dangerous episode ('auxit'), it seems to follow that *anceps* must primarily intensify *periculum* and mean something like 'critical' (*anceps* is listed in *TLL* 10.1.1467.71–2 under those terms 'quae periculum fere augent'); but, since the emperor in fact survived, *anceps* also functions as a sober (and almost self-reflexive) reminder that the episode was capable of more than one interpretation (*OLD anceps* 9). *uana rumoris* is a typically Tacitean variant on the Livian *uanus rumor* (Liv. 28.24.2, 33.44.7, 34.16.9); for the nominative use of the *ab urbe condita* construction see 3.24.1n.

praebuitque ipsi materiem cur amicitiae constantiaeque Seiani magis fideret At the end of the book Tib.'s friendship with Sejanus will be formally celebrated and cemented by an *ara amicitiae* (74.2); the disastrous nature of the minister's friendship, foreshadowed there (74.5), runs as a theme through Book 6 (7.2, 8.1–2, 14.1, 29.3). Surprisingly *constantia* seems not to be coupled thus with *amicitia* elsewhere, but cf. Cic. *Fam.* 5.8.5 'non solum amicitiae nostrae sed etiam constantiae meae causa'. On T.'s use of *materies/–a* see 1.32.1n.; *m. praebere* = 'to provide a reason' is regular, but *m.* followed by *cur* is unique (*TLL* 8.463.46ff., 465.44).

uescebantur in uilla cui uocabulum Speluncae, mare Amunclanum inter <et> Fundanos montes, natiuo in specu The background to this episode has been fully explored by Champlin (2013) in one of his brilliant contributions to the study of the Tiberian principate. If Suetonius is correct in saying that Tib. dined at Spelunca shortly after leaving Rome (*Tib.* 39 'paucos post dies'), one infers that he travelled directly down the Via Appia roughly a hundred miles south as far as Fundi, where he turned aside onto the coastal road which leads to Spelunca. Suet. says that Spelunca was part of a *praetorium* or imperial villa complex (ibid. 'in praetorio, cui Speluncae nomen est'), an estate which Tib. is likely to have inherited from his grandmother, Alfidia, who came from Fundi (Suet. *Tib.* 5). The estate evidently took its name from the grotto or natural cave which, like Marsden Grotto in the North East of England, faced out to sea from the shore-line and was a prominent feature. The cave is now famous for the series of monumental sculptures whose remains were discovered there sixty years ago and which were based on scenes from the *Odyssey* (see also A. F. Stewart, *JRS* 67 (1977) 76–90). Most (but not all) scholars agree that these sculptures were commissioned and positioned by the *princeps* himself, an expert in the details of Greek mythology (58.1n.) and inspired by his fascination with the *Odyssey* (which he could quote at will: 38.1n.), as if seeing in the hero a replica of himself, an island-dweller and wanderer (58.3; 6.1.1nn.), always searching for an elusive destination. Diners at the grotto had only to turn round to see, less than twenty miles away across the sea, Mons Circeius, identified as the home of Circe; to their right lay the town of Formiae, home of the Laestrygonians: Tib.'s grotto lay on the hero's original route and was a compellingly romantic location, a *lieu de mémoire* in a landscape of allusion.

mare Amunclanum inter <et> Fundanos montes T. elsewhere uses both *et* and *–que* with *inter* in anastrophe, as Orelli's collection of exs. makes plain; modern edd. prefer Bezzenberger's *et* because the word might easily have been omitted after *inter*.

It has to be said that T.'s orientation for Spelunca, though true, is very strange. Fundi is a well-known town on the Via Appia almost directly north of Spelunca, although T. with characteristic obliqueness refers not to the town itself but to the mountains surrounding it. The *mare Amunclanum* or *sinus Amyclanus* (Plin. *NH* 14.61) takes its name from a town (Amy(n)clae) which in the elder Pliny's time – and *a fortiori* in T.'s – had long since ceased to exist (*NH* 3.59, 8.104) and of which the location is unknown today. The assumption (see *BA* Map 44: D3) is that the *sinus Amyclanus* lay to the east of Caieta and hence that Amynclae lay to the SE of Fundi in the neighbourhood of Formiae, the next town along on the Via Appia, although Martial confusingly describes Amynclae in terms of Fundi, not Formiae (13.115.1 'Fundanis ... Amyclis'). T. thus appears to be locating Spelunca in terms of two oddly identified points on the Via Appia; but, since this section of the road is inland and bypasses Spelunca entirely, one would never know that the *princeps*' grotto was by the sea. On Amynclae see also Harrison on Virg. *Aen.* 10.564.

59.1–2 Eius os lapsis repente saxis obruit quosdam ministros: hinc metus in omnes et fuga eorum qui conuiuium celebrabant Suet. has guests killed as well (*Tib.* 39): 'incenante eo complura et ingentia saxa fortuito superne dilapsa sunt, multisque conuiuarum et ministrorum elisis praeter spem euasit'. The dining area seems to have been just outside the mouth of the cave (Champlin (2013) 211): a substantial rock-fall at the cliff face would explain why some persons were killed and some not; it would depend entirely on where each person happened to be at the time.

59.2 Seianus genu utroque et manibus super Caesarem suspensus M reads *uultuque*, which, unlike the two instrumental ablatives by which it is surrounded, would be abl. of respect: either Sejanus had his face suspended over that of Tib. or *suspensus* is literal with *genu* and *manibus* but metaphorical with *uultu* ('with anxiety written all over his face'). Neither of these interpretations can be paralleled or seems at all likely, and in 1989 I suggested emending to *utroque*: Sejanus is crouched over his master. T. elsewhere places this adj. before the noun, as does Statius in a comparable phrase (*Theb.* 6.679–80 'humique | pressus utroque genu'), but the proposed order is otherwise acceptable (cf. Hyg. *Astr.* 4.2 'genu utrumque', Plin. *NH* 11.250 'in ipsa genus utriusque commissura').

opposuit se incidentibus sc. *saxis*. It is difficult to see how Sejanus' action could afford any real protection against any but the smallest flying stones; he is not mentioned in Suetonius' account of the incident.

a militibus qui subsidio uenerant Soldiers are again mentioned at 67.1, and we may assume that they were constantly in the immediate vicinity of the *princeps* to protect him. Cf. also 6.15.2n.

Maior 'more influential' (*OLD magnus* 12a, *maior* 6a).

59.3–60 Accusers, Sejanus and Nero Caesar
Although it seems natural to infer from the preceding section that the following events took place after Tib.'s departure for Campania, of which the seemingly inevitable consequence is that Nero Caesar had accompanied his grandfather on his journey (so e.g. Seager 270 n. 88), Rome seems the more likely backdrop for the street scenes, the repeated encounters with Tib., and the assembly of family members (60.2). Indeed the whole section appears (as it were) unchronological and extended, a generalised description stretching back before Tib.'s departure (59.3 *Adsimulabatque . . .*) and after it, as Sejanus, who was with Tib. at Spelunca, no doubt commuted to and fro between the capital and Campania. Only with *Fine anni* (61), a marker of narrative time rather than of 'real' time, do we return to the main storyline. (See also Koestermann on 60.2.)

Wherever the section is set, there can be no doubting its graphic brilliance. Sejanus not only takes on the principal role himself (59.3 'partes') but his fans (60.2 'fautores'), as if they were mere puppets, are manipulated to play their supporting roles too (59.3, 60.2). The street scenes are as vivid as any drama, a comedy for the spectators but a tragedy for the victim, in whom alarm induces hallucinations (60.1 'diuersae . . . sollicitudinum formae'). The *princeps*' grimness is genuine, his beaming false; no matter what Nero does, he is regarded as guilty. Even his wife betrays his night-time confidences, while his brother Drusus, treated by Sejanus like a hungry dog, is thrown the sop of supplanting him ('spe obiecta principis loci').

59.3 **Ad**s**imulabatque uindicis partes a**d**uersum Germanici stirpem** 'And he had been affecting the role of champion against the stock of Germanicus' (for the tense see above). M clearly reads *iudicis partes*, which Walther defends as follows: 'subornabat qui Germanici stirpem accusarent apud se et Tiberium . . ., ipse deinde cum Tiberio consultabat de criminibus et rogatus sententiam dicebat, tamquam ab omni partium studio alienus'. Although he did not quote it, Walther evidently envisaged a scenario such as that described at 11.3.1, where Claudius asks Vitellius his opinion about the doomed Asiaticus; but it seems to me impossible for the reader, who has not encountered a scene like that hitherto, to infer such a scene from the single word *iudicis*. Furneaux takes a similar view to Walther and compares 15.69.1 'non crimine, non accusatore existente, quia speciem iudicis induere non poterat'. Yet that passage is quite different from ours here. In Book 15 the would-be judge is Nero, who as emperor has the power to act as he likes: he would have preferred to pass judgement on Vestinus (and, of course, condemn him), but, in the absence of charge and accuser, there is no case to judge, and so he simply has him eliminated. But Sejanus has no power of his own, and pretending to act as a judge does nothing to further his ambitions; besides, the notion of judicial impartiality combines oddly with *aduersum*, which is naturally taken to mean 'against', and is not borne out by the subsequent narrative (59.3–60.3). Muretus' *indicis* is no improvement: Sejanus had others to do his informing for him, and his transmission of their information to Tib. was in no way a pretence. D. R. Shackleton Bailey ('Tacitea', in *Filologia e forme letterarie: studi offerti a F. Della Corte* (1987) 4.63–4) proposed *uindicis*, which gives Sejanus the role of acting as Tib.'s champion against the house of Germanicus during the *princeps'* absence from Rome; but his championing was of course a charade, because he was really clearing the way for himself. *uindicis* makes good sense, and Borzsák was right to print it.

su**bditis qui accusatorum nomina s**u**stinerent** Both *sustinerent* (*OLD* 5b) and *nomina* (*OLD* 15a) maintain the metaphor of play-acting: as is made clear in the sequel, these men in reality are Nero Caesar's freedmen and clients, whose loyalty to their patron ought to be absolute; but their ambition for power leads them to 'keep up their roles as accusers', prepared to bring formal (and false) testimony against him. *subdere* in the sense of sinisterly supplying agents and the like seems to be a Tacitean peculiarity (*OLD* 6; Malloch on 11.2.2); there is perhaps a suggestion that these men are Sejanus' puppets, manipulated by one who was himself playing a role (for the image see e.g. Muecke on Hor. *S.* 2.7.82).

proximum successioni Nero Caesar, born in AD 6, was a year older than his brother Drusus (60.2, below).

quid in praesentiarum conduceret 'what was appropriate at the present time' (*OLD conduco* 6b). Ritter wished to emend to *in praesentia* on the twin grounds that *rum* was wrongly repeated from *plerumque* and that *in praesentiarum* is simply too bizarre. It is true that there is a line-break between *praesentia* and *rum* in M, but it nevertheless seems wrong to change a word which occurs once each in Cato, Fannius, Nepos and *Rhet. Herenn.* before T. and becomes much commoner in later Latin (*TLL* 7.1.673.72–674.5). For various hypotheses concerning the origins of the term see G. Serbat, 'Un mot populaire ancien chez Tacite: *impraesentiarum*', in *Mélanges de littérature et d'épigraphie latines, d'histoire ancienne et d'archéologie: hommage à la mémoire de Pierre Wuilleumier* (1980) 325–30.

apiscendae *potentiae properis* 'hastening to acquire power': *properus*, another favourite term (52.1n.), is not elsewhere followed by a gerund(ive) (*TLL* 10.2.1988.36); whether the case is gen. or dat. is unclear. For *apiscor* see 3.31.2n.

ut erectum et fidentem animi ostenderet Pichena wished to read *animum*, but the gen. of reference (or perhaps locative: see Oakley on Liv. 6.36.8) with *fidens* is supported by Virg. *Aen.* 2.61 (where Horsfall's long n. mistakenly says that T. has the abl. here) and with *erectus* by Sil. 13.188. See also K–S 1.446–7. For the omission of *se* cf. 1.35.3n. *exstimulare* is nowhere else constructed with an indir. command (*TLL* 5.2.1911.71).

uelle . . . exercitus These arguments recall those addressed by the army to Nero Caesar's father, Germanicus, whom he strikingly resembled (15.3): cf. 1.35.3.

neque ausurum contra Seianum, qui nunc patientiam s_e_nis et segnitiam i_u_uenis i_u_xta insultet *patientia* is here 'apathy, passivity' (*TLL* 10.1.713.10–21; *OLD* 3c); *segnitia* suggests not only the idleness of youth (cf. *H.* 4.5.1) but also actual cowardice (*Agr.* 5.1n.). *contra*, though evidently regarded as the preposition in *TLL* 2.1257.30–1, is adverbial (as Plin. *NH* 32.53 'nihil contra belua audente'): 'nor would Sejanus dare any opposition' (for the adv. preceding an acc. cf. e.g. Cic. *Sest.* 103, *Bell. Alex.* 24.3, Liv. 7.39.17 'ni uenire contra exercitum . . . audissent'). Sejanus' alleged timidity seems contradicted by the contempt which he is said to be showing for Tib. and Nero Caesar alike ('qui . . . insultet'): perhaps the emphasis of the relative clause falls upon *nunc*, suggesting that his present abuse is mere braggadocio; things would be very different if Nero Caesar were to act.

The transferred use of *insulto* + acc. is an imitation of Sall. *H.* 2.23 M = inc. 42 R 'multos . . . bonos insultauerat' (*TLL* 7.1.2045.28–31).

60.1 Haec atque talia audienti For this formula see 6.22.1n.

uoces procedebant contumaces et inconsultae *procedebant* adds to the picture of Nero Caesar as lacking wilful intent. The verb is very rare of utterances but before T. cf. Sen. *NQ* 4 *praef.* 15 'nullum uerbum mihi quod non salua bona conscientia procederet excussum est' (*TLL* 10.2.1499.13ff.). For *contumacia*, also used of his mother (12.3), see Vielberg 173.

quas . . . auctasque cum deferrent The guards elaborated the statements between receiving them and passing them on: cf. the treatment meted out to Nero's brother, Drusus Caesar (6.24.1–3). *quas = et eas.*

diuersae insuper sollicitudinum formae oriebantur means 'in addition different kinds of anxiety arose' and is illustrated by the following sentence (*Nam*); but the reader is confronted momentarily by a scene like that described by Virgil in the unforgettable passage of *Aeneid* 6 where the ghostly personified forms of Grief and Care, Fear and Death, 'terribiles uisu formae' (277), rise up and terrify the hero. For *oriebantur* cf. Cic. *Acad.* 1.26 'ortae animantium formae earumque rerum quae gignuntur e terra'.

60.2 salutatione reddita 'after exchanging greetings' (Oakley on Liv. 9.6.12).

inceptum sermonem abrumpere Cf. Virg. *Aen.* 4.388, Sen. *Ira* 2.24.1 'ille me parum humane salutauit . . . ille inchoatum sermonem cito abrupit . . . illius uultus auersior uisus est', Quint. 4.3.13 'abrupto quem incohauerat sermone', Suet. *Tib.* 21.2.

***in*sistentibus contra *in*ridentibusque qui Seiano fautores aderant** *fautores* continues the theme of play-acting introduced at 59.3 above: Sejanus was there acting a part himself, but Roman actors were often also impresarios, and here he is the producer of a cruel comedy of which his supporters are bystanders, mocking the victim in the various scenes. *fautores aderant* recurs at 12.1.2 'huic . . . illi . . . fautores aderant' and is perhaps Sallustian (cf. *J.* 103.7 'fautor . . . adsit'), but in our passage the verb suggests 'being present as a spectator' as well as 'providing support for' (*OLD adsum* 5, 11a); the dat. *Seiano* is to be taken equally with *fautores* and *aderant* (cf. 6.36.3n.). For *insistentibus* cf. *TLL* 7.1.1923.80–1924.3.

Enimuero *T*iberius *t*oru̱u̱s aut falsum renidens u̱u̱ltu To the derision of the mockers are now added Tib.'s smiles – or his grim look. Smiling at people defined one as not being a tyrant (Plato, *Rep.* 566D προσγελᾷ τε καὶ ἀσπάζεται πάντας, ᾧ ἄν περιτυγχάνῃ, καὶ οὔτε τύραννός φησιν εἶναι); but the smiles of Nero's grandfather are characteristically false, and they alternate with the grim look of the tyrant (*Agr.* 45.2n.). T. perhaps borrowed some of his brilliant cameo from Sil. 13.374–5 'inde minaci | obtutu toruum contra et furiale renidens'; he was in his turn followed by Amm. 14.9.6 'toruum renidens'. Ritter wished to delete *uultu*, on the grounds that one does not smile with one's *uultus* and that the word started life as a marginal gloss on *toruus* but was absorbed into the text; but cf. Apul. *Met.* 3.12.1 'hilaro uultu renidens', Macrob. 1.2.10 'statimque uultu renidens' (also M. Beard, *Laughter in ancient Rome* (2014) 72–4, though she seems sceptical about whether Romans smiled at all). Whether *enimuero* = 'and in fact' (*OLD* 2) or 'on the other hand' (*OLD* 3) is not altogether clear (2.64.3n.).

seu loqueretur seu taceret iuuenis, crimen ex silentio, ex uoce Since speech defined a person as free (*Agr.* 2.3n.), it was dangerous to speak in the presence of the man who considered people his slaves; on the other hand, silence could be interpreted as an accusation of tyranny. Cf. Sen. *Contr.* 6.8 'Varius Geminus apud Caesarem dixit: "Caesar, qui apud te audent dicere magnitudinem tuam ignorant; qui non audent, humanitatem"'. *loqueretur* and *taceret* are frequentative subjunctives (6.4n.).

cum uxor uigilias, somnos, suspiria matri Liuiae . . . patefaceret His wife was Julia, daughter of Livi(ll)a and Drusus (Tib.'s son), whom he had married in 20 (3.29.3n.). *uigilias* and *somnos* are elliptical for the night-time revelations (in words or dreams) of Nero's periods of waking and sleeping; *suspiria* is presumably an exaggeration, like *Agr.* 45.2 'cum suspiria nostra subscriberentur'. Nipperdey–Andresen argue that *patefaceret* does not denote any hostility towards her husband: like everyone else, Julia is being manipulated, in this case by her mother.

in partes sc. *suas*, 'to his own side'.

spe obiecta principis loci Although *spem obicere* is a regular phrase (cf. Oakley on Liv. 6.14.12), the verb is also the *mot juste* for throwing food to a dog (e.g. Phaedr. 1.23.4, Sen. *Const. Sap.* 14.2, *Ira* 3.37.2, [Quint.] *Decl.* 298.10 'sicut muta animalia obiectis cibis in istam cecidisti seruitutem'): Sejanus treats Drusus like a hungry dog whose instincts can be used against him (see also below, 3n.). For dog imagery see R. Brock, *Greek political imagery from Homer to Aristotle* (2013) 118–19, 163–4, Fantham 112.

si priorem aetate et iam labefactum demouisset Nero Caesar is seen as an older and already unstable building which is occupying a desirable site (cf. Cic. *Phil.* 4.13 'quae numquam ui ulla labefactari potest, numquam demoueri loco'; Fantham 130). For *labefactum* see 6.29.3n.

60.3 Atrox . . . ingenium . . . accendebatur Livian (3.11.9), as also are *atrox ingenium* (7.4.3, 8.21.1) and *ingenium . . . accendi* (3.45.6).

cupidinem potentiae recurs only at *H.* 2.38.1 and is evidently the Tacitean form of others' *cupiditas p.* (Cic. *Off.* 1.26, Sen. *Const. Sap.* 2.2, Suet. *DJ* 50.1). See 1.3.6n.

solita fratribus odia See 3.8.1n.

promptior Neroni The dat. after *promptus* is common (46.2n.), but of a person is extremely rare: cf. Fronto p. 249.7–8 vdH² 'alieis non amantibus . . . promptus' (*TLL* 10.2.1888.10–14).

ut non in eum quoque semina futuri exitii meditaretur For similar metaphors see 27.1n., 6.47.2n.

praeferocem et insidiis magis opportunum Although *praeferox* is not used of animals apart from the elephants at Auson. *Epist.* 11.13 (p. 206G), and although the (more or less) set phrase *insidiis opportunus* (again at *H.* 3.20.2) is usually used of people or places, nevertheless both expressions would be equally suitable for sustaining the metaphor of Drusus as a dog (above, 2n.): 'Ferox' is regarded as a good name for a dog at Col. 7.12.13, while *insidiae* is the regular term for animal traps (*OLD* 3).

61 The end of the year

61 Fine anni excessere insignes uiri See 3.30.1n. for obituary notices at the end of a year.

claris maioribus quam uetustis Asinius Agrippa, consul in the previous year (34.1n.), was grandson of Asinius Pollio and M. Agrippa, both *noui homines*. His parents were Asinius Gallus and Vipsania, daughter of Agrippa and Caecilia Attica; since Vipsania's first marriage had been to Tib., he was also half-brother of Drusus, the *princeps'* recently deceased son. For the omission of *magis* or *potius* see K–S 2.463.

Q. Haterius Since his wife is thought to have been another daughter of Agrippa called Vipsania (Syme, *AA* 145–6), he was related to Asinius Agrippa above (see 44.2–3 for another obituary of relatives). Suffect in 5 BC, he was now almost 90. In T. he appears 'as a model of rash candour and flattery' (*BNP* 6.1 [2]); see 3.57.2n.; Syme, *TST* 88.

eloquentiae – quoad uixit – celebratae The younger Seneca referred to the 'rapidity' of Haterius, 'suis temporibus oratoris celeberrimi' (*Ep.* 40.10), a verdict of which T.'s could be a pointed variation. *eloquentiae . . . celebratae* is surprisingly unparalleled; *quoad uixit* (a very common phrase) is explained by what follows.

monumenta ingenii eius haud perinde retinentur *monumenta ingenii* is a standard expr. for 'literary works' (e.g. 15.41.1, *Agr.* 2.1 and n.); *monumenta . . . retinentur* recalls Cic. *Mil.* 104 'animi monumenta retinebitis': for *retineo* of retaining in the mind or memory see *OLD* 12. For the elliptical use of *haud perinde*, of which T. is fond, see 2.88.3n., where G. notes that 'Different ideas need to be supplied according to the context'; here Jackson has 'are not retained in equal esteem', but other supplements are also possible, e.g. 'are not retained as might have been expected'.

impetu magis quam cura uigebat This lapidary assessment is borne out by the much lengthier critique provided by Haterius' contemporary, the elder Seneca (*Contr.* 4 *praef.* 6–11), in which there are two occurrences (§§6 and 9) of the term *impetus*; the technical rhetorical meaning of the term is 'impulse' (see M. Winterbottom in *Ethics and rhetoric* (ed. Innes, Hine and Pelling, 1995) 313–22), but, since the word can be used of the violent movement of water or rivers (*OLD* 1), it also looks forward to *profluens* below. *uigere* can be used of literary survival (*OLD* 3b) but here refers to excellence in a particular field (*OLD* 2b).

utque aliorum meditatio et labor in posterum ualescit Strictly speaking, it is the *products* of *meditatio* and *labor* which survive to posterity, a similar ellipse to that which most scholars see at *D.* 30.2, 'eam disciplinam qua usos esse eos oratores accepimus quorum infinitus labor et cotidiana meditatio et in omni genere studiorum adsiduae exercitationes ipsorum etiam continentur libris' (the only other occasion on which these two terms are combined). If *labor* recalls the Callimachean πόνος, *meditatio* suggests the reflection and care of the Callimachean ἀγρυπνίη (for these terms see e.g. N. B. Crowther, *Mnem.* 31 (1978) 33–44; Brink on Hor. *AP* 291), although each had long since become the common parlance of literary criticism in general (see also next n.). That the clause constitutes 'Tacitus' testimony to his own quality' was suggested by Syme, the famous last words of whose *Tacitus* are perhaps also self-referential: 'Men and dynasties pass, but style abides' (624 and n. 3; cf. *TST* 89). *ualescere*, found earlier only at Lucr. 1.942 = 4.17 (a famous passage) and a favourite of T. (8×), occurs only in these two authors in classical Latin.

sic Haterii canorum illud et profluens cum ipso simul exstinctum est T. alludes to Cicero's appreciation of the orator Carbo at *De Or.* 3.28 'profluens quiddam habuit . . . et canorum' (Syme, *Tac.* 324, 727), except that for *quiddam . . . canorum* he has substituted the equally Ciceronian *canorum illud* (Cic. *Senec.* 28). *canorus* in Cicero, as elsewhere, is a term of praise, but can also be used of 'empty sound' (Hor. *AP* 322 and Brink's n.); *profluens* sums up Seneca's final words on Haterius (*Contr.* 4 *praef.* 11 'multa erant quae reprehenderes, multa quae suspiceres, cum torrentis modo magnus quidem sed turbidus flueret', an allusion to Horace's Callimachean criticism of Lucilius at *S.* 1.4.11 'cum flueret lutulentus, erat quod tollere uelles'): for this and related metaphors see G. Hays, 'Flumen orationis', in G. R. Wieland, C. Ruff and R. G. Arthur (edd.), *Insignis sophiae arcator* (2006) 1–27. It was always an author's fear that his works would not outlast him (e.g. Plin. *Ep.*

5.8.6 'ne tantus ille labor meus . . . mecum pariter intercidat'; R. Mayer, 'Pliny and *gloria dicendi*', *Arethusa* 36 (2003) 227–34).

62–67 THE YEAR AD 27

This year's narrative is the shortest in Book 4 and one of the shortest in the extant *Annals* (see 6.28–30 intro. n.); like the narrative of AD 23, it is concerned exclusively with domestic affairs.[117] The first two thirds of the narrative are devoted to twin disasters, one man-made (62–3) and the other natural (64–5). The collapse of a jerry-built amphitheatre, which is described at some length in terms reminiscent of a military disaster (62.1–63.1), is followed by precautionary measures for the future (63.1 'in posterum'), the generosity of leading men, and a comparison with the old days (63.2). Next a devastating fire at Rome, which is described scarcely at all (64.1), is followed by the generosity of the *princeps* (64.1–2), of which the future commemoration (64.3 'in posterum') leads to a comparison with the past and an antiquarian excursus (64.3–65). These disasters, deliberately presented as parallel to each other (cf. 64.1), constitute the central panel of an elaborate ring structure which began with Tib.'s dedication of Campanian temples in the previous year (57.1) and ends with a return to those same temples at 67.1 (see *Tac. Rev.* 149).

The final third of the year's narrative is taken up with accusations (66) and Tib.'s withdrawal to the island of Capri (67.1). The latter, the most momentous event of the reign, is marked by a formal description of the island as if it were a foreign country (67.1–3), underlining in narrative terms the increasing alienation of the *princeps* from his people.

62–63 Disaster at Fidenae

62.1 M. Licinio L. Calpurnio consulibus The former is M. Licinius Crassus Frugi; he was son of the consul of 14 BC and, after achieving considerable military distinction, was executed by Claudius. See *RE* 13.338–45 = Licinius 73 (Groag), *PIR* 5.37–9 no. 190, *BNP* 7.538 [II 9]; Syme, *AA* 488 (index). The latter is the former Cn. Calpurnius Piso, son of the consul of 7 BC, who was compelled to change his *praenomen* after his father's disgrace (*SCPP* 98–110; 3.17.4 and n.): he went on to become proconsul of Africa in 38/39 or 39/40. See 3.16.3n., also *RE* 3.1383–4 = Calpurnius 76 (Groag), *PIR* 2.69–70 no. 293, *BNP* 2.1001 [II 20]; *AA* 379, 477 (index). Neither man will reappear in the extant *Annals*.

---

[117] It is misleadingly categorised by Ginsburg 54, 139.

ingentium bellorum cladem aequauit malum improuisum At 32.1 (above) T. had lamented the absence from his narrative of *ingentia bella*; here he explicitly compares a local calamity to the disaster which attends great wars, a comparison which he implicitly repeats at the end of the episode (63.2 'magna post proelia') and underlines by further references to its disastrous nature (63.2 *cladem*, 64.1 *clades*). The military analogy is sustained throughout, and, since the disaster involved the collapse of a building, the closest parallels are with the besieging of a city, for the description of which Quintilian offered detailed instructions at 8.3.67–70 (see further below). Suetonius, who places the collapse after Tib. had first crossed to Capri (*Tib.* 40), says that Caligula saw it as the pre-eminent disaster of Tib.'s reign and lamented that his own principate had no comparable misfortunes (*Cal.* 31 'principatum . . . Tiberi ruina spectaculorum apud Fidenas memorabilem factum . . . atque identidem exercituum caedes . . . incendia . . . optabat'). *malum improuisum* recurs only at 13.57.3, where it refers to the outbreak of an unnatural and terrible fire.

eius initium simul et finis exstitit T. uses *simul et* (as he uses *simul ac* and *simul –que*) in various ways (G–G 1506a–b). Sometimes he is co-ordinating two virtual synonyms (as 2.5.1 'dolo simul et casibus'), sometimes two antonyms (as 1.51.1 'profana simul et sacra'), but sometimes he seems to be stressing the virtual simultaneity of two different terms (as 15.48.1 'coepta simul et aucta coniuratione', 'no sooner begun than enlarged'). This last appears to be the sense here: 'its beginning and ending presented themselves simultaneously'. Since the statement closely resembles the topos 'they knew they were at war only when it was over' (e.g. 3.47.1 'ortum patratumque bellum'; cf. Vell. 129.3n.), it is appropriate to a 'military' narrative (see previous n.).

coepto apud Fidenam amphitheatro The town was 5 miles N of Rome on the Via Salaria; Horace implied that it was deserted in his day (*Ep.* 1.11.8), but a municipal senate and local magistrates are attested in the second century AD (*ILS* 6223) and later. The name of the town is usually plural, as Liv. 5.54.1; another exception is Virg. *Aen.* 6.773 (see L. Quilici and S. Quilici Gigli, *Fidenae* (1986) 40–1: for some other towns which are found in both singular and plural forms see Oakley on Liv. 8.25.4. *apud* = 'near' (*OLD* 1a).

coepto . . . amphitheatro reads more naturally as an aoristic abl. abs. than a dat. with *subdidit* below, though the matter is disputed. Some scholars have objected to the order of the first three κῶλα of this sentence. Transpositions have been proposed by Ernesti (*Atilius quidam libertini generis coepto apud Fidenam amphitheatro quo spectaculum gladiatorum celebraret, neque . . .*) and Wex (*coepto apud Fidenam amphitheatro quo spectaculum gladiatorum celebraret, Atilius quidam libertini generis neque . . .*);[118] but, since *quo . . . celebraret* is to be taken closely with *coepto . . . amphitheatro*, the transmitted order is perhaps to be regarded as an extension of the idiom whereby the subject of a sentence can be placed within an abl. abs., as *Agr.* 25.4 'diuiso et ipse in tres partes exercitu incessit' (n.).

libertini generis This expression, which is found again at 2.85.4 'quattuor milia libertini generis' and Suet. *Aug.* 44.1 'quosdam etiam libertini generis', may mean either 'of the freedman class', as seems generally thought, or 'of freedman parentage', as Damon translates. If the former is correct, scholars have been worried by the statement of Suetonius that Claudius gave to the freedman Harpocras 'spectacula . . . publice edendi ius' (*Claud.* 28), which could be taken to imply that in Tib.'s time freedmen were banned from putting on shows. Lipsius sought to avoid this difficulty by proposing that any such ban did not apply to towns other than Rome; but, since *publice* must mean 'at public expense' (*OLD* 1b) rather than 'in public' (which would be redundant in the context of *spectacula*), it is clear that Claudius' measure is irrelevant to projects such as that of Atilius, which relied entirely on private money. Atilius is otherwise unknown.[119]

quo spectaculum gladiatorum celebraret The verb is fairly common in inscriptions relating to *spectacula* and the like, but its meaning here is disputed. If the reference is to crowding the amphitheatre with people, which seems to be the view in *TLL* 3.742.83–4, one would expect the verb to be passive, which indeed Wex proposed to write. It therefore seems more probable that the verb is equivalent to *ederet*, which is likely to be the meaning at Val. Max. 2.4.4 'circensi spectaculo . . . quod primus Romulus raptis uirginibus Sabinis Consualium nomine celebrauit' (the point is presumably that Romulus put on the first show, not that he was the first to pack a circus). The two other literary exs. of the phrase are Cic. *Sest.* 124 'id autem spectaculi genus erat quod omni frequentia atque omni genere hominum celebratur, quo multitudo maxime delectatur' and Tac. *A.* 11.22.2 'P. Dolabella censuit spectaculum gladiatorum per omnes annos celebrandum'. Whether *quo* is to be regarded as the conjunction (cf. 30.1n.) or the rel. pronoun is unclear.

There is a vast bibliography on gladiators and amphitheatres etc.: see e.g. G. Ville, *La gladiature en Occident des origines à la mort de Domitien* (1981), esp. 225

---

[118] F. C. Wex, *Spicilegium in Cornelio Tacito* (Schwerin 1859) 5–7.

[119] Note that J. Cels-Saint-Hilaire has argued that the term *libertinus* should be understood more widely to include *peregrini* who had been granted Roman citizenship (e.g. 'Les *libertini*: des mots et des choses', *Dialogues d'Histoire Ancienne* 11 (1985) 330–79, 'Le sens du mot *libertinus*, i: quelques réflexions', *Latomus* 61 (2002) 285–94).

and 430–2; G. Tosi, *Gli edifici per spettacoli nell'Italia romana*, Vol. 1 (2003) (67 for Fidenae); Carter and Edmondson 555–8; www.oxfordbibliographies.com (Kathleen Coleman, 'Arena Spectacles').

neque fundamenta per solidum subdidit 'he did not underset the foundations through firm ground': *per solidum* (like *fundamenta subdere*) is an unparalleled expr. but is presumably clarified by Vitruv. 1.5.1 'fundamenta . . . fodiantur ad solidum et in solido'. See also next n.

neque firmis nexibus ligneam compagem superstruxit 'nor did he superimpose the wooden framework with reliable ties.' Wooden amphitheatres had long since given way to those built of stone but were still sometimes used even under the empire, e.g. *CIL* 3.6832 (Pisidian Antioch), 13.1642 = *ILS* 5639 'Ti. Claudius . . . Capito sacerdos Aug. theatrum quod Lupus Anthi f. ligneum posuerat d.s.p. lapideum restituit' (Gallia Lugdunensis). Atilius used wood because he could not afford the alternative and was trying to make a quick profit. At 13.31.1 T. famously writes that in AD 57 'pauca memoria digna euenere, nisi cui libeat laudandis fundamentis et trabibus quis molem amphitheatri apud campum Martis Caesar exstruxerat uolumina implere, cum ex dignitate populi Romani repertum sit res inlustres annalibus, talia diurnis urbis actis mandare', but his objection in that passage seems not so much to the technicalities of building as to the application of panegyric to trivia; and in any case none of T.'s language in the present passage seems esp. technical (indeed for *firmis nexibus* cf. Stat. *Theb.* 6.889).

non abundantia pecuniae nec municipali ambitione sed in sordidam mercedem According to the traditional scholarly view of such matters, in local towns there were three types of gladiatorial (and other) shows: (i) public shows, which officials such as magistrates were obliged to put on, partly at least at public expense;[120] (ii) 'private' shows, which an individual would put on to display his generosity and munificence; and (iii) shows which were put on entirely for profit, for which the present passage of T. is the principal evidence. (i) is irrelevant to the present passage; the two rejected reasons (*abundantia* and *ambitione* are causal abl.) relate to (ii) and are contrasted with (iii). Thus the consul of AD 81 commemorated by means of an inscription the amphitheatre which he had built at Urbs Salvia in Picenum (*AE* 1969–70, 183): [*L. Flauius – f. V]el. Silua Nonius Bassus cos . . .pec(unia) sua, solo suo, [amphitheatrum faciundu]m curauit et parib(us) XXXX ordinar(iis) dedicauit.*[121] Since such undertakings were increasingly competitive, it was important not only to mention personal expenditure but also to give prominence to the benefactor's

---

[120] For the equivalent of these shows in the capital see 11.22.2, 13.5.1.

[121] The text is reconstituted on the basis of two other inscriptions, fragmentary but evidently identical, found nearby.

name. 'Le nom de celui . . . qui a financé la construction figure souvent au nominatif, en tête de l'inscription. La dédicace représentait . . . un moment de grande fierté pour l'évergète. L'organisation d'un spectacle était pour lui une des meilleures façons de se gagner la reconnaissance de l'ensemble de la communauté, représentée par la foule dans les gradins' (G. Chamberland, 'La mémoire des spectacles: l'autoreprésentation des donateurs', in *L'organisation des spectacles dans le monde Romain* (ed. Coleman and Nelis-Clément, 2007) 261–303, at 278). Hence *municipali ambitione* probably refers to the courting of local townspeople, as commentators say, although other interpretations (such as boosting the profile of one's local town) are theoretically possible (cf. perhaps the gladiatorial rivalry which breaks out at 14.17).

Such considerations were not relevant to Atilius and his construction: since he had no access to substantial resources, he was interested in the third type of operation described above; but here a modification in the traditional tripartite division of spectacles has been proposed by G. Chamberland, 'A gladiatorial show produced *in sordidam mercedem'*, *Phoenix* 61 (2007) 136–49. Questioning the sparse other evidence for 'profit-making' shows, he argues that municipal officials and the local élite would almost certainly have been excused the entry fee to any show and hence that there was no such thing as a show put on *entirely* for profit, as T. has been taken to imply. It was in order to reduce this loss of potential profit that Atilius built his amphitheatre within easy reach of Rome, so that the proportion of fee-paying spectators from out of town would be all the greater.

In sordidam mercedem is an emendation by Pichena. M reads *in sordida mercede*, which, though defended by Ritter, makes no sense, whereas *in mercedem* is a regular phrase meaning 'for a reward' *vel sim.* (cf. 11.6.2, Sall. *H.* 1.13 M = 1.14 R, Liv. 21.43.7 'in hanc tam opimam mercedem', 39.28.6, Sen. *Ben.* 4.1.2, Gell. 5.3.1; and compare *non in quaestum tamen aut mercedem* at *G.* 24.1 and *in quaestum* at *Agr.* 19.4). As Walther remarks, it would be easy to miss or omit the macron over the final syllable of each word. *sordidam mercedem* is a Livian expr. (44.25.9)

62.2 Adfluxere auidi talium There is a certain *hauteur* about T.'s description, suggesting a dislike of gladiatorial spectacles similar to that of Cicero (*Att.* 2.1.1), Seneca (*Ep.* 7) and the *princeps* himself (1.76.3–4, Suet. *Tib.* 47); T. did, however, attend the races (Plin. *Ep.* 9.23).

imperitante Tiberio procul uoluptatibus habiti *uoluptates* here has the quasi-technical meaning of 'organised entertainments' (*OLD* 4), a meaning which became increasingly common under the empire. T.'s choice of wording almost suggests that Tib. positively forbade or at least discouraged such entertainments; if this was actually the case, it was presumably a gradual procedure: despite trouble in AD 14 (cf. 1.54.2 'alia Tiberio morum uia, sed populum per tot annos molliter habitum *nondum* audebat ad duriora uertere'), actors were not banished from Italy until 23 (above, 14.3).[122] There is in any case some irony in T.'s statement if, as Suetonius reports, Tib. appointed a minister to supervise his own private entertainments (*Tib.* 42.2 'officium instituit a uoluptatibus'). For the *princeps*' general meanness see Suet. *Tib.* 34; for *imperitare* see 3.4.1n.

uirile ac muliebre secus recurs in T. at *H.* 5.13.3 'multitudinem obsessorum omnis aetatis, uirile ac muliebre secus, sexcenta milia fuisse accepimus', an ex. which Furneaux categorises as an 'accusative of description'. On the grounds that nomin. *secus* does not occur until late Latin, the phrase is generally taken the same way in our passage, qualifying the unexpressed subject of the sentence; but the nomin. *secus* is found in Varro (ap. Gell. 3.10.7) and in the prose of Ennius (*Varia* 70V: see Adams (2016) 13–14): it has therefore been argued by J. T. Ramsey, who drew attention to these instances, that in our passage it is a nominative phrase in apposition to the subject and that T. is using a deliberate archaism (*Philol.* 149 (2005) 321–7). Although it is true that the other exs. of the same expr. cannot be nominative (Sisenn. F90C = 80P 'in muro uirile ac muliebre secus populi multitudine omni conlocata', Sall. *H.* 2.70.1 M = 3.10.1 R 'magna gloria concurrentium undique, uirile ac muliebre secus, per uias et tecta omnium uisebantur', Liv. 31.44.4 'ut Philippi statuae imagines omnes nominaque earum, item maiorum eius uirile ac muliebre secus omnium tollerentur delerenturque', Amm. 16.11.9, 18.8.13 'confluente ex finitimis uirile et muliebre secus', 27.10.2, 29.6.8 'praedas hominum uirile et muliebre secus agebant'), our example is different, as Ramsey observes, in that nominatives both precede (*auidi* ... *habiti*) and follow ('omnis aetas').

ob propinquitatem loci effusius Presumably the amphitheatre's proximity to Rome is meant; we know esp. from the case of Pompeii that ambitious entrepreneurs would advertise in neighbouring towns in order to attract as many spectators as possible (see Carter and Edmondson 545 with further refs.). For the adv. cf. Liv. 3.26.7 'ubi effuse affluant opes'.

unde grauior pestis fuit H. Sauppe wished these words to be the conclusion of the preceding sentence rather than (as commonly printed) the beginning of a new one.[123] Yet, although there is self-evidently a close connection between the greater attendance (*effusius*) and the greater loss of life (*grauior pestis*), his repunctuation requires both the deletion of –*que* (below) and that readers supply the subject of the sentence (which now begins with *conferta*)

---

[122] In AD 19 there was passed the *senatus consultum* from Larinum, forbidding members of the upper classes to appear on stage or in gladiatorial shows (B. Levick, *JRS* 73 (1983) 97–115).

[123] *Quaestiones criticae* (Göttingen 1886) 21.

from *pestis* in the previous sentence, which is awkward. The advantage is thus outweighed by the disadvantages.

The expr. (again at 2.47.1, of a nocturnal earthquake) seems Senecan: cf. *Ep.* 14.6 and esp. *Octav.* 240 'haec grauior illo pestis'. *pestis* = 'destruction, death-toll' (*OLD* 1).

dum ruit intus aut in exteriora effunditur . . . spectaculo intentos aut qui circum adstabant, praeceps trahit atque operit Although the divisions between the two groups of victims are not absolute, *ruit intus* and *praeceps trahit* apply principally to the spectators on the tiers inside the building, while *in exteriora effunditur* and *operit* apply principally to the bystanders outside: in other words, this is a complicated ex. of so-called 'double zeugma' (1.55.1n.). For *ruit intus* cf. H. on *H.* 1.35.1 and Lucr. 6.726 there quoted (*moles ruit* is at Sil. 17.556); though *in exteriora* is found elsewhere (Cels. 8.1.16, 23), it is 3× in Seneca. *spectaculo intentus* is Livian (4×); *praeceps* is of course adverbial (adj. at Sil. 17.122 'siluas ac saxa trahens per deuia praeceps').

immensamque uim mortalium Servius on *Aen.* 4.132 remarks that Virgil's similar use of *uis* 'plus est quam si diceret "multitudo": unde Sallustius "qua tempestate ex ponto uis piscium erupit"' (*H.* 3.66 M = 3.86 R); the expr. *uis mortalium* is unparalleled in classical Latin, but, just as *uis* suggests the life-force and identities which have been destroyed, so *mortales* underlines the precariousness of life (cf. 40.1 and esp. 68.3; in general see 6.22.1n. and Oakley on Liv. 6.16.4). *immensam* is literally 'immeasurable': it hints at the 'inexpressibility topos' (so many died that the numbers were impossible to deal with) and at the horror of the scene (body parts and mutilations made counting impossible); but T. does give a round total for the dead and injured at 63.1 below.

62.3 ut tali sorte has caused trouble: is it to be taken with what precedes or what follows, and, either way, what does it mean?[124] The current view is that it should be taken with *cruciatum effugere* and means 'so far as was possible in such a fate' (Jackson), although 'as happens in such circumstances' or 'as was to be expected in such circumstances' seem equally possible (cf. 1.65.1 'utque tali in tempore').

miserandi magis quos . . . noscebant Cf. Liv. 5.42.4–5 'quocumque clamor hostium, mulierum puerorumque ploratus, sonitus flammae et fragor ruentium tectorum auertisset, pauentes ad omnia animos oraque et oculos

[124] Wopkens suggested that we repunctuate the sentence ('ut tali sorte cruciatum effugere, miserandi magis . . .') and understand *ita* before *miserandi*, but such an elliptical use of the correlative construction seems rare elsewhere and not to be found in T. (G–G 1711b).

flectebant uelut ad spectaculum a fortuna positi occidentis patriae nec ullius rerum suarum relicti praeterquam corporum uindices, tanto ante alios *miserandi magis*, qui umquam obsessi sunt, quod interclusi a patria obsidebantur omnia sua cernentes in hostium potestate' (the Gallic occupation of Rome). See also below.

abrupta parte corporis See G. W. Most, '*disiecti membra poetae*: the rhetoric of dismemberment in Neronian poetry', in *Innovations of antiquity* (ed. Hexter and Selden, 1992) 391–419. For the general liking of scenes of gore and carnage see e.g. Fantham on Sen. *Tro.* 1110–17.

qui . . . ululatibus et gemitu coniuges aut liberos noscebant The cross-sections of society which flocked happily and anonymously to the spectacle (62.2) have become the husbands, wives and children whose terrible mutilations prevent them from comforting one another at their time of greatest need; and the forthcoming list of other relatives and intimates adds to the horror. The sufferings of women and children are a standard feature of disaster narratives such as those of besieged cities (Quint. 8.3.68 'infantium feminarumque ploratus') and Polybius famously criticised historians such as Phylarchus who indulged in them too freely (2.56.7–8): see above and e.g. Oakley on Liv. 6.3.4; Paul (cited at 32.1n.); A. Rossi, *Contexts of war: manipulation of genre in Virgilian battle narrative* (2004) 40ff. Particularly close to our passage is Pliny's account of the aftermath of the eruption of Vesuvius (*Ep.* 6.20.14 'audires ululatus feminarum, infantum quiritatus, clamores uirorum; alii parentes, alii liberos, alii coniuges uocibus requirebant, uocibus noscitabant; hi suum casum, illi suorum miserabantur');[125] cf. also Liv. 10.33.2, 22.5.4. For *ululatibus et gemitu* cf. esp. Virg. *Aen.* 4.667 (and Pease's n.), Curt. 4.15.29. *noscebant* = 'kept on recognising' or 'tried to recognise'; *poscebant* was suggested independently by Neue (6) and J. J. Hartman (*Mnem.* 22 (1894) 357).

hic . . . ille, alius . . . lamentari Koestermann remarks that the 'Unruhe' of the scene is matched by the *uariatio* of the expression, comparing Sall. *C.* 61.8 (the aftermath of the battle).

etiam quorum diuersa de causa amici aut necessarii aberant pauere tamen 'even those whose friends or connections were away for some other reason [sc. than the gladiatorial show] nevertheless panicked'.

---

[125] Doederlein refers to this as 'a clear imitation' of our passage and uses it to support the view (taken also by Pluygers) that *qui . . . noscebant* refers to a separate group of people from the mutilated; but it seems odd to say that the uninjured were '*more* to be pitied' than those who had fallen to their terrible deaths, and in any case Pliny's letter precedes the composition and publication of the *Annals*.

nequedum comperto quos illa uis perculisset For such abl. abs. as *comperto* see 1.66.2n., Malloch on 11.26.3. For *uis percellit* cf. Lucr. 6.310–11, Cic. *Sest.* 140, *Marc.* 17, Liv. 10.28.12, Apul. *Apol.* 12.

latior ex incerto metus 'In ancient as in modern times the unknown proverbially caused more fear than the known' (Oakley on Liv. 9.24.8, quoting this passage); for *latior* cf. *H.* 4.33.3 'latiorem . . . terrorem' (and H.'s n.); for *ex incerto* see Oakley on Liv. 6.23.2 *Addendum* (4.525).

63.1 obruta is evidently substantival, 'debris, rubble' (*OLD* 3a), though seemingly not recognised as such in *TLL* 9.2.151.35ff.

saepe certamen si confusior facies, sed par forma aut aetas, errorem adgnoscentibus fecerat 'and often there was a quarrel whenever too mangled a face, but the appropriate shape or age, led to error in those identifying [sc. the corpses]'; *par* means that the *forma* or *aetas* of any given corpse corresponded with the *forma* or *aetas* of more than one individual during life. Questions of identity, which feature prominently in drama and evidently played their part in declamation ([Quint.] *Decl.* 388.17–18 'quomodo autem potuit confusa facie agnosci? aetas, inquit, conueniebat; . . . statura'), are guaranteed to raise the emotional tone: in addition to 1.62.1 ('ossa, nullo noscente alienas reliquias an suorum humo tegeret, omnis ut coniunctos, ut consanguineos, aucta in hostem ira, maesti simul et infensi condebant') cf. Curt. 8.3.13, Luc. 3.756–61 'quis in urbe parentum | fletus erat, quanti matrum per litora planctus! | coniunx saepe sui confusis uoltibus unda | credidit ora uiri Romanum amplexa cadauer, | accensisque rogis miseri de corpore trunco | certauere patres', Stat. *Theb.* 12.33–7 'at circum informes truncos miserabile surgit | certamen qui iusta ferant, qui funera ducant. | saepe etiam hostiles (lusit Fortuna parumper) | decepti fleuere uiros; nec certa facultas | noscere quem miseri uitent calcentue cruorem'.[126] *confusior* is well chosen to describe a face which has been so mangled as to be indistinguishable, exactly as in the passage of pseudo-Quintilian above (the term has both meanings: cf. *OLD confundo* 7); Borzsák prints his own emendation *contusior*, for which he argued in *Gnomon* 63 (1991) 23, but the form is unattested.

Quinquaginta hominum milia eo casu debilitata uel obtrita sunt This total corresponds to modern estimates of the capacity of the Colosseum. Suetonius puts the number of dead at 'more than twenty thousand' (*Tib.* 40). For the language cf. Plin. *Ep.* 8.17.5 'multi eius modi casibus debilitati, obruti, obtriti, et aucta luctibus damna' (of flooding).

---

[126] The last two examples are owed to Professor R. G. Mayer.

cui minor quadringentorum milium res The omission of *quam* in comparative expressions is common but more usual with ages (e.g. Plin. *Ep.* 10.79.1 'cautum est . . . neue sit in senatu minor annorum triginta') than with other numerical genitives (K–S 2.473). The sum of 400,000 sesterces is the same as the minimum capital qualification for equestrian status (Demougin, *OE* 76ff.).

firmitatis T. normally prefers *firmitudo* (3.6.2n.).

63.2 patuere procerum domus, fomenta et medici passim praebiti For the scene cf. Just. 28.4.5–6 'patentibus omnes domibus saucios excipiebant, uulnera curabant, lassos reficiebant'. *proceres* is generally more common in poetry than prose but is greatly liked by T. (see Oakley on Liv. 9.18.7 for some statistics).

quamquam maesta facie *facies* is readily used of places (thus *urbis* at Sall. *C.* 31.1 and Ov. *Tr.* 4.6.45; cf. 67.2n.) but *maesta* personifies (cf. Luc. 8.69–70, Sen. *Med.* 790, the latter of the moon), as if Rome were in sympathy with its inhabitants. For a picture of a city (Tusculum) going about its 'normal' business see Liv. 6.25.8–10 (cf. 74.3n. below).

ueterum institutis similis, qui . . . cura sustentabant The reference seems to be to 480 BC (cf. Liv. 2.47.12 'saucios milites curandos diuidit patribus'). For *ueterum institua* cf. 3.5.2n. (but note that the sing. *institutum* is twice in Cic. *Fin.* at 3.5 and 5.23); for *cura sustentabant* cf. Vell. 114.1 'cuius salus ac ualetudo non ita sustentaretur Caesaris cura'.

64–65 Disaster at Rome

64.1 Nondum ea clades exoleuerat, cum . . . In T. an inverted *cum*-clause is introduced by *nondum* again only at 6.25.1 'nondum is dolor exoleuerat, cum . . .' (where see n.); the present ex. is followed (below) by a '*ni* de rupture', a combination which Chausserie-Laprée finds esp. effective (671).

cum ignis uiolentia urbem ultra solitum adfecit, deusto monte Caelio Since T. has just described the disaster at Fidenae in some detail, he limits the second disaster to a brief notice and instead concentrates (below) on the *princeps*' response: he thus eschews the irony whereby the victims of Fidenae, seeking medical help in the capital for their wounds (63.2), found themselves in another disaster zone. For the constant menace of fires in Rome see 6.45.1 'Idem annus graui igne urbem adfecit, deusta parte circi' (and n.), 15.38.1 'Sequitur clades . . . omnibus quae huic urbi per uiolentiam ignium acciderunt grauior atque atrocior' (the Great Fire). For *ultra solitum* cf. 6.50.3, *H.* 1.18.1, Plin. *NH* 18.361. This particular fire is also mentioned at Vell. 130.2

(see further below) but is absent from Suetonius, whose account of this period is otherwise close to that of T. Varro associated the phrase *ignis uiolentia* with the name Volcanus (*LL* 5.70 'ab ignis iam maiore ui ac uiolentia Volcanus dictus').

feralemque annum *ferebant* The subject has to be extracted from *uulgo* below. For *feralem* cf. [Quint.] *Decl.* 12.4 'feralis anni' (*funesti anni* at Cic. *Sest.* 59).

ominibus aduersis Cf. *Vir. Ill.* 31.1 'aduersis ominibus . . . progressum'.

qui mos uulgo For T.'s attitude to the *uulgus* see 5.4.2n.

fortuita ad culpam trahentes The antithesis *fortuita ~ culpa* is conventional (Vell. 118.4n.; Braund on Sen. *Clem.* 1.2.1). For *traho* = 'assign X to Y', 'interpret X in terms of Y', see *OLD* 20b.

ni Caesar obuiam isset tribuendo pecunias ex modo detrimenti Tib. responds to the fire as spontaneously as to blighted harvests and maritime disasters (4.6.4 'obuiam iit'). In the serious fire a decade later he set up a commission to estimate how much loss individuals had suffered (6.45. 1–2). For *ni* see 3.14.4n.

64.2 Actaeque ei grates apud senatum <et> ab inlustribus, famaque apud populum The transmitted text is undoubtedly very strange. The most obvious question is how *famaque apud populum* is to be construed; but A. Stein ('Zum römischen Ritterstand', *AJP* 67 (1946) 361–2) pointed out a more serious difficulty, which is that nowhere else in Latin are senators described as *inlustres*, a term conventionally used of *equites* and women (58.1n.; G–G 643b). Stein concluded that, as at 74.3 below, there should be a three-fold reference to 'senate, *equites* and people', which he brought about by inserting *et* or by simply placing a comma after *apud senatum*. His case seems unanswerable; the only issue is whether his proposed solution is adequate. The expression *actae . . . grates apud senatum* seems secure (cf. 15.22.1 'agendas apud senatum . . . grates'), and T. is very fond of prepositional *uariatio* involving *apud*; on the other hand, no precisely comparable example of the resulting *uariatio* is listed by Sörbom 46–7, and the use of *inlustres* alone to designate the *equites* seems odd (58.1 is not really parallel because of the presence there of *eques*). Given the strangeness of *famaque apud populum*, it is tempting to suggest that the corruption of the text extends to more than the mere omission of *et*. One obvious candidate for insertion would be the word *equitibus* itself, but for reasons of euphony we should not want the two abl. plurals juxtaposed (cf. 2.59.3). On the whole it seems safest to adopt the minimal change proposed by Stein, but this leaves *famaque apud populum* untouched. Scholars generally assume that *fama* is nomin. and that *ei erat* is to be understood (cf. 1.7.6 'mirus apud populum fauor', 1.33.2 'magna apud

297

populum Romanum memoria'); but we should not dismiss the possibility that the phrase is equivalent to *famāque populari erat*, a Ciceronian expr. (5×), which T. would therefore be varying. Either way, the repetition of *apud* remains as one final oddity. For *grates* see 3.18.3n.

sine ambitione Since *proximorum precibus* seems to correspond to *ignotos etiam*, it appears to follow that *sine ambitione* corresponds to *ultro accitos* and hence means 'without lobbying'; but 'without favouritism' cannot be excluded. Cf. Vell. 130.2 'qua liberalitate cum alias tum proxime incenso monte Caelio omnis ordinis hominum iacturae patrimonio succurrit suo!'

ultro accitos i.e. invited spontaneously by Tib. (*OLD ultro* 5b); the expr. (again at 11.36.3) seems Livian (1.35.3, 10.19.1).

munificentia See 6.45.1n.

64.3 ut mons Caelius in posterum Augustus appellaretur Suetonius tells it differently (*Tib.* 48.1): 'quod tamen beneficium tanti aesti- mauit ut montem Caelium appellatione mutata uocari Augustum iusserit'.

Iunii senatoris Unknown.

Claudiae Quintae In 204 BC, when the ship carrying Cybele's sacred stone became stuck in the Tiber, she is said miraculously to have got it afloat again (Liv. 29.14.11–12, Ov. *F.* 4.305–22, Plin. *NH* 7.120, Suet. *Tib.* 2.3; Powell on Cic. *Senec.* 45; *MRR* 1.304).

eiusque statuam . . . bis elapsam maiores apud aedem matris deum consecrauisse The statue's two escapes were in III BC and AD 3, whereas its consecration had been in 191 BC (Liv. 36.36.3–4 and Briscoe ad loc.): this is therefore one of those sentences where participle and main verb should logically be transposed ('eiusque statuam, apud aedem matris deum a maioribus consecratam, uim ignium bis esse elapsam'); this transposition is similar to, but not identical with, that illustrated at K–S 1.781–2; cf. also 20.1n. and 34.5n. above. The dates of the two escapes are given by Valerius Maximus in a chapter entitled 'De Miraculis' (1.8.11), a category of phenomenon to which Tib.'s *effigies* therefore also belongs.

augendam caerimoniam loco 'there should be an increase in sanctity for the place': the phraseology recurs at 3.61.2 (n.) but here has extra point in alluding to and explaining the proposed name *Augustus*, which was derived from *augeo* (cf. Maltby 66). There is no evidence that the proposal was ever carried out. For *caerimonia* see 1.62.2n.

65 Haud fuerit absurdum tradere The proposal that the Caelian Hill in future be called Mons Augustus (64.3) leads to a digression in which T. explains how the hill came to be called Caelius in the first place. Since some readers might have felt that the connection with the main narrative was too tenuous, he introduces the digression by an apologetic formula: some of his other digressions on 'cultural history' (as they are classified by Hahn 51ff., esp. 56–61) are similarly introduced: 3.55.1 'quaerere libet' (n.), 6.28.1 'cognitu non absurda promere libet' (n.), and 12.24.1 'noscere haud absurdum reor'. The phrase *haud absurdum* is used for an identical purpose at Vell. 38.1 'Haud absurdum uidetur . . . paucis percurrere'; the collocation originates in Sallust (*C.* 3.1 and 25.5, though in neither case in the context of a digression) and is found nowhere else, although *haud absurde* (which is used by Vell. to mark witticisms at 77.1 and 83.3) is used by T. to excuse digressive material at *H.* 3.51.2. On digressions see further 6.11.1n.

From the similarity of topic and wording (see nn. below) numerous scholars have believed that the present digression is somehow related to the speech which the emperor Claudius delivered in the senate in 48 on the admission of Gallic nobles to the senate (*ILS* 212). Just as *honestam . . . paupertatem* at 2.48.3 and *tutam . . . honoratamque sedem* at 2.63.2 seem to be genuine echoes of Tiberian speeches (see *PH* 374–6 for discussion), so T.'s familiarity with Claudius' speech is clear from the version which he presents later at 11.24 (see Malloch's commentary ad loc.), and Syme believed (*Tac.* 286, 709–10) that he consulted the speech directly when composing not only this present digression but also that on legislation in Book 3 (see 3.26.3n., 26.4n., 27.1n.). But this raises the question of why T. should be consulting now a text which would not become relevant until more than twenty narrative years later, when he was dealing with the Claudian books of the *Annals*. An answer to this question was proposed by G. B. Townend, who suggested that for his account of Tib.'s reign T. was using the history of Aufidius Bassus (*FRH* 1.518–21, 2.1000–7, 3.603–5; *LH* 69–70). Aufidius was a contemporary of Claudius and, when he came to describe the Caelian fire of AD 27, he will have made a point of inserting the antiquarian material on the hill which he had heard or read in the *princeps'* speech (so the argument goes). Many decades later, T. reproduced not only Aufidius' notice of the fire but also the antiquarian material from Claudius which accompanied it. Any Claudian echoes in T.'s digression are thus mediated by Aufidius' history. See G. B. Townend, 'Claudius and the digressions in Tacitus', *RhM* 105 (1962) 358–68. Alternative and more complicated scenarios were offered by Questa 231–2 and then in *L'Aquila a due teste: immagini di Roma e dei romani* (1998) 91–2; that there is no relationship at all between Claudius' speech and T.'s narrative is argued strongly by S. J. V. Malloch, 'The tradition about the *mons Caelius*' (forthcoming), whose paper should be consulted for all aspects of the story.[127]

---

[127] I am most grateful to Dr Malloch for sight of his paper before publication and for discussion of various issues.

montem eum . . . mox Caelium appellitatum a Caele Vibenna, qui dux gentis Etruscae . . . Compare the wording of Claudius (*ILS* 212, col. 1, lines 20–1): '*montem Caelium* occupauit et *a duce* suo Caelio ita *appellitatus*' (the last word is conventionally emended to *appellitauit*). *appellitare* occurs only in these two passages, if we exclude a few instances in the later authors Gellius (3×), Apuleius (2×) and Macrobius (3×) and the entry in Paul. Fest. p. 24L (*TLL* 2.272.76–82). It is nevertheless clear that T.'s version of events, while close to Claudius', is not identical: in Claudius it is Servius Tullius who occupies the hill and names it after his leader Caelius Vivenna; in T. it is Caeles Vibenna himself who is given the hill by Tarquinius Priscus and from whom it subsequently derives its name.

antiquitus Querquetulanum cognomento fuisse The digression begins and ends (~ *e uocabulo*) with nomenclature. We know that Callimachus wrote a work entitled *On the foundations of islands and cities and their name-changes* (Pfeiffer p. 339), and modern scholarship has demonstrated fully the extent to which *metonomasia*, aetiology and etymology fascinated the ancients and permeates their texts in a wide range of genres (see e.g. A. S. Hollis, *HSCP* 94 (1992) 278–9). T. himself explains the various name-changes of the River Rhine at 2.6.4, specialised local knowledge which he perhaps acquired while his father was procurator of the province of Gallia Belgica and the two Germanies (Plin. *NH* 7.76). The present digression, however, is marked as antiquarian (*antiquitus*), as befits material which the historian has in common with the emperor Claudius (a topic perhaps treated too ironically by Syme, *Tac.* 514–15). *Querquetulanus* is 'the name of various places and deities associated with oak-woods' (*OLD*); for *cognomentum* see Malloch on 11.4.1.

talis siluae frequens fecundusque erat *frequens* + gen. is hard to parallel (Col. 3.6.2 is quoted at *TLL* 6.1.1299.44–5, but the text is uncertain), whereas *fecundus* + gen. is at *H.* 1.11.1, Col. 9.4.2, 11.2.90, Plin. *NH* 33.78; such combinations are typical of T.

cum auxilium [appellatum] tulisset Lipsius' *tulisset* for the transmitted *tauisset* produces an extremely common phrase which T. uses again at 3.41.2, although Doederlein supported his own *<por>tauisset* by quoting Sall. *C.* 6.5 'auxilia portabant' (where see Mariotti's n.). Some scholars have emended *appellatum* to *appellatus*, on the grounds that Vibenna was summoned to bring help; but it is difficult to believe that T. would have written *appellatus* so soon after *appellitatum*,[128] and it seems safer to assume that the word originated as

[128] That Claudius has a similar repetition in successive lines (*ILS* 212 col. 1, lines 22–3) is noted by Ruperti in defence of Walther's *cum auxilium appellatum <i>tauisset* ('after his frequent journeys to seek help').

a scribal gloss on, or correction of, *appellitatum*. T. offers no explanation of the circumstances in which Vibenna brought aid to the Romans, either because the story was well known or because the various traditions were contradictory or otherwise unclear (next nn.). See T. J. Cornell, *The beginnings of Rome* (1995) 133–45.

seu quis alius regum dedit According to Varro (*LL* 5.46), the request for help came from Romulus, not Tarquinius Priscus; other kings mentioned in connection with the Caelian Hill are Tullus Hostilius (Liv. 1.30.1, Dion. Hal. *AR* 3.1.5) and Ancus Marcius (Cic. *Rep.* 2.33, Strabo 5.3.7).

nam scriptores in eo dissentiunt The reference to variant versions suits both the scholarly context (cf. e.g. Gell. 5.6.27 'super quo dissensisse ueteres scriptores accipio') and the emperor Claudius (*ILS* 212, col. 1, lines 16–17 '*nam et hoc inter auctores discrepat*', though on a different point). See also next n.

Cetera non ambigua sunt References to variant versions etc. are often accompanied by the one 'certain' version, e.g. 6.28.6 'haec incerta . . .; ceterum . . . non ambigitur' (n.), Liv. 4.55.8 'incertum diuersi auctores faciunt; illa pro certo habenda, in quibus non dissentiunt, . . .'. In general see Marincola 280ff., and note Oakley on Liv. 7.9.6.

unde Tuscum uicum e uocabulo aduenarum dictum The Vicus Tuscus ran SW from the Forum Romanum to the Circus Maximus along the western end of the Palatine (*LTUR* 5.195–7). The etymology given here differs from that of Livy (2.14.9: see Ogilvie's n.) but agrees with that of Varro as quoted by Serv. *Aen.* 5.560 'a quo in urbe Tuscus dictus est uicus' (from which it is clear that T. has adopted the appropriate aetiological manner and style: see further J. J. O'Hara, *True names* (²2016) 73–5 n. 329); see also C. Marangoni, *Supplementum etymologicum Latinum* (2007) 1.135–6. *aduena* occurs in the *Annals* only here and in the version of Claudius' speech at 11.24.4: although the word does not appear in the extant text of Claudius' original, it does appear in the Livian speech on which Claudius' speech is based (Liv. 4.3.13) and to which T. alludes in a 'window reference' at 11.24.1 (cf. C. S. Kraus and A. J. Woodman, *Latin historians* (1997) 99). *e(x)* is regular in etymologies (*OLD* 14d).

66 An accusation

T. begins with a medical bulletin on the plague of accusers, which was spreading and daily becoming more violent; but by way of illustration he provides only the single example of Quintilius Varus, attacked by Domitius Afer and P. Dolabella. Moreover he makes no mention of the charge brought against Varus; the trial was stopped by the senate; and there is no evidence that it was ever resumed. The episode thus exemplifies very well the classic Tacitean technique of creating an 'impression' which fails to be supported by the 'facts' provided (in the familiar formulation of Walker 82–137).

66.1 Sed ut studia *procerum* et largitio *principis* aduersum casus solacium tulerant After the digression in 65, *sed* returns us to the year's main narrative, the two preceding episodes of which are referred to by *studia procerum* and *largitio principis* respectively (cf. 63.2 and 64.1–2). T.'s language, esp. appropriate in view of 63.2, suggests medical treatment (e.g. Cels. 6.7.3 'commune . . . auxilium aduersum omnium aurium casus'; *OLD casus* 9b) and thus contrasts with the disease imagery in the main sentence (next n.). For *solacium ferre* see *Agr.* 44.5 and n.; for *solacium aduersum* cf. Sen. *NQ* 6.2.1 (and for the form *aduersum* see 3.14.1n.); for *proceres* see 63.2n.

accusatorum maior in dies et infestior uis sine leuamento grass-abatur *uis* can be used of the 'violent attack of disease' (*OLD* 9b), while *grassari* = 'to rage' is used 'esp. of diseases, conditions' (*OLD* 4); likewise *infestus* (*OLD* 4a) and *leuamentum* (8.3n.) are part of the same metaphor, and even *in dies* sustains the notion of a medical bulletin (cf. 14.51.1 'grauescentibus in dies publicis malis', Vell. 123.1 'ingrauescente in dies ualetudine'). There is no independent evidence to confirm or refute T.'s generalisation. For *infestus* see also 3.15.2n.

corripueratque Varum Quintilium, diuitem et Caesari propin-quum, Domitius Afer Quintilius Varus (for the transposition of names see 3.21.3n.) was the son of Claudia Pulchra (52.1n.) and her husband P. Quintilius Varus (ord. 13 BC), whose three legions were wiped out by Arminius in the Teutoburg Forest in AD 9. His grandmother was the daugh-ter of Augustus' sister (hence *Caesari propinquum*); he himself had at one time been betrothed to Germanicus' youngest daughter (Sen. *Contr.* 1.3.10). Nothing is heard of the family hereafter. See *RE* 24.987 = Quinctilius 28 (Hanslik), *PIR* 7.20 no. 29, *BNP* 12.337 [II 8]; Syme, *AA* 149, 315, 327, and Tables III and XXVI. For Domitius Afer see 52.1–4 and nn.; *corripio* is very often used of informers and disease alike (3.28.3n.). For the case see Rutledge 143–4.

condemnator is even rarer than *criminator* (1.3n.), not being found again until late Latin. For the case see 52.1–3 and nn.

parto nuper praemio i.e. for his partially successful prosecution of Claudia Pulchra (52.3n.); for the rewards to prosecutors see 20.1n.

plura ad flagitia accingeretur For the metaphor see Malloch on 11.28.1.

66.2 Publium Dolabellam . . . miraculo erat For Dolabella see 23.2n.; *miraculo erat* contrasts with *nullo mirante* above: what *was* astonishing was that the highly respectable Dolabella was prepared to attack a relative (next n.). For the acc. + infin. cf. Liv. 25.8.7.

claris maioribus et Varo conexus Dolabella's grandfather had been consul in 44 BC; his father had married a sister of the disgraced Varus, so he and the younger Varus were cousins (Syme, *AA* Table XXVI; stemma between pp. 24–5 in *PIR* 7). The two points of ancestry and relationship are repeated in *nobilitatem* and *sanguinem* below.

suam ipse nobilitatem, suum sanguinem perditum ibat The anaphora of *suus* emphasises the incredulity of contemporary observers, the horror of Dolabella's actions being underlined by *ipse*. The pronoun may precede (as *Bell. Afr.* 64.2 'ipse suam causam probauerat Caesari') or follow (as Cic. *Phil.* 2.56 'is non apertissime studium suum ipse profitetur?', Sen. *Ben.* 3.12.4 'beneficium suum ipse insequenti iniuria rescidit') the noun-phrase, but T. favours interposition, as here (cf. e.g. 3.24.2, 3.50.3, 3.66.4, 6.6.2, 6.14.1 'suam ipse ceruicem perfregit', *Agr.* 46.3). *sanguinem perdere* recurs at 16.16.1 and Quint. 10.1.115, while *perditum ire*, after two or three appearances in comedy, recurs 3× in Sallust and Livy respectively before such later authors as Gell. and Apul. (*TLL* 10.1.1274.1–5); here there is perhaps a varied allusion to one of the Sallustian passages (*C.* 52.12 'ne illi *sanguinem* nostrum largiantur et . . . bonos omnis *perditum eant*').

opperiendum imperatorem The *princeps'* absence, of which we are here reminded, often made the senate nervous or even rendered it impotent (see Talbert 169–70 for some similar cases).

quod *unum urgentium* malorum suffugium in tempus erat Since *urgere* is regular of disease (e.g. Cels. 2.1.6, 2.4.4, 4.7.5), and since *malum* regularly means 'disease' (*OLD* 7b), T. may possibly be returning to the imagery of §1 above; but the two words are also regularly combined in other contexts, e.g. in Cicero and Livy, and *suffugium* seems not to be used of escaping illness etc., but is more likely to be used of sheltering from hostile climatic conditions (e.g. *G.* 16.3). *in tempus* means 'for a time' (*OLD* 5a; 6.11.1n.).

67 *Tiberius withdraws to Capri*

The decisive moment of the *princeps'* withdrawal to Capri is marked by a description of the island which takes up two thirds of the year's final section (67.1–3), the last third being devoted to the tragic effects of his withdrawal on Germanicus' widow and eldest son (67.3–4). The description can be compared point by point with the rhetorical guidelines for the *laus locorum* found in Menander (see nn. below and on 55.3–4 above) but requires to be seen in the light of Tib.'s portrayal as an exile (58.2 'patria careret', 6.15.3 'ambiens patriam et declinans'): if he is in exile from his fatherland, it follows that his destination is a 'foreign' country, and R. F. Thomas (126–30) has argued that 67.1–3 is a passage of ethno-geographical description comparable in nature to that of Africa in the *Bellum Iugurthinum* (*J.* 17–19) and of Britain in the *Agricola* (*Agr.* 10–13.1). In this way T. not only underlines the increasing alienation of Tib. from his people but also provides for his readers in metonymical form the kind of *situs gentium* which at 33.3 he said he could not provide.

67.1 At Caesar dedicatis per Campaniam templis With these words we are returned to the narrative of Tib.'s departure from Rome which began at 57.1 'Caesar <proficiscitur> in Campaniam specie dedicandi templa'.

quamquam edicto monuisset ne quis quietem eius inrumperet Commentators have noted T.'s use of *eius* instead of *suam*, a type of substitution which is common both in T. (G–G 709b–10a, H. on *H.* 2.9.2) and elsewhere (K–S 1.610, L–H–S 175). The explanation and effect, if there is one, will vary according to context. It seems unlikely that the present example should be 'imputed to inattention' (2.36.2n.). Since *quis* is subject of the *ne*-clause, perhaps T. wished to avoid any possible ambiguity, although in the corresponding passage of Suetonius a reflexive is used (*Tib.* 40 'urbe egrediens ne quis se interpellaret edixerat'). Or perhaps we are to imagine that T. is formulating the edict in his own words or that *edicto monuisset* is shorthand for a third party (e.g. Sejanus) issuing the edict on Tib.'s behalf. Admittedly such interpretations as the latter conflict with the view of Syme, who, noting that T. is 'careful to emphasize the strain of violence in Tiberius', implies (but does not actually say) that *inrumpere* is an example of his 'unbridled language' (*Tac.* 701). For *inrumpere* see also 2.11.3n., although the present example is metaphorical.

   In his desire for *quies* Tib. had Augustan precedent (Sen. *Brev. Vit.* 4.2–4 'Diuus Augustus, cui dii plura quam ulli praestiterunt, non desiit quietem sibi precari et uacationem a re publica petere; omnis eius sermo ad hoc semper reuolutus est, ut speraret otium: hoc labores suos, etiam si falso, dulci tamen oblectabat solacio, aliquando se uicturum sibi. In quadam ad senatum missa epistula, cum requiem suam non uacuam fore dignitatis nec a priore gloria discrepantem pollicitus esset, haec uerba inueni: "Sed ista fieri speciosius quam promitti possunt. Me tamen cupido temporis optatissimi mihi prouexit ut, quoniam rerum laetitia moratur adhuc, praeciperem aliquid uoluptatis ex uerborum dulcedine." Tanta uisa est res otium ut illam, quia usu non poterat, cogitatione praesumeret. Qui omnia uidebat ex se uno pendentia, qui hominibus gentibusque fortunam dabat, illum diem laetissimus cogitabat quo magnitudinem suam exueret. Expertus erat quantum illa bona per omnis terras fulgentia sudoris exprimerent, quantum occultarum sollicitudinum tegerent'); the difference is that Tib., encouraged by Sejanus (41.3 'extollens laudibus quietem et solitudinem'), acted on his desires, and the *quies* which he announces here will soon be interpreted as *malum otium* when he reaches the island (3 below).

concursusque oppidanorum disposito milite prohiberentur contrasts vividly with the Tib. of earlier days in Rome (2.34.3 'processit Palatio, procul sequi iussis militibus. spectabatur occursante populo compositus ore et sermonibus uariis tempus atque iter ducens'). Although Suetonius agrees with T. on the nature of Tib.'s journey through Campania (*Tib.* 40 'toto itinere adeuntes submouerat'), he also says that Tib. had already arrived on Capri when he heard of the disaster at Fidenae, whereupon 'transiit in continentem potestatemque omnibus adeundi sui fecit' (ibid.).

municipia et colonias i.e. the Italian towns generally (1.79.1n.).

Capreas se in insulam abdidit Whereas great men were supposed to live their lives in the open (to Summers' n. on Sen. *Ep.* 43, a letter which almost constitutes a commentary on Tib.'s withdrawal, add Vell. 2.14.3),[129] the secretive Tib. hides himself away on the island of Capri (also below, 2n.); for the association of islands and exile (self-imposed, of course, in Tib.'s case) see Plut. *De Exilio* 602c–F. T.'s word order is slightly unusual (contrast e.g. 2.85.3 'in insulam Seriphon abdita est', 4.13.2, 4.71.4) and not only mirrors Tib.'s action ('mimetic syntax') but also serves to underline the fact that Capri is an island, one of the first points to be made when an author is presenting the situation (θέσις) of a place (Menand. 344.19–23 θέσιν τοίνυν χώρας δοκιμάζομέν τε καὶ κρίνομεν ὅπως κεῖται πρὸς γῆν ἢ <πρὸς> θάλατταν ἢ πρὸς οὐρανόν· . . . πρὸς δὲ θάλατταν, εἰ νῆσος), the topic to which T. devotes most of his description. According to the account of the island given by Strabo (5.4.8–9), whose geographical work was completed very shortly before Tib.'s withdrawal there (see 6.18.2n.), Augustus had regarded Capri as his personal possession and had built on it (τὰς δὲ Καπρέας ἴδιον ποιησαμένου κτῆμα καὶ κατοικοδομήσαντος): it was therefore a most suitable place for his adopted son to move to. Since *Capreae* suggests the etymology 'Goat Island', it was also an appropriately named domicile for a *princeps* whose alleged sexual proclivities led to his being called 'the old goat' (Suet. *Tib.* 45): see Champlin (2015) 222–3. For Tib.'s life on the island and the latter's various other associations see Bernecker 65ff., Houston, Syme, *RP* 6.409–20, Champlin (2013) 223ff.; also 6.1.1–2 and nn.

trium milium freto ab extremis Surrentini promunturii diiunctam T.'s readers 'would hardly have required the information that this island is three miles off the Campanian coast, opposite Surrentum.

---

[129] See 40.1n. (*quibus*) above for a related topos.

The detail, however, is demanded by the genre' (Thomas 126–7, comparing Plin. *NH* 3.82 'mox a Surrento VIII distantes Tiberi principis arce nobiles Capreae circuitu XI'). Phraseology such as 'separated by a strait' (e.g. Mela 2.122) is conventional in geographical passages; for *diiuncta* cf. *TLL* 5.1.1386.16ff. ('saepe in re geographica'; cf. *dirimere* at *Agr.* 23 and n.): the closest parallels to T. are in the *Verrines* (Cic. *II Verr.* 1.154 'freto disiunctus', 4.103 'insula . . . diiuncta', 117). See further 6.1.1n.; for the verbal hyperbaton cf. 3.1.1n.

67.2 Solitudinem eius placuisse maxime crediderim T. is in agreement with Suetonius (*Tib.* 40 'praecipue delectatus insula, quod uno paruoque litore adiretur, saepta undique praeruptis immensae altitudinis rupibus et profundo mari'), and, since *maxime* qualifies *placuisse* (G–G 792b), perhaps using the same source (cf. Suetonius' *praecipue delectatus*). For the solitude of the tyrant see *Agr.* 39.3 and n., Plin. *Pan.* 48.5 'tenebras semper secretumque captantem, nec umquam ex solitudine sua prodeuntem nisi ut solitudinem faceret' (both of Domitian). Again cf. 6.1.1 'solitudinem maris' and n. Conversely G. Parker argues that the island was relatively accessible ('Highways into byways: the travels of Tiberius', *Antichthon* 43 (2009) 64–78, at 69–70).

importuosum circa mare et uix modicis nauigiis pauca subsidia The description alludes to the rocky coastline for which the island was famous (see previous n. and 6.1.1n.); today the principal harbour is on the north shore (Marina Grande). It is generally, and no doubt rightly, assumed that here and at 12.20.1 T. is alluding to Sallust's ethno-geography of Africa at *J.* 17.5 'mare . . . importuosum', although the same phrase recurs in Seneca, another author whom T. often imitates (*Cons. Helv.* 7.8); for the appearance of the adj. in other geographical contexts see Thomas 131 n. 13. For *subsidium* in the concrete sense of 'harbour' see 5.8.1n.

nisi gnaro custode *custode* is collective singular (for which see Austin on Virg. *Aen.* 1.564); for the soldiers accompanying Tib. cf. 59.2, 67.1. The security of a place was one of the advantages recommended for praise by Menander (350.30, 351.11).

Caeli temperies hieme *m*itis obiectu *m*ontis, quo saeua uentorum arcentur 'In winter and spring the prevailing winds are north (*tramontana*), east (*levante*) and north-east (*grecale*), alternating with south (*ostro*) and the humid south-west (*libeccio*), and south-east (*scirocco*)' (J. Money, *Capri: island of pleasure* (1986) p. xv). This makes it difficult to know whether by *obiectu montis* T. means Monte Solaro, which rises above Marina Grande in the centre of the island but to the west of Tib.'s presumed villa complex, or the Monti Lattari range on the mainland to the east. For the phrase itself cf. Sen. *NQ* 4a.2.8 'Nilus alto ac profundo alueo fertur, ne in latitudinem excedat obiectu montium pressus', Gell. 12.13.27 'regiones quae Tauri montis obiectu separantur' (*obiicio* is another 'geographical' word: *OLD* 8d). *mitis* (*OLD* 7a–b) and *saeuus* (*OLD* 5) are often used of climate or the weather etc., but T. has characteristically varied the latter by means of his favoured neut. plural + gen.; cf. Val. Aedit. fr. 2.3 'uis saeua . . . uenti'. For the importance of climate in *descriptiones locorum* see 55.4n.; also next n.

aestas in fauonium obuersa et aperto circum pelago peramoena 'In summer westerly winds (*ponente*) prevail' (Money, loc. cit.). Similarly Strabo assures his readers that nearby Herculaneum has a promontory which faces the sea and catches the SW breeze (5.4.8 ἐκκειμένην εἰς τὴν θάλατταν ἄκραν ἔχον, καταπνεομένην λιβὶ θαυμαστῶς ὥσθ᾽ ὑγιεινὴν ποιεῖν τὴν κατοικίαν). Menander says that, if you are praising an island community, you should enumerate all the good things that come from the sea (348.25–7); he nowhere refers specifically to wind, which was, however, a standard topic in texts which describe places (Kienzle 25–8, 53): 'in Mediterranean countries it is as important to "catch" coolness as the sun' (N–H on Hor. *C.* 2.15.16, q.v.). *aestas*, a bold metonymy for 'the island in summer', is used similarly at 6.33.3 to mean 'summer weather conditions' (n.); here the usage is facilitated by *obuersa*, the appropriate word for a place which faces a prevailing wind (Ov. *F.* 5.381 'Pelion Haemoniae mons est obuersus in austros'). *pelagus* (again at 15.46.2, *H.* 5.6.2) is overwhelmingly a poetical word: the only prose author to use it at all frequently is the geographer Mela (*TLL* 10.1.989.66–9); *aperto . . . pelago* is almost exclusively poetic (Lucil. 1291, Virg. *Aen.* 5.212, Vitr. 5.12.3, Luc. 3.532–3, Val. Fl. 1.7, 4.678, Stat. *Theb.* 5.351). *peramoenus* occurs only here in classical Latin; the idyllic qualities of the island will be used against Tib. when he fails to attend his mother's funeral in 29 (5.2.1 'nihil mutata amoenitate uitae').

prospectabatque pulcherrimum sinum, antequam Vesuuius mons ardescens faciem loci uerteret Menander says that in describing bays you should praise their beauty (352.7–8 κόλπους ἐπαινέσεις εἰς . . . κάλλος), but of course the shores of Campania were in any case famous for their attractiveness (3.59.3n.). When Vesuvius erupted in 79, T. was in his early twenties, perhaps a military tribune in Britain (Birley (2000) 237–8). News of the eruption will have spread quickly and widely of its own accord, but almost three decades later T. would famously ask Pliny about the disaster so that he could include the information in his *Histories* (cf. Plin. *Ep.* 6.16, 6.20). Statius, writing in 95 at Naples, gives a brief but graphic account of the effect of the eruption on the landscape and implies that volcanic activity is still occurring more than a decade and a half later (*Silv.* 4.4.78–85). Furneaux believed that this ongoing activity explained the tense of *uerteret*, but an imperf. subjunc. can express a once-for-all event (e.g. Liv. 25.31.12 'paucis ante diebus quam Syracusae caperentur, T. Otacilius Uticam transmisit'), which seems the natural interpretation here.

facies loci/-orum is a common expr. (*TLL* 6.1.49.78–82; cf. 63.2n.) but perhaps still retained something of the original metaphor (cf. 14.10.3 'non, ut hominum uultus, ita locorum facies mutantur', also of the Bay of Naples). For the substantival use of the present participle see 12.1n. *prospectare* (again at 14.9.1 'subiectos sinus . . . prospectat', *H.* 3.60.1, 5.6.1) is another 'geographical' term (*TLL* 10.2.2204.49ff.).

Graecos . . . fama tradit Menander laid great stress on discussing the earlier settlers of a place (e.g. 353.6, 356.1ff.), and Virgil in his 'gathering of the clans' refers to the hero Telon, 'Teleboum Capreas cum regna teneret' (*Aen.* 7.735). This man is otherwise unknown before Virgil 'and, it is widely suspected, invented' (Horsfall ad loc., who sees *fama tradit* as an 'Alexandrian footnote', T.'s implicit indication that he is quoting the *Aeneid*). Whether *ea tenuisse* is due to the Virgilian line or to the verb's regularity in ethnographical contexts (*OLD* 8) is uncertain; *ea* must = 'those parts' or simply 'the island'. The Teleboans are a people of western Acarnania and the adjacent islands (*BNP* 14.220). Modern scholarship stresses the importance of the island's 'Greekness' to Tib. (e.g. Houston 182–3, Champlin (2013) 240–1). For *fama tradit* elsewhere in T. cf. *H.* 2.3.1 (the temple of Venus at Paphos), 4.84.3 (Serapis); for such phraseology in general see Norden's note on *Aen.* 6.14.

67.3 Sed tum Tiberius duodecim uillarum †nominibus et molibus† insederat Modern editors print the transmitted text without any indication that there may be something amiss with it, yet this is one of the most challenging cruces in Book 4.

(a) The first question to address is whether *insederat* (which may be from either *insido* or *insideo*) is here followed by the dative (as at 12.64.1) or whether we should understand a more regular acc. object (e.g. *insulam*), in which case *nominibus et molibus* will be abl. There is a problem either way, and in each case it involves *nominibus*. It makes no sense to say *either* 'he settled in the names of twelve villas' *or* 'he settled on <the island> in the names of twelve villas'.
(b) Many scholars have attempted emendations of *nominibus*: thus *munitionibus* was suggested by W. S. Watt (in our 1989 edition) and *moenibus* by R. A. Kaster (ap. Champlin (2013) 226 n. 58); but the difficulty with each of these, as with most of the older suggestions listed by Walther, is that they seem redundant with *molibus*.[130] In 1989 I suggested *amoenitatibus*, comparing, among other exs., *H.* 2.87.1 'uillarumque amoenitates': this makes good sense ('in twelve attractive and massive villas'), and *amoenus* and cognates are very often used of villas;

---

[130] An exception is Heinsius' *ignominiosis molibus*.

but the word is perhaps too far from *nominibus*, and the combination of abstract *amoenitatibus* and concrete *molibus* is arguably too awkward even for T. (exs. in Sörbom 75–6). (c) Martin (in our 1989 edition) suggested the deletion of *nominibus et*. This leaves us with the idiomatic *moles* + gen. (cf. e.g. 13.31.1 'molem amphitheatri', Plin. *NH* 36.88 'aedificiorum moles'; *TLL* 8.1342.10ff.), but it has to be admitted that the genesis of the proposed corruption is quite unclear.

(d) A further oddity is the reference to twelve villas. Capri is a very small island (only 3½ miles across, and 4 square miles in area), a significant portion of it mountainous: it seems implausible both that Tib. should want or require so many villas in so confined a space and that so confined a space could actually accommodate twelve villas of imperial dimensions.[131] Suetonius' reference to only one villa (*Tib.* 65.2) seems much more plausible. I therefore wonder whether T. wrote something like *duodecim uillarum <spatium> insederat* ('had occupied the area of twelve villas'; cf. 3.53.4 'uillarum . . . spatia'), *duodecim* being rhetorical for an indefinitely large number (cf. D. Fehling, *Herodotus and his 'sources'* (1989) 231). But, since this simply extends the problem of *nominibus* to *molibus*, I have decided to obelise the whole phrase, as in our 1989 edition.

The one villa to which Suetonius refers is called the Villa of Io or Ion (*Tib.* 65.2 'uilla quae uocatur Ionis'), although scholars have often emended the text to read *Iouis* or *Iunonis* or *Inonis* instead (Champlin (2013) 226–8). It is generally assumed that this villa is to be identified with the extensive remains of a building-complex in the north-eastern corner of the island (see J. H. D'Arms, *Romans on the Bay of Naples* (1970) 88–9, with plates 2–3, C. C. Mattusch, *Pompeii and the Roman villa: art and culture around the Bay of Naples* (2008) 24–6), part of which is thought to be the lighthouse referred to by Suetonius (*Tib.* 74) and Statius (*Silv.* 3.5.101). See the full discussion of Champlin (2013) 224–30, with further references.

quanto intentus olim publicas ad curas, tanto occultior in luxus et malum otium resolutus The appendix to the sentence conveys the transition from the description of the island to its effects on the *princeps* but raises problems of text and interpretation. The formulation *quanto* + positive ~ *tanto* + comparative, as here, is frequent in T. (see 1.57.1n.; G–G 1254a–b). In most cases the reader has to supply *magis* with *quanto*, yet it makes no sense to say 'the more secretly relaxing into luxury and evil inactivity, the more concentrated formerly on official concerns'. Gronovius solved this problem

---

[131] It should also be borne in mind that each villa would require an ample supply of water (M. Zarmakoupi, *Designing for luxury on the Bay of Naples* (2014) 145).

by emending *occultior* to *occultos* (for the writing of *r* instead of *s* see Koestermann p. x): this makes good sense ('as relaxed into hidden luxury as formerly concentrated on official concerns') but produces a construction otherwise unparalleled in classical Latin, since *quanto* + positive ~ *tanto* + positive (i.e. equivalent to *quam* ~ *tam* or *ut* ~ *ita*) is not found until much later (L–H–S 137). Most modern editors (Furneaux, Halm, Koestermann, Heubner, Borzsák) print Weissenborn's *occultiores*, but it is significant that none of those who translate this text (Jackson, Damon, Yardley) translates a comparative at all. The fact is that a comparative is not needed here; does that mean that, like Fuchs, we should follow Gronovius? This is what Walther did, while adding: 'nisi forte vocem *occultior* intelligas de Tiberio e conspectu hominum remoto et insula abdito. Tum *tanto* pertinet ad *resolutus*.' This interpretation, though rejected by Walther himself, seems to me the likeliest: it still leaves us with an unparalleled use of *quanto* ~ *tanto* (though seemingly accepted at K–S 2.485), but we should note *tanto pessimus* ~ *quanto . . . optimus* at Catull. 49.7–8, which is not essentially different; the sole advantage of this interpretation over Gronovius is that it does not require emendation. *occultior* is being used adverbially, as e.g. 12.1 and 40.5, and the sense is: 'more secretly relaxing into luxury and evil inactivity to the same degree as he was formerly concentrated on official/public concerns'.

Tib. was very conscious of the *curae* which he undertook on behalf of the *res publica* (3.54.5n.), and, although sometimes he had expressed his exasperation at their volume and frequency (3.35.1n.), his previous concentration on them was confirmed at the start of Book 4 (6.2–4 and nn.). Although *intentus ad curas* recurs only in T. (cf. *H.* 2.67.2, 4.2.1), the adj. perhaps recalls Sallust, in whom it is unusually frequent and characterises 'the good man' (R. Syme, *Sallust* (1964) 268). Suetonius says that a neighbouring island was called 'Apragopolis' by Augustus 'a desidia secedentium illuc e comitatu suo' (*Aug.* 98.4), but, according to Plutarch, Tib. was still overwhelmed by cares while on Capri (*De Exilio* 602E ἐκείνῳ μὲν αἱ τῆς ἡγεμονίας φροντίδες ἐπιχεόμεναι καὶ προσφερόμεναι πανταχόθεν οὐ καθαρὰν παρεῖχον οὐδ' ἀκύμονα τὴν νησιῶτιν ἡσυχίαν); here in T., however, the *princeps'* earlier concentration is contrasted almost chiastically with his 'dissolving' or 'slackening' or 'relaxing' into luxurious inactivity (*intentus* ~ *resolutus*, seemingly unparalleled), a contrast which is seen by Thomas in terms of environmental determinism: the 'balanced environment' generates in its inhabitant 'a low moral worth' (129). Words denoting looseness are typically associated with luxury and idleness (e.g. 11.31.2 'solutior luxu' and Malloch's n., *H.* 2.99.2 'soluti in luxum' and H.'s n.); Seneca regards it as paradoxical that so important a figure as Maecenas walked about the city 'solutis tunicis' and, when deputising for Augustus, issued the daily password when 'discinctus' (*Ep.* 114.6). *otium* is frequently associated with luxury: for the pair of nouns as found here cf. 1.16.2, *Octav.* 562, Flor. 1.24.8 (= 2.8.8), and for T.'s favoured *luxus* cf. 3.52.1n.

Manebat quippe suspicionum et credendi temeritas   *quippe* explains *malum otium*, an unparalleled expression: Romans took it for granted that inactivity was synonymous with dissoluteness (see above), but Tib.'s inactivity on Capri was positively *criminal*, because of the attacks on Agrippina and Nero.

One of the topoi of περὶ φυγῆς literature is that a change of locality does not lead to a change of mentality (see e.g. Mayer on Hor. *Epist.* 1.11.27 or Summers on Sen. *Ep.* 28; Tosi 48–9 §108). The topos, whose use can vary according to circumstances (consolatory, admonitory etc.), is perhaps hinted at by *manebat* here: Tib. is in exile (58.2 and n.) in a 'foreign' country, but the change of location has no effect on his mental rashness. For the *uariatio* of noun ~ gerund see Sörbom 111–12.

turbabat   Some scholars think that the verb is used absolutely or that we should understand *eum*, but it is most natural to regard *quam* as its object: since *suspicionum et credendi temeritas* is equivalent to 'his rash suspicions and beliefs', T.'s point is that Sejanus so confused the one with the other that Tib. no longer knew what to believe and what to suspect.

non iam occultis . . . insidiis   T. seems to intend a comparison with the methods used primarily against the young Nero alone at 59.3–60.1 above, although the difference between the two passages does not appear substantive and one might even be justified in talking in terms of a 'doublet': in particular Nero already has *custodes* attached to him in the previous year (see further next n.). Whether this awkwardness of presentation is connected to the 'unchronological' nature of 59.3–60 on the one hand (see intro. n. there) and/or to Suetonius' different chronology for these same events on the other (see below on *eaque . . . obiciebantur*) is unclear. For *occultis . . . insidiis* cf. H. on *H.* 3.68.1.

67.4 Quis additus miles . . . uelut in annales referebat   Since *additus miles* seems to be a cross-reference to 60.1 'adpositi custodes', *additus* must be attributive ('The soldiers attached to them were recording . . .'). *in annales referre* ('to write down in *annales*') occurs elsewhere (Liv. 4.34.6, 43.13.1–2, Plin. *NH* 33.18, *HA Iul. Capitol.* 3.1) but its application here is obscure. Does *annales* denote a work of importance, as 13.31.1 (and cf. 4.32.1n.), or does it connote daily minutiae, as Semp. Asell. F1 'annales libri . . . id est, quasi qui diarium scribunt'? Cf. also 6.24.1. For *quis* see 3.28.2n.

introitus   'visitors', an abstract for concrete for which the only parallel seems to be Ov. *F.* 1.138 'ianitor egressus introitusque uidet' (*TLL* 7.2.78.32).

ultroque struebantur qui . . .   *ultro* = 'in addition to everything else' (*OLD* 3a) and marks the difference between the victims' present treatment and that at 59.3ff. *struo* is not normally used of people (*OLD* 6b) but cf. 11.12.1 'strueret crimina et accusatores' and Malloch ad loc.; see also 38.2n. above. The sentence is chiastic with the preceding and the three infinitival commands (below) are arranged in the order ABBABA.

qui monerent perfugere ad Germaniae exercitus 'to advise them to flee to the armies in Germany': the infin. after *moneo* (again at 16.11.1, *H.* 4.33.1, 5.24.1) is rare in earlier prose but more common hereafter (*TLL* 8.1411.27ff.). For the resonance of 'the German armies' see 5.10.2n.

celeberrimo fori 'in the most crowded part of the forum': the very unusual substantival use of the neut. sing. (for which cf. Apul. *Apol.* 16 'in propatulo et celebri') is T.'s variation on standard phraseology (the superl. adj. is often found in inscriptions, e.g. *SCPP* 171 'in urbis ipsius celeberrimo loco', with Eck et al. 269).

effigiem . . . amplecti On this form of 'asylum' see 3.36.1n.

auxilio uocare recurs only at 12.45.1, Virg. *Aen.* 5.686.

eaque . . . obiciebantur Suetonius mentions two of the three charges but associates them with Agrippina alone and seems to link them with her banishment in 29 (*Tib.* 53.2 'nouissime calumniatus modo ad statuam Augusti, modo ad exercitus confugere uelle, Pandatariam relegauit').

68–75 THE YEAR AD 28

Earlier in Book 4 T. had warned about the nature of his forthcoming narrative: a city in mourning, a *princeps* uninterested in foreign glory, savage orders, continuous accusations, false friendships, the destruction of the innocent (32.2, 33.3). All these warnings are realised in the final year of the book.

The year is organised on the same pattern as AD 24. Two domestic sections (68–71 and 74–5) frame a section of foreign affairs (72–3), in which the Frisian revolt disconcertingly fails to provoke the appropriate Roman reprisals (73.3 'neque dux Romanus ultum iit') and instead results in the Frisian name being celebrated across Germany (74.1 'Clarum . . . Frisium nomen'). The two domestic sections mirror each other, in that a more substantial episode is followed by a much shorter notice of a traditional kind: on the one hand the death of Julia, Augustus' granddaughter, suggesting the end of a link with the past (71.4); on the other hand the marriage of the younger Agrippina to Cn. Domitius Ahenobarbus, who as parents of the emperor Nero symbolise the grim future (75). The first major episode (68–71.3) is the entrapment and execution of Titius Sabinus, whose crime, mentioned at the very start, is his friendship with Germanicus (68.1 'ob amicitiam Germanici'). Since the attack on Sabinus was decided four years earlier but cynically deferred until now (cf. 18.1, 19.1), its narration here has a retrospective aspect; but a forward reference to his accusers' eventual punishment (71.1) alerts the reader to an impending sequel. The second major episode describes the newly acquired power of Sejanus (74), which we are invited to see as the achievement of ambitions conceived three years earlier (41.1–3); but a reference to the fatality of his friendship, here mentioned at the very end (74.5 'infaustae amicitiae'), reminds us that his manipulations will have violent consequences in the future. In both episodes the tension between closure and anticipation is perfectly judged for the end of a book.

68–71 Domestic Affairs

Most of this section is taken up with the case of Titius Sabinus, the last case in the book 'and also the most dramatic . . . The picture of Sabinus, bound and helpless, dragged to his dungeon as a sacrifice to the virtually deified Sejanus, lives in the reader's mind when the circumstances of many other cases have been forgotten'.[132] Sabinus was targeted because he had been befriended by Germanicus and had stayed loyal to the family after Germanicus' death (68.1 *amicitiam, sector . . . comes . . . post tot clientes unus*, 68.3 *amicus*): with a cynicism typical of tyrannies, it is friendship – on this occasion naturally false – which Sejanus' agents use as their method of trapping him (68.4 'speciem artae amicitiae', 'quasi ad fidissimum'). Sabinus is deceived into revealing his 'treachery' in the presence of hidden witnesses (69.1–2); and no sooner has Tib. responded to the revelations than the victim is executed (70.1). The general panic attending these events (69.3, 70.2) is a reflection of that experienced by the tyrant himself, on which Sejanus intends to capitalise again in due course (70.4, 71.3).

68.1 Iunio Silano et Silio Nerua consulibus For C. Appius Iunius Silanus, son of the consul of AD 10, see 6.9.3n. About P. Silius Nerva, son of the consul of AD 3 and nephew of the Silius of 18.1–20.1 above, little is otherwise known: see *RE* 3A.1.95 = Silius 22 (Nagl), *PIR* 7.2.277 no. 727 (stemma on p. 271). If we exclude AD 29 as a special case (5.1.1n.), T. again uses *et* rather than the regular asyndeton to join the consuls' names only at 14.29.1 and 15.23.1, a variation found also in Livy. When the elder Pliny tells the story of the faithful dog belonging to one of Sabinus' slaves, he too uses *et* in providing the same date (*NH* 8.145 'Appio Iunio et P. Silio consulibus').

---

[132] Walker 104–5; cf. also Heinz 58–62, J. Blänsdorf, 'Die Kunst der historischen Szene in den "Annalen" des Tacitus', *Latomus* 53 (1994) 771–4.

foedum anni principium incessit Since these words are equally applicable to a weather report (*OLD foedus*[1] 2a, *incedo* 6a 'to arise, come on'), the effect of the appended abl. abs. is maximised; much less suspenseful are 16.13.1 'tot facinoribus foedum annum etiam dii tempestatibus et morbis insigniuere', Liv. 8.18.1 'foedus insequens annus seu intemperie caeli seu humana fraude fuit'. *anni principium* is resumed ring-fashion at 70.1 'Sed . . . incipientis anni', where we learn that the actual date was 1 January; the intervening narrative relates to a period before the start of the present year (see also next nn.), a similar, but not identical, technique to that used in AD 23 (see 4.1n.).

tracto in carcerem inlustri equite Romano Titio Sabino In keeping with the ring composition (last n.) the victim's imprisonment is returned to at 70.1 'trahebatur damnatus'. For Sabinus see *RE* 6A.1569 = Titius 39 (Stein), *PIR* 8.83 no. 270, *BNP* 14.744 [Titius II 4]; Demougin, *PCR* 222 no. 258; for his case see Rutledge 144–6. For *inlustri*, which here contrasts with *foedum* (cf. 15.32), cf. 58.1n.

neque enim omiserat . . . percolere The pluperf. tense indicates that reference is being made to an earlier period than the beginning of the year; *adgrediuntur* (below) is subsequent in time to *omiserat* but also prior to the start of the year. Since Sabinus' case had been decided but postponed four years earlier (18.1, 19.1), the events described in 68–9 'may have spread over a considerable part of the intervening time' (Furneaux). See further below, 2n. (*Compositum*). After Plautus, *percolere* seems not to be found until Caesius Bassus (*Gramm. Lat.* 6.264.23 K), T. and the younger Pliny (*TLL* 10.1.1216.5–6).

sectator . . . comes Cf. Cic. *Rab. Post.* 21.

unus 'the only one remaining.' The use of *post* here is, if not identical with, at least very similar to that mentioned at 40.2n.

68.2 Latinius Latiaris See 6.4.1n. for the problems of this man's nomenclature.

Porcius Cato Suffect consul in 36 and *curator aquarum* in 38, the year in which he came to grief: 'not necessarily from the ancient consular family' (Rodgers on Front. *Aq.* 102.6). See *RE* 22.218–19 = Porcius 33 (Hanslik), *PIR* 6.366–7 no. 856, *BNP* 11.636 [II 1]; Syme, *AA* 222–3.

Petilius Rufus was perhaps the father of Q. Petilius Cerialis Caesius Rufus (14.32.3), who was twice (or perhaps even three times) consul, and ninth governor of Britain: see *Agr.* 8.2n.; also *RE* 19.1150 = Petillius (Swoboda), *PIR* 6.99 no. 262. The name is spelled 'Petillius' on inscriptions, but T.'s editors conventionally adopt Lipsius' emendation of M's *petitius*. For another such case see 6.28.1n.

M. Opsius Possibly an ancestor of the Neapolitan senator M. Opsius Navius Fannianus (*IG* 14.719): see *RE* 18.758 = Opsius 1 (Hoffmann), *PIR* 5.3.456 no. 126.

ad quem non nisi per Seianum aditus Sejanus had added to his earlier influence (2.3) because he now controlled also physical access to Tib., as he had planned (41.2 'sua in manu aditus'): see 70.1, 74.3, 6.8.2 'ut quisque Seiano intimus, ita ad Caesaris amicitiam ualidus', Juv. 10.91 'summas donare curules' (Syme, *RP* 3.1148). The repetition of *non nisi per Seianum* by *neque Seiani . . . nisi* (below) emphasises the fact that along every avenue one encountered Sejanus; for the metaphor *ad consulatum . . . aditus* cf. Cic. *Mur.* 17, Liv. 6.37.7 (and Oakley on 6.35.3).

Compositum sc. *erat*, continuing the flashback which started with *neque enim omiserat* at §1 above.

qui modico usu Sabinum contingebat Cf. Ov. *Ex P.* 2.5.6 'fuerim quamuis modico tibi iunctus ab usu'; also Curt. 7.6.11 'libertatis modico et aequali usu'. *contingebat* = 'was in contact with' (*OLD* 2b).

strueret dolum . . . accusationem inciperent The three stages of the plan (here in the verb–noun arrangement ABBABA) correspond to this and the two following paragraphs. For *strueret dolum* cf. Sen. *HO* 1468 (*Phaedr.* 828 'instruitur . . . dolus').

68.3 quod non . . . florentis domus amicus adflictam deseruisset The metaphor (again at 71.4 below) is that of a tree or plant, once thriving but now laid low (cf. Col. 2.16.2 'quod [sc. pratum] . . . tempestatibus adfligeretur'): other exs. at Cic. *Quinct.* 93, *Att.* 3.10.2, Nep. *Att.* 11.4 'non florentibus se uenditauit, sed afflictis semper succurrit', Liv. 7.20.5, 28.41.17, Sen. *Tranq. An.* 5.3.

honora For this poeticism see 1.10.7n.

ut sunt molles in calamitate mortalium animi Cf. Caes. *BG* 3.19.6 'mollis . . . ad calamitates ferendas mens'. For *molles . . . animi* see e.g. Mariotti on Sall. *C.* 14.5; for *mortalium* see 62.2n.

audentius iam onerat Seianum, saeuitiam, superbiam, spes eius 'The return to the historical present marks the change of subject again to Latiaris' (Furneaux). *onerat* = 'he loaded with abuse': normally the abuse is expressed by an abl. (e.g. *probris* at Liv. 26.3.5), but not here or at *Laus Pis.* 99 'onerare nocentes' (*OLD* 6b, which is clearer than *TLL* 9.2.634.22ff.). For the collocation *saeuitiam, superbiam* cf. 6.31.1n.

68.4 tamquam uetita miscuissent 'as though they had exchanged treasonable confidences' (*OLD* ueto 1d, misceo 10). The confidences are naturally not treasonable for the informers, as is explained by Dio 58.1.1–2 in his account, which he places at the later meeting described at 69.1–2 below.

speciem artae amicitiae The episode illustrates in classic fashion the *fallaces amicitiae* about which T. warned at 33.3. For *arta amicitia* cf. 2.66.2, Val. Max. 4.7.3, Apul. *Apol.* 58.

quasi ad fidissimum deferre For *fidus* see 3.46.4n. The arrangement has again been mannered (ABABBA).

69.1 loco . . . seruanda . . . facies For *facies* see 67.2n.; for *seruanda* cf. Luc. 9.978, Sen. *Clem.* 2.5.5, *NQ* 3.3.1, Front. *Strat.* 1.1.9.

si pone fores adsisterent The door was too natural a place for over-hearing conversations (Plaut. *Merc.* 477, *Truc.* 95). The verb is subjunctive because the clause represents the conspirators' thoughts (cf. *metus*). For the archaising *pone* cf. 2.16.1n.

metus uisus, sonitus aut forte ortae suspicionis erat From *ortae suspicionis* it is clear that *uisus* and *sonitus* are gen. sing. Since T., seemingly like other authors (cf. *TLL* s.v.), does not construct plural *metus* with a dependent genitive (G–G 830b), it appears that Rhenanus' change of *erant* to *erat* is likely to be correct.

It is worth noting that a more regular manner of expression here would have been *metuebant ne uiderentur* etc., just as, two sentences earlier, one might have expected *quonam modo ea a pluribus auditoribus acciperentur* instead of *quonam modo ea plurium auditu acciperentur*. The concentration of verbal abstract nouns is remarkable and indicates that T. is here writing in what D. R. Langslow has called a 'nominal' or 'noun-based' style, characterised by compression, as opposed to a 'verb-based' style, characterised as descriptive and uncompressed (*Medical Latin in the Roman Empire* (2000) 378–9). Langslow sees the nominal style as lacking in variety, but of course T. is not a technical writer and famously varies his manner of expression throughout his narrative: for him the nominal style is itself a manifestation of variation. It is interesting that in the case of Thucydides 'it is the abstract nouns which catch our eye most often' (K. J. Dover, *Thucydides* (1973) 11, with some exs.): this is perhaps just coincidence, but it was after all Thucydides who stood at the head of the dissenting tradition of historiography to which T. belonged (*RICH* 40–7, 117ff.) and who was another master of *uariatio* (J. Ros, *Die METABOΛH (Variatio) als Stilprinzip des Thukydides* (1938)).

Tectum inter et laquearia tres senatores haud minus turpi latebra quam detestanda fraude sese abstrudunt *latebra* (*OLD* 1b) and *abstrudunt* (cf. Vell. 129.3 'uelut serpentem abstrusum terra') combine to describe the three former praetors as animalish predators, crammed into a disgusting lair (for *turpi* cf. Sen. *Tro.* 504) and waiting to pounce; the lair is mirrored in the anastrophe of *inter* ('mimetic syntax'), for which see 5.1n. Commentators refer to Val. Max. 6.7.2 and App. *BC* 4.44, where a similar hiding-place is used as a refuge, like a priest hole in post-Reformation England (see further J. Osgood, *Turia: a Roman woman's civil war* (2014) 118ff.). False walls could also be used for entrapment (Thuc. 1.133, Cic. *Top.* 75), giving real point to the phrase *tectum et parietes* at §3 below.

foraminibus et rimis aurem admouent T. catches all three in the ridiculous posture of simultaneously putting an ear to every possible crack; *aurem admouere* is a set phrase but naturally at home in stories of deception (e.g. Ter. *Phorm.* 866–9 'ad fores | . . . ire perrexi, accessi, adstiti, | . . . aurem admoui . . . | hoc modo sermonem captans').

69.2 in cubiculum trahit 'The *cubiculum* is the room for secret activity' (A. M. Riggsby, '"Private" and "public" in Roman culture: the case of the *cubiculum*', *JRA* 10 (1997) 36–56, at 44). *trahit* does not of course mean 'dragged' here but 'brought him along' (*OLD traho* 2a).

instantia See 6.48.2n.

adfatim Only here in T.; see further Oakley on Liv. 9.35.4.

Eadem ille et *diutius*, quanto maesta, ubi semel prorupere, difficilius reticentur The simplest way of interpreting this sentence is to assume that T. has omitted not only a verb of speaking, as often (1.31.5n.), but also *tanto*, another frequent omission (6.17.3n.). Hence: 'he spoke similarly and at greater length, corresponding to the greater difficulty with which laments, when once they burst forth, are left unsaid'. But Manutius' *quando* for *quanto* is very tempting.

prorumpo, which is rare of speech and before T. seems so used only at Sil. 3.699 'uox prorumpit in auras' (*TLL* 10.2.2162.43–4, 2164.37–8), is common of water (ibid. 2162.54ff.): laments are seen in terms of a series of waves; once the first ones have burst forth, there is no stopping those that follow (lamentation, to which Sabinus' outpourings are likened, was conventionally hard to control: see N–H on Hor. *C.* 2.20.23). The substantive use of *maesta*, previously at Luc. 7.382 and Sil. 3.504, is favoured by T. (*TLL* 8.49.28–9).

69.3 suumque ipsi dedecus narrauere In their anxiety to curry favour with Sejanus (68.2) disgrace marks their behaviour as much as it did that of Visellius Varro in the case with which that of Sabinus was originally linked (19.1 'odiis Seiani per dedecus suum gratificabatur').

Non alias magis anxia et pauens ciuitas A tyrant's subjects are conventionally characterised by fear (7.1n.), as is the tyrant himself (below, 70.4n.).

317

For such superlative expressions as *non alias* see 3.11.2n.; for the two adjs. cf. Sen. *Vit. Beat.* 15.3 'uita anxia, suspiciosa, trepida, casum pauens'.

<cautissime> agens aduersum proximos M's nonsensical *egens* is conventionally emended to *tegens*, following Lipsius, but, since the verb is not usually found with persons as its object, it is difficult to understand *se*, which Vertranius therefore supplied (Müller preferred *sui*, on the basis of 4.1.1 'sui obtegens'). R. H. Martin noted that *cautus* is the appropriate word for being on guard against treachery and is elsewhere followed by *aduersus* (Liv. 38.25.7 'consuli parum cauto aduersus conloquii fraudem', Val. Max. 3.8 *ext.* 5 'aduersus Heraclidem et Calippum . . . insidias ei nectentes cautior esset'; cf. 6.5.1). A scribe might perhaps have omitted *cautissime* between *ciuitas* and *–gens*, and T. is exceptionally fond of combining *agere* with an adverb; the combination with *caute* is found in Cicero (*Caec.* 15 'nihil satis caute . . . posset agi'), and, although T. does not use the superlative form of *caute* elsewhere, the expression is unexceptionable (Plin. *NH* 15.12 'qui cautissime agunt'). The cynical suggestion that people were 'behaving most cautiously of all towards their nearest and dearest' is both typically Tacitean and exactly right in the context of Sabinus' entrapment. For the form *aduersum* see 3.14.1n.

congressus, conloquia, notae ignotaeque aures uitari T. depicts a society in which natural social groupings are collapsing and the isolation of the ruler (cf. 42.1) is reflected in that of individuals – with the significant qualification that, as remarked by the French thinker Saint-Simon, in an absolute monarchy it is only the ruler who can soliloquise out loud (quoted by Rutherford 17 n. 49). For the combination of *congressus* and *conloquia* (again at *H.* 4.64.1) cf. Cic. *Phil.* 9.2, 12.26, Liv. 7.40.3, Mela 1.47. The 'complementary opposites' *notae ignotaeque*, a common coupling, express totality (Wills 571–2): *everyone* was avoided (for T.'s favoured metonymy of *aures* cf. 29.3n.; for *uitari* cf. Sen. *Ep.* 43.4).

etiam muta atque inanima, tectum et parietes circumspectabantur The conceit is not simply that 'the walls have ears' but that they can speak and thus repeat what they have heard: for this complex of ideas see Fraenkel on Aesch. *Ag.* 37, Dyck on Cic. *Cael.* 60; Otto 266, Tosi 106 §230; Santoro L'Hoir 166–7.[133] *muta atque inanima* (again at *H.* 1.84.4) is a fairly common

---

[133] In *The Times* for 20 January 1992 an article on informers in the former East Germany by the brilliant Bernard Levin was accompanied by a Peter Brookes cartoon depicting two apprehensive women walking alongside a wall which is topped with barbed wire and has grown a pair of very large ears. The conceit, albeit differently applied, also featured in numerous posters in World War II.

combination (Cic. *Verr.* 5.171, *ND* 1.36, *Rhet. Herenn.* 4.66, Quint. 5.11.23, 5.13.23); *tectum* and *parietes* are commonly combined from Cicero onwards (e.g. *Verr.* 5.184).

70.1 Sed Caesar sollemnia incipientis anni kalendis Ianuariis epistula precatus We are hereby returned to the narrative of the begin-ning of the year which we left at 68.1; everything in between, as we have seen, is a flashback. *sollemnia incipientis anni* is a reference to the *uota pro salute rei publicae*, which were offered on 1 January each year (Weinstock 217–19) and are to be distinguished from the *uota pro incolumitate principis* (17.1n.).[134] Although *sollemnia* is a regular term for new-year rituals (Cic. *Quir.* 11, Liv. 9.8.1, 21.63.7), there is no parallel for its coupling with *precari*, perhaps implying the oddity of performing the rituals by letter. We know that in the interests of confidentiality some of Tib.'s letters from Capri were written in his own hand rather than dictated (Sen. *Ep.* 83.15), but naturally we cannot know the format of this particular letter. For the tyrannical symbolism of letters see 6.2–14 intro. n.

uertit in Sabinum Ironically the *princeps'* ominous habit of changing topic in the middle of a letter (for which see 6.15.2n.) would later be used to accuse Sejanus himself (Dio 58.10.1). Neither here nor at 68.1 is any formal charge mentioned, and it is not clear whether there was even a formal trial (see *nec mora* below).

libertorum sc. *suorum.*

haud obscure i.e. in contrast to his usual obscurity (31.2n.).

trahebatur sc. *in carcerem*: cf. 68.1 'tracto in carcerem'.

nec mora quin decerneretur So too Dio 58.1.3 ἔς τε γὰρ τὸ δεσμωτήριον αὐθημερὸν ὁ Σαβῖνος κατετέθη, καὶ μετὰ τοῦτο ἄκριτος ἐφθάρη, τό τε σῶμα αὐτοῦ κατὰ τῶν ἀναβασμῶν ἐρρίφη καὶ ἐς τὸν ποταμὸν ἐνεβλήθη.

quantum obducta ueste et adstrictis faucibus niti poterat 'with as much effort as he was able, given that his clothing was drawn over [sc. his head] and his throat bound': the clause qualifies *clamitans.* The head was covered, usually (it seems) by the wearer of the clothing himself, as a sign of impending death (R. Waltz, *REL* 17 (1939) 292–308): with *obducta* we have to understand *capiti* (cf. Curt. 6.5.27 'uestis non tota Amazonum corpori obdu-citur', *Ciris* 342 'genis obducere uestem', where Lyne refers to the discussion of the expr. in his Intro. p. 42). *adstrictis faucibus* (metaphorical at *Aetna* 562) is

---

[134] Ritter's contention that *anni* is to be taken not with *sollemnia* but with *kalendis Ianuariis* seems connected with his strange belief that the senate did not meet on 1 January; on the contrary, for a full account of the meeting see Talbert 200–2.

explained at §3 below by *laqueus*, which does not imply hanging but strangling (cf. 5.9.2): cf. Juv. 10.88 'ceruice obstricta' and Courtney ad loc.

inchoari annum An expr. found only in T. (*Agr.* 25.1n.).

has Seiano uictimas cadere The Roman year was officially opened by a sacrifice of young bulls to Jupiter on the Capitol (Weinstock 217–18); Sabinus' pathetic cry is that he himself is taking the place of the bulls (for *cadere* as a technical term of sacrificial victims see *OLD* 9b) and Sejanus is being substituted for the deity (for Sejanus' 'divine' status see 2.3nn., 74.2–3nn.), a combination of perversions which Tarrant compares with Aeneas' 'sacrifice' of Turnus at the climax of the *Aeneid* (see his n. on 12.949 'immolat').

Independently of each other, P. L. Corrigan (*RhM* 136 (1993) 330–42, at 339) and Ll. Morgan (*CQ* 48 (1998) 585–7) have argued that T. has put into Sabinus' mouth a bitter pun: Sabinus describes himself as being sacrificed to Se-ianus, the privative *se-* suggesting the antithesis of Janus, the god who gave January its name.[135] The notion is self-evidently attractive, but involves some special pleading. Corrigan argues only that Janus was a favourite god of Augustus (not Tiberius), while Morgan says that Janus was especially associated with the year's new consuls and, as a god of time, with the recording of the new consuls. Although it is true that it was the new consuls who sacrificed the bulls to Jupiter, T. makes no reference to the consuls in the immediate context: their only mention is as a date two chapters previously (68.1n.). Other problems are (i) that the principal divinity of 1 January was Jupiter, not Janus, (ii) that T. expressly mentions 1 January ('kalendis Ianuariis'), and (iii) that Janus' festival did not take place until the Agonalia on 9 January.

70.2 *Quo* intendisset oculos, *quo* uerba acciderent, fuga, uastitas The subjunctives are frequentative (Carmody 83); *intendisset* is pluperfect because it refers to the time before Sabinus' head was covered: hence perhaps 'wherever he had directed his gaze, there had been flight, and wherever his words fell, there was desolation' (i.e. 'double zeugma': 1.55.1n.). Although *fuga* and *uastitas* are combined elsewhere (Cic. *Verr.* 4.114 (cf. *Dom.* 17), Liv. 8.9.12), C. L. Whitton has suggested (*CT* 349) that T. has taken his 'piquant' phrase 'from Pliny's evocation of more recent fear' at *Pan.* 48.3 'nec salutationes tuas fuga et uastitas sequitur: remoramur, resistimus ut in communi domo, quam nuper illa immanissima belua plurimo terrore munierat, cum uelut quodam specu inclusa nunc propinquorum sanguinem

---

[135] Prof. Reeve points out to me that *hasce Iano* was suggested for *has Seiano* by A. Scholte, *Dissertatio literaria continens observationes criticas in Saturas D. Junii Juvenalis* (1873) xi.

lamberet, nunc se ad clarissimorum ciuium strages caedesque proferret'. *accidere* is regular of utterances and the like but seems not to be used of *uerba* elsewhere (*TLL* 1.290.83–291.29).

id ipsum pauentes quod timuissent For other such plays cf. *H.* 1.81.1 'cum timeret Otho, timeretur', 1.88.2 'quanto magis occultare et abdere pauorem nitebantur, manifestius pauidi'; for the fear to which the subjects of a tyrant are conventionally prone see 7.1n.

70.3 ubi ... uincla et laqueus inducantur The verb suggests the introduction of a new practice (*OLD* 5), as *H.* 5.5.1 'hi ritus ... inducti'; for *uincla et laqueus* cf. Ov. *Met.* 11.252. For the form *uinclum* see 3.28.3n.

quo tempore uerbis etiam profanis abstineri mos esset *etiam* is to be taken with *uerbis*: cf. Ov. *Fasti* 1.71–2 'prospera lux oritur: linguis animisque fauete; | nunc dicenda bona sunt bona uerba die' (and G. Appel, *De Romanorum precationibus* (1909) 187–8, quoting our passage); also Plin. *NH* 28.22 'primum anni incipientis diem laetis precationibus inuicem faustum ominamur'.

non <im>prudentem Tiberium tantam inuidiam adisse Without Rhenanus' emendation the transmitted text is contradicted by *quaesitum meditatumque* immediately below; the same error occurs at 1.70.3. Contemporaries are repeating the point already made at 31.2 'quo magis mirum habebatur gnarum meliorum . . ., tristiora malle. neque enim socordia peccabat'. *adire* here = 'to submit to, endure' (*OLD* 11); *inuidia* as object seems unparalleled (*TLL* 1.627.46).

quaesitum meditatumque As subject we seem obliged to understand *id*, referring to Tib.'s courting of resentment ('inuidiam adisse'): perhaps 'it was chosen and premeditated' (for the expr. cf. Gell. 1.7.4 'pleraque omnia ueterum litterarum quaesita, meditata euigilataque erant').

ne quid impedire credatur quominus noui magistratus, quo modo delubra et altaria, sic carcerem recludant 'to prevent the belief that there was anything to stop the new magistrates from opening up the prison in the same way as they did shrines and altars'. Trials and the like were banned on holy days (Cic. *Div.* 1.102 with Pease's n., *Leg.* 2.19 and 29 with Dyck's nn.) and specifically on 1 January (Ov. *Fasti* 1.73–4 'lite uacent aures, insanaque protinus absint | iurgia: differ opus, liuida turba, tuum'), although Tib. evidently had a precedent in Marius (Plut. *Mar.* 45.3 ὕπατος μὲν οὖν ἀπεδείχθη τὸ ἕβδομον Μάριος, καὶ προελθὼν αὐταῖς Καλάνδαις Ἰανουαρίαις, ἔτους ἀρχῇ, Σέξτον τινὰ Λικίννιον κατεκρήμνισεν). Suetonius extrapolates from Sabinus' case (*Tib.* 61.2 'animaduersum in quosdam ineunte anno nouo'). For the opening up of temples cf. Ov. *Fasti* 1.70 'et resera nutu candida templa tuo'.

70.4 infensum rei publicae Since this expr. recurs only at 6.24.1, another imperial missive, perhaps we are to understand a Tiberian idiolect, although *infensus* is one of T.'s favoured words (3.15.2n.).

adiecto trepidam *si*bi uitam, *s*uspectas inimicorum in*s*idias Tib. will come to regret this incautious admission, since it provokes a response from Asinius Gallus (71.2), which in turn elicits an implied reaction from Tib. (71.3 and nn.). For the period of time involved in such exchanges with Capri see 6.5.2n. (where add A. Kolb, *Transport und Nachrichtentransfer im römischen Reich* (2000), K. A. Raaflaub and J. T. Ramsey, 'Reconstructing the chronology of Caesar's Gallic Wars', *Histos* 11 (2017) 3–11).

The tyrant is typically characterised by fear and suspicion (e.g. 53.2, 67.3, 71.2, Plato, *Rep.* 579B, 579E, Xen. *Hiero* 2.18; Tarrant on Sen. *Ag.* 72–3 (also for the reciprocal fear of the tyrant's subjects)). For such one-word abl. abs. as *adiecto*, which seems unparalleled, see Malloch on 11.26.3. For *trepidam . . . uitam* cf. 14.59.1, Gratt. 13, Sen. *Ep.* 15.9, *Vit. Beat.* 15.3.

neque tamen dubitabatur in Neronem et Agrippinam intendi sc. *compellationem* from *compellato* above: 'yet there was no doubt that the accusation was being aimed at . . .' (*TLL* 7.1.2115.68ff.). The fact that Tib.'s alleged targets were common knowledge provides the ironical background to Asinius Gallus' motion below (71.2).

71.1 suum quaeque in *a*nnum referre 'to assign individual items to their own year' (*OLD refero* 9), a different meaning of the verb from that at 67.4 (n.); for plur. *quaeque* = *singula*, more frequent from Livy onwards and a mannerism of the elder Pliny, see L–H–S 199.

***a*uebat *a*nimus *a*ntire** 'Ardent language, abstraction, and alliteration combine to produce a striking expression of Tacitus' eagerness to race ahead in his narrative', says Damon (*AHC* 356); she notes that *TLL* 'lists no parallels for this usage' of *antire*, although the verb is used by T. in other passages where there are racing metaphors (3.47.3n., 3.66.4n.). T. perhaps has in mind Cic. *Phil.* 5.13 'auet animus apud consilium illud . . . dicere', although the same phrase is used in another racing metaphor at Hor. *Epist.* 1.14.8–9 'tamen istuc mens animusque | fert et auet spatiis obstantia rumpere claustra'. Lucian in his *How to Write History* refers to the historian's mind being carried along on horseback (45 ἐφ' ἵππου ὀχουμένη τότε τῇ γνώμῃ), Isocrates evidently described Theopompus and Ephorus as differently tempered horses (Cic. *Brut.* 204), and Quintilian talks of reining in the horses that are running away with the writer (10.3.10 'ut . . . ferentis equos frenis quibusdam coerceamus'); for many other similar metaphors see E. Norden, *Die antike Kunstprosa* (repr. 1958) 1.33–4 n. 3. For the 'speedy writer' in general see Vell. 41.1n.

The tense of *auebat* is explained by T.'s seeing things from the reader's point of view; the mood indicates that his desire was real: it was the actual race on which he did not embark ('I was keen to race ahead, <and would have done so,> had it not been my intention to write annalistically').

exitus quos . . . habuere is an allusion to the obituary formula *hunc exitum habuit* (Vell. 53.3n., 72.1n.). Anticipatory notices are relatively rare in the *Annals* (6.32.4n.); this one is combined with a cross-reference forwards (*in tempore trademus* below), another relatively rare feature (6.22.4n.). For *memorare* (above) see 3.24.3n.

Latinius He was killed in 32 (6.4.1 and nn.).[136]

flagitii eius repertores Although T. likes to mark innovations in crime and the like (cf. 11.2n., 34.1n.), this phrase will soon adapt itself to the gastronomic metaphor which develops below: for the importance of inventiveness in cooking and preparing dishes see e.g. Hor. *S.* 2.4.74 'primus et inuenior'; C. J. Classen, *CQ* 28 (1978) 340 n. 58. The Romans talked metaphorically of 'cooking up a plot' etc. in the same way as we do (see Oakley on Liv. 8.3.2).

incolumi Tiberio, qui . . . adflixit The relative clause is not specific to the present case but is a generalised reference to Tib.'s behaviour. For the *uariatio* of abl. abs. ~ temporal clause see Sörbom 117.

scelerum ministros is a common expression of abuse, 'accessories in crime' (*H.* 4.27.2 and H.; Vell. 83.1n.), but, since *ministros* can also designate a person who serves at table (*OLD* 1), the phrase in this context, as also at 6.36.3 (n.), suggests the serving up of crimes as if they were dishes of food (next n.).

plerumque satiatus et oblatis in eandem operam recentibus ueteres et praegraues adflixit Once he becomes glutted with the confections served up by his previous 'cooks' (*satiatus*; cf. 1.75.1 'nec patrum cognitionibus satiatus'), and fresh persons have presented themselves for the same job (*OLD opera* 7a), the *princeps* dashes down his former servants as old and past their prime (cf. Liv. 44.4.10 'Romanus imperator maior lx annis et praegrauis corpore'; Vell. 76.1n.). For similar metaphors in Book 6 see *PH* 339–60.

has atque alias sontium poenas in tempore trademus The fates of Latiaris' three co-conspirators will have been told in the part of the *Annals* which is now lost. It is thought that Porcius Cato was punished very shortly after his appointment as *curator aquarum* in 38 (see Rodgers on Front. *Aq.* 102.

---

[136] The OCT reads *Latinius* at 68.1 but *Latinus* here, the latter therefore presumably a misprint (so D. R. Shackleton Bailey, *Two studies in Roman nomenclature* (1991) 29).

6–7); nothing is known of the other two. For the forward cross-reference see on *exitus* above; for *sons* see Malloch on 11.26.2.

71.2 cuius liberorum Agrippina matert*era* *erat* Gallus' wife had been Vipsania, the former wife of Tib. (cf. 1.12.4), daughter of Agrippa, and half-sister of Agrippina. She had died in 20 (3.19.3n.). Gallus' children included the consuls of 23 and 25. For Gallus himself see 6.23.1n.; his relationship to Agrippina is mentioned here 'to aggravate the baseness of his conduct' (Furneaux).

ut metus suos . . . amouerique sineret *metus amouere* is a perfectly normal expr. (Ter. *Andr.* 180, Cic. *Clu.* 159, Quint. 4.1.20; cf. *OLD amoueo* 4), but, since the verb can also be used of removing people (*OLD* 1), Gallus' unctuously worded question lets it be known that he knows what lies behind the *princeps'* original admission (70.4 and nn.).

71.3 Nullam aeque . . . quam *d*issimulationem *d*iligebat Passages such as this have required reconsideration in the light of the knowledge that on the *Tabula Siarensis* Tib. himself went out of his way to deny that he was dissembling (IIb.16 'ipse se uelle non dissimulare eodem libello testatus').[137] The likelihood seems to be that he had a reputation for *dissimulatio*, was aware of it, and attempted to counter it (see 3.2.3n.). *ut rebatur* is to be taken with *ex uirtutibus suis* ('of his self-styled virtues'); *diligere* recurs only at 6.51.3 and 15.63.2 in the *Annals* (Syme, *Tac.* 345).

eo aegrius accepit recludi quae premeret Dio heads his account of Tib.'s reign with the statement that the *princeps* did not think it right to reveal his thoughts (57.1.2 τό τε σύμπαν οὐκ ἠξίου τὸν αὐταρχοῦντα κατάδηλον ὧν φρονεῖ εἶναι· ἔκ τε γὰρ τούτου πολλὰ καὶ μεγάλα πταίεσθαι καὶ ἐκ τοῦ ἐναντίου πολλῷ πλείω καὶ μείζω κατορθοῦσθαι ἔλεγε); in the present case, of course, Tib. was himself responsible for letting his guard slip (70.4n.), and it cannot have improved his mood that Asinius Gallus picked up on his words. This characteristic secretiveness (see also *Ann. 3*, p. 513; *Ann. 5–6*, p. 325) contrasts strikingly with the confessional aspects of the last years of the reign (e.g. 6.6. 1–2nn., 6.38.3n.).

mitigauit Seianus It was, of course, Sejanus who was driving the attacks on Nero and Agrippina (67.3–4). The verb perhaps activates the latent sense in *aegrius* above: cf. Cic. *TD* 3.53 'dies . . . quae procedens ita mitigat ut isdem malis manentibus . . . leniatur aegritudo'.

[137] The precise meaning of the passage is disputed: for discussion see A. Sánchez-Ostiz, *Tabula Siarensis: edición, traducción y comentario* (1999) 238–42. It is difficult to see how *dissimulare* can be translated as 'exaggerate' (J. B. Lott, *Death and dynasty in early imperial Rome* (2012) 95, 231).

ut . . . opperiretur 'to await the outcome of': the verb is a favourite of T. (Malloch on 11.12.2) and this particular meaning of it is uniquely Tacitean (2.69.2n.; *TLL* 9.2.749.17–22). Halm (*Beiträge* 15–16) argued for the transmitted *aperirentur*, which seems far less appropriate in the context. For the *uariatio* with *amore* above see 8.2n. For *cunctationes* see 11.1n.

gnarus lentum in meditando . . . Sejanus was already alert to this behaviour in AD 15 (1.69.5 'peritia morum Tiberii odia in longum iaciens, quae reconderet auctaque promeret'). For *lentus in* + abl. see 3.70.2n.

ubi prorupisset 'whenever he burst forth': for the metaphor see 5.3.1n.

tristibus dictis atrocia facta coniungere The destiny of Achilles was to be 'a speaker of words and a doer of deeds' (Hom. *Il.* 9.442–3), and the speedy translation of thought into deed was attributed to Hermes (*Hom. Hymn* 4.46 ὡς ἅμ᾽ ἔπος τε καὶ ἔργον ἐμήδετο κύδιμος Ἑρμῆς). These heroic ideals echo down through classical literature (e.g. Sall. *C.* 1.6 'priusquam incipias consulto, et, ubi consulueris, mature facto opus est', with Vretska's many parallels), while the combination of words and deeds became proverbial (Tosi 435 §930). But the *princeps'* words illustrate his characteristic *tristitia* (6.40.2n.) and his deeds are heinous (*atrocia*): cf. Suet. *Cal.* 29.1 'immanissima facta augebat atrocitate uerborum'. For *coniungere* cf. Vell. 79.1 'consultisque facta coniungens'; *tristia dicta* is otherwise poetic (Lucil. 1014, Virg. *Aen.* 2.115, 10.612, Sil. 7.548, 11.84), whereas *atrocia facta* is not (Liv. 28.29.5, Val. Max. 9.11.2).

71.4 Per idem tempus Iulia mortem obiit As if reaffirming the annalistic nature of his narrative, to which he drew attention at 1 above (n.), T. closes his section of domestic affairs with that most annalistic of elements, the obituary notice (3.30.1n.). The fact that the obituary is placed here, rather than at the end of the year, allows him to give exclusive prominence to the marriage which concludes both the year and the book (see 75n.). For the younger Julia see 3.24.2–3nn. For *per idem tempus* see 3.29.1n., 6.10.1n.

conuictam adulterii With D. Iunius Silanus (3.24.1–3nn.). If T.'s reference to 'twenty years' (below) is a true figure and not a round number, Julia was banished in AD 8. 'The date thus furnished makes her exile coincident with that of Ovid, which has been thought to be connected with it' (Furneaux).

in insulam Trimerum, haud procul Apulis litoribus These words give rise to problems of nomenclature and number (see, briefly, H. Philipp, *RE* 7A.1.156). Like T., the majority of ancient authors refer to only one island, which they call *Diomedea insula*; but some authors refer to two, of which the second is called Teutria by Pliny (*NH* 3.151), while Ptolemy (*Geog.* 3.1.69) refers to five. There are in fact three islands (apart from some rocks), so perhaps *Trimerus* designates a three-part archipelago. Because the modern name for the islands (just north of the Gargano Peninsula) is Tremiti, Freinsheim emended to *Tremetum* here; but, where so much is uncertain, it is perhaps wisest to retain the paradosis; indeed T.'s explanation of the island's position is perhaps due precisely to the general obscurity surrounding it (see also 67.1n. *trium*). Trimerus, a name otherwise unattested, is adopted at *BA* Map 44: H1. The place was again used as a penal establishment by Mussolini; for Julia's confinement there see Drogula 234.

exilium tolerauit The expr. (earlier at Curt. 8.3.2, Sen. *Cons. Helv.* 9.7) recurs at 1.53.4, 6.3.3, 14.62.4. For the verb see 3.1.1n.

Augustae ope sustentata For Livia see 5.1.1n. *sustentare* is elsewhere coupled with *opibus* (2.40.3, Caes. *BG* 2.14.6, Cic. *Fam.* 4.13.1, *Aetna* 557) but never with sing. *ope*.

quae florentes priuignos cum ... subuertisset, misericordiam erga adflictos ... ostentabat *florentes* presumably refers primarily to Gaius and Lucius Caesar (cf. 1.3.3, Dio 55.10^a.10), but Livia was also thought responsible for the death of the banished Agrippa Postumus (1.6.3, with *Tac. Rev.* 23ff.). Her role as a *perfugium* is mentioned at 5.3.1 (n.), but, apart from Julia here, T. gives no other instance of her helping her *priuigni*. The horticultural imagery of *florentes* ~ *adflictos* (cf. 68.3n.) is sustained by *subuertisset* (cf. e.g. Col. 11.2.44 'lupinum ... aratro subuertit', Luc. 3.436 'subuertere siluam'); the subjunctive is surely not that of repeated action (so Nipperdey-Andresen, Furneaux, Carmody 110, Koestermann) but indicates that *cum* means 'although'.

72–73 Revolt of the Frisii

This episode, lacking the drama and suspense of chh. 23–6 or 46–51, bears out the complaints which T. had made earlier (32.1–2) about the lack of glorious warfare. It begins with a reference to 'nostra ... auaritia' (72.1) and ends with Roman soldiers dying in a barbarian manner (73.4 'mutuis ictibus'). Within this frame every positive is succeeded by a corresponding negative. Drusus' mild treatment of the Frisii is followed by Olennius' unrealistic harshness (72.1); Apronius' admirable counter-measures are nullified by misguided tactics (73.1–2); the victory of the Fifth Legion cannot disguise the facts that the Roman dead fail to be buried and that in a further engagement the Romans lose heavily (73.3–4). Flight and fear punctuate the narrative (72.3 'fuga praeuenit', 73.2 'pauore fugientium', 73.4 'proditio metuebatur'): the second of these expressions derives from Livy's account of the battle of Cannae (22.47.6) and, together with some other hints (72.3n., 73.3n.), perhaps indicates that that famous defeat was at the back of T.'s mind.

72.1 Frisii 'Modern scholars universally locate them in the coastal region north of the IJsselmeer, the modern provinces of Friesland and Groningen; archaeological evidence suggests that by Roman times they may also have spread east of the IJsselmeer into Noord-Holland' (Rives on *G.* 34.1, q.v. for further details and bibliography; also Malloch's full nn. on 11.19.1, where the Frisii reappear).

pacem exuere . . . quam obsequii impatientes A 'headline' statement (45.1n.), to be elaborated in the narrative which follows. T.'s reference to 'our greed' recalls his famous statement in the *Agricola* (13.1): 'ego facilius crediderim naturam margaritis deesse quam nobis auaritiam'. For the *uariatio* of causal abl. ~ participle, as 2.1.2 'haud perinde nostri metu quam fidei popularium diffisus', see Sörbom 89.

tributum iis Drusus iusserat The elder Drusus, Tib.'s brother, had annexed the Frisians in 12 BC (Dio 54.32.2). *iusserat* = 'had prescribed': for the constr. see *OLD* 4a; it is unknowable whether the *ut*-clause below depends on *iusserat* or is epexegetic of *tributum* (described as 'acc. praeparativus' in *TLL* 7.2.580.79; no classical parallel).

modicum pro angustia rerum 'modest in proportion to their straitened circumstances': this is a further case where other exs. of the phrase are plural (*D.* 8.3 'angustiae rerum', Cic. *Sull.* 78, Caes. *BC* 3.15.3); cf. 71.4 above and 74.3 below. It is perhaps worth noting that Drusus' moderate behaviour 'pre-echoes' that of T.'s father-in-law in the *Agricola* (*Agr.* 4.3 and n., 19–20.1 and nn.). When T. in this episode registers Olennius' harsh treatment of the Frisians and Apronius' various deficiencies, we should remember that he had as his personal yardstick a man who was both a benign provincial governor and an outstandingly successful general – at least if his account in the *Agricola* is to be believed.

in usus militares coria boum The Roman army could not have functioned without a large and regular supply of leather, which was used for e.g. reins, belts, shoes, defensive gear and, above all, tents. See C. van Driel-Murray, 'The production and supply of military leatherwork in the first and second centuries AD: a review of the archaeological evidence', in M. C. Bishop (ed.), *The production and distribution of Roman military equipment* (1985) 43–81 (our passage mentioned fleetingly at p. 61 and nn. 79, 81). One of the Vindolanda Tablets (343) refers to the existence of a tannery at Cataractonium (Catterick, in North Yorkshire) during the period when T. was active as an author: cf. lines 15–16 'coria que scribis esse Cataractonio'.[138]

---

[138] Since the beginning of the twentieth century Catterick has again been a military base, the evocative names of its present buildings recalling memorable battles of the Great War.

Olennius e primipilaribus Olennius, who as a re-employed *primipilaris* will have enjoyed equestrian status (Demougin, *PCR* 223 no. 259), is the first of four unfamiliar names in this section, the others being Cethecius Labeo (73.3), Baduhenna and Cruptorix (73.4). Norden (285) remarks on the unusual military and topographical detail of T.'s account, concluding that he is indebted to the elder Pliny's *Bella Germaniae* (1.69.2n.).

terga urorum delegit, quorum ad formam acciperentur 'selected aurochs' skins as the model according to which they [the oxhides] would be accepted' (cf. *OLD ad* 34–8). Caesar has a famous description of these beasts (*BG* 6.28; see also next n.), which are also mentioned by Pliny (*NH* 8.38); for the occurrence of *uri* in Virgil see Mynors on *G.* 2.374. The aurochs was last recorded in Poland in the early 17th century.[139]

72.2 ingentium beluarum feraces saltus T. characterises Germania as 'siluis horrida' (*G.* 5.1 and Rives ad loc.); the elder Pliny says that forests 'totam reliquam Germaniam referciunt' (*NH* 16.5); Livy was so impressed by reports of the 'Germanici saltus' of his own day that he obtrudes a reference to them into his narrative of late fourth-century Italy (9.36.1); these writers in their turn look back to Caesar, for whom Germany is a land of 'endless forests' (C. B. Krebs, '"Imaginary geography" in Caesar's *Bellum Gallicum*', *AJP* 127 (2006) 111). The principal forest was the Hercynian Forest, described by Caesar as being of indefinite extent (*BG* 6.25.4; cf. Plin. *NH* 16.6) and hence home to the kind of beasts which inhabit the edges of the world (6.25.5): 'genera ferarum nasci constat quae reliquis in locis uisa non sint' (cf. H. Shadee, *CQ* 58 (2008) 178–9). Caesar proceeds to list three types of beast (6.26–8), of which the aurochs (previous n.) is one: see H. Aili, 'Caesar's elks: interpolation, myth, or fact?', *Eranos* 105 (2009) 4–17. T.'s present clause belongs to this tradition; *ingens belua* is the phrase used by Seneca to describe the monstrous marine bull at *Phaedra* 1047. See further B. Günnewig, *Das Bild der Germanen und Britannier: Untersuchungen zur Sichtweise von fremden Völkern in antiker und moderner wissenschaftlicher Forschung* (1998).

modica domi armenta sunt *modica* contrasts with *ingentium* above: the problem is not that the Germans have few herds but that the animals in the herds are smaller than the prescribed size. This is made clear at *G.* 5.1 'plerumque inprocera [sc. pecora]: ne armentis quidem suus honor aut gloria frontis; numero gaudent'.

[139] The Wikipedia entry is most informative and has a variety of illustrations. Re-wilding projects are said to be trying to recreate the aurochs and reintroduce it into Europe.

boues ... agros ... corpora coniugum aut liberorum seruitio tradebant 'The periphrastic use of *corpora* with the genitive is popular in dactylic poetry because it eases versification' (Skutsch on Enn. *Ann.* 88), but here the language suggests the formulae of the *deditio* (cf. Liv. 8.19.12 'agros ... corpora ipsorum coniugumque ac liberorum suorum in potestate populi Romani esse futuraque') and a bleak future of physical labour and sexual exploitation. *tradebant* is to be taken with all three accusatives, but *seruitio* only with *corpora*.

72.3 qui tributo aderant 'who were attending to the <requisitioning of the> tribute', a dat. of purpose similar to 12.69.1 'cohortem quae ... excubiis adest'.

patibulo adfixi The practice, which is typical of barbarians (1.61.4, 14.33.2), no doubt appealed to them, as it was also the punishment which the Romans inflicted on rebellious provincials.

castello cui nomen Fleuum According to Mela (3.24) the same name was given both to a lake into which the right-hand branch of the Rhine debouches and to an island in the middle of the lake (see *BA* Map 10: B4); according to Pliny (*NH* 4.101) it was the name of a mouth of the Rhine. Any connection between the *castellum* and any of these names, to say nothing of the modern off-shore island of Vlieland, is quite unclear: for some idea of the various hypotheses see E. Janssens, 'Le Castellum Flevum', *Latomus* 3 (1939) 107–10. See also below, p. 330 n. 140.

haud spernenda illic ciuium sociorumque manus litora Oceani praesidebat *ciues sociique* in its various forms is an expr. found above all in Livy (18×), one of whose exs. occurs in his narrative of Cannae (22.49.15). In the *Annals* it recurs at 1.11.4 and 13.8.2 and refers, as here, to legionaries and auxiliaries (seemingly misunderstood by D. B. Saddington, 'The Roman *auxilia* in Tacitus, Josephus and other early imperial writers', *Acta Classica* 13 (1970) 104). For *haud spernenda ... manus* see *H.* 2.11.2 and H. ad loc.; for the 'Sallustian' acc. after *praesidere* see 5.1n.

73.1 L. Apronio See 4.13.3n. and 6.30.2n.

uexilla legionum e superiore prouincia The four legions from which the detachments (*uexilla*) could come were II Augusta, XIII Gemina, XIV Gemina and XVI Gallica (see 5.1n.).

utrumque exercitum ... intulit i.e. his own army from Lower, and that summoned from Upper, Germany. *inferre* is an exceptionally common verb in military contexts but almost always has words such as *arma* or *bellum* as its object; apart from *acies* at 2.17.3 the very few other personal exs. are in verse, and *exercitum* is without parallel at all (*TLL* 7.1.1380.23–31).

soluto iam castelli obsidio et ad sua tutanda degressis rebellibus
ad sua tutanda presumably implies that the Frisians were expecting Roman reprisals (which indeed will soon materialise): this explains why T. later refers to the 'enemy rear' (2 'terga hostium') and says that they are 'arranged in line' ('acie compositi').[140] For *soluto . . . obsidio* see 3.39.1n.; for T.'s use of *tutor* see 3.28.1n.

Igitur proxima aestuaria aggeribus et pontibus traducendo grauiori agmini firmat It is because the Frisians have withdrawn to their heartlands that Apronius 'therefore' (*igitur*) needs to tackle the estuaries which are nearest to them (*proxima*) and by which they were presumably protected. The 'heavier column' which requires the construction of causeways and bridges across the estuaries is presumably being compared proleptically with the *ala* of Canninefates and the unit of German infantry whose ability to negotiate the shallows (2 *uadis*) means that they do not need to wait upon the engineers but can be ordered to attack the enemy rear 'in the meanwhile' (2 *interim*); it is nevertheless not clear when, or indeed whether, we hear of this heavier column again (see further below, 2n.). Estuaries, vividly described by the elder Pliny (*NH* 16.2), were regarded as particularly treacherous (Veg. *Mil.* 4.42; cf. 3.7), so Apronius' preparations are irreproachable. For *aggeribus et pontibus* cf. 1.61.1 'pontesque et aggeres umido paludum . . . imponeret'; for bridges alone see 2.8.2–3.

73.2 repertis uadis Apronius again acts wisely, since familiarity with the terrain was naturally desirable in a general (*Agr.* 5.1n.).

alam Canninefatem An *ala* was a cavalry unit of auxiliary troops, nominally 500-strong but, even if at full strength, probably no more than 480 and subdivided into 16 *turmae* (*BNP* 1.417–18); see further below. The Canninefates lived west of the Frisii, on the other side of the IJsselmeer, sharing with the Batavi the 'island' to which the latter gave their name (*H.* 4.15.1; Malloch on 11.18.1).

qui iam acie compositi pellunt turmas sociales equitesque legionum subsidio missos 'And they, now arranged in line, repelled the allied squadrons and the legionary cavalry sent to help them' (*subsidio missos* applies only to *equites . . . legionum*). *turmas sociales* is a varied way of referring to the above mentioned *ala* (Sörbom 24; for *turmae* see 25.2n.). Each legion would

---

[140] It was observed in the earlier nineteenth century that, in a passage indebted to his predecessor Marinus, the geographer Ptolemy lists side by side two places in Germany called Φληούμ and Σιατουτάνδα (*Geog.* 2.11.12), of which the latter looks suspiciously like a misguided transliteration of T.'s *sua tutanda*; for discussion see Norden 284–6.

have attached to it a cavalry unit of c. 120 men which was distinct from the mounted auxiliaries: here *legionum* presumably refers to the four legions of Lower Germany (I, V Alaudae, XX, and XXI Rapax: see 5.1n.).

tum tres leues cohortes . . ., dein . . . alarius eques If these forces comprise the 'heavier column' which had been waiting for the engineering work to be completed (1 above), as is perhaps suggested by *tum . . . immissus*, it is confusing that the cohorts are described as 'light'.[141] *alarius* is also confusing, since it might seem to imply a connection with the *alam Canninefatem*, which, however, was already engaged in the action. (*alarius* is an emendation but it is difficult to see what else T. could have written.)

ac rursum duae 'and another two' (*OLD rursus* 5aα).

pauore fugientium 'terrified runaways.' The expr. occurs in Livy's Cannae narrative (22.47.6) and recurs at *H.* 2.26.1.

73.3 Cethecio Labeoni The form of the man's name as given in M is defended by Syme, *TST* 67, and endorsed by H. Solin and O. Salomies, *Repertorium nominum gentilium et cognominum Latinorum* (1988) 54.

quintae legionis V Alaudae, from Lower Germany.

ille i.e. Labeo.

uim legionum implorabat It was standard practice to rely initially on auxiliary troops and to call upon the legions only if necessary (see *Agr.* 35.2n.).

fessas uulneribus Although this expr. is found elsewhere (Sil. 7.707) and occurs once in Livy's first decade (4.41.7; *uulnere* at 1.25.11), its other three appearances are late in Book 22, one of them in the Cannae narrative (22.49.5 'pepulerunt tamen iam paucos superantis et labore ac *uulneribus fessos*').

neque dux Romanus ultum iit aut corpora humauit Pichena proposed *Romanos*, 'sed Tacitus reprehendere voluit L. Apronii socordiam atque ignaviam, Romano duce prorsus indignam' (Orelli). When in Domitian's reign the Nasamones, a Numidian tribe, were similarly provoked to revolt, killed the tax collectors, and inflicted a defeat on the governor as he ventured on reprisals, the governor avenged the defeat savagely and thereby delighted Domitian (Dio 67.4.6). Clearly T., who had celebrated the brutality of which Agricola was capable (*Agr.* 18.1–4), expected the same of Apronius. For the

---

[141] The 'legionary strength' mentioned at 73.3 below no doubt also qualified to be described as 'heavier', but it was summoned by a different leader (Labeo) to meet a subsequent crisis ('dubia suorum re . . . uim legionum implorabat'), whereas *traducendo grauiori agmini* implies a force which Apronius had intended to commit all along.

horror attaching to lack of burial (1.60.3, Cic. *Inv.* 1.108 'inimicorum in manibus mortuus est, hostili in terra iacuit insepultus') see e.g. Vell. 53.3n., N–H on Hor. *C.* 1.28.23, Pease on Virg. *Aen.* 4.620, Horsfall on Virg. *Aen.* 2.646, 3.62, 6.328; and note also 6.23.1n., 29.1n. Philosophers could of course deny the importance of burial (e.g. Sen. *Ep.* 92.34–5).

praefectorumque The term for officers commanding units of legionary or auxiliary troops (*OLD* 3a). For Livy's habit in his later books of classifying and sometimes naming officers who had died in battle see Oakley on 9.38.8.

73.4 compertum a transfugis For the importance of deserters as a source of information see N. J. E. Austin and N. B. Rankov, *Exploratio: military and political intelligence in the Roman world from the Second Punic War to the battle of Adrianople* (1995) 67–73.

apud lucum (quem Baduhennae uocant) T. regularly associates barbarians with groves, esp. as scenes of horror or ritual or both (G–G 785a–b; Rives on *G.* 9.2). Baduhenna is presumably a local goddess. *uocant*-formulae and their equivalents are a feature of ethno-geographical contexts (3.43.2n., *Agr.* 10.4n.) but their punctuation can pose problems. Since they are very often parenthetic (cf. Vell. 102.3 'in urbe Lyciae (Limyra nominant)', 107.1 and n.; for exs. from Curtius see W. Havers, *Glotta* 16 (1927) 118), it seems reasonable to think that some relative examples may also be parenthetic rather than defining; but consistency is impossible and each case should be considered on its merits: thus *castello cui nomen Fleuum* at 72.3 above but *templum (quod Tanfanae uocant)* at 1.51.1. For parenthetical relative clauses see *Tac. Rev.* 92 and n. 26.

pugna . . . extracta is another Livian expr. (23.47.4).

quondam stipendiarii i.e. he had formerly served in the Roman army (cf. 2.10.3 'qui Romanis in castris ductor popularium meruisset').

mutuis ictibus They die in a barbarian manner (cf. 50.1, 50.3; 3.46.4n.), although note the contrived death of Petreius at [Caes.] *Bell. Afr.* 94. The episode concludes with chiastic assonance (*pro–metue– ~ mutui–. . . pro–*).

74–75 *Sejanus and a wedding*

Just as Book 4 began with Sejanus and a seduction (1–3), so it ends with Sejanus and a wedding. At the start of the narrative we were told merely that Sejanus, a master of cunning second only to Tib. himself (1.2), was set on *regnum* (1.3); the central section of the book's narrative, where his relationship with Tib. is described (39–41), ended with him formulating in detail his stratagems for sidelining the *princeps* and taking power into his own hands (41.1–3); now, in a final section which clearly looks back to 41.1–3, those initial ambitions have been fulfilled: he is treated as if he were a god, and it is he, not Tib., who is the centre of everyone's attention (74.3). All that remained to be acquired was formal recognition and official status – which he seemed to be on the point of receiving three years later, when there was recited in the senate the letter which sealed his fate. That story was told by T. in Book 5 and is now lost, but is foreshadowed here by reference to the *grauis exitus* which was hanging over the minister's unwitting friends (74.5). Their many deaths are the cataclysm brought about by his fall, duly noted at the start of Book 4 (1.2 'pari exitio uiguit ceciditque').

The wedding of Cn. Domitius Ahenobarbus and the younger Agrippina is presented as a happy contrast to the aftermath of Sejanus (75 'Ceterum . . . celebrari nuptias iussit'); but 'the names were enough' (Syme, *Tac.* 267). Their son, not mentioned, will be Tib.'s counterpart in the last books of the *Annals*. 'An Neronem extremum dominorum putatis?', asks Curtius Montanus two years after Nero's death (*H.* 4.42.5). 'Idem crediderant qui Tiberio, qui Gaio superstites fuerunt, cum interim intestabilior et saeuior exortus est.'[142]

74.1 Clarum inde inter Germanos Frisium nomen The notion that

a Roman defeat brings distinction to Rome's opponents (Vell. 105.1n.; Oakley on Liv. 9.1.1) is a motif of Livy's Cannae narrative (22.39.8, 22.43.9, 22.50.1). T. later refers to the 'natio Frisiorum, post rebellionem clade L. Apronii coeptam infensa aut male fida' (11.19.1 with Malloch ad loc.).

dissimulante Tiberio *damna*, ne cui bellum permitteret T. had earlier complained of a 'princeps proferendi imperi incuriosus' (32.2); here Tib. does not attempt even to recoup his losses but simply conceals them. The motivation attributed to him is one which was explored fully in the *Agricola* (39–41), viz. the fear that a general, if successful, would win *gloria* and so might be seen as a rival; cf. also Corbulo at 11.19.3 (and Malloch ad loc.). Tib. had again dissembled, but differently, about the revolt in Gaul in 21 (3.47.1n.). For Tib.'s *dissimulatio* see 71.3n.

Neque senatus in eo cura, an imperii extrema dehonestarentur It was of course true that Augustus' division of the empire into imperial and senatorial provinces (for which see e.g. Talbert 392ff.) restricted the senate's jurisdiction to the lands encircling the Mediterranean, while the *imperii extrema* fell to the emperor; but it is typical of the author's cynicism to see the division in terms of failure of responsibility. *in eo* is prospective, as at 40.1 above,

---

[142] An allusion to Macer's speech at Sall. *H.* 3.48.9 'finem mali credebatis; ortus est longe saeuior Catulus'.

a regular formulation when *cura* is followed by an indir. qu. (*TLL* 4.1457.18ff.). For *dehonestare* see 3.66.2n.

pauor internus occupauerat animos It was a commonplace of ancient thought that an *external* threat helped to preserve domestic harmony and social cohesion (Oakley on Liv. 6.27.7); in the case of Rome this *metus hostilis* is most commonly represented by Carthage (Paul on Sall. *J.* 41.2). T.'s point is that external threats are now ignored because society is gripped by the *domestic* fear that conventionally attends despotisms (7.1n., 69.3n.). Such sentiments are often expressed in medical terms (e.g. Liv. 6.31.4 'ut ciuilia certamina terror externus cohiberet'; *OLD cohibeo* 5b), and so it is here: see *OLD occupo* 4b, *internus* 1a. The metaphor is sustained by *remedium* immediately below.

74.2 quamquam diuersis super rebus consulerentur T. evidently envisages the scheduled *relationes* being superseded by the vote in favour of the two altars (below); it is unclear whether, as Orelli seems to imply, we are to imagine that this resulted from a member speaking 'off the question' (for which procedure see Talbert 257–60). At any rate the *quamquam*-clause emphasises the single-minded *adulatio* of the senators, in the same way as the diversity of city life at §4 below is used as a foil for the focussed concentration of the waiting crowd.

aram clementiae, aram amicitiae effigiesque circum Caesaris ac Seiani censuere The anaphoric reference to each altar is ironically punctilious. *clementia* was one of the virtues claimed by Tib. (see *Ann. 3*, p. 513; *Ann. 5–6*, p. 325) and it had featured on the coinage of (probably) 22 (3.68.2n.); the Altar of Clemency is thus the culmination of a process, but its proposal in the present year is entirely belied by the entrapment and execution of Titius Sabinus (70.1–3, where prisons and altars are pointedly compared in terms of their accessibility). The Altar of Friendship is also climactic, since the relationship of Tib. and Sejanus has been a major theme since the start of the book (1.1, 7.1, 39–41 (note *pro amicitia* in Tib.'s letter at 40.7), 59.1–2) and will linger long after the latter's death (see 5.6.2n.). It has been argued by K. K. Jeppesen that the Grand Camée de France is to be dated to the present year, that its two principal male figures are Tib. and Sejanus, and that the female figure between them is the personification of Amicitia ('Grand Camée de France: Sejanus reconsidered and confirmed', *MDAI (RA)* 100 (1993) 141–75; also Birley (2007) 137–8 and Champlin (2012) 371–2). For the repetition *–am am–* see 13.2n. above; *circum* presumably means 'on either side' (*OLD* 3b).

crebrisque precibus efflagitabant, uisendi sui copiam facerent Although Tib. proclaimed his mortal status (38.1 and n.), people might naturally react to him as if he were divine (38.4; cf. 3.70.2n.); as for Sejanus, his divine status was implied at the start of the book (2.3) and again, most recently, at the start of this year's narrative (70.1): see also Juv. 10.62 'adoratum populo caput', Dio 58.2.7–8, 4.3–4, 8.4, 11.2. It was therefore inevitable that both men should be prayed to, and in the appropriate manner; and the subsequent narrative shows that the prayers are partly successful ('satis uisum *omittere* insulam et in proximo Campaniae *aspici*'). This context indicates that the prayers in question here are cletic prayers, in which divinities are asked to 'leave' their current location (often, as here, an island: see N–H on Hor. *C.* 1.30.2) and to present themselves (i.e. to become *praesentes dei*) at the location specified by the suppliant (see F. Cairns, *Roman lyric* (2012) 199–201). Although *praesens* is less intrinsically suggestive of visibility than its Greek equivalent ἐπιφανής, it is clear from the exs. assembled by Brink on Hor. *Epist.* 2.1.15 (§1, p. 50; cf. also p. 53) that the god's *praesentia* not only implied revelation but often was conjoined with a reference to it. This is exactly what the senators are praying for here; their explicit request for the pair's visibility rather than their mere *praesentia* is no doubt to be explained by the fact that the 'look' of a ruler was of crucial importance (Vell. 94.2n.): the senators were anxious to see whether Tib. and Sejanus would be looking kindly on them (cf. 3.53.1n. for reciprocal gazing). *precibus efflagitare* is Ciceronian (*Leg. Agr.* 2.3; cf. *Sest.* 25). It is tempting to suggest the insertion of *ut* before *uisendi*: at *TLL* 5.2.188.30–2 only Suet. *Tit.* 5.2 is quoted as a parallel for *efflagitare* + subjunc., and in that passage *ut* is transmitted as a variant for *aut* (the latter printed by Kaster in the OCT). For the peculiarity of *uisendi sui* referring to more than one person see K–S 1.746 (top); Pease on Cic. *ND* 2.124.

74.3 Non illi tamen in urbem aut propinqua urbi degressi sunt There would nevertheless be later occasions when Tib. approached the city (6.1.1, 15.3, 39.2 and nn.); for *propinqua* see 6.1.1n. and 6.44.2n. For *degredior* = 'to depart for' see 2.69.2n., *Agr.* 6.1n.

in proximo Campaniae aspici The sing. *proximum* + gen. seems unusual (*TLL* 10.2.2035.28ff.); for other rare singulars see 72.1n.. For *aspici* see on *crebrisque* above (2n.).

anxii erga Seianum, cuius durior congressus After the preceding plurals referring to both men ('uisendi sui copiam facerent', 'non illi . . . degressi sunt') it is striking that the reference here is to Sejanus alone: his earlier ambitions of sidelining Tib. have been fulfilled (41.1–2), and *he* is now perceived to hold the future of individuals in his hands (cf. 68.2). *durior* hints at the doorkeepers (below) protecting access to the great man (cf. Sen. *Const. Sap.* 14.2 'fores quas durus ianitor obsidet'): whether we are to understand *quam Tiberii*, underlining the reversal which has taken place, or *quam antea*, contrasting with the earlier accessibility which Sejanus had come to resent (cf. 40.5,

41.2), is unclear. *anxius* is not elsewhere constructed with *erga* (*TLL* 2.202. 84–203.1), a preposition of which T. is fond (2.2.3n.).

per ambitum The proverbial bribability of doorkeepers (Hor. *S.* 1.9.57, Juv. 3.184–5) contributes to the theme of reversal: *ianitores* had a very low status in the hierarchy of domestic slaves (McKeown on Ov. *Am.* 1.6, intro. n.), yet here they are exercising power over senators and equestrians (above).

societate consiliorum Although Dio has a different picture (58.5.2 σπουδαί τε καὶ ὠθισμοὶ περὶ τὰς θύρας αὐτοῦ ἐγίγνοντο), T.'s phrase seems to mean that the waiting hopefuls shared with one another their plans for achieving access to Sejanus (cf. *consilia sociare* at *H.* 2.74.1 and *miscere c.* at *H.* 2.7.2, both with H.'s nn.); in theory the phrase could refer to their sympathy with Sejanus' own plans, but such a point seems redundant in the context: they would not have travelled to Campania to see him if they had not been prepared to go along with his plans.

foedum illud in propatulo seruitium Since *in propatulo* is explained by *ibi campo aut litore iacentes* below, the primary meaning of the expr. must be 'out in the open' (*TLL* 10.2.1951.32–4); but, since the relationship of the people to Sejanus is presented in religious terms (above, 1n.), there is perhaps also the metaphorical suggestion of a temple forecourt (cf. Cic. *Verr.* 4.110 'ante aedem Cereris in aperto ac propatulo loco'; *TLL* ibid. 6–7). *illud* seems to focalise the scene through Sejanus, expressing his contempt for 'that servile crowd' hoping to see him. This ex. of sing. *seruitium* in the concrete sense of 'body of slaves' (*OLD seruitium* 3), elsewhere in T. only at 1.23.1 and 12.17.1, is miscategorised in G–G (1480a), where it is however shown that his use of the plur. in this sense is extremely common; for his use of the word in its abstract sense see 3.45.2n. For *foedum* cf. Flor. 2.18.2 (= 4.8.2) 'foeda seruitia'.

Romae sueti discursus ... quod quisque ad negotium pergat For the to and fro of city life cf. Catull. 15.7–8, Hor. *Epod.* 4.9, Liv. 6.25.9 'uulgus aliud ... huc atque illuc euntium, qua quemque suorum usuum causae ferrent' (Tusculum). For *negotia* as emblematic of the city see 41.3n.

campo aut litore iacentes is the first of a series of three opposites ('noctem ac diem', 'gratiam aut fastus') which are reduced to sameness by the expressions *nullo discrimine* and *iuxta*, not only emphasising the lengths to which the devotees will go but also contrasting with the diversity of city life above (*discursus, incertum, quisque*): this crowd has only one aim – to see Sejanus. Given the earlier association of Sejanus with the divine (above), *iacentes* suggests a posture of religious supplication (*OLD* 3b), while the shore, as an archetypically marginal area, underlines the desperation of the hopefuls. Juvenal portrays the shores of Italy as filled with Domitian's *delatores*

(4.47–8), and in AD 28 the crowds were no doubt infiltrated by Sejanus' informers.

gratiam aut fastus ianitorum perpetiebantur Doorkeepers were conventionally haughty (Sen. *Const. Sap.* 15.3 'ianitoribus turbam uenali fastidio derigentibus'), but Sejanus' reflected the *adrogantia* of their master (above). *perpetiebantur* is not so much zeugmatic with *gratiam* as heavily ironical: the doorkeepers' condescension was as intolerable as their disdain (cf. 6.8.5 'libertis quoque ac ianitoribus notescere pro magnifico accipiebatur'). See also Mayor on Juv. 3.184.

74.5 quos *non* sermone, *non* uisu dignatus erat The anaphora reflects the repeated refusals transmitted by the janitors. *dignari* is a verb very frequently used of divinities (many exs. in *TLL* 5.1.1141); here Sejanus is perhaps taking a leaf out of his master's book (Suet. *Tib.* 53.1 'nec ullo mox sermone dignatus erat', of Agrippina). For *non uisu* cf. Dio 58.5.2 δεδιέναι μὴ μόνον μὴ οὐκ ὀφθῇ τις αὐτῷ, ἀλλὰ μὴ καὶ ἐν τοῖς ὑστάτοις φανῇ.

ma̲le alacres 'misguidedly enthusiastic' (*OLD male* 9a).

quibus *in*faustae amici̲tiae grauis exi̲tus *im*minebat Although *grauis exitus* occurs in other earlier authors (Cic. *Div.* 2.22, Ov. *Met.* 10.8, Stat. *Theb.* 2.17), scholars have seen an allusion to Juno's comment on her favourite Turnus at Virg. *Aen.* 10.630 'manet insontem *grauis exitus*'; similarly friendship with the 'divine' Sejanus will bring disaster to many who before his fall thought themselves blameless (5.6.2, 6.8.1, 6.8.6 and nn.). *infaustae amicitiae* brings to a simultaneous close both the main theme of the episode and its religious language; the expr. is unparalleled, but cf. *infaustos . . . amores* at 2.41.3 (n.).

75 neptem Agrippinam The younger Agrippina (53.2n.) was now about thirteen.

cum coram Cn. Domitio tradidisset The betrothal evidently took place locally, in Campania or on Capri. Cn. Domitius Ahenobarbus, son of L. Domitius Ahenobarbus (cos. 16 BC) and Antonia maior (44.2n.), was described about this time by Velleius as 'nobilissimae simplicitatis iuuenem' (2.10.2; cf. 72.3) and later by Suetonius as 'omni parte uitae detestabilem' (*Nero* 5.1). He became consul in 32 (6.1.1, where see n.), escaped charges in 37 (6.47. 2–3 and nn.), and died in late December of 40. 'A nasty fellow' (Syme, *AA* 185; cf. 483 (index)).

celebrari nuptias The placing of Julia's obituary at 71.4 (above) allows T. to devote the final position in both the year and the book to this marriage notice, which thereby gains in emphasis and ominousness. The marriage produced the future emperor Nero, of whom we have already been put in mind at 53.2 and of whom his father is said to have remarked that nothing could be born of himself and Agrippina 'nisi detestabile et malo publico' (Suet. *Nero* 6.1). For foreshadowing at the end of a year see also 3.29–30 (and Ginsburg 46–8).

super uetustatem generis Three generations are summarised at 44.2 (nn.); see also Syme, *AA* Table VIII.

sanguinem here combines the notion of 'blood regarded as running through a family and expressing relationship' (*OLD* 8a) and the common metonymy of a 'person standing in blood-relationship' (*OLD* 10).

auiam Octauiam et per eam *Augustum auunculum* praeferebat Since Octavia was Augustus' sister, *auunculus* here means 'great-uncle', as at 3.4 above. See Syme, *AA* Table III. *praefero* = 'to boast of', 'to present <as credentials>', as 14.53.5 'longa decora praeferentes', Sen. *Clem.* 1.9.10 'agmen nobilium non inania nomina praeferentium' (*TLL* 10.2.612.64ff.).

INDEXES

I GENERAL

2 LATIN WORDS

3 NAMES

All dates are AD unless otherwise specified